CONTINENTAL PHILOSOPHY

For my mother, Adele T. Schroeder,
and in fond memory of my father, Ralph W. Schroeder
and of my brother, Richard A. Schroeder

WILLIAM R. SCHROEDER

CONTINENTAL PHILOSOPHY

A CRITICAL APPROACH

Blackwell Publishing

BLACKWELL PUBLISHING
350 Main Street, Malden, MA 02148-5020, USA
108 Cowley Road, Oxford OX4 1JF, UK
550 Swanston Street, Carlton, Victoria 3053, Australia

First published 2005 by Blackwell Publishing Ltd

Library of Congress Cataloging-in-Publication Data

Schroeder, William Ralph.
Continental philosophy : a critical approach / William R. Schroeder.
p. cm.
Includes bibliographical references and index.
ISBN 1–55786–880–8 (hardcover : alk. paper) — ISBN 1–55786–881–6 (pbk. : alk. paper) 1. Philosophy, European. 2. Philosophy, Modern. I. Title.

B791.S246 2004
190—dc22

2004011693

A catalogue record for this title is available from the British Library.

Set in 10/12.5pt Meridien
by Graphicraft Ltd, Hong Kong
Printed and bound in the United Kingdom
by MPG Books Ltd, Bodmin, Cornwall

The publisher's policy is to use permanent paper from mills that operate a sustainable forestry policy, and which has been manufactured from pulp processed using acid-free and elementary chlorine-free practices. Furthermore, the publisher ensures that the text paper and cover board used have met acceptable environmental accreditation standards.

For further information on
Blackwell Publishing, visit our website:
http://www.blackwellpublishing.com

CONTENTS

ACKNOWLEDGMENTS

I owe special debts to Frithjof Bergmann, Richard Schacht, and John Coker for reading parts of the manuscript at various stages of development and offering helpful comments. Also I would like to thank Larry May and three other anonymous referees for Blackwell Publishing, whose comments proved stimulating and helpful. I would especially like to thank my research assistant for 2003–4, Charlotte Frye, for reading the final versions of each chapter and making useful suggestions. I thank the University of Illinois Research Board for supporting her. I also thank the University of Illinois for granting me a sabbatical leave in 1999–2000 to work on this project.

I have drawn on 30 years of teaching the subjects discussed in this book, but even with such extensive experience, I cannot hope to do complete justice to all the figures treated here. That would require several lifetimes. Also, length considerations forced me to be highly selective in areas that might have received more extended treatment. A number of sections had to be dropped or reduced to make the finished manuscript a reasonable length. In the middle of the project, I was asked to co-edit Blackwell's *A Companion to Continental Philosophy*, and editing those essays certainly deepened my understanding of many figures discussed here.

Finally, I would like to thank the students, both graduate and undergraduate, who asked intelligent questions in my classes on this material. My hope is that this book will stimulate deeper understanding and assimilation of the Continental philosophical tradition and thus will enable the next generation of students to make more creative and better-informed contributions to, and use of, this tradition.

PREFACE

Post-Kantian Continental philosophy is currently experiencing a malaise – perhaps even a crisis. Both poststructuralism and postmodernism climaxed some years ago, and no replacements are on the horizon. Though those movements still have adherents, they can no longer claim to be the cutting-edge. Indeed, that edge has disappeared. Continental scholars seem to be waiting for a new movement to emerge while continuing their historical research. Few attempt to use established insights to address current problems or to advance new answers to old quandaries. Some may hope that philosophy is finally ending after all, but most are simply treading water – unsure how to proceed. This book seeks to shatter the malaise. So I shall begin by examining it further.

Both poststructuralism and postmodernism had withering effects on earlier movements in Continental philosophy. They trumpeted a paradigm shift in philosophy, abandoning the tasks of previous movements and substituting their own agendas. Poststructuralism proved especially destructive. It rejected structuralism for postulating universal, unconscious rules governing mental operations when structuralists should have realized that the complex dynamics of human action cannot be explained in this way. It dismissed phenomenology for failing to establish the accuracy of its reflective self-descriptions and the universality of its discoveries. Instead of allowing that the mind might know itself directly, poststructuralists insisted that consciousness always exists at a distance from itself and is conditioned by factors it cannot fathom. They challenged the phenomenologists' claim to self-knowledge. They also chided hermeneutics for presupposing that organic unity is a necessary condition for adequate interpretations. Instead, they advocated an interpretative creativity that would rival that of artists – the more flamboyant and outrageous, the better. They eviscerated existentialism for its humanism and individualism, instead insisting on the "death of the subject" and the rootedness of persons in social relations. Arguing that "man" is no longer a viable philosophical concern, poststructuralists insisted on the dominating influence of power and historically specific rules governing agency and thought. Because they rejected historical dialectics – whether based on economic forces or a self-developing pattern of concepts or types of consciousness – poststructuralists abandoned Hegel and Marx. They viewed the totalizing feature of dialectical systems –

their claim to incorporate all other positions – as repressive because it allegedly ignores everything that fails to fit the system. Poststructuralists also questioned the dialectician's claim to occupy an absolute standpoint that could adjudicate all others. Though they praised Nietzsche, they ignored his efforts to revitalize philosophy to overcome the crisis of nihilism. Instead, poststructuralists welcomed and fueled it. Foucault's epistemic breaks, Derrida's *différance*, and Deleuze's rhizomes challenged aspirations to provide unchanging truths that characterized previous Continental movements.

Beyond these criticisms, however, neither poststructuralism nor postmodernism produced a widely accepted program for Continental philosophy despite modest efforts to do this. Foucault's late ethics of freedom seemed to be a rehashed version of existentialist authenticity, subject to the same objections. His theory of power seemed unhelpful in analyzing specific struggles and failed to justify new goals through which a convincing critique of the current order could be mounted. It applied equally to all political possibilities and so favored none. This became obvious during the rise of postmodernism, whose proponents seemed almost infatuated with the current era and thus abandoned the search for alternatives. Because it could be used against any author, Derrida's deconstruction also left philosophy stalled – spinning its wheels uselessly – even if this was not his actual goal. Deleuze introduced an alternative vision of philosophy (as conceptual creation) and attempted to renew process-philosophy, but he won few adherents, and even his disciples had difficulty applying his insights. Collectively, however, the poststructuralists silenced all other contenders in Continental thought (an ironic result given their opposition to silencing minorities). Though partisans of other approaches continued their investigations, few believed their efforts would influence the future of Continental philosophy.

Of the major movements in Continental philosophy since 1960, only the French feminists produced a program for renewing culture and philosophy. Although they learned powerful critical techniques from Foucault and Derrida and used them effectively to attack patriarchy, they also used the resources of other major Continental movements to create a new vision of feminine possibilities: feminine writing, feminist ethics, feminist epistemology, and the distinctiveness of women's experience. Resources from phenomenology, hermeneutics, Marxism, Nietzsche, and existentialism were quietly employed to elaborate these new positions. The difference between the French feminists and their poststructuralist contemporaries is that they found ways to nurture social change. Instead of relying exclusively on critiques of past philosophy and social science, they proposed alternative positions, defended new cultural goals, and founded a movement to realize them. Though poststructuralists imagined political alternatives, their efforts yielded few results because their critical strategies undermined their own constructive ideas. Even the achievements of French feminism, despite its high aspirations and multiple fronts, were modest. Though it showed that much classical thought failed to incorporate the experience of women, the ramifications of this were unclear. Was the tradition to be dismissed entirely or merely supplemented?

Also, feminism's cultural goals were limited by its celebration of difference, an ideal that resists centered hegemony, but otherwise offers minimal direction. Its praise of multiplicity and decenteredness threatened to dissolve the sense of agency and responsibility that political movements require.

Why did the poststructuralist critique succeed in silencing the rest of Continental philosophy? My hypothesis is that defenders of earlier movements failed to counter-punch because they already sensed serious flaws in their positions. These doubts prevented partisans from rallying to the defense of their movements. Let me briefly indicate some of these only half-acknowledged problems.

Though Hegel offered many powerful insights into modernity, philosophical dichotomies, and social recognition, Hegelians had lost confidence in the Concept – the underlying patterns defined in the *Logic* that allegedly inform Nature and Spirit. Without confidence in that central core of Hegel's system, only piecemeal contributions to current problems were possible. Hegelians withheld possible responses to poststructuralists' attacks on the dialectic because they had already abandoned it in spirit.

Marxists, already on the defensive because of the tyranny and inefficiency of existing Communist governments, began to doubt Marx's economics – the heart of his system. They questioned whether Marx's historical predictions would ever be confirmed since capitalist economic principles were being deployed even in the most entrenched Communist countries. Though they continued to use Marxist tools to analyze current cultural problems and Marx's ideals to challenge contemporary capitalism, Marxists' answers to poststructuralist objections were half-hearted because they doubted Marx's humanism and the presumed primacy of economic production. Moreover, Marxist alternatives to capitalism simply disappeared.

Nietzscheans maintained Nietzsche's critical vision (the revaluation of all values and the critique of morality and modernity), but they balked at his "aristocratic radicalism" in politics and culture. They vacillated over his critique of equality, his constructive perfectionist ideals, and his vision of a new culture based on an order of rank. They believed that Nietzsche correctly diagnosed modernity's discontents, but they could not ratify his prescriptions. They fared better than partisans of other movements because poststructuralists reinterpreted Nietzsche rather than rejecting him. Though they embraced his alleged critique of reason, even poststructuralists ignored his challenges to equality, freedom, and fraternity.

In a similar fashion, Freudians sensed the difficulty of confirming or disconfirming Freud's speculative hypotheses, and life-philosophers doubted whether life could bear the philosophical burden they had placed on it. When Deleuze attacked Freud for presupposing an ideal of coherent selfhood – instead of acknowledging the potential curative value of schizoid experience – or when Foucault challenged Freud's repressive hypotheses about sexuality, Freudians seemed paralyzed. Moreover, when Foucault showed that life (like labor and language) threatened the importance of the category "man" as a useful philosophical theme, life-philosophy itself was targeted. Only Deleuze used Bergson to discover a path to a new vision of process and becoming.

Poststructuralists ratified the hermeneutic claim that cognitive frameworks play a constitutive role in human experience, only to reject the constitutive role of subjects and authors. They thus challenged the interpretive standard of organic wholeness and the importance of authorial intent. Yet hermeneutic theorists had already abandoned the importance of authorial self-knowledge when they sought to understand authors better than authors understood themselves. Also, their emphasis on cognitive backgrounds often overshadowed whatever conscious purposes authors might bring to their creations. Without authorial coherence, the justification for organic unity as the guiding ideal of interpretation collapsed. Any basis for responding to the poststructuralist attack was undermined by assumptions they already accepted. Hermeneutics prepared the way for its own demise.

Phenomenologists like Sartre and Merleau-Ponty had long been aware of possible Derridean objections to their methodologies. Merleau-Ponty examined the grounds of self-reflexivity in the lived body's relation to itself in his last, unfinished work, *The Visible and the Invisible*. Sartre anticipated Derrida's key point that consciousness cannot be self-identical, but pursued his phenomenological descriptions nonetheless. Phenomenology renews appeals to experience while remaining an a priori discipline, and it claims its descriptions have universality even if made from a single person's viewpoint. These claims seem incompatible. Sartre neglected to show how reflection could be properly purified, and Merleau-Ponty's conception of ambiguity seemed too unstable to answer poststructuralist attacks. Such paradoxes stifled effective responses from phenomenology's defenders. They sensed that their methodological foundations were shaky, despite Herculean efforts by Husserl and Heidegger to ground them.

Existentialists could have claimed that poststructuralists attacked only a caricature of their position, but other weaknesses loomed. They understood (with Foucault) the limits that facticity imposes on human life, and they recognized (with Derrida) the human tendency to fall into self-deception and self-oblivion, but their own ideal of authenticity failed to ground new cultural ideals (no vision of community was offered) and foundered on its own formalism (many dubious character-types were compatible with authenticity). Existentialists portrayed the gritty realities of human existence more vividly than poststructuralists or postmodernists, but once the focus of Continental philosophy had shifted from experience to language (as a result of structuralism), this advantage disappeared. Philosophical anthropologists could have answered poststructuralism's attack on the importance of "man" and "subjectivity" because they effectively blended the first- and third-person viewpoints. But few philosophers adopted this movement's approach after the war; so this response was never offered.

Structuralism provided tools for its later progeny, but this did not exempt it from their devastating attacks. Partisans of structuralism sensed the modesty of their actual achievements. After several decades of research, they had suggested a number of ways in which Saussure's and Lévi-Strauss's paradigms might be extended, but no consensus concerning the success of these extensions had been achieved. No one in Continental structuralism (including Lévi-Strauss and Lacan) produced an underlying grammar for any symbol or sign system, including language itself. At best, only sketches and fragments were offered. The American linguist Chomsky was most successful in realizing structuralism's goal, but Continental structuralists largely ignored his accomplishments. Also, insights derived from Wittgenstein and Austin raised doubts about whether an underlying *langue* (constitutive system) existed even for language itself, much less for derivative symbol systems. Many structuralists (e.g., Barthes) shifted gears to mesh with new poststructuralist directions, thus acknowledging the force of their criticisms. Hence structuralists also suffered from self-doubt. Poststructuralism was correctly seen not as an inheritor of structuralism's aims, but as a rejection of its program. Structuralism thus succumbed to the paralysis poststructuralism imposed on other movements in Continental philosophy.

Although these problems may be serious, they need not be fatal. I believe that much resilience remains in virtually all the movements of Continental philosophy. Demonstrating this is one goal of this book. I acknowledge that any revitalization of Continental philosophy cannot ignore the poststructuralists' challenges, but poststructuralism itself exhibits significant flaws. For example, Foucault forgets the impact of his own episteme when claiming to provide "objective" descriptions of the background assumptions of previous epistemes, and his theory of power forecloses alternative political goals because social systems cannot help but be oppressive on his view. Also, his late idealization of self-critical, self-creating subjectivity revivifies the very "subject" he declared dead. Or I might argue that Sartre and Merleau-Ponty anticipated Derrida's argument against self-presence; yet they drew less skeptical conclusions than he does. Heidegger does the same for the ontology of presence. The real question is thus whether Derrida's skeptical conclusions follow from his premises, and this is at least arguable. Similarly, Deleuze clearly articulates an alternative model of ontological relations (rhizomes vs. organics), but he does not show that this model is broadly applicable. He seems to forget that the mere conceivability of an alternative is no guarantee of its applicability. Though Lyotard realizes that certain opposed language games have little common ground, he fails to show that each side must capitulate to ultimate disagreement, instead of seeking plausible procedures of adjudication. Finally, Baudrillard discovers some genuine insights into the current era, but these alone do not vindicate the evaluative conclusions he draws, nor do they preclude contrasting perspectives. I could argue that his survey of the present era is truncated and blinkered. Thus, since neither poststructuralism nor postmodernism is without flaws, I have chosen not to limit this survey to only the most recent Continental figures (or to the twentieth century). Instead, I propose to re-examine the entire post-Kantian tradition – reconsidering the major objections to these movements and providing a richer appreciation of their achievements and future possibilities. I will then reconsider the current situation in Continental philosophy, once this reassessment is complete.

Now that the passion for poststructuralism and postmodernism has waned, I believe the time is ripe for taking stock, for systematic re-evaluation, and new creativity. The allegiances of students and scholars may have loosened sufficiently to allow receptivity to new assessments. Partisans within each movement may be ready to explore new options – opening new horizons and articulating better-defined disagreements. One goal of this book is to begin this process. Continental philosophy has periodically reinvigorated itself by rethinking its own past. This has typically happened when new movements, seeking to supersede established ones, minimize earlier achievements in order to inflate the need for new solutions. In addition, new movements often adopt an apocalyptic tone that claims special privileges for their innovations. In contrast, I explore potential paths toward the future by underlining the virtues of previous figures and movements, as well as acknowledging their potential problems. Throughout this book, I try to forge a standpoint that both celebrates and criticizes each position. I underline their virtues and acknowledge their apparent flaws. I invite scholars to collaborate in this millennial reassessment, while hopefully providing a reliable survey for newcomers.

Although the book's organization may seem chronological, the project is systematic rather than historical. I make no attempt to include every possible figure, and I say little about historical influence or biography. *Most importantly, I reject the guiding assumption of many histories of thought – that more recent theories are better ones.* Instead, I review the major currents of post-Kantian Continental thought so that their contributions can be compared and assessed. (You might imagine that I invite the proponents of each standpoint to gather at a round table, which privileges none but allows each to have full voice in the discussion.) I provide the best summaries I can (in limited space), note crucial disagreements, indicate major contributions, and assess their potential flaws. Some readers will benefit from the summaries (especially students and others new to the field); others will no doubt challenge and augment my assessments (other specialists); still others will benefit from the comparisons, the analysis of decision points, and the concluding discussion of the contributions of this tradition (philosophers working in other traditions). This project seeks to benefit all three audiences.

Each chapter opens with a summary of the most vital contributions of a specific figure or movement, continues with an expository interpretation, and concludes with a brief assessment. The opening arias motivate and structure the chapters. The expositions are not intended to be controversial or innovative, but neither do they merely restate received canonical interpretations. Above all, I aim for reliability and accessibility. I hope that specialists who have spent years on one of these figures will find my treatments to be fair, even if compressed and lacking nuance. The assessments are intended to stimulate further critical thought. They invite students to articulate their own objections more fully, and they invite further analysis and discussion by specialists. Too many surveys offer only an endless summary of positions; the assessments included here should provide some perspective. I indicate some major strengths of Continental philosophy as a whole in the book's conclusions. The Introduction is a highly compressed prologue that cannot possibly do full justice to the figures and movements considered. Primarily, it anticipates later developments by indicating points of contrast and contention. It suggests that post-Kantian Continental philosophy emerged as an organic response to problems in Modern philosophy and in Kant. This may help philosophers in other traditions identify important similarities and differences between Continental philosophers and those with whom they are familiar.

Throughout the book, I use "Continental philosophy" to include significant nineteenth- and twentieth-century contributions from both the German and French traditions. Many twentieth-century figures cannot be appreciated without comprehending their nineteenth-century predecessors, and these earlier figures have continuing relevance today. Also, I give equal weight to figures from the first half and those from the last half of the twentieth century, even though the later thinkers claim to supersede the former (or even to refute them). Because of space considerations, some figures and movements have been given more cursory treatments than I would have preferred (e.g., German Idealism before Hegel; Western Marxism; Structuralism; Philosophical Anthropology), and others had to be left out entirely (e.g., Brentano; literary philosophers like Unamuno, Camus, Cioran, Bataille, and Blanchot; and Continental philosophers of science like Canguilhem). I concentrate on major contributors to the movements rather than dwell on lesser figures. This selectivity allows richer treatment of important figures, an approach that best serves most readers. This project's systematic architectonic and orientation toward the future also justify such selectivity. I group thinkers systematically, rather than temporally, in order to highlight relevant similarities. Also, after the Introduction, I present each thinker/movement using the present tense because I believe that each movement remains vital to present philosophical concerns.

In the United States, philosophy has too long been divided into two indifferent – or sometimes antagonistic – camps: Analytic and Continental. In the last decade, Analytic philosophy has become more open-ended, its reigning assumptions challenged or rethought. It still prizes clarity and argumentative rigor; it still focuses on conceptual elucidation; but it has broadened its horizons – abandoning its isolation from empirical research, the dilemmas of practical life, current cultural issues, and everyday life. This new openness may offer a perspicuous moment for its adherents to consider the virtues and achievements of Continental philosophy, for they may discover that many of their current strategies have been anticipated, and may be instructed by the other tradition's results. I have tried to create a jargon-free, unpretentious, even humble introduction to Continental philosophy for such readers. They may discover new ramifications of these figures and movements as they consider their relevance to their own specialties. In addition, Continental scholars too often limit themselves to exposition and scholarly commentary. I would argue that they must now use the tradition's best achievements to propose solutions to current philosophical problems. (And they could certainly benefit from a study of Analytic approaches to these problems.) My effort to demonstrate the value of the Continental tradition to non-specialists will hopefully strengthen the rapprochement that is already occurring.

Two large goals govern the project, and they take center stage in the Conclusions. First, I attempt to locate the major fault-lines of opposition among the major players in post-Kantian Continental philosophy. The comparisons among the various movements offered near the end of many chapters help define and highlight central disagreements. Some specialists may believe that the debates on these "decision-points" have already been won. My purpose is to challenge this impression and suggest that many core disagreements remain unresolved. Their resolution will determine the future course of Continental philosophy. At minimum, clarifying these "decision-points" will provide partisans with an opportunity to hone arguments for their favored solutions and to reconsider their soundness. Second, I indicate some important contributions of Continental philosophy to various sub-fields of philosophy (e.g., ethics, politics, epistemology, philosophy of mind). This may encourage philosophers in other traditions (especially the Analytic tradition) with these specific interests to explore certain figures in greater depth. If it cannot prove the relevance of its insights to other traditions, Continental philosophy's impact outside its circle of scholars will be marginal. My goal is to revitalize all movements of Continental philosophy. The concluding section on "decision-points" is thus primarily for specialists and advanced students; the one on "specific field contributions" is largely for philosophers in other traditions and for general readers.

I also include a concluding section that continues the argument of this Preface. It shows that many poststructuralist arguments against earlier movements are unsound or problematic, and it thus attempts to further lift the chill that poststructuralism visited on other Continental positions.

Although I use standard labels to designate various movements in post-Kantian Continental philosophy (e.g., "hermeneutics," "existentialism," "postmodernism"), and although I take these labels seriously enough to indicate the common features they seem to identify, I believe they cannot bear much weight. Intellectual historians often create such categories after the fact. Creative thinkers are usually motivated by *issues* and rarely identify themselves as members of *movements*. Thus, thinkers grouped together with these labels may often have significant differences as well as similarities, and often a single figure (e.g., Heidegger) makes major contributions to several different movements (e.g., hermeneutics, phenomenology, and existentialism). *Individuals* make the real philosophical advances; the usefulness of grouping individuals into movements varies. In one case, I simply invented a classificatory name to cover several philosophers who have some interesting common features, but who are not traditionally grouped together (Schopenhauer, Freud, and Bergson). In general, I do not include quotations from the philosophers themselves, though I assume many readers will study texts by these authors as they read this book. In the notes I indicate passages that support my interpretations, but I refrain from documenting every claim. I offer suggested readings (primary and secondary) at the end of each chapter, but these are not intended to be exhaustive, and I limit them primarily to English-language sources.

This is a Hegelian project – tempered by a Foucauldian sensibility. I do not presume that Continental philosophy has achieved a new synthesis (hence, my attempt at assessment and exploration), and I am not clearing the ground for my own new standpoint (since different approaches may be needed to make useful contributions to different current problems). Nonetheless, I do seek promising, critically informed paths forward. I review the entire history of the tradition, without assuming that newer movements successfully refuted or even directly challenged earlier movements. Like Foucault, I reject the presumption of historical progress and acknowledge potential epistemic breaks. Like Hegel, I think something powerful can be learned from each movement. But, like Nietzsche in relation to diverse perspectives, I seek a *just assessment* of the contributions of these movements. I reconsider the value of each. I do not attempt to offer final judgments; instead, I hope to engage readers in the assessment process so that Continental philosophy can become stronger by engaging their objections.

INTRODUCTION

Many important questions for post-Kantian Continental philosophy were raised by Kant, Fichte, Schelling, and their predecessors in the Modern period (1650–1800). Thus, brief sketches of those positions will supply some background. My goal here is to introduce the main themes of this book, not to fully explicate these earlier thinkers. These sketches are only springboards to clarifying the responses of later figures. Consequently, I will review only the major themes explored by Descartes, the Empiricists, the Rationalists, the French Enlightenment, Rousseau, the Romantics, and Kant.[1] In each section I emphasize key points that were later challenged or rethought by post-Kantian Continental thinkers. Then I will briefly sketch some initial reactions to Kant by Fichte, Schelling, and Hölderlin to provide a transition to the figure that truly inaugurates the contemporary period in Continental philosophy, Hegel. As the Modern period developed, its philosophers depicted persons to be increasingly distant from ultimate reality. They also construed mental capacities – such as reason, desire, imagination, and emotion – to be in conflict with each other. This increasing inner disharmony and widening separation from ultimate reality is the condition Hegel sought to overcome.

DESCARTES

René Descartes's (1596–1650) major contribution is difficult to appreciate today because everyone takes it for granted. He urged that individuals rationally determine their own beliefs, rather than automatically accepting religious authority, tradition, or common sense. For him, this is an ethical *imperative*: accept beliefs only if they can be certified through rational argument. Descartes believed that rationality, deduction, analysis, and clarity would be sufficient to justify the existence of God, morality, and common-sense beliefs. His imperative reinforced the individualism inspired by the Reformation. It implied that rational individuals bear responsibility for their beliefs, which they must evaluate using logic and evidence alone. Descartes's system derives from a fundamental belief that the world has a mathematical structure; he sought to describe physical nature as matter in motion. He makes room for new scientific approaches to studying nature by rejecting conflicting metaphysical assumptions.

In his *Meditations on First Philosophy* (1641), Descartes sought *certainty* – absolutely unquestionable foundations for knowledge. He made significant advances in mathematics, and was impressed by its deductive beauty. Starting with self-evident truths, he hoped to deduce, and thus to ground, commonly accepted beliefs. To discover those truths, he rejected any claim that could reasonably be doubted. But what are reasonable doubts? If a claim *could be* wrong under *any* circumstances, then he rejected it. Hence, he discarded most *empirical* statements because they could be illusory (e.g., he might be dreaming). He even jettisoned most *mathematical* truths because there might be an evil trickster consistently deluding everyone about them (thus, 2 + 2 might in fact be 5, even though everyone believes it is 4). Descartes raised the standards for knowledge so high that only *indubitable* claims could satisfy them, and then he sought to rebuild everyday knowledge on these secure foundations. Such elevated standards often engender deep skepticism because so little can satisfy them. Perception, memory, values, other people, and even science may fail the test. Descartes's strategy can be self-stultifying because the rebuilding process typically depends on dubitable claims and thus cannot be completed.

Descartes believed that each individual's own mental states could provide a source of indubitable knowledge. These are known so intimately that nothing could seriously challenge them. (Even if you doubt your experience, the doubting itself is an indubitable experience!) Thus, for Descartes, people have *privileged access* to their own mental states. They know their present experiences better than anyone else can know them and better than they can know anything else. Descartes extends this certainty to the self that allegedly possesses such states even though it may not be experienced directly. Conscious states and the self thus become indubitable building blocks from which all knowledge of the world, other people, mathematics, God, and science must be derived.

Unfortunately, this claim divides human beings from within. Not only do people possess occurrent conscious states, they also have bodily states that must be described in physiological terms. But such states – such as heartbeat, metabolism, brain activity, and hormonal functions – are not directly accessible to consciousness. Hence they are known only secondarily, and their relationship to consciousness is mysterious. For Descartes, the physiological processes of the body become dubitable appendages to conscious states. He must solve the problem of how conscious states are related to bodily states – e.g., how neurons firing in the brain are related to conscious thoughts or how the experience of willing an arm movement is related to the muscle movements that result. Descartes believed the body to be part of the mechanical, material world and the mind to be a distinct, independent sphere. They constitute two separate realms, governed by two different types of law.

Thus, Descartes emphasized two distinctions that still preoccupy Continental philosophers: appearance/reality and mind/body. These distinctions establish gulfs that later thinkers must bridge. He also postulates the epistemic primacy of the self and the first-person standpoint, which ground the modern notions of subjectivity and individuality. In addition, Descartes contends that persons have "innate ideas," concepts that do not derive from experience but nonetheless organize it. His best example of this is the experience of an object that remains identical across a change in all of its properties (e.g., a piece of wax that changes its shape, color, texture, smell, and location). The observer can intellectually grasp the identity of the wax despite the fact that none of its observable properties remains the same. This suggests that humans impose some categories on experience (here: thinghood), rather than deriving them from experience. Descartes thus anticipates Kant's claim that an unconscious system of categories organizes experience and Hegel's claim that such a system informs all spheres of reality – including nature, mind, and history.

Finally, Descartes created a method of analysis that reduces complex propositions to a minimum of clear and distinct components in order to achieve philosophical clarity. In considering philosophical problems, he proceeded from the simplest issues to more complex ones, hoping that answering the former would provide insights necessary to resolve the latter. This method assumes that issues are discrete and can be resolved in isolation – without considering their systematic ramifications. In addition, he thought physical systems, or wholes, could be reduced to the mechanical operations of their parts. His reductive method was rooted in these ontological assumptions. Many later Continental philosophers argue that philosophical problems cannot be isolated in this fashion and that only by considering their systematic relationships can adequate solutions be discovered. Philosophy's questions are so interlocked that answers to any one must take account of the ramifications for many others. They also argued that living organisms cannot be reduced to the isolated mechanical operations of their parts.

Continental philosophers thus challenge Descartes's analytic method and his foundationalism. For example, Hegel's dialectical understanding of reality takes everything to be a moment of an organic whole. Reducing the world to its simplest atomic parts distorts dialectical unities because organic wholes are *more* than the sum of their parts and because their properties are *emergent.* The parts can adopt entirely new functions if the whole requires this to achieve optimal responses to the environment; thus, the functions of parts may change in different situations. Also, organic elements are not isolated because a change in one generates a compensatory change in all the others. Not only Hegel and Marx, but also hermeneutics, existential phenomenology, and structuralism elaborate this dialectical model of reality. It demands new forms of knowledge and an appreciation of the systematic connections among philosophical issues.

Beyond this, many Continental figures reject Descartes's foundationalist program and his ideal of individually certifying knowledge-claims. Hegel, Marx, Nietzsche, hermeneutics, and poststructuralism all defend approaches to knowledge that require integrating many perspectives, allowing them to mutually refine and enrich one another. The Continental tradition (excepting Husserl) challenges confidence in self-evidence and seeks procedures to improve human knowledge that deploy more modest epistemic criteria. Some Continental figures challenge the primacy of theoretical reason over practice or lived experience. Finally, some argue that knowledge requires specific social conditions and thus deny the self-sufficiency of the first-person viewpoint when isolated from its social background.

Many also question Descartes's claims about occurrent mental states. For example, many Continental philosophers acknowledge unconscious elements of human experience (for which privileged access is lacking). They also argue that background conditions that cannot be discovered even indirectly through retrospective self-examination shape experience. Special procedures for uncovering these conditions are required. Many also reject the "substance" analysis of the self either by locating selfhood in expressive actions, in the relationships among mental states, or in social recognition. Some even reject Descartes's *cogito*, the view that mental states are sufficiently self-transparent to produce immediate self-warranting knowledge. They claim that since mental states become manifest only in expressions, the owner's access to them is no better than that of other people; both self and other must interpret observable actions to comprehend the self. Derrida even suggests that the *cogito* is a myth by showing that persons only experience traces or echoes of their own states, rather than undergoing and comprehending (or possessing and knowing) them simultaneously.

Lastly, many recent Continental philosophers repudiate Descartes's mind-body dualism and its dismissive conception of embodiment. Rather than reduce the mental to the physical, however, they reinterpret the body as a primordial tool through which persons grapple with a world of tools, and thus they see the body and the world as mutually constitutive and interdependent. Some also suggest that many mental states are continuous with animal and vital capacities and thus that human mental capacities develop from them. These alternative positions emerge in Marx, Nietzsche, existentialism, and philosophical anthropology. Descartes's claim that some "ideas" are innate and universal is developed and defended by Kant and by some structuralists, but challenged by Marxists, poststructuralists, and hermeneutic thinkers who believe all concepts are historically constituted. Descartes's philosophy thus provides both a foil and a resource for later Continental thought.

EMPIRICISM AND THE RISE OF SCIENCE

Descartes's main motive for distinguishing mind from matter was to legitimate a mechanical interpretation of matter and thus to facilitate scientific progress. Empiricism – primarily in Locke (1632–1704), Berkeley (1685–1753), and Hume (1711–66) – defended the assumptions and methods of science and developed a complementary theory of mind. Oddly, as scientists made significant strides in explaining nature, Empiricist philosophers became more skeptical about the foundations of scientific thought. Making science's assumptions explicit revealed some serious problems. Hume, for example, came to doubt whether causes really exist and whether induction could be legitimated. He believed that humans attribute causation to regularly recurring events that are constantly conjoined. The only defensible empirical claim is that one event typically (not necessarily) *follows* another (rather than being *caused* by it). Similarly, there could be no experiential assurance that future conjunctions of sensations will resemble past ones. At best, this would only be a contingent fact. Likewise, he came to doubt the existence of a self that unifies experiences because he could not discover it in experience. (Later Hume reversed himself, suggesting that experience does not always speak with one voice.) Hume's skepticism epitomizes the entire Empiricist movement.

Three claims define Empiricism: all knowledge derives from experience – typically from sensory experience; the mind is a "blank slate" prior to experience so that concepts emerge via abstraction from and association among sensations; and sensations are atomic and simple or at least can be reduced to atomic and simple elements. By grounding all knowledge in sensory experience and suggesting that experience may only represent or mirror the external world, Empiricism reinforced Descartes's first-person standpoint and his conception that persons have privileged access to their own sensations. However, by denying the existence of innate ideas, Empiricism departs from Descartes by limiting the importance of reason. "Concepts" derive from associations of similar experiences. If certain concepts – such as causality or the self – are not directly experienced, then they may have no genuine application. Empiricism generally assumes that the mind's structure derives from experience; since it lacks structure prior to experience, different cognitive organizations may result from different arrays of experience. Different cultures and civilizations thus may acquire different concepts because they interact with different environments. The only explanation for similarities in cross-cultural concepts is a common material world that engenders experience. If this common world were lacking, then intercultural and even interpersonal understanding might become impossible. The third claim – concerning simple, atomic "ideas" (raw elements of experience) – denies that experience possesses any organic wholeness. Relationships among experiences must be established externally by comparison with previous experiences. Close attention to experience, however, may reveal essential interconnections, especially when "experience" is broadened to include imagination, desire, emotion, and volition. This atomistic analysis is often extended to social theory by interpreting individuals to be the fundamental social atoms of society and taking all social relationships to be the result of explicit contracts. Although this individualistic position can ground fundamental human rights, it often remains oblivious to the need for strong institutions to guarantee such rights.

For Hume, custom and tradition provide structure to the mind by guiding the manner in which experiences are organized and synthesized. Common-sense concepts embody the accumulated sum of experiences assimilated by prior generations. New generations may supplement them, but must not ignore them. Custom and tradition, however, have no greater authority than the experiences they summarize. Should entirely new kinds of experience emerge (for example, as a result of new instruments like the electron microscope or new technologies like magnetic resonance imaging), then customary habits of thought would require appropriate modification. Most Empiricists sharply distinguish facts and values. Value judgments derive from "irrational" elements of the mind such as feelings, emotions, or attitudes, which lack experiential validation. Purely descriptive and verifiable, facts are statements that allegedly conform to experience. Many Empiricists insist that evaluative claims cannot be derived from mere facts; they are emotional reactions to facts, which may readily differ for different persons. (Only if ethical claims could be reduced to people's actual desires or to the maximization of actually experienced pleasures could Empiricists find them defensible. This is why later Empiricists, e.g., James and J. S. Mill, gravitated toward utilitarianism in moral theory.) Empiricists generally interpret the mind to be passive, imprinted with representations of real objects. Reason's major function is to discover similarities and differences among representations. In this way it creates concepts (through grouping similarities into types) and modest generalizations (noting constant conjunctions) to better organize future experience.

Hume's doubts about causation, induction, and the self can also be directed to the "laws" of logic and to the sanctity of the individual. The exact status of logical laws vexed Empiricists. They should regard them as generalizations from actual thought processes (which are frequently flawed), but logic's certainty seems more deeply rooted than this. Skepticism about the foundations of logic also threatens the legitimacy of scientific reasoning. Also, since causation is essential to the mechanistic world-view, Hume's skepticism threatens this as well. Similarly, Hume's doubts about the existence of distinct personal selves threaten the legitimacy of individual rights and the entire first-person standpoint.

Continental philosophers often claim that Empiricists overlook the temporal unity of and internal relations among experiences, and that they presuppose an arbitrarily limited conception of experience (atomistic sensations) and of their possible combinations (association). Phenomenologists, for example, discover a directedness (or intentionality) in experience and a complex nested structure among conscious states. These features are rarely acknowledged in Empiricism. They also insist on examining the full range of experiences, including emotions, intentions, valuations, and imagination, and on exploring the intersubjective sources of experiential unity (which are only minimally foreseen in Hume's notion of custom).

Because Empiricism produces skepticism about its own greatest achievement, science, some Continental philosophers develop an alternative conception of systematic knowledge. Hegel, Marx, phenomenologists, structuralists, and others explore alternative conceptions of a "scientific system," requiring an expanded rationality and revealing structural relations among phenomena that are neither causal nor conceptual. Continental philosophers also resist the sharp Empiricist division between appearance and reality. Although Kant adopted the Empiricist posture that appearances represent reality (and thus actual things in themselves cannot be directly known), many Continental philosophers reject this division. They insist that experience reveals reality as it is, or at least genuine features of and perspectives on it. For this reason, a taproot of realism flourishes in Continental philosophy. Initially, Kant and the German Idealists challenge Hume's skepticism about the self by reinterpreting its function, but this skepticism eventually resurfaces in existentialism and poststructuralism. Many Continental philosophers also reject the social contract as the source of social unity, arguing that culture is more deeply rooted in communal traditions than the notion of an explicit contract could ever explain.

RATIONALISM

Mathematical knowledge fascinated the Rationalists – Spinoza (1632–77) and Leibnitz (1646–1716) – more than empirical science. They valued the power of deductive argument from axioms (the manner in which Spinoza presented his philosophy), and they believed mathematics could discover the underlying structure of everything: nature, mind, life, and the cosmos. Spinoza was especially concerned to clarify the principles of intelligibility of all existence. The order of nature and mind are identical – a logical order – an order of necessity rather than contingency. Logical relations are not limited to propositions, but inform everything else. The Rationalists reject the notion of efficient causation, at least as a fundamental explanatory principle. They also reject sensory knowledge because it engages only limited parts of the body. Only when the whole body grasps the world as a totality and in its totality can genuine knowledge be achieved. Rationalists are less concerned with skepticism because they believe the intelligible structure of the universe can be known.

For Spinoza, mind and nature are parts of a single order because both have the same intelligible structure. Because he grasps this underlying unity, Spinoza is suspicious of rigid dichotomies. He seeks to resolve them by seeing them as opposite poles of a continuum or terms expressing an underlying unity. A single intelligible structure informs everything. It is self-sufficient and all-encompassing, but is simply the underlying rational order of all that is, rather than a personal or purposive force that transcends what is. Leibnitz sees all things as reflecting the larger whole, like microcosms within the macrocosm. He interprets the universe to be developing toward greater unification and order, thus facilitating deeper human understanding.

Spinoza articulated the ethical ramifications of such a system. Since all events are logically determined at least in their general outline, freedom in the ordinary sense of choice among open possibilities is an illusion. Spinoza reinterprets freedom as acting in accord with the necessity of one's nature and identifying with the rational structure of the whole. The task is to feel harmony with the order of things. His ethical ideals include humility, tolerance, and acceptance of this fundamental order. Because everyone's actions are determined, praise, blame, resentment, and hatred are unjustified. Facing life's vicissitudes with equanimity is a virtue.

Later Continental philosophers reacted against key Rationalist postulates while also acknowledging the power of their vision. Hegel sought to develop a system that unifies Spinoza's vision of the whole with a fuller concept of subjectivity that itself develops and matures over time. In order to defend such a system, Hegel had to create a distinctive logic, an alternative to the deduction of the Rationalists. But, like them, he believed that science made important but limited contributions to understanding the underlying rational unity of the whole. He sought to resolve dichotomies and conceptual oppositions in a way similar to Spinoza, but he also acknowledges the role of conflict and opposition in achieving deeper unities. Moreover, not only did Hegel try to incorporate all stages of the maturation of consciousness, he also included all spheres of culture in his system, including art, social life, history, and religion. One of the most important divisions within Continental philosophy is whether later figures follow Hegel's lead on this point or whether they see the cosmos (and humanity within it) in dispersion, disharmony, or chaotic conflict.

Even when later Continental philosophers see the world as ordered, they often see different principles of order – for nature, life, and mind. Even among mental states, different kinds of order seem to inform perception, imagination, volition, and thought, and phenomenologists seek to describe these differences. Life-philosophers believe the kind of organic unity Spinoza saw everywhere existed more fully and distinctively in the sphere of life. Hermeneutic and Romantic thinkers take art to be the best exemplar of organic unity.

Though Schopenhauer, and to some extent Freud, accepted Spinoza's determinism, few other Continental figures have followed this lead. Most have developed a conception of freedom as situated self-expression; free actions realize individuals' potential and bring them to fruition. People do not just express the ramifications of a pre-existing concept or underlying structural principle; they create themselves, at least to an extent, and responsibility for the course of the world lies squarely on humanity's shoulders. Human actions may facilitate the world's self-realization, just as the world shapes and conditions human action. Nietzsche agreed with Spinoza that overcoming resentment, hatred, and fear are essential to achieving ethical self-realization, but his argument for this did not depend on a deterministic outlook. He also agreed that overcoming reliance on praise and blame is an important ethical ideal.

THE FRENCH ENLIGHTENMENT

Voltaire (1694–1778), Denis Diderot (1713–84), Holbach (1723–89), and their compatriots stressed psychology and social theory over epistemology and metaphysics. They were deeply impressed by Newton's mechanical laws, and they imported many British Empiricist theories into the French tradition. They shared Rationalism's confidence in reason, but they sought to use rationality to discover solutions to social problems like poverty, injustice, and war. They sought a general improvement in the human lot through social and legal reform. Many were anti-clerical, and some were anti-Christian or at least skeptical of religion. Their naturalistic perspective rendered a personal God superfluous; nature's order did not require theological intervention or origination. Believing non-natural forms of explanation were unnecessary, they also rejected metaphysical speculation. Nature's orderliness inspired them to believe that humanity could emulate that order.

Those who still accepted God believed he had created a rationally intelligible and lawful world and then departed the scene. They felt God had no personal stake in humanity's fate and thus ignored human suffering. Such a God might have started the universe in motion, but humanity's obligation is to keep it running efficiently and to use nature's laws to enhance human welfare. Thus, whether they derived it from this Deist conception of God or from atheism, the French *philosophes* adopted an activist stance toward human social affairs. Humanity's task is to improve its own lot. Since such improvement is not guaranteed, it must be achieved through political leadership. The stability of the established social order is never assured; human actions sustain it and can thus overturn it if it no longer produces happiness. These thinkers valued religious toleration, peace, progress, cosmopolitanism, democracy, and basic human rights.

The French Enlightenment thus sought to increase human happiness, defined as an increase in pleasure or economic well-being for the greatest number of people. The modern rise of hedonism (the idea that pleasure is the only inherent good) and utilitarianism (the idea that actions are right only if they produce greater happiness for larger numbers of people) emerged in France first; the English utilitarians followed their lead in the nineteenth century. The French Enlightenment thinkers valued ordinary pleasures because they believed humanity to be an earthly natural species, with animal needs as well as spiritual ones. Many ethical thinkers dismiss the value of pleasure, but Enlightenment theorists make pleasure primary. They are *pure* hedonists, regarding all pleasures as equivalent, different only in quantity or degree, but not in kind or quality. They hoped that measurable improvement in the human condition would result from defining goodness in these mundane terms. They sought to promote pleasure – as well as reduce suffering – in all areas of social life: family, work, voluntary associations, community, law, and government. Four leading French Enlightenment figures were Voltaire, Diderot, Holbach, and Condillac.

Voltaire (François-Marie Arouet) struggled against judicial arbitrariness throughout his life. He learned Newton's physics when he was exiled to England and became the first of several French *philosophes* – passionate, freethinking critics of established institutions. He was a playwright and an historian, as well as a businessman and free-thinker. His histories explored popular movements, as well as the arts and sciences, not merely kings, political intrigue, and wars. His popular novel *Candide* (1759) lampooned Leibnitz's optimistic position that this is the best of all possible worlds. Voltaire vividly depicted the horrors of human history and the unjustified suffering of even remarkable people. When he retired, he launched several intellectual campaigns. He argued that Christianity had had reprehensible effects on humanity and that its destruction would be necessary if a humane and rational society were to emerge. He insisted that most Christian doctrines are either absurd or immoral, citing Christianity's historical exhortations to violence and war. Voltaire also worked to free several famous prisoners whom he believed to be unjustly accused and wrote a comparative study of legal institutions in order to justify French judicial reforms.

Diderot expanded a publisher's idea for an *Encyclopédie* (1751–80; 35 volumes) into a tool for challenging the monarchical order. The *Encyclopédie* brought Enlightenment thinking to the general reading public in the guise of expert knowledge on various topics. Diderot himself firmly believed in the efficacy of the scientific method to discover the important truths of nature. He demonstrated a lively interest in technology, explaining the operations of many practical devices in the *Encyclopedia*. He also commented extensively on art and literature, wrote important novels and plays, and produced learned studies of individual pathologies and mental abnormalities. He challenged the need to believe in God and questioned the value of Catholic supervision of everyday life. He defended the view that matter is already infused with mind or spirit (exhibiting a kind of sensitivity and dynamism) and thus that life and mind simply exhibit higher degrees of order. Along with Condillac, he analyzed knowledge into component sensations and their perceived similarities with, and differences from, previous sensations (indicating a great distrust of abstractions), and thus continued Voltaire's effort to import of British conceptions into French philosophy. For Diderot, art enhances the perception of complex relationships and charges them with emotion. He shows that discovering scientific hypotheses requires poetic insight, but also insists that speculative theories be tested experimentally. Like most members of the French Enlightenment, he was unable publish his most controversial books during his lifetime.

Diderot and Voltaire laid the groundwork for the more uncompromising materialism of Baron Paul von Holbach, who fashioned it into a world-view. For Holbach, there is only matter in motion. Because humans are part of nature, they are microcosms of its processes. Living organisms require no additional principles of explanation. He argues for determinism and suggests that personal choices always seek the chooser's greatest advantage. He denies human immortality and the soul's existence, in addition to challenging the foundations of theism, Deism, and Christianity. Holbach claims that Christian morality is not essential to a just, rational, and humane social order because ordinary people will voluntarily limit their egoistic impulses in order to live peacefully together.

The basis for the Enlightenment's belief in equality is the fact that human minds are blank slates at birth and thus identical, thereby warranting equal treatment for all. People can be trained through proper exposure to stimuli. Etienne Bennot de Condillac (1715–80) simply adopts Locke's associationistic psychology, which held that all knowledge derives directly from sensations and their observed similarities. Because human nature is malleable, Condillac hoped education would produce human progress. Claude-Adrien Helvétius (1715–71) added to this the importance of just and humane laws to properly train and discipline human behavior, claiming that strong, rational institutions could produce humane citizens. Both regarded education and politics as sources of human improvement; and both defended utilitarianism. Montesquieu

(Charles de Sécondat, 1689–1755) supplemented their reform programs a massive historical study of political institutions in a wide variety of cour and cultures. Examining several different types of law (international, political, and civil) and political organization, he contributed to the emergence of social science and clarified important institutional conditions of human well-being. He defended practices that would satisfy genuine human needs, not merely unreflective surface desires, and favored a government with limited powers that would include a strong executive and a democratically elected legislature to check the executive's powers.

The French Enlightenment thus united the best tendencies of Rationalism and Empiricism. They retained the Rationalist faith in reason without deifying mathematics or indulging in metaphysical speculation. Yet they also learned to attend to individual and historical experience from the Empiricists. To this they added a toleration of religious differences, a focus on social and personal improvement, and a faith in humanity's capacity to plan and control its own destiny. They believed the universe to be rationally ordered and were confident that reason could comprehend this order. Discovering laws of nature could increase human happiness, encourage peaceful coexistence, reform the legal and political systems, and limit the influence of the Church in everyday life.

Some major thinkers of nineteenth-century Continental philosophy developed the anti-theist, anti-Christian elements of the French *philosophes*, viz., early Hegel, Marx, Nietzsche, and Freud. Thereafter, the role of God in Continental philosophy becomes less important. Some later figures retain the *philosophes'* naturalism (notably Marx, Nietzsche, and Freud), but their mechanism is regarded as too reductive and limiting – indifferent to the unique features of living organisms. Later Continental reservations about the egoism and atomism of British Empiricists also applied to the French appropriation of these ideas. Confidence in reason and empirical science waxes and wanes throughout the history of Continental philosophy, as does belief in reason's ability to improve humanity's lot. The French Enlightenment laid the foundation for the French Revolution, whose liberal ideals and humanism remain important through the mid-twentieth century, when it is challenged by the poststructuralists and postmodernists. This is perhaps the most significant break in recent Continental philosophy. Following Nietzsche, the poststructuralists revalue the ideals of liberty, equality, and fraternity and question humanity's self-determining power.

CHALLENGES TO THE ENLIGHTENMENT: ROUSSEAU AND ROMANTICISM

Jean-Jacques Rousseau (1712–78)[2] wrote contemporaneously with the Enlightenment thinkers, and although he accepts some of their positions, he inaugurates a new direction by challenging several of their doctrines: that history has produced improvements in human happiness and morality, that civilization and science are essential to such progress, and that a mechanistic understanding of nature is sufficient. Rousseau created a new vision of nature, suggesting that an emotional attunement to it can transfigure human existence. Because he idealized the "state of nature," he produced a re-evaluation of civilized life, suggesting that many features of civilization – especially property ownership, the division of labor, and the need to impress one's fellow citizens – corrupt the natural goodness of humanity. By re-establishing humanity's attunement to nature, he sought to restore that natural goodness.

Rousseau saw nature as a rustic, colorful realm with which people can commune and revitalize themselves. Beautiful and nourishing, nature is not a mystery to be deciphered (or a force to be tamed) by reduction to mechanistic laws. It establishes limits to human action, and the human body becomes strong and skillful by acknowledging those limits. Rousseau's pre-social, state-of-nature humans are rugged and healthy, independent, amoral, sexually unselective, and simple. Possessing minimal linguistic skills or theoretical intelligence, they lack the capacity to invent, but they are neither immoral nor vicious. They live in relative isolation, but during their chance encounters, they exhibit an open-hearted natural sympathy. Civilization represents a fall from this condition of innocence in two ways. It creates many dubious motivations – greed, envy, domination, other-directed pride, and shame – which produce various artificial needs, maladies, and discontents. In addition, because civilized life reduces hardship, humanity's natural strengths atrophy, and people become overly dependent on one another. Civilization produces a loss of natural self-esteem, replacing it with anxieties about others' evaluations.

Rousseau imagined a more probable genealogy of human culture than those envisioned by Hobbes or Locke. Moreover, he deepens his analysis by exploring the birth of several human capacities and institutions – language, emotions, rationality, inequality, and government. He divides cultural history into four stages. First, small settlements develop, offering individuals some degree of security and social intercourse. Here, families are the fundamental social units, and the primary division of labor is sexual. Humans retain their natural skills and enjoy the benefits of community without much loss. Natural inequalities of talent exist, and a primitive economic division of labor develops between toolmakers and the farmers who use the tools. These initial settlements retain a symbiosis with nature and improve security. Second, larger cities develop in order to protect against natural disasters. Property is instituted, and a greater division of labor emerges. Property allows natural inequalities of talent to become permanently entrenched, enabling people to become more selfish and more conspicuous in their public displays of wealth. Romantic love becomes one means by which women can dominate men in the domestic sphere. Asymmetries of wealth produce inequalities of power, and these may lead to class struggles. This second stage remains pre-political, however. When conflicts threaten communities, legal agreements resolve them without protracted struggles. Third, new political institutions emerge to protect existing property relations, institutionalizing unequal distributions of wealth. The wealthiest now rule with legitimate authority. The poor may gain modest security, but they sacrifice their right to a fair share of the wealth, mocking the state's claim to provide equal rights. Everyone becomes trapped in a system driven by greed that produces universal deception, other-direction, anxiety, and unhappiness. The wealthy fear losing their possessions and power; the impoverished feel resentful and disenfranchised.

Rousseau postulated a fourth stage in which the social contract would be renegotiated, and persons would become genuine participants in determining the policies and laws of the city-state. Direct participatory democracy would produce genuine freedom because citizens would collectively create the laws they must obey. Rousseau thus articulates a new conception of freedom. Instead of limiting personal freedom, democratically determined laws become freedom's necessary condition. Civilization finally produces benefits that may justify its existence. Rousseau distinguishes between enacting laws and administering them, suggesting that administration be delegated to respected, wise leaders. But enacting laws is a task for all citizens acting in concert; such participation will create a social unity and self-realization that could never be achieved in the state of nature. Rousseau believed that full democratic participation requires a small city-state. Citizens must be able to discuss and deliberate together collectively in order for the resulting legislation to be self-expressive.

Rousseau invented an approach to education that sought to resurrect humanity's natural virtues. He urged that children develop their talents and inquisitiveness through direct interaction with nature, solving the problems it sets for them. The educator's task is less to mold children by imposing conventional patterns than to stimulate their natural potentials – finding tasks that challenge and integrate these talents. He favored practical insight into nature's order over reading books and memorizing formulas. Educating the senses, the body, and character should take precedence over training the intellect. He noted that children must traverse various stages before reaching maturity, and advised that they be allowed to do this at their own pace and in their own fashion. Since he believed that the natural functions of men and women differ, he recommended a different educational regimen for women, emphasizing their nurturing abilities. Rousseau thus sought to counteract the evils of modern civilization through educational reforms. He structured education to prepare men for communal political participation and women for empathetic child rearing and companionship.

Rousseau also defended a different kind of aesthetic value from the one embraced by the Enlightenment, championing Italian over French opera (both as composer and critic). French opera is academic, complex, refined, full of mathematical harmonies, and populated by superior, heroic characters. Italian opera, on the other hand, is popular, accessible, full of easily remembered melodies that speak directly to the emotions, and is populated by ordinary, familiar characters. Italian opera evokes genuine feeling and has a universal appeal. Audiences can relate directly to its music and stories regardless of their education or refinement. Rousseau also favored participatory arts – like festivals, dances, and games – over spectator arts like theater. He embraced Italian opera because it evokes natural sympathy and emulates spontaneous attunement to nature. He thus sought to reform human culture through new forms of education, art, and political participation. Collectively crafted legislation would nurture a new kind of freedom and self-realization, while his favored forms of education and art would restore lost natural virtues.

Rousseau's concept of political participation influenced Kant's ideal of rational autonomy and provided a new justification for participatory democracy. Hegel and Marx later reinterpreted and extended Rousseau's participatory ideal, as did Hannah Arendt in the twentieth century. The Romantics and Schelling later ratified Rousseau's empathy and respect for nature. In addition, Rousseau's stance on artistic value remains a viable option today, and both Hegel and Western Marxists defend his claim that art is a culture's self-expression. Finally, in his hands the method of historical genealogy became a critical tool – a way of underscoring the potentially regressive results of history. Later, Nietzsche and Foucault refined and strengthened this method of challenging Enlightenment claims of historical progress. Even though Rousseau valued reason, it was the reason embedded in the beauty of nature that he loved. Nature demands a fundamentally different response from the prediction and control sought by natural science. Though Rousseau was unable to justify this alternative response, Schelling and Hegel later provided it with a rational foundation. Finally, Rousseau's challenge to the value of theoretical reason in education as well as his emphasis on the ethical importance of natural sympathy were central to the development of Romanticism and one strand of Continental ethical theory.

Romanticism – here represented by Herder (1744–1803),[3] Hamann (1730–88), and Goethe (1749–1832) – arose first in Germany as a reaction to the Enlightenment's confidence in reason and to the rise of mechanistic science, which reduced nature to mathematical formulas. The Romantics saw nature as a vast self-regulating organism. They stressed the value of emotions, artistic intuition, and human uniqueness – challenging hedonistic definitions of happiness. They contended that specific cultural traditions, distinctive local languages, and unique geographies more deeply condition communal life than reason's abstract rules and universal prescriptions. They valued the exotic, the primitive, the exceptional, and the irrational in human psychology, culture, and art, but they also saw some common features among people – e.g., the capacities for feeling, imagination, and sensation. They studied conditions for spiritual growth in both individuals and cultures, but also saw that cyclic decay is frequent. They challenged the assumption of historical progress with this cycle metaphor and with their belief that every historical era makes distinctive contributions.

The Romantics rejected the universal validity of the mechanistic assumptions of Newtonian physics. They offered skeptical rebukes to reason's claim to absolutely certain foundations. Insisting that knowledge encompass all aspects of human life – including art, morality, and religion – they argued that creative imagination and artistic insight are effective means for comprehending nature and humanity. Nature exhibits awesome beauty that inspires glorious poetry and soulful resonance, yet also embodies perilous dangers that may crush cities and threaten civilizations. The Romantics also foresaw the potential for chaos and social disorder, instead of the cultural harmony posited by Enlightenment reason. Technology could be a source of dull, routinized existence and a flattened, vapid sense of reality. They also feared that scientific determinism might undermine human freedom entirely. By construing nature more organically, the Romantics sought an almost spiritual bond with it.

They also challenged reason's usefulness in human affairs. Excessive rationality can deaden people's humanity, leaving them incapable of compassion, imagination, or subtlety. Emotion creates compelling social bonds and motivates exceptional human effort. Emotion inspires where reason stunts; emotion elicits moral responsiveness, while reason's principles are often ineffective in motivating moral action. The Romantics believed that nature's organic unity includes humanity and that thinkers (especially scientists) are artistic creators of reality, not merely discoverers of pre-existing reality. Though they sought to overcome some philosophical dichotomies central to Rationalism and Empiricism, some continued to divide the human psyche – opposing emotion and intuition to reason and thought. Herder, however, explored a holistic theory of mind that sought to integrate these apparently opposed states. And the nature to which poetic insight can be attuned remains distinct from the nature studied by scientists. Goethe tried to use scientific methods to produce a more holistic comprehension of perception that would correct and enrich the overly atomistic theories of the Empiricists.

The Romantics underlined the exotic and the unique in human nature and culture. These features defy rational analysis. Exploring the maturation of persons and cultures, they created a new literary genre – the *Bildüngsroman* – to examine this process in depth. A person's distinctive character emerges through complex interactions with nature and culture. When Enlightenment social theorists explained human actions, the Romantics contended that the laws they used were limited to stereotypical responses/situations and were incapable of grasping unique responses or atypical situations. They missed the contingency and complexity of human action. Thus scientific models often yield limited, artificial conclusions in human studies. The Romantics sought epiphanies – syntheses of cognition and intuition that would illuminate art, politics, and social life.

For the Romantics, each culture has its own traditions, language, character, and mentality. Consequently, social understanding must be contextual, utilizing the historical development of the culture. Each culture exhibits distinctive types of self-understanding, solutions to life's mysteries, and responses to the human constants of birth, childhood, marriage, child-rearing, and death. Scientific approaches often remain oblivious to historical context and contingencies, imposing a conception of universal human nature on all cultures. The Romantics scrutinize such universalistic claims carefully. Their heirs created a new approach to the study of persons and cultures that aimed to clarify the unique features of human action and culture: hermeneutics. Herder articulated some important general intuitions about the interpretive process that were later incorporated by Schleiermacher and Dilthey.

The Romantics claimed that growth requires struggle because it involves overcoming opposition. Such challenges may enliven heroic natures, but they can crush ordinary people. Moreover, the Romantics realized that victories are often temporary; even so great an empire as Rome fell, and its demise was followed by centuries of chaos and darkness. Insisting on the power of art to discover unique, nearly inexpressible truths, they acknowledged the rarity and preciousness of this capacity. They can be dismissive toward philistines. The pride of scientific reasoning is that it is accessible to all who educate themselves to it; any trained observer can verify its experiments and reasoning, and anyone can learn its method and results. But artistic insight and creativity are rarer and more mysterious, less readily shared. Such "privileged knowledge" can support an elitist, anti-democratic politics, but Herder resisted such tendencies, defending liberalism, egalitarianism, republicanism, and democracy. He also sought to make philosophy more accessible to ordinary people by explicitly rejecting the use of technical jargon.

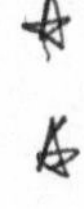

The legacy of Romanticism for post-Kantian Continental philosophy lies in its conceptions of self-expression and harmony and its stress on uniqueness and individuality. Self-expression plays a central role in the ethics of Hegel, Marx, and the existentialists, and existentialists also stress the central importance of individuals in opposition to rational systems of thought. These traditions typically seek to overcome the experience of disharmony with nature and culture, and they buttress the holistic vision of the Romantics. Romanticism challenges the dominance of natural science as a form of knowledge, and its effort to make art and literature – emotions and imagination – central to the knowing process also remained influential, especially to Hegel, Nietzsche, Dilthey, Scheler, and Heidegger. The goal of achieving harmony with nature and culture is retained by Hegel, Nietzsche, Heidegger, and Merleau-Ponty. While most Continental philosophers abandoned the idea that nature itself is the Absolute, they continued to explore the ways person and world co-constitute each other and thus cannot be conceived independently.

KANT

Immanuel Kant (1724–1804) hoped to resolve several contradictions between previous philosophical movements. He sensed the difficulties inherent in both Rationalism and Empiricism and tried to bridge the chasm between them while also circumventing Hume's skepticism and Romanticism's abandonment of reason for intuition. Like the Romantics, Kant argued for limits to pure reason, but unlike them he celebrated the achievements of scientific rationality. Although he embraced the scientific world-view, he believed that morality and aesthetic judgment could also be given rational foundations. His system reconciled determinism with human freedom, which he made the core of morality. He assigned creative imagination the role of uniting the two dimensions of reason – pure and practical. Kant also sensed that the French Revolution signaled the dawn of a new era, and felt that philosophy should provide guidance to this new age.

Kant defended his central claims in three books: *Critique of Pure Reason* (1781; revised 1787), *Critique of Practical Reason* (1788), and *Critique of Judgment* (1790). "Critique" here means both "to determine the limits of" and "to provide foundations for." Each book established the limits beyond which reason cannot legitimately go, yet also created solid foundations for it in the areas to which it can be justifiably applied. He believed that reason has an inveterate tendency to overstep its limits and engage in unverifiable, paradox-ridden speculation. He sought to terminate this temptation by demonstrating the anomalies of reason's exceeding its proper limits. His central claim was that reason *constitutes* the world of experience, as well as the moral world of ultimate ends; it does not merely inhabit a pre-given, pre-established world. This was Kant's "Copernican" revolution, which relocates the source of the coherence of experience from the object to the subject. It implied that reason could ground its own operations and justify its claims to knowledge; it need not depend on tradition, habit, dogma, or convention. Kant made many important advances, but he also left many unanswered questions. His immediate successors saw themselves as completing his project by resolving problems he neglected. I will sketch both his achievements and his system's problems.

In the *Critique of Pure Reason* Kant's central task was to show that the mind actively organizes everyday perception even though it is typically unaware of this ordering activity. Kant argued that human minds share universal structures that organize the perceived world by applying forms and categories to raw sensory input. Mental functions unify the perceived world through forms of intuition (space and time) and categories (cause, substance, etc.). Thus, the unity of the perceptual world is due not to its own inherent stability but to the necessary imposition of order on initially chaotic sensory streams. Kant also tried to show that his ordering functions supply the *only possible* coherence humans can impose and thus that everyone experiences a similarly ordered world, at least in its general outlines. Central to this argument is the "transcendental unity of apperception," which sustains the continuous operation of the forms and categories. Kant claimed that the functioning of these categories is a priori (i.e., prior to experience, rather than derived from it) since they are a precondition for the organization of experience. He also insisted that what exists prior to the operation of the categories (things-in-themselves) cannot be known; their nature lies beyond the limits of pure reason. Thus, though everyone is assured of constituting the world in a way similar to everyone else, no one has access to things-in-themselves (noumena), the entities that are the source of experience. Kant thus split the difference between Rationalism and Empiricism, positing a central role for "innate" ideas (categories and forms), but also defending the objectivity (or at least intersubjectivity) of the experienced world and the necessity of sensory input. Kant believed he had discovered a definitive answer to skepticism (since the mind cannot organize the world other than it does), but some contemporaries believed his position actually strengthened skepticism, at least about ultimate reality (things-in-themselves), because he claimed that it is forever inaccessible.

Kant suggested that the unity of this unconscious organizing activity is sustained by the transcendental ego. This too cannot be experienced (and thus is noumenal), but is a necessary condition for the proper operation of the categories. Since number is one of the categories, the transcendental ego is prenumerical and thus might be unindividuated. It might therefore encompass many empirical egos. Kant did not suggest this himself, but this is one possible way to interpret his position, one pursued by Fichte and Schelling. The empirical ego consists of a person's explicit memories, dispositions, character traits, volitions, beliefs, and desires. It is individuated, and it may have different degrees of coherence. The transcendental ego is otherworldly, like the noumena that are prior to experience, and for this reason it is also beyond deterministic causation because "cause" is a category imposed on experience. Thus, it guarantees the human autonomy so central in Kant's ethics. The transcendental ego also grounded the claim that all persons are ends in themselves. Even if it is not experienced, it must be respected, and it may support a rational faith in immortality. But this postulated ego removes humans from the natural order and leaves the relation between the transcendental ego and the empirical ego mysterious.

Kant distinguished the understanding (which is the synthetic activity of the categories on sensory input) from pure reason, which is speculation about the relationships among the categories themselves. The operation of the understanding produces substantive empirical knowledge, but the operation of pure reason does not. For Kant, pure reason requires critique because it often exceeds the boundaries of what anyone can genuinely hope to know. Kant demonstrated many different *antinomies* of pure reason, in which he shows that equally plausible arguments can be given for a metaphysical thesis *and* its contrary. His conclusion is that pure reason cannot decide between such conflicting claims, and indeed that no position on such issues can be correct because the questions are unanswerable. Kant hoped to halt these fruitless speculations. The most that pure reason can provide is a defensible set of *regulative ideas* – general cognitive goals that express plausible expectations about the order of the universe. By imposing limits on philosophical speculation, Kant inaugurated the task of ending abstract speculation in philosophy.

In ethics, Kant pursued a new approach. Instead of defining right action as action that produces the best consequences (thus making its rightness conditional on really achieving those consequences), he sought an unconditional source of duty in reason itself. To act rationally is to act autonomously – according to a valid maxim. Maxims are valid if they pass the universalization test – that is, if everyone in that situation can will them consistently. This "categorical" imperative will allegedly provide clear guidance concerning which actions are right or wrong. For example, if someone is considering whether to break a promise gratuitously, her maxim is "break promises whenever it is convenient." But if *everyone* were to act on this maxim, then this would undermine the entire institution of promise-making, and promising would become impossible. Thus, when universalizing a maxim leads to a practical contradiction, then any act based on such a maxim is wrong. Only actions based on maxims that can be universalized are right and dutiful because their motives have been purged of egoistic interests. Rational autonomy is good in itself; so it can support an objective notion of duty – acting solely on the basis of reason. Because all persons are capable of becoming purely rational, Kant concluded that all are worthy of respect and should be treated as an ends in themselves.

In addition, Kant insisted that truly moral actions must be performed solely because duty requires them and not because the agent desires to do them. Relying on desire cannot guarantee an unwavering commitment to duty. In opposition to the Empiricists, Kant believed that reason can motivate moral action on its own. Ultimately, his ethics is rooted in the agent's motivation. Kant thought the will could be pure only if it is entirely free of desire and inclination – because these introduce contingencies and dependencies. Kant sought an almost Buddhist withdrawal from chance and emotions. By disassociating from desires and needs (the empirical ego), persons can identify with the transcendental ego and achieve full autonomy and purity. An agent's will becomes free only when it acts like any rational person would act, and such rational actions are absolutely valid. Other agents can choose to join this moral world insofar as they too act in accord with reason's demands. Obeying duty produces freedom because reason generates its own law – rather than following externally motivated laws. When the action is motivated by purified reason (purged of all desire), then Kant believed it would be genuinely self-determined. In a fully ethical community, all persons determine themselves to act rationally and freely in this way. Kant claimed that achieving this rational autonomy is a continuous task of self-perfection. That is one primary duty; another is to contribute to other people's happiness.

Unfortunately, there is no guarantee that someone who acts according to this stringent conception of duty will achieve happiness in her lifetime. Consequently, Kant postulated the existence of a God who will assure the ultimate happiness of such people. Moreover, in order to insure that such happiness can be appreciated, Kant claimed that the soul (the transcendental ego) must be immortal. Thus freedom (autonomy), God, and an immortal soul are necessary preconditions of morality. If morality is to be legitimate, these preconditions must be accepted. This was Kant's rational faith. These religious postulates were needed solely to support morality. Both God and the soul are noumenal and hence cannot be known. They require faith. Kant believed that no other features of God could be known. He did not notice that insuring such a reward for moral goodness means that the dutiful person cannot be known to choose duty solely for the sake of duty, rather than for the reward of eternal bliss. Kant's postulate of immortality thus created a tension in his theory of moral motivation.

Finally, Kant looked to creative imagination and aesthetic judgment to unify the operations of understanding and reason, the phenomenal and the noumenal realms. For Kant, aesthetic contemplation involves disinterested delight: it has no goal outside itself (and thus it tutors people to comprehend moral autonomy). Because it is disinterested, its results will usually be shared, not because of a common imposition of categories but because idiosyncratic factors have been expunged from the evaluation. In aesthetic judgment, reason thus operates freely, in a kind of play with itself. Judgment is also needed to understand organic wholes, like animate organisms. Kant thought the basis for this a priori sense of organic unity is the experience of intentional action, which organizes and integrates a plurality of factors seamlessly. Kant denied that these unities require any new principles of order. Finally, he suggested that the unity of nature is a regulative goal that science will probably confirm, rather than a constitutive rule of reason that is imposed on experience.

Kant also defended two important political goals. First, following Rousseau, he hoped that nation-states would become republics, with significant political participation. Then the public law – not just the moral law – would derive from freely adopted legislation by citizens. Second, he suggested that these republics create an international league of nations to regulate international affairs through law rather than violence. He believed that perpetual peace could be a realistic possibility.

Kant thus noted that people are capable of two perspectives on themselves. They embody the perspective of natural science and causality which is produced by the operation of the categories of understanding, and they also can adopt a transcendental perspective in which they are rational and self-legislating, which is produced by purging the empirical ego of its idiosyncratic elements and acting on this purified will. Kant follows Rousseau in thinking that democratic participation in politics can transform public law from an external coercive force to a free, self-expressive union of citizens. But even if humanity were able to create a moral and political world order, it would still inhabit a noumenal world that it did not create and cannot know. Humanity is capable of significant achievements, but it also must live within real limits.

Overcoming this divided condition is the central goal of the philosophical systems of Fichte, Schelling, and Hegel. Fichte rethought Kant's moral theory; Schelling reconceived Kant's philosophy of nature; and Hegel reworked everything. Kant's conception of an unconscious universal system of categories is further developed by structuralism. Phenomenology continues Kant's investigations by clarifying relationships between mental acts and their objects. Nietzsche and Gadamer further explore the role of creative imagination in relating theoretical and practical reason. Sartre follows Kant in making freedom the heart of his ethics, and Foucault adopts Kant's ideal of self-criticism.

PROBLEMS WITH KANT'S SYSTEM

Kant's philosophy seems like a towering achievement today, but it was hotly debated in his day, and many weaknesses became apparent as a result. These weaknesses paved the way for Fichte's and Schelling's efforts to repair Kant's deficiencies, and eventually for the system that truly inaugurates contemporary Continental philosophy – Hegel's. I will indicate some of these weaknesses so that the goals of Kant's successors can be better understood.

The deepest problem concerns the status of noumena (things-in-themselves), especially the fact that they are supposed to *cause* sensory input when cause is allegedly an a priori category that can only be applied *after* such input is received. Since the concept of cause only organizes input phenomena, speaking of causal relations between noumena and human organisms should be unintelligible (not to mention that it violates Kant's stricture against claiming to know anything about noumena). Kant never successfully relates consciousness and fundamental reality. Noumena remain mysterious, and ultimately Kant fails to answer skepticism.

Equally important are the internal disharmonies that plague Kant's system. Though aesthetic judgment is supposed to unify reason and understanding, arguably Kant neglects to show how this happens. Moreover, Kant seems unable to unify the major fractures between theoretical and practical reason, science and morality, desire and pure will, and the transcendental and empirical egos. Though Kant needs these divisions to preserve science and morality, many critics believed that he sidestepped rather than resolved their tensions. For example, how does noumenal free will produce bodily action in the phenomenal world of empirical causes? Or what kind of human sciences are possible if an important element of persons is noumenal? In addition, Kant provides no explanation for why there are twelve and only twelve categories, nor why they are the only categories through which the mind might organize sensory input. Post-Kantian philosophers sought to formulate a more integrated system of categories while answering the questions Kant left unaddressed.

A third problem involves the relationship among the transcendental egos of different persons and between the transcendental ego and the empirical ego of a single person. If the transcendental ego is noumenal and thus unknowable, how can Kant know that it individuates like empirical egos (like human bodies)? Perhaps it is a higher-order subject that unites individuals into larger wholes. Beyond this, even if phenomenal experience is constituted by the operation of the concepts, this cannot be the manner in which the *transcendental* egos of other people are encountered and justified. Others' transcendental egos cannot be experienced; they are beyond experience, like all transcendental entities. But other people cannot be regarded as fully human unless they possess similar transcendental functions; yet how can Kant claim to know this if transcendental operations are beyond experience? Thus, Kant is threatened with solipsism (and his ethical kingdom of ends may implode) unless he can demonstrate what he insists is impossible: that other people's transcendental egos can be known.

Questions about the role of reason and the independence of the categories from historical/cultural influences suggest additional problems. Some of Kant's heirs believed that pure reason might achieve more than Kant expected. Perhaps they could resolve the antinomies or integrate the categories into a unified system. Though the metaphysical dilemmas that motivated Kant to impose limits to reason could not be ignored, some still defended philosophical speculation. In addition, Kant claimed that his categories ground history, culture, and language like all other empirical phenomena, but perhaps alien cultures, non-European natural languages, and domineering historical forces can transform the categories themselves. Kant avoided this possibility by insisting that the categories are a priori, universal rules of the human mind, but can this claim be proven? Perhaps even the deepest elements of human understanding are affected by historical factors and social conditions. Many later Continental figures acknowledge such influences.

In ethics, many maxims that might inform the same action – some of them completely contradictory – seem capable of passing the universalization test. Thus Kant's test fails to provide sufficient concrete guidance because it does not explain how to identify the unique maxim of the act. Moreover, the notion of practical incoherence or "contradiction" on which the universalization test depends is poorly explicated. (If everyone were to lie, would the practice of talking dissolve? Isn't some degree of lying the normal case?) In addition, critics doubted whether people could divorce themselves from their desires in the way Kant's ethics demands. If this requirement is impossible to fulfill in practice, can it be taken as a legitimate moral ideal? To do so would imply that a serious ethical person would experience endless frustration and disillusionment, possibly resulting in the complete rejection of morality. In addition, when Kant tries to insure that those who live for duty's sake alone will eventually be rewarded with eternal happiness, he violates his own motivational strictures because his postulate encourages moral agents to seek this reward rather than be motivated by duty alone. If happiness (or the satisfaction of desires) is alien to morality, then why should Kant care whether there is any guarantee of happiness for dutiful agents?

Kant's system answers questions generated internally by his own assumptions. But can the philosopher's standpoint be shown to develop out of the everyday, common-sense standpoint of ordinary life? Why should the results produced by a grand system like Kant's matter to everyday practice and science? Kant's successors sought to demonstrate a clear path between everyday experience and the philosopher's standpoint so that the results of the latter would have value for the former. Similarly, Kant's God was consigned to the relatively minor role of sustaining morality. Kant's successors sought a concept of the Absolute (or infinite) that would inform and incorporate all spheres of the finite: nature, consciousness, reason, history, social life, and art. They rejected Kant's division between ultimate reality and the spheres of finite life. By permitting unresolved divisions between kinds of rationality (theoretical, practical, aesthetic), Kant fails to integrate the various dimensions of human life. His successors sought to comprehend its fundamental structures and to integrate them.

Though Fichte sought the fundamental principle in the dynamics of the ego, Schelling described distinctive principles informing nature and art and integrated these with Fichte's principles of self-consciousness.[4] Hegel discovered a conceptual system informing all these areas (and more) and showed how ordinary consciousness could comprehend this conceptual system for itself (and as its own principle of development).

FICHTE

Johann Gottleib Fichte (1762–1814) developed a system in which every claim flowed from a single principle. The system was perpetually reworked in order to better approximate an ideal form for its presentation. He discovered his fundamental principle at the core of Kant's system: the transcendental unity of apperception, the source of self-identity. One of Kant's central claims is that the unity of the perceived world presupposes the unity of the ego – the ego sustains the world's coherence. Fichte discovered a different way to show the relative dependence of the world on the transcendental ego. He interpreted this ego as a dynamic, active process that is both self-aware (subject) and self-expressed (object) at once. It establishes its existence as it acts; for this reason it is not dependent on anything else, and thus is "absolute." This "self-positing," active ego is prior to the distinction between subject and object, knower and known. It is grasped through an *intellectual intuition* that reveals the underlying structure of reality. The transcendental ego authorizes itself to institute norms that will govern empirical action. Fichte thus extended Kant's metaphor for understanding – that it organizes and unifies the world – to *practical action*, for the *will* gives shape and order to the world even more directly than the intellect does. This "shaping" metaphor allowed Fichte to unify all mental operations (thought, action, creativity) under one basic concept: *striving*. The transcendental ego strives to realize itself in all human activity: knowing, acting, and creating. Because striving characterizes both desire and reflective rule-following, it provides foundations for a unified theory of human nature, a way of integrating duty and desire.

Because his philosophical goal was to unify subject and object, Fichte considered the possibility that subjectivity might be derived from the structures of objectivity. He called this alternative "dogmatism," and rejected it because he believed it would ultimately lead to determinism, reductionism, and the death of subjectivity. Like Kant, Fichte defended human freedom against determinism. He believed that persons possess indubitable awareness of their own freedom as they strive to realize their goals; these are everyday empirical glimmers of the deeper operations of the transcendental ego. His task was to elucidate the facts of ordinary experience – including the apparent independence of the objective world and the body's adaptation to it – using the operations of the transcendental ego. He offered several different "deductions" of these everyday facts. I will describe only one of these here.

The transcendental ego exists only in striving for self-realization, in pure activity; it has no existence prior to its activity and thus is not a substance. It exists by constantly striving for self-actualization, thus "positing" itself. But it cannot realize itself without opposition and something to shape. The transcendental ego (which is pre-personal and unindividuated) thus requires the not-I (the objective world) because the not-I provides a medium in which to express itself and a resistance that makes its operations meaningful. The tendency of these two extremes (I and not-I), however, is to oppose and destroy each other; so the transcendental ego consciously limits itself (thus producing empirical egos) and limits the not-I. It thus both distinguishes and relates empirical egos and the world, allowing them to condition one another. Empirical egos are unaware of these prior operations of the transcendental ego; yet philosophy can discover their necessity through intellectual intuition. Empirical egos naively strive to realize themselves without any awareness of the transcendental ego, but their striving realizes that of the transcendental ego. Thus, philosophical intuition contributes both to humanity's mature awareness of its own underlying unity with the world and to the developing self-awareness of the transcendental ego. Humans experience a world that seems independent even though its existence serves the transcendental ego. The deep connection between empirical human beings and the transcendental ego lies in the experience of striving itself. By realizing their ends, individual persons enhance the maturation and self-understanding of the transcendental ego.

Like Kant, Fichte believed that the highest form of freedom is achieving goals that are inherently good, that are not merely particular expressions of desire, but manifestations of autonomy. He valued striving for its own sake because it embodied pure freedom. The actualization of the transcendental ego is thus a continuous process of striving and transformation, a process that unifies actions with their achievements, producing harmony between subject and object. The heart of morality, for Fichte, is conscience, in which empirical egos become aware of the transcendental ego's striving for autonomy and strive to emulate it. Ethical debate helps individuals to discover inherent goods; conscience shows how to achieve them. Individuals elevate themselves to moral personhood through participating in this self-expressive process. Fichte deduced some very general duties from the preconditions of striving; for example, since action requires a healthy body, it should not be harmed or mutilated. Full ethical action, however, cannot occur in isolation; it requires mutual recognition of the autonomy of self-conscious persons.

Individuals can enhance the transcendental ego's freedom by creating moral communities that produce mutual recognition among their members. Recognition also produces communal identity and thus enhances each member's self-consciousness. Recognition arises through a mutual process of appeal. Each appeals to others to limit themselves so that everyone's freedom will have opportunities for self-expression. When others respond to this appeal, they act freely; so they can also be recognized while they acknowledge the appealer's freedom. Thus, both the appealer and the responder realize each other's freedom. They establish norms mutually by recognizing each other as legitimate creators of norms. Recognition allows the group to enact laws in which all members can experience themselves expressed (thus, free) and to establish a system of rights. The state exists to protect such laws and individuals' rights to act according to their consciences. The state is also obligated to assist citizens' self-realization through education and by providing work suited to their individual talents. This essentially intersubjective realization of self-consciousness is one of Fichte's great contributions to the Continental tradition. Hegel developed and expanded this idea, and several other Continental theorists identified additional internal relationships between people (e.g., Scheler, Heidegger, and Sartre).

Fichte also developed a theory of historical development in which freedom is gradually realized through increasingly rational action. Primitive humans strove to achieve various goals unreflectively. Then an authoritarian minority imposed a single will on the masses. This, in turn, produced a rebellion that challenged the minority's dominance. After a period of struggle, people come to recognize each other's freedom, which produces the social basis for rational policies and the state. Finally, the state encourages the full realization of a moral community and facilitates individual self-expression.

Fichte thus created the groundwork for Hegel's theory of recognition and theory of history. He also demonstrated one possible way of achieving harmony between subject and object, a goal pursued by many later Continental movements. Fichte's conception of striving anticipates Schopenhauer's metaphysics of will and Marx's claims that praxis is the essence of humanity and that history is the collective praxis of human communities. His support for a state-organized economy provided an early rationale for the socialist ideal. His theory of self-consciousness anticipates later discussions of this capacity in phenomenology (in Scheler, for example) and existentialism (especially in Sartre). Sartre developed Fichte's emphasis on human freedom.

Fichte emphasizes the operations of subjectivity (the transcendental ego) in unifying mind and world. Schelling stresses the organic quality of nature to achieve the same goal.

SCHELLING

Friedrich Wilhelm Joseph Schelling (1775–1854) was a friend to both Hegel and Hölderlin (they were roommates in school). He was a genuine prodigy with widespread interests and a fertile mind. He had strong ties to August and Friedrich Schlegel and Novalis (proponents of the Romantic world-view), and he arrived at Jena in 1798 as Professor (at age 23) just before Fichte was forced to resign on trumped-up charges of "atheism." In his twenties, Schelling published several systems of philosophy. He helped Hegel obtain a minor university post in 1801 and co-edited the *Critical Journal of Philosophy* with him from 1802 to 1804. Although Schelling incorporated Fichte's striving, self-expressive ego, he also sought to integrate nature, art, history, religion, and myth into his system.

Two central differences between Fichte and Schelling concern nature and art. For Fichte, nature was little more than an inert realm that offered resistance to moral action, but for Schelling nature exhibited an inherent, dynamic, self-organizing quality that anticipated the structure of self-consciousness. This self-ordering allowed Schelling to construe nature and mind as manifestations of the same self-active principle. Schelling's early systems developed this view of nature as implicit mind. In addition, Fichte believed the truest form of self-realization was moral self-perfection, while Schelling gave artistic creation this status. The artist's finished creation endures and exhibits an organic unity unparalleled by moral achievements, and it deepens the artist's self-understanding. Schelling interpreted the Absolute's self-realization on this model of artistic creation, instead of using Fichte's model of moral striving.

Although Fichte started from the transcendental ego's self-active nature, he acknowledged that a similar unification of subject and object might be achieved by starting from the not-I (or nature). Schelling asserted the equivalence of these starting points, and thus rejected the transcendental ego's primacy. Because Schelling conceived nature to be self-active (implicit mind), he believed that one could experience the unity of the transcendental ego with nature through intellectual intuition. Schelling conjectured that mind and nature are exemplifications of a single dynamic principle that divides itself into subject and object and then reunites them. Schelling noted that an artistic idea takes root in the artist's mind and in the artistic object simultaneously, each refining the other during creation. Since art realizes the artist's self-consciousness and shapes materials into coherent unity, art integrates mind and nature by making them express each another.

Schelling concluded that the primordial principle (or Absolute) is an intermingling of subjectivity and objectivity, which when expressed as nature allows objectivity to predominate, but when expressed as mind allows subjectivity to predominate. Subjectivity and objectivity are alternate perspectives on the Absolute. Art shows how the real and ideal are united in the present, an achievement that Fichte had to postpone into the indefinite future – when a moral community of mutual recognizers could be achieved. The Absolute cannot be known because knowledge presupposes the division between subject and object. Instead, the Absolute had to be intuited rather than proven, like the idea animating an artwork must be intuited, rather than deduced. Schelling sought to dissolve philosophical problems, rather than solve them on their own terms. The presuppositions that generate the problem must be challenged, and change at the most basic philosophical level only happens via a change in perspective, which is achieved only through intuition, not argument. Schelling believed that art is superior to philosophy because it exhibits a concrete intelligence, rather than abstract understanding: it *recreates* the world, rather than merely understanding it (theory) or transforming it (moral action).

Schelling interpreted nature as an organic whole – stressing organisms' life cycles and maturation. He interpreted nature in a way that revealed a self-relatedness that is typical of mind (self-loss and self-recovery); mind simply amplifies the negation and reintegration in this self-relation. Schelling's central category in elucidating nature was force, and he used it to unite various natural sciences. He conceived force as pure activity, much like Fichte conceived the ego, and this allowed him to interpret nature (object) and self-consciousness (subject) as manifestations of one principle. Nature consists of a myriad of conflicting forces which eventually reach equilibrium. When this happens, nature elevates itself to a new level of complexity, and the conflict of opposing forces recommences. The lowest levels of mind develop from the highest levels of nature. Intellectual intuition makes this identity of nature and mind fully explicit, and this allows the empirical ego to experience a harmony with nature that is impossible to experience on the mechanistic model of nature favored by Newton and Kant. Schelling also believed that nature becomes richer and more complex as it develops (as does self-consciousness); in this way too they are structurally similar.

Schelling defined the transcendental ego using the principle of identity (I = I). Hegel later pilloried this "identity" claim as a reductive and superficial form of unity ("the night in which all cows are black"), but Schelling gave the formula an active interpretation. Identity is self-activity, in which something achieves full self-expression. Schelling believed that an intellectual intuition would be necessary to comprehend these dynamic identities and to grasp the interlocking self-organization in nature, art, history, and self-consciousness. "Development" plays a key role in Schelling's entire system, as it does in Hegel's. Schelling organized mental capacities in ascending order to explain the development of human cognition. Beginning with sensation, he proceeded through imagination to reflection, and finally to will and reason. Sensory feeling exhibits the most unmediated relationship humans can have with nature, and the higher-order mental functions achieve more mediated forms of connection. Schelling thus took some initial steps toward a phenomenology of spirit in Hegel's sense. Like Fichte, Schelling also developed a theory of stages of historical development, with a final stage – a full realization of freedom – defined by a world-federation in which every citizen participates.

In a late essay on freedom, Schelling investigated the problem of evil. He believed that evil must exist if real freedom and moral goodness are to exist. Humanity must be capable of choosing evil in order to be able to choose the good. But since God is the source of all that exists, he must contain some element of evil in order to create it. Yet if God is perfect, he cannot be evil. So there must be a dark part of God that is prior to God. God must therefore have a ground that allows light and dark to coexist but that is not identical with God (who must be all-light). Thus, God has an element of non-identity or difference within Himself. Humanity too has a dark element – blind impulse – that is opposed to freedom and reason. Schelling interpreted evil to be the means by which God redeems creation and recovers unity with himself. Humanity is the means of overcoming evil and thus participates in God's self-realization. Humanity must overcome evil if God's unity is to be restored. These abstract theological speculations demonstrate humanity's role in God's reconciliation with existence. They also indicate how ultimate reality (or the Absolute) can be conceived as already fractured or divided within itself and thus in need of reunification and why human self-realization is the primary means by which the Absolute recovers its self-identity. These features also become important in Hegel's system.

Schelling's belief in the importance of art both drew on and reinforced similar views in the Romantic movement. This emphasis continued in later Continental thinkers like Schopenhauer, Nietzsche, Heidegger, and Lyotard.

Schelling's notion that philosophical problems must be dissolved rather than solved anticipates similar views in Hegel, Nietzsche, Heidegger, and Derrida. His understanding of the continuity of mind and nature is developed by the later Continental movement, Philosophical Anthropology, and by the phenomenologist Merleau-Ponty. Hegel owes more to Schelling than he sometimes admits, even if he stresses the centrality of reason and philosophy over intuition and art. Schelling himself drew on key insights reached by Hölderlin, and to close this introductory survey, I turn to his position.

HÖLDERLIN, NOVALIS, AND SCHILLER

Schelling borrowed some of his ideas about nature and art from his friend, the poet Friedrich Hölderlin (1770–1843), and another poet, Novalis (1772–1801). Hölderlin loved Greek culture and the polis, and he also saw nature as a living organism. He saw an important paradox in Fichte's position: since Fichte's ego needs to posit the not-I (world) as resistance against which to realize itself, if that ego fully realized itself (thus conquering the world entirely), then it would cease to exist. Hölderlin saw that human life oscillates between a pre-reflective sense of immersion in the world (an innocent harmony with it) and a reflective sense of distance from the world and oneself. Humans live both viewpoints simultaneously. Self-consciousness is pulled in both directions, toward unity and toward withdrawal; it must learn to abide with this dissonance, which cognition cannot resolve. Only the beauty of art and poetry can render this dissonance tolerable; it allows humanity to see the way that the reflective and the pre-reflective develop each other, even if no final resolution is possible between them.

In addition, Hölderlin realized that self-consciousness cannot be the most fundamental being. Since it exists divided within itself between an I-subject and an I-object and can only exist in relation to an object, there must be some more basic sense of unity that accounts for self-identity over time. This unity cannot be known directly because knowing presupposes a differentiation between subject and object; the unity can only be intuited with the help of art. It underlies not only all experience of self-identity, but also all experience of identity in general. Thus, it attunes one to being itself, not only to one's own being. This "ground" is a precondition for reflection that can only be suggested or hinted or intuited, not explicitly, rationally demonstrated. To the extent that one can recover contact with this primordial unity, it is transformative. Not only does it make possible a sense of harmony with nature; it provides direction in one's life: one seeks to recover this unity. Art and beauty allow people to experience this deeper unity, and this experience awakens people to what is truly important in their lives. Two everyday experiences can suggest this primordial experience: love and art. Love binds one to the beloved without erasing his or her sense of difference. Beauty makes visible a unity that underlies what seems merely fragmentary and disconnected; it refashions the everyday world.

Novalis (Friedrich Leopold Freiherr von Hardenberg), also a notable poet, believed people could have a felt intuition of their own being, and he too believed it could not be given further philosophical elucidation. This experience emerges in a form of pre-reflective consciousness as it confronts the givenness of the I. In reacting to this givenness, consciousness objectifies the I, making access to its true nature impossible. The being of the I is beyond words, primarily because it is eternal, while ordinary human life is temporal. Because this self-givenness cannot be further elucidated, it cannot serve as a first principle in philosophy; one can only acknowledge one's distance from it and learn to accept it. In comparison with this self-givenness, actual human life is always contingent, incomplete, and finite. Because of this, the only possible form for philosophy is the fragment, a partial capture of an elusive experience that can never be completed. Novalis developed a theory of literary interpretation that utilized the same principle: interpretations can only be partial perspectives on the full meaning of the text; interpretation is thus a never-ending task. Novalis also believed distinctive philosophical insights could emerge as people "thought together" in intensive discussion; he called this practice symphilosophy and contrasted its potential with the abstract thinking that often is produced by philosophers working in isolation. Finally, he saw that much of everyday life was repetitive, task-oriented busy-work, and he sought a more authentic form of living in the world that seriously confronted the truth of the human condition, that acknowledged that self-being is both given and elusive and that a new form of self-directness (or freedom) could emerge from this acknowledgment.

No less devoted to clarifying the role of art in human cultivation was Johann Christoph Friedrich von Schiller (1759–1805). Schiller believed art's central task is to transform human faculties through the appreciation of organic unity. Ultimately this would create deeper connections between individuals and their communities. He praised poetry for depicting inspiring myths that can guide the future. He notes that philosophers must begin from first principles that cannot be rationally defended, and claimed that only poets could provide the necessary intuitions to make such principles compelling. Schiller believed art's role in culture is a harmonizing one, and its role in the lives of individuals is to encourage self-integration because it can unify reason and sensibility. Thus, art avoids the twin excesses of intellectualism and sensualism. Crucial to art is the free play of the imagination, which releases consciousness from the limitations of both reason and sensation. This free play responds to reality's givenness, but nonetheless responds creatively, thus completing or refining the merely given. Actuality is a combination of what imagination makes of the sensory givens; it is neither merely given nor wholly created; instead, it combines both forms of consciousness. Art, for both Schiller and Schelling, is the richest expression of human life, a creation that expresses the core of human uniqueness.

HEGEL

CORE CONTRIBUTIONS

Kant left the German Idealists a system riddled with dichotomies that threatened to undermine his achievements. Fichte, Schelling, and Hölderlin struggled to bridge those rigid oppositions. The first of Hegel's important contributions is to complete that project by showing how those dichotomies could be overcome. He resolves oppositions such as individual–society, desire–virtue, mind–world, reason–passion, god–humanity, and even subject–object, in various ways: sometimes by showing that the opposition itself is unstable and vanishes, sometimes by demonstrating that each term presupposes the other and thus cannot be conceived in isolation, sometimes by discovering the underlying whole from which both terms derive. These dichotomies often reinforced the very skepticism that Kant sought to overcome; Hegel's resolutions produced philosophical renewal. If individuals and societies, for example, presuppose each other for their complete realization, individuals must creatively sustain social order, and social order makes possible the full realization of individual freedom. This conclusion alters the landscape of social philosophy. If the world's depth and complexity derive both from mind's cognitive amplifications and practical transformations, while the mind's categories and practical capacities exist because of the world's structure and resistance, then they sustain and enrich each other. If Hegel's stand-in for God – the system of categories which inform all spheres, including nature, history, society, consciousness, and logic – requires humanity's comprehension in order to come to fruition and self-comprehension, and if humanity can only reach that high pinnacle by achieving the cognitive, ethical, and social maturation enabled by that system of categories, then ultimate reality and humanity co-constitute each other. Transcending these dichotomies creates new ways of doing philosophy – which consign analysis and distinction-making at best to the first phase of serious philosophical investigation.

Hegel's second contribution is to provide an educational pathway toward the standpoint from which the truth of his system can be appreciated. This is the project of his first book, *Phenomenology of Spirit* (1807).[1] There he shows that his philosophical standpoint and conclusions derive from the inadequacies of previous positions and also that his system retains their best insights. The historical-cultural and cognitive development of humanity are necessary to achieve Hegel's philosophical standpoint, but individuals can retrace in their own maturation the steps by which human history made Hegel's achievements possible. Moreover, he notes that this path is treacherous, even if its final achievement is harmony. Indeed, it involves conflict, struggle, and despair as the hopes and assumptions of previous forms of life (and intellectual outlooks) are dashed and disproven. From these ashes emerges a stronger, suppler system that can perhaps withstand skeptical objections. Hegel makes philosophy accessible to any serious thinker; yet he shows it to be an adventure – requiring insight and boldness. Previous philosophers made little effort to provide a bridge between everyday thought and their own conclusions. Hegel sought to subsume everyday understanding as well as previous philosophical outlooks. Moreover, his approach to history allows him to articulate the achievements of previous eras and forms of life while maintaining a progressive vision that sees history culminating in the realization of freedom, the most revered modern ideal.

Hegel's third contribution is the idea of an underlying dynamic system of categories that informs the development of many spheres of reality: nature, social life, world-history, art, religion, philosophy, and personhood itself. This system integrates Hegel's insights into each of these spheres and allows him to articulate a unique approach to each – based on the logical development from simple to complex, from unmediated to mediated. Some critics believe that Hegel's system is too diagrammatic and abstract and that he often forces the content of these spheres into rigid forms. But he strives to enter into the concrete elements of each sphere in order to discover the central oppositions and presuppositions that give his patterns purchase. Although he did not publish treatises on all these spheres, he did produce his *Encyclopedia of Philosophical Sciences* (1817),[2] which includes his system's logic, its applications to nature, psychological development, and cultural development, and his *Outlines of a Philosophy of Right* (1820),[3] which includes its application to social-political theory. His students preserved his rich analyses of religion, art, and the history of philosophy. Hegel reinvigorates the ideal of a truly systematic vision in philosophy, which cannot be equaled by isolated treatments of problems or concatenations of pithy insights.

Another important contribution is to social theory – the concept of recognition. Through recognition, individuals can achieve social unity and in the process attain a new level of personal development. Hegel shows that social unity need not come at the price of individuality. He thus explores issues in social ontology – e.g., the nature of social bonds, the fundamental constituents of culture, and the presuppositions of law and legitimacy. In doing so, he establishes the foundations of sociology. For Hegel, social life is an essential part of philosophy because ideas and forms of life depend on social structure and practices. He rejects several simplifying assumptions made by many social theorists – a reliance on methodological individualism and psychological egoism – and their failure to understand how individual action and social structure support and require each other. His innovations in social theory insured that Continental philosophy would remain in critical dialogue with the social sciences – contributing to their development, enhancing their self-understanding, and overcoming their shortcomings.

A fifth contribution derives from his reflections on the historical development of Europe, which allowed him to determine the unique features of the modern era – still in many respects our own era. Hegel realizes, for example, that the notion of an individual is a modern achievement, as were many of his own conceptions (e.g., development, supersession). Moreover, his historical reflections allow him to describe some key problems of modernity: the dangers of alienation, the domination of instrumental reason, poverty, unemployment, and nationalism. Though he does not always find their solutions, at least he locates many crucial problems. He also identifies the governing ideal of modernity – freedom – and provides a deeper analysis of its nature and conditions. He argues that freedom requires self-realization and self-expression – a harmony with one's surroundings – not just the absence of obstacles, the fulfillment of desires, or the provision of choices. This allows him to achieve a critical perspective on the significance of democracy, capitalism, revolutionary fervor, bureaucracy, and work in modern life. Thus, Hegel insures that the problems and aspirations of modernity will become central issues for later Continental philosophy.

LIFE

Born in 1770 in Stuttgart, Hegel was an excellent student who received a scholarship to study at a famous seminary in Tübingen. There he befriended the poet Hölderlin and also Schelling, who rose to national fame quickly. After his university studies, Hegel served as a private tutor in Berne (Switzerland) and Frankfurt. In this period he sketched his early ideas on religion and ethics in essays published posthumously as *Early Theological Writings*.[4] When his father died in 1799, leaving him a modest inheritance, he decided to join Schelling at the University in Jena, also the center of Goethe's influence. Hegel published some modest essays in a journal he co-edited with Schelling, and lectured privately, without an official university post. He worked on early versions of his system during this period. His first major publication was the *Phenomenology of Spirit* (1807), which he finished just as Napoleon invaded Jena. Even though Napoleon closed the university, Hegel was enthusiastic about his leadership. He later accepted a position as headmaster at a high school in Nuremberg (1808–15), where he attempted to distill his complex ideas for students at that level. While there, he published *The Science of Logic*[5] in three volumes (1812, 1813, 1816). On the strength of this work, in 1816, he was finally appointed Professor of Philosophy at Heidelberg. There he published his *Encyclopedia of Philosophical Sciences* (1817; revised 1827 and 1830), as a textbook to supplement his lectures. With his reputation finally rising, he was called to Berlin to accept a chair in Philosophy in 1818. He lectured on philosophy of history, philosophy of religion, philosophy of art, and the history of philosophy, and published his *Philosophy of Right* (1820) to accompany his lectures in political philosophy. His students preserved these lecture cycles, and in this form they were published after his untimely death in 1831. He had served as rector of the University of Berlin for one year.[6]

THE PHENOMENOLOGY OF SPIRIT

The *Phenomenology* (1807) is both an introduction to Hegel's system and an application of its main ideas. It is a daunting book. Part of its difficulty lies in Hegel's use of abstract concepts to discuss several different positions simultaneously, making the book seem overly compressed. Moreover, Hegel's language is alien and technical, often reading like a foreign language even in translation. In order to provide an overview of the book's purposes, I will concentrate on the relatively accessible Introduction and the first half of the Self-consciousness section, perhaps the most famous section of the book.

Hegel's introduction

The aim of the book is to exhibit the path by which anyone who thinks seriously can reach the standpoint that will yield knowledge of ultimate reality. This path contains five major steps: Consciousness, Self-consciousness, Reason, Spirit, and Religion, each of which is both a way of knowing and of living. The person who takes this journey learns from every step, but none is fully successful in its own terms. These internal failures drive the earnest traveler further along the road until Hegel's standpoint is reached.[7] In retrospect, the traveler learns that the journey contains clues to the nature of ultimate reality and is actually governed by its patterns. The elucidation of ultimate reality – the system of concepts that informs nature, mind, and history – is reserved for *The Science of Logic*. The *Phenomenology* discovers the standpoint from which the *Logic* can be understood, and provides some of its substance.

Hegel's main achievement is to show that most ways of knowing/living fail on internal grounds. Each has its own standard of success, and each finds itself lacking on that basis.[8] Thus, Hegel rejects the typical critical strategy of using external standards to evaluate different ways of knowing/living. Rather, he shows that each fails to meet its own standard and that these failures ultimately lead to his own standpoint, which successfully satisfies its standard. Hence the *Phenomenology* is an ordered presentation of stages in the development of knowing/living; the failure of each plausibly leads to the next step, until a final step yields Hegel's own perspective. Hegel thus "derives" his own perspective from the previous failures. Each new stage emerges with its own new standard, creating a new strategy for knowing/living. The new stage/standard is a logical development of the dissolution of the old one.[9] Hegel calls this pattern "determinate negation," meaning that the failure of each stage leads in a specific direction. The full development of these stages often takes several moves, since different strategies for satisfying the standard are tried before failure is acknowledged. Acknowledged failure produces what Hegel calls "experience" (used in a sense typically opposed to "innocence").[10] The *patterns* of development within each of these stages are similar, but this is discovered only at the end of the process through retrospective review.

Thus the book has two standpoints: the standpoint of the person undergoing the developments and the standpoint of the person who recalls these developments and recognizes their patterns.[11] Within the first, the lessons of earlier stages are lost, as is consciousness of any patterns informing the development. Each new stage presents itself as the "truth," and the person taking the journey throws herself into its assumptions. The narrator of the book (the second standpoint), however, has already experienced the major stages and thus can comment on their patterns and relationships.[12] The narrator makes sense of the development by noting parallel patterns of development among the different stages. For the first standpoint, the path through the *Phenomenology* is a "highway of despair" because it seems like every step fails, but for the narrator – who sees the connections and patterns – the path unfolds "rationally" as each dissolution produces positive results that supersede shortcomings of earlier stages.[13]

The *Phenomenology* thus has both a linear and a hierarchical structure. It is linear in that each stage of knowing/living leads plausibly to the next, but it is hierarchical in that structural similarities inform the development of each major step.[14] Discovering these similarities is one requirement for achieving Absolute knowledge, the final stage. The steps in the journey include: Consciousness, Self-consciousness, Reason, Spirit (ethical stances rooted in social-political institutions), and "Religion" (expressive depictions of these stances, including art and ritual).[15] These terms have special meanings for Hegel. Consciousness, for example, is an orientation that regards the world as wholly external and independent of itself. Self-consciousness is an orientation that regards the external world as a manifestation or expression of mind. Thus, Consciousness takes objects as essential and itself as inessential, while Self-consciousness takes itself as essential and worldly objects as inessential. Reason is an orientation in which both mind and world are regarded as equally essential, neither being what it is without the other, and each a partial element in a larger whole. Spirit seeks the same harmony with the world as Reason, but actively seeks to maintain this harmony through social institutions. Religion and art create images, myths, and expressions that illuminate Spirit's ethical forms of life.

The many sub-stages that Hegel analyzes are too numerous to summarize, but here are some examples of the overall dynamic. Consciousness searches for a unified, independent object that sustains its own identity. Initially, unmediated sensuous apprehension seems like it might discover such an object, but instead of reaching a bare particular with a coherent identity, it discovers only a universal form that is satisfied by every object (a "this").[16] The same result occurs when a merely conscious being seeks unmediated access to its own mental states (it discovers only a universal "I") and to the temporal moment in which the "I" and the "this" meet (finding only a universal "now").[17] Instead of discovering an independent sensuous unmediated particular, it finds only all-encompassing universal forms (this-here-now). Consciousness then proceeds to common-sense perception and discovers that the ordinary notion of a thing oscillates between a single self-sustaining particular and the many universal properties that it somehow interlaces. The perceptual object thus shifts from a bare particular to a collection of properties to an ambiguous mixture of both. Perception thus also fails to discover a coherent object.[18] Finally, consciousness posits unperceivable scientific constructs – like force – which allegedly resolve the ambiguities of perception and produce stable, unchanging entities. But these scientific constructs also become unstable: a single force becomes a dynamic play of forces; a single law becomes a multiplicity of laws; a hypothetical, supersensible world becomes an inverted world. Finally, consciousness realizes that scientific "objects" reflect its own dynamism and then realizes that they simply mirror its own structure, which is the transition to Self-consciousness.[19]

Self-consciousness begins with the standard that worldly objects are simply pale reflections of itself and strives to prove this by taking action – either by consuming the object in desire, by gaining recognition from other conscious beings, by demonstrating the dominance of its critical powers, or by projecting itself as God.[20] Again, all Self-consciousness's efforts fail to demonstrate its primacy. It then morphs into Reason, which sees both its object and itself as equally essential and strives to demonstrate their harmony, first through observation, then through action, and finally through a synthesis of each resulting in artistic and ethical individuality.[21] But individuals in isolation cannot achieve complete harmony because it must extend to other people, not just the natural world. Thus, only communally organized individuals can complete the harmony that constitutes Reason's standard, and Reason must become Spirit.

Spirit seeks to complete this unity of subject and object in the social sphere. Hegel explores whether the family and the city can provide the mutual recognition necessary to provide this unity. Initially, the world of traditional customs shows promise, but customs – because they develop contingently over time and thus can easily be inconsistent – eventually conflict, leading to a breakdown of custom-governed social unity.[22] This yields a broken social world of atomized individuals, who eventually must recreate social unity by sacrificing themselves to the social ideals that inform the feudal system and its corresponding religious order. But a world dominated by two different principles of order (secular/sacred; State/Church) cannot achieve unity or harmony. Both the Enlightenment and the French Revolution destroy this separation of principles by rejecting both and searching for a new foundation for community. They eventually produce socially acknowledged, principled individuals who internalize social rules through rational assent. Hegel believed that a social order that could command the rational assent of these socially mature individuals was ready to emerge and would harmonize their interests by achieving mutual recognition.[23] In his book on ethics and politics, *The Philosophy of Right* (1820), Hegel proposes specific legal and political institutions that would produce this result.

Politically engaged, autonomous individuals seek to produce a social order that can truly unify them, and they can learn how this might be achieved by examining artistic creations and religious myths. Hegel thinks both provide forms that, when properly understood, suggest conditions for social unity that have evolved from previous historical eras.[24] Understanding the implications of these artistic and mythic expressions and translating them into concepts is one task of philosophy, which facilitates the transition to Absolute knowledge. Both religion and art reveal how to create unity within multiplicity. For example, the Christian myths of incarnation, self-sacrifice, and ascension suggest one kind of unity (of God externalizing himself and recovering himself).[25] Hegel's logical forms incarnate themselves in nature and history, seeking to achieve self-comprehension; humanity must abandon its sense of isolation from nature and history in order to discover those forms. When mature humanity fully comprehends them, humanity "ascends" to a higher level, and the forms become fully real because they are recognized by a humanity whose maturation they have guided. Absolute knowledge synthesizes several threads from the previous stages of development.[26] Hegel does not try to explicate the full content of Absolute knowledge in the *Phenomenology*; instead, he simply describes the resolutions achieved by this new standpoint and the preconditions for articulating that content. *The Science of Logic* and the *Encyclopedia of Philosophical Sciences* elaborate it.

Not everyone achieves the final stage. Many falter along the way because they fail to take the standard internal to their own current stage seriously. So although their experience indicates that this standard is not satisfied, they avoid this conclusion by ignoring their experience's significance. Deceiving themselves about the conflicts within their stage of knowing/living halts their development. They smugly believe they are successful when in fact their standard remains unsatisfied. Such self-deception is difficult to overcome, and Hegel makes this a central issue for later Continental philosophy, especially in Marxism (false consciousness) and existentialism (bad faith).

Hegel rejects skepticism because it imports standards that the stage it criticizes does not acknowledge. The skeptic typically relies on elevated standards of knowledge – *so* elevated that almost nothing can satisfy them. Thus, the problem lies not in the challenged stage – it never aspired to such elevated criteria – but in the skeptic's standards. Instead of such merely external criticisms, Hegel discovers *internal* criticisms, based on the stage's own standards.[26] Moreover, skepticism leads nowhere; once it rejects a position, it can only wait patiently until new positions are asserted.[28] But the internal dissolutions of Hegel's stages of knowing/living always lead toward new stages, which emerge from the ashes of previous ones. This conception of internal dissolutions that lead toward new positions – each providing a link in a chain of development – is a central innovation of Hegel's *Phenomenology*.[29] This developing pattern is what Hegel means by "dialectic."

The *Phenomenology* covers many philosophical orientations, too many to summarize here. Rather than give a cursory – and therefore unhelpful – summary of the entire book, I will sketch the main points of the first two stages of the Self-consciousness section, perhaps the most famous one.[30] This strategy will help clarify the book's virtues.

The Self-consciousness section

Hegel organizes his discussion into several parts: an introduction describing the standard of Self-consciousness and its initial object, life; a first attempt to satisfy the standard – desire; a narrator's intervention describing the ideal encounter between two self-consciousnesses; and a description of the actual events of an encounter between two self-conscious beings *at this stage of development.*[31] I will discuss them in turn.

Self-consciousness's goal is to establish its own primacy and thus to show that external objects are dependent on itself. Self-consciousness thus initially assumes it is embodied in whatever is not itself; when it is conscious of an object, it believes the object to be itself externalized.[32] This realization was the concluding moment of the previous section of the *Phenomenology,* when consciousness concluded that the concepts that govern natural science are its own creations and thus that the basic constituents of objectivity are creations of subjectivity (thought). This realization motivates the transition to Self-consciousness because when a merely conscious being finds itself expressed in this way, it becomes self-conscious. But now Self-consciousness must prove its presumptions by *demonstrating* (rather than simply believing) that the world just is itself manifested, by showing the transitoriness of the object through practical action – consuming or reshaping it. Thus, Hegelian Self-consciousness is more active than Hegelian Consciousness, which remained passive and contemplative – searching for a stable, coherent object.

Before examining the first stage of Self-consciousness, desire, Hegel discusses the object of self-consciousness, which has undergone a comparable increase in complexity, exhibiting a self-relatedness similar to self-conscious beings – life. For Hegel, life is a synthesis of (1) the life-energy embodied in all life-forms, (2) the distinct species that embody that life-energy, and (3) the cyclic process by which living beings return to organic matter at death, later to be used in the birth of new life-forms. Life is thus the self-sustaining cyclic totality that connects life-energy and its manifest life-forms.[33] The various species are to life-energy what individual members are to the species; the species (and life-energy) articulate(s) themselves (itself) into its various individual members (or life-forms) and these individuals procreate to maintain the life of the species. Hegel's concept of Spirit is exactly parallel to Life, but the "terms" it integrates are individual, self-conscious beings who recognize each other as such and thus establish a social bond. Spirit is the process by which self-conscious beings achieve reciprocity, harmony, and social unity.[34]

Hegel's discussion of life can also be read as a description of the way a self-conscious being discovers its own attachment to a living body, which converts its intentions into real-world changes. On this reading, self-consciousness would learn its own dependency on the body when trying to assert its independence through desire.[35] Both readings are plausible.

The first moment of Self-consciousness is *desire*. Desire emerges because the object's apparent independence challenges self-consciousness's sense of primacy. Desire must prove the dominance of self-consciousness by destroying/consuming the desired object. By assimilating the object, self-consciousness proves its superiority.[36] But this proof is both short-lived and deceptive. First, another external object soon challenges self-consciousness, and it must assert itself again, and again – without achieving any definitive proof of its primacy. Second, the fact that self-consciousness must negate objects in the first place acknowledges that they have *some degree* of independence. If objects were fully dependent, action would be unnecessary. For both reasons, self-consciousness fails to prove its primacy through desire.[37] In order to rectify desire's failures, the self-conscious being must discover something that can *negate itself*, that will acknowledge its own dependence without requiring self-consciousness to constantly assert its superiority. The only possible candidate for such a self-negating entity is another self-consciousness.[38] Hence social interaction becomes the next step by which self-consciousness seeks to establish its own dominance.

Hegel then examines interpersonal interaction to determine whether Self-consciousness can achieve its goal there. His discussion has two parts. The first part is a narrative interpolation – not experienced by the self-consciousness undergoing the maturational experience of the *Phenomenology*.[39] It shows what an encounter between two self-conscious beings could produce if it achieved full fruition. The second part explicates the actual experience of self-conscious beings in this phase. The interpolated ideal would fulfill the standard of Self-consciousness, but it is not achieved yet. When it succeeds, "Spirit" emerges and unites self-conscious beings.[40] Genuine sociality or solidarity develops through the mutual recognition that I call "*pure recognition*."

Hegel says that pure recognition has three moments, which can be distinguished analytically but are not really separable; both parties simultaneously experience them. In the first moment, each self-consciousness experiences the other as a living being. In order to experience identity with the other, however, each must temporarily abandon its sense of self-sufficiency and independence – the hallmark of Self-consciousness. By losing themselves, both can identify with the other.[41]

In the second moment, each self-consciousness tries to recover itself by asserting its distinctiveness, but because the other reasserts her distinctiveness as well, each retains a sense of identity with the other.[42] Both continue to see their own actions reflected in the other's actions. This allows each to *reinforce* the other's self-assertion by recognizing him/her as self-conscious. The other's recognition of self-consciousness makes possible self-consciousness's full self-recovery. Thus, a full realization of self-consciousness requires another's cooperation. The major transition occurs when a merely surmised sense of identity with the other becomes explicitly affirmed, but, to succeed, this identification requires corroboration by the other. Moreover, in this process self-consciousness acknowledges the self-consciousness of the other, since to assert his identity with her is to assert her identity with him.

In the third moment, each experiences him/herself as socially acknowledged, and this produces a bond between the reciprocating pair. Both experience an identity with the other; as the other's potential foreignness is superseded, solidarity emerges.[43] The bond coalesces because in each moment a sense of identity with the other is experienced; the encounter is an action and event in the life of both self-conscious beings, created by both together and producing something that neither could produce alone. Each partner mirrors the actions of the other, and each is elevated and confirmed while also elevating and confirming the other.[44] Neither loses; both achieve the goal of self-consciousness.

Through pure recognition, then, the sense of completion and harmony of both self-conscious individuals increases, and both experience an encompassing social unity – the community of mutually recognizing self-consciousnesses.[45] This community embodies Spirit. At this early stage, recognition ratifies each participant's self-consciousness; but later the same process can ratify each person's intelligence, moral earnestness, and artistic creativity. Spirit makes individuality socially real. The process of recognition thus becomes central to the development of fully human beings. Recognition becomes the guiding motivation of social life.

The *actual experience* of self-conscious beings at this stage is somewhat different, however. Each one refuses to sacrifice his existing sense of independence, refuses to lose himself and accept an initial identity with the other person as a living being.[46] Instead, he sees only *himself* as fully self-conscious and the other as *merely* a living being. The goal then becomes to prove that he is the *only* self-conscious being, that the other is too attached to life to be truly self-conscious (independent). Both self-consciousnesses in the encounter see each other this way, and this leads them to struggle to the death. Each tries to prove that he/she alone is self-conscious, and each tries to force the other to acknowledge her/his dependence on life (mere consciousness).[47]

Self-consciousness proves himself to be more than a living being by risking his life; this is why the initial struggle must be to the death. The goal is not to kill the other, but to force her to acknowledge that she is merely a living being, not a fully self-conscious being like himself. In effect, each demands that the other deny his/her self-consciousness. In order genuinely to risk his life, however, he must allow his life to be genuinely threatened. The initial outcome of this struggle is the death of one of the participants. Death proves to the survivor that self-consciousness is dependent on life after all. The dead body does not acknowledge the victor's primacy; it merely lies mute. This result does not satisfy the standard of Self-consciousness; it merely replicates the result of desire. In order to prove himself self-conscious, he needs the other to deny herself continuously by recognizing his supremacy. So during the next battle, the goal becomes forcing the other to submit, rather than killing her. The other then becomes his slave, and he becomes master.[48]

The experience of self-consciousness now becomes split into two halves: master and slave. The master seems to satisfy the standard of Self-consciousness.

Since the slave transforms the world by executing the master's wishes, the master need no longer experience the independent object of desire. Indeed, the world is not merely consumed, but is redesigned in accord with his own plans and thus given the shape he commands. This reinforces his sense of self-sufficiency and primacy and extends his sense of confirmation. To the extent that the problems of desire remain, only the slave experiences them. Moreover, through regular service and continuous recognition of the master's superior status, the slave reinforces the master's supremacy. Thus, the master seems to solve the problems of Self-consciousness and to satisfy its standard.[49]

Still, a fatal objection exists. The recognition of the master by the slave is worthless because the slave is not truly equal and self-conscious. When the slave submits in the battle, she can no longer truly recognize the master. The slave's recognition is no better than a pet's; the master may experience a diminished sense of himself in the slave, but this neither satisfies the standard of Self-consciousness nor achieves the reciprocity of pure recognition.[50] To achieve harmony with the social world, the master needs the recognition of other masters. With them, however, he must always do battle, and either dominate them (rendering their recognition irrelevant) or be dominated by them (becoming a slave himself). Mastery is thus an unsatisfactory solution. What of the slave?

The slave experiences a self-realization sufficiently rich to continue the story of Self-consciousness. To be sure, she is not recognized by anyone, and this motivates development to a new phase of Self-consciousness (stoicism). But she does discover a world transformed by her own hands, retaining the shapes she imposes on it through work. Unfortunately, she does not will this shape; the master does. So the slave does not exactly externalize her own will, but she learns that *activity* is essential to transforming the world. She only needs to assume the planning role herself. Moreover, during the battle, the slave experiences herself profoundly because it shakes her to her roots. Because her life is threatened, she loses attachment to particular roles or characteristics – discovering a selfhood that is independent of her embodiment. Because of this fear, Hegel thinks the slave gains a deeper, clearer sense of herself than the master. The master still feels identified with the skills that insured his victory, but he does not discover this abstract, unlimited sense of selfhood. Finally, under the tutelage of the master, the slave learns discipline; she conquers desire's tendency to consume everything. She learns that creatively transforming the world – shaping it to human goals – provides a deeper sense of self-expression than consumption. The slave thus transcends the stage of desire. Through work, fear, and discipline, she becomes the foundation for the next stages of Self-consciousness.[51]

The slave's self-consciousness is thus more mature than desire's. The slave still fails to satisfy self-consciousness's standard because she does not achieve genuine social recognition. In its next phases, self-consciousness will retreat into itself and try to become an entirely self-sufficient person (stoicism); when this fails it will seek self-realization not in negating other people or worldly objects, but in negating its own thoughts and principles (skepticism); and when this fails, it will finally seek recognition from a transcendent Other (God) (the stage of Unhappy consciousness). I shall not recount the remainder of this story, but I hope this detailed analysis of desire, pure recognition, and the master-slave interaction shows how Hegel analyzes specific stages of experience, how new standards evolve from the collapse of previous stages, how sub-stages fail to meet such standards, and how later stages retain the best elements of earlier ones, while encountering new dilemmas and gaining new insights.

Some additional implications can be drawn from this story. First, Hegel shows that self-conscious beings only become fully actual through the recognition of other self-conscious beings. Other people are essential for one's own full development; so he proves the adage that "no person is an island." Moreover, if Hegel's analysis is correct, then recognition is a central goal of social interaction. The experience of recognition need not be a zero-sum game – one person's gain does not have to be another's loss. Both can achieve recognition together, if they abandon their initial claims to distinctiveness. When Hegel examines human interaction, his questions are less epistemological than ontological. He abandons the question of justifying knowledge of others; in effect, he assumes humans know and experience others in various ways. Instead, he explores the conditions affecting the direction and outcomes, the dynamics and motivation, of social interaction. This is a fertile area of research that was pursued by Heidegger, Sartre, and Merleau-Ponty.

Hegel also suggests that self and other – like self and world – develop together; both achieve self-consciousness through each other's joint action, producing communal solidarity. Finally, Hegel offers a social ideal that is realizable, even if not always easy to realize. Such communal unity does not require anything so powerful as mutual love; recognition will suffice. Love creates a different kind (and perhaps higher level) of social bond, but that deeper unity is not necessary for the effective functioning of communities and social groups. Hegel explains how and why struggle sometimes emerges between individuals and between groups, but he also shows that it can be productive and that it need not dominate every social interaction. Interpersonal relations (in pure recognition) need not be a war of all against all, as they are in the battle to the death. But he acknowledges there is a level of social existence in which such conflict is endemic; insight, risk, and sacrifice are required to overcome it.

PHILOSOPHY OF HISTORY

For Hegel, "Spirit" is ultimate reality. It is a dynamic, self-active, all-inclusive whole. It realizes itself by expressing itself in various spheres: in the dynamic relation of categories to one another (Logic); in the relationships among inorganic elements and organic species (Nature); in the hierarchy of capacities in individual minds (Mind); in the progressive maturation of individuals toward an adequate philosophical standpoint (Phenomenology); in the relationships among social, economic, and legal institutions within a modern state (Politics); in the relationships between various cultural expressions in history (Art,

Religion, and Philosophy) and, finally, in the relationships among principles embodied in historical cultures (History). Spirit cannot comprehend itself (and thus cannot fully exist) without expressing itself. When self-conscious beings achieve full comprehension of Spirit, they attain Absolute knowledge. For Hegel similar logical patterns inform the development in all these areas. By discovering those patterns, philosophers discover a sphere's rationality, which reveals itself more completely as the sphere becomes more like Spirit. In reviewing history, Hegel seeks the deeper rational pattern operating in the rise and fall of nation-states. Finding similar patterns is the task of Hegel's political theory, aesthetics, philosophy of mind, and logic.

History integrates the partial expressions of Spirit, including philosophical standpoints, cultural expressions, and political institutions. These dimensions can be studied in isolation, but their actual development occurs interactively in history. Nation-states are the vehicles of the historical process because they embody substantive principles in laws and institutions.[52] Change is the dominant fact of history, but change also involves purification and rejuvenation.[53] Important achievements made by earlier civilizations are not always lost; they may be retained in later cultures. Hegel claims that history is goal-directed – leading to full human freedom. Identifying this goal allows Hegel to treat history as a rational process. As freedom becomes better realized, history becomes more rational.[54] Hegelian freedom requires a harmony between citizens and their institutions, which is achieved when institutions express citizens' rationality. For Hegel, history is progressive, but its development is not necessarily smooth or unilinear.[55] Indeed, typically it progresses only through conflict (negation) and resolution. States develop internal rifts (often resulting from differing interpretations of the state's purpose); overcoming these tensions creates unifying principles that realize history's movement toward freedom.

Philosophers discover history's logical patterns only through retrospective elucidation. They do not create these patterns; they articulate them. Such patterns are not evident to the leaders or the states that produce historical change.[56] Each stage of historical development represents a partial achievement of freedom, but most are partial failures as well. The failures must be overcome, but typically this does not occur within the same civilization. Instead, a new state, which retains the achievements of the previous stage, advances toward a richer realization of freedom. History is philosophically comprehended when its patterns are clarified. History only partially embodies Spirit because it retains some contingency. Eventually Spirit must seek more adequate self-comprehension by examining the patterns in higher cultural spheres: art, religion, and philosophy.

What is Hegel's basic story? How is freedom more adequately realized as history proceeds? Hegel elucidates four major phases: Oriental, Greek, Roman, and German.[57] In what Hegel calls the "Oriental" world (including China, Japan, and Persia), only the ruler is free; ordinary citizens are immersed in the natural processes of life. Most people lack distinct individuality and independent self-consciousness; because of tradition they follow the laws imposed by the ruler. No rational assent is involved. Either a sense of familial duty (China) or caste obligation (India) governs their actions. The ruler is sustained by his subjects and has absolute power over them. In Persia, the ruler is obeyed because he embodies a principle, and this represents a modest advance in rationality.

In the Greek world, individual city-states pursue their own destiny, and in many instances their citizens rationally determine that destiny through democratic participation. Nevertheless, the Greek world still depends on slaves. Indeed no direct democracy could exist if the citizens did not have the leisure to discuss public policy. Hence slavery is no mere coincidence, but rather an essential element in Greek democracy. Freedom can exist only for some in this phase. Greek citizens identify with their cities; city and citizen exist through each other. Greeks typically identify completely with their city's actions. Each city's laws embody its customs, but typically these customs are *not* rationally examined or justified. Eventually, conflicts among them emerge, leaving citizens in tragic situations in which they are unable to coherently satisfy different laws' requirements, fated to violate one or another. Moreover, even Greek citizens are not fully free because they obey laws from habit, not for rational reasons. Sometimes oracles, rather than critical reflection, are consulted to determine the proper course of action. Only if citizens follow rational social regulations because they express their own rationality can their actions be free.

In the Roman world, individual citizens are recognized, but only in an abstractly formal way. Roman power crushes the diversity of states, reducing them to subservient status. Property owners' legal rights are recognized by the state, but these rights coexist with the factual powerlessness of most individuals. Though Roman law allows some political representation, emperors still retain absolute authority. This produces outward conformity to laws combined with a spiritual retreat from public life into self-sufficiency (stoicism) or self-critical self-examination (skepticism). Eventually it produces the Christian bifurcation of nature/spirit. Christianity progresses by challenging the moral basis of slavery, claiming that everyone is equal in the eyes of God. It also imagines an alternative sphere in which persons achieve genuine solidarity through common love of God – the spiritual community. And although there is an organized system of rules to follow – thus overcoming the pure contingency of oracles – the rules are mere edicts of the Catholic Church. The Church dominates its subjects as forcefully as the Roman emperors dominate theirs. A tyranny that annihilates individual conscience dominates both Church and State in the Roman era. Thus, it too provides only imperfect freedom.

Finally, in what Hegel calls the "Germanic" world – the essential moment of which is the emergence of Protestantism, which promotes individual self-determination of belief – many limitations of the Roman world are overcome. Not only does Protestantism recognize distinct interpretations of faith, it also pressures political authorities to promote toleration of differences. Since humans share the capacity for reason, modern legal and social institutions must conform to rational principles, not abstractly or formally, but through judicious modification of traditions and customs. Traditions and customs embody the accumulated rationality of past political systems and thus must not be dismissed arbitrarily (as they were during the French Revolution). Rather they must be progressively transformed so that they better embody the aspirations of rational citizens. Hegel outlines such political institutions in *The Philosophy of Right* (1820). When individuals can self-consciously affirm their laws and institutions (when they accord with their rationality), then they will both be free and fully actualized. Hegel did not foresee additional developments in the principle of freedom, but he believed the modern era's institutions could become more rational. Though history may not have reached "completion" in his time, the necessary requirements for achieving freedom were evident.

Hegel claims that the actual developments of world history cannot be judged morally. Serious moral evaluation *presupposes* a rational social order; morality is not sufficiently robust by itself to vindicate such critical evaluation.[58] This severely limits moral evaluation of political institutions, at least prior to the realization of a rational social order. For Hegel, morality concerns individual actions; it cannot properly assess larger social developments. Constraints on the political order exist, however, since it must inspire citizens' rational assent. Hegel is a reformist, not a revolutionary. He has an abiding respect for history's achievements.

POLITICS AND ETHICS

A particular ideal of freedom guides Hegel's politics. Individuals exhibit Hegelian freedom when they experience themselves in harmony with the social order; i.e., when they experience themselves becoming universal through it and experience it becoming real through their own actions.[59] Achieving this harmony requires cultivation, a well-ordered state, a rationally organized civil society, a supportive family life, and recognition of property rights and individual conscience. Hegel shows that several institutions are necessary to produce this freedom. He underlines the importance of property, classes, and professional associations – guilds and unions – institutions in which individual and group interests are interwoven and unified in civil society and in the state. A good society creates richer humanity in its members. Hegel believes that modern culture has the potential to implement these rational social institutions, but modern prejudices also erect significant obstacles to achieving them.

Hegelian freedom differs from common-sense conceptions. For example, it does not involve minimizing obstacles or doing what one desires. First, although particular obstacles may be eliminable, some kinds of obstacle will always remain. Second, even if people enact their desires, this does not always yield or derive from harmony with social institutions – families, guilds, and the state. It often expresses an isolated, socially alienated type of individuality, and thus would indicate a lack of freedom. Hegel's freedom is also quite different from making arbitrary choices that allegedly define the chooser's identity.[60] Again, arbitrary choices derive from a lack of harmony with institutions; when such harmony exists, individual actions embody family affiliations, professional duties, and social laws. These define agents' social essences, and acting in accord with them expresses their deepest freedom. Finally, although

Hegelian freedom embodies the goals of Self-consciousness, it is the kind of self-consciousness that is *created by* social recognition – through family, co-workers, and fellow-citizens. Such self-consciousness does not require distancing oneself from institutional practices or distinguishing oneself from others. It is compatible with social solidarity because it is reinforced by acting in accord with institutions and norms. Free actions express the agent's social identity. Hegel's point is that people realize themselves as individuals within institutionalized social settings, not in isolation from them. Freedom is not opposed to social unity, but is an expression of it.[61]

Hence Hegel's ethics and politics are intertwined. He cannot conceive of a valid individual ethics in isolation from a rationally ordered community.[62] He considers two spheres that yield only partial freedom: formal legal property rights and isolated individual morality. Then he describes social institutions that make genuine freedom possible – family relationships, the professions, and the state. The ideal social order integrates individuals and institutions in self-expressive harmony in all three dimensions.

The sphere of abstract legal rights primarily involves property rights, and owners achieve minimal recognition from other owners when their property rights are respected.[63] To be recognized in this sphere requires owning property. Hegel suggests that some form of property is essential to anyone's social identity. Not only does it provide a medium of self-expression; it also facilitates minimum mutual recognition.[64] In respecting others' property, people acknowledge their social standing and individuality.[65] Communal property is inadequate, according to Hegel, precisely because it fails to provide this socially recognized individual identity. Hegel suggests that impoverished people who own nothing will experience themselves as socially unreal and alien.[66] Hence, a rationally ordered society will ensure that all members possess some property.[67] Criminal behavior often violates property rights in some fashion; crime thus severs the criminal from this basic form of mutual recognition. This disharmony must be rectified if criminals are to re-establish their relationships to the community. Punishment permits this restoration. For Hegel, punishment does not abrogate the criminal's rights, but restores them.[68] Punishment not only rights the wrong and rectifies the loss; it also allows the criminal to reconstitute the mutual recognition that grounds social relations.

The second sphere of partial freedom is individual morality and conscience. Hegel believes that this sphere dominates modernity because it lacks fully rational institutions and effective social integration. Individual morality delimits an individual's moral vocation and concerns her purity of heart.[69] Typically, objective social laws and customs supervene on and provide content for this kind of morality, which can sometimes ignore the requirements of specific social roles. Conscience tries to emulate the requirements of communal morality by positing very abstract imperatives (e.g., Kant's categorical imperative), which usually produce sham limitations. Typically, such imperatives are purely formal and can sanction almost any action; also these formal "laws" provide little guidance in difficult situations of value conflict. Whether a particular action is certified depends entirely on how the maxim informing the action is formulated, and most actions can be made acceptable by reinterpreting the maxim they embody. Individual morality may produce more active consciences, and it may even encourage improved attention to ethically relevant factors in situations.[70] But it does not supply the direction provided by the laws and customs of a well-ordered community; these are objective and mutually recognized in a way that no purely individual ideals can be. Moreover, in a well-ordered society, instead of being limited or stifled by laws, citizens are expressed by them. Their freedom becomes actual when they obey such laws because their social identity is embodied in them.[71] Genuine ethical life requires a rational community of mutual recognition.

For Hegel, social institutions constitute a person's ethical content, the milieu in which values become real.[72] He examines three distinct types of institution: the family, civil society, and the state.[73] A person's self-consciousness is realized in different ways in each of these spheres. The ethical bond of the family is love; altruism is its principle – each member contributes to the well-being of other family members.[74] Pure recognition in families creates organic groups, which cultivate sympathy. But isolated families lack organic bonds to one another; hence, ethical relations between families must be insured by other social institutions and ethical principles. Since family affection cannot be generalized to everyone, Hegel believes that love cannot be the basis for social ethics in larger communities.

Hegel regards civil society as a sphere of universal egoism in which members pursue their own interests and satisfy their individual needs. Yet each depends on others' productive activity, and everyone's work also satisfies others' needs. This interdependence is the essence of free economic activity.[75] The social institution that organizes this sphere is the professional guild. Guilds organize workers of similar talent and training to produce collective benefits. Membership in guilds certifies workers' recognition by their peers, and different guilds may collaborate for mutual benefit. Guilds are necessary because civil society often isolates and atomizes its members. Work makes people experience their dependence on other workers (both to complete their products and to produce needed goods that they cannot), and workers' demand for new products increases as they become habituated to a certain level of satisfaction.[76] Hegel foresees that consumer society will have difficulty achieving equilibrium because new needs are constantly created. For this reason civil society requires regulation by a rational state. Left unregulated, civil society would allow great wealth to accumulate in the hands a minority at the expense of the majority – increasing social polarization that would undermine mutual recognition. It also would encourage colonial exploitation and economic imperialism in order to maintain a continuous supply of needed raw materials. Hegel also understands the benefits and costs of workplace division of labor and a consumption-based economy. Division of labor turns laborers into quasi-mechanical appendages of machines even though it enhances productivity.

Hegel believes that these criticisms of civil society demonstrate the need for a rationally ordered state that embodies universally accepted laws and supersedes the principles of family life and civil society and the moralities of property rights and conscience.[77] Hegel's state has a single executive – a specific leader whose actions establish decrees and laws – his actions express the will of all citizens.[78] Hegel stresses the importance of social classes in the formation of representative institutions. The agricultural class has a conservative function; the business class, an innovative function; and the bureaucracy, an integrative function.[79] The bureaucracy interprets and applies the laws, working for the common good. Members are chosen on the basis of merit alone and are tenured so that they can remain uninfluenced by transient public opinion or wealth. They resolve conflicts in the best interests of all concerned and formulate policies that everyone can accept.[80]

The bureaucracy settles disputes among professional guilds that civil society cannot resolve on its own. Its power is checked by voluntary associations whose purpose is to apprise the bureaucracy of the consequences of planned actions. This process prevents the bureaucracy from becoming isolated and unresponsive, and it encourages expression of particular interests, which then must be addressed by the bureaucracy.[81] The unifying tasks of the state are thus not performed by the executive (whose function is almost ceremonial) or the legislature (which has only an advisory function), but by the bureaucracy that actually creates collectively recognized directives. These provide citizens with a sense of identification with state actions. They recognize each other to be embodied in those actions and thus are free in abiding by them.

Such a felicitous arrangement of institutions is not yet realized by any actually existing state. Hegel indicates the direction history must take if it is to realize such universal freedom. The state lifts people out of the parochial concerns of their own property, family, and profession, but it benefits from the different types of recognition and solidarity produced in these sectors. Since individuals can lose their connection to the state by remaining immersed in their parochial interests, sometimes a crusade that re-establishes individuals' dependence on the state is necessary. Hegel believes that war can sometimes serve this political function.[82] It transforms the complacency of various subgroups, reawakening their reliance on the state's ability to defend its territory. Like the battle to the death which causes its participants to fear for their lives and thereby to discover their abstract self-consciousness, so too war can reawaken people's awareness of their larger purposes and historical tasks. When countries declare war, Hegel believes that neither side can be entirely right. Both assert the justice of their perspective. War determines which perspective must yield. Despite this modest praise of war, Hegel still seeks international institutions that would sustain peace and world unity through culture, mutual recognition, and reason.[83]

AESTHETICS

If history and the progression of ethical principles embodied in states and social institutions constitute embodied spirit, then art, religion, and philosophy constitute Absolute spirit, the sphere in which the unifying processes of reason and history become self-conscious to humanity as a whole. Thus, the three forms of Absolute spirit seek to express the same reality, but they do this in different ways. Art presents these truths to sensuous perception; religion allows them to be felt, experienced, and imagined; while philosophy presents them in conceptual form, the form most appropriate to their content.[84] For Hegel, art expresses harmony and unity – whether among the structures and materials of architecture and sculpture, the sounds of music, or the narrative developments of drama and poetry. The value of a particular work of art depends on how well it embodies the Idea (the normative whole that provides orientation to an era and organizes its tensions; in the modern period this is the unity of subject and object, spirit and nature, and concept and reality). The goal of art is thus neither mimetic (of external perceptual reality), nor expressive (of an artist's vision). It embodies a unifying, fundamental cultural principle of which the artist is barely conscious.[85]

Art thus discloses (or reveals), rather than describes, these unifying cultural truths for specific eras. It makes them manifest through the depictions of human bodies, faces, characters, scenes, or events. Artists idealize the human figure to suggest the distinctive kind of freedom humanity seeks – a freedom in which oppositions are overcome and reconciled and in which humanity finds itself at home.[86] Art seeks to present the human in perfected form, whether in the idealized poses of Greek sculpture, in expressive faces and noble postures of classical portraits, or in the reconciliation of opposites achieved through narrative literature. It dwells on the distinctive features of humanity because the dynamic of self-consciousness is the process of overcoming oppositions, a process fully realized in the Idea.[87] Art brings this freedom to intuition, allowing it to be contemplated for its own sake. Humanity discovers a distinctive kind of necessity – an organic relation among parts – in the best works of art. This unity is also exhibited in infinite freedom. However, artists do not explicate it or show how it may guide human life; those functions belong to philosophy and religion, respectively.

Hegel distinguishes three distinct periods of art: the symbolic, the classical, and the Romantic. Specific arts flourish during each period: architecture is the exemplary symbolic art; sculpture, the dominant classical art; and painting, music, and poetry are defining forms of Romantic art.[88] Since the Idea (and reason) develops in history, the unity that art strives to embody changes over time, and this explains the distinct periods of art. Symbolic art develops primarily in Egypt in the building of pyramids, temples, and obelisks. In that era, ultimate truth was experienced as *beyond* the world, and symbolic art gestures beyond itself to intimate this hidden presence. Symbolic art presents the Idea as a mystery, as if ultimate reality cannot be fathomed by humanity, as if humanity can only behold the Absolute in awe.[89] Symbolic art evokes such awe and reverence.

Classical art emerges when ultimate reality becomes more accessible, when the unifying Idea is represented by human-like individuals in the form of the Greek gods. Greek sculpture embodies this Idea through human forms. Spiritual freedom is expressed in bodily poses, and complex relations among the gods can be depicted in myths and stories. Unfortunately, like the contingent multiplicity of customs governing the Greek city-states and the contingent diversity of (and strife among) city-states at the height of Greek civilization, this era never achieves complete unity. Hidden contradictions and political disharmony undermine it. The Greek world offers an inadequate expression of the unified whole that Hegel sees history striving to produce. Still the Greek gods are idealizations of humanity, and their nobility and grace can be effectively represented in statues. Greek poetry and drama present human affairs as expressions of larger conflicts among tempestuous deities, and reveal the sources of human tragedy and the reasons behind the Greeks' self-destruction: the opposition between divine law and human law which remains unresolved. Art achieves a kind of perfection during this era because the Greek Idea is expressible in human form. But as the Idea evolves (becoming more spiritual and complex), art becomes less effective in disclosing it since perceptible forms are less adequate to represent it. Romantic art must acknowledge the superiority of religion and philosophy for expressing the modern Idea.[90]

In the modern era, the Idea incorporates the inwardness of self-consciousness and the search for harmony with reality. Romantic art seeks to evoke that inwardness.[91] But perceptual objects (rather than myths or concepts) are inadequate means for embodying the dynamism of subjectivity and for showing its unity and reconciliation with the world. Music can express the inwardness of feeling, painting the inwardness of character, and poetry the subtleties of human interaction, but none of these arts can exhibit the way subject and object (individual and society) might be united. This requires the imagistic myths and communal rites of religion and the conceptual comprehension of philosophy. Nonetheless, Romantic art does depict human complexities – and inwardness – both in the expressiveness of paintings and the self-awareness of literary characters. In this way, Romantic art fulfills art's general aspiration – to disclose and behold the distinctive features of its age. Spirit becomes concrete in Romantic art; the other-worldliness of symbolic and classical art is overcome.

Unfortunately, Romantic art extols a defective conception of freedom, one closely related to satisfying contingent desires, experiencing chaotic selfhood, and self-distancing (dissociation).[92] Hegel believes these conceptions of freedom are immature and inimical to achieving the kind of self-possession, coherence, self-direction, and social unity that he takes to be essential to modern freedom. Romantic art overemphasizes the self-dividing features of modern culture. It lacks confidence in the unifying wholeness that Hegel thinks is the essential feature of modernity, accepting the spirit of alienation rather than striving to overcome it and achieve reconciliation. Because Romantic art blinds modern humanity to its highest possibilities, religion and philosophy are needed to express this Idea more adequately.

Hegel finds much to appreciate in modern art nonetheless. It reveals the spiritual in the everyday while dispelling illusions, and it exhibits a realism that is consonant with Hegelian reason. It invites reflection on artistic means of representation and thus encourages deeper philosophical reflection on the function of art in culture. Finally, it indicates the divisions of modern social life, revealing the oppositions that must be overcome if the modern Idea is to be historically realized.

Hegel's discussions of both the various types of art and its historical development are rich and subtle, informed by illuminating discussions of many concrete cases. My brief summary does not do justice to the details of his analysis. At best it sketches his views on the guiding principles of each historical era. Hegel sought to provide both a systematic theory of art and penetrating insights into particular artworks. I will not attempt to summarize his discussions of religion and philosophy, both of which are extensive and subtle. Instead, I will turn to his analysis of the capacities of individual minds, his "philosophy of mind" in the modern sense. This dimension of Hegel's thought offers important contributions as well.

PHILOSOPHY OF MIND

Hegel's philosophy of mind differs from traditional theories in two ways: it does not try to reduce higher mental capacities to lower ones (even though it remains naturalistic), and it orders human capacities by showing how they contribute to humanity's highest mental function – rational comprehension.[93] Instead of deriving mental functions by causally reducing them to the simpler processes (and ultimately to physical processes), Hegel shows how mental functions fulfill themselves by producing more sophisticated, complex mental operations.[94] Hegel's conception of a "science" of mind is unrelated to empirical scientific models; instead it seeks to elucidate the unified whole that overcomes dichotomies and oppositions among simpler functions. This unified mind realizes itself by dividing itself and then overcoming those divisions.[95] Humanity's mental powers yield comprehension of ultimate reality; Hegel shows how this is possible.

Hegel's philosophy of mind actually concerns the constitution of spirit: pure self-generating activity that determines itself and reorganizes itself. Spirit exists in both individuals and communities, but here Hegel focuses on individual capacities. He insists on the continuity of nature and spirit: spirit is the most organized form of nature, while nature is the least organized form of spirit. Both nature and spirit have developed over time into more complex forms; both build on their earlier stages. For Hegel, spirit does depend on nature (this is most evident in the functions of the body), but new principles of organization emerge at the higher levels of spirit's development.[96] On the extreme ends of the nature-spirit spectrum are a nature that has minimal internal coherence (its changes derive primarily from outside itself) and a spirit that is entirely self-organized and self-produced. The transition between nature and spirit occurs in living beings – animals – and the functions that humanity shares with them: sensation.

Sensation is the least spirit-like capacity of the human organism. It is not cognitive, but is the basis for all cognition. In sensation, spirit is most dependent on its environment and the body. Even at this primitive level, however, the organism limits the degree to which it gives itself to sensation; the role sensation plays in experience depends on the overall state of the organism when it is experienced. The content of sensation is given, but spirit generates its own content out of these found materials.[97] When sensation dominates a phase of experience, then spirit is less integrated, active, and creative in that phase. The next stage of mental organization is feeling, which is a spontaneous, non-cognitive synthesis of sensations. Feeling is simultaneously self-feeling, while sensations themselves are anonymous.[98] Standard patterns of response, or habits, allow persons to distance themselves from both sensation and feeling. Their urgent demands are controlled by habits. Just as habits allow the organism some degree of control, the self emerges as the organism distances itself from its habits.[99] Selfhood is self-relatedness; when the organism gains the power to transcend or refashion its habits, selfhood emerges.[100] The self is an organizing principle of habits, and it gradually realizes that the lower-level capacities – especially feeling and habit – are self-constituted at a preconscious level.

Hegel acknowledges a role for intuition, in which consciousness directly grasps the features of perceived objects as organized wholes. Intuition is manifest in self-feeling, in attention, and in the experience of flowing time. It grasps the object intuited as distinct from itself, yet imbued with structure like itself. It grasps its objects as particulars, not as universals. Just as sensation provides the basis for feelings and selfhood, so intuition provides materials for higher-order mental operations that supplement feelings with fantasies and memories.[101] Recollection abstracts the presented object from its given context in space and time; it can single out features of the object that seemed insignificant in the actual encounter and allows them to be considered independently of the presented object.[102] Imagination produces new images on the basis of previous experience, but they have no necessary order or rationality. Imagination can make certain properties symbolize an entire class of presentations, and this capacity is essential to the use of language.[103] Memory is a higher capacity organizing received contents; it is both made possible by language and enriches the development of nascent linguistic capacities. Words themselves must be remembered if language is to develop, and this involves more than just remembering a sound. When the organism becomes capable of distancing itself from its own use of words, when it becomes capable of reflecting on the relations among words, it becomes capable of full-fledged thinking.[104] The connections among words are organized in conceptual relations when thought realizes its goal.

Rational thought, for Hegel, is isomorphic with self-experience; it realizes itself by unifying individuals into classes, thereby creating unity. Concepts actively integrate their instances, and the instances achieve completion through conceptual organization. Concepts themselves are active, calling for supplementation by additional concepts until a systematic rational totality of concepts emerges. Reason develops when thought discovers laws and structures that are common both to itself and the world. Thought itself is an active, self-dividing, and self-unifying process, not unlike the operation of self-consciousness described in the discussion of the *Phenomenology of Spirit*.[105] In addition to discovering these self-active concepts (concrete universals), Hegel believes thought is expressed in distinctive kinds of judgment and inference. Judgments discover unifying third-terms that link apparent opposites. The subject and predicate in judgments are not really distinct, but establishing their identity is informative and illuminating. Inferences establish deep links among concepts, and philosophy is the highest achievement of thought because it uncovers the logical structure of the conceptual whole that informs all sectors of reality. This conceptual whole is a self-contained, self-explanatory system that unfolds itself once apparent conceptual oppositions are properly overcome.

THE PREFACE TO THE *PHENOMENOLOGY* AS A TRANSITION TO THE SYSTEM

The Preface to the *Phenomenology of Spirit* clarifies Hegel's general philosophical aspirations and provides a transition to the system as a whole, for which I will provide only a brief sketch. The Preface has two major goals: to distinguish Hegel's enterprise from other approaches to philosophy and to explain his important innovations. The first might be called the Preface's critical dimension, and the second, its constructive dimension. They elaborate Hegel's ultimate philosophical goals.

Hegel criticizes many commonly accepted approaches in philosophy. These include a reliance on common sense, on feelings or intuition, on abstract formulas like the principle of identity, on arguments, and on foundational principles. For example, against accepting common sense, Hegel argues that reasoned defense is needed to legitimate a philosophical position. Common sense's homespun formulas often conceal deep prejudices. Also, he thinks philosophy's results should be systematic rather than the random nuggets of "wisdom" common sense offers.[106] Similarly, Hegel rejects the Romantic faith in "intuition" or intense feeling as a basis for philosophical insight because they are often mistaken, and even if accurate, they provide no genuine comprehension of their insights. Mere intuition and feeling are empty unless their results are rationally confirmed and organized into a coherent system of results.[107] He also contests the value of abstract formulas – such as Schelling's principle of identity (A = A) – as ways of unifying diverse truths. Such formulas gain universality at the expense of significant content; they thus lack genuine explanatory power. They say nothing specific about the contents they allegedly subsume because what they assert can be said of anything.[108]

Hegel also suggests that argumentation alone is typically an inadequate approach to clarifying ultimate reality. When arguments are critical, they often lead nowhere. At best, they show that a conclusion is unproven, not even that it is false. They rarely contain insight into the truth. When arguments are positive and defend substantive conclusions, then they invariably rely on premises that must remain undisputed for the purposes of the argument. Such premises then must be defended by further arguments. Thus, arguments ultimately depend on foundational premises.[109] This is Hegel's primary objection to mathematical argument in philosophy: some claims must be taken as axiomatic and thus unchallengeable. But this requires accepting as given what ultimately must be defended. Postulating axioms also presupposes that the philosopher occupies a stable standpoint, but Hegel thinks deep philosophical insight transforms investigators (and criteria of truth), first shattering, then reconstituting them anew. Hegel calls this process "experience." Because it allows premises to remain unchallenged, the argumentative approach inhibits such experience and thereby undermines philosophical discovery.[110]

What then will constitute an adequate philosophical approach? Hegel's answer involves three key principles: the identity of substance and subject; the truth is the whole; and a deep connection between thought and being. Each point needs clarification. When Hegel asserts an identity claim, he does not intend a simple equivalence. Hegelian identity results when two terms that were originally thought to be distinct and independent are shown to be two aspects of a larger whole. The two terms are different expressions of the whole, dissolving and merging into one another, and thus cannot be independent. Hegelian identity is thus a dynamic process in which each term becomes the other. The dynamic unity underlying both terms is the ultimate reality; the whole is not fully actual until the identity of the apparently opposed terms is shown.[111] This general analysis of Hegelian identity can be clarified by explicating the identity of substance and subject.

To claim that substance and subject are identical is to assert at least two propositions. First, ultimate reality has a relatively stable aspect and a developing aspect; the first aspect expresses and understands itself through the second. The two aspects are not ultimately distinct; they are two dimensions of the same ultimate reality. But they can be studied separately in logic, on the one hand, and in nature and culture, on the other. Both nature and culture are embodiments of the categories in the *Logic*. Moreover, even the "unchanging" aspect is dynamic (the categories of Hegel's logic develop out of each other), and the "changing" aspect has relatively stable material forms (e.g., biological species in nature, human capacities in mind, and social institutions in culture). Hegel's key assertion thus is that ultimate reality has a substantive (unchanging) and subject (changing) aspect, each of which requires and amplifies the other.[112]

Second, the logic governing ultimate reality's development is similar to that governing the manner in which any individual mind comes to comprehend ultimate reality. Hegel's proposition thus also says that being and knowing develop according to similar patterns, that knowing is essential to the development of being, and that the development of being is essential to the development of knowing. Thus, knowing and being cannot really be isolated from each other. Coming to know itself via individual minds is necessary for the completion of ultimate reality. And knowing is not complete until it reaches full comprehension of ultimate reality. The process by which humanity comprehends ultimate reality is another instance of the dynamic logic governing that reality. The completion of each is necessary to the completion of the other, and the pattern governing each is the same; the two (knowing and being) are thus not ultimately distinct, but are two sides of the same process. Moreover, as each develops, it produces further complexities in the other so that each side remains adequate to the stage of development achieved by the other side. Knower and known thus interlock and become two aspects of one complex process.[113]

Reason's goal is to comprehend this dynamic identity between substance and subject. Reason comes to fruition only when it grasps this deep identity, producing harmony between knower and known. Once achieved, the knower never need experience the known as alien; the known always is an expression or embodiment of patterns and principles that govern the knowing process. Knowledge thus becomes absolute when this dynamic identity is grasped; and ultimate reality becomes absolute when it knows itself in this rich, complex manner. Ultimate reality contains a drive to complete itself, a drive that informs knowledge's drive to satisfy its standard and ultimate reality's drive to embody itself in many different spheres in order to achieve full comprehension of its patterns and principles.

Hegel's second key principle is that the truth is the whole. The first principle can help clarify this one. "Truth" here means completed reality; it is the finished whole, including both the subject (knowing) (changing) and substance (known) (relatively stable) sides. Not only is truth the whole system, it incorporates its own developmental process. All the phases of development must be comprehended before the whole is completed. The truth is not merely the conclusion that culminates from the steps required to reach it; those steps are woven into the conclusion, and the conclusion is not fully comprehended until it is seen as a supersession of those steps. The whole incorporates and supersedes its partial moments.[114]

This unity is realized when each sphere is related to the totality that subsumes it. "The truth is the whole" thus also means that ultimate reality informs everything, i.e., nature, mind, political institutions, science, art, religion, and philosophy all exhibit similar logical patterns. Moreover, these spheres also reflect each other. Hegel's system allegedly offers the key to every sphere of reality. Grasping the way in which the underlying concepts inform these spheres and understanding their structural isomorphism form the path to "Absolute knowledge." Such knowledge becomes universal in that all people can confirm it for themselves. Humanity can unify itself if people recognize themselves in Hegel's system.

The third principle articulated in the Preface concerns the relation of being and thought: they are identical.[115] This is just a different formulation of the first principle about substance and subject. But understanding this formulation is crucial to understanding what is called Hegel's "idealism." The main point is that being (ultimate reality) and thought are not distinct, but Hegel does not seek to reduce one to the other. He is not saying that organic nature or human maturation or social institutions are mere ideas; he suggests that all of them are to different degrees adequate expressions, or externalizations, of the basic patterns exemplified by the system of concepts. The dynamic that governs the different spheres of being thus expresses the dynamic governing the relationships among concepts; however, understanding the different spheres of being is the only way of elucidating these conceptual patterns.

Thus, none of the spheres of reality is unreal, insignificant, or illusory; all are essential to comprehending ultimate reality. Each exhibits the relationships that illuminate being/thought to different degrees. Comprehending one sphere will facilitate comprehending the others; comprehending all will make ultimate reality lucid to itself. Hegel's idealism does not deny the reality of any sphere of being; it asserts the isomorphic character of all spheres and articulates their underlying unity.

Philosophy begins by establishing sharp distinctions between whatever appears different and separable. These distinctions seem stable to philosophical understanding. Hegel believes that reason must proceed further, however. Reason looks beyond the distinctions to see the underlying whole that unites the apparently isolated terms. They are then seen to be artificial abstractions, moments of an underlying system. In grasping the whole, reason transcends mere thoughts and discovers genuine concepts.[116] Reason then realizes that its concepts form an integrated system that must express and comprehend itself. The conceptual system embodies itself – first in nature, then in the capacities of mind, and finally in social institutions and cultural history. The concepts and their embodiments form the basic divisions of Hegel's *Encyclopedia*.

THE SYSTEM

Because full understanding of Hegel's system would require detailed commentary, my treatment of it will be brief. The system contains Hegel's logic, his philosophy of nature, and his philosophy of spirit (which includes philosophical anthropology, philosophy of mind, and the analysis of social and cultural institutions). Given the critical conclusions of the Preface described above, Hegel's logic must be self-founding and also demonstrate the inadequacies of the partial forms of rationality embodied in science and previous logics. His logic in effect develops dialectically out of the shortcomings of alternative forms of rationality, shortcomings that are demonstrated on the basis of standards internal to those forms of rationality. Moreover, his logic must have material or substantive implications if it is to contribute to demonstrating the unity of thought and being sketched above. The *Logic* consists of three parts, each of which is concerned with a type of rational assessment: being (the sphere of finite beings and their relationships); essence (the sphere of appearances in relation to reality); and concept (the sphere of purposes, ends, and the norms governing them). The larger message of the *Logic* is that rationality is a human creation – developing in history – that creates its own standards of normative assessment. This view displaces the view that the principles of logic derive from some objective, independent source (either beings or essences, for example). The "concepts" or thought-patterns articulated in the *Logic* are expressed in human comprehension of nature, in our understanding of mind or spirit, and in objective cultural institutions and creations.

Hegel's philosophy of nature is not meant to compete with scientifically validated results, but it does seek to remain compatible with them. It illuminates what must be true of nature if scientific inquiry is to be possible. He abandons Schelling's effort to provide quasi-scientific explanations of how various dimensions of nature (physical, chemical, biological systems) are related. He believes there are several broadly conceived natural kinds that any philosophy of nature must acknowledge, but he also insists that philosophy of nature cannot be done a priori. It depends on the purposes for which humans pursue natural inquiry because these purposes organize the whole enterprise of scientific explanation. He explores the differences among mechanical systems (which can be understood purely quantitatively), physical systems (which require complex experimental investigations to understand), and organic systems (which are self-organizing and contain a principle of explanation within themselves).

He also explores the most general features of spirit, the most important of which is that it is self-interpreting and thus distinguishes itself from nature over the course of history. For Hegel, the nature/spirit distinction is not an ontological one; he is neither a monist nor a dualist, neither a naturalist nor a theorist of emergence. The core of spirit is the norms it creates to organize itself and collectively govern its actions. Those norms are embedded in traditions that are regularly reinterpreted and refashioned in accordance with revised and renewed self-interpretations. The task of spirit is to improve its self-expressiveness and rational coherence; if it does this satisfactorily, then it becomes freedom. Freedom itself is a normative status collectively produced in specific cultures; persons become free in so far as they are recognized as having this normative status. (I described this process above in the discussion of pure recognition.) To maintain itself, freedom must be embodied in institutional forms, and I sketched some of Hegel's favored institutional forms above in the discussion of the *Philosophy of Right*.

ASSESSMENT

Hegel is the point of departure for this survey because he integrates Fichte's and Schelling's insights, while resolving the paradoxes Kant's system. Nearly every later Continental thinker either develops or contests Hegel's achievements. Hegel abolishes the thing-in-itself and shows that the whole historically developing world exhibits a rational structure that is isomorphic with the development of self-consciousness. His core achievement is his system; it informs every element of his philosophical thought. Marx looks for such a system governing socio-economic life. Even those who challenge reason's importance find an underlying order informing desire, will, or conscious experience (Freud, Schopenhauer, and Bergson). Nietzsche abandons Hegel's system, but nonetheless seeks to overcome apparent opposites by allowing perspectives to supplement each other. Many hermeneutic thinkers rely on Hegel's notion of organic unity to establish a defensible conception of interpretation. Existentialists assert the importance of individuals against thought-systems, but they also elaborate a holistic and systematic vision of human existence. Phenomenologists seek an underlying rational order to experience, even if they discover such an order in different ways from Hegel. Structuralists make the same isomorphic assumptions about the structure of mind and the structure of reality (especially culture). Finally, the poststructuralists and postmodernists rely on Hegel's analysis of negativity, even if they reject his systematic vision. The animating impulse of their philosophical stances is to overcome Hegelianism. So Hegel either contributes to or is a central target of his Continental heirs.

The system is also Hegel's greatest weakness. While one cannot help admiring his ambitions, few will accept every Hegelian solution to his metaphysical questions. Many are stimulated by his penetrating insights in specific areas and his seminal innovations, but few accept the totality of the system or even its main components. Hegel's critique of other approaches to philosophy remains powerful, however. Most Continental philosophers still reject the project of discovering foundationalist premises or relying on common-sense intuitions or Romantic inspiration. Most acknowledge that genuine philosophy is systematic in that it must solve a variety of philosophical problems with an integrated set of assertions that mutually support each other, even if they do not strictly imply each other. Moreover, Hegel's version of systematic thinking is prone to difficulties because if one step fails, then the whole system seems to falter. The audacity of his system raises the question whether philosophy should aspire to that kind of tightly integrated system ever again. Hegel's conception of reason – a capacity that overcomes apparent conceptual oppositions by discovering underlying integrative unities – remains compelling. One may question whether every conceptual opposition will yield to reason in this way, but Hegel successfully shows that many such oppositions do. Finally, Hegel's belief that a philosophical starting point can be vindicated if the system circles back around to subsume it may be problematic because too many ways to subsume a starting point exist. The circuit may be either incomplete or too easily completed.

One of Hegel's deepest assumptions is the claim that alienation can be cured if one sees otherness as like oneself, if one sees oneself expressed or embodied in the other. This assumption motivates Hegel's key metaphysical conclusions (e.g., demonstrating that both subject and object are in a complex way identical) because he seeks to make humanity again feel at home in the natural and cultural world. But perhaps this assumption is flawed. Perhaps something stronger is needed to transcend alienation. One can feel alien among others who are experienced as like oneself. Their very similarity can produce alienation. Perhaps this point becomes clearer if one asks whether pure recognition would produce the deepest human bond. Reciprocity and mutual recognition can generate deep commitment, but so too can antagonistic challenge from someone who is experienced as different (either higher or lower). This challenge can be the source of a different kind of human bond and a different kind of honor among antagonists. In fact, probably neither of these relationships alone would provide a fully self-expressive connection to the social world. Both may be necessary, and by extension both a sense of difference and a sense of identity with the various spheres of reality may be necessary for complete human freedom.

Hegel makes significant strides toward providing a new kind of logic of thought and a new understanding of relationships among concepts. He also indicates some illuminating ways to explore the logic of being (dynamic relations among entities in different regions of being). But not only does he not show that all regions of being follow the same logic (e.g., do the forms of absolute spirit – art, religion, and philosophy – really follow the same patterns of development?), he also does not convincingly establish that the logic of thought and the logic of being are identical. This is why so many today are unable to experience Hegel's confidence in his system. Hegel opens an array of probing questions in this area, but he does not consider that there may be a variety of logics of thought. In addition, he illuminates the substance of the many fields he discusses (social institutions, art, religion, etc.) in an exemplary fashion. But he is also constrained by the requirements of his system. Sometimes the system may limit his ability to clarify the distinctive elements of specific fields; it can become a formalistic framework that hampers deeper insight.

Hegel's philosophy of history articulates one possible narrative of human development – the gradual realization of freedom. Progress toward this goal is not easy and not without setbacks, reversals, and challenges. But perhaps there is more than one narrative, and perhaps they interweave in complex ways. Perhaps the achievement of freedom comes with more devastating prices than Hegel is willing to acknowledge. Perhaps the value of his harmonizing freedom can be questioned, even if it has been an important goal for humanity so far. Perhaps humanity should consider new goals, creating its own narratives, as it better understands the paradoxes of modernity. To grasp Hegel's pattern, one has to observe history from a high altitude. From there, other possible narratives may become evident. Someone might even argue that the narrative Hegel tells requires this distant standpoint. The closer historical observers are to actual events, the less evidence of a larger pattern there may be.

Finally, Hegel's emphasis on supersession suggests that there are no ultimately irresolvable conflicts/oppositions, and thus no insurmountable tragedy. This may be overly optimistic. One view of tragedy is that the situation forces the hero to choose between two equally important values: the realization of one destroys the other and vice versa. No ultimate synthesis is possible. Only one path can be taken. Hegel believes that the conflict between divine law and human law produced tragedy in the Greek era and that, once this conflict is acknowledged, the Greek world had to shatter. But he thinks divine law and human law can ultimately be reconciled in a different way in a later era. Thus the tragedy that destroyed the Greek world can be overcome. Precisely this assumption may be wrong. Naturally, the critic must demonstrate the irreconcilability of the tragic conflicts that inform modern life, but if there are such conflicts, then Hegel's confidence in rational supersession may be questioned.

These are some possible reservations concerning Hegel's position. Still, the scope of his vision is breathtaking, and the subtlety of his execution is impressive. Hegel establishes so many new directions and revises the tasks of philosophy in such basic ways that the Continental tradition continues to benefit from rethinking and reassessing his vision and his project.

MARX AND WESTERN MARXISM

MARX: CORE CONTRIBUTIONS

For at least the last 150 years, capitalism has been the dominant economic force throughout the world. Marx not only offers an analysis of the functioning and dynamics of capitalism, he also offers a critique of it and gestures toward an alternative. His critique still retains significant power, and the ideal in terms of which this critique is made remains attractive and compelling, incorporating some of modernity's most promising possibilities. Like Hegel, Marx believes that human nature is historically conditioned, but for Marx, economic institutions are the primary factors in this process. Thus, he traces much of the selfishness, isolation, and alienation that modern people experience directly to the structures of capitalism, and he argues that a new stage of economic development (socialism) will produce a qualitative transformation in human existence. Marx hopes for an everyday life that can finally take advantage of the technological developments introduced by capitalism, a life that exhibits self-expressiveness, solidarity with others, and aesthetic engagement with nature and culture.

Marx's second major contribution is an activist conception of philosophy; his formula is that philosophy's goal must be to change the world, not merely to understand it.[1] Taken seriously, this new task would require philosophy to engage in sociological and social-psychological analysis, as well as incorporate the historical and economic understanding already introduced by Hegel. Moreover, philosophy would have to learn to influence the popular imagination, shaping people's vision of themselves and their future, motivating them and providing them with tools with which to make major social changes. In this way, Marx seeks to realize one of the promises of Enlightenment thought: that humanity assume control of its own fate through sustained application of reason. Marx's activist vision of philosophy goes well beyond anything inherited from previous Western traditions, however, and many later movements in Continental thought retain this goal.

A third contribution is an interpretive perspective that has come to be called "the hermeneutics of suspicion." Because Marx sees all cultural institutions – including political representation, democratic ideology, laws, property, religion, philosophy, and art – as integrally connected to the ascendancy of capitalism, and because he reveals some deep flaws in the capitalist order, his analysis requires a reconsideration of the value of these institutions. He suggests that perhaps the whole system of democratic institutions is merely a smokescreen by which the wealthiest class maintains its dominance. Similarly, he claims that popular religions are merely mechanisms for tricking people into accepting their assigned positions in an unjust social order. In addition, academic and artistic work may simply be activities by which the best and the brightest are wedded to the status quo and thus prevented from leading any serious revolt. Perhaps economic "developments" are not simply accidental, but rather are induced to serve the interests of the rich. Marx may not prove that his suspicions are correct, but he demands that they be seriously considered and evaluated, and his interpretive stance forces one to look for suspicious elements in any historical development.

Fourth, Marx insists on the central importance of productive life (i.e., work) in human existence and culture. Though previous philosophers had argued for the importance of practical reason (ethics), few had stressed the central importance of productive activity – activity that contributes to sustaining the existence of the species and individuals. Concentrating on this element of human life allows Marx to provide insightful explanations of historical changes. Even if the central role he assigns to the economic system in the analysis of culture is overstated, productive activity's importance in human life throughout history seems assured. Certainly in the capitalist era, work has become pervasive in the lives of nearly everyone, and Marx is the first to realize that if people's relationship to their work is strained, the rest of their lives will follow suit.

Finally, though many of his predictions about the development of later stages of capitalism were mistaken, he nonetheless did see some important trends: the concentration of power in an ever-smaller number of corporations, the gradual reification or commodification of most natural resources and human talents, and the realization that neither democracy nor human rights by themselves will guarantee a just social order. Though capitalism may not have undermined itself from within as Marx predicted, he still identified many of its trends and problems correctly.

LIFE

As a university student in Berlin, Marx (1818–83) studied law and philosophy, but his radical political activities prevented him from being seriously considered for an academic career in Germany. Turning to journalism, his editorials sharply criticized the existing order, and for this he was exiled to Paris in 1843, where he wrote his early philosophical manuscripts (not published until 1930). There Marx met Friedrich Engels (1820–95) with whom he co-wrote several books (including *The German Ideology*, written in 1845–6, and *The Communist Manifesto* (1848). After the emergence of a counter-revolution to the Paris revolt of 1848, Marx and his family were forced to escape to London. There he lived in great poverty, and three of his six children died. Nonetheless, he continued his studies of economics and history, eventually completing the first volume of his masterpiece, *Capital* (1867). Only this volume was published in his lifetime. He maintained vital relationships with existing revolutionary movements in various European countries – offering advice, writing pamphlets, and arguing with other radical thinkers. He founded the International Workingman's Association in 1864 and nurtured it through nearly a decade. When his wife died in 1881, followed quickly by the death of his eldest daughter, Marx weakened and died in 1883. After his death, Engels edited and published the remaining volumes of *Capital*. Yet many of Marx's essays remained unpublished for 50 years. He wrote some historical studies, *The Civil War in France* (1871) and *The Eighteenth Brumaire of Louis Bonaparte* (1852), indicating how his general approach to history could be applied to the study of particular periods and contexts.

EARLY MARX: ALIENATION AND CAPITALISM

Some commentators think Marx's early writings are discontinuous with his mature essays, but I believe that the two periods exhibit important continuities. Although Marx's early manuscripts were not published until the 1930s, they contain vivid formulations of many objections to capitalism that inform his later work. The moral fervor of his challenge to capitalism is perhaps more evident in the early writings, but so is his general outline of the social conditions that might rectify those problems. I begin with Marx's analysis of alienation, the criticisms of capitalism that follow from it, and the ideals presupposed by these criticisms. Once the substance of his early writings is clear, I will examine his materialist theory of history and his later economic critique of capitalism.

Alienation is not just a state of discomfort or separation, but a violation; it implies a normative requirement that the separation should be overcome. This requirement may arise from transgressing human dignity or from stifling self-realization. For young Marx, alienation is not just a condition that certain people experience in a given culture (objectively described); it is also a condition that calls for revolution because the humanity of those alienated is compromised. No one should have to endure such alienation; the more widespread and overwhelming the alienation, the more corrupt the economic and political order that creates it, and the greater the demand that this order be overthrown.[2] Marx distinguishes five types of alienation: alienation from the product of one's labor, from the productive process, from one's species being, from other people, and from oneself.

Alienation from one's product has two variations.[3] In the first, instead of embodying creative self-expression or genuine desire, one's product has no relation to one's own will. It reveals one's enslavement because the product embodies the will of the capitalist who forces one to produce it. The more energy one expends in work, the less one's life is really one's own because one's energy is absorbed by the product and stolen by the capitalist. This type of product alienation would exist even if people were fairly compensated for their work and even if they were allowed to keep their products. The product is alien because others will its creation. In the second variation of product-alienation, the finished result is simply taken, and one is not fairly compensated for one's efforts. Here, even though the product may have some self-expressive relation to one's talents, the usurpation of the product by the capitalist produces the alienation. In effect, the product is stolen, no longer one's own. Because the capitalist keeps the profit, the worker earns only subsistence wages. Often both types of product-alienation occur together: not only has the worker not chosen to produce the product, but the finished result is expropriated as well.

The more alienated people are from their products, the more alienated they become from the *process* of production.[4] Labor becomes so routinized and mechanical that few find it self-expressive, and the work process becomes so relentless and numbing that few see their labor as their own. Marx uses both criteria for genuinely self-realizing work: self-willed and self-expressive. For Marx, practical action should be an expression of one's creative powers and should lead to a sense of self-embodiment. Instead, most people are bored and exhausted by their work, lacking any commitment to it, finding nothing of themselves in its results. When one's relation to the process is so dispiriting, then one rarely experiences any identification with the product.

Human life is productive activity: people must produce to survive. They realize themselves through their work, and testing their talents on challenging tasks enhances their humanity. Marx calls features of life that are essential to being human "species being."[5] If people's productive lives are alienated, then they lose their humanity, becoming reduced to the status of animals or machines. In addition, humans are essentially social; to be human is to exist in solidarity with a community. But the system of capitalist production engenders a competition that undermines any sense of fraternity. Capitalism produces egoistic individuals who are trained to be indifferent to the fate of others, trained to pursue their selfish gain at the expense of others. So even the most basic forms of communal life are destroyed by capitalism.[6] This alienation from other people also undermines everyone's species being.

Finally, many in the capitalist system are alienated from themselves.[7] They have no sense of individuality and no way to express it even if they did. Their everyday lives are usurped; their social relations are polluted by competition; their activity is routinized; and their products are stolen. Under these conditions people lose all self-respect and self-esteem. Because their productive lives are inhuman, they lose all sense of their own humanity as well. Their work and lives become spiritless: they are drained without being revitalized; they are dispossessed and never restored. Under capitalism people experience themselves as lifeless, passionless, and spent.

Marx next connects these dimensions of alienation to the necessary, defining features of capitalism. If he succeeds, then he will have a forceful critique because he would have shown that capitalism is unable to change to become more humane. Then a radical alternative would have to be created in order to transcend this alienated condition. That alternative must show how to overcome alienation systematically for large numbers of workers, and it must produce an entirely different sense of work, community, humanity, and self. The central features of capitalism on which Marx concentrates are private property, the division of labor, exploitation, and the workplace.

Private property is the institution by which the economically privileged class maintains itself over time.[8] It allows systematic advantages to be created within one generation and then expanded by using these advantages to elevate future generations. Marx thinks private property is inherently unjust; collective forms of property ownership produce fairer distribution. Private property drives people to take advantage of others and increase that competitive advantage over time. It insures some people will begin life with unfair advantages, and teaches them to increase those advantages in order to benefit their children. Without this driving force toward inequality, Marx believes that a system of production can be fair and just, socially harmonious and cooperative.

A second essential feature of capitalism is the division of labor, which reduces work to small, repetitive tasks.[9] The assembly line is exemplary in this respect. The division of labor forces workers to specialize and thus to ignore their full range of talents. Even if the specialized task they are assigned is initially interesting, the fact that they must repeat it continuously throughout the day gradually drains it of value and meaning. Because their other skills atrophy, workers become stunted. The capitalist system forces them to disengage from serious commitment to work, engendering both process and product alienation.

A third defining feature is exploitation. Marx believes that the value of a product is not equivalent to the price it can garner on an open market, but rather is directly related to the amount of labor-power invested in it. The capitalist pays the lowest wage possible and sells the product for the highest price possible. Skilled labor-power makes possible the higher price, but labor is not properly compensated for its contribution. The profit goes to the capitalist who thus systematically exploits his workers – the true source of the product's value.[10] Their life-energy, their creativity, their physical and emotional powers are absorbed by products which are sold by the capitalist to benefit himself. Under capitalism, laborers can never be compensated to a degree equal to their real contributions because this would eliminate profit, and profit is the motor of the capitalist system. In effect, wherever there is profit, there is also exploitation. Capitalism is built on systematically extracting excess labor-power from workers.

Finally, there are always more workers than jobs, which allows capitalists to reduce wages to subsistence level, to fire workers who make trouble, and to force people to work harder for ever-lower compensation. Marx claims that the logic of capitalism is thus to reduce workers' wages to a minimal level and to remain oblivious to those who live with poverty, misery, and disease.[11] This underclass shows workers their fate if they refuse to work or if they protest the conditions of production. Capitalism thus requires a downtrodden class that instills fear into workers and that can be used to minimize worker privileges. The alienating conditions of production are thereby maintained by the misery and poverty of the underclass. There is little opportunity to improve one's initial lot in life by rising to the capitalist class.

Private property; division of labor; exploitation; subsistence living: these are the defining conditions of capitalism that Marx links directly to alienation. They virtually assure a condition of slavery for most workers. Private property creates product alienation and alienation from others. The division of labor creates process alienation, and exploitation destroys workers' species-being. Taken together they maximize self-alienation. These defining features of capitalism must be transformed to create a productive system that can overcome alienation. Marx's discussion of capitalism presupposes some crucial values. He sees capitalism as essentially unjust (private property, exploitation), inhumane (division of labor, subsistence living) and alienating. Justice, humanity, and self-expression thus provide the evaluative foundation for his early critique of capitalism.

Marx's critique relies on the ideals that his alternative system should strive to embody: self-expressive creativity (the opposite of alienation), full sensuous appreciation of the world, and social relations built on respect and cooperation.[12] Through self-expressive creativity, workers realize themselves – the totality of their talents and passions – in their work. Their products concretize them like artists' creations embody their vision. Work thus becomes a living expression and affirmation of the worker. It would derive from genuine inspiration, rather than survival needs or greed. Production would be organized so that individuals could develop a wide variety of talents and make a diversity of products (e.g., Marx imagines people hunting in the morning, drawing in the afternoon, and pursuing philosophical discussion in the evening). Moreover, people would work both for their own exhilaration and for the benefit of the community. Self-expressive work would thus produce social recognition as well as individual self-realization.

Marx contends that when life is driven by survival and is experienced as a rat race, people's ability to perceive the world is sharply limited. They apprehend only those qualities most relevant to their tasks. A different system of production would allow workers to perceive the world completely, aesthetically responding to nature, culture, and history from many perspectives and possessing the leisure to explore them. Instead of simply consuming objects and neglecting nature, Marx thinks people will appreciate life more fully. In effect, truly aesthetic perception would become typical, and new forms of social interaction would emerge that would amplify one's sensuous and intellectual relations with the world. Everyday life would be richer and more wondrous.

Finally, Marx's alternative would produce a radical change in social relationships. Instead of competition, envy, and resentment, his system would encourage cooperation, mutual respect, recognition, and community – a world in which people relate to one another as ends in themselves, not as tools for their own ends. This means people will create products that will be valuable to others and will freely offer them for others to use and appreciate. They will experience the social significance of their productive activity, which will reconnect them with their species-being. This will allow people to recognize and confirm each other. Social respect and community will evolve naturally, and laws need not be imposed simply to prevent crime, inhumanity, or class conflict, because the new economic system will eliminate these indignities.

These ideals reinforce each other.[13] Self-expressive work will create people who are better able to recognize each other's value and appreciate it. Those who are recognized by others will be better able to see the value of the work they produce and thus can better experience self-realization in their products. Those who experience social recognition will be better able to appreciate others' diverse perspectives and thus achieve a wider range of intellectual and sensory perspectives on the world themselves. Richer perception will allow full appreciation of others' contributions and thus will promote richer forms of recognition. Fuller perception will also encourage more refined, self-expressive activity, partly by enabling people to better comprehend themselves, but also by encouraging them to see their achievements in new ways. Taken together these ideals provide standards for evaluating a new socio-economic order. Such criteria are notoriously lacking in Marx's late writings. These ideals still animate his later critique of capitalism, but he is less explicit about the positive directions he hopes socialist societies will take. These ideals offer positive reasons to seek a new order and provide revolutionaries with some political direction.

THE MATERIALIST CONCEPTION OF HISTORY

In his middle period Marx developed a "materialist" conception of history, which is allegedly opposed to Hegel's "idealist" theory of history. Marx believes that he sees the true motor of history more clearly than Hegel – productive forces and class conflict. He claims to have inverted Hegel's "ideas" in favor of earthly economic factors.[14] Marx's theory can be organized into three elements: some basic principles, a theory of statics and dynamics, and an analysis of the historical stages of production. This theory prepares the way for Marx's detailed analyses of capitalism's internal contradictions in later works, especially the three volumes of *Capital*.

Here are the main principles of Marx's materialist conception of history:

1 The human world (i.e., economy, society, law, state, technology, and culture) is a product of human activity, which is embedded in social relations that are products of previous human activity.[15] These social relations are reproduced – and sometimes transformed – through human activity (which Marx calls "praxis"). Praxis and social relations change together; sometimes the social relationships limit the possible responses available to individuals in particular

situations, and sometimes individuals transform social relations by contesting or refashioning them.

2 Instead of providing the most accurate description of the world as it is, the best theory of history enables a new economic order to be born.[16] A theory's truth concerns its practical results when actively pursued. (This is one Hegelian meaning for "truth.")

3 Social relations determine consciousness, thought, and ideals, not the reverse.[17] Certain types of social order create specific types of individual (e.g., self-interested competitive individualists are created by capitalism).

4 An economic "base," consisting of the forces and relations of production, governs the totality of social relations in any particular era.[18] These are the ultimate determinants of change in all other social relations (e.g., political, familial, or legal relations) and in individuals (e.g., in their thoughts, ideals, or myths). Changes at the higher, dependent levels always result from more basic economic changes, which are not always readily apparent until they manifest themselves in other spheres.

5 The full implications of a mode of production (a system defined by specific forces and relations of production) must be exhausted before that mode self-destructs and a new one can take its place, but the dissolution of the old mode produces the intellectual, moral, and practical tools necessary to create the next mode of production.[19] Societies cannot "leapfrog" stages of economic development; the struggles of each stage, including capitalism, must be endured to reach the culminating stage of history: communism.

Praxis is thus the "matter" to which Marx's "materialist" theory of history refers. Economic production is primary, but praxis includes all human activity. Social relations provide a context for such activity and the tools for their own transformation if they contain contradictory demands. Since Marx seeks to promote social change, he values theories only if they facilitate it. He is impatient with descriptive theories that yield no insights into mechanisms of change. Probably the vaguest word in Marx's vocabulary is "determine." It has been taken to mean "causally necessitate" or simply "provide a condition for" or even "is a factor that bears on." Marx's position gains plausibility as the interpretation of this term is weakened. His basic idea is that changes in social relations should explain changes in ideas and that shifts in economic relations should explain shifts in all other social relations. But Hegelians might argue that ideas – especially ideals or poetic metaphors – can have great impact on the success of historical undertakings. Moreover, Hegel typically refers to an encompassing social constellation when he uses "idea." Marx may reply that such success actually is due to some underlying change in social relations that correlates with the ideal. This kind of reply makes Marx's theory difficult to test because some underlying factor can always be posited to explain any apparent counter-example. Accepting it can then become a matter of faith. Similarly, historical cases in which important social changes that seem unrelated to underlying economic change seem to exist, but Marx can always offer similar caveats.

Another issue that affects the meaning of Marx's theory is how broadly to interpret the concept of economic "base." For example, in a fully industrialized society, does the agricultural economy still form part of the base? In a predominantly service or "information-oriented" economy, does the industrial element still form part of the base? Marx is able to clarify the concepts of "forces and relations" of production for earlier pre-capitalist societies. But modern capitalism is extremely complex, with a variety of forces and relations interweaving to generate production. Exactly what constitutes the base in such a complex system? In addition, the claim that stages cannot be leapfrogged has certainly been challenged by a number of socialist societies (e.g., Russia, China). They have attempted a transition from an agrarian economy to a socialist economy without traversing the capitalist stage. Though some Marxists might challenge their chances for success, Marx himself seems more open-minded about the necessity of passing through intermediate historical stages. These interpretive debates constitute one major dimension of Western Marxism, which challenged the Orthodox Marxism produced by the Russian Revolution.

Historical materialism: statics and dynamics

Marx begins from the premise that practical activity aimed at survival is the motor of history. Sometimes satisfying subsistence needs creates additional needs, and these can also play a role in historical development (e.g., the need for specific tools to maintain a certain level of productivity). The mode of production is the economic organization by which such needs are satisfied. Marx privileges the need to survive over all other needs, e.g., for recognition, for community, for harmony with nature, which can be pursued only if survival is assured.[20] Every society has a mode of production; for this reason Marx thinks human life is essentially social (not, for example, because humans are raised in families, but because survival requires communal forms of praxis).

The mode of production can also be defined as the relationships among all forces of production, e.g., natural resources, labor-power, and technology. All modes of production, including capitalism, have depended on the division of labor and consequently on class division and class conflict.[21] Such divisions exist between masters and slaves (or apprentices), men and women, city and country dwellers, landowners and serfs, and capitalists and laborers. The division of labor within a mode of production creates fundamental inequalities between classes, some of which are privileged because they are supported by the labor of others. Marx contends that the entire political and legal organization of society exists to legitimate and reinforce this class domination. Moreover, the dominant ideas of an era aim to justify this domination.

Marx realizes that some ethical and religious ideas compensate for economic powerlessness and subordination. The hope for an afterlife of heavenly rewards encourages widespread passivity, acceptance, and resignation. Though these ideas sustain the dominant order, they may not be created by the privileged class. The ideas that most strongly support capitalism in this era emerge from classical economics. Its assumptions about human motivation and markets re-inforce capitalist class domination. Thus, Marx attacks capitalist economic theory as forcefully as its economic institutions.[22]

Marx's writings are ambiguous concerning the relationship of the superstructures to the economic base. In his theoretical formulations of historical materialism, he states that the causal influence between the economic base and the political and ideological superstructures is one-directional. The base must explain all superstructures, and every change in the superstructures must be explained by a change in the base. But in his concrete historical studies (e.g., *The Eighteenth Brumaire*), the issue is less clear. There, when he is forced to address history's complexities, he allows changes in ideas or non-economic institutions to causally act on the base and produce significant changes. Some degree of relative independence of the superstructures seems inevitable because historical actors are not always aware of their own class interest and thus may allow ideas or institutions to influence them in ways that are contrary to those interests. (They may do so even if they are aware of them, but this only shows the deeper limits of Marx's theory.)

The central materialist thesis about dynamics is that transformations in the institutional or cultural superstructures of a society derive from changes in the mode of production (the economic base). In its strongest form this would mean that all changes in the mode of production would have superstructural ramifications and that no change in the superstructures would occur without some motivating change in the economic base.[23] Changes in the base occur when changes in the forces of production (technology, training of labor, new natural resources, new scientific knowledge) alter existing relations of production. This creates a "contradiction" in the base that leads to fundamental change. Although human actions produce these changes, its agents are not always aware of these implications. Thus, the mode of production may change without anyone realizing this has occurred. In addition, the direction of fundamental change is established by the existing historical context – existing class relations.

Marx suggests that all history prior to the Communist revolution is the pre-history of genuine humanity because the division of labor (and related exploitation, alienation, oppression, and inequality) has prevented the full realization of human capacities and genuine human community. After the revolution, once new economic institutions are created, human life will be qualitatively transformed. Truly human history will begin when people make history with greater self-consciousness and when their fullest powers are engaged in the process. Marx thinks that the revolution will not be possible unless the capitalist mode of production has produced its deepest contradictions and thus has reached maturity. A mode of production can be transcended only after it reaches its apogee; it then implodes and is replaced by an entirely new mode of production that rises from its ashes. Thus modes of production in Marx develop from each other's demise, just as stages of consciousness did in Hegel's *Phenomenology of Spirit*. Later stages usually retain many positive features of superseded ones.

Historical change occurs through class struggle, and group praxis is necessary to transform the mode of production. The class that Marx expects to fight the Communist revolution is the working class – the industrial proletariat.[24] Marx thinks that the conditions of the proletariat must reach a nadir worldwide before workers will revolt against capitalism. This will not be a peaceful process; many people (especially capitalists) will die. Marx had great confidence in the revolutionary potential of the proletariat because under capitalism it allegedly becomes a universal class – a class that can express *everyone's* interests. When the proletariat wins victory, Marx expects class conflict to end; no other class will emerge because the exploitation produced by the division of labor and the inequalities perpetuated by private property will cease. Alienation will be overcome.

The state pretends to represent the general interest of all citizens, but Marx believes it exists only to benefit the ruling class. All appendages of the state – the military, the judiciary, the legislature, the executive, and the bureaucracy – cooperate to dominate and confuse the subordinate classes. The bourgeois state must be destroyed if the bourgeois mode of production is to be destroyed. Similarly, the dominant ideas supporting the bourgeois order must be dismantled, and new ones must be erected. The revolutionary class cannot be expected to conform to the ethical and legal imperatives of the outmoded order. It will create its own ethical and legal ideals and a more modest state apparatus and system of education. When ideas that challenge the status quo become accepted, the capitalist order will begin to crumble – undermining itself from within. But revolution will be complete only when the economic forces and relations of production are thoroughly transformed, and the communist mode of production emerges.

The Communist revolution will require coordinated actions by workers throughout the world, revolting together in a large number of capitalist countries. It cannot succeed if the revolution is restricted to a relatively backward country (like Russia) or if it occurs only in one country (even an advanced industrial country). It must occur in many advanced capitalist countries at once.[25] This is why Marx sought a worldwide labor movement and created a loose federation of revolutionary parties to guide that movement. The goals of the Communist revolution remain similar to Marx's early aims: full expression of the creative powers of individuals; strong communal bonds; the abolition of private property and inequality; the gradual withering away of the state; and full human control over nature and over the future.

The historical stages of production

Marx adopts Hegel's phases of history, and some of his main points about them derive from Hegel; but Marx gives the economic base greater importance in shaping each phase.

In the Asiatic mode of production of migratory pastoralism, there is a harmony between city and country. The tribe owns productive forces collectively, and the community as a whole (embodied in a tribal leader) dominates its individual members.[26] Membership in the tribal community makes people human. Unaffiliated, isolated individuals can neither own nor possess anything. Tribal leaders are united through loyalty to a national leader (despot), and local tribes are related to the despot as tribe members are related to the tribal leader. Land cultivation and barter is restricted only to acknowledged tribal members.

The Greek-Roman mode of production is organized around the city. The city is the concrete expression of social unity; the surrounding farmland is subordinate to it. Commonly owned property is distinguished from privately owned property (that belongs to families); and the common lands sustain the city.[27] Each city maintains its cohesiveness by differentiating itself from other cities; only through opposition to other cities is a sense of unity/identity maintained by each particular city. In this phase men live divided lives: a private life in the household and a public life of participation in city decisions. Women are confined to the household. All surplus labor is devoted to military service and city defense. The key element in this mode of production is the city as a whole; individuals contribute to its greater good. War sometimes drives cities to conquests that they cannot sustain in the long term.

In the Germanic (or feudal) mode of production, dominance shifts to the countryside. All property is private and organized into feudal estates, and thus concentrated amongst a small number of landowners. Heads of families own the land, and communal unity across estates is virtually non-existent.[28] Peace and trade exist only through explicit agreements between estate owners. Feudal lords are thus independent centers of production. In the towns this organizational form governs in the guilds that organize individuals by skill and profession. Historical traditions, common language, and customs promote social harmony. Occasionally, several estates share some territory, e.g., for hunting, but this has no larger implications for the mode of production. Here, too, individuals are subordinate to families, but there is greater division of property into independent landholdings.

In the capitalist mode of production, many types of division of labor exist: production/commerce; artisans/industrial mass production; homeland/colonies; and capital/labor, which dominates this phase. As the whole world becomes gradually more interdependent, individuals become more isolated from one another. Production begins to assume a life of its own regardless of the human consequences to workers, who are impoverished, exploited, and dehumanized.[29] No common ownership exists in this phase; all forces of production are privately owned and organized. Moreover, independent means of subsistence (such as rural family farms or individual tradesmen) lose viability, no longer functioning as serious alternatives to industrial mass production. Labor is reduced to labor-power; anyone not owning property is reduced to an industrial laborer.

MARX'S ANALYSIS OF THE CAPITALIST MODE OF PRODUCTION

In the last period of his career Marx analyzed the dynamics of the capitalist mode of production, its internal contradictions, and the ways it might be transformed into socialism. Because of space limitations, I will not explicate Marx's entire three-volume work, *Capital*, but I will indicate some of its main claims. Three features of this late work can be distinguished: a critique of bourgeois economic theory, a critique of capitalism, and an elucidation of capitalism's contradictions.

Concerning bourgeois economic theory, Marx makes several points.[30] He first denies that there are universal laws of economic behavior, since human actions within each mode of production differ, and they will change again after the capitalist mode is superseded. At best, current economic theory might describe the laws governing human behavior under capitalism. Bourgeois economics tries to naturalize these laws, making them seem eternal rather than historically restricted. Second, he notes that a system in which individuals are forced to contract their labor for any price just to survive is an historical aberration. In previous economic stages, other social units – e.g., the family, the city, the guild or manor – protected individuals by offering a safety net. Third, Marx suggests that any mode of production is always in flux, and hence accurate theories explaining economic phenomena at one time might not apply at other times. Economic theories must continually explain changes within the mode of production in order to maintain their validity. Because there are multiple interests and classes in capitalist economies, bourgeois economic theory must monitor crosscurrents, tensions, and internal oppositions. It cannot expect to describe a static system that will continue unchanged across time, even if this is often how it presents itself in both the macro- and micro-economic models.

Marx's fourth major point is a Hegelian one: bourgeois economics acts as if production, consumption, exchange, and distribution are isolated and distinct. But in fact these phenomena interlace in ways that make distinctions among them difficult to maintain. For example, consider production and consumption. All production consumes both labor and raw materials, and much consumption produces labor-power for the future. Moreover, the goal of most production is consumption, and the goal of most consumption is further production. Finally, producers seek to create the ideal consumer, defining the proper style of consumption. In this way, consumers are produced as well as the products they purchase. Moreover, consumption styles determine production. Ordinary consumers may accept mass-produced goods, but refined consumers may require more stylish products. Thus consumption and production are intertwined – directly, as means to ends, and as determinants of each other. Similar arguments can be given for the relations among the other terms. Such fluid concepts require a more supple rationality. Regarding some terms as dependent variables and others as independent variables will only generate misleading results.

Finally, bourgeois economics gives pride of place to production and entrepreneurialism. But it everywhere minimizes the role of labor in production and in computing exchange value. Exchange value is the relative value of one product in relation to all others. Without some means of comparing products, only the market can determine exchange value. But the common element in products is labor-power and time; it can create a basis for exchange values so that such exchanges can proceed fairly.

With such criticisms Marx challenges the aims and results of bourgeois economic theory. Some of his arguments are perhaps more effective than others, but in his last period he realized he had to attack not only the capitalist mode of production, but also the correlated "science" that describes and justifies it. He contends that economic theory is not necessarily improving over time; it simply is concerned with different modes of production, and it may conceal the dynamics of capitalism even as it reveals the true colors of capitalists.

Marx also introduces some new criticisms of capitalism. For example, he compares the circulation of capital with the circulation of consumer goods. The latter at least satisfies genuine desires. But the former's only goal is blind increase in capital formation, greater profits, and ultimately more capital circulation. The primary core of Marx's economics is the labor theory of value, which states that the value of any product is directly proportional to the amount of labor time required to make the product.[31] For Marx, economic value is produced by workers who add value to raw materials; a product's final value includes the many accretions of value added in production. But capitalism represents this value as a raw fact, as something arbitrarily assigned to a good by the market. This conceals the commodity's value in relation to the labor process, thus preventing workers from comprehending their contributions to production.

Marx also shows how exploitation occurs. By extracting surplus value from the laborer, the capitalist is able to keep profits and invest them in further capital formation. Surplus value emerges from the additional hours a day worked beyond what is necessary to replenish a worker's energies to work another day.[32] The capitalist also increases his profit by increasing the productivity of labor by investing in machines. In using these machines, laborers become their appendages, and their minds are deadened by repetitive mechanical operations. Capitalists divide the laboring process so that no meaning or self-expression remains in work. Machines may even usurp the creative elements of labor, thus further alienating workers.

Marx isolates two processes by which capitalism contributes to its own downfall. The first is the creation of international institutions. Capitalism needs international mechanisms for importing natural resources that can be fashioned into industrial products. Often this requires direct or indirect colonization. But it also depends on an international market for its finished goods in order to reap the benefits of mass production. These international systems require international means of communication that are available to workers as well as capitalists. They also create an international proletariat that gradually recognizes that its own interests transcend the artificial boundaries of nation-states.[33] Thus, capitalism creates the means by which a revolution can be planned and executed through raising workers' class-consciousness. If workers worldwide realize they are systematically reduced to poverty, then class-consciousness and solidarity can develop, making revolution possible.

In addition, Marx argues that capitalism is plagued by a long-term tendency toward reduced rates of profit.[34] Since profit is wrested primarily from labor and since machines continually replace labor, this reduces the opportunities for extracting profits. In the short term, this tendency is countered by several other trends: increasing the productivity of labor, reducing wages below subsistence level, using the reserve labor of the unemployed poor to intimidate workers, expanding markets through foreign trade, and relocating production to foreign countries to use cheaper labor. These counter-tendencies allow capitalism to maintain modest profits, but the basic direction is clear. Soon there will be no way to increase profits because the supply of cheap labor will be exhausted. Thus, capitalism undermines its ability to extract profit, the motor of the entire system.

Finally, Marx elaborates some conditions of the communist mode of production. Transitional programs would include free public education, graduated income taxes and an inheritance tax, collectivization of farming and manufacturing, and the centralization of credit.[35] Crucial turning points in the transition include the abolition of private property and the reconstitution of work. Once the revolution occurs, Marx expects an end to class division and class conflict, an overall reduction in laboring, a comfortable life for all so that people can participate equally in the new order, and the institution of common ownership of the means of production. Finally, work and leisure will become realms of freedom in which everyone can develop their creative powers for their own sake, rather than for material gain or another's profit. However, Marx does not indicate how the revolution will produce these outcomes. In this final period, his ideals remain similar to those that inspired his youth, but he still neglects to think through the effective means to achieving them. The ultimate goal becomes clearer, but the transition from the revolution to the new communist mode of production does not.

ASSESSMENT

First, one must acknowledge that many of Marx's predictions about capitalism have not come to pass. It has not produced its own demise and is unlikely to do so. The rate of profit has not fallen over time; large numbers of producers have not fallen into the working class; though income differentials between the richest and poorest groups have widened, typical workers under capitalism now can make a living wage and enjoy a diversity of benefits unanticipated by Marx. In general, real wages have not continued at a subsistence level, but have modestly improved, partly as a result of the efforts of union movements and socialist-democratic parties. Full political revolutions have only occurred in relatively *less* advanced countries – like Russia, China, and Cuba – not in the advanced capitalist countries as Marx anticipated. Capitalism still remains subject to business cycles, and its wealth may still be produced through the exploitation of labor in poorer nations, but the deep system-crises that Marx predicted have not emerged, and this casts doubt on the general analysis he provided.

Moreover, though Marx is perhaps less responsible for this, the transition to actual socialist states did not produce many of the idealistic changes he anticipated. Neither alienation, nor the division of labor, nor exploitation, nor injustice disappeared; indeed, in some cases they may have increased. The state did not wither away; if anything, it became stronger, more centralized, more bureaucratic, and more totalitarian than states operating within capitalism itself. Marx's failure to examine the problems of making the transition to socialism caused many to reject his goals. Marx would probably have lamented this fact even more than the first.

A third problem lies with the base-superstructure model of historical explanation, especially when the base is interpreted in a straightforward economic sense. In different historical eras, probably many different dimensions of culture have constituted the primary organizing institution of social life. In some eras, religious institutions and myths have dominated; in others, artists and artworks; in yet others, economic structures broadly conceived. Today media structures or perhaps technology may organize social life in advanced cultures. In fact, in some eras even postulating a single "base" structure may be misleading, since different levels of culture interact and mutually influence each other, and a major part of historical explanation is understanding how these factors interact.

A fourth problem concerns the justification Marx offers for his ideals of self-expression, solidarity, and justice. At least in the early manuscripts he tries to derive these ideals from claims about human essence, which suggests that these features are unique to human beings and thus distinctively valuable to them. However, features that are unique to humanity are not necessarily valuable. Humans may also be unique in their capacities for cruelty, self-hatred, or indifference, but these capacities do not gain value just because they might be part of humanity's essence. So while the ideals that Marx relies on in developing his critique of capitalism are important, his justification for them seems weak. Moreover, he may wrongly isolate capitalism as the predominant source of alienation, oppression, and exploitation. Certainly, these conditions existed in prior economic systems (systems including slavery, for example, and feudalism), and in some cases, more explicitly. This is not to deny they also exist under capitalism, but overcoming them may require more thoroughgoing reform of culture than simply transforming the capitalist economy.

Finally, Marx's willingness to dismiss the importance of democratic and bourgeois legal institutions may have made it easier for his followers to engage in the excesses of power to which they were disposed. Hegel believed these institutions needed some supplements and revisions, but he did not think they could be dismissed altogether. Marx too quickly asserts that the state is simply the pawn of the ruling classes, and in fact it has sometimes served this function, but it has also played many different historical roles in mediating class conflict. Marx also failed to see the emergence of a state bureaucracy after the revolution that would re-establish hierarchies of power similar to those that existed under capitalism. Again, the ill-advised rejection of bourgeois legal rights may have contributed to the ease with which these invidious political developments became possible. Nothing in his theory prevents political excesses in implementing his goals. For all his praise of praxis and revolution, Marx was remarkably short-sighted about the political effects of his proposals.

WESTERN MARXISM

Two generations span the period between Engels's death and the beginnings of "Western" Marxism.[36] Those of the first generation – Labriola (1843–1904), Mehring (1846–1919), Kautsky (1854–1938), and Plekhanov (1856–1918) – knew Engels and corresponded with him. Some were philosophers or journalists; others were militants. Each participated in the revolutionary movement in his own country and used Marxist theory to influence events. They sought to systematize historical materialism into a comprehensive theory of humanity, society, and culture that could rival other social theories in scope, coherence, and justification.

When the second generation emerged, capitalism was undergoing serious transformations and was experiencing challenges to its hegemony. A full-fledged Communist revolution succeeded in Russia in 1917. The second generation included the leaders of the Russian revolution – including Lenin (1870–1923), Bukharin (1888–1938), and Trotsky (1879–1940) – as well as leaders of socialist or Communist parties in other countries (e.g., Rosa Luxemburg (1871–1919) in Poland and Germany and Hilferding (1877–1941) in Germany). These figures published their treatises as revolutionary activity increased throughout Europe during the aftermath of World War I. Their theoretical work focused on two issues: the newest phase in the development of capitalism (monopoly capitalism) and the political strategies needed to produce socialist revolutions in different cultures.

Capitalism mutated in ways unanticipated by Marx, and his ideas had to be reinterpreted in the light of these events. Some second-generation Marxists studied the importance of the agricultural sector; others, the realm of finance; still others, the relevance of tariffs, international trade, and trusts in capitalist development. Still others explored how various ethnic subcultures (not just workers) might contribute to revolutionary transformation. Finally, some examined the role of imperialism and colonialism in maintaining capitalist domination. Through these efforts, Marxist theory became more complex and supple, better able to comprehend the distinctive features of each country's historical and social context. In addition, they refined Marx's political theory and tactics, yielding a better understanding of the role of the state and a more astute grasp of workers' organizations (trade unions and political parties).

With the outbreak of World War I, however, fissures began to develop within Marxism. Some Marxists sided with their own nations rather than support the international working-class movement. Moreover, the war produced a series of crises in Russia, which culminated in the successful revolution of 1917, in which Lenin's party took power. The establishment of a socialist state in a primarily agrarian, underdeveloped country like Russia was not predicted by Marxist theory. Moreover, Marx had little to say about the actual process of creating a socialist state. Lenin and Trotsky addressed these problems in the first decade after the revolution. International capitalism was not content to abandon Russia; it made various efforts to destabilize and undermine the new revolutionary regime. The Russian leaders were preoccupied with the sheer survival of their revolution. Other revolutionary insurrections arose in central Europe, and many of these were suppressed with military force.

When Lenin died in 1924, Stalin eventually consolidated power in Russia by 1927. He created a police state answerable only to himself, which vested all power in the hands of his bureaucracy. Lenin's revolutionary institutions were either abandoned or suppressed. Stalin killed all other contenders for Communist party leadership, eventually assassinating even Trotsky. Most importantly, party intellectuals in Russia and in the official Communist parties throughout Europe were censored, repressed, and forced to obey Stalin's dictates. The effects of this intellectual repression were dramatic. Russia became an intellectual wasteland, and European Communist parties became Stalin's mouthpieces. Stalin's version of Marxism became orthodoxy, and no opposing tendencies were tolerated. In order for serious Marxist thought to continue, it had to emerge outside the official Communist parties. Thus, "Western" Marxism really means non-Stalinist Marxism deriving from Western Europe.

Western Marxists can be divided into three groups: Hegelian Marxists (Lukács, Gramsci); members of the Frankfurt School, founded in 1924 (Critical Theorists such as Horkheimer, Adorno, Benjamin, and Marcuse); and more recent figures who challenge or inherit these traditions (Althusser,[37] Habermas). Hegelian Marxists rethink Marx's relation to Hegel, discovering important connections between them. They initiated a broader reconsideration of Hegel for all areas of Continental philosophy. The Frankfurt School formed as Fascism was growing in Germany. This group developed "Critical Theory," and they produced important social research on authoritarianism and on capitalist economy and culture. Horkheimer was one of the movement's directors and did some of his best work with Adorno. Marcuse and Benjamin were important contributors. Marcuse sought to integrate Marx with Freud; he became a leading theorist of the "New Left" during the 1960s. More recent figures, such as Habermas, reconsider the assumptions and foundations of earlier traditions of Western Marxism to determine whether it can remain relevant in the current historical era.

The broader picture

Here is a partial list of the leading contributors to Western Marxism, by country.

In *Germany*, Marxism remained alive in the "Critical Theory" developed by the Frankfurt School, whose members included Max Horkheimer (1895–1973), Theodor Adorno (1903–69), Herbert Marcuse (1898–1979), Ernst Bloch (1885–1977), Walter Benjamin (1892–1940), and, eventually, Jürgen Habermas (b. 1929).

In *France*, Marxism played a central role in Alexandre Kojève (1902–68), early Merleau-Ponty (1908–61), late Sartre (1905–80), Simone Weil (1909–43), Henri Lefèbvre (1901–91), Lucien Goldmann (1913–70), Cornelius Castoriadis (b. 1922), Louis Althusser (1918–90), Nikos Poulantzis, Andre Gorz (b. 1924), Ernesto Laclau, and Chantal Mouffe.

In *Italy*, Marxism was rethought by Antonio Gramsci (1891–1937), Galvano Della Volpe (1895–1968), Lucio Colletti (1924–2001), and Antonio Negri (b. 1933).

In *Eastern Europe*, it was reinterpreted by Georg Lukács (1895–1971), Karl Korsch (1886–1961), Mahailo Markovic, Gajo Petrovic, and Ernst Mandel (b. 1923).

In *England*, cultural studies emerged in the work of Raymond Williams (1921–88), Stuart Hall, Perry Anderson, E. P. Thompson (b. 1924), Immanuel Wallerstein (b. 1930), and Terry Eagleton (b. 1943).

In the *United States*, the most prominent Marxist theorist is Fredric Jameson, though several émigrés eventually found asylum here during World War II. All but Marcuse returned to Germany after the end of the war.

Western Marxism developed during the rise of counter-revolutions throughout Europe after 1917. The development of Fascism, the rise of nationalism, the emergence of state-guided capitalism, the inflexibility and repressiveness of Stalinism in Russia, the outbreak of World War II and the rise of communism in less developed nations like China, Cuba, and Vietnam all had to be explained and understood. Moreover, after World War II, capitalism mutated again into consumer capitalism and mass society. The late twentieth century brought the rise of international corporations, whose power surpasses that of any nation-state. New developments in the arts arose – modernism and, later, postmodernism. The revolutionary potential of working-class movements in capitalist democracies was weakened by new institutions that created a social "safety net." Later, the union movement was marginalized and broken, primarily by conservative governments. Many hard-won union benefits were reduced or eliminated altogether.

There were also important theoretical developments. The publication of Marx's early philosophical manuscripts made possible a better retrospective understanding of his theories in relation to previous philosophers, especially Hegel, but also Kant and Spinoza, and this produced a re-evaluation of his achievements. Simultaneously, a worldwide rejuvenation of interest in Hegel occurred, partly in order to understand how Marx's early thinking developed out of Hegel. This effort to interpret Hegel more sympathetically was led by Kojève and Hyppolite in France, Lukács in Hungary, and Marcuse in the US. Hegel's early political writings and Jena manuscripts received serious scholarly attention, highlighting his similarities with Marx.

In addition, many new theoretical movements arose after Marx's death, many of which are discussed in this book: psychoanalysis, phenomenology, existentialism, structuralism, as well as logical positivism and empiricist social science. Some Western Marxists attempted a synthesis of Marx and Freud (Marcuse is often interpreted this way). Sartre himself attempted a synthesis of Marxism and existentialism. Adorno reacted forcefully against Husserl's efforts to make philosophy into a strict science and against Heidegger's existentialism. Lukács, on the other hand, can be interpreted as appropriating Heidegger within his own Marxist framework. In general, Stalinist Marxism simply rejected the value of these movements, but the Western Marxists could be fairer in assessing them. They strengthened Marxism by challenging and appropriating the best insights of these movements. Thus, both practical realities and theoretical innovations influenced the development of Western Marxism.

CORE CONTRIBUTIONS

Western Marxists take epistemological issues more seriously than Marx and address them with more sophistication than Engels. Unfortunately, their language can often be abstract, academic, and tendentious. They do mount a serious challenge to the dominance of positivist social science, arguing that social theory should have some transformative social aims and that it should at least examine potential horrors and tensions in the existing political-economic system. They also defend, and sometimes exemplify, a model of a committed intellectual who addresses both theoretical and practical problems that prevent successful social movements from emerging and succeeding. Though some Western Marxists tend to be isolated from larger political movements, they search for ways to nurture them by maintaining a critical perspective on the current stage of capitalism.

Western Marxists challenge Marx's economism, and for this reason they often examine social superstructures (ideology, art, media, and culture generally, as well as the state and legal apparatus) more carefully and insightfully. Many saw in modern art a renewal of hope for progressive social transformation. Many wrote treatises in aesthetics; some wrote books specifically devoted to new developments in particular arts, like music and film. Some return to a Hegelianism that sees an underlying unity to all spheres of culture, including the economy. Others retain a looser notion of dialectical integration among various spheres of culture, in part to provide some autonomy to those areas that might lead the way out of dark times. Like Marx, they all stress the importance of challenging the reigning ideology of capitalism, sometimes unmasking its distortions and other times using it to criticize capitalism's existing economic practices. Most importantly, they defend the view that humans make history; people are not mere pawns of historical forces. They may need a rich analysis of the current historical moment in order to move history in desired directions, but Western Marxists take one of the their main goals to be providing this comprehension.

In the midst of serious crises – in history (the rise of Fascism), in Marxist theory (the resilience of capitalism; the co-optation of the working class), and in Marxist practice (the betrayal of Marx's ideals by Stalin) – they make a valiant effort to save what is still viable in Marx's thought while abandoning positions that can no longer be maintained. They continue to seek ways of producing less alienated lives, and they offer conceptual explorations that show how traditional Enlightenment values – liberty, equality, fraternity, reason, and happiness – can still contribute to progressive social change. They strive to rectify the purely formal interpretation of these ideals that dominates bourgeois ideology. They continue Marx's project of seeing through the smokescreen of capitalist self-justifications and distortions. If workers have become unreliable agents of social transformation, they look to other groups (e.g., Marcuse's efforts to create an umbrella organization of disaffected groups) or they create distinctive institutions (e.g., Habermas's communicative public spheres or Gramsci's organic intellectuals) to fulfill this function.

My discussion of this complex movement will be limited. I offer modest summaries of four major figures, each coming to prominence in a different generation, each representing a different aspect of Western Marxism: Gramsci (Hegelian), Horkheimer (Frankfurt School), Marcuse (the New Left), and Habermas (the current era).

GRAMSCI

Influenced by the Italian Hegelian Benedetto Croce (1866–1952) and by his organizational work for the Communist Party in Turin, Antonio Gramsci (1891–1937) emphasizes the centrality of human action in changing history and criticizes orthodox Marxists for believing that capitalism will collapse of its own accord. People make history in specific historical circumstances, which themselves have been made by previous generations. The world is humanly produced, and people contribute to history in light of values guiding their actions.[38] Revolutionary transformation cannot occur without powerful motivations, and self-interest is rarely sufficient to produce major cultural, political, social, and economic changes. The superstructures – especially ideology – shape people's motivation and determine the experienced legitimacy (or lack thereof) of the dominant order. Gramsci stresses the importance of superstructures and civil society in achieving successful change. He notes that Marxists often fail to criticize the underlying legitimating ideology of capitalism, and this allows capitalists to present their own interests as universal ones ("what's good for big business is good for the nation"). Bourgeois values remain dominant because the masses continue to live by them. Revolutionaries must reshape cultural institutions, not just economic institutions, to create permanent change.[39] This means refashioning education, journalism, the arts, religion, and the media. Because Gramsci regards these factors as equally central to a society, his position recalls Hegel's, who construed all elements of a culture to be parts of an organic whole. Gramsci relies on this organic metaphor.

He distinguishes between traditional and organic intellectuals, for example. "Traditional" intellectuals characteristically remain aloof from the political and social struggles of their times, pretending to occupy a supra-historical standpoint. "Organic" intellectuals emerge from these struggles and derive important insights from participating in them.[40] Intellectuals are typically rooted in a specific class or subgroup; they help define the self-images and aspirations of these groups. Gramsci thinks the working class can and does produce its own leaders, organizers, and creative minds. Their task – if they are to succeed in building a long-lasting revolution – is to unite the working class and to forge alliances with other classes by offering a more compelling and attractive world-view than capitalists. This inclusiveness is required by new stages of capitalism, which gain greater penetration into the popular mind, co-opting even many workers. Their job requires persuasion and imagination as well as criticism and creativity. Organic intellectuals not only create new theory; they also learn how to use it in creating concrete historical change. One test of effective thought is its ability to harness energies that will make social change possible.

Thus, a critique of the capitalist world-view can play an important revolutionary role. Only if the shortcomings of the existing order are widely acknowledged will an alternative be given a serious hearing. Central to Gramsci's analysis of culture is his concept of ideological hegemony. This exists when a system of ideas so dominates the popular consciousness that force and violence are unnecessary to maintain mass allegiance to the dominant order.[41] The hegemonic ideas allow the dominant class to rule with legitimacy and consent, making repression unnecessary. The so-called ideological superstructures do not merely "reflect" the economic base, but actively sustain it. The hegemonic ideology typically draws institutional support from education, religion, and popular culture, and is embedded in "common sense." If this dominant ideology can be shaken, then a mass movement to transform the economic mode of production can succeed. Without such a critique, only a minority movement can threaten the elite, and it can become just as oppressive as the existing order. Gramsci's political strategy expresses his democratic vision of the new society. Ideology organizes the way ordinary people see themselves and act. Hegemonic ideology becomes "naturalized," accepted as the obvious and correct way to live; its power derives from its unreflective acceptance. Workers may internalize it even if it opposes their interests. Hegemonic ideology also produces passivity toward existing power structures. It must not only be rejected; it must be superseded if a revolutionary movement is to sustain long-term change. Organic intellectuals help produce this new ideology in the course of challenging the dominant order.

Gramsci insists that real people make revolutions in risky historical circumstances; they do not happen because of scientific laws of history. Classical Marxism failed to predict that a revolution would occur in Russia, but it happened nonetheless because of the astute leadership of Lenin and the Bolsheviks. Revolutionary movements often cannot wait for the economic factors to ripen; serious political opportunities must be seized.[42] Gramsci rejects the notion that a vanguard party should determine when the time for revolution is right. He believes that democratically organized councils engaged in continuous dialogue with the masses are needed to sustain revolutionary momentum. Sometimes economic factors seem ripe for change, but the dominant order's ideological factors still command allegiance. The best hope for lasting revolution is a simultaneous challenge to both base and superstructures.[43] An organic transformation can occur if this strategy succeeds on both fronts. Gramsci expects revolutionary activity will be supported by the masses when their hearts and minds have been converted. He solicits support from avant-garde artists, educators, and popular heroes. An internal critique of capitalist ideals that yields more vital and inspiring future goals can produce ideological change.

Gramsci believes that Lenin's "vanguard party" concept shows little promise of success in the rest of Europe. He distinguishes between a "war of movement" and a "war of position."[44] The war of movement consists of direct military assault on the state with the aim of overthrowing political power and eventually reorganizing economic power relations. A war of position strives to build mass consensus around a new set of goals; it thus undermines the legitimacy of the hegemonic ideology. Gramsci gives priority to the war of position because social relations and identities are reconstituted in this process. This change is needed because capitalist ideas now dominate nearly all institutions of civil society. Challenge is needed on many fronts. Revolution consists of significant changes in both institutions and ideals; it develops nascent possibilities in the old order and refashions them into a new vision. The transfer of state power is only one moment in this total process; it can happen with less violence and greater democracy if it occurs gradually by reshaping social institutions. In the past, capitalism dominated by masking its exploitation and pretending to satisfy people's needs. This strategy must be exposed and shown to favor limited, minority interests. Social transformation will only be complete when economic, political, social, and ideological relations are transformed and when alternative institutions successfully realize its newly forged social goals.

Gramsci's conception of rationality or truth is exploratory and open-ended. Because he thinks many positions are likely to contain some element of truth, he thinks the rational thinker will give each position its due. Each standpoint may contain features overlooked by others, and the best view is the most complete and coherent one.[45] Gramsci also believes that history's direction is determined by many collective wills seeking to realize their guiding ideals. The best theories not only command agreement, but also effectively produce needed changes. For Gramsci, the creative philosopher must find ways to transform these guiding values through metaphors that will energize the masses. History may limit what can be achieved at a given time, but thought and action must seize the opportunities history offers. Change will not emerge if the necessary political and intellectual leadership is lacking. Theory and practice are thus interwoven; theorists find the best possibilities that can be realized in the current situation, while agents re-examine theorists' goals and create new identities in the course of producing historical change.

Gramsci insists that human nature is not fixed, but constantly open to transformation. The human condition in any given era is only a point of departure, not a finished fact.[46] Human agents acting collectively have the capacity to refashion human possibilities. Rather than insuring "progress," history offers only a process of becoming. How progressive its results are depends on the victorious groups. In addition, individuals are constituted by their social relations, which in turn are transformed by political alliances and history. No one exists in isolation; people are defined by the group actions in which they participate. Individuals can change themselves only by changing their surrounding social relations; this is why political and social theory – not just economic analysis – are so important.[47] The goal of philosophy for Gramsci is to find the constructive potentials in the existing order – as well as its contradictions – in order to inspire and guide serious change. In addition to arguing that civil society and ideology must be taken seriously, Gramsci transforms Marxism by importing more flexible political strategies, making it a living theory that must evolve with historical practice and development, and showing how it can better analyze new stages of capitalism.

HORKHEIMER

One goal of the Institute for Social Research – an interdisciplinary group of like-minded social theorists initially located in Frankfurt, Germany – was to relate philosophical theories to empirical research. Its members believed that empirical research must be guided by philosophical questions and that socioeconomic philosophical theories require empirical testing. They criticized narrowly conceived, positivist empirical research in the social sciences because it assumes that social reality is fixed (and need only be described, rather than transformed), and they created research programs that sought to accurately comprehend the historical forces operating in their era.

Max Horkheimer (1895–1973) was the most important director of the Institute and the founder of the movement called "Critical Theory." Horkheimer became Director of the Institute in 1931, a dark period in German history: Hitler was rising to power, a worldwide depression had created great suffering, and the only alternatives to Fascism were monopolistic capitalism and Stalin's totalitarianism. Gone was Gramsci's optimism that people could take control of their historical destiny through collective action. Many socialist movements throughout the capitalist world had been brutally suppressed, or workers had been co-opted by new government programs (e.g., social security, minimum wage, and banking reform laws) or by nationalism. Even worse, many Germans supported Hitler's rise to power, and this appeal required explanation. Horkheimer's goal was to protect *some* hope for positive historical change and to comprehend the forces producing the current situation. Because the times were so antagonistic to socialist goals, he argues for a critical perspective on the current order.[48] Not only its ideology, but its institutional supports require analysis. Unless its contradictions can be dissected, the masses might simply capitulate to the "inevitability of the way things are." The possibility for radical social change would disappear.

Horkheimer agrees with Hegel that internal criticisms of theories – those rooted in the criteria of evaluation propounded by the theory – are the most effective. He agrees with Gramsci that historical change only happens if human beings act to produce such changes, but he no longer sees any revolutionary potential in the working class, and thus rejects Marx's claim that historical progress is inevitable. He acknowledges that history is a totalization in process, but thinks it may never be completed. He seeks a dialectical analysis of each part's relationship to the cultural whole. Like Gramsci, he believes that a potent critique of bourgeois ideology could be derived from commonly accepted Enlightenment ideals (freedom, justice, equality).[49] He agrees that ideology often is concealed by formulas that seem natural and inevitable to the ordinary person (e.g., the inevitability of egoism, the abstract freedom to sell one's labor-power or not). Ideology substitutes limited special interests for the general interest and presents current historical practices as inevitable. Critical Theorists must contest such ideologies by unmasking them, demonstrating historical alternatives, and analyzing the contradictions informing the present. One aspect of this unmasking operation shows how the typical formulas supporting capitalism really mean the opposite of they seem. Thus, a "free economy" often means near-monopolistic control in which the state is prevented from limiting powerful corporations; "fair exchange of labor on an open market" typically means exploiting laborers for the lowest possible wages, etc.[50] Horkheimer hoped such ideological unmasking would awaken the masses to their true condition.

He notes that the various social sciences (economics, psychology, sociology, anthropology) are guided by different methodological and metaphysical assumptions and that adjudicating these different paradigms is difficult. An impartial observer cannot always tell which research programs are the most promising. Thus, empirical social science pursues many different experiments, rarely achieving coherent results. On the other hand, social philosophy often explores questions of essence without examining the empirical data. Horkheimer sought to rectify this isolation of social theory from social research by developing the theoretical implications of the best empirical studies in order to unify them into a larger framework that would reform Marxist theory and using social theory to generate culturally useful empirical research programs.[51] He also suggests that if research leads to positive social change, this would confirm the theories it propounds. Thus, his goal was to create a real interchange between philosophical social theory and empirical research. He assembled a group of diverse thinkers to create this interchange and execute the research programs they collectively decided would yield useful results.

This research program requires historical study as well. Examining specific societies in specific eras, Horkheimer sought to clarify connections among their economic organization, psychic structures, class relations, political-educational-cultural institutions, and ideologies.[52] He uses survey research to study current trends and statistics to better comprehend existing historical records. On the basis of this research effort, Critical Theorists could work toward better-confirmed, politically effective general theories. Rejecting the task of providing metaphysical comfort and "meaning," Horkheimer's main goal was to discover illuminating theories that could facilitate social transformation.

Positivist social science simply describes and explains the existing order; Critical Theory highlights the flaws in that order and sketches historically achievable alternatives.[53] Critical Theory emphasizes that social reality is made rather than given, while positivist social science treats society like nature – as a fixed reality that can only be explained, rather than transformed. Because social reality is constantly changing, responsible Critical Theorists must recognize structural changes. In addition, Horkheimer expects Critical Theory to challenge mainstream social science by reviewing and assessing its results. He rejects the view that social science must have only one set of methodologies because alternative methods often yield illuminating contrasts. He also insists that theories not be accepted solely on the basis of experimental confirmation or abstract criteria (e.g., simplicity), arguing that political effectiveness is also relevant.[54] Positivist social sciences typically serve ideological functions that must be unmasked.

The criteria by which Horkheimer evaluated the present order are similar to Marx's: genuine self-realization that overcomes capitalist alienation for all social agents; a social order that is rationally governed and consciously directed by its members through collective decisions; and a work system that would pay living wages and offer opportunities for self-development.[55] Most of the other members of the Frankfurt School accept these evaluative criteria, but they differ in their estimates of their achievability. Unlike them, Horkheimer says little about aesthetics or high culture (art, music, literature). Marcuse does examine art and also tries to integrate Marx with Freud and some tenets of existentialism.

MARCUSE

From 1928 until 1932, Herbert Marcuse (1898–1979) assisted the existential philosopher, Martin Heidegger,[56] after receiving his doctorate in literature in 1922. Later, he published several books on Hegel, was among the first to appreciate the importance of Marx's early manuscripts, and attempted to integrate Freud's and Heidegger's theories with Marxism. He joined the Frankfurt School in 1933 after becoming disenchanted with Heidegger's support for the Nazi party. He fled from Hitler to the US and later accepted affiliation with the Institute for Social Research, which had by then relocated to Columbia University in New York. Starting in 1941, he worked for the US government's secret service to resist Fascism, continuing until well after the end of the war. As a result, he knew details about Stalinist Russia that allowed him to publicly challenge that country's legitimacy as a Marxist society. Instead of returning to Germany after the war, as did many other members of the Institute, he joined the philosophy faculty at Brandeis University in 1958 and eventually moved to the University of California at San Diego in 1965. His later writings, especially *One-Dimensional Man* (1964) and *An Essay on Liberation* (1969), helped stimulate the rise of the New Left in the 1960s, whose critique of the dominant order Marcuse sharpened and elaborated.

Marcuse integrates elements of existentialism and Freud with Marx by relating alienation to existential inauthenticity[57] and to Freudian repression.[58] Heideggerean inauthenticity involves living one's life according to established norms and abdicating one's own possibilities for self-determination. Alienated individuals blindly accept the economic routines of capitalism and typically feel controlled by impersonal forces. Becoming authentic would thus involve overcoming alienation and rejecting the routines of the established system. However, Marcuse believes that the essence of humanity cannot be defined ahistorically (as Heidegger sought to do); it must be situated and re-envisioned in each historical era.[59] By "essence," Marcuse means the best human possibilities, rather than "the necessary conditions of being human," as Heidegger did. Still, Marcuse's Hegelian historicizing of human essence offers an important challenge to Heidegger. Moreover, alienated individuals typically repress their deeper need for libidinal satisfaction, a need Freud believes is universal. Marcuse suggests that Freud's eros can be a source of creativity, free play, sensuality, and joy; thus, it can become a drive that challenges capitalist alienation.[60] Marcuse believes that Freud missed its critical potential. Repressive self-denial allows people to tolerate their alienated, repetitive lives. By rejecting this repression, individuals can transcend their alienation, actively pursue their need for joy, and discover the possibility of genuine freedom. Both authenticity and eros can release imaginative possibilities that reveal more promising futures. This new sense of direction can mobilize enough energy to power a mass movement for social change.

Like Horkheimer, Marcuse challenges two of Marx's key tenets, i.e., that the proletariat is the only candidate for leading a revolution and that capitalism will eventually suffer self-destructive crises. Not only has capitalism survived the Depression and two world wars, it has co-opted workers through appeals to nationalism and through improved standards of living. Revolutionary change is no longer assured. Capitalism still produces the means of its own supersession (primarily through creating technology that could satisfy basic human needs on a mass scale), but these must be utilized in service of a new aesthetic. Today a mass movement for change will need the support of minorities, outsiders, disaffected intellectuals, professionals, and artists, as well as workers.[61] Radical leaders must learn to speak to the concerns of all these groups and forge solidarity among them. To provoke a crisis of legitimacy, Marcuse encourages people to reject the current order: refusing its incentives and sanctions while seeking the means to create more fulfilled lives, individually and collectively.[62] His vision allowed the political and counter-cultural elements of the New Left – which rose to prominence in the 1960s and '70s – to forge a coalition.

Marcuse's best-known treatise is *One Dimensional Man* (1964). There he shows that capitalism flattens everyday life to a "one-dimensional" existence, anaesthetizing people and concealing their lack of freedom and joy via subtle institutional controls and consumerism.[63] Capitalism implants "false needs" in people – desires they would not have if left alone – and induces them to waste their lives working to satisfy them.[64] The state is highly bureaucratized, dividing people into interest groups so that larger unities of opposition cannot form. In addition, many liberal-democratic institutions fail to provide the freedom they promise.[65] Most work is deadening; even successful capitalists often question the value of their success. Elections, which are supposed to offer people the opportunity to determine their collective destiny, often fail to offer significant choices among candidates or ideologies, and their outcomes are usually determined by manipulative, hypocritical advertising campaigns. Though everyone has the right to speak, few critical voices are taken seriously, and few alternatives to the status quo are even proposed. Popular culture merely distracts people from their alienation, and the mass media numb people into resignation. They manage and manipulate public opinion, rather than encouraging reflection, critique, and creative options. A culture that pretends to offer unlimited freedoms thus in fact produces despair, boredom, and resignation. The real potential for democratic participation in determining the historical future is subverted. The existing system is militarist, brutal, and ugly; yet it reproduces its values in conservative majorities.

Marcuse's alternative vision includes self-realizing work, sensuous appreciation of nature, full exercise of one's talents, and communal solidarity. He supplements these with Freudian pleasures, existential authenticity (realizing one's human essence), and Hegelian dialectical rationality.[66] Some of these ideals will require aesthetic reimagination, but some can be revitalized from past eras. Together they constitute a new sensibility, a genuine alternative to the competitiveness, selfishness, and indifference of the status quo. Seeking to restore critical thought, Marcuse urges people to reject the routines of the current system because they fail to provide genuine satisfaction. Not just alienated workers, but anyone disaffected from the system can become a positive force for change. Fragmented forces of social rebellion exist, but they must learn to unify and cooperate.

Marcuse appeals to the emancipatory possibilities of art and memory to supply alternatives to the existing order.[67] Art makes the familiar strange, and the best artworks challenge accepted pieties and ingrained habits. Art can stimulate both memory and imagination, allowing people to recall or project moments of personal joy and collective achievement. These can provide a basis for challenging the current stage of capitalism. Art alters what can be conceived. In addition, historical recollection awakens people to the fact that social life is created, not given; it too offers alternatives that can challenge the current order. Marcuse is critical of social science because it invites acceptance of the status quo through its emphasis on description and explanation. He doubts that social science can become critical in the way art is. For this reason he seeks a new aesthetic sensibility to support his radical agenda.

HABERMAS

In his essay "Tasks of a Critical Theory of Society," Jürgen Habermas (b. 1927) reviews the differences between his own research program and Horkheimer's earlier one. He suggests that basing normative objections to capitalism on Marx's historical dialectic (that ideal human possibilities will eventually emerge historically) is a questionable strategy because Marx's predictions have been unreliable. Habermas is more concerned to let individuals determine and pursue their own visions of the good life, and he tries to defend a more limited set of procedural requirements that will facilitate democratic determination of collective goals.[68] He also notes that Horkheimer's emphasis on family structures that allegedly nurture docile personalities is less relevant today, both because families are less authoritarian and because peer groups have taken over many socialization functions. More significant is the disjunction of experience across generations because of the speed of technological change. Adolescents are worse at coping with their everyday problems because their parents are simply unable to guide them.[69] Also, against Horkheimer's exclusively negative assessment of the mass media, Habermas stresses their positive potential for creating forums for communal democratic discussion.[70] Although he agrees with Horkheimer that workers have been partially co-opted by capitalism, he notes the new emergence of protest groups addressing quality of life issues (e.g., the environment, health care, and control of technology). Moreover, the methods and channels for contesting the current system no longer center on class conflicts, but instead are drawn from diverse generations, subcultures, and ethnicities. Indeed, some counter-institutions (e.g., Green parties) have surfaced to unify these diverse protests.[71] Finally, Habermas believes that philosophical theory has a different role to play in contemporary intellectual life. It can function as a creative resource for the development of new concepts and theories, which may eventually lead to new sciences, and it may mediate the diverse forms of rationality and diverse interests in pursuing knowledge, thus contributing toward a more coherent intellectual culture. Philosophy cannot any longer claim to provide foundations for other disciplines or to produce a single rationality that can unify all others.[72] Habermas thus defends the importance of rationality and theory construction in philosophy, while producing reasonable foundations for his more limited political program.

Habermas attempts to revitalize commitments to reason and democracy in an era that regards them with cynicism. He finds deep connections between them, because democratic participation in public forums is essential to improving rational arguments since they can correct for ideological distortions resulting from dogmatism and taken-for-granted assumptions, and because rational collective discussion improves democracy's outcomes. Public discussion can play a social function similar to the function that psychoanalysis can play for individuals; both overcome self-deception, bias, and irrational attachments to beliefs.[73] In Habermas's ideal dialogue situation, participants reach agreement based on cogent argument, careful examination of evidence, and listening to all viewpoints. Each participant retains autonomy while gradually discovering solidarity by participating in the discussion. Rather than achieving a mutual interpenetration of identities – as can happen in Hegelian recognition – Habermas's intersubjectivity maintains a respectful distance among participants and primarily concerns belief formation and collective determination of policy. Because this communicative rational process is necessarily intersubjective, Habermas claims to break with the individualistic knowing subject that he believes has dominated Continental philosophy since Kant and to achieve a genuinely intersubjective foundation for both ethical and political decisions.[74]

Habermas's ultimate aim in rethinking rationality and democracy is to provide an effective critique of capitalism. He notes that even Marx missed the significance of communicative reason because of his central emphasis on work and production, which are governed by purposive rationality. Rational consensus derived from public discussions can better ground serious critique of the current order. And to the extent that this order stultifies communicative reason, it oppresses everyone. In addition, Habermas engages in a continuous critical dialogue with prominent approaches in social science and social theory (including hermeneutics, systems theory, functionalism, structuralism, and poststructuralism). He identifies their shortcomings and gradually builds a framework that can supersede them.[75] Just as Marx targeted classical economics as the advertising agent of the capitalist order, so Habermas charges a variety of social theories with complicity in maintaining oppression. Yet he also learns from their mistakes and incorporates their best insights into his position.[76] He refashions many of the themes discussed by the previous generation of Critical Theorists and responds to central developments in recent analytic and Continental philosophy (e.g., especially action theory and hermeneutics).

Habermas agrees with some hermeneutic thinkers (especially Gadamer) that an interest-free standpoint in social inquiry is impossible and thus that all knowledge is conditioned by interests. He distinguishes three types of such interests: prediction and control (the interest that governs most positivist sciences); mutual understanding (which is essential to the development of all inquiry as well as to interpersonal comprehension within and across cultures; this interest infuses many of the human sciences); and personal and social emancipation through distortion-free dialogue (which is made possible by self-examination and mutual criticism).[77] These latter two interests are just as important in producing knowledge as the first, but the first has typically dominated the others, especially in the sciences. The three interests may produce different kinds of knowledge, but all of them are important. Any theory of knowledge that ignores one of them cannot be adequate. Still, Habermas challenges the relativism implicit in the hermeneutic claim that interests condition knowledge by insisting that certain universal preconditions for the success of communicative reason exist and by showing that all three types of knowledge-interest exist in all cultures. Communicative reason need not be confined to public, political forums; it can contribute to transforming the workplace, the university, and professions as well (encouraging greater worker-management discussion of corporate policies, greater student-faculty cooperation in educational improvement, and greater professional-client discussion of project goals). Moreover, Habermas challenges hermeneutics directly by positing the third form of self-critical rationality and a fundamental interest in *distortion-free* communication and self-understanding. This makes actual interpersonal dialogue (not merely imaginary scenarios) essential to his position because each participant's conclusions must respond to challenges from other participants in order to insure that everyone's assumptions are tested. Though hermeneutic thinkers typically seek an empathic grasp of others in their own terms, Habermas insists that persons must directly challenge one another's arguments and evidence in order to achieve genuine, rational consensus. Understanding and agreement must be reached through open discussion with those to whom the resulting policies and practices matter.

This focus on communicative, emancipatory reason allows Habermas to challenge traditional epistemology, which postulates isolated subjects relying only on their own sources of evidence and insight. This individualist approach to knowledge typically overlooks distortions that derive from unexamined assumptions. When unfettered discussion occurs in an ideal speech situation, everyone interested in the outcome scrutinizes all participants' potential biases. In the ideal speech situation, each participant has an opportunity to speak, to react to the ideas of all the others, and to ratify each step on the path to agreement. This full discussion of presuppositions, issues of fact, forms of reasoning, and evaluation of potential outcomes produces a deeper examination of everyone's reasoning than can be achieved by any single person alone. Intersubjective democratic discussion thus promises a convergence toward truth than is unavailable within an isolated individual. These discussions address not only future policies, but also existing practices in government bureaucracies, the workplace, and other institutions. Each participant appeals to the uncoerced assent of all other participants. Habermas seeks to create a variety of public spheres at both the local and national levels, through the use of media and through face-to-face discussions.[78] Moreover, all conclusions are subject to continuous review and further analysis in order to insure that vital objections have not been overlooked. Habermas's focus on democratic discussion, however, produces a theory centered on the formal procedures that will guarantee such discussion, leaving matters of substance (political, economic, and cultural) to the decisions of the participants themselves. He thus accepts a much humbler role as a social-political philosopher.

The social and economic policies of the current capitalist order have rarely been subjected to such interpersonal scrutiny. Capitalism has undergone crises in legitimation (e.g., depressions and wars) and its reigning ideologies promulgate distortion, through which the interests of a specific class or small group of people are represented as the universal interest (or the good of the smaller group is promulgated as the good of the whole).[79] Although the media and political leaders may strive to conceal these crises, critical discussion among the populace can uncover them if it is allowed to develop. Until local and national public spheres are created in which the goals and policies of corporations and the state can be discussed, the current order is likely to benefit only a minority of citizens. Moreover, both capitalism and the welfare state are dominated by instrumental rationality; the two other types of reason (mutual understanding and emancipatory discussion) – and the interests they serve – are ignored. Only by responding to the additional interests implicit in these types of rationality and through critical discussion with those affected by its policies can the capitalist system and liberal state regain some legitimacy. Habermas uses the concept of the life-world of the social participants to provide a basis from which they might challenge the ideology and assumptions of the capitalist order.

Habermas defends the important Enlightenment ideals of truth, justice, and autonomy by showing that they can emerge from collective discussion in ideal speech situations. Participants must remain autonomous and must appeal to the unbiased rationality of the other participants. Indeed, all participants must commit themselves to four criteria of evaluation: comprehensibility, truth, sincerity, and social relevance or appropriateness.[80] Any claim can be challenged on any of these grounds. These values are thus presupposed by Habermas's best mechanism for achieving knowledge and consensus. They are conditions of possibility for communicative reason and thus are binding on every inquiry. When these values are respected, Habermas argues that participants in ideal speech situations can achieve consensual agreement on the basis of argument and reasons alone. By participating in such public discussions, each citizen is forced to take account of the perspectives of other citizens and to see issues from a diversity of relevant viewpoints. By allowing agreement to emerge gradually, on the basis of mutual discussion and challenge, autonomy can be respected even as solidarity is gradually achieved.

ASSESSMENT

Each of the Western Marxists contributes to the development of Marx's thought. Gramsci stresses transforming popular ideologies and creating viable leaders to improve the chances for a stable socialist transformation that would more successfully achieve Marx's goals. Horkheimer challenges positivist social science and creates a path through which Critical Theory and empirical science can work together to understand the current stages of capitalism and to discover effective mechanisms for change. Marcuse utilizes insights from more recent theorists (Freud and Heidegger) to buttress Marx's arguments against alienation and to create a viable ideal of freedom, while also providing a basis for uniting a wider diversity of groups dedicated to social transformation. Finally, Habermas employs his considerable understanding of contemporary philosophy and social theory to provide a basis for assessing the strengths and weaknesses of late capitalism, while also creating a better justified, more democratic vision of social criticism and cultural change. These Marxists thus continue to mount searching objections to everyday life under contemporary capitalism, and they strive to forge viable institutional mechanisms to propagate needed social transformations.

SUMMARY

The main problem for Marxism now is the lack of a significant movement to implement its goals. Marxist theory has always been informed by politically transformative praxis, but there are at best only marginal efforts to achieve major social change today. Moreover, the failure of Marx's predictions concerning capitalism suggests that his economic theories have significant flaws. No one can pretend that Marxism is better grounded epistemologically than current alternatives in social science or that Marxism is a more "scientific" approach to society.

The basic situation is that socialism has not yet proven to be a viable alternative to capitalism, but capitalism remains a deeply flawed way of organizing a culture. Two tasks are necessary: finding ways of transforming capitalism in the direction of Marx's goals from within and finding ways of mobilizing people to identify and rectify their discontents, thus allowing them to actively shape their collective destiny. This will require a better critique of capitalist ideology than so far has been forthcoming from Western Marxism. It will also require imagining alternative institutional futures that acknowledge that state socialism is no longer a viable option. This may require a return to utopian thinking that is informed by an analysis of current historical realities.

The Western Marxists perhaps better understand the operation of capitalist superstructures (e.g., ideology, law, the state, art, administration, education) than Marx did, but this improved understanding has not produced many effective mechanisms for social change. Both Gramsci and Habermas realize that the road to Marx's goals may require a radically different strategy from the one suggested by Marx – ideological and institutional evolution rather than militant revolution. Moreover, for all their efforts to provide a "Critical Theory," Western Marxists have not made many advances in justifying Marx's ideals. Marx's own efforts were murky at best, but Western Marxists seem to assume that no further justification is needed. Here serious philosophical thinking about foundations might provide deeper comprehension about the nature of the goals themselves as well as the means to realize them. Though they continue to search for viable institutional alternatives, Western Marxists have not yet found a path that can begin to actualize Marx's goals.

LIFE-PHILOSOPHY AND SUBCONSCIOUS FORCES: SCHOPENHAUER, FREUD, AND BERGSON

CORE CONTRIBUTIONS

Hegel and Marx examine the ways in which social and economic institutions constitute human beings, demonstrating that an encompassing, dialectical historical process provides an often-unacknowledged milieu for humanity. The three philosophers explored in this chapter – Schopenhauer, Freud, and Bergson – highlight the ways in which an encompassing *life-process* constitutes a similar milieu. Unlike Hegel and Marx, who see a rational pattern to the historical process, these thinkers believe that the life-process lacks rationality and shapes human existence unconsciously. Thus, they relegate reason – even in an expanded Hegelian sense – to a subordinate role. Because the life-process dominates human existence, reason is its servant. If humanity is rooted in the life-process, then humans are continuous with other animals, equally driven by instincts and governed by habits. This "naturalizing" attitude remains one important current in Continental philosophy, continuing in Nietzsche, philosophical anthropology, Merleau-Ponty, Deleuze, and Le Doeuff. It opposes another current, which sees human beings as discontinuous with the rest of nature (much of hermeneutics, phenomenology, existentialism, and structuralism).

Because life operates behind reason's back, humanity's access to its own existence is often incomplete. The life-philosophers believe that central features of human life are unconscious. Life is a subterranean ocean in which humanity swims, sustaining the social, economic, and cultural currents that organize human existence "from above." Although people are often unaware of this life-process, this stupor can be rectified through a special access called "intuition." Schopenhauer thinks humanity can grasp the operations of a primal, universal Will and its ordering Ideas through *aesthetic contemplation*. Freud holds that one can grasp the dynamics of instincts and their vicissitudes through psychoanalytic "insight." Finally, Bergson believes that intuition reveals the flow of lived temporality and that this binds people to life's creativity. This "intuition" is a non-conceptual vision into the underlying forces governing all life. Intuition provides a merging with the life-process which grasps it from within and which abandons the objectifying, distancing preconditions of most forms of knowledge. The life-philosophers' elucidation of this distinctive access to life is an important strength of this movement.

The figures in this movement split between those who seek to "dumb-down" and flatten the internal organization of the life-process and those who see it as self-organizing and exhibiting an intelligence or purposiveness of its own. For Hegel, life provided a model for clarifying dialectical self-organization. Bergson (and later, Dilthey) retain this self-organizing, creative feature in their models of life. (Nietzsche also retains this vision in his picture of life as will to self-organization and self-overcoming.) But Schopenhauer and Freud posit a blinder, less directed life-process. Neither of them accepts the progressive interpretation of the temporal dynamic in Bergson (and previously, in Hegel and Marx). They see life as an endless struggle of forces or energies that just continues, without leading to any better outcome. Other life-philosophers accept or build on Bergson's vision.

Schopenhauer and Freud sharply differ from Hegel and Marx in their goals for ordinary humans. Schopenhauer believes that life involves endless suffering. The only sensible response is ascetic detachment, but only a few saints will succeed in this, and then only because they have a biologically inherent capacity for such withdrawal. Freud also thinks humanity's best hope is modest everyday satisfaction; most people will be lucky to control their destructive impulses. However, Bergson believes more creative achievements are possible, even though tradition and habit may resist them. Most people in fact abide by habitual patterns. These philosophers' "ideals" pale in comparison to dreams of a humanity "fully at home in the world" (Hegel) or achieving "full self-expressive activity" (Marx). These lowered expectations constitute one major current in Continental thought thereafter.

Yet all three thinkers acknowledge the inspirational power of exceptional persons. Both Schopenhauer and Bergson stress the value of saintly exemplars. Freud and Bergson stress that special interpersonal "insight" is possible through psychoanalytic insight (in the first instance) or through co-inhabiting temporal flux (in the second instance). Even Schopenhauer allows for a distinctive interpersonal knowledge when the illusory boundaries of individuation dissolve via sympathetic identification with others. Thus all acknowledge that persons can provide spiritual rejuvenation to one another and that some have the possibility of significant ethical achievement. The real task for those sympathetic with these higher aspirations is to discover ways of making these higher possibilities more achievable for greater numbers of people. This is one of Nietzsche's central tasks, and other major figures continue this project – e.g., Heidegger, Sartre, Merleau-Ponty, and the French feminists.

Like Hegel and Marx, life-philosophers identify constitutive relations between individuals and other people. Schopenhauer believes that individuation itself is illusory and hence that sympathetic identification with others is possible. In effect, all wills – regardless of appearances – embody one Will. Freud shows how the super-ego – the psychic factor responsible for moral imperatives – results from internalizing parental demands. Thus, individual conscience contains inescapable voices derived from others. Bergson holds that societies shape the moral personalities of their members by creating ingrained habits and stigmatizing neighboring groups. Societies thus establish an exclusive, "closed" morality and static religion. Only exceptional individuals can transcend these social limits. This deep interwovenness among persons is central not just to this movement, but also to the whole Continental tradition. Individuality is typically conceived as a mere modification of a more deeply rooted sociality.

While previous thinkers in the tradition emphasize history, these life-philosophers stress the importance of everyday lived temporality. It becomes the key to understanding the ongoing flux of experience (or the gaps in that flux deriving from unconscious pressures). Freud postulates a continuing pressure of the past in the present via unconscious mechanisms. Although Schopenhauer recoils from the eternal recurrence of desire, he acknowledges the importance of time as an organizing category of lived experience (even if he contends that such experience is illusory on some ultimate level). Bergson regards the understanding of time's flux in experience and of experience's unification of itself in time to be central issues solved by his overall position. The centrality of time in everyday experience remains a central issue in the work of Husserl, Heidegger, Merleau-Ponty, Derrida, and Deleuze. Solving the problems associated with lived time becomes one of the major tasks of twentieth-century Continental philosophy.

SCHOPENHAUER

Arthur Schopenhauer (1788–1860) was an independent scholar (living on a family inheritance after his father's suicide), who had an abortive university career. He scheduled his lectures at the same time as Hegel at the University of Berlin in 1820, at the height of Hegel's fame, and when they drew very few students, his teaching career faded. His main books included *The Fourfold Root of the Principle of Sufficient Reason* (1813) and *The World as Will and Representation* (1818). They gained only modest recognition during most of his lifetime, though they became very popular during his last decade. He continued to rework his main treatise by adding new material in later editions. His father was a wealthy businessman, with whom he traveled widely and from whom he developed a cosmopolitan standpoint. His mother had a literary sensibility and wrote scores of romance novels, but she wanted little to do with him after her husband's death. Schopenhauer's core ideas derive from Kant, Plato, and Eastern religions, such as Hinduism and Buddhism. He reintroduces many Kantian dualisms that Hegel had sought to overcome. For him, philosophy derives from humanity's metaphysical need for answers to questions about themselves and the universe, but in contrast to religion, philosophy defends its answers rationally.

His central claim is that all events – both human actions and natural changes – are expressions of a single underlying Will, which lacks rationality and purposiveness and seeks only continued self-perpetuation.[1] This Will is a single unity; that individuals are apparently distinct is ultimately an illusion. He reaches this conclusion by reinterpreting Kant's noumena/phenomena distinction. Instead of accepting that only phenomena can be known, in contrast to things-in-themselves, Schopenhauer believes humanity's direct experience of its own will permits contact with this primal Will,[2] which often remains unknown to those whose lives it dominates. What Kant called "phenomena" – spatio-temporal perceptual appearances organized by concepts – Schopenhauer regards as illusory projections. They too are expressions of Will, but they possess no ultimate reality. The Will, when embodied in human actions, continually strives to overcome a sense of emptiness that always recurs from failing to adequately satisfy one's desires. Thus, Schopenhauer argues that human life is an endless round of striving, struggle, disappointment, and despair, which ultimately leads nowhere.[3] Rationality, coherence, and order are products of human intellect and exist only among phenomena; the ultimate thing-in-itself, Will, has no rational direction; it is haphazard and without any explicit goal. Schopenhauer arrives at this conclusion by generalizing the experience of introspection. In inward self-awareness, no spatial or causal relations exist among mental states; yet there are constant urges. He thus extrapolates to the nature of the primal Will by examining his own will. Ordinary human beings typically remain tethered to this wheel of appearances, rarely glimpsing the ultimate reality of Will informing their actions. Schopenhauer's cosmic vision anticipates later philosophers of the absurd (e.g., Camus, Cioran).

Schopenhauer dismisses appearances because they are derivative, shaped by concepts of space, time, and causality. These concepts (ordering mechanisms) also create the illusion of individuation, which allows diverse human wills to oppose one another despite being expressions of a single Will.[4] Schopenhauer elaborates a theory of the grounds (reasons) phenomena give to one another (e.g., causes, warrants, proofs, motives); understanding these grounds and their spheres of application yields everyday and scientific knowledge.[5] In addition to the primal Will and its expression in appearances, there are Ideas, which are sensuous, perceptual models organizing appearances. Ideas can be grasped only when humans release their attachments to willing; Ideas resemble Platonic forms, but are more sensuous.[6] They are grasped through a distinctive form of *intuition* – not thought or cognition – that is achieved in the experience of art.

The human condition is typically one of endless striving, failure, and dissatisfaction. Even if some desires are satisfied, this is evanescent, and then even more desires emerge. Schopenhauer believes a modest kind of salvation is possible, but it cannot be achieved voluntarily. It requires quieting one's attachment to Will through contemplation of or identification with ultimate realities.[7] The Will is manifest directly in bodily expressions, and the body fully exhibits the Will. Though humans can reason in addition to willing; their wills are entirely explicit in bodily behavior. Different persons have different characters, but these are not subject to transformation through human volition. The operations of the Will in human life can be grasped only retrospectively. Given people's acceptance of their individuated condition, they typically misunderstand the source of their actions and their true purposes, making their self-interpretations nearly always unreliable. Schopenhauer believes that love, for example, is an elaborate ritual that serves only the survival of the species by inducing procreation; it typically fades after children have arrived.[8] Also, attachment to egoistic appetites – to individual will in opposition to other wills – is ultimately based on the illusion of distinct individuality.

Schopenhauer distinguishes two possible human types: those who embody ordinary consciousness and those who achieve "higher" (or "better") consciousness by grasping deeper metaphysical truths about the Ideas and the Will. Higher consciousness is an achievement of genius, a rare commodity. Genius is expressed in saintliness (withdrawal from the Will) and in creating art and music (which unveil the Ideas and the secrets of the Will itself).[9] It does not require conceptual sophistication or scientific knowledge; these concern only appearances and remain divorced from ultimate reality. Saints and artists achieve a sympathetic union with the Will by abandoning their individuality. For those immersed in ordinary consciousness, however, life is driven by physical need and the sexual urge to procreate. Schopenhauer believes that sex provides no lasting satisfaction and no transcendence of individuation. He anticipates Freud by interpreting the sexual drive to be behind many diverse human activities. Unlike Freud, however, he does not think humans can control their sexual or destructive drives; at best they can limit their damage. People cannot change what they are, only become resigned to it.[10] Those who achieve higher consciousness do so because of inborn genius, not because of personal effort. Higher consciousness is a matter of grasping reality as it is, and only artists and saints are capable of this.

Through creating and appreciating art, humans can transcend their attachments to appearances, disconnect from the Will's sufferings and their false sense of individuation, and contemplate the Ideas or the Will itself. Schopenhauer follows Kant in thinking that art requires disinterested contemplation or at least a state in which interestedness and individuality are minimized. Those who contemplate art overcome their particularity and gain an impersonal vision of ultimate reality.[11] Representational artists achieve a sympathetic union with the Ideas, and their works allow audiences to approximate this union. For this reason, Schopenhauer values representational art, which better captures the Ideas that inform and organize appearances. Art yields an intuitive knowledge that provides deeper truths than the sciences, which rely on concepts (and experiences) that distort the primal Will and the Ideas. These truths cannot be captured in ordinary concepts; they can only be intuited; comprehending them produces peace. Since space and time are produced by the subject, the Ideas are timeless, though they still participate in the subject-object distinction. Deeper truth than even the Ideas reveal is achieved through the creation and appreciation of music, which makes possible a sympathetic union with the primal Will itself. Schopenhauer regards music to be the highest form of art, requiring the greatest genius to create. It exhibits the essence of Will directly without being dominated by it.[12]

Schopenhauer's ethical goal is to abandon the cycle of desire and satisfaction. Rules and principles are irrelevant in ethics; character is essential.[13] Rational acts are not always the best acts, and rationally effective means may be evil, thus undermining the value of their end results. The good person sees through the illusions of individuation to achieve sympathetic union with others' suffering. This may be the best people can offer each other.[14] Attachments and desire lead only to greater suffering. The road to redemption requires contemplation, resignation, and release. Detaching oneself produces a spiritual transformation that allows one to transcend egoism and merge with reality. This self-transcendence can only be achieved through faith. However, for saints and artists who ascend to higher consciousness, their experience of the Will redeems appearances, because they allow the Will to see appearances as its own projection. Will gains explicit self-consciousness through this human achievement. Though this does not alter the dream-like nature of appearances, it does redeem them.[15] The Will discovers its own expressiveness through human intuition. Thus, human saintliness and artistry have larger metaphysical significance, if they come to full fruition.

Schopenhauer is often regarded as a pessimist, and certainly, in contrast with Hegel and Marx, his ideal for humanity is modest. Ordinary life is full of suffering, pain, dissatisfaction, and ceaseless desire. Yet sainthood can be achieved by dissociating from one's desires, contemplating the Ideas, abandoning optimistic illusions, and merging with the single Will. Geniuses achieve rare insight into underlying reality, allowing them to achieve a kind of eternity.[16]

Freud retains these reduced hopes for humanity. All that most people can achieve is an uneasy compromise between the demands of the id, reality, and the super-ego. Freud retains Schopenhauer's belief that willing is fundamental and that unconscious forces govern the will. Instead of a single will that manifests itself in diverse events, Freud posits opposed instincts of creation and destruction. Freud also challenges Schopenhauer's fatalism and his assessment of art.

II. FREUD

Sigmund Freud (1856–1939) trained as a medical doctor in Vienna, specializing in neurophysiology. Initially he studied aphasics and hysterics. Visiting France in 1885 to learn how Jean-Martin Charcot treated these disorders, he discovered the therapeutic potential of hypnosis. He saw that hysterical symptoms can be released and reconstituted through hypnotic suggestion, and this suggested that "ideas" might have independent psychic force. Freud collaborated with an older colleague, Josef Breuer, on his first book, *Studies in Hysteria* (1895). These cases demonstrate the importance of early childhood trauma on the formation of later symptoms. Through letters and discussions with another doctor, Wilhelm Fliess, Freud formulated a model for mental functioning in the unpublished "Project for a Scientific Psychology."[17] This was Freud's first attempt to create a single theory that could explain both normal and pathological functioning, a lifelong ambition. In the next decade (1900–9), Freud discovered the crucial insights that ground psychoanalysis, which are defended in two key books: *The Interpretation of Dreams* (1900) and *Three Essays on the Theory of Sexuality* (1905). He also published several case studies. These works demonstrate Freud's growing confidence, his sharper understanding of unconscious functioning, and his ability to illuminate everyday life. In the next decade (1909–19) Freud wrote and published popular introductions to his new discipline: *Introductory Lectures on Psychoanalysis* (1917) and *Five Lectures on Psychoanalysis* (1910), published additional case studies, and composed many of his "meta-psychological" papers, in which he makes a number of theoretical advances. In his final period (1919–38) Freud introduced several theoretical changes that were strongly contested by other psychoanalysts, the most important being his postulation of a death instinct – a drive toward destruction – in addition to eros (or creation). This allowed him to explain the importance of aggression, a fact that Hitler's rise to power vividly demonstrated. Freud also applied his theories to many diverse topics, e.g., to the function of civilization, art, group behavior, and religion.

General theory of mind

Instead of summarizing the many revisions of Freud's theories, I will concentrate on his mature formulation. For Freud, mental life results from conflicts among several psychic structures: the id, the ego, and the super-ego. The id is the oldest; it includes urges inherited from previous generations and instincts that regularly seek to discharge themselves, producing satisfaction. The ego emerges from the id, and responds to the demands of the external world – natural and social – in order to limit the demands that the id and the world make on each other (e.g., by withholding satisfaction from the instincts and filtering stimuli penetrating the id). The ego's goal is the preservation of the whole organism; to achieve this, it controls voluntary movement and processes external stimuli.[18] It seeks changes in environmental stimuli that are advantageous. It also controls the id by postponing instinctual satisfaction until favorable situations emerge and by selecting which impulses can be satisfied. The ego seeks pleasure and avoids pain; pleasure results from a relaxation of tension produced by stimuli. An increase in pain produces anxiety in the ego.[19] During sleep the ego's defenses are weakened, and the id can dominate the psyche's functioning. Finally, as a result of parental influence, the super-ego emerges from the ego, imposing rigid restrictions on it and limiting the satisfaction permitted to the id. If the ego disobeys its commands, it may punish the ego.[20]

The ego's task is thus to mediate the demands of the id, the super-ego, and reality, reconciling their demands with one another. The super-ego derives primarily from parental imperatives, but teachers and surrogate parents may also be internalized. While the ego meets present worldly demands, both the id and the super-ego represent past influences. As the locus of basic instincts – sex and aggression – the id is unconcerned with the ego's preservation or with consequences; it seeks only release of its tensions. The ego is cautious, always seeking the least perilous method of satisfying the id. The super-ego imposes limits on the id, and the ego must enforce those limits. Freud's two basic instincts are Eros (including self and species preservation, the love of objects and oneself) and Thanatos (including aggression and destruction).[21] Eros has the power to periodically overcome Thanatos, but aggression cannot long be denied. If it is denied external targets, it will turn against the ego itself.

The unconscious, repression, and everyday life

Hysterical symptoms, everyday slips and missteps, and dreams offer Freud evidence for unconscious drives. He notes that hysterical symptoms result from wishes that are incompatible with other desires or with the person's ethical self-image. Because of such conflicts, the offending wish is repressed – eliminated from conscious awareness, but not rejected altogether. It remains active, seeking an opportunity to fulfill itself surreptitiously. The hysterical symptom is its disguise, and it usually produces more pain than acknowledging the original wish would have done.[22] Because consciousness does not recognize the original wish implicit in the symptom, neither the passage of time nor critical self-consciousness will cure the symptom. Only if the sufferer connects the symptom with the original wish, and acknowledges it, can the hysterical symptom be cured. Sometimes this acknowledgment must occur under hypnosis, and often the wish must be discovered this way too.

Freud also shows that unconscious wishes express themselves in a variety of everyday phenomena, such as jokes, slips of the tongue, and behavioral "accidents."[23] Some jokes are substitutes for revenge and barely conceal their intent. The motive for the joke and the revenge is the same, but the joke partially conceals the intent. Losing or breaking objects, slips of the tongue, forgetting requests, and bungled actions – when studied closely and in context – may also express unconscious desires. Such everyday phenomena show that repression operates even in normal personalities, not only in hysterics. Freud eventually argues that every psychic event is meaningful, that nothing happens by chance or accident.

Freud's best evidence for the unconscious and repression, however, derives from dreams. Interpreting dreams is the royal road to knowledge of the unconscious.[24] By clarifying the logic of dreams, Freud discovers keys to many psychic pathologies. Dreams function like symptoms and thus contain clues to the origins of patients' problems. Freud notes that some dreams' meanings are transparent, especially in children's dreams. Their dreams fulfill daytime wishes that remained unsatisfied. Freud claims that all dreams have this structure: they fulfill unsatisfied wishes.[25] When adult dreams fail to fit this pattern, they are distorted. The manifest dream results from performing complex psychic operations on latent dream content. These operations conceal the unconscious wish so that it cannot be recognized by consciousness. Distortion is necessary because the ego resists such wishes. Since the ego's forces of repression weaken during sleep, the wish can manifest itself in dreams. Dream analysis reveals that specific repressive processes transform latent wishes into manifest dreams and that many of these processes are universal.[26] Dreams use symbols that often occur in fairy tales and myths, and the meanings of such symbols are typically the same in both contexts. Such myths and tales can be analyzed using Freudian procedures; they are interpreted as if they are the manifest content of dreams.

What then is the logic of dreams? First, events are frequently condensed. This means that one object or event in the manifest dream often synthesizes fragments of many distinct objects or events at the latent level. Also, brief episodes in manifest dreams can encapsulate extended sequences of latent events. Second, psychic intensities are often displaced. This means that objects that seem peripheral in the manifest dream can be central in the latent content, and objects that are highlighted in the manifest dream can be unimportant in the latent content. The id's main goal is to discharge its energy; it succeeds even if the ego believes the manifest dream. Finally, ordinary logic has little purchase in dreams: contradictory states of affairs can exist side by side without requiring reconciliation or adjustment. Similarly, contraries are often treated as identical in the unconscious so that an event in the manifest dream can have the opposite meaning at the latent level.[27] These are just some of the operations involved in dream work.

Childhood sexuality and the Oedipus complex

Freud also clarifies the erotic life of children. Suggesting that many neuroses can be traced to disturbances in the erotic impulses of childhood, Freud insists that children have active sexual desires. Adults cannot confirm this using their own memories, however, because childhood eroticism is typically repressed. But direct observation reveals children's sexual intensity. Most of their sexual urges must be repressed because they cannot obtain legitimate satisfaction in reality, and these repressed desires can later become the source of neurotic symptoms.[28] Only by understanding the relationship of the symptoms to the original desires, and allowing them to be acknowledged and released, can the therapist cure the symptoms.

Childhood sexuality is not initially centered on the genitals. Instead the mouth, the anus, and the skin are sexually charged. Simple bodily contact produces pleasure, and sucking is the first form of autoerotic behavior.[29] Eventually the genitals do become charged, and masturbation becomes a second source of children's autoeroticism. In addition to autoerotic urges, children experience other-directed desires, both erotic and destructive. Children may wish to cause or receive pain, to look or be seen. These early urges may not be solely heterosexual; they may target the same sex too, even if such urges are not sanctioned by society. These multifocused drives initially seek to discharge themselves independently, but by puberty the child's erotic impulses are integrated around the genitals, which serves species-reproduction. At puberty, other-directed sexual desires typically displace autoerotic urges, and most early sexual impulses (for example, the child's desire for its mother) have long been repressed. Then, too, many social institutions (e.g., morality, education, and law) regulate the expression of adolescent erotic impulses. These controls limit the recovery of repressed childhood impulses. Freud claims that there is an ordered course of development in childhood sexuality that reaches a climax at the fifth year (the Oedipal period), followed by a seven-year period of repression and latency, finally resulting in a second flowering of sexuality during puberty.[30]

Every stage of this process contains pitfalls that can produce potential pathologies. If a stage is arrested or fixated or blocked, this can cause major personality defects later. Similarly, most sexual aberrations germinate during this period. For example, if early sexual drives remain isolated from later genital integration, perversions may develop, e.g., various fetishes. Similarly, if the child initially chooses a love-object of the same sex, this affinity may re-emerge during puberty, leading to adult homosexuality. Freud certainly broadens the use of the word "sexuality" in exploring childhood desires, but he discovers new territories for observation and analysis.

Narrating from the viewpoint of small boys in the fifth year, Freud describes an allegedly universal complex – the Oedipus complex – that is crucial to later moral development.[31] Later Continental philosophers (e.g., Deleuze and Irigaray) challenge the universality and necessity of this complex. And French feminists harshly criticize Freud's willingness to mechanically apply this model to women, instead exploring the many, unique ways women traverse this period of sexual development.

For Freud, all infants experience the mother's breast as their first erotic object, their initial source of nourishment and pleasure. Indeed, infants do not distinguish between their own bodies and the breast. Eventually this difference emerges, and the infant's bond with the breast transmutes into a connection with the whole mother as caretaker. Mothers thus become every child's initial love object.[32] During the phallic phase (between the age of 4 and 5), the young boy masturbates – using his mother as a fantasy object. Seeking literally to copulate, he may try to seduce her and often demands her rapt attention. He wishes to replace his father in her affections and may display his genitals to her. The father is experienced as a rival to be eliminated despite his size and authority. Once the mother realizes she is the target of the boy's desire, she typically rejects his affections and forbids masturbation. If the young boy accidentally observes the mother's genitals, he may experience fear of castration, which is what he thinks has happened to her. She may threaten this explicitly, or the boy may simply fear this punishment from the father. This fear can become his obsession.

This castration anxiety alters his relationships with his mother and father and later on with men and women generally. The boy has two options: to continue challenging the father by seeking copulation with the mother (this option is usually renounced because of the castration threat) or abandoning his desire and passively emulating the mother to gain the father's affection (but this accepts castration and effeminacy). Typically, he renounces desire for the mother entirely. He may continue to fantasize about her, but the usual response is to identify with and emulate the father.[33] The father's commands are internalized as part of the super-ego, making this Oedipus complex essential to moral development. These events are then repressed, but the conflicting crosscurrents of desire remain active in the unconscious. The boy's overt sexual initiative recedes into latency until puberty. According to Freud, the way this complex is resolved determines psychic development into adulthood.

Girls experience these events differently, according to Freud.[34] Like boys, girls are initially attached to their mothers as providers and sources of oral satisfaction. Freud's two questions concern how and why girls typically switch their object-love to men and how their center of sexual pleasure shifts from the clitoris to the vagina. Freud answers that when girls learn they lack a penis, this is experienced as a loss resulting in envy of the boy's penis, producing inferiority about their clitoris (which is allegedly seen as a degenerate penis). This felt inferiority produces both self-hatred and resentment of the mother for failing to give her a penis. This hatred leads the young girl to reject her mother and embrace her father, provoking a change in affections from women to men. But since she already experiences herself as castrated, she has no castration anxiety and thus no motivation for releasing her childhood attachment to the mother. "Normal" femininity is achieved only if her penis envy transforms into a desire for a baby. The baby functions as a surrogate penis for the girl. She then begins to compete with the mother for the father's sexual attentions (the female version of the Oedipal situation). Rejecting her own clitoris, she abandons masturbation, and this allows her to feel vaginal pleasure during intercourse.[35] Since the motivations for transcending the Oedipal situation are weaker, girls develop weaker super-egos and, consequently, they supposedly lack the severe, impersonal moral consciences typical of men. Instead, women's ethical sensibilities privilege affection and social connectedness. Additional sex differences resulting from this divergent development include: a greater narcissism leading to a stronger need for love; increased vanity to compensate for felt inferiority; and a weaker capacity to sublimate drives, which leads to rigid character formations earlier than in men.

How psychoanalysis works

The ego's task is to resolve the demands of reality, the id, and the super-ego and still preserve its own organization and strength. Mental illness occurs when the ego is too weak to do this. Withholding satisfaction from the id is its most difficult task, but the imperatives of the super-ego can also be debilitating. Even though their agendas differ, the id and super-ego often make common cause against a weakened ego. If they destabilize its organization, they can then have free rein. Therapists must strengthen the ego, helping it to resist the demands of the id and super-ego – thereby rebuilding its relation to reality.[36] Patients must provide honesty and cooperation in recounting their dreams and free associations, while therapists must offer expertise in interpreting unconscious material to illuminate the ego's weaknesses and to determine how best to rejuvenate it.

Freud doubts that psychotherapy will help psychotics because their relation to reality is too disoriented. With neurotics, however, improvement is possible because they can learn to accept a therapist's help.[37] If they stop judging themselves, their unconscious desires can become accessible, and their egos can gain strength. Therapists can formulate hypotheses about their weaknesses. In addition, therapists often benefit from transference – the transfer of emotions directed toward important figures in the patient's past (usually parents). Whether the transferred affects are positive or negative, they are informative.[38] Positive transference provides patients with greater motivation to cooperate with therapists since they want to win their approval. Also, patients must learn to surrender the demands of the super-ego to therapists; the therapist-parent can then re-educate the patient about more realistic self-demands.[39] But Freud's therapeutic goal is to facilitate independence, not to offer another model to emulate. The psychoanalyst must constantly remind the patient that the feelings transferred derive from their past relationships. By identifying the sources of transference as it happens, therapists help patients to release troubling emotions.

Therapists can strengthen weak egos in several ways. Improving the patient's self-knowledge can provide greater self-control.[40] Therapists examine dreams, free association, slips and everyday mishaps, and transference. Freud urges therapists to be judicious in communicating their interpretations; the goal is to encourage patients to discover the necessary conclusions independently or at least to contribute insights essential to resolving their problems. The *process* of self-discovery can be as restorative and its *results*. Also, patients can confirm analysts' insights when offered at propitious moments; they may even consciously remember crucial repressed events, which can release the symptoms. A second strategy is to elicit the expression of repressed materials. Often the ego exhausts itself in maintaining these repressions, and when they are released, the ego can recover those energies.[41] Frequently, the ego fears insight; here therapists must supply reassurance and support. Once the repressed desires are explicit, the ego can respond to them explicitly – either allowing them limited expression or rejecting them rationally. In either case, the ego is strengthened because it no longer drains itself in repressing the desire.

Therapists must remain mindful of patients' ambivalence and work to overcome the ego's fears, which become manifest in several ways.[42] One is severe guilt deriving from the super-ego. Often neurotics improve after experiencing objective misfortune because they feel such sufferings are sufficient to atone for past sins. Another is the inversion of self-love into self-hatred and self-destructive behavior. When the destructive instinct targets the ego, therapy often cannot protect against the onslaught. Such patients cannot aid their recovery because they feel that they do not deserve it. These sources of resistance are difficult to defeat. Reassurance can help patients to benefit from therapy.

The goal is to strengthen the ego sufficiently so that it can acknowledge the id's urges and respond to them directly. By replacing internalized parental figures, therapists help patients achieve realistic self-evaluations. They can then adopt better responses toward previously repressed desires: they may rationally reject them, replacing repression with explicit disavowal; they may allow the repressed desires to be productively expressed in sublimated, acceptable ways; finally, they may allow the illicit desire some direct satisfaction, accepting their urges and challenging socially imposed limits.[43]

Some applications

Freud extends his ideas in many directions. Here I will briefly consider four: civilization's psychic costs (*Civilization and its Discontents*, 1930), mass psychology (*Group Psychology and the Analysis of the Ego*, 1921), art (various writings), and religion (*Future of an Illusion*, 1927).

Freud doubts civilization's ability to produce greater happiness than suffering. He evaluates civilization by measuring its effects on individuals, who have three sources of pain: bodily decay, natural catastrophes, and oppressive power. With respect to disasters and aging bodies, people can only resign themselves to reducing some sources of suffering without eliminating them entirely. From social relations, however, people hope to eliminate all suffering, striving to live peacefully and lovingly with everyone. For Freud, this is an unrealistic – even misguided – hope.[44]

Civilization's function is to increase humanity's control over nature, but the processes that create civilization cause significant frustrations. Civilization arises through sublimating instinctual energies of love (sex) and aggression (destruction), reducing psychic energies available to individuals and exponentially increasing super-ego dominance. Civilization utilizes the love instinct to unify wider groups of people, and it controls aggression through the super-ego. Both strategies amplify individual unhappiness and weakness.[45] Extending love to everyone debases the notion of love because not everyone deserves to be loved and because love can only embrace a limited number of people. Even if love is restricted to the nuclear family, civilization demands repression of childhood sexuality and promotion of heterosexual object-choices and monogamy. Freud thinks these demands are too high; the repression required is too great. Similarly, civilization can never eliminate all aggression since it is an innate drive. It achieves control only by allowing substitute aggression (e.g., stigmatization) against foreigners or subgroups and by reinforcing the most aggressive psychic force, the super-ego.[46]

Civilization does alleviate some unhappiness by creating technologies to increase control over nature; by facilitating order, cleanliness, and beauty; by educating peoples' higher capacities (for art, philosophy, ethics), and by regulating social relations. But civilization blossoms only when the group is experienced as stronger than the individual. Freud hypothesizes that personal freedom is greater outside civilization but that people exchange their freedom for security and justice. Civilization represents a compromise between the needs of the group and the individual, but, especially in recent times, the civilizing process has gradually become oblivious to individual happiness. Common work and affection among families initiated civilization; it relies on the same psychic bonds as the family, but it dampens individual satisfaction by prohibiting incest, forcing parents to work outside the home, and enforcing monogamy.[47] It also reduces interfamilial aggression by directing individuals' aggression against themselves via their super-egos. The super-ego borrows energy from the ego, thus weakening its ability to cope with other demands. Because these sublimations of love and aggression are not compensated, individuals readily become neurotic. Freud thinks civilization itself is a collective neurosis because it is a poor solution to the problem of suffering, producing more unhappiness than the original suffering it was designed to alleviate.[48]

Freud's social psychology is closely related to his individual psychology, perhaps because his system already relies on social (familial) relations to explain individual development. He believes that groups maintain cohesion through love of leaders and of cohorts, just as families remain united through love of parents and siblings. To be sure, behavior in crowds is often irrational, immoral, and intolerant, but Freud explains this as a regression to earlier stages of psychic development, prior to super-ego formation.[49] Regression allows primitive fantasies from the unconscious to be unleashed. Moreover, the love that binds groups, like most love, has another face – hatred. This hatred is expressed in intolerance of outsiders as well as ambivalence toward leaders and fellow members.[50] Groups disintegrate when the love that binds them disappears, when leaders no longer inspire loyalty and when camaraderie evaporates.

Freud examines the process of artistic creation and the content of specific literary works in order to confirm his theories about the human condition. He compares the creative process to dreaming, especially to daydreaming and children's play. In play, the players create artificial rules, following them with great seriousness. In fantasies, present wishes recall past moments when such wishes were fulfilled, and this in turn allows the daydreamer to project future worlds in which they might be realized again. Art functions similarly in that the artist experiences a present wish that arouses memories that suggest a means for fulfilling the wish. The artwork provides that fulfillment, though this is concealed by work's formal structure. The audience values the artwork for the same reason: it offers symbolic satisfaction of a universal wish.[51] Freud analyzes artworks by determining the underlying wishes they express and their means of satisfaction. Art operates in a fashion parallel to the symbolic processes that allow a manifest dream to express a latent dream. Identifying these processes is Freud's characteristic approach to interpreting art. He also examines specific literary works to elaborate his ideas (e.g., the Oedipus story).

Freud's main point about religion is that it derives from a reanimation of childish illusions that everyone experiences. He notes that culture is rarely successful in taming the forces of nature – death, catastrophe, and illness – leaving people vulnerable and anxious. Religion's origin lies in this helplessness, which resurrects the infant's helplessness. Like the infant who produces fantasies to counteract his dependency, adults project gods to protect them.[52]

Children already experience religious awe, fear, and passivity in the face of their fathers; these experiences are simply projected on a larger canvas by religious adults. Though Freud distinguishes between illusions and delusions, as the argument proceeds he concludes that religion is delusional. It serves mankind badly and produces few improvements in humanity's lot. Science offers a better hope for the future because it relies on evidence, observation, and mutual criticism, while religion resists rational scrutiny.[53] Freud suggests that religion exacerbates individual suffering because it reinforces an already harsh super-ego through guilt and blame.

Bergson's position has several similarities with Freud's. He too understands the importance of instinct in guiding behavior, defends a multilayered conception of self, and stresses the past's domination of the present. However, Bergson examines the vast *pre-conscious* realm – events that *can* become conscious but typically *do not* – rather than Freud's *unconscious*. For Bergson, the past weighs on the present through *habit*, though he acknowledges that many memories are filtered ("repressed") because of irrelevance. Finally, Bergson's deep self is a *personal self* that emerges through full contact with the present, rather than the instinctual drives of Freud's id.

III. BERGSON

Born in Paris, Henri Bergson (1859–1941) was appointed a professor at the Collège de France in 1900, at the age of 41. His lectures were immensely popular, and his major books – *Time and Free Will* (1889), *Matter and Memory* (1896), *Creative Evolution* (1907), and *Two Sources of Morality and Religion* (1932) – established his reputation. A diplomat as well as a philosopher, he was awarded the Nobel Prize for Literature (1928) and advocated the formation of the League of Nations.

Like Freud, Bergson respects empirical science. Even though he specifies a distinctive task for philosophy, he wants it to remain compatible with the best scientific findings of its time. Nonetheless, his central theme derives from a critique of the scientific notion of time, which presupposes an external, third-person standpoint, quantitative measurements, and discrete temporal points – each entirely like the others. This view construes time as a fourth "dimension," extending the metaphor of spatial dimensions. Although this scientific conception has produced many practical applications, in fact it is inadequate.[54] In its place, Bergson offers a model that construes time as a flux of moments – each internally related to the others and interpenetrating all the others – that flows progressively. This lived experience of time, which Bergson calls "duration," can only be accessed through "intuition" from a first-person perspective. Lived time preserves pasts and projects prospective futures in every present; indeed, past-present-future interlace in lived time, producing an indivisible process.[55] Time does not flow only through individual lives; it also encompasses everything else. In this generalized form it becomes Bergson's fundamental concept: *élan vital* (vital spirit). Lived duration provides each

person some access to the creative current of life that pulses through every living thing. The vital spirit is creative, opening new possibilities and directions for development in all species.[56]

Science cannot comprehend lived duration because it uses abstract concepts that cannot explain the subtleties of experience. Though it requires empirical observation, Bergson claims that its ability to grasp ultimate reality is deficient. Since science cannot illuminate duration, philosophy's task is to elucidate this distinctive realm. Direct intuition of duration's flux is Bergson's philosophical method. He construes science to be a refinement of practical intelligence, which aims to satisfy human needs through prediction and control. Intuition, on the other hand, is a non-objectifying sympathetic merging with duration that reveals its distinctiveness.[57] It exhibits the essences of given objects because it is disinterested and non-perspectival, and intuition's ability to grasp synthetic wholes becomes evident in apprehending art, especially music.[58] (In these ways, Bergson's intuition resembles Schopenhauer's aesthetic contemplation, just as *élan vital* resembles his Will, with a more positive accent.) This methodological reliance on intuition makes Bergson a forerunner of existential phenomenology (see chapter 6), which also distinguishes its methods from empirical science and claims deeper insight into lived experience. Bergson, however, acknowledges that the results of intuition may be *less reliable* than scientific experimentation. Intuition substitutes for intelligence in areas where it is unsuited, but its efforts yield less adequate knowledge.[59] Bergson's intuition does not reveal the eternal truths of classical metaphysics; rather, it illuminates becoming, spontaneity, and creative flux directly – the fundamental metaphysical realities.

In human life, lived duration produces creative self-development; actions reshape past tendencies in order to improve future results. Bergson's theory of evolution construes *life's* temporal flow in the same fashion, though its direction is not predetermined, and it advances by major leaps rather than by small steps.[60] As with a person's confrontation with the present situation, evolution can produce surprises. Bergson criticizes Darwin's model of evolution for regarding organisms as mere aggregations of parts, rather than synthetic wholes, and for its inability to explain the complexity and integration of organisms. More importantly, Bergson suggests that the central process of evolution is *division* (fission) rather than *combination* (fusion).[61] Evolution produces distinct lines of organic life, each of which advances by large leaps along its own path. Organic structures undergo refinement and then suddenly produce entirely new structures that constitute major improvements. This evolutionary drive toward increased structure and creative transformation is the *élan vital* governing life. Though it allows for contingencies and setbacks, it eventually presses forward.[62] Bergson notes, however, that positive changes require supportive environments. Creative leaps are never assured; they must be nurtured.

Bergson distinguishes three lines of organic evolution: plants, animals governed by instinct, and animals utilizing intelligence.[63] Plants are inherently conservative and repetitive. Instincts enable fixed behavioral responses in the presence of specific triggers. The success of insects suggests that instincts can effectively sustain a living species. Intelligence allows for diverse responses to similar stimuli, depending on the context and the goals of the organism. It often requires trial and error and may create the tools needed for success. Instinct responds to specific features of the stimulus and cannot delay or alter the organism's response-pattern, while intelligence can intercede between stimulus and response to evaluate the features of the situation that are most relevant to the organism's goals. Its outcomes are less assured than those of instincts, but it adapts and improves by evaluating its responses. Both instinct and intelligence motivate human actions; each compensates for the limits of the other.

Parallel to the instinct/intelligence distinction is another one that organizes Bergson's analysis of freedom (in *Time and Free Will*): habituated-mechanical-stereotypical action versus self-expressive, self-defining action.[64] Habituated actions are almost impersonal and automatic; the agent is virtually passive in relation to them. They "happen" instead of being chosen; the person remains uninvolved. They approximate "instinctual" responses, but they are socially ingrained, rather than biologically predetermined, patterns. Self-expressive, self-defining actions are experienced differently: the subtleties of the situation are assessed, and the whole person is involved in the response. In such actions persons redefine or discover themselves. Their outcomes cannot be predicted, and they embody genuine selfhood. They are free not because they are uncaused or self-caused, but because they bring the person to fruition. They may not involve extensive deliberation or rational assessment, but their agents are truly expressed in them. Free actions in this sense are rare, and most actions fall between the endpoints of purely habituated response and fully self-expressive involvement. Bergson regards only the most self-expressive actions as genuinely free.

Bergson insists that the classical positions on the free will issue are unhelpful. First, many classical positions (such as determinism and libertarianism) presuppose a retrospective, third-person, objectifying standpoint on actions, thus analytically isolating their elements (motive, means, end) from the flux of pre-reflective life. When actions' moments are temporally isolated in this way, the question of whether actions have causes seems answerable. On Bergson's view, action is a synthetic whole, all of whose parts interanimate each other. Agents do not cause free actions; they are more fully involved and expressed in free action.[65] Bergson supports this position by showing that mental states in general cannot be quantified or divided into discrete, isolated parts of the temporal stream. The pre-reflective temporal flux transforms itself when confronting new situations; responses call upon the agent's entire past and commit the entire future. The "moments" of action reshape each other, and the deep, personal self gradually emerges through this interaction.[66] In effect, for Bergson, mental states are not the kinds of thing that can have causal relations to one another because such relations presuppose only externally related components. Since Bergson argues that the entire stream of mental life is internally related, the usual causal analysis gains no purchase. Only if a spatialized, illusory understanding of time is accepted can the free will issue seem problematic. Nonetheless, Bergson distinguishes between free and unfree actions without depending on the notion of cause.

A related distinction in Bergson's analysis of human capacities is habit memory versus experience memory.[67] Habit memories insure that the body responds in specific ways in well-defined situations. Bergson's analysis of mind emphasizes the lived body (the first-person standpoint), the vehicle by which action is realized, as opposed to the objectified body (the third-person standpoint), which is studied by scientists. The lived body explores various possible responses to an event and selects relevant features of the situation to which to respond. It is the repository of habit memory. Experience memories are called forth by present situations, making present (in imagination) events that are charged with meanings. Naturally, many of these memories are irrelevant to the present situation and so must be ignored or repressed; so they are filtered for practical relevance. Bergson's main innovation is to claim that the agent's entire past is ultimately accessible to experience-memory, but much is temporarily repressed in response to current situational demands. Central to the free/unfree distinction is Bergson's division between surface/deep self. The surface self is attuned to immediate practical demands. The deep self separates itself from these demands, allowing contemplation of its past. Both selves are abstractions from the real organic whole of the person's lived temporality, just as lived body and experience memory are moments of the person's *vital spirit*. Bergson's deep self is disinterested, like the subject of Schopenhauer's aesthetic contemplation, but it is personal and individuated in a way opposite to Schopenhauer's subject.

Both dimensions of the self operate in typical cases of perception. Perception appropriates some elements of the given situation, but it also incorporates some elements from experience memory, which supplement the features given to perception. Typically, perception assimilates present stimuli to the agent's experiential past. Bergson believes that the objects of perception are neither fully independent objects (realism) nor mere mental representations (idealism); they have their own distinctive status that is neutral to the subjective/objective distinction. Perception transcends purely mental contents, and many perceptual qualities are genuine qualities of the world, but perceptual objects are not entirely independent of the subject because experience memory contributes to them.[68] Perception fuses the exploration of the actual world with experience memories. (Proust highlighted this process in his novels.)

Also related to the instinct/intuition distinction is Bergson's analysis of closed and open morality. He rejects philosophical efforts to rationally ground morality; reason is not the true source of values, and such efforts to justify them only lead philosophers to misunderstand value.[69] The finest morality – open morality – represents the vital spirit operating in humanity. It is best understood through its contrast with closed morality, which is custom-based, dogmatic, conservative, and rooted in habituated traditions that are internalized by an in-group that defines its identity in opposition to an out-group, e.g., one nation or ethnic group against another. Closed morality requires rules and maxims, but its real foundation is the established authority of the in-group. Its dominant emotions are fear and guilt (related to betrayal and transgression), and its dictates are presented as absolute commands, regardless of situational complexities.[70] Too often moral philosophy simply codifies and systematizes these rules. Open morality, on the other hand, is inclusive, incorporating all human beings; its source is the inspirational power of model persons. Through such model persons, the *élan vital* of humanity leaps forward creatively, rather than reactively. Open morality appeals to humanity's higher aspirations; its predominant emotions are joy and enthusiasm. It is also situational, allowing that different contexts may call for different responses and recognizing that attention to the specific features of the context is necessary to discover the optimum ethical response.[71] Bergson uses the symbolic metaphors of the open hand versus the closed fist to capture the difference between these moralities.

He also distinguishes two types of religion in a similar fashion: static and dynamic religion.[72] Static religion protects individuals against intellectual skepticism, overwrought egoism, the fear of death, and despair, which may be reasons for abandoning ethical responsibility altogether. Static religion attempts to answer these sources of disillusionment: it offers heavenly rewards to convince egoists that acting morally is advantageous, magic rituals that pretend to control fate, faith to quell doubts about God's existence, and the afterlife to silence fears of death. Still, the main effect of static religion is to reinforce the status quo, requiring adherence to very modest demands. Dynamic religion reaches for higher possibilities, relying on saintly individuals to inspire others by their example. Bergson believes that basic human needs must be satisfied before people are able to respond to these exemplary figures. He identifies God with the creative spirit (*élan vital*) that animates his entire philosophy; it is neither personal, nor omniscient, nor all-powerful, but it can be a genuine creative force that operates through evolution and the best exemplars of humanity.[73]

COMPARISONS

Although these thinkers have many affinities, their differences are equally striking. Central are their differing attitudes toward the life-force itself: Bergson's stance contrasts sharply with Schopenhauer's, while Freud's lies in between. Schopenhauer's Will is an all-consuming force that uses people without purpose: for him life is ultimately no good. The only logical response is life-denial, withdrawal, asceticism, and passive contemplation. Bergson's *élan vital* is a creative, progressive force that impels species and individuals in more promising directions. Therefore, he embraces the life-process and seeks union with it through intuition. Although life embodies many instinctual processes, these often *facilitate* creative response to the present. Freud stands closer to Schopenhauer's attitude toward life; consciousness is dominated by unconscious drives, but at least life's core drives include a creative principle as well as a destructive one. Life is a ceaseless struggle between love and aggression, creation and destruction. People can gain some understanding and control of their behavior (through therapy) by becoming conscious of early traumas and repression, thereby strengthening their egos. Yet Freud is not optimistic about the prospects for human happiness. Neither Schopenhauer nor Freud envisions anything similar to Bergson's open morality, which draws inspiration from heroic figures and embraces all of humanity. Schopenhauer admires saintliness, but only because it overcomes the illusion of appearances, desire, and individuation. Since these thinkers evaluate the encompassing life-force differently, their preferred responses to life and outlooks for humanity differ. Life-affirmation in Nietzsche, Camus's resistance to the absurd, Deleuze's enthusiasm for energetics, and Irigaray's embrace of the distinctively feminine all derive from or react to these stances.

Three other differentiating issues remain important for later Continental philosophy: science, freedom, and time. These thinkers constitute exemplary alternatives on the value of empirical science to philosophy. Hegel and Marx created "scientific" systems, but they did not create new empirical sciences (though both made major contributions to the emergence of sociology and the other social sciences). Their dialectical picture of history and reality produced an entirely new conception of "science." Life-philosophers react to *empirical* science. Schopenhauer dismisses it because it concerns only illusory appearances, not ultimate reality. Art offers a better path to that. Bergson takes empirical science seriously, accepting many of its results but challenging its concepts and interpretations, especially its assumptions about time and matter. Bergson also believes intuition provides philosophy with an independent field to map (the flux of experience); it may be more fundamental than science, but is at least independent of it. Bergson, like Hegel and Marx, argues with scientists about the proper interpretation of their results. Freud reveres empirical science as the only path to genuine knowledge, and strives to render psychoanalysis scientifically legitimate. He stresses the role of observation, evidence, hypothesis testing, and confirmation. Although his success in making psychoanalysis scientific is debatable, this is certainly his goal. Even when his explanations are teleological, he acknowledges the ideal of scientific explanation. Later Continental philosophers typically follow Bergson's lead – finding a distinctive task for philosophy while critically assessing the claims of empirical science. Bergson's organic understanding of temporal flux makes his vision at least compatible with dialectical thought.

Freedom is another differentiating issue. Both Schopenhauer and Freud believe human behavior is determined. Schopenhauer thinks that character determination is so complete that responsibility is unintelligible. Even those who are able to withdraw from Will's seductions are fated in the sense that only they have sufficient inborn capacity to succeed. Even then, the capacity may not be realized. Withdrawal from the Will constitutes a kind of salvation (liberation), but the agent alone cannot consciously effect it. Freud believes most of human behavior is determined by unconscious drives, but the ego can be sufficiently strengthened to resist them and achieve some modest degree of self-control. Success usually requires the intervention of therapists however, and even then self-control will always be threatened and partial. Bergson acknowledges that most human behavior is governed by habit and thus is not free. He insists on the possibility of genuine freedom, however, when actions engage and express the deep self. Free action makes contact with the creative life-force within oneself, and this possibility remains open to everyone. Schopenhauer is ultimately fatalistic. Later Continental philosophers rarely accept this position. Most acknowledge that manifold factors influence human behavior, but they also insist that freedom is both possible and desirable. Even poststructuralists acknowledge freedom's value.

Finally, these life-philosophers disagree about the status of time. Both Hegel and Marx make time and dialectical progression essential features of ultimate reality. Bergson takes this trend to its logical conclusion, declaring duration to be fundamental, and supporting this with a process-metaphysics. Schopenhauer demurs, however, arguing that time is but a construction of human subjectivity, and thus applicable only to appearances. He posits a timeless realm of Will and Ideas, which transcends mere phenomena. Schopenhauer is among the last Continental thinkers to defend this Platonic position. Most believe time is a fundamental condition of ultimate reality. Freud, for example, believes the past remains active in the present via the struggle between the ego and the id. However, even in Freud, the struggle between the creative and destructive drives is eternal, not genuinely affected by history. The narrative of these conflicting forces in particular persons is central to Freud's psychoanalysis, but time does not transform the basic instincts themselves. No narrative organizes their struggle; they engage only in endless conflict, like the primeval forces of order and chaos in some early Greek thinkers. Many Continental thinkers follow Bergson's example, though most challenge his progressive interpretation of duration; they may acknowledge that progress is possible, but it is won only through sustained effort.

ASSESSMENT

The vision of the life-force that these thinkers promulgate becomes more plausible as this tradition progresses, and Nietzsche brings the interpretation of life to a culmination. Schopenhauer's notion that life is blind desire, responsible for both human action and appearances, seems unhelpful both as an account of human action and of appearances themselves. He regresses to many Kantian dualisms that the Continental tradition as a whole strives to overcome. Freud's vision of life as a continuing struggle of drives toward unification (love) and dissolution (aggression/death) also seems to oversimplify both the dynamics of animal species and human psychology. Moreover, Freud's claim that hedonism is the central principle governing human psychology also seems like a regression to pre-Kantian views of human motivation that both Hegel and Marx had superseded. Nietzsche's view that life and human action are dynamic and self-organizing and that they seek greater self-enhancement or internal coherence ("power") at least contributes to and develops the richer understanding of human motivation and life that had been achieved in Schelling and Hegel. Bergson's conception of life as *élan vital* is richly informed by wide-ranging observations of all forms of life and retains important features of Nietzsche's picture. Many current thinkers (philosophers and scientists), to the extent that they think life has an overarching lawfulness at all, conceive it to be Darwinian. Bergson defends an important contrasting picture and offers considerable supporting evidence that challenges Darwin's hypotheses directly.[74]

The other major theme unifying this group of thinkers – that there are many unconscious factors operating in human action and experience – seems correct. However, many of these factors operate at what Freud would call the pre-conscious level, rather than the repressed unconscious level. All three figures show that many psychic operations transpire beneath the surface of consciousness, and Bergson and Schopenhauer show how the human capacity for intuition can make these deeper levels more accessible. Thus, they suggest that though much of human experience is implicit, it can be made explicit through special attention and careful description. Freud makes a reasonable case for his less accessible level of psychic forces, but even he thinks astute therapeutic insight can make those forces explicit as well. Thus, though they all believe that everyday self-knowledge is severely limited, they all suggest that it need not remain forever impoverished. Viable steps can be taken to broaden its scope, even if they may not always enable greater control over these forces.

These thinkers also suggest that naive realism about perceptual objects at least must be qualified because perception is nearly always intermingled with memories, fantasies, and wishes that overlay the given elements of perception. Beyond this, even these given elements are filtered for relevance to the practical goals the organism brings to the situation. Thus, they challenge the claim that interest-free, direct observation of the perceived world is possible.[75] Nietzsche and Gadamer press this argument further. At the same time, both Bergson and Schopenhauer defend a capacity for intuition that can sharpen one's self-perception. Self-perception is no doubt infused with some of the same fantasies and memories as world-perception, and self-perception remains a task to be achieved, rather than something that can be taken for granted. But these thinkers show that the two types of perception are more similar than is usually thought, each subject to the same epistemic weaknesses and potential for improvement.

Some important reservations about each thinker should be considered. Wherever Nietzsche came to disagree with Schopenhauer, a philosopher from whom he learned much, Nietzsche's position seems superior. Not only is his vision of life more plausible, his response to life also seems more apt. Humans are tougher than Schopenhauer suggests. Though life may be an endless struggle and frequently disappointing, many take up life's challenge and work to overcome failures. Why withdraw from life, even on Schopenhauer's vision of it, if one can enhance and enrich it through one's own life? Even if life on its own is "blind," perhaps humanity as a whole can compensate for that blindness with its intelligence. Moreover, Schopenhauer's fatalism is questionable. Bergson's claim that freedom emerges gradually as a person's deep self or character becomes more explicit seems both more true to lived experience and more enabling of human excellence. Bergson's position allows him to acknowledge that many actions are habituated and that many determinants condition action, but freedom remains possible and a viable ideal. Though Freud had a largely deterministic vision of human action, even he acknowledged the possibility of self-possession and self-control.

With respect to Freud, the central problem is his system's claim to scientific status. This has been challenged, despite Freud's efforts to defend himself. Freud allows himself too many auxiliary hypotheses in the face of problematic evidence. Moreover, the therapeutic results of Freudian practice are often disappointing, and the assumptions of the theory are too completely protected from serious challenge because his postulates about the unconscious are difficult to verify. Similarly, the universality of many of his claims about sexual and psychic development is arguable. Later feminists show that very different patterns of psychic development apply to women's experience. And similar challenges may emerge from any culture that has a family structure that differs from that typical of the West. Finally, Freud's reservations about the value of civilization are perhaps overstated, and his methods of interpreting literature seem reductive and over-simplifying. He is right to question the value of civilization, but he is too quick to dismiss the achievements of the ascetic ideal and insufficiently attentive to the ways in which contemporary culture incites a variety of pleasures. Certainly Western civilization's sublimation of aggression remains incomplete, but the question concerning the value of civilization, and modernity more generally, requires more careful and more thorough discussion than Freud offers. He initiates an important inquiry that remains to be completed. To approach complex works of literature as if they are dreams fails to do justice to literature's cognitive value and its artistic significance. Literature can compete with Freud's system not only in clarifying human experience, but also in illuminating life, nature, and social life.

I have fewer reservations about Bergson, and there is much to praise in the overall direction of his position. He defends a holistic picture of the universe, based on a new metaphysics of processes and theory of intuition. These ideas have promise and should be further developed; they have not yet been given due consideration. Bergson discovers a distinctive task for philosophy that allows it to remain critically engaged with contemporary science, but requires it to remain attuned to science's most recent developments. The phenomenologist Maurice Merleau-Ponty continues this direction of research. Most of the distinctions Bergson drew seem illuminating and useful. They may need further refinement, but they seem to be on the right track. Like Nietzsche, he is both critical of an absolutist ethics of obligations and seeks to explore a different kind of ethic of aspirations. Both of them believe that philosophical ethics must be completely rethought. Overall, Bergson offers a vision of human existence and lived experience that is deepened in hermeneutics, phenomenology, and existentialism. His positions and arguments thus provide an important impetus for later movements in Continental philosophy.

NIETZSCHE

CORE CONTRIBUTIONS

Nietzsche (1844–1900) is at once a trenchant critic of modern values and institutions and an insightful visionary, proposing new approaches to ethics, knowledge, art, culture, and philosophy. He challenges the value of both religion and traditional morality – interrogating the still-dominant values of this era: reason, freedom, equality, and sympathy. Finding these values flawed, he proposes a new goal for mankind: self-perfection. Achieving this will require a multi-perspectival approach to knowledge and bold philosophical vision.

Nietzsche anticipated the death of (or loss of belief in) God and foresaw its potential nihilistic consequences, but nonetheless he urges humanity to overcome this loss by remaking *itself* into something godlike.[1] He strives to counteract nihilism and decadence by calling humanity to a new mission – to redeem life by achieving greatness.[2] Nietzsche claims that both religion and traditional morality are inimical to this goal.[3] By also showing that the motives and consequences of living in accord with religion and morality (in the traditional sense) are often *immoral*, he criticizes them on *internal* grounds. Traditional morality typically buttresses faltering Christian ideals, and Nietzsche proposes new values (and a new relationship to values) to supersede them.

Nietzsche challenges many of modernity's deepest assumptions, e.g., the belief that humanity over time is improving in wisdom, refinement, and moral sensitivity. Instead he finds opposed trends toward specialization of knowledge (in both science and scholarship), mediocrity, and pursuit of easy pleasures. He contends that nearly all modern developments are inimical to the human excellences he sought to promote – challenging the democratic and egalitarian values that have governed political thought since the French and American revolutions.[4] He rejects the view that humans are essentially self-conscious, rational, self-determining creatures, arguing instead that biological drives, the body, and cultural backgrounds govern human development and that natural factors explain the dynamics of human action.[5] He even reconsiders the value of truth itself, noting that sometimes illusion may be necessary to achieve greatness and that pathways to truth are more treacherous than is often assumed.[6] Though he may have doubts about truth's absolute value, he steadfastly pursues it. The test of a person's mettle, for Nietzsche, is the amount of truth she can bear.[7]

Against this background picture of modernity's decadence and of religion's and morality's inability to counteract it, Nietzsche proposes his alternative: the promotion of human greatness. Success will require a rejuvenation of humanity: revitalizing strength, passion, self-control, foresight, the sublimation of drives, individual style, grace, life-affirmation, and strengthening distinctive virtues in different types of individuals.[8] He seeks a tougher, truer, more spirited relation to life that will enrich humanity. Nietzsche creates a psychology that shows how to transmute the questionable givens of human nature into heroic virtues. This requires a new conception of selfhood and agency, of motivation, and of the ways social, natural, and educational environments can support human achievement. Humans must comprehend and refashion their earthly roots – their instincts, drives, genetic endowments, culturally inherited habits, diet, geography, and the challenges and vicissitudes of life – in order to make themselves higher and nobler.[9]

This goal will also require new forms of knowledge and philosophy. Nietzsche argues that all knowledge is perspectival, but instead of drawing skeptical conclusions from this premise, he infers that continuously improving knowledge/wisdom can be achieved by multiplying perspectives, triangulating them in relation to each other, using each to supplement and correct the others – gradually integrating the results.[10] Gaining knowledge requires the resources of many disciplines; no single approach is sufficient. Truth-seekers will have to become more versatile, master many disciplines and methods, learn artistic creativity and balanced judgment.[11] Nietzsche also defines new cultural roles for philosophers in addition to pursuing this perspectival approach to knowledge: cultural physician, genius of the heart, value-legislator, and revaluer of values. Cultural physicians examine the strengths and weaknesses of past cultures in order to enhance and refashion the current one – diagnosing its specific flaws and offering prescriptions.[12] Geniuses of the heart see deeply into their fellow-humans, finding ways to overcome their resistances and inertia, inspiring them to greater achievements.[13] Value-legislators create guiding values for the future and establish the necessary institutions to support them; they gain the strength and insight to do this from revaluing and testing various past, and proposed future, values.[14]

Above all, Nietzsche seeks to overcome the negative attitudes people have to themselves, to other people, to nature, to the cosmos, and to time. So many people – even the most promising ones – learn to hate themselves and resent the achievements of others. Gradually they come to hate life and then cannot take advantage of its opportunities. They collapse when the world offers resistance instead of rising to its challenges. Nietzsche shows people how to make the most of the hand they have been dealt – identifying alternative cultural institutions that would support this new affirmation of life.

LIFE

Born in 1844, Nietzsche was the first son of a Lutheran minister; his sister, Elizabeth, was born two years later. His father died prematurely before Nietzsche was 5, and a younger brother died before he was a year old. Between the ages of 14 and 20, Nietzsche attended a well-known boarding school that specialized in classics, Pforta. There he established a small group of friends devoted to music composition, poetry, and intellectual discussion. Initially, he studied theology at the University in Bonn, but within a year, at 21, he moved to Leipzig to devote himself to classics, soon becoming the favored student of the senior professor, Ritschl. On his recommendation, Nietzsche became Professor of Classical Philology at Basel, Switzerland, at the unbelievably young age of 24, without yet having completed his dissertation. There he became associated with Richard and Cosima Wagner, whose influence shows in his first major published book, *The Birth of Tragedy* (1872). Though Nietzsche had in the interim received his doctorate on the basis of published articles, classics scholars did not receive this first book warmly. Throughout his life, Nietzsche was hampered by severe migraines and a variety of other illnesses. But he was still able to publish four essays that he later collected in *Untimely Meditations* (1873–6) and the first volume of *Human, All Too Human* (1878). At the age of 34, having taught at the university for ten years, Nietzsche resigned his appointment for health reasons. He spent the next ten years living an itinerant lifestyle on a modest university pension, publishing roughly one book a year, although none achieved success during his lifetime. He fell in love at least once (with Lou Salome), but his proposal of marriage was declined. He also struggled with his sister over her marriage to a well-known anti-Semite, Bernhard Forster. In 1889, att the age of 44, Nietzsche suffered a severe mental collapse, the causes of which are uncertain. He lived another 11 years, but never regained lucidity, even though several unsuccessful attempts were made to treat him. Nietzsche lived his last years in silence, first with his mother, then with his sister, who oversaw the publication of his last books (composed and completed in 1888 before his collapse), *Twilight of Idols, Antichrist,* and *Ecce Homo,* and who created the compilation of notebook entries called *The Will to Power*.

ON READING NIETZSCHE

Many of Nietzsche's works – *Human, All Too Human* (1878–80), *Daybreak* (1881), *The Gay Science* (1882), *Beyond Good and Evil* (1886), and *Twilight of Idols* (1889) – consist of fragments: loosely organized vignettes on a variety of topics. Two early books – *Birth of Tragedy* (1872) and *Untimely Meditations* (1873–4) – and two late ones – *Genealogy of Morals* (1887) and *The Antichrist* (1888) – consist of continuous essays, but this is the exception rather than the rule. (*Thus Spoke Zarathustra* (1883–5) is a narrative and prophetic work that straddles this distinction.) This writing strategy makes organizing Nietzsche's ideas on a given topic difficult. The interpreter must integrate all the fragments on similar topics, keeping in mind their original context and their order of publication. In addition, Nietzsche often states apparently contradictory views (even in the same book) in order to force the reader to explore the issue with him and resolve the apparent contradictions. He also approaches topics from many different perspectives to gain a comprehensive overview. Sometimes he is even deliberately misleading to insure that only kindred spirits will comprehend him. Some philosophers complain that Nietzsche fails to offer arguments for his views. I find this objection to be mistaken. Nearly every fragment contains arguments; sometimes premises are implicit, but he seeks to convince, not to pontificate. Indeed, Nietzsche often develops so many different arguments for his conclusions that isolating the pivotal ones is hard. Because his supporting arguments derive from many types of evidence, even when some of his arguments are questionable, the overall impact of his multi-pronged defense remains powerful.

Even if many textual problems can be explained, Nietzsche's views still remain puzzling. For example, though he adopts an anti-theist stance, he also seemingly creates new myths – the *Übermensch* (highest human beings) and eternal recurrence – which could be regarded as religious symbols for a postmodern era. Certainly his thought has mythic dimensions even if his metaphors are this-worldly and his philosophical views are rooted in earthly nature. Also, Nietzsche's belief that humanity must transcend *ressentiment* seems incompatible with his own apparent hatred toward Christianity, morality, and his socialist contemporaries. But close inspection of his critical assessments reveals that he gives his opponents their just due, indicating strengths others had overlooked, at the same time as he reveals crucial weaknesses. Often Nietzsche adopts an almost clinical gaze on those he criticizes (including his youthful self) – seeking the psychological motivation, as well as the reasons, for their mistakes. Occasionally Nietzsche's proclamations seem like *ad hominem* arguments, but since he insists that philosophies symbolize and encapsulate their creators' lives, an examination of those lives may be relevant to evaluating their ideas. Also, for Nietzsche the motives for holding a view are important for assessing its value. Finally, for all his aspirations toward truth, Nietzsche is sometimes too willing to assert what can only be regarded as speculative hypotheses, the evidence for which is weak and even the meaning of which is unclear (e.g., eternal recurrence).

THE DEATH OF GOD AND THE STRUGGLE AGAINST NIHILISM

Nietzsche sees that God was no longer a credible idea to educated, thoughtful people, and he realized this collapse of faith would gradually spread to the masses. Earlier thinkers had made their peace with the death of God, but Nietzsche realizes that this loss would be a defining cultural and intellectual event and would require major adjustments in humanity's forms of life.[15] Indeed, the consequences of this loss extend to every field: political and social theory, psychology, anthropology, art, history, and economics, as well as philosophy. He predicted that great dangers would threaten mankind during this period of adjustment; people would be tempted by nihilism – the view that nothing has any value, meaning, or power to motivate greatness through self-sacrifice.[16] As ruinous as Nietzsche felt Christianity had been during its long reign, he feared nihilism even more because it insidiously enervates all striving for human excellence. Indeed, Nietzsche's dominant philosophical project can be interpreted as a heroic effort to forestall, circumvent, and transcend nihilism, by providing humanity with meaning and direction during a period of potential drift and uncertainty. His solution is to invite individuals to become godlike – realizing their greatest potentials.[17]

Nietzsche is unique in defending not just atheism (the belief that there is no God) but also *anti-theism* (the view that belief in God is destructive to the believer). Theists readily entrust humanity's future to God, often abdicating their own responsibility for creating that future.[18] For Nietzsche, the death of God is not just an intellectual event; it is a species-defining cultural event, and it demands a dramatic response. Otherwise, the loss of God may destroy any possibility for realizing humanity's greatness. Feuerbach and Marx had shown that God is a projection based on human need and that religious belief has specific social and psychological functions – to reduce fear of the unknown and to gain a sense of control over nature. Nietzsche agrees, but also adds that theism is spiritually debilitating. Though he provides intellectual arguments for rejecting theism, his main objections are ethical.

Nietzsche's intellectual arguments develop those of Enlightenment skeptics: the punishments religion imposes are based on assumptions for which little evidence can be given, e.g., the existence of heaven and hell, eternal bliss, original sin, and final judgment. The harsh vengeance these concepts imply seems incompatible with the moral aspirations of Christianity. Also, once a religion is established, its priests manipulate its doctrines to dominate the everyday lives of its believers.[19] For example, the religious obsession with the soul encourages indifference to the needs and health of the body. In philosophy, the concept of God is used to solve problems that philosophers cannot answer more inventively – concealing weaknesses in their philosophical systems. In effect, it forestalls serious inquiry at those junctures where deeper philosophical analysis is most needed. Such intellectual arguments may justify skepticism about God's existence. But Nietzsche's ethical arguments overturn theism – showing that people must learn to live without belief in God because it debilitates them, insuring that greatness will elude them.

Ethical arguments against theism

Nietzsche contends that most religions – especially Christianity – displace the *inherent* value of acting nobly, encouraging people to act ethically only to achieve some reward (entrance into heaven) and to resist evil only to avoid horrible punishment (hell).[20] Nietzsche believes that such incentives undermine ethical action because it should be indifferent to rewards and punishments. Moreover, the otherworldly focus of most religions encourages adherents to ignore this world – to abandon their responsibilities and ignore their failures here – because they can be compensated or forgiven in the next world.[21] Equally suspect is the belief that a last-minute conversion can atone for a lifetime of heartlessness and lassitude, as if deathbed conversions can eliminate responsibility for such failings. For these reasons, Nietzsche believes most religions mock ethical seriousness because they undermine its presuppositions: that virtue is its own reward, that this world is where ethical action is needed, and that every action matters.

In addition, many religions idealize asceticism – opposing natural human impulses, e.g., sex, pride, self-assertion, and joy in achievement.[22] Nietzsche thinks these natural impulses are incipient sources of excellence. Religion's primary tactic is to extirpate or annihilate them, producing people who are either divided within themselves (insofar as they maintain some identification with their impulses) or hate themselves (because they cannot overcome them). Self-contemptuous people reject life and act spitefully. When others reciprocate, anger, hatefulness, and resentment escalate, creating poisonous social relations.[23] Religion's victims eventually come to hate life itself – not just themselves. Nietzsche believes that the best relationship to natural passions is sublimation – redirecting and guiding them toward higher goals.[24] Nietzsche celebrates these impulses because they provide the energy necessary to achieve greatness.

Beyond this, Nietzsche shows that Christianity's emotional ambiance is dominated by sin, guilt, suffering, penance, atonement, and despair. Thus, its psychic landscape is desolate, without vitality, passion, light-footedness, or playfulness – characteristics that Nietzsche believes are essential to higher achievements. This emotional ambiance devastates the faithful, shattering their self-confidence and inspiration. Moreover, historically, religion is responsible for many ethnic wars and hatreds, and soldiers (and terrorists) infused with holy righteousness are more efficient killers. Of course, priests might argue that religion offers "metaphysical comforts" to the masses, making their modest lives meaningful and providing them with hope. But Nietzsche often thinks that illusory hopes are problematic and that religious meaning depends on indefensible assumptions. Without metaphysical comforts, people would be forced to push themselves to achieve meaningful lives. Nietzsche concludes that the psychological and historical consequences of theism have reduced humanity's capacities for excellence. The demise of such a corrupting institution should be greeted with joy.

Nietzsche also challenges Christianity's embrace of "slavish" values – values that sustain the weak, the failures, the inept, and the mediocre. Nietzsche holds that the concept of "good" within a *slavish* system of evaluation is *derivative* – defined solely in opposition to whatever it calls "evil" – and that "evil" maligns noble traits that enhance human flourishing and exceptional achievement.[25] Slavish value systems sanctify humility, passivity, pity, lassitude, dependence, non-responsiveness, and procrastination. These "values" lead humanity down a path opposite from the one Nietzsche embraces. They sustain those who avoid the challenge of greatness, who shun danger, and who mindlessly conform. Slavish values encourage dependence on higher powers, keeping people in a helpless condition.

As an alternative to theistic ideals, Nietzsche defends a distinctive array of values: real achievements in this life; graciousness and gift-giving abundance; sensuousness, joy, delight in the present; health and strength and spirited vitality; affirmation of oneself, this life, and this world; independence and the power to achieve self-transformation. Nietzsche seeks to strengthen, refine, cultivate, and elevate human capacities, not to debilitate and weaken them as many religions do. His virtues promote the enhancement of life and humanity, guiding it toward higher achievements. In his fictional prophet, Zarathustra, Nietzsche created a model for his new direction, a spokesperson for these new ideals, and perhaps an inspiring myth. Nietzsche replaces dependency on religion with a guidebook for the self-transformation of humanity. Above all, he wants to avoid the harmfulness of nihilism.

Resisting nihilism

Nietzsche's diagnosis of the consequences of the death of God was surprisingly prescient; they are still gradually unfolding over a century later. One result is that values seem foundationless and all ways of life seem equivalent – the most radiant, ennobling achievements seem to merit no greater admiration than anemic failures. In addition, long-term, multi-generational tasks (e.g., space travel) no longer motivate dedication, and striving for self-perfection seems ridiculous to those seeking money, fame, or power. When the myth of God disintegrates, the earth becomes a tiny chunk of granite supporting insignificant life-forms. Humans born in declining or impoverished cultures can only curse their fate; no redemption from above or vindication from the future will arrive. Since modern culture is decadent and since reinvigorating it is too large a task for a single individual, the death of God can produce hopelessness, futility, inertia, and weariness. These effects worsen the cultural quicksand into which modern humanity is sinking, making the achievement of higher humanity extremely difficult.

This general condition of enervation requires ever-stronger narcotics to make life tolerable. People seek artificial stimulants, filling their empty lives with intoxicants, mysticisms, sexual frenzy, fanaticism, jingoism, and workaholism. They exhaust their flagging energies by seeking meaning in activities that cannot provide it. People sacrifice themselves to these false gods rather than transforming themselves. Instead of learning to confront tragic suffering and life's hardships directly, instead of seeking a genuine solution to the loss of meaning, they pursue paths that yield only disillusionment.

The next stage of nihilism truly frightens Nietzsche. He expects that many will decide to admit defeat, to protect their small comforts, and to live only for the moment. Nietzsche calls this option the "Last Man."[26] These "last humans" seek small pleasures, are easy-going, conformist, uninvolved and uninspired; they let others be and pass them by; they refuse to react – indifferently blinking at the passing scene. The "last humans" lack passions, loves, cares, and aims, and thus are diametrically opposed to Nietzsche's *Übermenchen* (of which there are many types). Nietzsche's doubts about modernity seem justified because last humans are proliferating in the current era. Only the most overwrought and extreme music, art, news, and lifestyles produce any reaction at all. Passivity, indifference, and lifelessness – almost an inability (rather than a refusal) to act – constitute the dominant attitudes. Nietzsche desperately seeks to avoid this result.

Nietzsche distinguishes between active and passive nihilism.[27] Passive nihilism simply surrenders to this condition, accepts exhaustion and weariness, and says "no" to life. Active nihilism attempts to destroy the vestiges of Christian-moral values so that something new might emerge. Active nihilism alone is not constructive, but at least it initiates the critical work necessary to stimulate a revaluation of values, and this in turn may enable the construction of a better, stronger culture. Active nihilism dispenses with illusions and strives to see the world as it really is. Nietzsche regards it as a transitional phase. Christianity played a similar function: even though it had many flaws, it also produced positive results, allowing more promising human possibilities to develop. Nietzsche seeks to reshape modern cultural trends so that they will contribute to his goals for humanity.

What are these goals? Nietzsche summarizes them in his *Übermensch* ideal, which is an earthly ideal that can be realized in many different ways. It challenges people to fully develop their talents, and this requires self-comprehension (both of one's strengths and weaknesses) and self-will (the capacity to alter one's habits and patterns of behavior). "Higher humans" must continuously challenge themselves to outdo their best achievements, to push themselves toward their highest possible accomplishments in the areas they value most. The *Übermensch* ideal requires individuals to affirm life despite its challenges, setbacks, and sufferings; to integrate their passions so that they collectively sustain their chosen tasks; and to function as models for others.[28] It requires self-sacrifice and dedication, not a life of small pleasures and amusements. It may produce some joy and exhilaration, but it will also encounter suffering and struggle – risking self-destruction to achieve self-transcendence. It offers much to others without seeking any return and without feeling any loss.[29] Many different values can be legitimately pursued under the banner of this ideal, but they must be higher values. Nietzsche challenges people to become godlike, thus rendering their former dependence on God superfluous.

CRITIQUE OF MORALITY AND REVALUATION OF VALUES

When Nietzsche criticizes "morality," he means the Kantian heritage of Christianity, with its weighty sense of duty, obligation, and responsibility. He also challenges specific virtues associated with Christianity that often define being "moral" (e.g., altruism, compassion). He does not reject ethics altogether; indeed, his own alternative to nihilism is a constructive ethical stance. But because he rejects core elements of traditional Western morality, some commentators see a contradiction in his ethical perfectionism. The response is that Nietzsche's ethics offers an alternative to traditional morality that overcomes its flaws. I will first discuss his three strategies for criticizing "morality" and then explain his method for revaluing many "moral" values.

Nietzsche offers a three-pronged critique of morality: first, he suggests that morality is misguided or misdirected; second, he shows that morality depends on non-moral, or even immoral, factors; finally, he shows that the standard supporting arguments for morality are flawed. Each prong includes several sub-arguments.

The misguidedness of morality derives from its other-directedness and its presumed dominance over other types of personal evaluation. The other-directed focus of morality can be shown in two ways. On the one hand, moralists concentrate too much on *judging* other people (instead of embodying excellence themselves). They arrive after an action has already occurred to assess its rightness – often seeking reasons to condemn rather than praise.[30] Only rarely do moralists investigate the conditions that make moral excellence possible; instead, they focus on failures and blame. Moreover, the moral judge tends to condemn the unique and the unusual because moral values derive from group norms.[31] This judgmentalism unleashes the moralist's urge to punish, but Nietzsche is highly skeptical of the effectiveness and presuppositions of punishment.[32] Moral "judges" derive from angry fathers, angry Gods, or wrathful principles – all demanding atonement and fostering guilt. Such judgmentalism is often rooted in hatred of life's natural drives or in resentment of other people's advantages. For Nietzsche, such motives are ethically corrupt; they pollute the outcomes of moral judgments, making them immoral.

On the other hand, moralists emphasize duties to other people almost exclusively, remaining silent about duties to oneself.[33] Nietzsche believes that ordinary socialization implants social obligations into individual psyches deeply enough. People do not need the added sledgehammer of morality to pound them in further. Nietzsche thinks that duties to oneself are too readily ignored because morality protects other people primarily and overlooks the sacrifices in personal excellence required to achieve this. Nietzsche would reverse this emphasis: better to achieve radiant personal virtue than to become compulsively concerned about others.[34]

In addition, morality assumes the authority to judge every person's life – dominating all other standards of evaluation. Consider that a complete evaluation of a person would require assessing her wisdom, intelligence, and sensitivity; her political astuteness, interpersonal relationships (friends, lovers, family), and professional achievements; the unity, splendor, and coherence of her life; her vigor and joy in living, physical grace and beauty, and the range of talents she has perfected. Her moral tenor is but one element in a complex story. But moralists insist that it is the definitive criterion of personal value;

moral failure is allegedly identical to personal failure.[35] Nothing else matters. This arrogance is unwarranted. In a sense, everyone – no matter how ordinary and wooden – *can* be evaluated morally. Because many will not score well on these other, non-moral standards, morality insists that it should be the primary criterion of personal value, thus demoting these other standards. Nietzsche asks only that morality play a restricted role in personal evaluation, that non-moral evaluative standards be given due weight in this process. The moral standpoint yields misleading conclusions about a person's overall value.

The second prong of Nietzsche's critique of morality argues that morality is immoral. He defends this by showing that morality often derives from dubious motives. Nietzsche notes that the main motivation for acting morally is fear – of the wrath of God, of punishment, of bad consequences, or of others' disapproval.[36] But actions motivated by fear cannot be moral, for this would make morality into a domineering tyrant. Acting freely would be impossible under such conditions. Morality presupposes freedom, and fear undermines it. Fear-based moralities thus are immoral. In addition, tradition-based morality typically seeks to make people behave robotically and uncritically. Moralists often strive to inculcate customary or habituated responses. Such responses prevent full appreciation of the ethically relevant features in the situation. In effect, such morality demands ethical insensitivity so that its subjects act more reliably.[37] Hence morality again seems to defeat its own presuppositions. The motivation for ethical action should be the inherent worth of the relevant values, and ethical responses should derive from sensitivity to them. Thus, both in its motivation and the kind of action it inculcates, morality undermines itself, making its adherents immoral.

Another argument for the immorality of morality appears in *Genealogy of Morals*. There Nietzsche examines the origins of the moral point of view, which he traces to a "slave morality" created by people who were ill-suited to life – those who were failures, weak-willed, untalented, or unsuccessful. They reacted against a different human type who demonstrated talent, assertiveness, success, and strength. This type embodied what Nietzsche calls "master morality," whose proponents value whatever produced joy or delight, self-expression and life-affirmation, and whatever improved their capacity to live well. Their virtues were pride, strength, passion, power, and exuberance. They were indifferent to the opposite experiences, avoiding such states not because they were *evil*, but because they were unhealthy and self-destructive. Master morality's terms of evaluation are good and bad, where "bad" had no moral overtones.[38]

Nietzsche surmises that the birth of specifically *moral* forms of goodness and virtue occurred when the priests who ministered to the unsuccessful slavish types inverted the valuations celebrated by strong, healthy human types. Their will to dominate designated the non-moral, noble values "*evil*." The vituperative resentment implicit in this term is the source of the negativity and the judgmentalism operating in morality.[39] Whatever lacks these "evil" values is "good" for the slavish types; their "goodness" is wholly derivative, praising weakness, humility, suffering, passivity, resignation, and self-denial – living long rather than living well. Nietzsche wonders how such "virtues" could become dominant, how they could gain ascendancy when they so clearly inhibit the highest human possibilities. His answer is that the priests inverted master morality's values through a kind of ideological maneuver. They created an array of counter-ideals that shattered the self-confidence of the noble types, and this allowed the priests to achieve some degree of cultural ascendancy. The base, priestly virtues became "moral values"; this is one reason why Nietzsche regards "morality" with contempt. He argues that "morality" is typically opposed to the achievement of human excellence and concludes that it has been a disaster for humanity.[40] Entirely new modes of evaluation must be created.

In addition, moralities are not designed to correct themselves, like science. They take currently accepted obligations to be absolute, dismissing all innovations or alternatives as evil and immoral. Thus, ethical innovators and visionaries are almost always castigated by their contemporaries before their insights achieve broad acceptance; often they are ostracized and tortured.[41] Nietzsche also notes that most people who claim to be moral really do not deserve the accolade, arguing that people must be capable of doing great evil and nonetheless still choose the good in order to merit praise. Most "moral" subjects are so habituated to it that they rarely imagine any alternatives and are incapable of anything risky. They take the path of least resistance by conforming to tradition's demands. They do not choose to be moral in the sense of rejecting an alternative that they might have seriously pursued. Nietzsche thus questions whether morality's adherents really deserve to be called moral.[42]

The third prong of Nietzsche's critique of morality is more philosophical. He raises doubts about the evidence and general arguments used to defend morality. For example, moralists rarely address the question: why be moral? Indeed, any answer to such a question must lie outside the limits of morality if the fallacy of circular argument is to be avoided. Morality cannot be self-justifying. But what sort of argument might justify it? Prudential grounds are both insufficient (because sometimes doing the wrong thing is to a person's advantage) and regarded as immoral. Aesthetic grounds are unlikely to be sufficiently strong and may justify alternatives to morality (e.g., being a refined person is not enough to be a moral person, and it points in a direction different from morality). No factual conditions can mandate acceptance of morality. So Nietzsche's question intensifies: what sort of non-circular argument can justify being moral?

Many moralists defend their imperatives by appeals to intuition or common sense. Nietzsche believes both are expressions of past prejudices. Common sense is what a new idea becomes when it achieves wide acceptance, often becoming oversimplified as it does so. Similarly, intuitions often derive from habituated responses, or else they express reactions that people think they *should* have (rather than the ones they actually have; the two can be difficult to distinguish). So Nietzsche rejects both intuition and common sense as sources of moral justification because they merely summarize past prejudices.[43] Moral rules are frequently justified by the social harmony they create, but this often necessitates sacrificing individual excellence, and Nietzsche wonders whether the price is worth the benefit. Moreover, he questions whether following specific moral dictates really produces long-term social good. He notes that morality may even be inimical to society in the long run because culture thrives on competition. Thus, the ideal of social harmony may be self-stultifying. Nietzsche therefore distinguishes conditions that produce social harmony from those that produce individual excellence, arguing that morality favors mediocrity rather than talent and achievement.[44]

Nietzsche also opposes Kant's universalization test – the claim that the maxim of a moral act must be capable of being adopted by everyone – as a criterion for moral obligation. Hegel rejected Kant's test because he thought the law-tester could unfairly influence its outcome by cleverly formulating the action's maxim. The very same action can be judged moral or immoral depending on how its maxim is formulated. Nietzsche faults Kant's test because he thinks people should follow *different* maxims. A promising virtue for one person may be harmful for another.[45] Nietzsche thinks that different human types require different ethical codes, each facilitating the specific virtues of that type. Thus, the claim that an agent's maxim cannot be universalized is irrelevant to Nietzsche; he expects this, even welcomes it. It shows that ethical guidelines must become more limited, nuanced, and attuned to the specific requirements of individuals.

Nietzsche also rejects the utilitarian principle that right actions produce the greatest good for the greatest number of people. He believes that the good is fragmented and multidimensional; because different people should pursue different goals, there is no single value that should be maximized for everyone. Moreover, goodness is certainly not equivalent to a quantifiable experience like pleasure or happiness (or even power). In addition, utilitarianism requires that every individual's good be counted equally in any calculation, and Nietzsche doubts whether everyone should count equally when weighing long-term consequences. Those with better chances of realizing human excellence perhaps should count for more.[46] The value of equality derives from the Christian notion that every believer is equal in the sight of God; the death of God means that this value needs to be reconsidered.

When morality requires justification, often it invokes transcendent (otherworldly) grounds or a questionable theory of human nature (e.g., reason is the only uniquely human faculty). Moral educators rely on inculcating habits or principles, neither of which is sufficient to produce venerable persons. Nietzsche believes that the only defensible basis for an ethics that can motivate self-perfection is a naturalistic one. Life and humanity exist; their enhancement and elevation can be readily defined. His naturalism starts with the human potential a given culture possesses, and then shows how to refine it. A naturalistic ethics uses culture to refashion natural givens, but realizes that success will require several generations, not a sudden conversion. Nietzsche also suggests that if a person's ethical values are so alien that they require justification, then they are probably unsuited to his type. The virtues informing a person's actions should motivate through their own inherent value and radiance, and thus should need no justification. A more complex human psychology will also be required to provide better ways to achieve self-perfection. Armed with such a psychology, Nietzsche's naturalistic ethics can transform human life.

Central to Nietzsche's ethical project is his revaluation of values, the methods for which require clarification.[47] He examines particular values from many different perspectives. Initially, he considers the characteristic *motive* for embracing a value, criticizing motives such as self-hatred, weakness, resentment, or life-negation. Then he examines the typical *effects* of embodying that value – on the agent, on other people, and on the culture. His main questions here are as follows. Does it contribute to the realization of human excellence? Does it generate inspiration? Does it produce greater cultural coherence? He also studies the typical *style* with which the value is lived. Some values are better realized by some agents than by others. For example, sympathy can be a burden on those to whom it is offered if the sympathizer demeans or trivializes their suffering. Some people offer it lightly, respectfully, without causing humiliation. Thus, only those who can offer it in this manner should embody sympathy; otherwise it can be ruinous to personal relationships. Nietzsche also examines *possible alternatives* to a value in the situations in which that value is typically pursued. Often he is able to imagine a new virtue that preserves the enhancement produced by the older value, but corrects its flaws. Sometimes other, already existing virtues offer more promise than the one in question. Nietzsche believes that these subtle comparative studies of the value of different values (and virtues) are important because they help produce deeper insight into their specific benefits and costs. Next, he considers the *type of person* that typically embodies the value. Is it pursued by strong, healthy, assertive, talented people or by other types? Nietzsche clearly articulates the kinds of people he wants to promote (*Übermenschen*), and if those types are drawn to a particular value, that itself is a sign of its worth. Finally, he examines the typical *lived experience* of a value – how does it feel to enact that value? Is it enlivening, uplifting, energizing, and intensifying? Does it encourage higher pursuits and elevated feelings; does it reinforce psychic integration, power, and health? If the answers to these questions are "yes," then the value's value is higher.

Nietzsche thus examines the motives, effects, style, and lived experience of a value, and also studies alternatives to it and the kinds of people who typically embody it. In this way he provides a rich analysis of its potential strengths and weaknesses. He tries to use all these perspectives to study each value. Sometimes these different criteria imply different conclusions. For this reason Nietzsche rarely dismisses a value *entirely*, but instead raises doubts about unconditional adherence to it, restricting its applicability. He also provides recommendations about who should pursue a particular value, and when, how, and why. The overall goal of his revaluations is to provide deeper and more concrete insight into the situations in which pursuing a value makes sense for particular persons (and when not). These restricted conclusions flow logically from his complex evaluation process. Nietzsche examines specific values, in specific constellations (like Christianity's pity, love of one's neighbor, and turning the other cheek; or the Enlightenment's reason, objectivity, and tolerance; or modernity's liberty, equality, and fraternity). He interrogates even his own virtues (friendship, gift-giving virtue, love of the future, and hardness toward oneself) using this process. The overall goal of this revaluation is deeper insight into the proper rank-order of values. He envisions a long-term period of ethical experimentation to fully assess the wide diversity of values.[48]

CONSTRUCTIVE ETHICS: LIFE-AFFIRMATION, POWER, INDIVIDUATED VIRTUES

Nietzsche's central ethical claim is that different individuals should devote themselves to different virtues because their talents and psychic constitution will be better suited to realizing some virtues rather than others. He wants everyone to strive to realize their best possibilities, i.e., their strongest loves, their greatest inspiration, and their deepest cares.[49] He also wants people to make steady progress, to remain committed over time, and to develop the strength and integration to gradually adopt harder tasks and higher aspirations. People should love their virtues with the same devotion parents give to their children. Above all, Nietzsche seeks to insure that people can *successfully* realize at least some of their aspirations; to shoot too high and fail risks disillusionment and self-hatred. Better to build slowly and succeed than to take on too much too quickly.[50] Part of the ethical task is self-discovery; part of it eventually becomes self-creation, but most of it consists in the daily pursuit of one's distinctive tasks.

Successful self-cultivation should be exhilarating, but Nietzsche also urges continuous self-overcoming – pressing on toward higher goals once a plateau is attained. Self-perfection involves giving style to one's character – treating one's life as a work of art, striking a balance between sharp contrasts, and maintaining proportion while taking risks. Stylization requires psychic organization, awareness of limits, concealing imperfections, highlighting strengths, and sublimating drives. It takes advantage of natural strengths and masters instincts by redirecting their energy toward higher purposes, rather than dominating or destroying them. It uses passions in the service of self-elevation, rather than allowing them to pull in contradictory, countervailing directions and thus to cripple serious achievement.[51]

Nietzsche defends various specific virtues: pursuing the broadest range of talents, depth and subtlety of intellect, serenity in the midst of harsh challenge, integrity, delicacy, vitality, courage, hardness toward oneself, friendship, devotion to the future, perceptivity, truth-seeking, and a willingness to risk everything in order to progress to new plateaux. He does not believe principles facilitate self-development; instead, he concentrates on habit-formation, education, self-understanding, and supportive natural and social environments.[52] He disdains breast-beating; the hardest demands should be met without pomp or fanfare, without complaint or heaviness. He expects people to remain attuned to their goals without losing their equilibrium. This requires grace and inner strength. His virtues and advice seek to overcome nihilism, prevent world-weariness, depression, despair, self-hatred, and life-negation. To counter this "spirit of gravity," he embraces vitality, focus, pride, wisdom, and self-love.

Two of his touchstone virtues are life-affirmation and character strength (one interpretation of the "will to power"). Life-affirmation embraces the life-process even when it is harsh or cruel. Life-affirming people know the dangers and amorality of life, understand the painful, messy, harsh, and uncertain process that life is, but nonetheless bravely stride forward – giving as good as they get, fighting the good fight without hesitation or self-pity.[53] They pursue their tasks wholeheartedly, realizing that success is not entirely in their hands. Life-affirmation allows people to overcome their own limitations and the mediocrity of their contemporaries. It involves emulating the creative play of life, progressing despite its vicissitudes, and retaining focus in the midst of suffering and setbacks. Life-affirming people function as models for others, offering inspiration and strength, allowing others to draw on their passion without feeling any loss or demanding any return.[54] Their lives redeem the life-process.

Life-enhancement also requires psychic and cultural integration. Nietzsche often speaks of the "will to power," and some interpreters believe this means dominating other people. But this is largely mistaken. The "power" he means is character strength – the ability to control one's actions, to succeed in the face of adversity, to create order amidst potential chaos.[55] Passions and instincts typically pull in contradictory directions. The will to power resolves these contradictions, producing energy where there might have been enervation. Powerful people achieve as much breadth as possible without being destroyed by its pursuit. Power involves organizing the drives, attaining self-control, success even in difficult tasks, and overcoming internal obstacles so that conquering external obstacles is easier. Such power can be given a social interpretation, but in that context it seeks to order the diverse forces within a culture, creating a social whole that contributes to the full achievement of the culture's goals. The drive to dominate others is often a sign of weakness, not of power.

Another virtue Nietzsche praises is the capacity to endure the idea of eternal recurrence.[56] Nietzsche uses "eternal recurrence" to define a new relationship to time. It substitutes for the claim that life is justified only if a specific end is realized, only if a specific future goal is successfully achieved. It proposes a cyclical view of time in contrast to a linear one. Eternal recurrence thus opposes the eschatological view of history, and gives meaning to the *process* of pursuing goals, rather than the final result. Believing in the factual truth of eternal recurrence is less important to Nietzsche than living with sufficient verve, high-spirits, and intensity that one *would be willing* to affirm one's life even if one had to live it over and over again, eternally, just as one has lived it. Eternal recurrence functions as an invitation to make present moments as meaningful as possible, so that they need not be justified by the future. Being able to affirm one's life even if it recurs eternally is a test that Nietzsche thinks only the highest and best lives can pass. He uses it to separate exemplary people from less successful types. It also balances his own commitment to future goals (the *Übermenschen*). Eternal recurrence highlights the present and the *process* of living; with it, Nietzsche seeks to unify being and becoming.

Nietzsche's constructive ethics thus combines three different elements: a naturalist basis, an aesthetic impulse, and an intuitionist moment. The naturalism derives from his view that life already strives to integrate, organize, and transcend itself; all life already seeks will to power and self-overcoming.[57] Nietzsche's ethics simply amplifies and makes intentional a direction life already adopts, however haphazardly. His metaphors of flourishing, enhancement, and integration of diversity express this naturalism. The aesthetic impulse valorizes creativity and stylization.[58] This supplements naturalism because life itself rarely finds the most creative paths on its own. These must be discovered, cultivated, and willed. The aesthetic impulse is also expressed in giving style to one's character, a regular pattern of self-discipline. Indeed virtually all higher achievements must overcome internal and external resistances. So even if nature provides their basis, individuals must assume nature's givens and creatively discover the means to realize them. The intuitionist dimension of Nietzsche's ethics involves the capacity to appreciate the full range of higher values. Higher persons are able to intuit or "smell" falseness, artificiality, or impurities in potential virtues.[59] They must "sense" the virtues that make their highest achievements possible. These intuitions are not fixed or static; they can be refined and sharpened, and serious ethical life requires a continuing effort to enhance these capacities. A penetrating grasp of genuine value is like the ability to appreciate color; some painters are able to refine their color-sensitivity to a remarkable degree, but many people barely register color subtleties at all. Similarly, some people remain indifferent to value discriminations, and consequently their intuitions remain unfruitful and inchoate.

ART

Nietzsche values art's ability to transfigure human life, the world, and the life-process. Art's emotional and spiritual powers – not its representational ability or its sensuous pleasures – fascinate him. He evaluates art in the perspective of life, and his main question is: does art contribute to life-enhancement and to achieving human excellence? He realizes that art can be a resource to help defeat nihilism or a palliative that exacerbates it. His first major publication, *The Birth of Tragedy* (1872), concerns the function of Greek and Wagnerian art in their respective cultures. There he clarifies both the audience's and the artist's relation to artworks. In later works he continues to explore art's relation to culture. His strategies for evaluating artists, art, and artistic genres provide a model for examining other cultural institutions.

Understanding *The Birth of Tragedy* requires appreciating Nietzsche's vision of life. Begin with the now famous cliché – "life is hard; then you die" – and then add "those you love often die prematurely; natural disasters can occur anytime; disease or accident may ruin your best years; often you will be misunderstood and judged a failure; and your deepest insights will rarely be shared." Add to this the fact that living is a constant struggle; challenges, tests, and competitors emerge at every turn; there is rarely enough money, time, or energy to do things right. Nietzsche's question then becomes: can art enhance life despite these terrors, harsh realities, and hardships? He answers that it can elevate life by transfiguring it. Both art and life are informed by two principles – the Dionysian and the Apollonian.[60] The Dionysian principle is associated with drunken ecstasy – a loss of individuality and a union with life's grandeur and power. The Apollonian principle is associated with dreams – the creation of beautiful forms that evoke order, balance, and harmony. Life embodies both principles; sometimes people discover a joy in existing that results from ecstatic immersion in the life-process; sometimes life transmutes itself by revealing a crystalline and geometric face. Art thus extends and amplifies life's existing dynamics, using these processes to transfigure a culture's sense of life. Art contributes to a culture's ability to comprehend its distinctive virtues.[61]

Art alters both the artist and the audience. Whenever art weakens, dispirits, or sickens an audience, then it is bad art. But art can inspire, strengthen, and enliven an audience both by presenting beautiful forms that enhance its resolve to face life's challenges or by forging a unity with the life-process that allows audiences to co-feel life's power and awesomeness.[62] The best art does both at once. Nietzsche thinks Greek tragedy managed to do this. Tragedy overcomes nausea and paralysis; it functions as a tonic and stimulus by making an affirmation of life possible while squarely facing its terrors. It overshadows both the palliatives of religion and the naive optimism of science – providing an aesthetic justification of life, seeing life as a kind of cosmic game.[63] Art transmutes the terrible into the sublime, the horrifying into the magnificent, and the painful into the stimulating. It encourages unity with the life-process even when it is harsh, and it allows people to embrace life even when they see through art's veils to the ominous forces underneath.

In later works, Nietzsche still admires art's ability to transfigure life, but he becomes uneasy about depending on such transfiguration. He also begins to value facing the harsh truths of life directly, and this makes him more uncertain about art's illusions.[64] He continues to examine the cultural functions of art, and he still rejects art that debilitates life or that depends on emotional excesses.[65] He also criticizes forms of art that have no transformative power, that merely seek to represent or entertain. Nietzsche lauds art when it provides style, order, and coherence to the conflicting forces of an age or when it gives unity to the flux of experience without denying life's tenuousness. He elaborates a concept of decadence, both in civilizations and in the arts, and shows how decadence in one stimulates and accelerates decadence in the other.[66] He embraces art that functions as a stimulus to life, that imposes a perspective on life, and that creates deeper bonds with life. He also defines a concept of "grand style" that initially is embodied only in great art, but which can then be transplanted to great individuals. Grand style requires a discipline that cultivates inner richness, mastering chaos through strength and organization.[67]

HISTORY

Because developmental theories of history were so central to Hegel and Marx, concrete historical studies proliferated throughout the nineteenth century, and history became an independent discipline in its own right. Nietzsche is among the first to raise critical questions about this result. He wonders whether this newly achieved historical sense will enable greater human achievements or undermine them, concluding that the historical sense can become a cancer that stultifies creative political action or a stimulus to further achievement. Situating a trend in an historical context often reveals its contingent nature, showing its dependence on specific factors. As a result, the trend seems less remarkable, less distinctive, and less compelling. For Nietzsche, the study of history is useful primarily to stimulate future accomplishments, and as a way to relate past achievements to future goals. Historical study should be a point of departure for an active transformation of the present. If it kills the urge for renewal or if it makes cultural enhancement seem impossible, then it must be challenged.[68]

Nietzsche examines three different types of history in his early essay, *On the Uses and Disadvantages of History for Life* (1874): monumental history, which discovers past actions that can serve as examples for future goals; antiquarian history, which preserves and reveres past actions as forerunners of present achievements; and critical history, which reveals flaws in past accomplishments in order to open new possibilities in the present.[69] Each of these types of history can have beneficial and detrimental effects. Monumental history highlights the best exemplars from past eras to inspire those who despair over the present, allowing current leaders to draw inspiration from past heroes. But monumental history works only if it stimulates current political action. If instead it encourages leaders to rest on the laurels of the past's great movers, then it undermines present efforts. Or if it overly adulates past heroes in a way that causes present leaders to feel inferior, then this may weaken their resolve.[70] Antiquarian history portrays the present as the outcome of past achievements, encouraging a reverence for the traditions that made the present possible. But this type of history can easily become idol-worship, suggesting that the present is inevitably inferior by comparison. Instead of eliciting gratitude for the past, antiquarian history may enshrine it in a reverential aura that suggests unsurpassability. This may enervate present leaders and may even invite shame over present accomplishments because they seem unequal to the glorious past.[71] Finally, critical history challenges the value of the past, dissolving its captivating power, by showing that better options are possible. In effect, it overcomes the adulatory effect of antiquarian history, at the risk of becoming ironic and disdainful toward all historical action. If the best attempts of past leaders are still riven with flaws, perhaps no current action will escape future reservations. Critical history produces a skeptical stance toward all leadership, which may undercut current efforts at cultural transformation.[72] So all three types of historical study have dangers, and all three have important uses. The value of historical study depends on its actual effects.

Nietzsche notes that achieving a just historical perspective – one that achieves a balanced comprehension of the positive and negative accomplishments of each era – is extremely difficult.[73] The historian tends either to invest too much value in the past or to refuse the value it is due. Adequately assessing the past requires penetrating insights of a culture's best thinkers. Fairly assessing the past is essential for the architects of the future, because their task is to preserve its truly important accomplishments while creating new solutions to unsolved problems. They must achieve a delicate balance that integrates the best of the past with the future.

Especially in the early stages of a culture's development, illusions may be necessary to its flourishing. As it reaches maturity, it may become sufficiently robust to confront the naked truth about its own past. Historical study often dismantles illusions and forces cultures to acknowledge past flaws. If this happens too soon, the culture may lose self-confidence and fail to reach its highest capabilities. Historical study may also so overload people with data that the culture's broad goals get forgotten. Or historians can infect a culture with doubts and irony that render its members incapable of taking their destiny seriously. These effects can weaken the culture's stamina and undermine its ability to make a distinctive contribution. Nietzsche suggests that the Greeks, at their height, were not very concerned with history, and for that reason they become a richer, more vital culture. The past can tyrannize the present and future, and historians sometimes encourage this. Nietzsche counsels resistance to these dangers of historical study.

Historical studies can contribute to the enhancement of life and culture. They can facilitate the understanding of exemplary human beings, challenging the present to think more creatively about the future; and they can force present actors to think more effectively, discovering necessary means to successfully realize their goals. Historical examples can also motivate self-sacrifice. Hence cultures must learn both to forget and to remember.[74] A culture achieves unity by building on its true strengths and discarding (or compensating for) its weaknesses. Vital cultures improve on the great deeds of their past heroes, drawing inspiration from them while refusing to be eclipsed by them. Leaders who create a culture's future must reinterpret its past, just as individuals must reshape and transfigure their natural talents. For individuals and cultures, Nietzsche seeks a movement toward perfection rooted in reality – that is neither impossible dream nor idle delusion, that stretches the limits of the achievable, but does not break during the process of accomplishment. When historical study serves this goal, it is productive.

CULTURE AND POLITICS

Nietzsche's theory of culture is better developed than his political thought; I will therefore concentrate on his analysis of culture's aims, preconditions, and elements. Culture is a social organization whose aim is the production of individual greatness.[75] It seeks to enhance genius by refining and transfiguring the givens of nature. Nature already exhibits an implicit will to power; culture sharpens it, guides it, and makes it more intentional, completing nature's nascent efforts to produce humanity's best exemplars. Higher cultures stimulate the perfection and integration of many drives, talents, and perspectives – keeping them in proportion and under control even when they threaten to destroy each other. Culture consists of the community of those who rise to the call of perfecting themselves; they constitute a republic that communicates and inspires across continents and historical eras.[76]

Nietzsche believes that long-range thinkers and strong-willed visionaries are necessary to successfully produce such a culture. Their most important task is to learn (and teach others) to conquer adversity, to rise to challenges, to endure suffering, and to overcome obstacles. Creating culture may require cruelty, both to oneself and to others.[77] This cruelty results from breaking illusions, demanding ever-greater efforts, and refusing everyday pleasures; often the cruelty can be sublimated, but it cannot be ignored. Even the best human creations derive from questionable sources. He also suggests that genuine culture may require a kind of slavery, though he thinks most workers in the current age live in worse conditions (by their own choosing) than did Greek slaves. He may mean only that those with great talents must rely on those with modest talents to supply their basic needs. Nietzsche thus acknowledges that even though a vital culture may facilitate individual self-perfection, it still is rooted in struggle, violence, illusion, and harshness. He thinks this is part of the life-process; the task is to find the internal strength to respond to its challenges. To reach their goals, vital cultures may have to use questionable means (Nietzsche thinks nearly everything great has been achieved via questionable means).

Early Nietzsche suggests that anyone who rises to the call of self-perfection thereby becomes a member of a culture, but even at that stage he realized that not everyone would so respond, only the most energetic.[78] Later he suggests a class system based on an order of rank, in which the highest and best have the greatest responsibilities, but also are expected to make the greatest sacrifices.[79] The higher depend on the cooperation of the lower to sustain their modest needs; in return they enshrine the culture with their best efforts toward greatness. Nietzsche expects the highest to facilitate each other's achievement through competition and mutual challenge.[80] He notes that vital cultures have specific missions and yet finite energies and resources with which to accomplish them. Hence they must not allow themselves to be deflected by petty issues, enervating wars, or wasteful decadence, and they must also be strong enough to resist domination by a single charismatic hero. Though vital, higher cultures may produce many heroic figures, their power is limited by other heroes; at best they can only establish sects of followers. Culture allows higher humans to esteem themselves, to pursue their talents intensely and fully, and to experience the inherent joy of self-perfection.

Cultures can be more or less healthy or decadent. They become decadent when individuals are too exhausted to attempt great things, when there is debilitating internal conflict, when people lack direction or focus, when they abandon themselves to the present, and when they hate themselves and the entire life-process. Healthy cultures exhibit the opposite tendencies (vitality, harmony or productive competition, exemplary leaders, future-orientation, and individual and collective self-esteem), and also create sciences that seek to enhance greatness, an economy that provides for people's needs without dominating their everyday lives, and a spirit of life-affirmation.[81] The highest task for the state is to protect the vitality of culture, but it must not weaken or distract those it seeks to protect. Education is crucial to the vitality and success of culture; it must instill both strength and discrimination, insight and knowledge of the conditions of self-realization, challenging people to push themselves to their limits. Education must teach people to assimilate their own experience, to become "naturals" at their best talents. Finally, it must inculcate a spirit of mutual challenge and support, teaching people to respect and learn from their enemies as well as their friends.[82]

Nietzsche's political views are far less organized. He explicitly acknowledges that his political stance cannot be readily categorized: neither conservative (he realizes that history cannot be turned back), nor liberal (whose policies often encourage decadence), nor revolutionary (because they often produce more harm than good). He seeks a new kind of political order that will support the realization of higher humanity (who will be of *many* kinds, exhibiting *diverse* virtues). For Nietzsche, the highest exemplars of humanity should guide its future development; they bear the greatest burdens of decision-making. Their leadership is legitimated less by mass consent or representation than by merit. He questions many modern political ideals and institutions: doubting democracy's value because it entails rule by those who are least knowledgeable and least committed to the future; favoring equality only among equals, not among all citizens; rejecting inalienable rights; claiming that rights and duties codify specific power relations that often change over time; challenging the effectiveness and value of punishment.[83] He rejects victims' demands to redress past exploitation, because everyone can be shown to descend from an exploiter if the historical record is examined extensively enough. He hopes for a different kind of society in which all classes are concerned for the long-term advantage and enhancement of all the others. He rejects socialism because its implementation would require terrorism and despotism and would only produce an unproductive backlash.[84] He values challenge and opposition as a stimulus to greater achievement; though wars can sometimes function as such a stimulus, often they exhaust the energies of a culture and squander its resources. He acknowledges that everyone must own some property to maintain a stake in the political system, and he expects leaders to create conditions that allow everyone the opportunity to perfect themselves.[85] He thus challenges many current political presuppositions, but the political institutions he would support are less well defined. The tasks and basic conditions of culture are clearer, but even there Nietzsche is often short on specifics and details.

HUMAN LIFE AND CONSCIOUSNESS

Nietzsche rejects the Cartesian view that we know our conscious states directly, arguing that major psychic forces – instincts and drives – operate beneath the level of consciousness.[86] Moreover, he notes that many urges that rise to consciousness have social functions rather than individual ones; that is, typically people notice features of experience because they are socially relevant.[87] A background hum of pre-conscious activity is never noticed, and a deeper level of psychic activity is virtually inaccessible because people lack the concepts and discriminative abilities to clarify them. Adequately understanding the mind requires examining evidence from multiple viewpoints: history, physiology, philosophy, sociology, and psychology. Most of the revelations of "self-consciousness" are filtered through common-sense categories that oversimplify complex processes. For Nietzsche, consciousness itself is a simplifying medium; these simplifications may be necessary for practical action, but often they belie the real sources and dynamics of psychic operations.[88] Nietzsche rejects claims that take consciousness and self-consciousness to be mere epiphenomena because sometimes their guidance and direction produce greater coherence, order, or balance in the psyche.[89] But neither are they the sole source of psychic strength or order. Effective willing involves a confluence of multiple centers of power; thus, self-conscious decisions are not the sole determinants of action because the rest of the psyche must support self-consciousness's chosen aims if they are to be realized.[90]

The body plays a central role in psychic activity, according to Nietzsche; its nutrition, environment (natural and social), exercise, health, and development condition all mental functions.[91] The body has both physiological and psychic dimensions; its psychic elements are drives, which aim to increase and organize energy to achieve greater strength, integration, and domination over other drives. Drives thus tend to increase their power, and their energy provides the psyche with its strength and health. Drives can be enhanced, directed, nurtured, and ordered, or they can be weakened, discharged, ignored, and allowed to counteract each other. Drives can be subsumed by other drives and sometimes ordered by self-consciousness. The number and strength of a person's drives determine the type of person she can become because they set limits to what she may achieve. Drives thus constitute a person's psychic "substance." Their strength depends on productive challenge and opposition as well as overall psychic integration; within an atmosphere of healthy competition multiple drives can enhance each other. If life lacks challenge, then drives may degenerate. If, on the other hand, life is so burdened with challenges that the drives become exhausted, then weakness and decline will also result. Drives seek increased organization and strength in all forms of life; this is Nietzsche's organizing empirical hypothesis – the "will to power." People seek greater power in order to achieve more difficult goals.

Nietzsche offers the will to power in contrast to the commonly accepted will to pleasure or will to survival. Nietzsche notes that people will sacrifice survival and pleasure to achieve great things. Organisms that desperately cling to life have already become decadent. Moreover, the will to power determines what is pleasing; hence the will to pleasure is entirely dependent on the will to power.[92] If, for example, I take celibacy as an aim, then sexual arousal would offer no pleasure, and copulation would be unfulfilling because my will to power commands that such stimuli be experienced as painful. Pleasure derives from achieving significant goals, which are determined by the will to power. Nietzsche offers some penetrating observations on social relations, on psychic expression, on art, and on everyday life that demonstrate the centrality of the will to power in motivating human behavior. He also believes it applies to all species of life and can even be extended to interactions of inorganic matter. These extensions may be less plausible. Even the universal application of the will to power in human behavior is questionable, but Nietzsche's hypothesis can be refined or qualified with fuller examination of the evidence.

Nietzsche denies that there is a unifying self that organizes drives or determines action.[93] People achieve psychic integration when either one drive dominates or when several drives strike a power-sharing arrangement. Typically, domination by any single drive is constantly challenged; other drives vie for control of the organism. Even the concept of "drive" is probably too simplistic; really there are diverse strivings, which consist of complexes of feelings, values, images, "commanding thoughts," and habits, etc. The aim of every striving is to transcend itself by producing an even more highly organized and richly structured pattern of response; it sacrifices itself in order to achieve this higher degree of coherence. For Nietzsche, the self is a complex assembly of competing strivings of this type; they alternate commanding authority in different situations. When there is a clear ordering of such strivings, greater psychic unity emerges. Nietzsche does not favor unity for its own sake, though he does admire it. His ideal is the deepest unification of the widest variety of opposing strivings. The more contradictory the drives that are integrated into a unity, the more power an individual exhibits.

Nietzsche discovered many psychic processes that Freud later named and made famous. For example, Nietzsche identifies sublimation, repression, substitution, projection and introjection, inversion, and the importance of sexuality in character formation. Nietzsche does not detail the dynamics of sexual development in the way Freud did, but he notes its importance for even the highest and most spiritual levels of the psyche. Nietzsche offers a more elaborate theory of sublimation than Freud; he relies on this process to transform mundane drives into refined aspirations (e.g., sex into romantic love). He indicates several types of repression: one is needed after the deed; one is effected before the deed, and one is achieved in the course of the deed.[94] His examination of *ressentiment* suggests how often people adopt attitudes toward others that initially are directed at themselves, and vice versa. He realizes that drives often target substitute objects in order to discharge themselves and that drives that initially oppose the world can suddenly turn inward and attack other drives instead (e.g., unsuccessful attempts to harm another can lead to harming oneself). Nietzsche also clarifies several psychic phenomena to a much greater degree than previous theorists: *ressentiment*, pity and sympathy, the hypertrophy of one sense or talent that causes many others to atrophy. He also anticipates Scheler's later concept of spirit as "the life that cuts into life" in order to guide and transmute it. Finally, he doubts the explanatory power of psychic causation (or any causation), but, apart from the will to power, he does not elaborate the relations that can obtain between different elements of the psyche.

EPISTEMOLOGY AND METAPHYSICS

Nietzsche stresses that interpretation is the central cognitive process in all knowledge because every phenomenon is examined from a perspective that limits what can be discovered within it. Nietzsche uses "interpretation" to signal this limitation.[95] He does not mean, however, that all interpretations are false. On the contrary, most interpretations clarify some feature of the phenomenon; the epistemic task is to integrate multiple perspectives and to compensate for their limitations. The fullest comprehension requires that various perspectives correct and supplement one another and that new corrections emerge when additional illuminating perspectives are discovered.[96] Nietzschean perspectives are less analogous to visual points of view than to different disciplines exploring the same facts (e.g., if history, psychology, ethics, economics, and sociology were to examine Goethe's life). Nietzsche's interpretive truths are fallible, open to revision, tentative, and only as powerful as the perspectives they integrate. They can be dangerous and unsettling; for Nietzsche, one measure of spiritual height is the amount of truth a person can bear.[97] In order to discover such truths, the interpreter must see with many eyes, from many perspectives.

Nietzsche also reconsiders the value of truth. Sometimes he thinks truth must be trumped by other values, but such instances are rare. He rarely withholds potential truths because they are unpalatable, and he sometimes asserts extreme hypotheses to force the reader to determine more reasonable, plausible claims in response. Truth's value is most questionable when it opposes life-enhancement, when wisdom overburdens life, and when living fully requires ignoring troubling truths. Sometimes pregnant falsehoods make great cultural progress possible. Still, even when cultural growth trumps truth, the falsehood that produces such growth does not thereby become true. Ultimately Nietzsche is surprisingly consistent in advocating wisdom and truth even when they increase the difficulty of affirming life or achieving excellence. Achieving excellence while still facing truth squarely defines higher human beings.

Nietzsche notes that language can sometimes be philosophically misleading, suggesting that many philosophical mistakes derive from an uncritical confidence in grammar.[98] Often philosophers read grammar into the nature of things; for example, the subject-predicate form of assertions seems to imply that there must be a doer behind every deed, an empirical ego (if not a transcendental one) that functions as a referent for the subject-term "I". Had the grammar of European languages been different, the urge to posit an autonomous self that governs human actions would be reduced. For similar reasons, philosophers assume that things are isolated particulars, rather than complex bundles of relations. In addition, Nietzsche asserts that many ordinary language distinctions perform social functions. The point of language, after all, is to communicate with others. He concludes that common-sense categories often miss experiential features that are rarely communicated (subtle feelings, original thoughts, creative visions, or unique virtues).[99] Often this means even the person experiencing them will not recognize them. Nietzsche believes that philosophers must forge new linguistic tools and new metaphors to achieve more accurate understanding of human life, culture, and nature.

Like Marx, Nietzsche critically evaluates various types of knowledge and methods for gaining it. I have already discussed his assessment of history and art; he also interrogates science, philosophy, and morality as forms of knowledge. He identifies the many purposes knowledge serves, purposes often unrelated to the discovery of truth. Often dominant groups (e.g., priests) maintain their domination through esoteric knowledge, and sometimes-specialized methods secure that monopoly. Nietzsche suspects that most forms of knowledge serve some special interests and oppose others. He demonstrates this "hermeneutics of suspicion" when he examines religion in *The Antichrist*. Knowledge is never pursued in a vacuum, and it is not achieved by adopting a "disinterested" viewpoint. It is motivated by drives, and they limit what can be discovered in any single perspective. Though these limitations are not always invidious, they show that knowledge's pursuit is more variously motivated and requires a greater range of perspectives than many epistemologists have assumed.

In his *Nachlass* (unpublished writings), Nietzsche explores imaginative metaphysical speculations that are less obvious in the published works. He rejects the notions of substance and essence. Instead he prefers a metaphysics of processes and flux and of multiplicities of forces and their relations. Most of these metaphysical hypotheses are not directly confirmable, but he sketches a naturalistic system that seeks to explain observable phenomena. Nietzsche claims that human senses, like any interpretive perspective, tend to oversimplify the phenomenal field; they miss most of what they do not expect to see, and most of their expectations are established by culture and social traditions. Thus, sensory "knowledge" is anything but direct confrontation with the given; it must be critically evaluated and supplemented by other perspectives just like any other source of knowledge. Nietzsche believes his own hypotheses integrate the variety of perspectives he explores, but his arguments for this are often sketchy. On metaphysical issues, Nietzsche's critiques are more penetrating than his constructive ideas; the latter are suggestive, but they are not well developed or fully defended.

NEW PHILOSOPHERS

Throughout his intellectual life, Nietzsche strove to redefine the philosophical enterprise. His goals for philosophy are directly related to his cultural aspirations. Many characteristic assumptions of past philosophy must be rejected: its agenda of defending "morality" (narrowly construed) at all costs, its rejection of the body and change, its lack of historical perspective, and its subservience to grammar.[100] Nietzsche does not dismiss past philosophy entirely; indeed he identifies several figures that exemplify what philosophy should become: Heraclitus, Empedocles, Montaigne, and Schopenhauer. Each of them embodied some key features that define Nietzsche's "philosophers of the future."

There are four key features: a cognitive element that elaborates the most effective way to determine truth; a cultural reconstruction element that includes a diagnostic part (for the present) and a legislative part (for the future); an existential element that describes the self-transformation necessary for serious thinking; and an educative element that facilitates a similar existential transformation in others when their time has come. The existential transformation is necessary to achieve the proper cognitive standpoint to approximate truth; the disciplined search for truth provides the strength and vision to legislate for the future and critically evaluate the present, and these elements taken together produce the skills necessary to educate others to become philosophers.

The cognitive task of Nietzsche's new philosophers involves synthesizing multiple perspectives.[101] They must first examine the phenomena using diverse approaches (e.g., those of the saint, artist, traveler, scientist, historian, poet, skeptic, moralist, free spirit, and seer) and then find ways to integrate the results.[102] They also need to consult the various sciences (e.g., physiology, psychology, anthropology, sociology, and economics), each of which offers a perspective that must be weighed against the others. Further, they must apply different cognitive skills (e.g., analysis, calculation, genealogy, thought-experiment, comparative cultural study) and allow different drives to inform their inquiries. Determining the complete truth about the phenomenon requires integrating the most insightful results from all these perspectives. New philosophers must transcend their era's prejudices and regularly reconsider their own assumptions.

The unique task of Nietzsche's new philosophers is cultural reconstruction. They must be prepared to legislate new values for the future, shaping humanity's future by offering it inspiring goals.[103] Strength, creativity, vision, and spiritual health are preconditions for this task. New philosophers cannot prescribe, however, without an adequate diagnosis of the present; hence a full revaluation of current values is necessary. Its goal is to determine what is no longer worth pursuing, what should be superseded, and what should be preserved. Nietzsche himself exemplifies this function of new philosophers by lauding life-affirmation, the gift-giving virtue, and love of the future as guiding ideals. Not since Plato has any thinker given such a leading cultural role to philosophers.

A third condition required of Nietzsche's new philosophers is an existential transformation – a three-stage metamorphosis of the spirit that Nietzsche describes in *Zarathustra* and in the preface to *Human, All Too Human*.[104] In its initial stage, people dedicate themselves to the strongest loves and highest ideals of their youth. The intermediate stage brings a self-critique in which these youthful values are challenged – and even inverted – in order to gain new perspectives and to insure that judgments are sufficiently multifaceted and balanced. This stage is called the "free spirit," a high-altitude view of life that forces new philosophers to discover their true intellectual tasks. A final stage produces self-mastery – including vitality, courage, experimentalism, and creative vision – yielding the power and subtlety to forge new values for the future. Through this process mature philosophers compensate for their initial inborn deficiencies and demonstrate an ability to weather harsh spiritual crises. Although they must experience life's terrors, they must still be willing to affirm life. They also discover a new innocence and cosmic joy that is better attuned to life's amoral dynamics than other philosophical attitudes.

Finally, there is an educative element to Nietzsche's new philosophers. They must provide effective advice to those seriously pursuing self-perfection. Nietzsche himself offers such advice; it is often the most valuable component of his books. He explains how to give style to one's character, how to sublimate one's drives, how to organize conflicting drives, how to defeat nausea and other weakening forces within the psyche, how to manage failure and disappointment, how to face death courageously, how to defeat the spirit of gravity, how to give gifts in ways that allow receivers to accept them without insult or loss. Nietzsche calls this capacity "the genius of the heart."[105] New philosophers study how to overcome the frustrations of the everyday in order to stimulate personal experiments in producing higher humanity. New philosophers are never oblivious to the fate of others.

The last three of these factors are Nietzsche's new demands on philosophers. Nietzsche has confidence in their capacity to do great deeds – intellectual, cultural, political, and artistic. He encourages philosophers to become visionaries, sages, and spirit-guides as well as truth-seekers in his new, more challenging sense, urging them to transcend their musty scholarly molds. Nietzsche's philosophy cannot simply be summarized in a system of propositions; it challenges and inspires, offers a handbook for achieving excellence, and generates creative metaphors that shaped the future.

COMPARISONS

Nietzsche shares some common features with Hegel and Marx: the rejection of other-worldly explanations, the belief that human existence is deeply conditioned by the type of culture surrounding it; the goal of enhancing of human powers – intellectual, artistic, and ethical; and a vision of the future that can guide present humanity. His greatest disagreements with his predecessors concern the value of modernity, the plausibility of dialectics, and the viability of political revolution, the value of life itself, and the dominance of power over pleasure.

Naturalism is the attempt to understand life, humanity, and the cosmos in wholly naturalistic terms, without positing transcendent powers or metaphysical postulates. Hegel had already begun to naturalize religious claims by regarding them as metaphors that express the underlying social relations of the era. His "spirit" refers to the animating principles and ideals governing a particular social order. Marx, following Feuerbach, continues this effort to naturalize religious concepts by further questioning the transcendence of God. They suggest that humans project their own powers into God, thus alienating these powers and abdicating responsibility for developing them. Schopenhauer adds to this naturalization by embedding humanity in the processes of life and will. Nietzsche further elaborates it, both in relation to God and to received moral and political values. His hypothesis of the will to power provides a foundation for a non-metaphysical philosophy of nature and a this-worldly human psychology. Nietzsche treats humanity as continuous with the rest of nature, even though he also explores humanity's unique possibilities. He challenges Schopenhauer's negation of life and Freud's reliance on the will to pleasure.

Both Hegel and Marx insist that culture deeply conditions individual development – Hegel through the basic social organization of an era ("spirit"), Marx through the economic mode of production through which the rest of culture is determined. Nietzsche maintains this insistence on the importance of social institutions in shaping individuals and even consciousness itself. Nietzsche suggests that those elements that rise to consciousness and those which become expressed in language do so primarily because of their *social relevance*. Language, Nietzsche suggests, is central to the development of consciousness and reason, and language exists in order to facilitate social communication. Nietzsche can be critical of the leveling effects of certain social institutions, but he recognizes the centrality of culture both in developing higher human beings and in making *Homo sapiens* into human beings.

Nietzsche seeks a qualitative transformation of humanity. Even though everyone may not be capable of the highest achievements, he urges all to play their part in contributing to this transformation. This task involves perfecting the best human traits and developing each individual's best possibilities. The ideal informing both Hegel and Marx is harmony with all spheres of existence (de-alienation). Nietzsche stresses a psychic harmony that integrates and orders a variety of opposing internal forces. He also claims that full self-realization sometimes requires rising to the challenge of powerful oppositional forces. Hegel and Marx also recognized the importance of negation and opposition, but for them it is only a stage in the achievement of a higher unity. For Nietzsche opposition can be a permanent stimulus to improvement. Life is hard, especially on its most promising experiments.

Nietzsche rejects the optimism of both Hegel and Marx; he is vividly aware of the tragic dimension of human existence. Nietzsche believes that a hard-edged pessimism is a stronger and more energizing stance toward life and history than the optimism characteristic of Marx, and to some extent of Hegel. Marx and Hegel clearly see the slaughter that history has produced, but they think that future achievements can vindicate or redeem that slaughter and that history will reach a happy ending. Nietzsche is doubtful. His pessimism is not defeatist; he thinks people must strive to become everything they have it in them to become. But optimists think conflict, struggle, and the harshness of life can ultimately be eliminated. Nietzsche thinks life will always involve struggle and conflict. He differs from Schopenhauer in thinking that the conflict can be meaningful and productive. Nietzsche acknowledges that the achievement of higher humanity would be redemptive, but he thinks the Last Man, with his apathy and small satisfactions, is as equally likely an outcome as the *Übermensch*.

Both Hegel and Marx showed that most people often fail to understand the deeper principles that govern history, but Nietzsche anticipates Freud in thinking that this systematic ignorance extends to much of human psychic functioning, to the genesis of virtually all human institutions, as well as to many historical and social processes. Hegel and Marx also believe that self-consciousness plays a greater role in human life than does Nietzsche. Nietzsche thinks people are blind to almost everything around them, and for good reason, since really seeing all that is there – really achieving genuine knowledge of oneself, others, or life – is painful. Nietzsche believes that many cognitive processes simply cannot become accessible and that humanity is *better* for this. Much must operate by instinct, and many behavioral responses must be automatic if the species is to survive. Nietzsche thus reassesses the value of self-consciousness, even though he retains some role for it.

Nietzsche's central disagreement with many Continental thinkers is his skepticism about modernity: about modern institutions, ideals, and everyday life – equality, democracy, human rights, happiness, freedom, the greatest good of the greatest number, mass media, overwrought art, and mass education. Nietzsche cares primarily about human excellence – the perfection of many different human types – and he thinks many modern values and institutions are inimical to this process. Modernity's problem is that it exacerbates trends in Christianity that undermine human excellence. Its ideals derive from resentment against higher humanity. Nietzsche is not wholly anti-modern, however; he supports achieving more complete access to reality, enriching knowledge rather extending the reign of illusion.

Nietzsche also rejects the claim that human history exhibits unilinear progress and the concept of dialectic in which oppositions and challenges are always overcome by some new higher (and better) result. For Nietzsche, history often produces major periods of regress, and recovering from these setbacks is among the most urgent tasks of this era. This does not mean he thinks progress is impossible, but he certainly does not think it inevitable, and indeed insists that much history since the Greeks has been a long regress that must be altered and reversed. Nietzsche measures the quality of an age by the quality of the individuals in that age, and though some promising individuals have emerged in the modern era (e.g., Goethe, Schopenhauer), they are the exceptions. Just as Nietzsche questions this historical dialectic, he also challenges the philosophical dialectic, especially Hegel's view that concepts form an underlying system. Nietzsche substitutes his own perspectival approach to knowledge for the dialectic. Many perspectives are needed to clarify a phenomenon, but they do not yield an easy synthesis. Their conclusions remain tentative and open to supplementation. He does acknowledge that opposites often engender each other, but they exist in perpetual combat, rather than achieving resolution.

Nietzsche rejects Marx's claim that political revolution is the best solution to the problems of Western culture. Nietzsche thinks that cultural institutions, education, and ideals need to be transformed in ways that encourage rather than inhibit excellence and that individuals must undergo internal self-transformations. He thinks problems of poverty and alienation are relatively tractable in comparison with the needed renewal of the human spirit and the required revaluation of values. Similarly, a change in the state apparatus or even in capitalism itself may not produce the necessary renewal. In effect, Nietzsche challenges the values in the name of which any social transformation should be undertaken. Self-perfection is a more demanding goal than self-expression (de-alienation) even if creativity is an element of both. He also believes that most political revolutionaries are bombastic, bloodthirsty, and seething with resentment. Nietzsche's new philosophers exhibit greater psychic "cleanliness" and health; for this reason he thinks they have a better chance at success. Nietzsche also appeals to the best among humans, not to the masses, to guide cultural change.

ASSESSMENT

Nietzsche's position has some shortcomings. He does not, for example, provide a convincing portrayal of the future culture and society that would nurture the *Übermenschen* and allow them to live together in mutually enhancing ways. Also, he is perhaps too willing to dismiss ordinary people possessing modest talents. They may have more to contribute than he acknowledges, both in experimenting with new virtues and in stimulating those with greater potential. Nietzsche provides many specific recommendations to individuals for improving themselves, but his vision of future culture and society needs elaboration. What institutions would the new culture include? What can sustain them across the many generations required to realize higher humanity? How can the diversity of human types enhance (rather than resent and destroy) each other's achievements? How can they overcome the regressive tendencies of the modern era?

In addition, Nietzsche suggests that truth is achieved by adjudicating conflicting perspectives, giving each its due. How does this adjudication work in practice? Do Nietzsche's own conclusions derive from such an adjudication process? If diverse perspectives are necessary for discerning truth, how do they supplement one another to produce a coherent assessment? How are their results to be combined? Without additional analysis and examples, Nietzsche only provides the beginnings of a developed theory of knowledge, rather than offering an effective means of producing genuine knowledge/wisdom. Here, too, his key insights need more elaboration before they can be adequately evaluated.

Nietzsche has confidence in his newly minted concepts of the will to power, eternal recurrence, genealogy, the innocence of becoming, and love of fate. But what exactly is the status of these notions? Are they meant as quasi-empirical hypotheses that could be falsified? Or are they more deeply rooted than this, and then what evidence supports them? Does the will to power apply to all living species and individuals? Does it have any chance of explaining all physical phenomena? Is eternal recurrence just a myth that serves a function (to produce a test for personal strength), or is it a theory about the real structure of time? If reality is interpreted as process and becoming, why does this restore its innocence? If some phenomena have essences, does this mean innocence is lost? How penetrating a critical strategy is genealogy? Are Nietzsche's own genealogies plausible and convincing? Do they justify the value implications he seeks to derive from them? Perhaps his opponents can create counter-genealogies that would undermine his own ideals in the same way as his genealogies challenge morality. How does Nietzsche prevent love of fate from backsliding into acceptance of whatever happens? Can he combine the ethos of struggle for self-perfection with beatific equilibrium and joyful embrace of life's vicissitudes?

Nietzsche's position depends on a crucial assumption: that achieving some number of truly glorious human exemplars is a better response to the threat of nihilism than continuously elevating the regularly achieved degree of self-perfection among ordinary human beings. Traversing all three of Nietzsche's stages of development toward higher humanity is extremely demanding, but perhaps larger numbers could achieve it if culture were organized to enhance everyone, rather than concentrating on a select few. Early Nietzsche seems to have thought widespread response to his summons to self-perfection was possible. Perhaps it is, and perhaps humanity as a whole would be more magnificent if this happened.

Nietzsche also expects that major conclusions will follow from his philosophical critiques: his rejection of the God-hypothesis, of the substantial ego behind each deed, of individuated particulars behind each thing. Even if his objections hit their targets, the conclusions he draws from them may be premature. Does personal responsibility for actions disintegrate when the substantial self dissolves, or is it merely relocated as agency is given a different analysis? Even if there is no transcendent realm, will that provide sufficient reason for valuing this world, even if the Last Man were to dominate the earth? Would life still be worth affirming under such circumstances? Some of his alternative hypotheses seem better defended than others, for example, the will to power in contrast to the will to pleasure and will to survival. Nietzsche's critique of pleasure and survival as basic targets of the will is convincing, and his independent evidence for the will to power (at least in human nature) is considerable. In addition, his defense of the productivity of social conflict does vindicate his challenge to the ideal of social harmony. My point is that Nietzsche's inferences have to be examined as carefully as his critiques; sometimes he draws dramatic conclusions too hastily.

Finally, the effectiveness of some of his key doctrines can be challenged. Does eternal recurrence, for example, actually produce "the greatest weight"? Is there any reason to live differently even if one does believe it (if one has no awareness of previous cycles)? In addition, Nietzsche's notion of rank-ordering plays a central role in his later books. But since his notion of power is complex and variegated, there may be many different orders of rank, depending on which type of power or virtue is taken as the benchmark. If people will be differently rank-ordered on Nietzsche's different criteria of value, then his hierarchical vision of future society may need re-evaluation.

HERMENEUTICS

Central to both Hegel and Marx are their interpretations of history. Freud develops a complex theory of interpretation to uncover a person's hidden urges. Nietzsche claims that all knowledge involves interpretation and makes the mutual correction of perspectives essential for achieving truth. Thus, the fact that the theory of interpretation (hermeneutics) becomes a distinctive philosophical movement in the late nineteenth century is hardly surprising. Its task is to clarify the process of interpretation, its legitimate uses, its relation to scientific explanation, its validation procedures, and its value. Although issues of textual interpretation had been discussed for centuries within religious traditions, secular hermeneutics is primarily a post-Kantian Continental development that examines the logic governing the understanding and interpretation of human actions and artifacts (artworks, literature, history, complex personal interactions, group dynamics, rituals, symbols, laws, and individual lives). Understanding typically is implicit; interpretation is explicit. Hermeneutic thinkers sometimes begin by examining a specific type of interpretation (e.g., legal, historical, literary), and formulating its rules; sometimes they start from a general analysis of understanding and *derive* implications for various types of interpretation from that. I call the former approach "traditional hermeneutics" (Schleiermacher, Dilthey, Betti) and the latter "philosophical hermeneutics" (Heidegger and Gadamer).

CORE CONTRIBUTIONS

Hermeneutics makes several important contributions to Continental philosophy: it underlines the richness and complexity of experience, examines the significance of historicality and temporality for human understanding, explores the hermeneutic circle, indicates several crucial differences between natural and social science, and highlights the background assumptions that operate in nearly all forms of understanding.

Together with phenomenologists and existentialists, hermeneutic theorists explore the richness of lived experience, clarifying its full complexity. They maintain a clear distinction between theory and experience, viewing theory as abstract and simplifying and suggesting that experience is always subtler than any theoretical perspective can capture. One reason for this is that experience is dynamic while theory is static; another is that theory progresses via simplification and abstraction, which intentionally ignore unique features of an action. Still another is that many threads are woven together in any moment of experience, and theoretical analysis usually cannot reconstitute this interlacing. In addition to discovering subtle complexities of experience, hermeneutics identifies experiential constants.

Two such constants – essential to human understanding – are temporality and historicity. To live temporally is to experience one's life as a temporal flow: aiming at future goals, drawing on past achievements, and facing the situational present. Experience often involves unusual temporal transitions and complex temporal incursions like sudden influxes of memory, fugue-like flash-forwards, and surreal symbolic associations. Temporal beings regularly restructure their experience as they learn from new situations – refashioning goals and rethinking the past's relevance. To live historically is to be situated in an era governed by specific meanings, assumptions, and technologies. These condition one's access to other eras and other cultures. Hermeneutic theorists develop the implications of these constants for understanding human action and expression as well as human artifacts and historical events. For example, temporal distance affects every historical interpretation since the meanings informing prior eras are typically different from those of the interpreter. Even self-interpretation is retrospective, introducing narrative unities into experience that may belie the chaos of everyday life.

The hermeneutic circle is not vicious, but it is unavoidable. It implies that one's grasp of a text's parts will depend on one's grasp of the whole and vice versa. It allows interpretations to be refined and sharpened by allowing parts and whole to clarify each other. Thus, understanding proceeds in a continuous circular process of comprehending relationships among parts and wholes. This circle acknowledges the fallibilism that is now accepted in the sciences by granting that new interpretive hypotheses may better account for the text's elements (just as new theories may better account for experimental data). Thus, interpretations are subject to revision when new and intersubjectively convincing hypotheses are offered. The hermeneutic circle reveals the demanding tasks of the interpretive process: hypotheses must be fully developed and weighed against alternatives, and the significance of all elements must be determined. In general, the common idea that "everyone has his own interpretation" is dismissed, despite its apparent truth. Not everyone has a *considered* interpretation; not every interpretation meets serious tests of evidence; and some interpretations account for more of the text (and do so more illuminatingly) than others.

Partly because of the temporality and historicality of human understanding, some hermeneutic thinkers contend that the social or human sciences are essentially different from the natural sciences. They claim that the same methodology cannot work for both because humans operate differently from other entities. Social science must develop its own distinctive methods because of this difference. Causal analysis, for example, is usually less informative and often reductive since the task of social theory is to understand the goals of human action in a way causal analysis cannot. Hermeneutic theorists also typically deny the existence of an absolute standpoint that might allow omnitemporal judgments. If theorists' judgments are historically rooted, they are biased by their era's assumptions. Natural scientists deny such biases and embrace the possibility of an absolute standpoint. Hermeneutics differentiates the study of the social from the study of the purely physical in other ways too: social theory seeks to clarify unique actions while natural science seeks to explain repeatable, typical events. Also, social investigators know more about the phenomena they seek to illuminate before they begin. Participation in human culture provides wide-ranging tacit knowledge that renders intelligible many everyday events. Social theorists' must *improve* on this tacit knowledge. Since natural scientists lack this tacit knowledge of physical events, their explanatory task is easier. *Any* lawlike understanding improves on humanity's tacit knowledge. The effort to produce this richer comprehension of human action and culture is an important achievement of hermeneutics.

Many hermeneutic theorists believe that enough common human nature exists across eras and cultures to allow some kind of mutual understanding across historical eras and between individuals living in different cultures. They suggest that the very fact of being rooted in a tradition constitutes a basis for understanding alien traditions. Hermeneutics acknowledges the importance of history by insisting on individuals' rootedness in historical tradition. Individuals' interpretive categories and criteria of relevance derive from these traditions, and they facilitate understanding of other individuals with a common history. One division among hermeneutic thinkers concerns whether this rootedness enables better interpretations or undermines them. Examining the relationship between historical background and social knowledge is another important contribution.

Philosophical hermeneutics suggests that cultural background and situational context are necessary for comprehending anything human. Without utilizing this background people cannot even describe events, much less explain them. Clarifying the processes enabling social knowledge requires assessing the role of these background conditions. One task of hermeneutics is to clarify differences between this background understanding and other kinds of knowledge. It contains implicit assumptions or presuppositions, often called "prejudices" or "horizons." Hermeneutic thinkers deny that an unmediated access to human phenomena is possible. This claim distinguishes them from phenomenologists (many of whom argue that some form of direct access to phenomena – at least some phenomena – *is* possible). An "interpretation" then becomes an amplification and refinement of these horizons. Often this refinement process can be very complex – involving many hypotheses – because the type of object interpreted can be very elaborate, e.g., a novel or an historical era. Interpretation generally involves a confrontation with otherness (something foreign to the interpreter's horizon) but from a standpoint that maintains the interpreter's perspective. This process transforms the interpreter and the object. The object gains something from having a new horizon applied to it, and the interpreter's perspective is enriched through encountering a unique object.

I shall concentrate on four figures: Wilhelm Dilthey, Martin Heidegger, Hans-Georg Gadamer, and Emilio Betti. Some secondary expositors trace the history of hermeneutics back to Aristotle, or at least to theorists who formulated rules of biblical interpretation. I will offer a sketch of one key precursor, Friedrich Ernst Schleiermacher, who addressed key issues in textual interpretation. However, the importance of hermeneutics as a philosophical movement did not emerge until Dilthey, who posited the need for a distinctive approach to human actions and historical events – one radically different from that taken by the natural sciences. Heidegger makes essential contributions to philosophical hermeneutics in his discussion of the existentials of *Dasein* (i.e., essential features of human existence) in *Being and Time* (1927). Probably the most famous recent thinker in this movement is Gadamer, a student of Heidegger's, who provides his own analysis of the interpretive process and locates it in a rich discussion of art, legal theory, and language. Finally, Betti synthesizes insights from Dilthey and Gadamer while trying to correct errors in both.

A PRECURSOR: SCHLEIERMACHER

Friedrich Ernst Schleiermacher (1768–1834) was Hegel's contemporary who had read Kant carefully and personally knew many of the writers of the German Romantic movement. Dilthey wrote a long biography of him that illuminates Schleiermacher's era and its institutions as much as his life and contributions. Two earlier figures made useful contributions to Schleiermacher: Friedrich Ast (1778–1841) and Friedrich August Wolf (1759–1824). Ast realized that texts have a linguistic (grammatical) dimension and historical conditions of possibility as well as authors.[1] Schleiermacher develops this observation by showing how texts are expressions/modifications of language itself as well as of their authors. Ast also realized that interpretation is a circular process that requires a "divinatory leap" in order to begin.[2] Schleiermacher extends this understanding of the hermeneutic circle and elaborates the concept of divination. Wolf distinguished specific types of interpretation (e.g., legal, historical, literary) from general hermeneutics, which seeks a global theory of understanding. Schleiermacher offers a general hermeneutics. Ast construed interpretation as a series of dialogues with authors in which interpreters work to expand their own horizons in order to incorporate authors' creative insights.[3] Schleiermacher includes this psychological dimension in his own theory of interpretation.

Schleiermacher's main question is not "what is the truth content of a person's text/speech?" but "what motivates the person to express those views at precisely that time?" His goal is thus less to understand the meaning of the text/speech than to understand its role in the life of its sources (author and language).[4] Interpretation reconstitutes creative expression in all its complexity, revealing processes often unconscious to the author. This requires grasping the organizing idea of the text, the way its parts contribute to that idea, and its place in the author's life.[5] Schleiermacher believes interpretation expands the *interpreter's* cognitive range to encompass the author's organizing ideas. Interpreters immerse themselves in an author so completely that they can re-experience the elements of her creative process and clarify their systematic relationships.

Schleiermacher identifies two "lives" to which any linguistic expression belongs: the life of its creator and the life of its language. Thus, there are two dimensions to interpretation: a psychological one and a "grammatical" one.[6] The grammatical question is: what motivates the emergence of this work in this language at this moment – that is, what stylistic developments and what rhetorical resources are transformed in the work such that it becomes a language-event? The psychological dimension concerns the transformations of the author that resulted from completing the work. Thus, any expression develops its author and its language, drawing on each, yet altering both. Neither of these dimensions is prior to the other; they are equiprimordial.

Each dimension requires two phases in the interpretive process: divinatory and historical.[7] The divinatory phase grasps the organizing principles of the work, which inform all its parts. The historical phase clarifies the ways the prior development of the author and the language make the work possible – the specific resources they contribute. Schleiermacher thus sees literary works as moments in the history of both authors and languages, drawing on the existing resources of each, but also expanding them.

Schleiermacher also elaborates Ast's discussion of the "hermeneutic circle." Within any text there is a mutual interanimation of parts and whole; thus, any thesis about the parts will be dependent on claims about the whole and vice versa. Interpretation is a circular process in which hypotheses about parts correct and refine hypotheses about the whole (and vice versa).[8] Interpretive intuitions about the basic themes of the work illuminate its relevant parts, and clarifying the contributions of the parts will sharpen understanding of its organizing themes. As interpreters' understanding of themes becomes clearer, so too will their grasp of its parts. The "divinatory" moment is Schleiermacher's answer to how the circle can be entered in the right way. It produces an interpretive hypothesis that can be tested against the text's elements. Schleiermacher notes that hermeneutic circles operate on many additional levels of the interpretive enterprise. They relate the language of this text to the whole of language at that historical moment, the specifics of this work to its literary genre, this work to the author's entire corpus, and authors' literary works to their lives.[9] These larger hermeneutic circles govern both the grammatical and psychological dimensions of the interpretive process. They imply that serious interpretation is a continuous process of clarification and self-correction. Schleiermacher also believed that no interpretation could be complete; the author's creative process will always exceed the interpreter's account of it.[10]

In addition, Schleiermacher notes several important problems for interpreters: For example, not all texts are organic wholes. Sometimes fragmentary or incomplete works require atypical interpretive procedures.[11] Also, interpreters must confine themselves to meanings established at the time of composition; they cannot use modern idioms to clarify texts from previous historical eras in which such idioms would be alien.[12] Beyond this, he notes the difficulty of viewing one's own interpretations objectively. After interpreters expand themselves to encompass the author's creative vision, they cannot easily transform themselves into critics to judge the viability of their hypotheses. They need the critical assessments of other interpreters in order to gain distance on their own conclusions. Finally, Schleiermacher realizes that the interpretive process involves significant effort and that some texts are not worth the effort.[13]

DILTHEY

Wilhelm Dilthey's (1833–1911) thought is wide-ranging, including both historical studies and theoretical essays. He believes that lived experience overflows all reflective efforts to comprehend it, but he nonetheless struggles to capture that flow and complexity as adequately as possible. He distinguishes human sciences from natural sciences, claiming that a special mode of insight called "*verstehen*" (to understand) is necessary in human studies. It tries to grasp an action or expression from the agent's standpoint, not from an impersonal, third-person viewpoint. Dilthey offers a quasi-Kantian critique of historical reason, which benefits from his mastery of historical writing. The concept of "world-view" is central in his historical essays. He distinguishes a variety of world-views and claims that each offers only a partial perspective, noting that none can integrate all the others. He thus denies the possibility of a Hegelian synthesis of perspectives. Dilthey contributes to clarifying the interpretative process, to distinguishing social from natural sciences, to understanding mental and social life, and to defining the types of understanding appropriate to human beings. I will summarize these contributions in turn.

Dilthey treats written texts as typical objects of interpretation. He regards texts as authorial expressions and interpretation as a method for comprehending authors' intentions. Interpreters begin with inspired guesses that are then confirmed/disconfirmed by examining the full text in depth. Methods of interpretation can be codified and taught to future generations; they include strategies for producing inspired guesses and for assessing them.[14] The best interpretive hypotheses emerge from a complete immersion in the texts, authors, and periods being interpreted. Dilthey emphasizes interpretive creativity as well as artistic genius.

Dilthey believes that interpreters elucidate authors like anthropologists clarify foreign cultures. He assumes that people are self-enclosed in the sense that individuals can directly intuit only their own mental states. Though states are embodied in expressions, action and speech provide only secondary access to them. His key assumption is that expressions differ from the states they express. The interpreter co-enacts these expressions in order to intuit the underlying states.[15] For this to be possible, human beings (in different eras, in different cultures during the same era, and in different subgroups within a culture) must be sufficiently similar. To defend this, Dilthey notes that humans live in the same material world and thus must develop similar means of comprehending it (number systems, logic, grammar), producing similar mental functions.[16] Cultural differences exist because specific mental functions are given different degrees of emphasis in different cultures. For example, some cultures accentuate perception, some imagination, some emotion, and some abstract thought. But all people experience all of these functions to some degree. This commonality provides the basis for intuiting others' states through their expressions. This claim of differential emphasis implies that interpretation can have important educational value. As people age, the range of their mental functions becomes limited to a certain repertoire because of specialization and habit; this causes other functions to atrophy. When interpreters empathize with artworks that embody these dormant mental functions, they can become revitalized. Interpretation can thus reactivate dormant mental powers.[17]

For Dilthey, understanding occurs when interpreters sympathetically re-constitute artists' intentions. Artists are not reduced to interpreters in this process; instead, interpreters expand themselves by re-enacting artists' creative intentions. Dilthey believes that fully adequate interpretations are possible only for the highest artistic achievements, e.g., poetry and philosophy. Because artists' uniqueness can be embodied in such expressions and because they are often sufficiently polished to fully express artists' intentions, they can completely embody their authors. If interpreters penetrate such works, they will transcend themselves.

Despite the fact that human life is rooted in nature and that many scientific approaches to nature can also be applied to human behavior, Dilthey believes that fundamental differences between the two spheres make understanding in the human sciences radically distinct from explanation in the natural sciences. One difference is that natural science seeks to subsume particular events under general laws; discovery and validation of such laws are the apex of natural scientific explanation. But in human studies (at least in interpretive human studies) the goal is to understand the uniqueness of the specific event – to clarify its complexity.[18] Even if laws could be discovered in the human sciences, they would be far less informative than in natural science because they would only explain what historical events have in common with similar events, not what is distinctive about these events.

A second difference is that socialized participants can understand social complexities without the aid of science. Humans already understand a great deal about social life before social theory begins. In examining natural phenomena, natural scientists lack the same rich antecedent knowledge.[19] The analytical and inductive procedures they use are necessary because such tacit knowledge is unavailable. In human studies, the task is to improve upon sophisticated, antecedent understanding, and this requires entirely different procedures from the explanatory forms used in natural science, which are typically reductive and abstract. Often it involves determining how complexes of factors interact in particular cases, or it may involve identifying unusual purposes or strategies.

Finally, social and human events are gestalts (organic wholes) in which the parts are internally related, whereas events in nature are usually related only externally.[20] Often the interpreter grasps the whole directly prior to any analysis into parts. Consequently, interpreters do not have to *construct* order in social and human studies; they only have to explicate the order already present. Thus, the human sciences operate with a different ontology, different kinds of antecedent knowledge, and different goals. Dilthey concludes that understanding in human studies is radically different from explanation in natural science. The cultural world requires distinctive categories of understanding, e.g., whole/part, duration, development, meaning, and value. These supplementary categories illuminate social life, even if they are not necessary to natural science.

Dilthey believes that psychology (i.e., the elucidation of mental processes and their relationships to the environment) must utilize every possible access to the mind: self-observation, the understanding of others, experiments, the comparative study of cultural institutions, examination of anomalous facts, and biographies. All these sources are needed to achieve a complete picture of the mind; no single approach alone is sufficient.[21] Dilthey claims that mental processes can be understood indirectly, by examining their products (actions, artworks, texts), or directly, through introspection. He also sees both a passive and an active element in mental operations. The mind adapts itself to the constant structures in the natural and social environment, and within limits the mind can also transform its environment by imposing its own goals. Thus, individuals develop both in response to external demands and to their own imperatives.[22] By comparing the expressions of different persons, interpreters can discern their dynamic principles and unique organizing goals. This is one of Dilthey's aims in writing biographies: to discover the individual's organizing purpose, which is partly given through adaptation to constraints and partly created by choice and design.[23]

Social structures also have complex relations to individual actions. Individuals internalize different types of social structure (e.g., religion, law, economy, art, or morality) differently; yet these structures coexist within individual psyches, often coalescing into organic unity. Interpreters sometimes can understand larger social structures through their effects on individuals, and they can understand changes in social structure by studying changes in individuals' actions. The study of the social and the individual are thus complementary, and historians elaborate both approaches. Like Hegel and Nietzsche, Dilthey seeks to clarify many types of mental functions – from the most rudimentary (instincts), to the everyday (perception and emotion), to the most refined (artistic creativity, philosophical thought). He sees an ascending hierarchy of such functions – from those humans share with other animals to those unique to humans.[24]

Dilthey also compares the processes involved in self-understanding and interpersonal understanding. He believes an implicit self-reflection exists alongside action, which allows unfolding plans to remain fluid and continuously adaptive to situational changes. Implicit self-reflection can be sharpened and made explicit through autobiography, but such explicit reflection must maintain contact with the fluidity of personal decisions, even as it reveals important changes and constants. But explicit reflection can become rigid and deceptive if it abandons contact with life's flow and turns temporal phases into isolated dimensions (past, present, future) that can only be connected artificially, intellectually, or by will. Such secondary reflection is always misleading and false.[25] The central fact of human life is lived temporality, which orients persons in three directions simultaneously: backward toward past meanings, forward toward future goals, and outward toward present demands.[26] One cannot alter the past, but one can reinterpret it. The openness of the future invites people to make choices that may reshape the present and reinterpret the past. Living is a mixture of passivity (accepting situational givens) and activity (using and transforming them).

Still there can be a viable form of self-reflection that is best embodied in autobiography and simply elaborates implicit, everyday self-reflection, as well as a flawed self-reflection that produces misunderstanding and falsification. The difference between them is their faithfulness to lived temporality. Rigid reflection freezes temporal vectors and then is forced to artificially reconnect them using concepts like cause and motivation. Fluid reflection maintains a contact with life's dynamics and renders explicit the complex, internal relations among temporal moments.[27] When reflection targets the past, it discovers the past's unity. When anticipating the future, it reveals a hierarchy of purposes governing choices. When addressing the present, it uncovers rival values that provide options within the situation. Often one value is violated in realizing another when there are hard choices. In actual living, all of these temporal vectors interfuse – interanimating and reinforcing one another. Autobiography can gradually make explicit this complex unity that constitutes a person's life.[28]

With respect to other people, Dilthey suggests that two levels of understanding are possible. The first is ordinary understanding of their expressions, and the second is deeper understanding of their organizing goals. In understanding expressions, interpreters can clarify another's thoughts, actions, or emotions.[29] Dilthey believes another's thoughts are the least personal, least distinctive feature of the person; hence, they are more readily understood. Actions are always revelatory, but each action reveals a different dimension of the person. Focusing too much on a single action can lead to misunderstanding the total person; actions must be compared with one another before the person's organizing goals can be grasped. Though emotions are the most revealing mental states, they can be opaque even to their owners. Emotions often express unconscious features of the psyche and thus can be difficult to comprehend. All of these expressions are grasped through analogies derived from the interpreter's experience: interpreters understand situations as if they were acting in them, and this imaginative immersion provides clues to understanding others' thoughts, actions, and emotions in these situations.[30]

Deeper understanding of others is achieved through empathy, through which interpreters strive to relive others' lives and reconstitute their dynamic choices. In this process interpreters' limits are expanded, and they discover human possibilities alien to their own lives. Interpreters understand their subjects when they have achieved sufficient comprehension to compose biographies of them. Understanding others' expressions remains external, but empathetic understanding penetrates people's lives as they live them. It can reveal their inner lives.[31]

Dilthey thus extends the scope and importance of interpretation significantly, making it the foundation of all social inquiry. He not only compares self-understanding with other-understanding, he also explores the complex relations between social life, historical institutions, and individual actions. He shows that social inquiry requires aims and methods that differ from those used in the natural sciences, and he also develops the psychological dimension of Schleiermacher's approach to interpretation. Heidegger elaborates Dilthey's claim that interpretation is essential to all human existence.

HEIDEGGER

Since Martin Heidegger (1889–1976) makes major contributions to three different movements in Continental philosophy, I will discuss them in this and the next two chapters, after providing an overall introduction to him here. *Being and Time* (1927) is Heidegger's major treatise; so I will concentrate on it. Many of his other books, seminars, and lectures explore claims initially defended there. His contribution to hermeneutics derives from the chapter entitled "Being-in," which elucidates several necessary conditions of being human. I will summarize this important section after providing a general orientation to Heidegger's project.

Heidegger examines situated practical activity, i.e., meeting various environmental demands using know-how. This is the most primordial manner in which humans exist. He challenges all philosophical conceptions that ignore the primacy of practical activity, especially the Cartesian subject-object picture, in which outer realities are "represented" in inner minds. Intelligence and intentionality are given new analyses in which principles, theories, and reason are minimized. Challenging the view that humans are hermetically isolated from one another, Heidegger situates persons in gradually learned public practices that provide the basis for all understanding and interpretation. They also are essentially oriented to one another and live their shared practices so completely that achieving a distinctive individuality requires a major self-transformation. Like Dilthey, Heidegger thinks humans are essentially temporal and historical, though he tries to develop concepts to clarify them that do not depend on "experience" or "consciousness."

The main question of *Being and Time* concerns the meaning of "to be" – the difference between being and not-being. Heidegger avoids the noun form (beings) and concentrates on the verbal forms (infinitive = to be; participle = being) to express his question. He thus reads "to be" actively – suggesting a process or event in which time is essential. Heidegger believes that his question (the meaning of "to be") has been abandoned in Western philosophy and that early modest attempts to answer it by classical Greek philosophers have been trivialized. Currently, professional philosophers resist even asking the question because they think it is either meaningless or vacuously general.[32] Like Freud meeting resistance in a neurotic patient, Heidegger thinks this resistance demonstrates that his question strikes a nerve, a flashpoint for the entire tradition. He believes that the pre-Socratics, who explored the question when it was still possible to take it seriously (e.g., Heraclitus, Parmenides), have been so badly translated or explicated that philosophers cannot benefit from their efforts. Heidegger sharply distinguishes the event or process of being (to be) from things (entities) that are.[33] Things are accessible and common and reassuring; people gladly ignore being by seizing entities. To the extent that humans have an implicit comprehension of being through their relationships with things, it is concealed by philosophy's indifference and people's absorption in practical affairs. As a result, their grasp of their *own* being is often deficient, and this makes an adequate grasp of being itself difficult.[34] A penetrating answer to Heidegger's question might transform both individuals' being and their relation to entities.

Heidegger offers several reasons to pursue his project. First, scientific understanding of any field of entities is conditioned by its fundamental concepts, which are conditioned by humanity's understanding of being. If its comprehension of being is deficient, then its comprehension of every region of entities (and thus every specific entity) will also be deficient.[35] Second, human beings care about their own existence, and their comprehension of being is integrally related to their existence. People *live* deficiently because their understanding of being is deficient.[36] Typically they live in a way Heidegger calls "inauthentic" – not-being-themselves. Their way of existing is dominated by how others live. Changing this condition – achieving authenticity – requires that people achieve a richer, more lucid grasp of (the process of) being. Thus, not only humanity's understanding of entities but also each person's way of living depends on perspicuously answering Heidegger's question.

Being is not an entity, but it manifests itself in encounters with entities, structuring them. Whenever people handle things (whether they see, touch, use, or destroy them), they implicitly understand being. Heidegger seeks to make this implicit understanding *explicit*. He clarifies being in part by clarifying humanity's grasp of and relation to things. One entity is privileged – human being – because it is *already there* open to entities, existing as it encounters them.[37] But people's implicit grasp of their own existence and their vague grasp of being as they encounter entities remain concealed. Partly this is because people construe their own being on the model of thing-being, overlooking crucial differences between themselves and things. Beyond this, they misconstrue the being of things. They use an inadequate model (thing-being) to understand their own existence, and the understanding of things determining that model is also flawed.[38]

The mistaken model is *presence* (becoming present). Something allegedly exists most fully when it is *completely present*. Heidegger challenges this model, suggesting that neither in persons' relationships with entities nor with themselves does presence play this central role.[39] When people are engaged with the world, surrounding entities play various functions; they are *ready-at-hand*. The more aptly they perform their functions, the *less present* they are, allowing agents to concentrate on their tasks. Worldly entities are typically encountered *as tools to be used* (not presences to be contemplated).[40] Only if tools break do they become glaringly present; only then do agents simply gape at them.[41] Since gaping is the orientation in which philosophers typically describe the world, their belief that presence is being's primary mode is understandable. For Heidegger, an entity's mere presence is a deficient mode of its *functionality*, the exception rather than the rule. The event of being is better revealed through proper functioning.

In addition, Heidegger notes that human beings characteristically interrogate themselves about their existence; they care how they are faring. This makes them essentially ontological because their existence is always an issue for them.[42] Just as philosophers have misconstrued entities, so too have they misinterpreted human being. Heidegger's project is to clarify the essential structures of human being and thus correct traditional misconceptions. Instead of explicating all its essential structures, however, he examines only those that are central to clarifying being. Heidegger he calls these essential structures "*existentialia*" (or existentials).

These structures organize humanity's orientation toward the practical world much in the way Kant thought his categories structured human perception and cognition. They operate in every mode of being human, and they condition every culture's practices. In action, existentials cannot be isolated, but they can be analyzed separately. Heidegger explicates several major existentials in Part I of *Being and Time*: worldhood, (instrumentality), being-with (solicitude), the impersonal self (*Das Man*), and being-in (disclosedness).[43] He integrates these structures into a unified whole with the terms "being-in-the-world" and "care." The important existential for hermeneutics is being-in, which structures practical understanding. I will clarify Heidegger's analysis of being-with and the impersonal self in chapter 6 (Phenomenology) and of worldhood and authenticity in chapter 7 (Existentialism and Philosophical Anthropology).

Heidegger's interest in the existentials of human being is not just theoretical; it is practical. Humans exist in two basic modes: being themselves (authentic) and not being themselves (inauthentic).[44] To be themselves is to pursue projects that are truly their own, that are explicitly chosen while clearly facing human finitude. Not to be themselves is to act as "everyone" acts, following the "normal" paths of the crowd. Inauthentic people are absorbed in everyday concerns and oblivious to long-term projects, becoming easily sidetracked.[45] Though people may choose authentically on occasion, Heidegger thinks most people typically live inauthentically. Thus, authenticity must be repeatedly recovered because of humanity's tendency to fall into inauthenticity. To live inauthentically is to live impersonally, though not necessarily without passion; those who live authentically live personally, staking themselves in their actions. Self-consciously committing themselves to chosen historical traditions, they make their own contributions to them.[46]

Two preliminary points can provide a transition to Heidegger's analysis of disclosedness and understanding (being-in). First, when discussing the process of questioning (in section 2) which arises in Heidegger's analysis of the question of being, he suggests that questioning is always implicitly guided by what it seeks. This is a key hermeneutic claim: questioning is organized by background expectations that determine acceptable answers and methods. He applies this general insight to his own project and concludes that his inquiry must be implicitly guided by being. Then Heidegger anticipates an objection: perhaps he is *presupposing* some conception of being since this background structures his questioning. This is Heidegger's version of the hermeneutic circle, and he asks whether it is equivalent to the fallacy of circular argument. "No!" he answers, the guiding expectation that structures questioning is unlike presupposing a premise in an argument, and answering fundamental questions requires not argument, but *insight*. Although a circle exists, he suggests it is not vicious. The task is to enter it in the right way – a way that deepens comprehension as the circle is traveled again and again.[47] Indeed, the circle deepens and sharpens the analysis as it reveals additional structures. The deep connection between human being and being is given; it must be explicated so that it is no longer concealed or dismissed. Once the connection is clarified, being itself will become more transparent.

Second, in section 3, Heidegger defends his project by noting that every science presupposes a basic experience of the being of entities it studies, and this experience is conditioned by the scientist's understanding of being. He even suggests that fundamental conceptual change occurs when this basic experience is transformed. Such background understanding guides even physics and chemistry. Being is the ultimate background behind all regional inquiries since science's grasp of any particular region will be flawed if its grasp of being is faulty.[48] Thus, Heidegger's investigation could transform all the sciences. In addition, he shows that all scientific inquiry is conditioned, just as Heidegger's is, and their mutual goal is to enter their circles in the right way. Heidegger's investigation thus serves as a model for all inquiry. Ultimately, this implies that unmediated access to things themselves cannot exist. Background presumptions condition any inquiry. This claim is central to philosophical hermeneutics.

Heidegger's discussion of interpretation is situated in his analysis of "being-in," one of the existentials of human being. Interpretation is one way to develop human "understanding," one of the three dimensions of being-in. The other two dimensions are moods (affectedness) and telling (discourse).[49] One of Heidegger's goals throughout *Being and Time* is to describe human life in ways that overcome the subject-object distinction. He does this by construing humans as purposive, tool-using creatures and the world as a system of tools.

Being-in is the background know-how that facilitates one's orientation toward this system of tools. It involves skills and practical familiarity, rather than theories and intellectual cognition. Of the three dimensions of being-in, the most difficult to grasp is telling, because language-use, assertion, and communication are only particular exemplifications of telling (another is "telling the time"). These three dimensions of being-in are irreducible and equiprimordial. The goal of Heidegger's discussion of being-in is to transform the traditional analysis of human understanding and to show how human action and the world fit together like hand in glove. I will first clarify the three dimensions of being-in and then turn to Heidegger's discussion of interpretation.[50]

Being-in is a person's orientation to a system of tools that offers itself to her use. This orientation is conditioned by the way the situation weighs on her, often manifested by her moods. Moods reveal how people are faring, where they are. According to Heidegger, persons are always affected by situations; moods are as inescapable as they are revelatory.[51] They are not merely personal, but social (e.g., the mood of an electorate), and sometimes historical (embodied in cultural sensibilities). Specific moods are internally related to specific types of understanding. Typically people remain oblivious to their moods even though their state of being is clearly exhibited in them. Moods express the quality of their attunement to the world and their aliveness to the demands of the situation. The kind of understanding that operates in theorizing involves a specific mood: tranquil tarrying. This is by no means the only mood, just as theory is by no means the only form of understanding. Moods reveal the fact that situations matter in specific ways; they are the conditions of possibility of this mattering.

"Understanding" is often analyzed as cognition. Dilthey already had challenged this assumption when he explicated a natural self-understanding that is part of living-in-time. Heidegger also rejects this cognitive analysis. In understanding, the practical possibilities of the situation emerge and stand revealed. Understanding indicates a person's preparedness for the situation, her capacity to navigate it.[52] Though manifest in a kind of vision, it is unlike perception or cognition. This pragmatic vision is manifest in *action*, in how one proceeds in the face of situational possibilities. The more fully a person seizes a situation, the more deeply she grasps its practical possibilities, and the more authentic her existence. This seizing of possibilities is rarely reflective, but it is purposive. It is made possible by one's familiarity with shared practices. Understanding discovers a limited range of options, which delimit one's room to maneuver in the situation.

"Telling" (discourse) is more basic than interpretation or assertion because it grounds any kind of meaning. For Heidegger, the foundation of meaning is the instrumental relationships among tools, which are socially determined. Telling registers the cultural comprehension of tools, situations, and their possible uses. It grasps the *articulations* of the world – the way it fits together – its joints. Expert use of tools derives from one's ability to tell what is needed in the situation. Neither these joints nor the telling that grasps them is linguistic or theoretical; it is practical and situated. This practical articulation is the basis for language and communication.[53] Words are not the only possible means of telling the possibilities of situations, but when telling is expressed in words, they become tools as well, functioning in specific practices. One's use of tools in response to situations also specifies telling. Both words and specific instrumental relations render the person's project transparent, embodying practical understanding. When the situation coalesces, when what to do and how to do it become clear, the necessary responses are already in motion. This coalescing of the situation happens in telling: sometimes in words, sometimes in crystallizations of tool-complexes. Telling is social; it makes mutual personal understanding possible, but it is not always directed toward other persons. It is embedded in any project that responds to a situation; it specifies the manner in which the project can be realized. Silence and attentiveness can embody telling, just as thought and speech can. A mechanic with a full grasp of her wrenches and a painter with a full grasp of his colors can *tell* how to fix this breakdown or to paint this scene. Language is only one way to express telling's realizations.

So the situation is fully revealed by moods, by possibilities, and by the command of tools embedded in telling what to do. *Interpretation* is one way to articulate this understanding; it works out a possibility projected by understanding. Interpretation attends to the situation and finds its way more explicitly.[54] Again, not all interpretation is verbal or even linguistic; nor is it always expressed in propositions. Sometimes specific actions function as interpretations; sometimes rehearsals of an action do so.

Heidegger suggests that interpretations consist of three elements: an as-structure, various fore-structures, and meaning.[55] The as-structure highlights the guiding possibilities of the situation, framing it. Interpretation makes this as-structure explicit (though not always verbally), while understanding simply accepts it unconsciously. The as-structure is manifest in how one responds to the situation. One can respond to an open field by cultivating it, creating boundaries to play a game, or building a home on it. The field can be lived as a farm, a baseball diamond, or a living space.

Interpretation also involves three fore-structures – fore-having, fore-sight, and fore-conception, which are also dimensions of understanding. Fore-having is the totality of involvements binding the agent to the situation; it includes all the concerns that are not active in the response taking shape. Fore-sight is the agent's organizing purpose, which establishes gradients of relevance for various features of the situation. Fore-conception involves expected results of various possible actions. Rarely are any of these fore-structures explicit in everyday coping, but they can be made explicit if actions are unsuccessful. They can be more or less adequate to the situation. In the case of building a home, fore-having includes all the functions the field must fulfill in relation to the home (aesthetic and structural); fore-sight makes certain elements of the field more important because they relate directly to the home's design; and fore-conception includes the expected results of different possible designs.

Meaning is the background from which interpretation derives. This includes the multiplicity of practices and skills necessary for coping with situations. These practices condition all specific purposes and instrumental relations. Meaning involves all the skills necessary to design and build the house, which in turn respond to the practical limits and potentials of the field. Thus, meanings can never be completely specified or objectified. They are only gradually revealed through circular elucidation that better adapts situations and purposes to one another.

The task of interpretation is to insure that the fore-structures guiding it are appropriate to the situation and phenomenon to be understood. All interpretations are unavoidably guided by fore-structures. This fact constitutes Heidegger's version of the hermeneutic circle. The as-structure can impose itself to different degrees. If it is highly attenuated; then the interpreter exhibits the attitude of pure theory – a "disinterested" gaping at whatever emerges from the situation. If it responds to the multiplicity of situational demands, then it yields an initial orientation. Interpretation occurs when the structures (as- *and* fore-) within which understanding is projected are made explicit – either verbally or behaviorally. Sometimes interpretations are expressed in assertions, sometimes in questions or commands, sometimes in behavioral responses, sometimes in silence and patience.[56]

Interpretations do not always emerge, but understanding always occurs. Both understanding and interpretation, as Heidegger construes them, are less dependent on language – especially written or spoken propositions – than other theories suppose. Heidegger examines human beings in their practical dealings with the world because every way of being human involves a practical orientation. Theory is just one form of practice. Interpretation is just one mode of understanding. Understanding always is deeply conditioned by mood and by social relations (via telling), and understanding is always practically engaged. These factors become more explicit when interpretation articulates understanding in particular situations. Heidegger claims that fore-structures always mediate interpretations, but they can be more or less appropriate to the situation; so interpretations can often be improved and sharpened. Finally, the interpretations that are expressed in language constitute only one class of interpretations, and even when language is used to express interpretations, it is functional language, not the abstract, contemplative language used by pure theory. Language – even instrumentalized language – is not the source of practical meanings and articulations; there are more basic instrumental units of meaning and telling which language discovers and makes explicit.

Heidegger's discussions of being-in show that understanding is rooted in practical coping, not theory or principles. It cannot be isolated from moods or the world's instrumental relations. His vision of human existence provides a new starting point for all human studies. His analysis of interpretation shows its embeddedness in practical life. Both understanding and interpretation are prior to assertion, to theory, and to explicit method. The task of interpretation is to explicate understanding with subtlety and thoroughness, enabling successful coping with the world.

GADAMER

Hans-Georg Gadamer (1900–2002) was Heidegger's student; he uses Heidegger's insights to deepen philosophical hermeneutics. His major treatise is *Truth and Method* (1960), but he supplements and applies his position in many other essays and books. Resisting several dominant trends in hermeneutic theory – e.g., assimilating the text to the interpreter, elaborating fixed interpretive methods, and exclusively focusing on authors' intentions – he provides a rich description of the process of interpretation and its effects on the interpreter. Although he doubts that correct interpretations of specific texts can be conclusively established, he nonetheless believes that texts press specific questions on interpreters. He urges interpreters to remain open to texts' challenges, allowing them to question entrenched assumptions.[57] Gadamer believes that past interpretive theories have sought to eliminate reliance on background assumptions in the hopes of finding a wholly objective, absolute standpoint. Gadamer rejects this aspiration because it neutralizes the power of the text.[58] Indeed, both aesthetic and historical consciousness, which aspire to pure contemplation, undermine the powers of art and history. He stresses that interpreters and texts have equal claims to truth; neither can be allowed to dominate the other. When interpreters relinquish their aspirations toward objectivity and acknowledge their assumptions, they can experience the text's challenges more fully. To be transformed by texts is the goal of genuine interpretive encounters.

Like Heidegger, Gadamer believes that everyone inhabits specific traditions, and, like Nietzsche, he thinks perspectives can never be transcended. Against traditional hermeneutics, however, he insists that this is beneficial: approaching texts from specific perspectives allows interpreters to experience their ramifications. Existing perspectives enable interpreters to pose specific questions and to discover those that motivated the text's creation.[59] The interpreter is historically situated, but so is the text; this gives each participant in the interpretive process a horizon/heritage. As interpretation proceeds, these horizons challenge and interrogate one another. The dialogic interpretive process produces *new* conclusions, *not* more self-conscious elaborations of the interpreter's prejudices. Gadamer encourages interpreters to allow the process to continue because no single interpretation can be absolute or ultimately finished. In the interpretive process a dialogue occurs between text and interpreter in which each undergoes challenge and recovery; each is altered or renewed in the process.[60]

Traditional hermeneutic theory suggests that interpretation is complete when the hypotheses of the interpreter explain the details of the text – when interpreter and text achieve equilibrium. Gadamer suggests that this equilibrium may never be reached in genuine interpretation. Noting that traditional interpretive theory presupposes an isolated interpreter reading the text, he claims that every interpreter emerges from a constantly renewed social tradition.[61] For Gadamer, the discovery of meaning derives less from interpreters' originality than from the interaction of the text's heritage with the interpreter's traditions. So, at best, any equilibrium between text and interpreter is temporary – subject to revision whenever the interpreter's traditions are enriched.

For Gadamer, the goal of interpretation is productive challenge – genuinely responding to the text's questions. Its value depends on its effect on the interpreter (and her readers). The *effect* of the text on a reader is central to its interpretation; it cannot be ignored or disregarded.[62] The text interacts not only with interpreters' *ideas*, but also with their feelings, hopes, goals, perceptions, and imagination. These influences are also part of its meaning and must be incorporated by any adequate interpretation. Still, such effects may differ in different historical eras, and since these various effects are essential to the text's meaning, texts have their own histories. Interpretation involves ongoing interrogation between the tradition guiding the interpreter and the tradition emanating from the text. The best result is an enhancement of both traditions, enriching each other but never merging. Gadamer calls this process a "fusing of horizons."[63] This fusion is not a higher synthesis – a single truth integrating two partial truths – but, rather, a reawakening of each tradition. Gadamer believes that adopting an impersonal, absolute standpoint undermines such fusions, thus stripping art, literature, and philosophy of their powers.

Gadamer examines language to provide clues to the interpretive process. For example, the experience of finding the exact words to express a thought is parallel to the experience of discovering the right question to ask a text. In both cases a sudden intuition of appropriateness emerges, and further productive thought becomes possible.[64] Promising questions allow interpreters to better comprehend texts, advancing their dialogue. Texts raise questions; pursuing them eventually reveals the text's motivating concern. Both text and interpreter respond to that concern. This process creates a reciprocity that provokes new questions. Gadamer values this mutual interrogation process, believing it should continue indefinitely. On this account, interpretation sharpens art's power, rather than dominating or muting it.

Gadamer accepts a key feature of Hegel's concept of experience, even if he disagrees about the possibility of "absolute knowledge" of a text. For both, a genuine experience disconfirms or negates one's fundamental assumptions, and this negation is productive – creating new perspectives and new tensions.[65] People also learn their own finitude through this negation; they learn that they live *within* time, within particular traditions. Gadamer insists that no one can escape history by standing outside it. Only by acknowledging their traditions can interpreters approach texts perspicuously.

For Gadamer, time is not a gulf to be overcome, but a supportive milieu that facilitates lucid judgments. One reason why current artworks are difficult to assess is that they have not passed the tests of time. Assumptions that condition current critics' encounters with such works remain implicit. Also the assumptions embedded in current artworks and interpreters are too similar; thus, only minimal mutual interrogation is possible. If all interpreters approach the text with assumptions, the salient question is whether productive assumptions can be distinguished from unproductive ones. The goal is not to suspend assumptions/prejudices, but to engage them completely so that they can be challenged in dialogue with the text. When this happens, the mutual challenge of the traditions produce new truths. Thus, effective interpretations are productive in both directions – yielding new experiences for readers and new implications for texts. They do not merely reproduce the intentions of authors or uncover general features of their eras; both these goals limit the text's power, rendering it marginal and inconspicuous.

In Gadamer's theory, dialogue governs the entire interpretive process. Dialogue entails risk, openness, and readiness for change. When the dialogue is serious, the horizons of text and interpreter interrogate each other and new revelations emerge. Gadamer believes that defining rigid methods for interpretation will nullify this process.[66] He thus challenges traditional hermeneutic theory by providing a deeper phenomenological description of interpretive experience and abandoning the dream of absolute knowledge. The analysis he provides allegedly applies to all forms of understanding, not just the interpretation of literature and art. Historical situatedness enables productive interpretive dialogues. He insists on the difference between text and interpreter and refuses to allow one to assimilate the other.

BETTI

Emilio Betti (1890–1968) criticizes Gadamer and revitalizes Schleiermacher's approach. Betti's central objection is that Gadamer does not distinguish between the text's *meanings* and its *effects*. He notes that readers can sometimes experience strong emotions during an apparent fusion of horizons, but these can result from *misunderstanding* the work. Interpreters may miss the text's irony, for example, or ignore whole sections of it. They may only seem to grasp the central questions motivating the work. Betti insists that interpretation requires adequate understanding of the complete work; without that, Gadamer's fusion of horizons produces minimal interpretive truth. A powerful encounter with a text *may* suggest illuminating hypotheses about its meaning, but it does not guarantee they will be adequate interpretations.[67] Betti thus stresses justifying interpretive hypotheses by relating them to the text, while Gadamer focuses on the processes by which such hypotheses are initially produced (e.g., fusion of horizons).

Betti's second objection is that Gadamer's approach does not allow texts to genuinely differ from interpreters' beliefs, despite his insistence on openness and joint interrogation. Gadamer says that interpreters must concede a presumption of truth to texts but that if they depart from interpreters' best judgments, then they may then search for psychological or sociological explanations of those claims. Betti suggests that Gadamer's "presumption" of truth is entirely circumscribed by interpreters' beliefs. So Gadamer actually reduces artworks to interpreter's assumptions despite contrary appearances.[68] Betti insists that the *meaning* of the text must be distinguished from its *truth*; this allows interpreters to ascribe meanings to a text that they do not accept. Interpreters can then maintain a clear distinction between their own beliefs and the text's assertions; discovering the latter is interpretation's goal.[69] Betti claims that when Gadamer confuses these two issues he mystifies interpretation. Gadamer might respond that when horizons fuse this distinction dissolves. The interpreter is then transformed by the text and forced to incorporate new claims to truth.

Betti also suggests that Gadamer overgeneralizes the type of interpretation used in law to other spheres.[70] Betti notes that *historical* and contextual factors must be distinguished from *contemporary* relevance. Contextual relations may condition the meaning of historical events, but contemporary significance is *not* typically relevant in the same way. *Legal* interpretations must continue to solve current cases that may not have been envisioned by the original lawmakers. Thus, contemporary applications are relevant to legal interpretation, but not necessarily for other types of interpretation – especially historical interpretation. Historical interpretation must try to understand the meaning of the past event in relation to *its own* context. Qua interpretation, history need not concern itself with the contemporary significance of past events. Betti accuses Gadamer of drawing global conclusions about interpretation based on the limited model of legal interpretation. This objection challenges the goal of philosophical hermeneutics – to produce a general analysis of understanding. Betti suggests that both understanding and interpretation are sufficiently different when applied to distinct spheres (e.g., texts, actions, artworks, historical events, and legal rules) that more specific interpretive theories will be needed in each case. Moreover, each type of interpretation requires familiarity with the sphere being clarified.

Betti and Gadamer disagree both about the proper description of the interpretive process and about its aim and justification. Betti thinks that meaningful forms are products of human activity and that understanding their meanings requires relating them to their creators. Since Betti sees interpretable works as specific creations of purposive agents, he concludes that uncovering their organizing thoughts should be interpretation's governing aim.[71] Yet Betti also realizes that interpretation is possible even if its creator does not intend the work or act as communication. Interpreters can treat artworks as symptoms or unconscious manifestations of creators. For example, interpreters may note the tentativeness accompanying a seemingly cheerful "hello," and rightly conclude that the agent is less enthusiastic than she appears. For Betti, interpretation aims at understanding an action's/text's meaning, which requires recovering its organizing idea or underlying unity.[72]

Moreover, Betti realizes that the meaningful forms (genres) can be interpreted by comparing them with other historical possibilities. This kind of interpretation clarifies the history of the genre and the manner in which specific works reshape it. In addition, interpreters can study the internal relations among types of genre (e.g., romantic comedy and melodrama) or of expressive possibilities in different media (e.g., film, television, and theater). They may even attempt the Hegelian project of understanding the logic of history and thereby produce an interpretive ordering of historical eras. These higher-order forms of interpretation transcend the relationship of works to creators/authors; indeed, they transcend authors completely. But these forms require special expertise – deep familiarity with the relevant forms. Interpreters cannot just seek "divinations" at this level and expect useful results. They must have rich experience with the genres they seek to understand and refined capacities for abstraction and generalization to make progress.[73]

Betti agrees with Gadamer that interpreters must remain open to the text's/event's full force, but he insists that they must experience the force of the actual work, not a fantasy-reconstruction. Thus, interpreters must grasp the text's/act's objective content without distortion and also fully confront the work – allowing it to transform them – once they understand it.[74] Betti's objective demand requires that interpreters relate the text/act to its creator – using the standard of internal coherence to achieve mutual illumination of part and whole. When necessary, they may also utilize relevant broader contexts, e.g., the creator's other works, life, and historical era. Although Betti would resist using coherence *alone* to substitute for relating the work to its creator, he acknowledges that coherence can enhance understanding of the creator's organizing idea.[75] Betti's subjective demand requires interpreters to incorporate the work's insights into their own world-views – assimilating them into their own webs of belief. Betti thus accepts Gadamer's demand that interpreters assimilate the ramifications of the interpreted text.[76] In this way, Betti seeks to integrate the insights of Gadamer and Dilthey – retaining both the subjective and objective requirements of interpretation. He recognizes that there are many diverse types of interpretation and that strategies appropriate to one type may not apply to others. His criticisms of Gadamer suggest that hermeneutics still has important questions to resolve.

COMPARISONS

Within the hermeneutic movement itself, the crucial disagreements among figures are interconnected. Some believe that meanings can be objectively determined and that specific methods are useful in determining those meanings. Within this side of the movement, some think objective meaning is linked specifically to authorial intention (the psychological approach) while others think it is linked to something like propositional meaning (and is thus independent of authors). Others believe that prejudices and historicity insure that encounters with interpreted events or texts will be unique for each interpreter. The first group believes that texts/events are comprehensible; their opponents believe comprehension dominates texts, forcing them into pre-established categories. The first group also sees interpretation as a more self-conscious extension of everyday processes of understanding. The second group insists, however, that the uniqueness of interpretive encounters require a special kind of openness – a willingness to be interrogated – which rejects objectifying methods. They construe interpretation as a unique opportunity for mutual transformation, and though the process may follow a pattern, it is not reducible to rules and methods. I have called the first group "traditional" hermeneutic thinkers; they often distinguish different types and regions of interpretive practice (e.g., literature, law, history). The latter group, "philosophical" hermeneutic thinkers, tends to assimilate all interpretation to one model because they derive their conception from a general theory of human understanding.

Betti and Gadamer are the best representatives of these two directions in contemporary hermeneutic theory. Gadamer is right to defend the text's otherness. Serious interpreters must grasp its subtleties and its structure instead of merely reducing it to their own perspectives. On the other hand, Betti is right to distinguish between the work's effects and its meaning. He shows that readers can have epiphanies while reading texts and nonetheless completely misinterpret them (sometimes even *because* they misinterpret them). Because Gadamer's fusion of horizons concerns the emergence of actual truths (rather than accurate hypotheses about textual meaning), it can only supplement the more basic process of interpretation itself. Determining actual truth differs from determining the text's meaning, and the latter is the project of interpretation, even if the former is central to philosophy. Betti offers an analysis of the objective and subjective requirements of interpretation that balances the dual demands of clarifying the text's meaning and remaining open to its challenges. The text's emotional, political, and perceptual effects may be elements to be accounted for by an adequate interpretation, but experiencing them is insufficient to produce an interpretation. Moreover, Gadamer's approach is ineffective when the interpretive target is what Betti calls higher-order expressive structures – like art genres or entrenched social institutions. In such cases, the effect of the object on the interpreter is less important than the internal relations among the structure's elements. Betti shows that different theories of interpretation may be more appropriate for different types of objects.

ASSESSMENT

Exploring the ramifications of the hermeneutic circle is one of this movement's important contributions. Still, given their grasp of the problems it creates, hermeneutic thinkers offer too little insight on how to enter the circle in the best way. Schleiermacher suggests that interpreters "divine" the whole and then integrate the text's parts around this insight. This suggestion offers little guidance on how to produce promising divinations. Dilthey addresses this problem by suggesting that interpreters empathize with authors' creative processes. This approach seems at once too limiting (restricting plausible interpretations to authors' world-views) and misdirected (focusing attention on authors rather than texts). The experience of interpretation involves transcending oneself toward the organizing principles of the text, not toward the creative processes of the author.[77] Texts may or may not express authors' intended meanings. Moreover, interpretation involves articulating nearly unconscious intuitions concerning not only the text's core themes but also its basic conclusions. Strong interpretations articulate this pre-verbal grasp of texts and illuminate their integrity and multifacetedness. This articulation is less a function of background perspectives that interpreters bring to texts and more a process of entering into the text's own governing conceptions. These observations may offer a more promising way to clarify the initial "divinatory" moment of the interpretive process.

Hermeneutics can focus either on specific types of interpretation (e.g., literature, history, or individual persons) or on interpretation/understanding in general. The latter inquiry supposedly yields general results that are applicable across all types of interpretation. I call the former types of theories "local" theories and the latter "global" theories. The methods and evaluative criteria for interpretation often differ depending on the type of interpretation involved. A local theorist tries to remain sensitive to differences in these different types. Global theorists assume that certain processes operate in all acts of interpretation – often deriving them from a universal model of cognition. Some hermeneutic theorists believe that a global theory is the Holy Grail, but I think the more promising strategy is to build solid local theories first, and then gradually work toward a global theory on these foundations. Many global theories are really hasty generalizations based on local theories, and these often produce mistakes at the global level. The difference between the two approaches, however, can only be a difference in emphasis because inevitably any serious theorist will work in both directions at once – clarifying both local strategies and global process – allowing each to inform the other. An insightful local theory will sometimes yield larger implications, and a global hypothesis may be useful and informative in many local contexts. Thus, even determining the most promising approach to hermeneutic theory involves the hermeneutic circle. The real tasks are to discover the generalizable intuitions in the more solidly grounded local theories and to test global hypotheses in a variety of local contexts, thereby correcting their over-simplifications.

Hermeneutics is most needed when examining mystifying actions and powerful artworks. Not only do these have the most to teach, they demand the most penetrating and creative interpretive efforts. Because it clarifies forms of understanding that always operate, regardless of the circumstances, philosophical hermeneutics is remarkably unhelpful in approaching truly challenging artworks and expressions. It does not illuminate the most creative forms of interpretation. But traditional hermeneutics also falls short in this respect because it does not attend to differences among local theories. Its methodological suggestions are often useful for one type of interpretation (literary or historical), but not for other types. Thus, a closer attention to actual practice of interpretation in its most complex and challenging cases (in all regions) offers the best means of progressing in hermeneutic theory.

Schleiermacher (and Ast) showed that the hermeneutic circle operates not only within the interpretation of specific texts, but also between the text, its genre, its language, and its era. However, the exact relation between genres and texts often remains unclarified. If a text is merely an exemplification of a genre, there is no value in studying additional examples, but if each text is a genre unto itself, there is no value in developing genre theory. An interesting solution to this problem can be found in the analysis of film interpretation provided by Stanley Cavell.[78] Cavell believes that narrative genres are myths or stories, consisting of linked passages. These passages are examined and challenged in individual works. When this process is successful, an equivalent passage is discovered that helps clarify deeper meanings of the original story. The members of the genre thus compete with each other to refine and reassess the organizing story; each of the instances interprets the original myth and thus comments on other instances. Thus, a circular relation exists between the motivating myth that defines the genre and the individual members of the genre. Each work in the genre brings the motivating myth to greater explicitness. This approach can also relate narrative genres to each other since, when passages are negated, new myths emerge that ground adjacent genres.[79] Such a theory of genre shows both that genres make individual works possible and that individual works contribute to the comprehension and refinement of genres. This approach clarifies entire genres, not just individual works.

Dilthey demonstrates that natural scientific approaches to social phenomena are unilluminating or over-simplifying. He also explores alternative interpretive approaches to social phenomena. Although hermeneutics has mounted reasonable arguments against natural scientific approaches, such approaches still dominate many social sciences. Hermeneutics' most promising stance here should be that interpretive approaches *supplement* quantitative approaches and often provide *deeper* comprehension of social action. Stronger claims may not be defensible. For example, Dilthey's analysis of purposes in social action may be compatible with causal analyses. Heidegger offers no argument to demonstrate that his assumptions about human being will lead to more insightful social analyses than the objectifying strategies of social science. He offers a coherent alternative, and he claims that the scientific approach is derivative, but he never develops the implications of these claims or tests their consequences for social inquiry. Some important contemporary social theorists have adopted interpretive methodologies (e.g., Clifford Geertz in anthropology; R. D. Laing in social psychology; Anthony Giddens in sociology), but they have not overthrown the ranking paradigms in their respective disciplines. They do, however, establish alternative paradigms, and the strongest support for hermeneutic approaches would be concrete studies that show where their methods can be most successful and why.

Heidegger and Gadamer show that interpreters always approach situations with background assumptions. They suggest that acknowledging these assumptions will intensify the interpretive encounter. They do not answer the objection that such background assumptions may be simplifying and selective, and produce only a partial access to the full phenomenon. Nietzsche recognized this possibility, and he showed how to compensate for it. He notes that any single perspective must be supplemented by additional perspectives. If perspectives simplify, the way to restore a more complete comprehension is to multiply perspectives and adjudicate them. Nietzsche's approach requires interpreters to transcend themselves and incorporate less familiar approaches to the world. In doing so they broaden their capacities for understanding. Gadamer should embrace such a goal. Perhaps this strategy will offer deeper and more significant results in all areas where hermeneutics can be used effectively.

Understanding and interpretation are not the only modes of access to the world. Description or direct intuition is also possible. The results of both processes are typically cast into language, but this does not imply either that direct intuition is impossible or that it presupposes implicit interpretive assumptions. People are capable of directly reliving their pasts; they may also attempt a retrospective interpretation of its direction and goal. The two ways of experiencing the past may even depend on each other, but they are distinct. Similarly an intuition of essences that does not depend on background perspectives or assumptions may also be possible. Interpretation is important and central to many forms of comprehension, but it is not the only – or even the primary – access humans have to the world, themselves, or social reality. Whether description/intuition or interpretation will produce more useful results depends on the purposes of the inquiry. No a priori argument can show that one approach will always provide better insight. Hermeneutics has shown that it can make important contributions to Continental philosophy, but it has not shown that it should be considered the most important – or even the most basic – approach to inquiry.

PHENOMENOLOGY

INTRODUCTION

Phenomenology is the disciplined investigation of fundamental structures and features of experience, basic types of experience, and various kinds of objects that are correlated with them. Examples of fundamental structures include the intentionality (or directedness) of consciousness and internal time-consciousness. Examples of basic features include a capacity to transcend the given situation and envision alternatives and an always pre-given world of tools and cultural meanings. Basic types of experience include perception, imagination, action, thought, emotion, volition, ethical responsiveness, aesthetic sensitivity, judgment, reflection, and various kinds of self-consciousness. Possible objects of consciousness include events, things, processes, images, concepts, projects, propositions, feelings, memories, fantasies, the body, other people, and groups. Objects can also exhibit different kinds of complexity – e.g., blackness, a blackboard, the fact that the blackboard is full of writing, the fact that the blackboard in this room is larger than those in other buildings, etc. Phenomenology clarifies the differences and connections among these diverse structures, features, types, and objects of consciousness.

Although this abstract definition sketches a general framework, the precise meaning of "phenomena" differs for different phenomenologists. The basic division is between transcendental and existential phenomenologists. Transcendental phenomenologists seek certainty and believe that a special procedure that requires bracketing belief in the existence of the external world will facilitate achieving it. Existential phenomenologists embrace the complexity of lived experience, believing that such bracketing is artificial and inimical to clarifying experience as lived. In addition, phenomenologists' attitudes, assumptions, and goals all influence the type of phenomenology they pursue. Common to all phenomenologies is a lucid description of the investigator's own experience; yet all phenomenologists also seek to transcend their idiosyncrasies in order to articulate universal features of experience. They rely on the confirmation of other investigators to determine their success in this respect. Where disagreements arise, further descriptions and closer comparisons may resolve them.

Central to nearly all forms of phenomenology is a process of *awakening*. Through disciplined effort, neophytes can gain access to previously unknown levels of experience that reveal philosophically important truths. These emergent levels contribute insights into mind and world while challenging common-sense assumptions that often produce misunderstandings. Thus, Husserl's formula "back to the things themselves" is widely accepted by phenomenologists, but the precise nature of the "things themselves" differs for different figures. This awakening process often has an ethical significance; it makes possible a fuller and deeper grasp of the world and consciousness, which contributes to living more truthfully and intensely. In general, phenomenologists avoid metaphysical hypotheses, instead offering lucid descriptions of experience, which often requires conceptual innovation. In order to illustrate the different types of awakenings, I shall clarify the process in six exemplary figures: Edmund Husserl (1859–1938), Max Scheler (1874–1928), Martin Heidegger (1889–1976), Jean-Paul Sartre (1905–80), Maurice Merleau-Ponty (1908–61), and Emmanuel Levinas (1906–95).

Husserl seeks to awaken people from the "natural attitude" by revealing the constituting activity of consciousness as it sustains and engenders the complexities of the experienced world. The natural attitude assumes that people operate amidst independent objects, which exist prior to consciousness, and that perception replicates the world as it is. Naive realism is its basic stance. Husserl challenges this orientation because he thinks consciousness contributes much of the "sense" persons give to the raw perceptual data and thus constitutes many complex facts of experience – such as the identity of objects across time, the differences between properties, relations, and objects, etc. For Husserl, the awakening process requires a procedure he calls "phenomenological reduction," which simply neutralizes or brackets the taken-for-granted objective existence of perceived objects.[1] This strategy puts all objects of all conscious acts on the same level and allows Husserl to study subtle differences among them. In addition, it supposedly neutralizes personal idiosyncrasies and cultural assumptions, thus reconstituting the investigator as a pure ego – without historically limiting determinants – and yielding access to universal structures of consciousness. These methodological steps allegedly show that consciousness plays a more active role in articulating and structuring the world than is assumed in the natural attitude. For Husserl, philosophical maturity requires intuiting and explicating all the conscious acts that sustain experience.

Scheler also questions assumptions derived from common sense and traditional philosophy. He claims that a searching description of experience can mount this challenge. For instance, he shows that most actions are motivated by values to be realized in situations. In order to grasp the essences of mental acts and their objects, Scheler thinks phenomenologists must learn to transcend life's demands – thus inhibiting drive-satisfaction – so that they can achieve greater insight into essences themselves. Immersion in life produces a drive to dominate the world that is characteristic of science. For him, phenomenology elevates people beyond this drive to control toward an intellectual grasp of essences for their own sake.[2] This step *prepares* phenomenologists for the ethical task of contributing to the realization of absolute being – a task he identifies as "metaphysics." This ascetic inhibition of drives thus prepares phenomenologists for serious ethical tasks and produces a deeper experience of reality.

Heidegger's phenomenology challenges the standpoint from which most past philosophical treatises have been written. This standpoint involves rational contemplation, which surveys the world in a cool, objective manner. The world that appears to this standpoint is one of pure objects – indifferent presences that passively await further investigation. This contemplative stance conceals the philosopher's antecedent involvement with the world (her cares) and the fact that her primary relation to worldly items is to use them as instruments. Heidegger notes that instead of neutral, indifferent objects, the world consists of tools organized in complex relations with one another, and instead of passive observers, persons are active participants in transforming the world.[3] Even pure theory is a limiting case of this practical orientation because it treats perceived events as grist for grinding out hypotheses. Once this fundamental practical orientation is acknowledged, then many other features of human life become visible. Heidegger's phenomenology elucidates these heretofore unnoticed, universal features. These insights facilitate a different way of living – a more authentic way – in which people seize their distinctive possibilities and refuse to be overwhelmed by everyday demands. This potential for achieving authenticity is one ethical implication of Heidegger's phenomenology.

The goal of Sartre's phenomenology is to overcome the illusions produced by reflection (introspection and retrospection) in order to uncover pre-reflective experience. He thinks that many philosophical theories originate in this problematic reflective standpoint and that support for these theories collapses as soon as it is challenged. For example, many philosophers believe that people have continuant selves that govern their actions and explain their distinctive choices. Sartre insists that this sense of self can be experienced only in reflection and that it is absent in pre-reflective experience and thus cannot have causal efficacy.[4] In fact, pre-reflective choices arise spontaneously, and such choices sustain whatever degree of personal unity exists. Instead of possessing essential natures, Sartre thinks persons choose their responses within historically defined situations and are responsible for these choices; to think otherwise is self-deceptive.[5] Thus, uncovering the pre-reflective level of experience reveals important ethical truths. The task of Sartrean phenomenology is to describe this level of experience accurately. Such descriptions clarify the nature of consciousness, its relation to the world, the experience of time, the nature of action, the body, relationships with other people, and human freedom and responsibility.

Merleau-Ponty's phenomenology is situated between two traditional philosophical positions, both of which he claims are misguided. The truth lies between them in a position that phenomenology makes accessible. The first mistaken view is empiricism, which operates with an atomistic concept of sensation that is not confirmed by physiological research and which is posited to satisfy artificial theoretical demands. The second mistaken view is intellectualism or cognitivism, which claims that the mind fashions reality through the imposition of categories on unstructured input. This view assumes that the unity and coherence of the world is produced by these categories. Merleau-Ponty uses experimental data to show that the perceived world has its own coherence and structure – prior to any categorial imposition – which guides and tutors the nervous systems of perceivers so that they can better and more completely grasp its details. Merleau-Ponty believes that perceivers *complete* the perceived world but that they follow the lead of an existing order, which itself is ambiguous and can be completed in various ways. Phenomenology elucidates these pre-reflective, dialectical relationships between the perceived world and the body-subject; it deepens philosophical understanding of perceived objects and the perceptual process.[6] The body-subject is an ordered system of habits for grasping the world. Sometimes, these complex reciprocal relationships become ossified, and this inflexibility invites the theoretical mistakes characteristic of empiricism and intellectualism. Phenomenology revitalizes a person's relationship with the world, and this, in turn, produces a more authentic way of living and perceiving: a way that continuously interrogates the world's structure and the culture's future.

Levinas's phenomenological approach is less systematic than others, but it has a distinctive aim and tenor. The aim is to defend the primacy of the ethical standpoint over the metaphysical-ontological standpoint, elevating the imperative to *respect* other people over the urge to *know or objectify* them. Levinas's point of departure is a critique of Heidegger (e.g., Heidegger insists on the primacy of the question of being, relegating ethics to a peripheral status). While Heidegger insists on the instrumental nature of the surrounding world, Levinas suggests that an immersion in the elements (water, air, earth), or even the experience of an impersonal rustling darkness (manifest in boredom, for example), are more basic than, and are fundamentally different from, practical, purposive action. Although both Heidegger and Levinas believe that the everyday sense of self is illusory, Levinas thinks only other people (not a more authentic grasp of one's own possibilities) can dispel the illusion. Levinas also tries to show, against Heidegger, that other people are essential to an authentic experience of time. Levinas insists that both desire and knowledge are inadequate ways to illuminate reality, since both seek to assimilate it. He thinks authentic experience emerges only when one accepts and acknowledges an unbridgeable difference between self and other and hence the transcendence of other people.[7] Responding to this essential transcendence produces the ethical current within Levinas's phenomenology. Levinas constitutes a pivot within phenomenology, anticipating key claims of poststructuralism.

CORE CONTRIBUTIONS

Phenomenologists challenge the relativism implicit in most historicism and hermeneutics by uncovering allegedly universal structures of experience – those common to all people, in all cultures, at all times. They claim that these structures are essential to human existence or consciousness, not produced by contingencies of culture or history. Phenomenologists strive to describe such structures accurately, rather than explain their genesis. For example, Husserl created the procedure of transcendental reduction to clarify acts that sustain the natural attitude; this is why he thinks that phenomenology can provide foundations for science – both by articulating the meaning of the concept "science" and by grounding the truths of logic on which all scientific reasoning depends.[8] Scheler eventually accepted the rootedness of mind (spirit) in life, but he also notes that imaginative variation can yield essential truths that transcend ordinary empirical claims. Moreover, Scheler believes that the diversity of human cultures produces positive contributions (they illuminate different sectors of an objective value hierarchy). Heidegger thinks his phenomenology reveals transcendental conditions of being human that exist in any type of person or any manner of being human. For him, fundamental ontology (the study of the conditions of possibility for revealing being) is prior to regional ontology (the study of specific sectors of existence), and phenomenology also pursues the most foundational investigations within regional ontologies, which clarify the fundamental concepts in those regions.[9] His results allegedly are prior to science and condition any empirical inquiry. Phenomenology thus articulates a defensible search for essences that has universal application.

Second, as one moves from Husserl through Sartre to Merleau-Ponty and Levinas, phenomenology becomes more realist in orientation, even though it operates primarily within the first-person standpoint. Rarely is this realism simply the naive realism of common sense; it is rooted in a dawning conviction that the world is both cultural and natural and contains features independent of consciousness. Husserl unquestionably accepts transcendental idealism, suggesting that much of the perceived world derives its meaning from transcendental consciousness; phenomenology for him becomes the task of tracing the paths by which the world's sense is constituted.[10] Scheler suggests that the realism/idealism controversy is misguided because it fails to distinguish existence from essence. Many objects of consciousness have essences (ideal conceptual definitions) even though they have varying types of existence.[11] For example, Scheler thinks specific values have essences and also have an existence-status similar to that of colors, but different from that of desks. He also thinks "reality" is a distinctive existential status uniquely associated with resistance to vital drives. Thus, an object is experienced as real only to the extent that it offers resistance to the fulfillment of vital drives. But much that *exists* does not necessarily resist these drives, and the question of how something exists is also distinct from the degree of its existential relativity. Scheler thus rethinks the realism issue, while showing that many types of object have independent existence. Like Heidegger he believes that various modes of existence can themselves be clarified phenomenologically.

Sartre guarantees the reality of "the external world" by sharply distinguishing its type of being from the being of consciousness and by insisting that consciousness is parasitic on it. Consciousness may be the source of the "meaning" objects can have, but this does not affect their independent existence.[12] Being-in-itself is self-identical, self-subsistent, and independent in a way conscious creatures can never be. Moreover, ordinary perceptual objects are independent of any given perspective on them, for Sartre, because they are not just the series of all possible perspectives on object, but the *principle* of that series, which itself appears. Merleau-Ponty clarifies the neurological basis for realism by citing experimental evidence which demonstrates that the neurological system tracks external objects, and he elucidates structures within the phenomenal field that are already given to consciousness.[13] Both Sartre and Merleau-Ponty insist that philosophy abandon the notion that the nervous system produces representations of objects, and both construe the mind-world relation in a more direct manner.

Despite this realist orientation, many phenomenologists accept an interactive relationship between object and subject, which acknowledges that these poles cannot be isolated from one another. (This is a twentieth-century version of Hegelianism.) Although Husserl accepts an intellectualism that gives consciousness the power to constitute the meaning and status of most objects, nearly all his heirs reject this. Scheler believes that both persons and world are participants in a fourfold hierarchy (sensory, vital, cultural, spiritual), and that at all levels subject and object participate in each other's full realization. Heidegger's reinterpretation of human existence as practically immersed in a cultural and instrumental context acknowledges both that cultural background shapes "subjectivity" and that human projects reshape the "environment." In fact, Heidegger attempts to eliminate the subject-object distinction in favor of a complex interanimation between agency and world. Though Sartre's dualism of consciousness and being-in-itself might suggest that he reintroduces a subject-object distinction, in fact Sartre strives to overcome it as earnestly as Heidegger. The world actually experienced is deeply interwoven with consciousness's structures, according to Sartre, and consciousness is always situated in the world.[14] Merleau-Ponty also develops the conception of an interwoven unity between organism and world, since the world contributes to the development of neural structures and since the organism's movements elucidate worldly properties that previously had been inaccessible. In effect, the concept of "intentionality" (or the directedness of consciousness) undergoes significant revision as phenomenology develops, and this produces a more concrete, interactive, situated conception of agency.

Correlative with this interactive co-constituting conception of subject and object is a common conception of the person (or groups or history) as a totalization in process – a perpetually self-unifying but never quite completed organic whole. This analysis is especially prominent in Sartre and Merleau-Ponty.[15] They construe persons as constantly self-restructuring wholes that must meet the demands of constantly changing, refractory environments. In practice, persons are hierarchies of projects that respond to diverse worldly demands. Both thinkers incorporate the notion of individual style – the manner in which persons characteristically address/participate in the world. Scheler also interprets persons to be expressive totalities, though for him their organizing principles are not self-chosen projects, but innate attractions toward specific values.[16] Husserl at least saw consciousness as an integrated system of operations, some of which are more basic in that others presuppose them. But he does not require that these operations be construed as a totalization, just as a coordinated system. He does clarify some important self-unifying operations of consciousness, e.g., time consciousness.

Phenomenology is primarily a *first-person* mode of inquiry. It describes the world from the perspective of the active, thinking, attentive individual. Never are the dynamics of human actions conceived from a third-person, external standpoint that would objectify both agent and world (the standpoint typical of empirical science). Even the complex world of social and historical relations is described from the standpoint of an individual participant. Phenomenologists discuss group actions from the standpoint of the individuals who execute and co-define the group's purposes. In his late works, Sartre explores how the characteristic first-person standpoint of phenomenology might be integrated with the characteristic third-person standpoint of Marxism.[17] Even Levinas – who requires persons to acknowledge transcendent other persons – always describes that transcendence as it appears to the experience of an individual. Thus, phenomenology might be described as the perspective of "subjectivity"; nonetheless it constantly strives to produce universal truths, clarify necessary structures, and reveal the world as it is.

Most phenomenologists emphasize the limitations of science because they believe either that it assumes a misguided standpoint or that it presupposes much that can be verified only by phenomenology. Phenomenologists conceive their discipline as fundamental. Husserl notes that science only produces probable hypotheses, rather than certain truths; moreover, he suggests that all sciences rely on principles of reasoning that must be grounded phenomenologically.[18] Scheler and Heidegger insist that science seeks to dominate and control the world in a way that opposes phenomenology's attempt to respect and articulate the world as it is. Both Sartre and Merleau-Ponty see science as an objectifying mode of inquiry that ignores the contribution of the scientist to scientific theorizing. Thus, Merleau-Ponty resists the metaphysical pretensions of science to reveal absolute truth, but, more than other phenomenologists, he believes phenomenology must be responsive to current empirical research. He realizes that his descriptions have empirical content, and thus he engages the sciences in critical discussion.[19] Scheler also stresses the highly mediated, symbolic relation between the constructs of science and lived experience, but he critically examines empirical research when he reviews possible positions on his central questions. Sometimes phenomenologists can be too dismissive of the results of science, but their goal is to redress science's rejection of the first-person perspective.

I have already mentioned the ethical significance of the awakening process. Generally, phenomenologists value an active, creative relation to the world, a relation that presupposes nothing and acknowledges the distinctive nature of consciousness. The ethical flaw most studied by this group of thinkers is self-deception – intentionally concealing important features of human life.[20] Sartre and Merleau-Ponty stress serious practical commitment in a world without absolute values. Scheler insists that there are objective values, but he notes that people participate in the life of values, making them real through their actions. Merleau-Ponty underlines the value of creativity by showing that an all-too-common tendency in human beings is simply to exemplify existing habituated structures of perception and response. Like Heidegger, his ideal involves consciously adopting an active historical tradition and creatively adapting it to the current historical moment.[21] Finally, Levinas insists that persons acknowledge the reality and distinctness of other human beings, which phenomenology makes vividly transparent.

SOME TYPES OF PHENOMENOLOGY

I divide phenomenology into the following types. The two main alternatives are transcendental and non-transcendental phenomenology. Husserl is the exemplary transcendental phenomenologist. Within non-transcendental phenomenology the main alternatives are hermeneutic and descriptive phenomenology. Each of these subtypes has a more abstract and a more concrete form. Heidegger and Schutz are exemplary hermeneutic phenomenologists; Schutz has the more concrete hermeneutic focus. Scheler and Sartre (and Merleau-Ponty and Levinas) are exemplary descriptive phenomenologists; The French thinkers embody the more concrete descriptive focus.

Transcendental phenomenology relies on some version of Husserl's transcendental reduction, which seeks to bracket the common-sense assumption that the perceived external world exists entirely independently. It does not doubt or disbelieve that assumption; it simply neutralizes it and then describes the resulting appearances as open-mindedly as possible (without presuppositions). Husserl calls this maneuver the "transcendental (or phenomenological) *reduction*" (because it steps back from or withholds the assumptions with which one typically grasps the world). Husserl thinks this reflexive maneuver will allow consciousness to achieve certainty because it avoids existential assumptions and because consciousness is supposedly transparent to itself. Moreover, the true criteria for independent existence will emerge more adequately when assumptions about them are neutralized. Husserl believes that such a maneuver will also remove personal idiosyncrasies from phenomenology's results, thus assuring their universality.

Husserl thinks that at minimum the transcendental reduction will make an accurate elucidation of all acts of consciousness possible, but he also believes that an intermediate sphere of entities he calls "senses" (or "meanings," using an analogy to the distinction between linguistic meanings and their referents), which emerge as a result of this maneuver, also can be described with certainty.[22] A "sense" is a way of taking an object, a description (or set of concepts) under which the object is encountered. Thus, for example, the same tree in a forest can be grasped as exhibiting a distinct shade of green, as an emblem of the lushness of nature, as symbolizing haunting majesty, as a promising target for clear-cutting the forest, as an element of an indifferent universe, as an aesthetic object suitable for painting, etc. Each of these are distinct "senses" through which the same tree can be grasped, and the senses can be described accurately without assuming anything about the existential status of the tree. So phenomenology becomes the study of mental acts, their various "senses," and the complex relations among acts and senses. Husserlian phenomenology describes and integrates the results of these studies. Sometimes it focuses more intently on mental acts themselves (Husserl calls this its "noetic" side), while at other times it addresses the senses through which acts intend objects (Husserl calls this its "noematic" side).

Non-transcendental phenomenologists disagree with Husserl about the efficacy of the reduction. They suggest that it alters the conscious state that it tries to describe and thus at least sometimes produces misleading results. For example, Sartre disagrees sharply with Husserl about the presence of an ego that organizes pre-reflective consciousness because he thinks the experience of an ego is *produced* by the reflective act; he thus denies that the ego exists in pre-reflective consciousness. Heidegger suggests that everyday life exhibits a far more practical orientation than Husserl believed. Neither Sartre nor Heidegger simply disagrees with Husserl; they both claim that Husserl was misled by the reduction. They also insist that it is unnecessary for achieving reliable, universal results. They show this primarily by example – offering insightful descriptions without relying on Husserl's reduction. They acknowledge that Husserl sometimes offers important, valid descriptions, but they reject his claim that reduction accounts for them. I will indicate other significant differences between Husserl and other phenomenologists below.

Within non-transcendental phenomenology, the main division is between the hermeneutic phenomenologists and the descriptive phenomenologists. Descriptive phenomenologists believe that persons can have unmediated access to many of their own conscious states and can thus describe them and their objects without interference from conceptual schemes, prejudices, or assumptions. Even though they grant that phenomenological results must be described in language, they insist that an effective user of the language can express these insights accurately. Hermeneutic phenomenologists reject the notion that consciousness's access to itself can be unmediated and insist that linguistic and conceptual categories will always be implicated in experience. Hermeneutic phenomenologists highlight the importance of antecedent linguistic, practical, and conceptual frameworks and insist that phenomenologists interrogate them via multi-perspectival forays into lived experience. Descriptive phenomenologists can acknowledge the reality of such frameworks, but they insist that consciousness can avoid their potentially falsifying effects when it describes its own operations. Indeed, they think that phenomenological descriptions can adjudicate debates between proponents of different conceptual schemes.

Schutz defends his hermeneutic orientation by suggesting that at bottom consciousness confronts a chaotic confusion of data on which it must impose interpretive order in order to produce any coherence at all. Thus, for him, consciousness creates all orderliness through interpretation. He thus interprets Husserlian "senses" like Kantian categories, except that they can be created, modified, and developed through experience. In addition, he insists that descriptions of consciousness are necessarily retrospective and thus are governed by present purposes.[23] He does not defend these claims, but his position requires them. Heidegger insists that all understanding is interpretive, and that every clarificatory enterprise is conditioned by the questions it poses. The questions determine the types of plausible answers and limit the relevant data.[24] He also notes that all understanding proceeds only in the light of certain interpretive expectations, which condition the results of the investigation.[25]

Scheler and Sartre, the descriptive phenomenologists, believe that consciousness experiences an antecedently ordered world and that the limits imposed by questions or expectations do not adulterate the phenomenologists' grasp of appearances. Scheler also thinks there is a realm of essences that informs existing things, a realm very much like Husserl's senses, except that only imaginative variation is needed to clarify it. Both Husserl and Scheler accept this method of clarifying essences. Imaginative variation envisions changes in all the properties of an object until its identity explodes; when that happens the altered properties constitute its necessary features or its essence. Sartre and Levinas think that proper attention can illuminate general structures of consciousness. Sartre also requires that reflective consciousness purify itself of false hypostatizations.[26] Sartre, Merleau-Ponty, and Levinas simply examine lived experience and describe its philosophically central features. Fully explicating these structures will challenge many common-sense assumptions and standard philosophical positions.

Although these differences in approach to the clarification of experience might generate incompatible results, in fact the varieties of phenomenology often supplement and strengthen each other. Their results do not coalesce with the precision of a jigsaw puzzle, but they often support and reinforce each other, rather than contest and undermine each other. Though there can be sharp disagreements between phenomenologists, these do not prevent mutual correction and development of each other's positions. Sartre, for example, draws heavily on hermeneutic approaches when he explicates methods appropriate for understanding individuals as hierarchies of projects. Though Schutz often focuses on the typifications or stereotypes through which people relate to one another, he effectively describes the subtleties of joint actions like making music as well. The basic approach of a phenomenologist thus does not preclude adopting alternative approaches if the inquiry is better served by doing so.

THE CONTRIBUTIONS OF THE FOUNDER: HUSSERL

Although his teacher Franz Brentano (1838–1917) and his contemporaries – e.g., Alexander Pfander (1870–1941) and Adolf Reinach (1883–1917) – examined experience introspectively, Edmund Husserl (1850–1938) refined the study of consciousness and established the discipline of phenomenology. His goal was to make philosophy into a rigorous science – with clear standards of evidence, intersubjectively verifiable results, and teachable research methods.

He sought to create an independent discipline that would solidify the intellectual foundations of all other fields. Above all, he sought to overcome skepticism by creating a method that would produce certainty.[27] He refashioned his method several times throughout his life in order to improve scholarly understanding of phenomenology. For example, he introduced Parisians to his aims and procedures by contrasting his approach with Descartes's *Meditations*.[28] He regularly rethought the foundations of phenomenology in order to keep the many ramifications of his research coherent. In addition to the many research paths Husserl blazed, his method was reinterpreted in a variety of ways by other talented philosophers (e.g., Heidegger, Sartre, Merleau-Ponty, and Levinas).

Husserl's position developed in several stages. Initially, the logician Gottlob Frege made an enormous contribution to Husserl by criticizing the psychologistic assumptions of his first book, *The Philosophy of Arithmetic* (1891). Husserl's response produced his first major formulation of phenomenology and a series of seminal contributions to logic in his *Logical Investigations* (1900). In this period, Husserl uses an egoless, act-object model of consciousness. His primary concerns are the theory of meaning and grammar, the process of abstraction, relations between parts and wholes, intentionality, and the nature of knowledge. After completing this book, he launched a detailed study of the internal experience of time's flow, a topic that fascinated many thinkers at the turn of the century (e.g., Henri Bergson, William James). Slightly more than a decade after his first major treatise, Husserl published *Ideas* (1913). This book introduces transcendental phenomenology, and thereafter the *phenomenological* (or transcendental) *reduction* becomes an essential ingredient in his phenomenological approach. In this period, he also shifts to an ego-act-(sense)-object model of consciousness and introduces the enterprise of clarifying essences (through imaginative variation). Husserl continues the studies initiated in *Ideas* and writes additional logical investigations from 1913 to 1929, capping this period with *Formal and Transcendental Logic* (1929). In 1929–35 he gave various lecture series, some of which were published posthumously, among them *Cartesian Meditations* (1931), *Experience and Judgment* (1948), and *The Crisis in European Sciences and Transcendental Phenomenology* (1954). In *Cartesian Meditations*, phenomenology becomes a study of the ego's capacities and structures, and the important theme of intersubjectivity is explored. *Experience and Judgment* introduces new fundamental distinctions. And in *The Crisis* Husserl offers a response to his most famous student, Martin Heidegger, whose *Being and Time* (1927) set German philosophy on a different path and influenced the direction of phenomenology after its publication. In addition to his many published works, Husserl left an immense number of unpublished manuscripts that fortunately were preserved, despite the rise of anti-Semitism in Germany.

Throughout all his phases of development, Husserl remains faithful to certain themes. He resists any approach that reduces philosophy to a branch of empirical science because he thinks philosophical truths must possess greater certainty than scientific hypotheses. Nonetheless, he respects the goal of science, which requires theories to have clear evidence supporting them. Husserl's ideal of evidence is self-evident givenness, self-evidence so vivid that anyone can verify its truth.[29] Phenomenological claims are supposed to exhibit this self-evidence. This prevents phenomenologists from relying on the opinions of experts or on tradition. Husserl explores the diverse kinds of intentionality among conscious states – the different ways consciousness can be directed toward its objects, and he formulates an expanding series of tasks for phenomenologists to complete. I distinguish five types of phenomenology that Husserl practiced over the course of his career. All of them presuppose the transcendental reduction.

The first type is *correlational* phenomenology.[30] This is probably the most generally accepted version of Husserl's discipline. With it, phenomenologists examine different kinds of mental act (e.g., perception, thought, imagination, or emotion) and the different ways their objects appear; they also explore different types and complexes of object that such mental acts can intend (e.g., a spatial thing, an animate organism, a psychic state, a cultural meaning or norm). Correlational phenomenology involves a close study of differences in types of mental act and also in types of object that can be intended in these acts. Late in his career, Husserl notes a central distinction between prepredicative experience (which intends everyday things and states of affairs) and predicative judgment (which intends propositions, assertions, etc., and is central to knowledge claims). He also studies purely formal relations, e.g., differences between universals and particulars, and between pluralities and totalities.

Husserl's second type is called "*eidetic*" phenomenology. "Eidetic" means "focusing on essences." The goal of eidetic phenomenology is to clarify essences (necessary and sufficient conditions) by imaginatively varying the different properties of an object until the key properties that cannot be varied without completely altering the object are discovered.[31] For example, if in studying the essence "cube," the length of one side is varied while the length of the other sides remains constant, then the cube "explodes" and becomes a completely different kind of solid. Thus, sides of equal length is an essential property of cubes. This procedure is very similar to the methods used in conceptual analysis in Anglo-American philosophy (i.e., elaborating imaginary cases that offer possible counter-examples to proposed statements of necessary and sufficient conditions); only they articulate conditions for the proper use of concepts, rather than the necessary properties of objects. Husserl insists that eidetic phenomenology can clarify essences even if there are no actually existing examples at a particular historical moment; examining merely possible individuals is sufficient. For example, the essence "science" can be clarified even if no discipline really embodies the conditions necessary for being a science at the time of the investigation.

Verificational phenomenology is Husserl's third type.[32] It depends on the important concept of "horizons." Whenever consciousness intends a specific kind of object in a specific kind of act, it includes perspectives on the object beyond those given directly. For example, when one sees a person acting (e.g., playing basketball), then he or she is given with a horizon (or penumbra) of possible future ways to continue the action (e.g., to pass, dribble, or shoot). These possibilities are given as part of the present perception of the person, but they are not given as fully or in the same way as the current phase of the action. And if one is *merely imagining* the person performing the same action, then the implicit horizon will contain many more possibilities because imagination is less stable than perception and often proceeds in wild leaps. These horizons are gradually confirmed or disconfirmed as one gains further experience with the object. Understanding how these unfolding patterns produce harmonious styles of verification for various types of act is the task of verificational phenomenology. It describes *the patterns of projected profiles* for each type of object and act. These "horizons" possess a variety of built-in limits. For example, if an object has a different color on its back side than expected, this may not disconfirm the object as a whole, but if the object suddenly changes into something entirely different (e.g., from a dog to a dinosaur), then one may be experiencing the object in a different mode than one assumed (imagining rather than perceiving it). Each type of act has its own pattern of horizons for similar objects.

Genetic phenomenology is a fourth Husserlian type.[33] Here Husserl suggests that various mental acts are preconditions for the possibility of other mental acts, and thus must exist prior to the others. Husserl claims that consciousness remains coherent because each new constitutional pattern achieved by the ego continues as an ever-renewable habit. Some of these patterns/capacities must develop earlier than others because they are the ones on which the higher-order capacities are based. He suggests, for example, that the mind learns to organize passively received data first, before it can create categorial structures of its own and thus take an active role in developing knowledge. In his last period, Husserl develops a conception of the life-world – an immersion in everyday life and practices – that he argues is primary. All higher-order acts of consciousness are traced back to their origins in this life-world. This development functions as an abstract model for the maturation of any possible ego; it does not describe the empirical development of a particular type of individual. By applying the procedures of imaginative variation to the development of the ego itself, Husserl defines an "essential ego," of which any actual (transcendental) ego will be simply an exemplification. Thus, genetic phenomenology studies the essential order of temporal development of act-types in the "essential-ego."

Just as some acts must emerge first in time, so too, at a given moment in time, some acts provide a foundation for higher-order acts. These cases involve highly complex acts. When perceiving another person, for example, Husserl believes one initially grasps her bodily behavior, which grounds a more elaborate perception of her mental state. The manner in which this complex act is organized will be described below. Husserl calls this fifth type of phenomenology *"static-constitutional"* phenomenology. It is static because it describes a complex system of related acts at a given time, and it is constitutional because it assumes that some acts presuppose others (not temporally, but logically).[34] The presupposed moments of the act are simultaneously interwoven with the higher-order moments in an elaborate structure.

CONCRETE PHENOMENOLOGICAL STUDIES

These abstract descriptions of Husserl's types of phenomenology hardly do justice to his many particular insights, which are their main payoffs. In order to better clarify the contributions of Husserl and other major figures of this movement, I shall examine their main conclusions on a single topic – intersubjectivity. I shall then clarify Merleau-Ponty's contributions to the analysis of perception.

Intersubjectivity (Husserl, Scheler, Heidegger, and Sartre)

Several phenomenologists have made significant contributions to the elucidation of intersubjectivity – the experience of other people. Each approaches the topic from a different angle; so it provides a helpful illustration of how the diverse types of phenomenology can supplement each other. Husserl, for example, clarifies the process that makes experiencing others as conscious beings possible. Scheler explores the ways in which the experiences of other people are deeply interwoven with one's own experience. Heidegger shows that most actions are already oriented toward other people and that most people's attitudes embody commonly accepted views. Sartre explores the radical change other people produce when they become *subjects,* rather than mere objects, of our gaze (the standpoint from which most philosophers have considered the "problem of other minds"). I will examine each of these positions in turn.

Husserl's descriptions are always given within the transcendental reduction, which means he never studies the actual existence of the objects he describes, but rather how they are given in experience, what "sense" or meaning they have and how that meaning is constituted. In the *Cartesian Meditations* Husserl makes phenomenology into an all-embracing study of the ego – its states, processes, and constituted meanings.[35] This leads him to wonder whether his position becomes a transcendental solipsism, which would eliminate the *possibility* of experiencing anything as another conscious being (because it would prevent the possibility of constituting the sense "other conscious being"). Since people indeed do have such experiences (and thus operate with such meanings), Husserl fears that this could become a fatal objection to his phenomenology if not answered successfully.

This meaning ("other conscious being") is important not only because it introduces an entirely new type of object, but also because it is presupposed in ordinary experience. For example, nothing could be grasped as existing independently if it could not be experienced as accessible to others at the same time.[36] In short, people could not experience the world as objective if they did not have the sense "other conscious being" available. Part of the meaning of "objective" is "capable of being experienced by others as well as oneself." Husserl believes that senses operate in layers, some of which are more basic than others. Thus, the sense "intersubjectively accessible object" requires an already constituted sense "other conscious being." In turn, the sense "other conscious being" is dependent on more basic senses already constituted in one's ongoing conscious life. His picture is that humans develop a variety of senses/meanings concerning consciousness as they live, and then they extend these senses to other people. Explaining this process clarifies the constitution of the sense "other conscious being." This is Husserl's approach to intersubjectivity.

In order to ensure that his analysis avoids an objection similar to the fallacy of begging the question (this fallacy would apply only if he were *arguing* for the *existence* of other persons), Husserl initiates a new reduction that is stricter than the standard transcendental reduction. He calls this new maneuver the "abstraction to the sphere of ownness (i.e., a sphere that presupposes nothing outside itself)." In effect, it neutralizes all higher-level senses that depend on the sense "other conscious being," such as "intersubjectively accessible object," "social group," "culture," etc.[37] Were he to use one of these higher-level senses in elucidating the constitution of the sense "other conscious being," he could be charged with utilizing a sense that depends on the one he is trying to clarify. Because of this, he abstracts from these higher-level senses to ensure that his description relies only on processes operating *within* the "sphere of ownness." But what is included in/excluded from this sphere? Husserl does not provide a basis for verifying his assertions about this, but he claims that the following elements remain after the abstraction: one's ongoing conscious states; the inherence of those states in a transcendental ego; the experience of senses independent of the sense "others" (which means all objects simply as they appear for oneself alone, including the other person's body); the senses related to the experience of one's own body – not as an independent, empirical object, but simply as a field of expression of one's own mental states.[38] Husserl here assumes that the entire transcendental sphere is *pre-social* – that it can be and is constituted solely by oneself. Thus, all social facts derive from this sphere of ownness.

Husserl must clarify two other basic capacities of consciousness – pairing and apperception – before he can produce his full analysis of the constitution of the sense "others". Pairing is the mutual interanimation of sense that occurs whenever one presentation is perceived as identical with another.[39] Thus, if a second tennis ball emerges from a can of three tennis balls that look exactly alike, then every property of the first will be transferred to the second. Pairing allows consciousness to learn from experience. If it did not occur, people would forever need to relearn everything anew because nothing discovered in previous experience would transfer to newly encountered objects. Husserl is ambiguous about the pairing process. Initially he says that full transfer of sense occurs only when one presentation is exactly similar to another. Later he says that there are degrees of pairing so that a certain amount of transferring can occur between roughly similar objects, but that the pairing process is halted when perceived dissimilarities arise. Moreover, pairing typically occurs when the objects paired are presented together and are experienced side by side. Memory elicits a different kind of pairing, but this case need not be examined here.

"Apperception" occurs most vividly when perceiving an object. If it is familiar – already experienced from a variety of viewpoints and distances – then whenever it is experienced from a perspective that conceals some of its features, these elements are typically *apperceived* or *appresented* simultaneously with the presented side.[40] Thus, apperception explains why people experience objects that have depth and continuity beyond what is given: the apperceived features are not directly presented but amplify the presented side of the object, like shadows amplify objects in sunlight. Husserl thus analyzes every "moment" of perception into a directly presented aspect and a series of appresented aspects, and, parallel to this, he suggests that every act of perception consists of a core of presentation and ancillary apperceptions that intend its appresented aspects. Thus, for example, if one knows that a particular person has tattoos all over her body, then even when one sees her clothed, the tattoos will be appresented simultaneously with the clothed body. Similarly, if one knows that a cube is colored mauve on the bottom even though its sides are black, then the mauve-colored bottom will be apperceived simultaneously with its black sides.

Husserl's analysis of how the sense "other conscious being" is constituted relies on these processes of pairing and apperception. The crucial factor is the similarity between the other person's perceived body and either one's own perceived body (grasped from one's own viewpoint) or one's own imagined body projected side by side with the other's perceived body. Initially, the presentation of the other's body is paired with a presentation of one's own body (however remote the similarity between the two bodies is, apparently). This pairing permits a transfer of sense from one's own body to the other person's body, which allows one to conceive the other's body infused with conscious states (like one's own), possessing its own ego (like one's own), and eventually constituting its own world.[41] In short, the other's body is apperceived with a consciousness like one's own because the similarity between the other's body and one's own allows a transfer of sense from oneself to the other. This transfer provides an apperception of the other person as conscious. For Husserl, the other's consciousness is never directly presented; only one's own consciousness can be "present in person." This is why the other person's consciousness is perceived in a different, more distant way than one's own: the other's consciousness is merely appresented while one's own is directly presented. If this were not true, people would be constantly confusing the sources of their conscious states (Scheler thinks people often make such confusions.).

Once another person is constituted as a conscious being, i.e., once one is able to perceive the other's body as at least *potentially* possessing mental states, then another step becomes possible. Husserl now tries to explain how people grasp others with the sense "really existing, independent consciousnesses." He is *not* showing that truly independent conscious beings exist (that would be to go beyond what can be shown within the transcendental reduction), but instead he shows how other bodies that are taken to be potentially conscious are seen as actually conscious. Here Husserl relies on a concept of *behavioral harmony*, which is presumably initially established on the basis of one's own case. Thus, if the other's body exhibits an appropriate degree of behavioral harmony over time, then one becomes capable of experiencing the other as an *actually existent* consciousness.[42] This allows one to transcend the sphere of ownness and to defeat the objection that Husserl's position commits him to transcendental solipsism.

Once other people are constituted as actual, then higher levels of sense-constitution (such as the intersubjective world) become possible. This does *not* happen by grasping the world as perceived by oneself and imagining another one perceived by others and then unifying them through a *synthetic operation*. Rather, just as the other person's body undergoes a modification of sense from "external object perceived merely by oneself" to "living body infused with consciousness," all worldly objects undergo a parallel modification from "object capable of being reperceived and reidentified by oneself" to "object capable of being grasped simultaneously and/or independently by others." Thus the world undergoes an enrichment of meaning analogous to that undergone by the other's body.[43] Others can then be constituted as having transcendental egos that constitute oneself in just the way one constitutes them. When this happens, Husserl believes that self and other undergo an experienced "equalization" and that both are grasped as constituting agents capable of *mutually* creating norms, symbols, and roles that establish a culture.[44] These descriptions and analyses provide only the barest outline of Husserl's theory of intersubjectivity. They are the dominant themes of *Cartesian Meditations*, but additional studies in *Ideas II* and *III* elaborate them.

Certainly, Husserl's analysis exhibits problems that are similar to objections raised to the traditional argument from analogy, which is sometimes used to attempt to "prove" the existence of other people. One problem is whether the other's body appears in a way that is sufficiently like the appearance of one's own body to be paired with it. (Within the sphere of ownness, one's own body is given as headless, backless, and neckless.) Another problem concerns whether the other's consciousness can be apperceived in the same way that unseen perspectives on objects can be apperceived because the other's conscious states can *never* be directly perceived (unlike the other perspectives on an object). Still another is whether the constituted other is really distinct from oneself, rather than a döppleganger – a projected duplicate of one's own experiences that cannot be experienced as genuinely independent at all. Finally, there are questions about the intelligibility of abstracting to the sphere of ownness and supposing that one's own conscious states could be coherently organized at all without others to explain and help produce that organization (through language, for example). These problems indicate the all-encompassing nature of the phenomenological reduction: it transforms the issue from being about the genuine existence of other people to being about how they merely appear. The entire discussion also shows how the constitution of the ego becomes a major theme of Husserl's later phenomenology.

Still, Husserl's analysis provides some insight into one way in which others might come to be perceived as persons. He proceeds carefully and explicates the tools needed for his analysis, which in themselves are fascinating (e.g., pairing, apperception). And some kind of interanimation of the sort he describes does develop when one strives to grasp the ongoing mental processes of another individual. One does not exactly formulate ongoing hypotheses that are either verified or revised. Instead, one projects one's sense of what the other person must be experiencing in the situation and allows his actual words and actions to revise this preliminary sketch. Husserl excavates the implicit conscious processes that operate in one form of intersubjectivity and clarifies the relations of these processes to other conscious operations. Having sketched Husserl's theory of intersubjectivity, I want now to explore some contrasting phenomenological approaches.

Scheler explicates the phenomenon of intersubjectivity quite differently. He wants to avoid assuming the primacy of the ego, and he begins with a thorough survey of the *possible* philosophical questions about other people. He highlights the ways others become manifest in their expressive behavior and the ways their mental states can penetrate one's own conscious life, often without one's explicit awareness.

Scheler formulates six questions.[45] What is the essential relation of the individual to the community? What is the justification for the claim to know the existence of other persons and/or the community generally (the traditional Cartesian, skeptical question)? What is the transcendental-logical origin of social consciousness generally (Husserl's question)? How does knowledge of others develop empirically in the lives of particular individuals (in normal and in pathological cases)? What are the metaphysical assumptions underlying the various positions concerning knowledge of other persons? What types of social relations have genuine value? Scheler distinguishes various elements within each of these questions and carefully differentiates them from one another. Only in this fashion can they be answered effectively.

He then challenges two central assumptions that guide most philosophical inquiry into other people: first, that one's own mental states are typically given more directly than others' states, and, second, that what is given most directly in grasping other people are their bodies.[46] Scheler notes that people experience a wide variety of conscious states, only a small subset of which really originates with themselves. For example, one argues for positions and accepts theories that one has assimilated from discussion with others. Similarly, one may pursue a long-term goal that was not really chosen, but rather was internalized from one's parents. Also, one may follow a particular course of action because it seems "required" or one's duty, but this frequently conceals implicit imperatives of other people. Finally, one may take certain emotions to be genuine self-expressions, but in fact one may have fallen prey to emotional infection just as the body can be invaded by physical infection. Other people (e.g., one's roommates or lovers) may be the source of one's depression, boredom, or anger, etc. – not in the sense that they cause one to respond this way, but in the sense that they are the true origin of the feeling that one unconsciously replicates. Thus, whether one considers beliefs, volitions, values, or emotions, experiences that might seem truly one's own (in the straightforward sense of originating with oneself) may in fact derive from others through psychic osmosis.[47] Moreover, one is frequently mistaken in one's attribution of such states. Quite commonly people introject states from others that they firmly believe are theirs, and they also project onto others states that are really their own reactions.

Drawing on these examples, Scheler concludes that people participate in a common stream of experience that is initially undifferentiated between themselves and others.[48] Only in the course of maturation do people become capable of differentiating states that are truly self-originated from those which originate in other people (and even adults regularly make errors about this). In effect, the primordial condition of consciousness is its permeability – its openness to others' experiences. Everything others feel, seek, and think is transmitted throughout one's psyche, and vice versa. To know one's own specific feelings, apart from the background noise of others' experiences, is a difficult adult achievement, at which some people never succeed. Scheler cites the examples of children and some primitive cultures to defend this point. They live within the stream of experience belonging to their families and clans, which itself is an eddy in the river of experience belonging to their culture. Though some theorists might argue that these "shared" experiences are simply reproduced between one person and others, Scheler suggests that an accurate elucidation of them demands a different analysis, which he captures with the "common stream" metaphor.

On the question of what is most primordially given in experiencing other people, Scheler suggests that people's actual mental states shine forth in their expressions, rather than simply being indicated by them.[49] Scheler thinks the particular joy another person feels is expressed directly in her specific smile, the particular sadness in his grimace. A witness experiences others' mental states themselves, not just behavioral effects indirectly related to them. An abstraction from actual experience is necessary to see others' expressions as *mere behavior* that might or might not correlate with "inner" states. Only if others' expressions are contradictory in some way does such abstraction become necessary. Thus, Scheler thinks others' expressions are unified wholes that include what is traditionally called both "inner" and "outer" manifestations of the state.[50] There may be cases when one must rely on *inference* to understand another's experience, but this happens only when her expressions are ambiguous or mysterious. Then one must await further experience with the person to clarify the situation, but even in such cases one relies on her future expressions to disambiguate one's present perception. Scheler thinks such direct insight into others' states is especially common with emotional states; cases in which inference is necessary typically concern their bodily states, e.g., bodily pain, headache, or hunger. Rarely does one need to compare the other's expressions with one's own in order to intuit their emotions. One simply perceives them directly, unless one is preoccupied or otherwise insensitive to their expressions.

Some will object that witnesses can often be mistaken about the states of others, but this is also true about knowledge of one's own states. Indeed, the depth and adequacy of one's access to one's own states is questionable because one is often mistaken both about their source and nature. This occurs when one lacks access to the expressive component of one's emotional state (e.g., one's own facial expressions or posture), and this means others can sometimes grasp one's states more adequately than oneself. Just as others may have motives to misapprehend the full complexity of one's state of mind, these same motives can color one's own reflexive self-awareness. One can be simple-minded, shortsighted, inarticulate, self-deceived, or simply biased in one's self-perception; these same conditions can affect one's perception of others. If anything, Scheler thinks others' emotional states are more difficult to misperceive than one's own states. By challenging the classical Cartesian positions on self-knowledge and knowledge of others, Scheler sketches the outlines of his own position. Though it needs further refinement and defense, his theory shows how astute phenomenological observations can transform deeply rooted theoretical presuppositions.

Heidegger's phenomenology seeks to let phenomena reveal themselves as they are. This means, in part, that he strives to find the right framework to illuminate the phenomenal field. He elucidates both the way humans exist and the ways worldly things exist, and he discovers that humans are deeply interwoven with the world. He avoids severing person and world in the way the "subject-object" framework demands. For him, worldly items are given primarily as tools, not as inert "objects. Humans are purposive agents situated amidst networks of tools. This practical orientation is one of the "existentials" Heidegger discovers. Existentials are necessary conditions of being human that are also essential features for understanding the process of being itself. Heidegger's elucidation of intersubjectivity explores two additional existentials, which condition all social relations – "being-with (*mitsein*)" and "the impersonal mode of selfhood (*Das Man*)."

Heidegger first notes that, contrary to the belief of many philosophers, other people are grasped as fundamentally like oneself, *not* as alien. They engage in similar tasks, use similar tools, and pursue similar goals. One encounters them while shopping, driving, working, and playing. Humans share the same functionally articulated world, and this world facilitates interpersonal understanding.[51] In addition, nearly everything humans do is *oriented toward* others in some fashion; this is the core meaning of "being with" others. Either one's product is destined for others' use (e.g., writing a book), or the tools and materials used were made by others (the computer, printer, pens, and paper), or one's interpretation of the task derives from others (the book contributes to an ongoing discussion of a certain tradition of philosophy). All actions are oriented toward others in one or all of these ways, even if one works alone in an isolated cabin.[52] Thus, the fact of being alone does not negate the truth that people are with others in Heidegger's sense, and if one is lonely, one is very much with them (oriented to them) in this sense. Human tasks gain direction in relation to other humans, and this fact constitutes an essential relation to others. Naturally, antagonism or envy toward others are also ways of being oriented toward them; so is indifference.

Heidegger's second existential is the *impersonal mode of selfhood*. Being with other people typically produces to a standard way of doing things: a characteristic handling of a tool, a typical formulation of an issue, a normal pattern of organizing the day, a standard response to specific situations. In each of these cases, people typically seek what everyone seeks, they choose what everyone chooses, they think what everyone thinks, and they feel as everyone feels. This is the impersonal mode of existing: each person lives as everyone else lives.[53] Since acting, thinking, feeling, and choosing are defining features of human life, to replicate others' responses is to have no distinctive selfhood of one's own, to be merely an exemplification of typical collective responses. Usually people do not realize they live impersonally. The second half of Heidegger's *Being and Time* shows how to achieve a different, more personal and individuated way of life that he calls "authentic" selfhood. His basic point is that this *personal* selfhood is an *achievement* – that it always transforms the more basic, impersonal mode of living and is always threatened by it. The average, everyday way of living is impersonal and thus not merely oriented toward others but also highly normalized: one speaks in the voice of others; one responds to current events as everyone responds; one values just what others value. Because people often live impersonally, Heidegger argues that achieving genuine selfhood is more difficult than philosophers like Husserl – who make the self their starting point – assume.

Beyond this, the quality of one's self-knowledge and of one's understanding of human existence and ultimately of being itself depends on one's mode of selfhood. Those who live personally or authentically can thus gain sharper comprehension of things themselves; those who live impersonally possess a weaker grasp of truth, largely because they rely on traditional frameworks and formulations and because they fail to approach their experience with open, attentive eyes.[54]

Taken together, Heidegger's and Scheler's insights show that other people are more deeply embedded in human existence than philosophers typically acknowledge. Indeed, the lives most people lead are simply expressions of some normalized way of living. Other people thus quite literally constitute one's experiences and responses. But everyone believes they live distinctive lives, make unique choices, follow their own paths. Heidegger suggests these beliefs provide a cover story for the real truth that socially constituted impersonal existence dominates everyday life. Heidegger makes no effort to show how this mode of selfness develops and changes, but he reveals a new way in which other people penetrate, structure, and sometimes govern one's existence. Sartre discovers yet a third way through which other people literally create a dimension of oneself.

Sartre also accepts the importance of practical orientations in human life, but he retains Husserl's framework of the directedness of consciousness. However, he strives to describe experience as lived, without engaging in the transcendental reduction. Like Heidegger he illuminates several unseen and theoretically important features of human existence. He criticizes classical philosophical investigations of intersubjectivity for using inadequate perspectives and assuming a dubious metaphysics.[55] Most philosophers have sought to *justify* claims that other people exist and have particular conscious states. To do this, they invariably *objectify* others because knowing something typically involves objectifying it. This is especially egregious in the case of other people because they can also be *subjects,* and when they are objectified, their subjectivity is concealed. Moreover, Sartre suggests that most philosophers approach the question of other people from a third-person viewpoint and assume a metaphysics of external relations. An "external" relation is one that does not essentially alter the terms of the relation (an "internal" relation does do this). Careful thought about the self-other relation reveals that other people essentially alter one's own existence when they become subjects. This means they are internally related to oneself. One readily grasps their power when philosophizing from the first-person, phenomenological viewpoint.

Sartre develops these claims by analyzing a crucial example. He examines the difference between seeing another as an object (say, walking across the street) and being seen by the other-as-subject (say, being caught looking through a keyhole). When one looks *at* others, one objectifies them. They do not threaten one's own projects; one may adapt to them, but one adapts to resistant obstacles in the world in the same fashion. When objectifying others, one often stereotypes them. But when one is objectified by another (when another person uses or scrutinizes one), then everything changes. One often abandons one's own project, experiencing *oneself* as an object *for* the other person.[56] That person imprints a definition on one that circumscribes one's options and creates a social identity. Sartre calls this objectified self one's "being for others"; I call it one's "social self." It is a real dimension of one's own existence, but others create it. It would not exist if they did not create it because only other people have the power to shatter one's projects. Others create an exterior, public identity that often remains mysterious to oneself. This social dimension is ultimately beyond one's control; one may attempt to influence its content, but success is never assured. Sartre thinks that others create this dimension simply by existing; they need not consciously objectify one. If their projects intersect with one's own, then inevitably they create one's social self because their reactions and judgments produce that definition. Thus, when Sartre clarifies the power of the other-as-subject, he shows that persons are internally related – that everyone's lives are essentially transformed because of their encounters with others.

This means that people have two dimensions – corresponding to a first-person viewpoint and a third-person viewpoint (a self for-oneself and a self for-others), and both are equally real. In the first-person viewpoint, one's life is always potentially in flux, open-ended, and subject to reinterpretation; in the third-person viewpoint, one's life seems fixed, predictable, and defined. Each viewpoint suppresses, but fails to eliminate, the other one; hovering in the background, it can re-emerge at any time. Typically, one viewpoint dominates in specific situations.[57] Indeed, Sartre thinks social life consists of struggles to control the social self imposed by others, and this requires seduction or domination. These struggles cannot succeed, however, because the other-as-subject is beyond one's control.[58] People can dominate (or seduce) others temporarily, but often the effort to control them motivates their escape (because it becomes transparent, and they rebel). People can also view themselves from the other's third-person viewpoint (reflection). Indeed, humanity's capacity for reflection derives from this radical transformation produced by others. Thus, one's ability to reflect on, objectify, and know oneself derives from others.

Sometimes people attempt to reject one of these viewpoints entirely, a strategy Sartre believes is self-deceptive, despite the intense conflicts between the viewpoints. The two visions of oneself can never be fully harmonized either. Some people attempt to become the selves other people define them to be, but they can never completely disappear into these masks. Others try to resist others' definitions entirely and live their own vision of themselves, but nothing ensures that others will accept this strategy. Moreover, in interpersonal encounters, at least in the typical inauthentic mode of living adopted by most people, Sartre believes a constant struggle to gain dominance ensues. In later works, Sartre explicates an interpersonal reciprocity that allows people to achieve mutual recognition and joint enhancement of authenticity.

For Sartre, knowing oneself or others presupposes the third-person viewpoint because knowing involves objectification. Truly comprehending others involves identifying their fundamental projects and showing how they inform their everyday lives. Even though this involves seeing people as goal-directed and self-defining, it remains within the third-person viewpoint.[59] If people seek to comprehend themselves, they must follow the same procedure and adopt the same standpoint. Someone might object, however, that different hypothetical fundamental projects could explain the diversity of someone's everyday projects equally well. Sartre answers this by suggesting that people have a "certainty" about their own fundamental project – an ancillary, inarticulate intuition of their basic choices. They do not typically explicate this intuitive sense, but they can use it to verify proposed hypotheses. So a Sartrean existential psychoanalyst will typically seek confirmation from the analysand before adopting hypotheses about him. This stance differs sharply from Freud's.

Sartre modified and supplemented his position in his later treatise, *Critique of Dialectical Reason* (1960). His approach there remains phenomenological but concentrates on group actions and group relations. In this early period, he shows that common ways of conceiving persons and personal relations must be rethought by providing incisive phenomenological descriptions of lived experience. Scheler establishes that experience is irradiated by other people's conscious states. Heidegger shows that other people suffuse one's practical life. Sartre demonstrates that others create a new dimension of oneself, for which one bears responsibility. Phenomenological description thus demonstrates that other people deeply penetrate all dimensions of consciousness. Self and other co-constitute each other in ways barely recognized by previous philosophers.

Perception (Merleau-Ponty)

Merleau-Ponty's main contribution is to illuminate lived perception. He thinks past philosophers have posited non-existent entities and processes in order to explain an artificially constructed sensory field. He rejects the existence of isolated, atomic sensations and the demand to postulate elaborate cognitive operations that unify such data. Such sensations and cognitive processes simply do not exist in lived perception. Since Merleau-Ponty also believes that all forms of reason and "logic" develop on the basis of the coherence of the perceived world, to misunderstand perception is to misconstrue the order from which rationality emerges.[60] He provides a careful description/analysis of perceptual experience.

In addition to the phenomenological description of lived experience, Merleau-Ponty draws on experimental research from psychology, psychopathology (neural disorders that can help clarify operations of the lived body), and child development. He also examines impressionism and other modernist art movements to illuminate the nascent structures of perception which they make explicit. These strategies are necessary to clarify perceptual processes because they dissolve as they complete themselves; phenomenological description articulates these processes as they occur. Like Husserl, Merleau-Ponty believes perceivers typically lose themselves in the perceptual process; phenomenology is necessary to help them recover the contribution of their lived bodies. Like Heidegger, Merleau-Ponty believes that perception is practical and interlaces person and world. Antecedent structures of the world are internalized through perception, and it gives the world its style and perspective. Merleau-Ponty differs from Heidegger in stressing the body-subject in everyday life – the set of habits that allow the body to accurately explore and grasp the perceived world.

Merleau-Ponty discovers that the perceived world already exhibits nascent structure. Humanity need not impose "form" on meaningless matter (data); instead, the perceptual field already contains implicit form/order. Meaning/order/structure already exists in the perceived; it guides the perceiver's efforts. These antecedent structures are systemic relations such that if one term is altered all the other terms change accordingly. The perceptual field consists of spontaneously organized wholes (totalities), which are incorporated in larger wholes and may contain subordinate wholes. The gestalt psychologists discovered one such structure: the figure/ground relationship. The ground always introduces an element of ambiguity into the figure, an ambiguity that calls for clarification by the lived body.[61] Moreover, perception does not operate primarily through the intake of peripheral excitations from the nervous system; rather, the lived body is typically already reaching toward the perceived as perception begins. These bodily movements interrogate the nascent structures of the perceived world in order to articulate them; indeed the perceptual world is continually illuminated as individuals mature. Thus, the lived body reacts *to* perceptual wholes and reacts *as* an organic whole.[62] The habits of the lived body are gradually augmented by implicit perceptual structures, and the perceptual field is gradually sharpened by the lived body. Through perception, person and world co-constitute each other.

The lived body itself is a complex network of habituated processes that develop in direct dialogue with perceived structures. They gradually become taken-for-granted, but they make possible a creative and personal response to the world. The impersonal structures operate in the process of perception and are augmented as they encounter the unique features of situations. This is when perception becomes creative and artistic. These creative patterns of response eventually become taken-for-granted habits, which are augmented again when the person confronts another unique situation.[63] For Merleau-Ponty, the lived body is the core of the person, yet always dependent on culture. It is a distinctive system of styles of revelation and elaboration that are transmitted by inaugurating new infants into the structures already grasped by the culture. Individuals in turn can then supplement those culturally transmitted structures and thereby enhance the culture's inheritance.

Merleau-Ponty offers some unusual analyses of qualities and things. He concludes that qualities are never simply visual, aural, or tactile; they integrate features from all the senses. Moreover, qualities can never be isolated from their context; the structures of the perceptual field condition every seemingly independent quality it contains. The qualities of an object can seem constant despite changes in the field because such changes are compensated by other ones.[64] Merleau-Ponty also notes that things are never entirely present and given. Instead they consist of visible features and invisible ones that are not simply imagined or projected, but are gradually revealed with greater experience of each type of thing. These are practical, temporal syntheses. Here Merleau-Ponty utilizes Husserl's notion of "horizon." A thing is analyzed as a complex temporal organization of profiles that are connected by a distinctive perceptual "logic" that produces time's flow. Every profile reveals the object as such, but none ever completely exhausts it. Perception is the process of living within this simultaneous presence and absence of the perceived, each sustaining the other.[65]

The lived body opens the organism to the perceived world. This "faith" in the reality of the world is deeper than, and supplies the foundation for, all other types of certainty. This faith acknowledges that the perceived world imposes structures on everyone and that this perceptual universality is different from common inferences to the same conclusion. Merleau-Ponty claims that few are confused by perceptual hallucinations and that global skepticism is rarely taken seriously. Skepticism engenders theoretical curiosity, but it does not and cannot dislodge this perceptual faith. To the extent that perceptual errors and illusions occur, only further perception can clarify the error, recognize how it arose, and situate it in more complex structures.[66] In the same way, reason and logic themselves are constantly in the process of self-correction (Euclidean geometry was corrected by more complex geometries; Newtonian physics was expanded by Einsteinian physics). Merleau-Ponty concludes that absolute certainty in the sense of self-evident, self-presence is impossible; there can be only a gradually improving grasp of the only world there is: the perceived world. Both philosophy and science attempt to elaborate this world.

The experience of objectivity develops through realizing that others perceive the same world. Their lived bodies are tutored in the same way, and they are guided by the same perceptual structures. These antecedent structures, however, are ambiguous. They must be completed by the lived body, and they allow for completion in different ways. Thus, different people can have different styles of perception, which then lead to different styles of expression (verbal and gestural). Just as cognitivism is wrong about the basic operations of perception, so too is it misguided about the basic processes of expression. People rarely know their thoughts explicitly prior to expressing them; they discover them in the course of speaking (or writing), and they constantly clarify them as they hear themselves speak (or write).[67] Similarly, to understand others is not to infer the intent that motivates their expressions, but to discover the pattern in the expressions that summarizes their intent. Each action further defines the project being pursued, both for oneself and for others.[68] Ethics requires acknowledging both the differences and the similarities among people. It accepts that the end of the action can never be separate from its means and the real consequences of an act reflect back on its moral value.[69] In effect, to act responsibly is to constantly steer, track, and readjust the action so that it actually achieves the best results possible.

PHENOMENOLOGY AND SOCIAL SCIENCE

Different phenomenologists adopt different attitudes toward social science. These attitudes depend partly on whether they expect to provide foundations for social science and partly on their familiarity with social scientific research. None simply accepts the truth of social science's hypotheses, but some take its results more seriously than others. Some treat social science dismissively because it cannot produce certainties (Husserl) or because they regard it as derivative and dependent on philosophy (Heidegger). Others treat social science with genuine respect, and even use its results to justify and elaborate their own positions (Merleau-Ponty). One key issue in this discussion concerns the relationship between empirical truths and conceptual or logical truths and whether there is any valid distinction between them. Another is whether the results of the first-person, phenomenological viewpoint and the third-person, objectifying viewpoint can be integrated.

Because social science operates within the natural attitude and at best establishes causal connections, rather than logical or conceptual relations, Husserl believes that phenomenology is better able to ground social science. It elucidates the concepts on which the social sciences depend; it vindicates their inference rules. It examines their presuppositions. Husserl is adamant that social scientists will contribute little to phenomenological research because they fail to adopt the transcendental reduction. Heidegger adopts a similar stance because he thinks phenomenology and fundamental ontology are more basic than science. They provide the core insights that generate new spheres of social inquiry. In addition to opposing traditional philosophy, Heidegger criticizes the common-sense assumptions accepted by many social theorists. Finally, Heidegger insists that humans can be adequately understood only if they are approached in a certain way. If science tries to objectify them – if it ignores the fact that they transcend given situations and are shaped by well-defined cultural backgrounds – it will produce misleading results. Both Husserl and Heidegger overlook social researchers' potential for creative insight into the phenomena. Sometimes, creative empirical research uncovers new concepts and social realities, and these innovations may contribute to the foundations of phenomenology.

Scheler and Merleau-Ponty adopt a different orientation. Both studied social scientific literature carefully, and Merleau-Ponty taught child psychology for many years. Because of their greater intimacy with actual social scientific work, they realized that social research is simultaneously conceptual and empirical and that creative thought is often stimulated by the questions posed by experimental data. Moreover, they both acknowledge that experiments can be philosophically innovative – opening new questions and discovering new phenomena. In these ways social scientists may contribute to phenomenology. Merleau-Ponty actually uses many results of the gestalt psychologists (which emerged in Germany in the 1930s and '40s – Kurt Lewin, Wolfgang Köhler, Kurt Koffka), showing that their work demonstrates the inadequacy of important classical philosophical positions and provides support for his distinctive analysis of perception.[70] Scheler distinguishes the attitude of phenomenology, which seeks to clarify essences themselves for their own sake, from that of social science, which seeks to control its objects of inquiry. He believes phenomenology can contribute to social research by challenging its commonly accepted metaphysical assumptions, but he also acknowledges that scientists can discover arresting facts that demand philosophical elaboration. Scheler also uses well-established social scientific results in his critique of philosophical stances, drawing extensively on sociology, anthropology, psychology, economics, and psychoanalysis. Scheler also emphasizes the powerful role of values in social life, claiming that social scientists often misconstrue their guiding role. Both Scheler and Merleau-Ponty are sharply critical of many social scientific hypotheses, but they realize that social theorists can contribute to philosophical debates.

Merleau-Ponty and Sartre both explore how the first-person (phenomenological) viewpoint and the third-person (objectifying, scientific) viewpoint can be integrated. Sartre tries to integrate given conditions with people's response to these conditions, which transforms (or sustains) them. Also he argues that most given conditions are created by previous generations (e.g., level of technology, class structure, operative norms and ideals). The creative transformation of these conditions is then deeded to future generations. Merleau-Ponty, on the other hand, respects existing social scientific research, while also urging scientists to remember their own role as acting subjects in creating scientific theories. He expects phenomenologists to acknowledge scientific insights, while subjecting them to intense critical scrutiny. Thus, for Merleau-Ponty, the empirical and the conceptual are deeply interwoven: new concepts stimulate new experiments, and new discoveries transform existing concepts. This implies that phenomenologists must make more serious efforts to understand the developing research in the sciences and to explore issues with their leading practitioners. Because of this orientation, Merleau-Ponty was better equipped to incorporate new developments in structuralism than Sartre was.

OTHER APPLICATIONS

In addition to the areas of intersubjectivity and perception, phenomenology has produced many additional applications in literary theory, aesthetics, social theory, and value theory.

Roman Ingarden (1893–1970) is perhaps phenomenology's most distinguished contributor to literary theory. He elucidates the nature of the literary text itself, conceiving it as a series of multidimensional layers, each of which demands a special kind of sensitivity: sounds and graphic shapes, the meanings of the words and sentences, the presentation of scenes (though various kinds of narration and description), and the total imaginative world the text evokes. These levels constitute ontological dimensions of the literary work.[71] Ingarden explores how the levels interact in the experience of reading. This study allows him to provide a detailed understanding of the ways the literary object is known and synthesized. Recently, an entire branch of literary theory has emerged to develop Ingarden's insights – reader-response criticism (e.g., Wolfgang Iser). Here the reader's experience of hypothesis formulation and testing is examined critically. Ingarden shows that simply *understanding* a literary work is a complex task.

Beyond reading and comprehension is the process of interpretation. Hermeneutics offers a complex analysis of this process. But its approach is intellectualist in that little attention is given to the emotional, perceptual, and volitional effects of literary works and their implications for interpretation. Even if the hermeneutic circle is a suggestive guide, fuller examination of the analytical and integrative processes used by interpreters is needed. Some attention to the differences in interpreting different genres (e.g., poetry, prose, drama, and film) could also be useful. A close phenomenological scrutiny of the interpretive process should deepen hermeneutic thought.

Finally, in *What is Literature?* (1947), Sartre shows that an examination of the writing process can also yield fruitful results. The style of the literary work can be related to the author's fundamental project. Thus an existential psychoanalytic grasp of an author can contribute to understanding specific literary choices. The kinds of appeal the work makes to the reader may also be explored. Sartre claims that imaginative literature appeals to the freedom of the reader to reconstitute the literary object, which can produce genuine reciprocity between authors and readers. Sartre takes some promising first steps, but phenomenology could contribute more to the analysis of the writing process.

In aesthetics, the primary contributors are Merleau-Ponty and Mikel Dufrenne (1910–95). Merleau-Ponty explores artistic styles in order to gain clues to various all-encompassing styles of life. In addition, he is fascinated by painting's ability to illuminate the actual structures of perception by concentrating attention on one sector, mode, or dimension of the perceptual process.[72] Dufrenne examines the creative processes of both artists and audiences for many different arts.[73]

In social theory, Sartre offers a new ontology of groups and their relationships to individuals in his *Critique of Dialectical Reason* (1960). He not only provides a typology of groups but also discusses the dynamics under which they undergo change. In addition, phenomenology might explore the dynamics of face-to-face relationships. The psychotherapist R. D. Laing (1927–89) and sociologist Erving Goffman (1922–82) illustrated how to do this in several books, especially, respectively, *Knots* (1970) and *Interaction Ritual* (1967).[74] Finally, in his interpretive sociology, Alfred Schutz (1899–1959) challenges many claims made by Sartre and Heidegger. Schutz is especially interested in the role of stereotypes and historicity in organizing social experience. Still another thinker who makes important contributions to understanding face-to-face personal relationships is Martin Buber (1878–1965). He develops the well-known distinction between I–It and I–Thou relationships.[75] There is an interesting phenomenological exploration of psychopathology as well, Eugene Minkowski's *Lived Time* (1933).[76] In that work he shows that breakdowns in the way people experience time are central features in nearly all psychoses.

Scheler defends a realist theory of value that roots their apprehension in human emotions. Emotions provide the means of access to various dimensions of an objective value hierarchy, which is gradually revealed over time and across cultures. Scheler explores the manner in which values inform action and the way in which they govern character.[77] In addition, Nicolai Hartmann's *Ethics*, vol. 2 (1926) also provides some insightful analyses of the classical virtues, together with a discussion of more recent virtues.[78] He defines and articulates the virtues predominant in the Greek, Christian, Modern, and Contemporary worlds.

COMPARISONS

Phenomenology underwrites no specific political goals, even if it does have an ethical thrust. Its fundamentally descriptive aim does not directly produce political consequences. It can explore the relations of persons to groups and groups to history, as Sartre and Merleau-Ponty did. Also, despite the importance of the notion of totalization in phenomenology, it offers no defense of a dialectical development within history itself (except a much looser version in Sartre and Merleau-Ponty), and this sharply differentiates phenomenology from both Hegel and Marx.

Unlike Nietzsche and Freud, phenomenology strongly emphasizes the operations of consciousness itself, including the implicit, pre-conscious structures that inform everyday life. The repressed unconscious or even the less submerged Nietzschean drives play no significant role in its investigations. Phenomenologists would consider them hypothetical constructs that distract from a full elucidation of the available phenomena. Indeed, Sartre contests the theoretical efficacy and justification of Freud's division of consciousness into two levels – conscious and unconscious. Both Husserl and Sartre treat consciousness as an almost *sui generis* dimension of human life, but Scheler, Heidegger, and Merleau-Ponty situate consciousness in a broader understanding of life and culture, a strategy common to Nietzsche and Freud. Phenomenology elaborates a more detailed, concrete analysis of specific types of conscious states, rather than the highly abstract models of consciousness offered by Nietzsche and Freud.

Although there is a type of phenomenology that can be called "hermeneutic," many phenomenologists would contest the standard hermeneutic position that all access to the world must be mediated or filtered by the background conditions of human understanding. The realist impulse that gradually emerges as phenomenology develops opposes the hermeneutic assertion that some form of interpretation intervenes in all conscious acts. Some phenomenologists think people can simply confront reality directly, without mediation or interpretation, and lucidly describe the results of this confrontation (e.g., Sartre, Husserl, and Scheler).

Existentialism derives from one subtype of phenomenology. Some phenomenologists, however, would not accept many key existentialist claims, even though Heidegger and Sartre are as central to that movement as they are to the development of phenomenology itself. Philosophical anthropology shares phenomenology's focus on lucid description of the defining structures of human life, but it seeks a more harmonious relationship with the sciences – especially biology and the social sciences. One way to understand the aspiration of philosophical anthropology is to see it as integrating the results of the first-person viewpoint so central to phenomenology with the third-person viewpoint so important in science.

ASSESSMENT

Phenomenology exhibits some specific weaknesses. The first-person approach used by phenomenologists should probably be supplemented by a third-person approach. Sartre begins to show how these two perspectives can be integrated in his methodological introduction to the *Critique of Dialectical Reason, Search for a Method*.[79] Merleau-Ponty addresses the issue, but his answer to how the two viewpoints can correct and enhance each other could be clearer. Phenomenologists have shown the value of the first-person approach; the task is to show how it can be integrated with the rest of scientific knowledge. Heidegger's and Sartre's dismissiveness toward science is unwarranted. Scheler and Merleau-Ponty are better models for developing a phenomenology that can work collaboratively with research scientists, much as current analytic philosophers are trying to work collaboratively with researchers in cognitive science and brain physiology. They are neither bullied by scientific theories nor dismissive in their criticism of them. They engage in constructive criticism of science on all levels, and then use important scientific results to refine philosophical investigation.

In addition, Husserl's transcendental phenomenology seems misguided. The bracketing or reduction procedure alters the lived experience to be described and leads to arbitrary postulates that are not confirmed in pre-reflective experience. Husserl's project aspires to an unrealistic degree of certainty that may be impossible to achieve; moreover, it assumes that an isolated, atomistic ego constitutes every possible object on its own. Although Husserl's project of providing absolute foundations for all other disciplines is tempting, it demonstrates *hubris*. Descriptive (non-transcendental) phenomenology makes solid contributions to many areas without these assumptions and invites collaborative work with researchers in other disciplines. Among non-transcendental phenomenologies, I prefer descriptive to hermeneutic approaches, primarily because the hermeneutic phenomenologists import a variety of dubious assumptions (e.g., the primacy of a conceptual background) into the analysis of lived experience. Scheler, Sartre, Merleau-Ponty, and Levinas all explicate distinctive dimensions of the phenomenal field. Heidegger certainly makes important contributions, but they can be recast into a descriptive framework that is less pretentious than his self-described quest for being.

Phenomenologists also expend too much effort showing that layer *x* is the most primordial or most foundational layer of experience. Primacy usually derives from the theoretical or practical purposes of the theorist; it is not an intrinsic feature of the phenomena. Perhaps questions of primordiality should not be abandoned entirely, but at least phenomenology should not define itself around them. Primordiality is essential to the project of building foundations for knowledge, a task abandoned by most post-Husserlian thinkers. In addition, this obsession with primordiality leads to indifference to other important structures and obliviousness to genuine complexities within the phenomenal field. Clarifying the entire realm of experience with penetrating acuity is a better goal. This stance may seem to make phenomenology a less rigorous approach to philosophy, but in fact it opens the path to richer and subtler contributions.

Finally, phenomenological insight – especially into the complexities and subtleties of experience – is often hampered by the metaphysical positions that guide the work of phenomenology's major theorists. Much about human experience is concealed by Husserl's belief in the self-presence of consciousness, by Heidegger's restriction to the ontological level of analysis, by Scheler's postulation of four levels of being, by Sartre's model of consciousness as nihilation, and even by Merleau-Ponty's desire to root his descriptions in the lived body. Perhaps such metaphysical hypotheses have guided each thinker toward important realizations, but the hypotheses themselves are less reliable than the realizations they make visible. Often their metaphysical pronouncements force phenomenologists to miss or ignore many key features of experience, and thus nearly every theorist's work needs revision and supplementation. A major task is to integrate the many insights of the key figures into a richer, more coherent vision of experience.

Heidegger and Sartre not only produced inventive phenomenological insights, they articulated a theory of human existence. That part of their theories became known as existentialism. To its central tenets I now turn.

EXISTENTIALISM AND PHILOSOPHICAL ANTHROPOLOGY

CORE CONTRIBUTIONS

Even if human nature is still a work in progress, the question concerning its distinctive features remains a viable and important one. One can explore this question cogently and carefully without presuppositions about the value and destiny of the human species. Despite the critique of essentialism in recent Continental philosophy, the question about human nature is still relevant as long as diverse cultures, sexes, and racial and ethnic groups are incorporated into the answer. The two movements examined in this chapter nicely complement one another in their approaches to this question. Philosophical anthropology uses the third-person perspective to examine the similarities and differences between humans and other animals, while existentialists use the first-person perspective to articulate the emotional and personal implications of being human as well as many of its universal structures. Each movement contributes a vital perspective on human life.

Both movements also seek to overcome the many dualisms that plague philosophical thinking about human nature, a goal to which Hegel made such important contributions. Such dualisms as mind/body, reason/passion, and self/other are at least reinterpreted in ways that allow significant reconciliation, and in some cases their opposition is virtually dissolved. Where Kierkegaard and Sartre and Scheler still see dichotomies, perhaps there is a distinction to be respected. Where Heidegger and the philosophical anthropologists build bridges across certain dualisms, perhaps a genuine synthesis is achievable. The two movements are united in seeing human existence as *eccentric*, as standing out from the surrounding world and transcending the given situation toward the future. Both also agree that human life is organized around practical action – though Scheler believes that the spiritual grasp of essences is humanity's distinguishing capacity and that humans act in and respond to the world differently from most animals. Sartre may have misunderstood the degree to which humanity's "world-openness" entails a complete transcendence of the given, but it certainly grounds an important type of freedom. When Heidegger, Merleau-Ponty, and Gehlen relocate the practical life of individuals in a context of ongoing habits and cultural traditions, they articulate defensible conceptions of freedom and responsibility.

In addition, the existentialists' vision of human existence as thrown and contingent – without antecedent meaning and purpose – seems plausible, especially after Nietzsche's caustic examination of religion's intellectual and ethical weaknesses. The philosophical anthropologists do not stress this feature, but their naturalism is compatible with it. Existentialists strive to strip away the metaphysical comforts and illusions that pacify human beings and thus to renew a sense of the adventure of existence – the sense that individuals can make a difference to the world around them. For their part, the philosophical anthropologists produce some innovative proposals for distinctively human capacities, including Scheler's analysis of the ascetic sublimation of vital drives, Plessner's exploration of laughing and crying, Goldstein's discussion of the abstract attitude, and Gehlen's stress on culture and language.

Both movements see humans as capable of transcendence, of distancing themselves from the present, and thus of shaping the world that in turn shapes them. Sartre's existential psychoanalysis seeks a new kind of comprehension that can account for this essential feature of action. He develops the notion of "understanding" already present in Dilthey. The more monistic-minded theorists in both of these movements also clarify important qualities of human action – its moods, its world, its holism, and its temporal structure. Both movements show that theory can provide insight into the lives of individuals by reflecting on the general nature of human life and the human condition. The abstractions they develop never lose touch with the concrete experiences they seek to illuminate.

Finally, both movements elaborate the sense of crisis concerning modernity first addressed by Hegel's system and developed and differently answered by Nietzsche. The existentialists believe that human beings are threatened with the loss of individuality and self-understanding and that this results in a misconception of the world and their relationship to it. The philosophical anthropologists identify an upsurge of Dionysian forces in human sensibility and attempt to develop the necessary theoretical tools to sublimate and redirect these forces. The existentialists develop a new ideal, authenticity, with which to combat this crisis, while the philosophical anthropologists create a vision of a total or holistic person and explore ways to fortify cultural structures that will enhance human development rather than undermine it.

EXISTENTIALISM

The two central figures of existential philosophy are Heidegger and Sartre. Karl Jaspers (1883–1969) is also important, but he is less frequently read today. Kierkegaard is often viewed as the movement's founder. I will begin by sketching some of the core tenets of existentialism; then I will explore some dominant themes in Kierkegaard. Finally, I will provide extensive expositions of early Heidegger and Sartre. My discussion of Sartre will concentrate on areas where he criticizes or supersedes Heidegger's insights. Heidegger's views changed significantly by 1945 when Sartre reached the height of his fame. Sartre's position also evolved toward a synthesis of existentialism and Marxism by 1960.

The similarities between Heidegger and Sartre illustrate existentialism's core tenets. Both thinkers contest the adequacy of Husserl's reflective viewpoint to describe everyday existence. They both think that access to a pre-reflective level of experience is possible, and both seek to articulate its main features.[1] In this way both create an existential phenomenology that is less concerned with certainty, methodological purity, and philosophical foundations, and more concerned with descriptive incisiveness, overturning traditional assumptions, and "living truth."

Both take human existence to be essentially temporal – persons always transcend the present toward the future and thereby organize the present via future goals.[2] Both think this process occurs in relation to a past that can be renewed or transformed. Sartre believes persons' past projects continue only if they are regularly renewed. People thus always escape the past and become capable of redefining themselves anew in the future. Heidegger insists that individuals are rooted in cultural traditions and thus that their projects are guided by past models or heroes.[3] Past traditions also organize the ways in which people interpret themselves and their basic possibilities. For early Sartre, the past is largely inert; it may limit human options, but it cannot determine behavior.

Both thinkers regard human life to be essentially practical – pursuing goals by utilizing whatever tools are available.[4] Both think humans live amidst practically structured worlds that reflect possible human purposes. Both take theory to be a form of practice and overcome the traditional dichotomy between them in that fashion. Unlike Sartre, however, Heidegger regards merely being present to things to be a degenerate practical orientation, and thus he regards the sheer being-there of things to embody an instrumental relation.[5] Because there are no mere objects, Heidegger overcomes the traditional subject/object dichotomy in this way. Sartre distinguishes the independent, raw being of inert matter from the tools that emerge out of it when consciousness brings purposes to the universe.[6] He thus retains a dualism between consciousness and matter. Ultimately, he may regard them as modifications of something more encompassing (being itself), but in practice the functional orientation of human beings restructures antecedently given, independent inert stuff. Both thinkers agree that this practical orientation to the world presupposes an implicit orientation to values, which therefore cannot be isolated from facts.

Both thinkers take the average, everyday human condition to be mystified. It can be revitalized only by apprehending a more primordial experience, which will allow people to recover an authentic relationship to themselves, the world, and other people. For Heidegger, this transformation is motivated by a different relation to death, which requires that the process of living be taken more seriously.[7] For Sartre, the experienced possibility of death cannot motivate this change. Rather, people must recover a living sense of their basic freedom, a freedom that always exists but often remains concealed through self-deception.[8] Both thinkers believe anxiety can be revelatory, and both think a more vivid sense of freedom emerges from understanding it.[9] For Heidegger, everyday mystification results from too great an involvement in immediate tasks that conceal more important goals. For Sartre, it derives from a belief that commonly accepted values are absolute, and thus that personal choices are dictated by them.

Finally, both stress the ultimate contingency of human existence – the fact that people are thrown into life without antecedent purpose or reason.[10] Both thus believe that people must give themselves goals and meaning, and the more fully they realize this, the more authentic they become. For Sartre, this contingency is a cause for celebration because it means people are free to create the best lives they can, but this freedom sharply increases the burden of their responsibilities.[11]

KIERKEGAARD

Søren Kierkegaard (1813–55) rebels against Hegel's systematic approach to philosophy – attacking him on a wide variety of fronts. First, he rejects Hegel's theoretical and systematic goals. Instead, he thinks philosophy should be concerned with ethical practice; it should speak directly to individual people and awaken them from their passive, slumbering lives. Although Hegel is mindful of existential concerns, his primary aim is to create a complete system that informs all spheres of reality and produces existential harmony. Kierkegaard is less interested in knowledge and system because he thinks these aspirations distract attention from the important task – to transform people's existence.[12] Hegel's reply is that *both* aims are important, and his goal is to show how both theoretical and practical goals can be realized in a unified system. Kierkegaard simply dismisses theoretical goals, as if they are irrelevant to philosophy. He offers his conceptual studies and psychological analyses primarily to serve his larger purpose of facilitating personal authenticity. While both Heidegger and Sartre accept Kierkegaard's aim, they also retain Hegel's theoretical and systematic aspirations.

Second, Hegel developed universal concepts, but Kierkegaard believes that such concepts cannot comprehend specific individuals and particular situations. Even though Hegel elucidated the concrete universals that inform particular eras, Kierkegaard insists each person lives the spirit of the age differently, and the task is to explore these diverse responses and their implications for individual lives. Hegel might justly retort that he examines a variety of styles of life in the *Phenomenology*. But Kierkegaard would reply that Hegel examines only idealized types and raises problems for these types that are limited to their role in his developmental scheme. To really explore those forms of life requires a more detailed examination of specific cases, unadulterated by the demands of the grand system. Kierkegaard's own discussion of the aesthetic, ethical, and religious lives uncovers a multitude of intrinsic problems and examines various efforts to avoid them.[13] Hegel, of course, does this too, but Kierkegaard would insist that Hegel's efforts remain sketchy and abstract, unconnected with the personal dimensions of these forms of life. Hegel might reply that the only possible way to study forms of life is to examine abstract types, insisting that Kierkegaard's portrayals are no less abstract, even if they are sometimes more detailed. Hegel might add that Kierkegaard's evaluations of his types are based on external criteria, rather than internal ones.[14]

Third, Kierkegaard claims that Hegel writes from an absolute viewpoint that forces readers to adopt his conclusions, rather than to discover their own positions by choosing among the alternatives examined. Kierkegaard thinks he sympathetically enters into the specifics of each form of life, indicating its problems, and then allows readers to draw their own conclusions. Indeed, he wrote under many different pseudonyms (concealing his actual identity) to encourage readers to arrive at their own judgments. Hegel's response would be that he (Hegel) articulates the standpoints of both the individual experiencing each form of life and the final result; in this way he depicts the existential crises of each form without becoming lost in details. This also allows him to provide commentary on the transitions between forms of life.[15] But Kierkegaard would answer that Hegel's studies involve too much retrospection – thus failing to give each stage its due. In addition, Kierkegaard believes that Hegel's absolute standpoint forces him to justify and legitimate his era's institutions, because he had to interpret them as the culmination of world history. Although Hegel may have been much more critical of his age than Kierkegaard suggests, many of Hegel's conservative students drew similar conclusions. So his actual position on this issue is at least arguable. Kierkegaard believes his age is deeply flawed, inviting people to live in smug self-satisfaction while they frittered away their lives in dalliances. He thinks philosophy should identify these tendencies and suggest alternative ways to live. Hegel explicitly resists formulating utopian alternatives, but he does see serious problems in his age as well.[16]

A related objection is that the dialectic within Hegel's system is too impersonal – pretending to discover a necessity that it cannot justify. Hegel implies that everyone will follow a certain developmental path based on the structure of the abstract types he describes, when in fact different people will resolve the issues within the various forms of life differently and may not emerge from these stages in the way Hegel expects. Some may continuously struggle within a form without ever superseding it. Kierkegaard rejects the claim that crises within each form are so determinate that they require specific resolutions which lead in inescapable directions. In effect, he rejects Hegel's concept of determinate negation. Hegel acknowledges that only people who take the standard of each form of life seriously will undergo the transitions he describes, but he also insists that the dialectical structure he uncovers is real.[17] He claims that the tensions within each form of life *are* resolved in specific directions, and he would suggest that this claim can be defended for each form of life (thus, blanket rejections will be ineffective). Individuals may come to the resolution of a stage at different rates, but he suggests that there are internal dynamics within forms of life that drive people toward specific resolutions.

Further, Kierkegaard thinks that Hegel's dialectic assumes that all oppositions can be rationally resolved through some higher standpoint – in a form of life that retains the strengths of the previous forms but resolves their problems.[18] Kierkegaard doubts that this is possible. He sees inevitable paradoxes and contradictions between different forms of life, and insists that ultimately unjustifiable ethical choices must be made between them.[19] This is perhaps their most fundamental disagreement, and again Hegel would insist that the allegedly irresolvable oppositions be examined in each case to determine whether a resolution is possible. Moreover, Hegel could suggest that if Kierkegaard wants to defend the ultimate superiority of the religious form of life over the others he must accept some weaker version of the dialectic. Though Kierkegaard claims that each person must make an ultimate choice between different forms of life, he also wants to hold that refusing to choose the religious life is a mistake. Hegel could also suggest that Kierkegaard searches for flaws or tensions within each stage that demand resolution leading to his version of Christianity.[20] So perhaps they do not disagree about this issue as much as Kierkegaard claims. Nonetheless, Kierkegaard would insist that even if there is some drive to move to the next type of life, that form does not retain the benefits of the previous form. Each stage has distinct virtues; no stage integrates the virtues of them all. Hegel might reply that evaluating this claim requires reflection about how the virtues of each form of life are described, and he would acknowledge that some features of previous forms are left behind, incapable of being preserved.

Ultimately, Kierkegaard believes Hegel's system induces lassitude. It eliminates the challenge of making necessary, vital choices that affect one's life and era.[21] These choices can be vividly experienced in the first-person viewpoint from which Kierkegaard writes. Hegel's third-person perspective is too reassuring; it obviates the urgency of personal choice. Moreover, because the system has a dynamic of its own, individuals' decisions seem less relevant. Even if individuals resist its currents, the river of the dialectic will ultimately reach its destination, reducing the burdens of the decisions that create each person's identity. Hegel might still reply that individuals must choose to take the form of life seriously for the dialectic to operate; their role would remain important. This entire dialogue between Hegel and of Kierkegaard can serve to introduce what he means by "existence."

Many kinds of thing exist: rocks, bacteria, cockroaches, dogs, chairs, computers, governments, and persons. Existentialists are not concerned with the meaning of "existence" that all these things can share. Rather, they attend to a meaning of "exist" that is unique to persons. It concerns *how* people exist: with what degree of passion, seriousness, and responsibility – with what effort to discover and live by their most important values. Kierkegaard extols these features of what later existentialists call "authentic existence." This ideal concerns not the content of people's choices and commitments, but the manner in which such choices are lived. Authentic existence becomes especially important if one believes that no objective grounds can be adduced to support fundamental choices, and this is Kierkegaard's key thesis. People who live inauthentically make their life-choices flippantly – without wrestling with the alternatives, without really caring about their significance, without realizing they are defining themselves in making such choices. Kierkegaard also challenges Hegel's conception of ethical life. He takes Hegel to claim that the good life requires living in accord with the duties of one's social role.[22] Such a life can involve detached, habituated responses, and acceptance of the status quo. Kierkegaard's notion of authentic existence rejects this depersonalization and awakens people to life's true meaning. Some conception of authenticity is central to each of the existentialists.

Unlike Hegel, who describes a wide variety of forms of life, Kierkegaard concentrates on three main types: the aesthetic, the ethical, and the religious. He also examines several variations within the ethical and religious forms.[23] He explores the distinctive features and paradoxes of each. They each define the good life (what is truly worth pursuing) in fundamentally different ways. Kierkegaard explores the tensions in each form of life, and he forces his readers to see the personal implications of choosing each way. Although some of the flaws he identifies might be considered internal flaws, most of them derive from external standards imported from the form of life he favors – the religious type (specifically Christianity).

The aesthetic life is devoted to the immediate: the momentary, the sensual, the whimsical, the new, and the challenging. It savors each moment, but pursues no larger organizing end. Kierkegaard's most dramatic example is the person engaged in periodic, repeated seductions – who appreciates each distinctive challenge, but cannot retain any joy in the conquest once achieved. Central to this way of life is the discovery of new experiences; its bane is the boredom of repetition.[24] Aesthetes make no effort to judge their actions in moral terms – remaining oblivious to moral standards. (They are not consciously evil; they are simply indifferent to moral evaluation.) Insofar as immoral actions offer a new kind of experience, they may taste them, but they do not dwell on them. Aesthetes depend heavily on good fortune, both to provide new experiences and to achieve success in relation to new challenges. They refuse to reflect on their lives as a whole, and they do not question their lives' ultimate meanings. Instead, they remain attentive to each passing experience – relying on chance to provide something to savor – hoping their own evanescent charms and talents will insure success.

Kierkegaard identifies several problems with the aesthetic way of life. First, its reliance on chance and on accidental talents means that it lacks ultimate control over its own success. Aesthetes easily fall into despair if they suffer serious injury or must endure highly repetitive experiences.[25] Second, their continuous pursuit of new experience creates a pervasive restlessness. Experiences can feel similar even if they contain some new elements, and this can produce unrelenting boredom. To take his main example, even if new victims of a seducer represent different challenges, the similarity of the process of seduction can blind the aesthete to these differences. Then this life can seem like endless repetition. Indeed, habitual success can produce this very experience.[26] Third, if aesthetes ever do reflect on life as a whole, they will experience a deep emptiness because their lives have no cumulative meaning, no unity, and no centeredness.[27] Here Kierkegaard seems to rely on a standard imported from the ethical form of life, rather than explore the paradoxes of the aesthete on the basis of internal criteria (which Hegel always sought to do). Kierkegaard's main objection, however, is that the satisfaction achieved by the aesthete is short-lived, unreliable, and unstable (an objection Hegel makes to a similar form of life – Pleasure and Necessity – in the *Phenomenology of Spirit*[28]).

Kierkegaard's second type is the ethical, which involves organizing one's life into a coherent whole through intense commitment to an ideal that takes account of one's talents and station, devotedly discharging the resultant social duties, and regarding people as absolute ends rather than as means to one's own pleasures. His key example is someone who enters into marriage – a long-term commitment to a person – with single-mindedness, sincerity, and the will to make the relationship last to the benefit of both parties.[29] Thus, people living ethical lives do not mindlessly accept socially prescribed duties, but attempt to put their personal stamp on each duty they acknowledge. They also define their own long-term ideals in relation to their commitments to other people, rather than simply seizing an ideal trumpeted by their culture. The ethical life is less concerned with successful results than with good-faith efforts, sincere devotion, and long-term dedication. Lacking from the ethical life is any conception of sin and paradox. The satisfaction achieved by discharging these personal commitments is palpable and self-sustaining; it is also more stable and less dependent on fate.

The ethical life thus synthesizes two elements: social norms and personal commitment. It must be distinguished from another form of social life that is central to Heidegger's existentialism: the impersonal or public mode of social existence. In this form of life, people conform to public norms – not because of conviction, conscious affirmation, or personal self-definition, but because of routine and social expectations. They act as everyone acts, unreflectively following whatever the masses embrace. Their behavior conforms to social rules, but the rules carry no personal stamp. This inauthentic existence Kierkegaard finds to be typical of his age, and even those who believe in a Christian God in this other-directed, depersonalized fashion are condemned.

Kierkegaard's objections to the ethical life properly understood are harder to explain, and they seem based even less on internal criteria than his objections to the aesthetic life. First, the ethical life can be lived in good conscience, without angst or doubt. Though many might regard this as a benefit, Kierkegaard regards it with suspicion because he is convinced of humanity's irredeemable sinfulness. In addition, the degree of passion and subjectivity a way of life can achieve is a function of its irrationality, paradoxes, and difficulty. Since the ethical life need not be paradoxical or irrational in this way, Kierkegaard regards it as less demanding and even less serious than the religious life. Finally, ethical persons may be divided by loyalties to conflicting values, rendering them incapable of acting as a unified whole. Only singular devotion to God can assure such self-integration.[30]

One of Kierkegaard's criteria for evaluating different styles of life is their self-sufficiency or independence from the vagaries of chance. But he rejects one ethical attempt to achieve this independence: stoicism. Stoics retreat from the world and attempt to remain indifferent to the results of their actions. They seek equilibrium and inner calm. This ideal is another way of avoiding Kierkegaardian authenticity. He values personal commitment, individuality, passionate devotion, and the willingness to risk oneself.[31] He believes that the inner fortress to which Stoics retreat empties them of genuine feeling and care. In addition, Stoics may falter if forced to endure long-term suffering (like Job's). Kierkegaard believes that only a relationship with a transcendent Deity will provide the strength to endure such suffering. This personal and passionate relationship to God is the core element of the religious way of life.

The religious life includes a feeling of sinfulness, an extreme sense of paradox, and a knowledge that ordinary social laws may have to be suspended in order to follow God's will. For Kierkegaard, the more irrational the faith in God, the more personal and authentic the religious faith because it lacks the support of objective reasons.[32] Kierkegaard insists that belief in the Christian God is paradoxical because it asserts that an eternal, transcendent God becomes incarnate and temporal. This paradox cannot be fathomed rationally; it can only be accepted through faith. Religious persons do not seek reassurance in proofs of God's existence or in well-digested catechisms that reduce their experience to simple formulas. Instead they struggle with the intellectual difficulties of believing in God and with the suffering involved in their consciousness of ineradicable sin. Crucial to Kierkegaard's notion of the religious life is feeling the continuous presence of God. Instead of foundering in uncertainty or skepticism, religious devotees welcome this continuous living presence and respond with constant devotion and awe. This living presence personalizes the devotee's relationship with God; everyday life becomes an expressive witness to that presence.[33] Religious devotees willingly disobey the requirements of social morality when God commands it – e.g., when God called Abraham to sacrifice his son Isaac.[34]

Kierkegaard contrasts two theories of access to Divine commands. Socrates believed his access to his inner *daemon* (an inner voice or guide) was reliable because he could remember a prior contact with an eternal reality to which his actions conformed. He was able to challenge the laws and customs of Athens because of his access to this reality. His task was to teach people how to recollect their relationship to this eternal realm. Kierkegaard's objection to Socrates' understanding of the religious life is that it is purely theoretical. In contrast, Christians' access to God's commands will forever be clouded because of their sinfulness. They cannot expect to achieve unity with God on their own through recollection. A Christian's relationship with God depends on His grace and forgiveness. There can never be final assurance or security. Christians thus experience constant uncertainty, despair, and crisis. Kierkegaard's preferred version of the religious life involves a continual struggle with the believer's own weakness and God's objective mysteries. A leap of faith is required, and this distinguishes the religious life from the ethical and aesthetic ways of life.[35] The more irrational the faith, the greater the authenticity (passionate single-mindedness) required to affirm God. Since Christianity is among the most paradoxical of religions, Kierkegaard prefers it to both Greek metaphysical spirituality and Jewish law.

Kierkegaard also develops a distinctive conception of truth. For him, truth is less a property of assertions than of how one lives. His conception shares many features with Hegel's conception of truth: realizing one's essential nature. For Kierkegaard, however, each person has a particular essence; only if one realizes one's distinctiveness does one live truthfully. Thus, the formula "truth is subjectivity" does not assert that truth is a function of the firmness or idiosyncrasy of one's convictions, and it does not make theoretical truth merely a subjective matter. Kierkegaard's truth is not a matter of beliefs or convictions at all. If one achieves authenticity, then one *lives* truthfully because one realizes one's personal essence.[36] In addition, Kierkegaard believes that achieving unity with ultimate reality is to achieve a truthful relation with ultimate Truth. Hegel accepted this as well, but for Hegel ultimate reality is a total system of concepts and its realization in nature, mind, and history; and unity with this totality requires conceptual comprehension. Kierkegaard insists that the Christian God is the ultimate reality, and unity with Him requires a leap of faith. Later existentialists develop this non-epistemic notion of truth, which involves a proper response to being (in Heidegger's case) or to human being (in Sartre's).

Kierkegaard contributes a number of crucial features to Heidegger's thought. In many respects, Heidegger simply secularizes Kierkegaard's insights. He retains, for example, Kierkegaard's notion of the essential self-relatedness of persons, the critique of the public or anonymous mode of existing, the analysis of angst (anxiety, dread), the ever-present tendency of human beings to fall (sin), and the general critique of the objective, third-person viewpoint in philosophy. In addition, Heidegger ratifies Kierkegaard's view that temporality is central to the human condition, though he jettisons Kierkegaard's longing for eternity, even as he retains his value of constancy. Instead of using the paradoxical features of the Christian God to heighten an individual's sense of existence, Heidegger uses a certain experience of death. Finally, like Kierkegaard, Heidegger seeks to articulate a viable conception of authenticity, though he does not think it requires a leap of faith.

HEIDEGGER

Although Martin Heidegger's (1889–1976) *Being and Time* is a seminal work for several movements examined in this book, it is the central text for existentialism. It provides philosophical foundations for important existentialist doctrines and deepens the analysis of its key concepts. It also contributes to existentialism's philosophical significance by challenging the adequacy of both common sense and traditional philosophical assumptions. Heidegger has deep reservations about academic philosophy because it seems untouched by the seriousness of the matters it explores. True philosophers are stirred by the questions they raise, and their insights should emerge from their most profound experiences. The reason academic philosophy has become moribund is that it no longer seriously interrogates its concepts or its assumptions. To recover the most basic experiences from which a more promising philosophy can be developed, the history of philosophy must be challenged and read in an entirely different spirit. Moreover, philosophers will have to discover the pre-philosophical roots from which the concepts used in ordinary and scientific comprehension grow. Unlike Husserl, who brackets all questions concerning existence to achieve greater certainty, Heidegger spotlights the question of being.[37] Like Husserl, Heidegger thinks philosophy can provide a foundation for rethinking the sciences, but he does not want philosophy itself to become a science. He believes that philosophy is a creative enterprise, like art. Unlike Kierkegaard, who is primarily interested in the distinctive existence that human beings possess, Heidegger seeks to clarify being itself and the way it becomes manifest in many types of entity, in addition to probing the specific character of human existence.

Heidegger believes the central error that plagues the entire history of philosophy since the Greeks is a mistaken conception of being. This conception emerges from a detached, theoretical relationship to the world. In that light entities appear like mere presences, and thus *presence* becomes the central metaphor that determines all philosophical conceptions of being. Something is known to exist only when it *presents* itself in person[38] (as Husserl would say); this applies to objects, persons, events, mental states, etc. But when anything is merely present, it is experienced in a detached fashion – simply there. In this orientation the most plausible way of relating to objects is to know them, and indeed the primacy of knowing in philosophy derives from this conception of being. In *Being and Time* Heidegger's main strategy is to show that common sense and traditional philosophical conceptions are degenerate cases of more primordial experiences.[39]

The experience of things as merely present is a degenerate instance of the more basic experience of tools. Tools become "merely present" only when they fail, e.g., when they break, are missing, or cannot operate. Then their raw presence suddenly emerges.[40] The more characteristic and all-pervasive way of relating to entities is through practical engagement. One does not typically stare at the keyboard: one types with it; or contemplate the car: one drives it. When engaged in practical tasks, one rarely perceives objects at all; one attends to the goal and the practical steps required to reach it. One remains ready to adapt to new situational developments and alive to the progress of each phase of the task. Heidegger's general term for this experience of entities is "readiness-to-hand," which philosophy has missed or forgotten.[41] Theory is just one practical way of exploring the surrounding world. It is "degenerate" because it loosens the characteristic practical relations between person and world. It thus isolates entities from their practical context and separates persons from their surroundings. When practically engaged, people are attuned to their environment; person and world interlock. Within this perspective, skepticism is unthinkable; nothing could be accomplished if the world were not ready to hand. These deep bonds to the world have been concealed by academic philosophy until now. To understand human knowing is to grasp the way in which skills smoothly interface with tools.[42] In terms that Gilbert Ryle adapted from Heidegger, knowing how is prior to knowing that.

Heidegger's main concern in *Being and Time* is human existence. This concern is prominent for two reasons. First, humans are the only entities that characteristically interrogate themselves about their existence, and thus human being is intimately related to being ("*Dasein*'s being is always at issue for it").[43] Second, the essence of human being is its existence.[44] This means that persons are uniquely capable of becoming who they are (or failing to). To do this they must actively pursue their distinctive possibilities, rather than allowing themselves to be distracted from them by a fascinating world, the Crowd (see below), or their own anxieties. Heidegger calls being-oneself, "authenticity," and failing-to-be-oneself, "inauthenticity." He claims these are descriptive rather than normative concepts,[45] but since the book is virtually a call to become authentic, they at least have normative overtones. Human beings exhibit an inveterate tendency to lose themselves by falling away from authenticity. The purpose of *Being and Time* is to counteract that tendency and show the path toward a fundamental transformation of persons, for only in the authentic state can humanity fully understand being itself and thus become capable of clarifying its meaning. The name Heidegger gives to the distinctive enmeshed attunement between persons and tools is "being-in-the-world." Being-in-the-world has three coextensive structures: Worldhood, being-with, and being-in.[46] They are unified by the fundamental fact that humans care about their projects, about others, and about themselves. Each of the three structures exhibits a distinctive kind of care. They are coextensive and equiprimordial and exist in every mode of being-human, in all cultures.

The traditional error committed by academic philosophy – interpreting being as presence – affects its analysis of human beings as well. Human existence is also typically understood as presence-at-hand. On this view, persons fully exist only if they are present to themselves, and others fully exist only if they are present (in person). The philosophical tradition thus construes persons as objects, and this leads to a misunderstanding of human existence. Just as objectifying things led to substance ontology, so objectifying persons leads to an ontology of the subject or ego.[47] On this view, persons are individuated either via empirical or transcendental egos. Because Heidegger thinks human existence is better understood – more primordially and truly depicted – as being-in-the-world, he rejects these hypothetical egos. He claims that in ordinary practical life there is no sense of an ego separate from the operative project. Personal and authentic existence has nothing to do with discovering an ego or becoming a subject. It involves pursuing projects which have their source in decisions made in the proper frame of mind. Heidegger's new way of thinking about being thus affects his vision of both worldly entities (now construed as tools) and persons (now construed as practical agents who work in collaboration with these tools) and their relationship (now construed as deeply interwoven rather than independent of one another).

Worldhood is a feature of human existence that makes complex networks of tools possible.[48] Each type of workshop has its own distinctive tools and requisite skills, and only people familiar with those tools will be "at home" there. This practical familiarity is virtually hidden from those who have it; moreover, they do not enunciate this understanding in rules or theories. They just know how to proceed, whatever the situation. Worldhood is the general capacity humans possess to learn new orientations in new instrumental contexts. This very general capacity is even more implicit than specific skills in the various kinds of workshops. But particular instrumental know-how and the general capacity that makes it possible are essential to human existence. Human life consists of practical projects. A project is a particular task with a specific end in view, guided by a purpose, in order to realize a value. Values are not mysterious elements added to factual states of affairs by human desires; they are built into practical contexts.[49] There are superior ways of handling tools and achieving purposes. The standard of excellence is part of the operational comprehension of the craft. Heidegger's new understanding of the being of entities thus returns values to their proper place in human life. He rejects their demotion to something dubious and unjustifiable, a misconception that results from present-at-hand ontology.

The second essential feature of being-in-the-world is being-with. People share the practical world of tools with other people. Their projects are essentially oriented to others, both because their products are destined for others' use and because they use the tools and materials made by others.[50] Since I analyzed this feature in depth in chapter 6, I will only review the key points here. Being-with is the fundamental condition, being-alone is merely a degenerate case of being-with (because the sense of loneliness refers to others' absence), and a person can be with others even when they are not in the vicinity. In addition, other people define the predominant uses of tools (via traditions), and they may also determine one's projects (through requirements or assignments, for example). Others can sometimes become so dominant that they literally take over the functions of the "self," as traditional philosophy understands them – assigning projects, establishing moods, delimiting possibilities, and numbing the intellect with idle chatter. Following Kierkegaard, Heidegger calls this way of being human the anonymous "They" or the Crowd or the *impersonal mode*. Achieving authenticity requires that one transform this impersonal mode of existence. Heidegger defines authentic forms of being-with others and working together. They involve revealing each other's possibility for authenticity and facilitating its realization, rather than intervening in people's lives to dominate them.[51]

The third dimension of being-in-the-world is being-in, which itself has three elements, all of which are interwoven with the practical orientation to the world. The three features are mood, understanding, and discourse; eventually,

Heidegger relates these features to the past, future, and present respectively. Since I have examined this structure in depth in chapter 5, I will only offer a summary here. Moods reveal one's relationship with the world and the past. If the past weighs too heavily, then it may eclipse one's own possibilities. Moods express the fact of being thrown into an already existing culture and history – with a trajectory already in process – whose direction cannot ultimately be justified. Understanding discovers future possibilities on the basis of an implicit sense of one's tasks and aspirations. It is an embodied or practical self-interpretation that orients everything one does, and it expresses one's sense of how to live. Discourse, in Heidegger's sense, is not always spoken or verbal, but it is socially constructed. It exhibits the ways workshops are organized and the means of distinguishing different tools and their components. Sometimes discourse hearkens people to their own possibilities; this happens most often when they are silent. Sometimes discourse clouds their access to their own possibilities, for example, when their talk becomes idle chatter. Idle chatter never discloses or reveals anything; the mere fact of speaking is its only concern; the content is irrelevant. Heidegger often praises reticence and silence as ways to escape the daze induced by idle chatter.

Just as idle chatter is the degenerate form of discourse, mood and understanding also have degenerate forms that encourage falling into inauthenticity: ambiguity and curiosity.[52] Curiosity explores surface possibilities without attending to the ways in which situations can lend themselves to the realization of authentic tasks. It distracts people from realizing their authentic purposes. Ambiguity is an understanding of the present in which all possibilities seem equal, anaesthetizing people's sense of their own distinctive possibilities. Because no option seems best suited to embody a person's unique task, he approaches the situation "in neutral" without seizing any definite direction. Instead of being-themselves, people react impersonally, like anyone would. Under these conditions, the Crowd conceals their distinctive projects and possibilities.

Heidegger defines authenticity simply as being-oneself, but this needs further elaboration. He suggests that authentic people are the sources of their projects. Instead of taking their cues from others, they bend situations to their own aims. People are the genuine source of their projects if they choose them in the right way: in reticence, in the light of their own finitude, with an acceptance of responsibility, and with a readiness for anxiety.[53] Reticence stills the voices of others that resonate within so that people can begin to hear their own voices. The experience of finitude – or the ever-present possibility of death – accentuates the importance of choices. It forces people to see that they cannot pursue an infinite diversity of paths; they must choose the one that matters most and dedicate themselves to it. People accept responsibility when they are answerable for their choices. And readiness for anxiety forces people to remain perpetually open to rethinking their projects and to acknowledge that they are contingent and ultimately unjustifiable. For Heidegger, authentic people fulfill three additional conditions: (1) they acknowledge the fact that they exist within a tradition and must either affirm or transform it in some fashion; (2) they decisively shape new situations to implement the projects they have chosen; and (3) they articulate to themselves the factors and conditions that moved them to choose one possibility over another.[54] Heidegger's ideal is a formal one. Many different goals – some of them heinous – can be pursued authentically. It does not limit the kinds of project people can choose, only the manner in which they enact them.

Heidegger claims that human beings have essential tendencies both toward authenticity and inauthenticity. They are essentially authentic in that they may recover their own possibilities and decide to enact them at any time.[55] The inherent self-relatedness (or "mineness") of human existence insures persons' distinctive possibilities can never be entirely concealed or silenced. On the other hand, the domination of the Crowd and the way in which the practical world can absorb one's attention – deflecting one from a sense of one's distinctive tasks – show that the typical or average way of being human is inauthentic.[56] People's pervasive tendency is to fall into inauthenticity, even if they always have the possibility of self-recovery. In the same way, humans exist always in both truth and untruth. When they live authentically, they remain attuned to the truth of human finitude and its contingent immersion in a tradition and in this historical moment. But experiencing this existential truth is an achievement; it must be wrested from the life of untruth that is the average, everyday state of inauthentic living.

In the second division of *Being and Time*, Heidegger reworks this analysis of human being, clarifying the unity of these structures. He elucidates the essentially temporal nature of human existence and shows that temporality can also be lived authentically or inauthentically. Heidegger thinks that only the proper relationship to death allows people to grasp the wholeness and finitude of life. He wants people to experience death neither as an objective probability that can be anticipated nor as an all-consuming, inevitable reality. Instead he wants people to remain vividly aware of death as a possibility because this forces them to remain cognizant of their finitude, which makes their choices more significant. In addition, Heidegger argues that while other people may substitute for many of one's social roles (taking over one's professional tasks, one's family responsibilities, one's friendships, and community roles), no one can replace another person in facing that person's own death. Since one's death is essentially related to oneself, other people cannot really help in facing it, nor can its *possibility* be denied. Death's possibility reminds everyone that they must determine their own lives. Thus, being-toward-death is individualizing; it shatters the easy acceptance of the anonymous Crowd and thrusts people toward authentic choices.

To live authentically is to live time differently. Instead of experiencing life stretching forward and backward in a sequence of similar moments, the future becomes life's essential dimension.[57] Authentic choices organize the future, rejecting the demeanor of passive waiting. But an authentic relation to the future engenders an authentic relationship to the past, producing the realization that human life is embedded in specific cultural traditions and limited historical options. Both futures and pasts are related to an authentic relationship to the present – in which people discover in a moment of vision the distinctive possibilities of this situation.[58] These temporal relationships constitute a single unified whole that arises from the proper orientation toward death as a possibility. They encourage people to discover their authentic choices in dialogue with past heroes – exemplary figures with similar goals.[59] They require people to acknowledge the contingencies of their traditions and the limitations of their control. This authentic experience of time can extend to an entire culture if a generation chooses its own distinctive possibilities for making history.

Elucidating these essential features of being human – Worldhood, entities as tools rather than substances, being-with, the various dimensions of being-in, authentic being toward death, authentic temporality, and the essential tendency toward falling – constitutes Heidegger's central contribution to existentialism. Heidegger gives new direction to the study of human life. Sartre develops this direction a generation later.

SARTRE

Several important conclusions define Jean-Paul Sartre's (1905–80) existentialism. I will clarify these first and then examine their supporting arguments. Sartre's analysis of raw being differs from Heidegger's tool-being. Sartre believes the cosmos is indifferent, superfluous, self-sufficient, and without concern for human purposes.[60] He agrees with Heidegger that the "world" consists of various relationships among tools that respond to and are organized by human purposes (individual and cultural). However, this practical system of tools overlays a raw being that has existed and could easily exist without any humans at all and without any reference to human purposes.[61] Heidegger, on the other hand, regards being (at least in *Being and Time*) as something active, which reveals itself to and conceals itself from humanity. Heidegger's conception of being borrows some animism from life-philosophy (Nietzsche and Dilthey) while Sartre's retains the flavor of indifferent materialism. He insists that purposes and meaningfulness are primarily human phenomena, created by cultures and individuals. These purposes are so predominant that they often conceal the underlying indifference of the universe. Sartre's existentialism highlights the fact that humans must create their identities – individually and collectively – by defining their own aspirations and goals.[62] Part of Sartrean authenticity is acknowledging the human origins of values.

Heidegger and Sartre agree that humans find themselves thrown into situations they do not create, situations that condition them and limit their options.[63] Sartre thinks that these limits are produced primarily by the actions of past human beings (who created the technology people now take for granted); so even if such limits exist, they are typically humanly made.[64] Neither Heidegger nor Sartre construes these limits as causal determinants. Sartre explicitly rejects this notion in favor of a concept he calls "motives," which emerge when actions are retrospectively examined for a rationale. Despite this "thrownness," Sartre insists that humans make themselves through their choices, for which they are responsible. They are not responsible for their *success*, but for their overall effort and their responses to inherited conditions (e.g., to resist, accept, or alter them). Choices define short- and long-term projects, and large-scale projects often subsume many smaller-scale projects, providing order to everyday life. Sartre rejects the claim that the material conditions can force persons to do something, because he regards consciousness to be a spontaneous, self-defining, *sui generis* phenomenon. Since consciousness just is the power to transcend the givens of any situation and objectify them, it can always negate these givens.[65] For Sartre, nothing grounds these choices; people posit the values by which they choose to live. This primordial freedom and responsibility is often concealed, however, by the fact that people mistakenly take values to be absolute and given. At some deep level people know better, but they often deceive themselves about the extent of their responsibilities.[66]

Most often people flee their sense of freedom into self-deception. Either they take the future to be fixed in the way the past is fixed (when they want to deny responsibility for their current actions), or they take the past to be fluid in the way the future is fluid (when they want to deny responsibility for their past actions). Many want to interpret actions to be mechanical, fixed, and necessary because this would eliminate their responsibility. Still another path to self-deception is to distance themselves from their situations to such a degree that no response seems required. They observe life from above and let events take their course. For Sartre, this distancing is an active stance, which must bear responsibility for refusing to change anything. Or people may take an active position and attempt to influence events in a way that backfires; then they may disassociate from the action, denying that they had any real part in it. Sartrean authenticity demands that people reject these self-deceptive maneuvers. It requires people to enter into the situations they inherit, actively choose the most promising response – realizing that values are contingent and self-chosen – and then willingly accept responsibility for their actions. Authentic people acknowledge that their actions function as examples for all humanity.[67]

Those are Sartre's major conclusions. He defends them through an analysis of the human condition and human action. Metaphysically, Sartre sharply contrasts two types of being – one belonging to things; another possessed by consciousness. Things include natural objects, like rocks and trees, which are self-sufficient, independent, complete, dense, solid, and will continue unchanged unless altered from the outside.[68] Human beings, on the other hand, are dependent, incomplete, empty, and may change from within anytime. Because humans must constantly "make themselves be," Sartre denies that the principle of identity applies to them.[69] Persons never are what they are; at best they constantly "have to be" what they choose. Since they constantly transcend what they have been, they always remain open to new projects and self-definitions. Sartre believes that inauthentic persons want to be like things, constantly escaping their open nature, or they want to retain their self-defining freedom *and also* exist as things – combining two essentially contradictory forms of being. This inauthentic aspiration is impossible to achieve;

people who seek it are "useless passions." Sartre also thinks that conscious beings ultimately depend on something outside themselves (something to be conscious *of*) because consciousness has no content of its own. Existing only to reveal objects, consciousness is dependent on those objects for its own existence.[70] Consciousness can be given a stable, thing-like definition by other people, but this never penetrates and qualifies consciousness itself; it surrounds consciousness like a sphere without ever truly determining it.[71]

Persons, for Sartre, have an ambiguous nature. In some respects they approximate the being of things – for example, in the given features of their bodies, in their pasts, in the historical realities they inherit. With respect to these features, persons are largely passive, though they can actively seek to transform or reinterpret them. In other respects, persons are completely open, for example, in their futures, in their professional roles, in the way they define various given situations. Sartre calls the former aspects "facticity," and the latter features "transcendence."[72] Because persons straddle both types of being, they easily confuse one with another; this is one major reason why self-deception is so common. They take their futures to be given in the way their pasts are, or they take their social definitions to be open in the way their futures are. They take their roles to be necessary when in fact their duties can always be reinterpreted. They take a past action to be as evanescent as a hypothetical imagined future when in fact the past action always remains part of their histories, even if later it motivates attempts at self-transformation. These are the structures and mechanisms through which self-deception operates.[73] Facing these ambiguities and acknowledging these structural differences is the first step toward authenticity.

How does consciousness constantly transcend the given situation? Sartre suggests that imagination is the catapult. People continuously project alternative possibilities for the given situation. There may be practical limits on what can be actually achieved at a particular historical moment, but these never prevent people from taking steps toward their projected possibilities. Sartre thinks persons are typically motivated by a sense of lack in the current situation; they attempt to realize specific transformations as a result of the values they posit.[74] This is what Sartre means by "choosing" – the projection of possibilities that, if realized, will transform or sustain the current situation. Sartrean choice does not require explicit reflection or deliberation over alternatives, and it may exist even when people sustain the status quo. That too is a choice, which happens by envisioning various ways in which the situation might become unstable and preventing them (say, working to maintain a vital marriage or a stimulating job). To choose is to project a goal on the basis of a value.

Every project responds to a specific situation. Situations are organizations of instruments and configurations of meaning. They never force people to respond in specific ways, though they can restrict available options. A person cannot, for example, fly overnight to Europe from New York if she lives in a time when airplanes have not yet been invented. We cannot now fly overnight to Mars. Thus, the situation may impose practical limits because of the level of technology available. Sometimes options are limited by the demands of other people or by the resistance of the materials with which one is working. Even if someone's life is threatened at gunpoint, however, he still has options – including dying with courage and honor.[75] If the tool with which one is working is inefficient, one can either choose to make do or abandon the task altogether. For Sartre, humans also have no pre-existent nature that determines their choices. They must constantly choose to sustain or alter their chosen projects; thus they continue to make and remake themselves.[76] Some people may be more talented than others in some areas, but how individuals develop those talents and even the extent to which they discover them is a function of their own choices. This is the meaning of existential freedom and responsibility. It is a limited freedom, only guaranteeing the opportunity to *try* to alter reality or one's own past history, but nonetheless significant enough to defeat protestations of helplessness.

This openness to the future and the gap between one's ongoing present projects and their future is just one of several gaps or "nothingnesses" that define the human condition for Sartre. At the most basic level, there is a gap severing consciousness's directed awareness of its object and its simultaneous ancillary (non-directed) awareness of itself.[77] Every moment of consciousness thus consists of two aspects that never quite coincide; this spacing within consciousness – later made so famous by Derrida – is already important for Sartre.[78] Another gap emerges when consciousness tries to take itself as its own object, either through introspection or retrospection. When it does this, consciousness seeks to adopt another person's standpoint on itself – thereby objectifying itself. Because this effort cannot wholly succeed, according to Sartre, reflective consciousness creates an illusory quasi-objectified vision of itself that it takes to be real and to antecedently inhabit all pre-reflective consciousness. For Sartre, this is the source of the belief in an empirical ego.[79] The gap between the aspect of consciousness reflecting and the aspect of consciousness reflected on is wider than the temporal (present-future) and simultaneous non-directed awareness gaps. Other people create the final gap at the heart of consciousness, when they transgress one's projects or judge one. They thereby create a structure that is continually supplemented and modified, but truly qualifies consciousness and perpetually haunts it.[80] This "socially created" self is always mysterious, however, because consciousness can never be sure of its exact content, and it is perpetually disorienting – so much so that the major theme of personal relationships is recovering control of this "social self."[81]

Sartre sharply differentiates the pre-reflective, pre-theoretical level of consciousness from the reflective level. Most people live on the pre-reflective level throughout most of their lives; it is the level of practical action, of perception and imagination, and ordinary problem-solving, and interaction with others. The reflective level emerges only occasionally, and need not emerge at all. When consciousness tries to take itself as its own object, then it "reflects."[82] Husserl's transcendental reduction is one kind of reflection, and it alters the consciousness on which it reflects. (One's objectified sense of self then becomes the center of attention, rather than the original object of pre-reflective consciousness.) Also, whenever one introspects to discover the specificity of one's experience or retrospects to discover a pattern in one's past actions, this involves reflection. Sartre believes the reflective act imposes different types of unity on pre-reflective states; for example, it often weaves a narrative that knits the past and present together. This narrative provides coherence, but Sartre thinks it belies the pre-reflective reality where consciousness is spontaneous and self-defining. At the pre-reflective level people have a sense of their goals, and they may be aware of the values from which they project those goals. But Sartre denies that they have any sense of self that authors their choices and subsumes the resultant actions. If people have an experience of self at the pre-reflective level, then it derives from the social self others impose, which may or may not be accurate.[83]

Sartre believes the illusions of impure reflection become obvious when people suddenly grasp pre-reflective consciousness in its naked state and thus recover from the narrative and thematic pretenses it creates. This is purified reflection, which dissolves the illusory psychic objects of impure reflection (the self, traits of character, affective dispositions, behavioral tendencies), and in which the spontaneity, freedom, contingency, emptiness, and self-transcendence of consciousness emerge vividly.[84] Sartre describes this moment of epiphany in his novel, *Nausea*.[85] The central character, Roquentin, undergoes the sudden transition to purified reflection and learns the basic Sartrean truths about the human condition. These quasi-objective psychic unities created by impure reflection have preoccupied psychologists in the past. Reflection leads people to invert all the real relationships within consciousness. Whereas reflection reports that the self is the origin of inherited dispositions that cause one to experience particular affective states in particular situations, which then cause a behavior response, for Sartre the truth is that there are only spontaneous behavioral responses in each situation which are later synthesized into thematic unities (after the fact) by impure reflection. The self is a fictional glue created to bind these fictional unities together. If Sartre is right about this, then many psychological "givens" are really constructions of over-active reflection, and psychological determinism is simply a mistaken inference from these illusions.

Just as Sartre retains a semi-Cartesian distinction between mind and matter in his division between consciousness and inert things, so too does he reinstall Descartes's distinction between mind and body despite adopting Merleau-Ponty's notion of a "lived body" that exists in dialogue with the practical world. The body as instrument and its world of tools function as a unified whole for Sartre, but in addition to this "subject-side" of the body there is also an "object-side" that exists primarily for others (e.g., doctors). This is the body that is fat/thin, tall/short, beautiful/ugly, toned/flabby; this is also the body on which surgeons operate. Sartre thinks that the two dimensions of the body are only contingently related to one another.[86] What the doctor sees may be unrelated to what one actually feels and is capable of doing. Sartre also privileges the practical, effective relation to the world that he takes to be characteristic of pre-reflective life. Many emotions, however, abandon this practical grip on the world and attempt to achieve goals in a "magical" fashion –

abandoning reliable means-ends relationships. Although emotions are still goal-directed, they are ineffective in achieving their goals.[87] Thus Sartre also retains a modified version of the reason/passion dichotomy.

One advantage of this modified dualism is its ability to justify the need for a distinct type of understanding concerning humans. Sartre elaborates this special understanding by clarifying his "existential psychoanalysis" as an alternative to Freud's. Its goal is to clarify persons by articulating the hierarchy of their projects, rather than the causes from which their actions allegedly spring.[88] The Sartrean analyst grasps higher-order projects by relating actions to goals and to the values informing them. Sartre claims that persons' goals have an organic coherence resulting from a "fundamental project." The notion of a "hierarchy of projects" is straightforward. For example, if a teacher creates a new course, then he is committed to preparing lectures, answering questions, setting assignments, providing feedback, and determining student grades. Similarly, if he seeks to be a philosophy teacher, this project integrates the task of teaching a wide variety of such courses over his entire life. The idea of a "fundamental project" is that all of a person's major goals (e.g., those that define her place in her profession, her personal relationships, her relation to oneself, her political commitments, etc.) are subsumed by one basic goal, of which she has some vague pre-linguistic comprehension.

Thus, to provide an "analysis" of an individual is to clarify the hierarchy of her projects and how it organizes her practical life. For the analyst, this is always a *hypothesis*, partly because it involves comparing diverse pursuits and finding their common theme, which requires interpretive leaps. Sartre insists that existential analysts must confirm their hypotheses by appealing to the implicit self-understanding of the analysand.[89] In addition, the analyst's task is to understand how these projects are pursued in practice, how they are modified as a result of the vicissitudes of the real-world situations, and how they change over time. Thus, in addition to clarifying the hierarchy of projects, the analyst must also rethink the analysand's life history as the basic project develops into various sub-projects over time. Though people may have an implicit grasp of their fundamental projects, they rarely have an explicit comprehension of them, and existential psychoanalysis makes this possible. If analysands acknowledge their hierarchy of projects, then they can decide whether they want to sustain those projects or abandon them.[90] Thus, even the most basic projects can be abandoned; this is essential to Sartrean freedom. Understanding the structure of a person's projects can help people change because it allows them to understand how certain, perhaps undesirable, patterns are sustained by higher-order projects and thus better locates which projects must be abandoned or modified in order to eliminate the pattern. This is an entirely different way of understanding persons than searching for external causes or even internal motivations for actions. Sartre rejects such deterministic approaches.

Though an analysand can attempt to interpret and understand herself in this way, nothing guarantees that her results will be superior to those of an analyst, because, in attempting to achieve this understanding, she adopts a third-person viewpoint on herself. Her implicit self-understanding will only offer provisional guidance in achieving an explicit linguistic formulation of her projects. Sartre's goal in creating existential psychoanalysis can be interpreted as an effort to integrate the analysand's first-person perspective with the analyst's third-person viewpoint. Sartre develops existential psychoanalysis in two distinct ways. First, he writes several biographical interpretations of famous French writers to show how the method can be applied in practice. He uses both their works (as expressions of their fundamental projects) and their lifestyles to illuminate this understanding.[91] He also uses the same approach in writing the first part of his own autobiography, *The Words*.[92] Second, he tries to provide a general typology of possible fundamental projects (by describing different possible relations a person can have to the world). Some of these types are: to seek complete union with raw being, to identify with nothingness, to live ambiguously between the two modes.[93] The project of authenticity involves internalizing the ambiguity of the human condition, understanding its elements, and acting in light of this self-comprehension. Sartre did not develop a distinctive therapy; though he explored the nature of self-deception, he left to others the task of helping people transcend it.

For Sartre, authenticity primarily involves acknowledging the realities of the human condition and explicitly accepting their consequences. This entails accepting the power to choose anew in each situation (refusing the various ruses people use to escape their freedom and responsibility), taking on the situation – rather than trying to ignore or distance oneself from it, and accepting responsibility for choices and the model they offer to others in similar circumstances. This early Sartrean version of authenticity is also primarily a formal ideal – concerning the manner of acting, the attitudes adopted before, during, and after acting. Later, Sartre introduces more substantive elements, which include a joy in the accurate revelation of being, a reciprocity among people who acknowledge and act to sustain each other's freedom, and an effort to provide better opportunities for authenticity to those dominated by totalitarian regimes. Sartre develops these additional features of his notion of authenticity gradually as he reflects on the possibilities for collective social life.[94]

In *Being and Nothingness* Sartre seemed to argue for the futility of all types of personal relationships. All the relationships he discusses fail to achieve the end they seek and even fail to sustain themselves.[95] (Sartre emulates Hegel's dialectic in his studies of concrete personal attitudes, like love and sexual desire.) The grimness of this view partly defines the ambiance of Sartre's existentialism. His later works, however, show that these early analyses are only partial descriptions – characterizing an inauthentic way of being (this was also suggested by a few carefully placed footnotes in *Being and Nothingness*[96]). Later, Sartre endorses the possibility of reciprocity between people when he examines the relationship between reader and writer. The writer appeals to the freedom of the reader to reconstitute the meaning he is striving to articulate, and the reader relies on the coherence of the writer while reconstituting the meaning of the text. In this way both reader and writer rely on each other's freedom in order to be fully free.[96] Using this relationship as a model, Sartre then argues that all expressive action appeals to the freedom of other people; it asks to be supported by others and given an appropriate response. The observers of the action may choose not to support it, but in responding at all, they acknowledge the person's freedom in proposing this goal. Their responses also appeal to the freedom of the original actor; they challenge the actor either to abide by the action or to alter its course in light of their responses. This mutual assumption of each other's freedom and the possibility of uniting in common projects constitute Sartre's version of Hegel's mutual recognition.[97] It adds a social dimension to his initial conception of authenticity.

PHILOSOPHICAL ANTHROPOLOGY

Philosophical anthropologists include both philosophers and scientists. In addition to developing analyses of central human phenomena (e.g., laughing and crying, asceticism, suicide, and boredom), they draw important theoretical and practical conclusions from scientific research. Though its core questions (what are humanity's distinctive features? what distinguishes humanity from other species?) have a long history, philosophical anthropology makes real progress on them by using recent scientific theories in biology, anthropology, psychology, culture theory, neurophysiology, and other relevant areas. Indeed, one of its goals is to integrate the many disciplines that investigate human life and reverse the fragmentation of human studies that typifies twentieth-century thought. Thinkers within this tradition do not limit themselves to scientific analysis, and they may draw different implications from the empirical research than the original experimenters. Their goal is to create a perspective and type of rationality that at least can initiate a synthesis (as well as a critique) of the existing disciplinary studies of human beings.

A dominant motif is rooting the whole person in the surrounding environment. They resist conceptualizing human beings as isolated, self-contained, atomic individuals. Instead they explore the complex ways in which persons are defined by natural and social contexts. As a result, they are less interested in individual uniqueness or in ideals like authenticity. They concentrate on clarifying humanity's common features, and they embrace social ideals like solidarity. Some possible candidates for common features are: upright posture, a lack of specific instincts, an unusually long period of infant dependency, and culture. They also resist the rationalistic view that human beings are cognition machines, preferring instead to explore the roles that irrational and unconscious factors play in human action. They develop a variety of new concepts to express distinctively human features (e.g., world-openness, sublimation, eccentricity). Since they situate human life in nature, culture, and history, they examine human embodiment, the role of institutions and tradition, and universal human capacities such as language use.

Perhaps one way to appreciate the difference between existentialism and philosophical anthropology is to consider that Sartre – in the later period of the *Critique*, when he sought to incorporate both first- and third-person viewpoints and the ongoing dynamic of history – saw his work as closer to the tradition of philosophical anthropology. Even though he still distanced himself from the analytical reason of science, he believed that supplementing the first-person, phenomenological viewpoint was necessary.[99] Usually when a thinker attempts to address humanity's relation to history and culture, to social groups, to language, and to biology, he moves toward philosophical anthropology. Many of these factors escape phenomenological description because they either operate in the background – beneath the level of explicit consciousness – or lie beyond the scope of merely individual consciousness and thus outside the range of phenomenological inquiry.

Scheler created the modern enterprise of philosophical anthropology in his last public lecture, which was published as a short book, *Man's Place in Nature* (1928).[100] The primary figure in this movement is Arnold Gehlen (1904–76), but valuable contributions were also made by Helmuth Plessner (1892–1985), Kurt Goldstein (1878–1965), Ernst Cassirer (1874–1945), Wolfgang Köhler (1904–76), Paul Schilder (1886–1946), and, more recently, Erwin Straus (1891–1975) and Michael Polyani (1891–1976). Gehlen was a Nazi sympathizer, and his views were neglected after the Nazis were defeated. This led many scholars to ignore the entire movement, thinking it was tainted with its leader's stain. In France, Merleau-Ponty used the research of many of these thinkers to develop his own understanding of human perception and cognition. In Germany, a serious re-evaluation of this movement has finally begun. In the US, Richard Schacht and Marjorie Grene have sought to cultivate interest in these figures. In the discussion below, I will concentrate on Scheler, Goldstein, and Gehlen.

SCHELER

Although Max Scheler (1874–1928) was primarily a phenomenologist, his last lecture inaugurated the new philosophical discipline of philosophical anthropology. As was his common practice, Scheler sketched an overview of possible positions in the essay "Man and History" before articulating his own views.[101] There he discusses five main positions and works to overcome their weaknesses, while constructing his own theory.

The first conception of human being is the Christian view, which asserts that human beings are creatures of God, have "fallen" as a result of their free will, but can be "saved" because a redeemer god-man died for their sins. The emotion that defines this position is fear – fear of God's punishment. The second conception is the Greek vision that sees human beings as rational/social animals who participate in a larger metaphysical order of nous. The order of human reason and that of the cosmos are identical; thus, insofar as humanity can become wholly rational, it unites itself with the eternal and unchanging cosmic order. The third conception of human being is the naturalistic one derived from science. On this model humans are purely natural beings like other animals. Human life is dominated by drives that interact to produce various intellectual capacities. Human knowledge results from discovering successful responses to problems. The fourth conception reverses the Greek interpretation of humanity. It elevates life over reason, devaluing reason in the process – treating it as alienating and impoverished. This conception praises life-values and extols identification with the life-process; it is a Dionysian picture of humanity, which claims that ecstatic states – dance, trance, and narcosis – can produce unity with the creative vitality of nature. On this interpretation, history's civilizing process represents regress rather than progress, undermining humanity's natural bond with life.[102]

Nietzsche's view emerges more vividly in the fifth conception – the historical task of creating the *Übermensch*. This position originates with disgust over current exemplars of humanity, and attempts through will and planning to elevate a wide range of human types – to produce god-like persons that will eventually replace human fantasies about God.[103] On this view, people have an historical responsibility to contribute to this elevation, both individually and collectively. This requires strenuous effort, will, responsibility, foresight, and detailed knowledge of human possibilities and psychology. History becomes the medium through which the *Übermensch* can be realized.

Scheler favors a sixth position. He thinks that it is more attuned to the historical developments of modernity and that it has a better chance of success than Nietzsche's dream of creating god-like persons. He calls this conception the "unified" or "total" person. Humanity exhibits a variety of contrasting features (e.g., reason/passion; masculine/feminine), and history has often emphasized one pole at the expense of the other. Scheler thinks the current age is compensating for these overemphases by discovering value in the other poles. He stresses the values in *each* side of these dichotomies and reconciles them by giving each its due. Scheler believes that capitalism has long emphasized ascetic values and that now the pendulum is swinging to restore Dionysian values. Thus, Scheler seeks to reconcile the Apollonian (demand for order and distance) with the Dionysian (demand for energy and identification), the Western drive to control nature with Eastern sympathetic union with it, life and spirit, reason and passion, male and female.[104]

Each of these dimensions is different, and Scheler seeks to reconcile the opposing poles on all of them. Full reconciliation would produce a "total" or "whole" humanity. He believes that the historical process is contributing to this goal. Biological evolution has taken humanity as far as it can; any future development must arise from cultural evolution. Becoming more fully human involves acknowledging and reconciling the poles of these classical oppositions, and this is an historical project everyone can embrace (and it allows every culture and subgroup to learn from every other one). He acknowledges the energizing power of life, but also insists that spirit direct this energy toward the best possible outcomes. This is just an initial sketch of Scheler's position. He examines human nature more thoroughly in his final essay: *Man's Place in Nature*. This book closely examines all forms of life in order to arrive at a more precise understanding of the differentiating features of humanity. The brevity of the book means that its arguments are sketchy, but Scheler appeals to a wide range of evidence from different sciences to render his position plausible. He demonstrates his seriousness by generously acknowledging a wide variety of practical capacities, social bonds, and even forms of cognition in non-human species. This strategy forces him to examine what is *distinctively* human in these areas (e.g., tool-use, cognition, and communication).

Scheler begins with a discussion of life in general, suggesting that all living species are animated by vital feelings and drives, which are sources of activity. These drives are typically goal-directed, but not necessarily conscious. They establish the orientation of the organism in its environment; even plants possess such an orientation in their tropisms toward light and nutrients. He suggests that plants have a drive for growth and reproduction, but not for power in Nietzsche's sense of self-organization and strength.[105] Plants, however, do not exhibit sensation, which requires some neural reporting from sensors to a central nervous system. He interprets sensation to be drive-motivated attention, and thus never purely passive. Sensation structures the environmental field according to the organism's vital values; it is guided by drives even prior to external stimulation.[106] Plants do exhibit directed behavior, but they do not animate themselves, make choices, or even exhibit reflex behavior. For Scheler, life is always *centric* – oriented toward the outside world. He suggests that plants react more "organically" than many animals because their parts are more interdependent. Moreover, he claims that the profusion of plant life in an environmental niche does not necessarily serve any evolutionary or practical function. Such cases show that life exhibits an impulse for fanciful play and aesthetic excess, and Scheler suggests that this may be a better candidate for a governing principle of life than survival.[107] He insists that vital drives operate in all organisms, including human beings.

Scheler notes that the world's relationship to drives is *resistance*; this root experience provides an organism's living sense of reality.[108] The last experience to be lost in extreme psychopathology, this experienced reality is much deeper than mere belief or intellectual conviction. Rarely are drives expressed or stimulated purely for the sake of pleasure alone; this is a late, decadent development. The expression of vital feeling produces inherent joy. Scheler believes that special effort to achieve pleasure compensates for deeper suffering. Hedonistic behavior thus is always indicative of a vital discontent; at best it offers a momentary palliative, but rarely addresses the true source of suffering.[109]

Instincts are purposive and meaningful. They respond to pre-set environmental triggers that are meaningful to the species, but the organism's response is automatic and unvarying, rather than voluntary and adaptable. It is a direct response to meaningful structure; no additional cause is needed. Instincts always serve the species, never individuals in their own right.[110] A complete expressive response emerges when instincts are triggered, but the response is not learned. One function of intelligence is to make instincts flexible in diverse situations, to guide them without succumbing to them. This is achieved primarily by sublimating them – redirecting them toward different goals.[111] When individuals are able to do this, they rise above mere species-life. This capacity for redirecting instincts may not be unique to humanity, but humanity can exercise it regularly. The more that instincts dominate, the less human is the organism.

Habits and conditioned reflexes involve goal-directed behavior that becomes organized and modified in response to past trials.[112] If spontaneous movements get rewarded, they tend to be repeated in expectation of the reward. When complex, directed responses develop, they can become habits. Sometimes habits emerge through imitation, and over time they can become social traditions – valued for their own sake – even if they no longer reliably achieve their original goals. Many animal species exhibit habituated social traditions, e.g., wolf packs and herds. Once established, tradition is taken for granted and appears timeless. The most direct way to undermine the power of tradition is to provide its genealogy; historical comprehension of a tradition reveals its limited purpose and invites its rejection when that purpose is no longer relevant.[113] Habits can be woven together by individuals who see how to unify them in unique situations; in this fashion the individual can advance the capacities of the species.

Next, Scheler considers practical intelligence. This is shared with the higher mammals, but it is central to humanity's inventiveness and historical development. Practical intelligence involves insight; it corrects for taking habits for granted. It grasps new meaningful structures in a situation and responds directly with a solution – resulting from an "a-ha" experience.[114] It does not require trial and error; and it functions by grasping meaningful wholes and their relationships. Sometimes the most effective response is not the habitual one; more creative actions are required. Practical intelligence discovers viable alternatives. The solution is not predictable because the individual did not know it beforehand. Creativity is engendered by a deep attunement to structural wholes in the environment.

So far Scheler has discussed capacities which humanity shares with other animals. Now he clarifies humanity's distinctive features, one of which he calls "spirit," though he does not mean either reason or practical intelligence. It includes conceptual thought and intuition of essences, but also the capacities for love, for preferring higher values, and for wonder and bliss.[115] Spirit transcends the life-process and has the capacity even to oppose it, though it also depends on life both for its existence and energy. Scheler thinks spirit distinguishes humanity in fundamental ways from other animals, primarily because humans exist in the world differently than do animals and because they have a self in a way animals do not. Spirit makes resisting vital drives possible; it allows humans to see *things,* rather than merely experience *resistances*. Humans can respond to objects independently of their drives; this allows them to distance themselves from the world – to be less compelled by its demands.[116] Other animals are fully immersed, unable to see objects per se, perceiving only configurations of meaning that are related to their drives. Humans possess a world; they do not just live in it.

In addition, humans experience selves in ways animals do not. For example, they have the capacity to identify and dissociate from their actions.[117] Not every action is experienced as owned/disowned in this sense, but many are. Animals lack this capacity; Scheler suggests that they live in a drugged state of consciousness – simply acting and reacting, sometimes choosing, sometimes solving practical problems – but never experiencing these capacities as distinctively themselves. Humans also can attend to the reports of their body-schemas and thus can achieve a degree of self-consciousness in a way animals do not. Animals receive such reports and act on them, but they do not objectify and reflect on those reports. Similarly, humans have a will that outlasts the energy of their drives and thus can sustain a continuous project across time, even if the project becomes tangential or inimical to their drives.[118] Persons can also respond to values, especially values higher than life. These capacities are organized by a distinctive center defining each person, which Scheler thinks is the core of human selfhood. This centeredness provides a lived spatiality for humans that animals lack, and allows them to coordinate highly complex sensory input. Persons can reflect on their own position – objectifying their situation and relationships.[119] The fact that humans transcend the surrounding world also makes humor and irony possible.

Spirit cannot be objectified, according to Scheler, only co-experienced. Humans do not learn others' personhood by judging, categorizing, or using them. They must co-experience other's conscious states through sympathy.[120] Spirit is manifest only through acts. The core of selfhood for Scheler just is the continuous self-execution of an ordered series of acts. People cannot introspect their own spirit; they can only recall their past sense of personal existence. Freely co-participating in others' tasks is the most direct way of knowing them. Ideation – the capacity to see particulars as exemplars of categories – is also essential to spirit. Humans grasp essences only by suspending practical demands in order to intuit the realm of essences.[121] People need not neutralize or bracket reality to grasp essences (as Husserl suggested); they can simply turn away from reality's immediate demands. They may still perceive reality, but they can look beyond it toward another realm.

Spirit nonetheless remains entirely dependent on life for its energy. The life-process must be sublimated and drive satisfaction must be deferred in order for spirit to develop. Life is dominant, but spirit can emerge out of life in favorable circumstances.[122] Spirit has its own distinctive nature and structure; it is not just a reconfiguration of life at a higher level. But it is helpless in generating its own energy; it must borrow this from the vital drives. The lower orders of life are the most vitally powerful; the higher orders of life depend on them. Spirit and will, once they develop, can guide the life-process, making it respond to and realize higher values. People may redirect drives, but this usually fails if they try to conquer them willfully; sublimating them by guiding them toward higher values affords greater success.[123] Scheler thus asserts that the passions (direct or sublimated) are the motive-force of history; ideas and values can guide these drives and can unify a cohesive social group. At best, spirit can only shape the overall direction of history. In different historical eras, different vital drives predominate.[124] Thus, no single "materialist" principle will correctly describe every historical era. Some eras may be dominated by the drive for survival, others by the drive to reproduce, still others by the drive for power and honor.

Scheler thus sees significant continuity between humans and other animals, but he also sees important discontinuities. He provides the basis for a new theory about what is uniquely human. Spirit and centered selfhood are the keys to that vision. Humans are not unique in using tools, in responding to meaningful forms in the environment, in communicating with others of their species, or even in practical innovative intelligence. Other mammals can do all these things. But animals lack the functions of centered selfhood, and they lack the ability to grasp essences. Elaborating these features constitutes Scheler's special contribution.

GOLDSTEIN

Kurt Goldstein (1878–1965) was a medical doctor who worked with brain-damaged patients after World War I. He brings the same sense of wonder to the study of neurology as does Oliver Sacks today. His two most important books are *The Organism* (1934) and *Human Nature in the Light of Psychopathology* (1940).[125] In this brief sketch, I will focus on the latter text. Goldstein is one of the original gestalt theorists, insisting that the organism is more than the sum of its parts and that it always meets stimulation as a whole, rather than as isolated neural circuits.[126] His orientation is empirical without being atomistic, attentive to subtleties in the research without being wedded to any particular philosophical interpretation of the data. He insists on the importance of basic models or "pictures" for ongoing empirical research, but he believes such models can be disproven by the data and is reluctant to postulate auxiliary hypotheses just to save a model that seems flawed. He seeks to account for the responses of individual organisms (persons), not for typical behavioral patterns of species.[127] He often dismisses simple quantitative correlations because he believes that the organism responds differently under different initial conditions and in different states of health. He first seeks to *describe* the pattern of responses in the individual before attempting any explanation of it.[128] He takes the viewpoint of the patient being described seriously, often relying on it to understand the kind of response adopted. Like Sartre, he thinks persons are totalities, and he seeks to describe the overall style of the person's responses and stance toward the world, rather than seeking causal laws that apply to all persons indifferently. He also believes that full self-expression is rarely achieved in part because individuals must limit their actions so as not to encroach too extensively on others.[129]

Goldstein's holism is limited to individual organisms. Though he does think one must locate the organism in its natural, social, and cultural environments in order to fully understand its patterns of response, he is not committed to the view that all environments (and history) are totalities. He does, however, insist that organisms react as totalities to meaningful stimuli. He thinks much neurological and psychological research goes awry because it attempts to isolate specific neurological circuits for experimental examination. This procedure necessarily falsifies the lived responses of persons in context. He suggests that the organism is always in a state of excitation, and thus perpetually active.[130] Its responses derive from changes in this activity, which involve the entire nervous system, not just the point of stimulation. In general, Goldstein posits a figure-ground relation in the pattern of stimulation as well as the pattern of response; the figure aspect cannot be isolated from the ground aspect in either case. In effect, the background of the stimulus conditions its meaning, and the background state of the organism conditions its response.[131] The organism as a whole can have different levels of excitability, and this is affected by the frequency of external stimulation. Nonetheless, usually the organism returns to a state of equilibrium when external stimulation ceases. This is the source of constancy in its response patterns. Goldstein also suggests that the organism never adapts to the environment passively when the environment undergoes significant changes; rather, it adapts in a way that will allow it to achieve its own optimal expression in the changed circumstances.[132] In short, the organism has internal patterns of preferred behavior that embody its own distinct individuality. Only if the organism is severely damaged does it seek mere survival.

If neurologists attempt to isolate neural circuits to study their patterns of response experimentally, then typically the neural responses will be stronger, longer, more rigid, and more determined by the stimulus than under conditions of everyday life because the rest of the organism's neural activity (the background) is eliminated.[133] Similar results occur if they examine the organism in reduced circumstances or states of illness. Such an "objective" approach is likely to yield misleading hypotheses both about the organism as a whole and about the way its parts work together. To exemplify how the organism develops as a totality, Goldstein uses the example of learning to ride a bicycle. The new bike-rider may practice the relevant skills separately, but simply adding these isolated skills together will not produce a successful rider. Rather, novice bikers must, through trial and error, modify incorrect movements in relation to one another in accordance with a felt sense of adequacy, until they get it right.[134] Too often researchers believe they must break down such integrated, holistic skills into analytical components in the name of "objectivity." Goldstein resists this atomistic demand, which he thinks has harmed the quality of neurological research.

Just as the sick or damaged organism operates at a lower level of functioning than the healthy organism, Goldstein believes that lower organisms operate at a lower level of functioning than higher organisms. He concludes that neurology cannot understand higher organisms on the basis of lower ones; it must do the reverse.[135] Understanding human organisms in context is important because they achieve the deepest integration; less developed organisms exhibit only partial integrations by comparison. Psychology must never understand human responses on the model of animal responses because the less integrated response is a simpler, reduced version of the more integrated response. In addition, Goldstein challenges the many versions of a theory of basic drives in human beings. Which organismic demands predominate a particular individual will vary with the individual and with the relation between individual and environment. The only common drive is to find the most preferred individual expression within whatever environment an organism inhabits – to express its own individual essence as fully as possible. In addition, Goldstein rejects the Freudian unconscious. He claims that all actions have three aspects: voluntary processes, somatic processes, and various moods and transient states that float across the surface of consciousness without always being registered or acknowledged.[136] All three aspects contribute to the total organismic response. Sometimes one of these elements predominates; for example, thinkers tend to foreground voluntary elements in their response to the world, while artists tend to foreground transient emotional elements. Nonetheless, in all actions all three aspects play a role.

Using these general methodological rules Goldstein examined various brain-damaged patients for whom he cared during and after the First World War. Though their patterns of response are simplified, this allows Goldstein to provide a clear description of key capacities they lack that may play a central role in normal human functioning. One such capacity he calls the "abstract attitude," a capacity that allows the organism to distance itself from the concrete demands of the situation, to appreciate general configurations in the environment, and to achieve the degree of organic centeredness necessary to performing complex tasks.[137] The abstract attitude is not correlated with any specific area of the brain, but with a higher level of functioning of the whole nervous system. When the organism is less integrated, it achieves the abstract attitude less readily. The loss of the abstract attitude produces odd deficiencies in the performance of practical tasks as well as syndromes such as infantile autism.

On the basis of his investigations, Goldstein draws a number of important conclusions. For example, he draws a distinction between drill and practice. Drill is repetition of a specific behavior that compensates for a lack of natural instincts in humans. Even here the mere repetition is not what makes drill effective; instead, insight is required to adapt the pattern of response to the situation properly. Practice, on the other hand, allows the organism to find responses that best express its own individual manner or style of approaching the world, and allows individuals to develop their abilities in that area to the fullest degree possible.[138] Practice thus helps the organism find its preferred pattern of response for that activity. Goldstein does not deny that drill can be important in the mastery of some crucial skills, but he believes that educators should find ways to allow individuals to practice a variety of skills in order to find the actions in which they can truly flourish.

He also claims that the effort to know something alters the phenomenon that the scientist seeks to know, including herself. As knowledge expands and becomes determinate, both knower and known are altered. In order to know another individual organism, one must observe its responses in a wide variety of environments. Only then will the full range of its preferred responses and the basic style of its response patterns become clear. Knowing other persons (or any organism) is a skill like riding a bike; it requires a coalescence of a variety of capacities and an intense sensitivity to the individuals to be known.[139] The knower must grasp the organism in a variety of contexts and remain open to the revelations of each. With careful attention, eventually the best hypothesis about the individual will emerge, and the synthetic patterns that define that individual's essence or preferred pattern of response will be identified. He also suggests that the value of knowledge is simply the intrinsic importance of grasping reality as it is, rather than achieving greater control over others, more effective manipulation of the world, or personal pleasure. Knowledge reveals the world as it is; it allows scientists to transcend the limitations of a single perspective. Learning is a continuing process that seeks to comprehend reality, but it is also a creative process that gradually locates essential connections in the subject matter via insight.[140]

GEHLEN

Like Scheler, Arnold Gehlen (1904–76) wants philosophical anthropology to maintain contact with the best work in the human sciences, using their results to frame its own questions and posing questions for them to answer. He thinks the key question of philosophical anthropology – what are the essential features of human life? – can provide a unifying impulse to the diverse researches in the social sciences. Like Dilthey, Gehlen seeks the basic categories that organize human existence and social life, the irreducible features that distinguish humanity from the rest of animal life. His central answer to the question is that humans are biologically ill-adapted creatures who are born helpless and thus depend on culture to solve problems of survival and adaptation to environmental changes.[141] In effect, humans are naturally impoverished; they lack the instincts that facilitate the survival of other species. Yet the cultural structures and traditions through which human existence is maintained are tenuous and – especially in the modern world – subject to continuous erosion. Gehlen fears that the corrosiveness of modernity might be disastrous for the species as a whole, and thus seeks to protect culture and tradition at any cost.[142] This accounts for his extremely conservative political views.

Gehlen believes that the human species has undergone minimal biological changes throughout history. Instead of producing linear development, history allows a diversity of human types to emerge. One of humanity's central features is its capacity for self-interpretation and self-orientation. This allows humans to distance themselves from their own actions. Action is the fundamental concept that defines humanity for Gehlen. It unifies the classical Cartesian oppositions between mind and body. Crucial to human action is anticipatory reflection in which people imagine scenarios beforehand, consider how they might unfold, and even approach the situation experimentally to discover a response that will produce success. Most actions discover their best means of achievement and their precise ends only as they are taking place; practical action thus exists in continuous dialogue with the situation.[143] Anticipatory reflection shows that humans live as much in the future as in the present; they stand out from situations, rather than becoming immersed in their immediate demands. Like Heidegger, Gehlen suggests that theorizing and cognition are forms of practical activity. He argues that the function of the intellect (and of all the cultural products it produces) is to gain greater control over the surrounding world. All actions involve a complex adaptation to the requirements of the situation plus a will to structure it creatively. Perception and behavior are integrated in the course of action, and this involves complex coordination between the lived body, perception, and feedback as the action unfolds.

Gehlen's central premise is that humans are defective as purely vital life-forms because they lack instincts that insure their adaptation to the environment. In effect, humans are born prematurely without the instincts that allow other species to survive. Infants are helpless throughout their first years of life, and they mature within cultural institutions and traditions, which must inculcate survival skills. Culture thus compensates for the vital defectiveness of humans. Because they lack a system of instincts, however, humans are "world-open." Their actions are freer, more plastic, capable of being shaped by culture, capable of undergoing development through challenge, imitation, and education.[144] Like Sartre's freedom (which brings burdensome responsibility), Gehlen's world-openness comes with a price: an excessive sensitivity to environmental stimulation and a surplus of internal impulses. The human organism is typically assaulted with sensory input that has no inherent survival function. Humans learn to filter much of this stimulation by fashioning symbols that reduce complex properties to simplified meanings. They then manipulate these simplified meanings, rather than the chaotic sensory stream. Gehlen calls this simplifying process "relief" or "disburdenment."[145] It allows humans to react with greater astuteness to the demands of the environment – nature and social. Gehlen praises any structure, tradition, or cultural institution that can increase this "relief." Culture also imposes order and coherence on the plasticity of human responses. Work, family, laws, marriage, and property all provide order to human activity, which is essential to the flourishing of the species.

Without culture, human life would be chaos of impulses and environmental overstimulation. Culture literally makes sanity and effective action possible. It is tenuous, however, and forever assaulted because of the constant innovation of modern technology. Moreover, modern values, like autonomy and human rights, invite people to criticize their institutions and traditions, and, whenever they are challenged, they can no longer function optimally.[146] They only provide "relief" for human agents when they are unquestioned and taken for granted. They offer the best solutions to typical human problems that have been discovered through history. As soon as traditions and institutions become scrutinized, they become one more site for the onslaught of stimulation. This weakness in modern institutions causes people to turn inward, experiencing anxiety and fragility. Because they must meet each new situation anew, without pre-structuring and filtering by institutions, their actions become uncertain and haphazard.[147] Because they do not develop consistent patterns of response, they build no character or mettle. Moreover, the incessant consumerism of the recent phase of capitalism undermines the ascetic restraint that made success in achieving long-term goals possible. For these reasons, Gehlen believed the current era of humanity is an especially dangerous one, and he embraced extreme political solutions to restore the power of tradition and culture. Without the second nature that culture provides, Gehlen feared humanity as a whole might perish.

In addition to this excess of external stimulation, Gehlen also claims humans are subject to an excess of impulsive energies. This accounts for humanity's rich fantasy life. Because impulses are constantly pressing and only one can be addressed at a time, fantasy develops as a secondary source of need-satisfaction. Culture also provides ordered opportunities by which groups of humans can satisfy such demands collectively without destroying one another (e.g., contests, play). Language also makes a central contribution here, as do tradition and habit. In addition to the excess of impulses, Gehlen suggests that many needs adapt to the specific limits of a situation and thus allow some degree of satisfaction even in an impoverished context. The notion of a "feedback loop," so important to information theory, was developed by Gehlen. The satisfaction of needs can be curbed, restrained, or sublimated in human beings. Many of the achievements of culture have been made possible by this ascetic possibility, which Gehlen admires.[148] One of his reasons for concern about modern humanity is its refusal to accept such asceticism and its pursuit of immediate gratifications. Though needs and impulsive energies seek satisfaction, not every action aims to satisfy needs. Many are pursued for inherent value and their "play" element.

Gehlen examines the role of language in human existence because of its importance to higher mental operations. He sought to understand how language is assimilated as the organism matures. The difficult task for the theorist is not to presuppose the linguistic or cognitive capacities that language makes possible in explaining its acquisition. Gehlen believes that sound is a distinctive element or world that humans inhabit. As with most actions, speech emerges through imitation and playful attempts to modulate this atmosphere of sound. Sounds are both produced and perceived, and like touch they are perceived as they are produced. Gradually sounds interlace with visual stimuli, and things begin to be named. Naming objects allows people to achieve distance from the immediacy of the world's demands.[149] In addition, verbal cries can function like behavioral gestures, which may be produced in play (for oneself) or with expressive intent (to command attention). When sound becomes gesture, then the communicative element of speech emerges. These are some conditions for the development of language. Gehlen believes language is essential to human flourishing.

World-openness and the constant excess of both internal and external stimulation thus constitute Gehlen's central themes. Culture and tradition control and structure this excess and allow vitally weak organisms to achieve remarkably successful adaptations. But the accomplishments of culture are tenuous in a way the achievements of instinct are not. They are especially endangered in modern conditions. Gehlen thus offers an analysis of the human condition diametrically opposed to that of Rousseau. The state of nature would be a condition of chaos and disaster for humanity. Only because humans have produced stable and coherent institutions can they truly flourish.

ASSESSMENT

Taken together, these two movements provide penetrating hypotheses about some essential features of human existence. The different perspectives they offer supplement each other, and those wishing to contribute to this inquiry today can draw on both movements.

Three common objections to existential philosophers are clearly mistaken. Neither Heidegger nor Sartre treats individuals as isolated atoms. Both see an essential social relatedness between self and other (Sartre) or self and cultural tradition (Heidegger). Both envision the possibility that individuals can enhance each other through achieving authenticity and mutual recognition. In addition, neither thinker offers an analysis of persons that is overly gloomy or dark. When they stress the difficulties of existence, they highlight human possibility and grandeur. Typically, however, they simply try to clarify the complex structures operating in each person and to draw plausible conclusions from this analysis. Finally, while both thinkers counsel taking existence seriously and living vitally, neither accepts either relativism or subjectivism about truth. Both believe their claims about human life have universal validity, and both appeal to their readers to confirm their claims for themselves.

Many thinkers in both movements show how to root human beings in surrounding environments (natural, instrumental, interpersonal, and cultural) without making them passive products of those environments. Both Sartre and Heidegger stress the role of facticity while asserting the importance of transcendence and purposiveness. The philosophical anthropologists offer a holistic conception of human existence that emphasizes its eccentricity while acknowledging the reciprocal influence of organism and environment. Humans develop standard patterns of interacting and structuring the surrounding environment, but these patterns can undergo change even as they create stability.

One weakness in existentialism is an overly formal conception of authenticity. Simply acknowledging one's freedom and responsibility, or making one's choices in the full awareness of the finitude of human life, is an insufficient ethical ideal. It may complement other ideals, and it may facilitate a new ethical awakening, but it is also compatible with heinous acts, and it may require a self-consciousness that is inimical to living in the most vital and passionate way. Sartrean responsibility seems empty because it is always present, even when the obstacles are high and the determining influences are strong. Even if he is right that we always have available choices, this fact is not sufficient for any significant concept of responsibility. Responsibility depends at least in part on the likelihood of influencing events and on mitigating background factors. Heidegger's notion of anticipatory resoluteness suggests spiritual intensity rather than substantive ethical accomplishment. One can act resolutely in light of one's chosen models and tradition and still choose badly – contributing to a tradition that is and was always corrupt (e.g., maintaining oppression). Nietzsche sought to give real content to his notion of higher humanity (and authentic individuality) by incorporating the values of life-affirmation, courage, vitality, self-overcoming, and aesthetic stylization. Sartre eventually saw this deficiency and sought to rectify it with a new conception of mutual recognition and an historical goal of providing the material conditions that could enhance freedom for everyone. But even these goals seem overly formal in contrast with the robust sense of "nobility" developed by Nietzsche. Some way of distinguishing good from evil goals would be an important supplement to existentialist authenticity.

In addition, both Heidegger and Sartre could be clearer on how authenticity is achieved in practice. Sartre suggests that a sudden achievement of purified reflection is needed, an idea that seems very similar to Heidegger's moment of vision. For both these epiphanies allow persons to constitute their identities and to grasp the full truth of the human condition. But these "lightning bolts" are rare in everyday experience, and some way of actively attaining them seems necessary. One might also question whether these self-constituting moments of choice are the whole story about authentic selfhood. Nietzsche, for example, located selfhood as much in talents and developing habits, as in aspirations and chosen ideals. Merleau-Ponty suggests that authenticity requires creatively transforming institutionalized patterns of action and thought, and he shows how this can and has been achieved in both politics and art by examining specific leaders and artists. Both suggest that individuals achieve authentic selfhood by modifying patterns of action they have already mastered; this position better illuminates how it can be achieved in practice.

A few additional specific criticisms might encourage some useful comparisons between these figures. For example, Sartre is more dismissive about emotions generally than he should be (they allegedly are a magical abandonment of instrumental orientation toward the world). Heidegger's theory of moods indicates both an understanding of their pervasiveness in human experience and the ways in which they can positively enhance one's insight into situations and one's future possibilities. Secondly, many of Sartre's claims about consciousness depend on the notion that certain types of experience exclude other ones (e.g., being an object for others excludes being a subject for oneself; imagination excludes perception). Sometimes Sartre qualifies such claims, but the complexities of experience suggest that these exclusivity claims do not hold universally. One can daydream as one operates in the world, and one can hear one's words from the other's viewpoint as one speaks. Thus, Sartre makes some simplifying assumptions that belie the actual complexity of experience. Finally, Gehlen is certainly right to insist on the ordering role of institutions in human life, but he misses the ways in which human action continues to sustain such institutions over time. They are always more open to change than he wants to allow. Gehlen also misses the resilience of humanity when institutions seem to implode, for example, during wars or natural disasters. Gehlen also needs to acknowledge that the habits produced by cultural institutions are not valuable in themselves; everything depends on the human results produced by the institutions. Defending institutions for their own sake is excessively formal in the same way that the existentialist ideal of authenticity is. Thus, the ordering role of institutions can be acknowledged without abandoning a critical perspective on them.

STRUCTURALISM

CORE CONTRIBUTIONS

Structuralism began in linguistics in the 1920s, and spread to literary and social theory in the 1940s and '50s while existentialism and Western Marxism were still dominant. It displaced existentialism as the favored movement among French intellectuals in the early 1960s. It continues to have some influence today because of the rise of cognitivism throughout the social sciences – especially in psychology, anthropology, and sociology. It also continues to exert some influence in linguistics and narrative theory, primarily through the work of Chomsky and Genette. It developed differently in different national contexts (primarily in Russia, France, and the US). No single figure dominates this movement in the way that Sartre and Heidegger exemplify existentialism. Saussure (1857–1913), Jakobson (1896–1982), Lacan (1901–81), Lévi-Strauss (b. 1908), Barthes (1915–80), Althusser (1918–90), Greimas (1917–92), Genette (b. 1930), Piaget (1896–1980), and Chomsky (b. 1928) all played pivotal roles throughout its history. Since genuinely innovative thinkers extended its basic principles, structuralism moved beyond linguistics into literary and social theory.

Structuralists typically attempt to uncover unconscious structures that organize and inform human activity. Usually these structures do not determine specific actions, but rather set limits on possible actions. The structures do not predict exactly what a person will do, but they establish boundaries for possible or intelligible actions (e.g., the laws of grammar set limits on the sayable without determining the said). Such structures are constituted by complex relational networks of terms, none of which is meaningful without the surrounding system. Structuralists claim that surface behavior is the result of complex transformations of simple underlying structures. Such structures are allegedly universal, e.g., rules of universal grammar that allow children to master the particular grammars of their distinctive natural languages; the rules that govern kinship relations and taboos. Because these structures operate unconsciously, structuralists challenge the claim that rational self-conscious subjects fully comprehend the sources of their actions.

One structuralist procedure is to locate a particular behavioral response within a small set of well-defined possibilities, the parameters for which are created by the structuralist. The parameters circumscribe the possible options, and this grid supposedly helps structuralists clarify the significance of the specific response. Alternative responses would have different meanings; so particular actions can be clarified by situating them amidst the other logical possibilities. The structuralist's task is to find illuminating parameters that define a logical space that specifies useful contrasts. Suppose, for example, that the game of chess allows for only four opening moves and that each of these moves exhibits a particular tactical approach to the game. By using this framework to understand a particular opening move, the strategy of this game could then be "explained." The implicit assumption is that specific opening moves are selected against an unconscious backdrop of other logical possibilities that give this move its meaning. This procedure can be used to study any well-ordered signifying system, whether it be clothing fashions, art styles, narrative genres, conversational maneuvers, cultural myths, or food menus. Central to the strategy, however, is the claim that the various logical possibilities have different meanings that can be understood only in relation to each other. Without this assumption, the illuminating power of the logical grid would be reduced, since the exclusion of the other options would be insignificant.

Structuralists typically examine sign-systems or meaningful expressive practices. But they are less interested in interpreting specific expressions than in elucidating their conditions of possibility. Thus, they try to uncover the unconscious codes that make the creation, transmission, and comprehension of meaning intelligible. They discover various types of code, but the most explanatory are generative rules. These consist in a small number of rules, which can operate recursively on strings of terms and thus can account for many possible expressions, e.g., the infinite number of intelligible sentences in English. Such generative rules define the limits of the system under study. Many codes studied by structuralists do not have the explanatory power of generative rules. Only Chomsky's linguistics has produced anything resembling such rules. But his example provides a standard against which the intellectual value of other types of structuralist analyses can be assessed.

Many structuralists challenge the value of historical explanation. Though they do not reject historical understanding entirely, they prefer to define the underlying structures that determine the state of a signifying system at a given time. If they can discover these, then a history of how this state was reached is superfluous. Consider a simple example. Suppose you know the rules of chess and walk into the middle of a game. You can understand the current state of the game and the variety of possible moves available given that array. You do not need to know the entire history of the game up to that point to determine which move would be most effective now. The underlying codes – in this case, the rules of chess and your informal inarticulate knowledge of chess strategy – provide the necessary understanding. Similarly, grasping the argot of a particular linguistic subculture requires full immersion in the use of its terminology at a given time. This provides a basis for comprehending the basic oppositions, distinctions, and relations among its terms. The visitor does not need to know the history of this argot across generations. Structuralist comprehension thus involves grasping the lawful relations among a system of elements at a given time. Saussure called this type of comprehension "synchronic" to distinguish it from historical, or "diachronic," understanding.

Structuralists thus seek a distinctive type of elucidation of moves within various expressive systems. They do not *describe* surface expressions, nor do they offer *causal* explanations for particular moves. Rather, they seek something more systematic and ambitious: a clarification of the *rules that constitute the system of meanings*, and beyond this, the rules that make all systems of that type (e.g., languages, kinship systems, fashion systems) possible. Such an analysis uncovers the underlying order (or grammar) of the system that is only implicitly understood by those who use it. Even if these rules do not determine the specific expression used on a particular occasion, they limit the kinds of expression that can be used; thus they govern both meaning production and comprehension unconsciously. Structuralists claim to achieve "scientific" understanding of expressive systems even though they make no reference to causal explanations or to their users' conscious intentions.

Structuralist systems consist of internal relations among terms. Internal relations define the terms they relate; the terms do not and cannot exist independently of the relations that constitute them. No term in such a system can be changed without a corresponding change in all the other terms. Such systems simulate organic systems. This is one Hegelian dimension of structuralism and a feature it shares with gestalt psychology. Structuralists differ from Hegel because they reject his view that expressive systems possess an internal dynamic – a moment of negation that originates within the system, which must then be overcome by the system. The system can undergo change, but typically changes are motivated from outside the system.

Although this introductory summary may seem abstract, I will present examples in the course of discussing some of this movement's major figures: Saussure, Barthes, Lévi-Strauss, Lacan, and Althusser.

SAUSSURE

Ferdinand de Saussure (1857–1913) was a linguist who taught initially at the University of Leipzig and later at Paris and Geneva. He developed his revolutionary views on language in a course of lectures given late in his life, *Course in General Linguistics* (1916), which survives mainly because of the conscientious efforts of his students. Understanding Saussure's contributions requires a clarification of some of his key distinctions, especially *langue/parole*, signifier/signified/referent, synchronic/diachronic, and syntagmatic/paradigmatic.

Saussure's central distinction is between *langue* (system of rules) and *parole* (speech acts). *Parole* consists of individual uses of language at particular times to make statements, ask questions, issue commands, etc. *Langue* is the underlying system – passively assimilated and not explicitly formulated by speakers – that makes these acts of speaking possible, intelligible, and meaningful.[1]

Saussure focuses on *langue*-systems for particular natural languages. Chomsky advanced this project by hypothesizing an inborn grammatical system underlying all possible languages. The language system is collective and impersonal in the sense that it is not created or altered by any one person. Even when a particular person initiates changes within *langue*, they must be accepted, acknowledged, and eventually used by other speakers in order to become institutionalized. Actually, *langue* consists of several systems of such rules governing phonetics, grammar, semantics, and even pragmatics. Just as chess has a set of rules that govern the actions of all chess players, so too does natural language have rules that govern all speakers. Often speakers learn these rules as they speak (and are corrected by others). When language is viewed from the standpoint of speech acts (*parole*), then individual creativity and intention seem important; but when the perspective shifts and to the standpoint of these implicit rules (*langue*), then individuals are just vehicles for their implementation.[2] They inherit rules they did not produce and will simply reproduce, even though they assimilate whatever rule-changes occur as usage changes. This systemic standpoint on language is Saussure's major contribution.

Language and every other expressive system consist of signs. Saussure gave a threefold analysis of linguistic signs: signifier/signified/referent.[3] Frege and Husserl adopted a similar analysis. Consider the word "red." The *signifier*, when written, consists of that configuration of marks on the page; they may be printed in different fonts or sizes or even handwritten, but as long as they maintain that general configuration, they exemplify the "signifier" of the sign "red" in English. The *signified* is the concept, situated within a system of color concepts in which red is differentiated from purple and orange (nearby) and yellow and blue (further away), through which a particular color is indicated when the sign is used. The *referent* can be any instance of the color red: his blood, this fire-engine, that tomato, or those strawberries. The concept "red" in fact includes a narrow range of colors, all of which are closely related on a continuous color spectrum. Concepts can usually be defined; referents are typically natural or created objects or properties of the world. A sign consists of a particular signifier (marks, sounds) linked to a particular signified (concept, meaning), which exists within a complex system of differentiations. For example, the written signifier "red" in English is importantly distinct from "rod," "rep," and "fed", each of which is linked to a different signified (meaning, concept). Also, the signified red is importantly distinct from all the other color signifieds – e.g., green, blue, orange, etc. Sometimes the same signified can refer to different objects – e.g., "the tallest person in the room" when spoken on different occasions or in different rooms, even though its meaning is constant across each use. Different languages typically use different signifiers for similar signifieds – e.g., in German "*rot*" and in French "*rouge*" are both associated with roughly the same signified as the English term "red." Especially in spoken language, the signifiers can sound exactly similar even though they are associated with different signifieds, e.g., "bare" and "bear"; the spoken context typically provides the clues necessary to determine which signifier is being used.

Thus, a sign consists of two linked aspects – a mark or sound and a concept or meaning – and these aspects exist within their own associated systems that determine their exact identity. For example, if English consisted of only three color signs -- red, yellow, and blue – then the range of colors included in the concept of each would be quite large. If, however, someone's active color language consists of 64 distinct color terms, then the range of colors included in the concept of any one of them would be much smaller, and her description of colors would be much more precise. Many writers confuse the Saussurian concept of "signified" with the referent of the sign; this is a mistake. The signifieds "the co-editor of the *Blackwell Companion to Continental Philosophy*" and "the author of *Sartre and His Predecessors: The Self and the Other*" *refer* to the same person (this author) even though they have different *meanings*. In poetry, signifiers (marks on the page or sounds) can sometimes be used to suggest supplementary meanings or even to emulate the referent (e.g., "whoosh," "crackle"). For Saussure, the central fact about signs is that the relation between signifier and signified is unmotivated, arbitrary, or purely conventional.[4] The marks "red" need not be associated with the color of tomatoes. Yet once a link between a signifier and a signified is established, it becomes so habituated and second nature to the language's speakers that it seems natural and unavoidable. Saussure insists on the conventional or arbitrary relationship between components of linguistic signs.

Saussure also utilizes a concept that he calls the "value" of a sign, which is its differential relation to other terms in the linguistic system.[5] Thus, in the example above, "red" in a 3-color-term language will have a substantially different value from "red" in a 64-color-term language. The value of a sign never exists in and of itself apart from the surrounding system. The system determines the value of each of its component signs, and if any term of the system changes value, all the other signs will change their values in a corresponding fashion. Saussure's formula for this is "in language there are only differences, no positive terms."[6] This explains the importance of comprehending the entire signifying system for Saussure because, in fact, no sign in the system can be understood unless its relation with other signs is understood. The question of whether a general "science" of signs (semiology) is possible depends on whether other signifying systems behave like languages or whether they are importantly different.

To study the development of a system over time, historically, is to examine it *diachronically*. But to study a system at a given time is to understand it *synchronically*. Saussure's aim is to show that language can be studied synchronically and that this is the most illuminating way to explicate it.[7] Synchronic analysis seeks to uncover the internal relations among the elements of the system. Instead of "explaining" a system, it clarifies the signs used by relating them to the signs not used. Absent terms illuminate present terms. Given this conception of synchronic analysis, structuralists can declare that system states have no motivational relation to one another, and they can thus reject the importance of history altogether. Although structuralists do not need to deny the relevance of history, their formal synchronic analyses assign no importance to the development of the systems they study. Saussure concentrates on synchronic analysis in order to overcome the dominance of historical and genetic research in linguistics. Structuralists can claim that their synchronic analyses are essential to accurate diachronic understanding because they help isolate the exact sites of system change. Still, when the linguistic system changes, the task of clarifying the new synchronic state of the system remains, and this is the structuralist enterprise.

Another important Saussurian distinction is between "syntagmatic" and "paradigmatic" analyses.[8] Typically, both are used together, but in some instances one is more useful. Syntagmatic analysis can be used whenever the expressive act requires a series of signs; this can be a series of words in a statement, a series of adornments in clothing, or a series of shots in a film sequence. Syntagmatic analysis examines the order of the signs. Often the same statement can be given quite different colorings if the word order is altered, or the same shots in a film can have different meanings if the order is reversed. Compare "The wise person is temperate" with "Temperate is the wise person"; the first is in classic declarative form and is formulaic, while the second is poetic and surprising. Also, syntagmatic analysis shows that some word orders are excluded (grammar). Paradigmatic analysis, on the other hand, examines the signs used in the expressive act against a background of possible alternatives in each position. Thus, instead of "person" above, the statement could read "woman" or "man" or "creature," each of which would produce a different meaning. Similarly, instead of "temperate," the statement could have used "intuitive" or "calm" or "empathetic" or "unselfish." "Temperate" gains its meaning in this context from the terms it excludes. Thus, signs not used clarify the signs that are used; absent signs illuminate present ones. Indeed, both types of analysis supplement each other, and the meaning of the expression is more fully comprehended when both are used.

An important implication of Saussure's theory involves learning a foreign language. One might think that learning another language is primarily a matter of learning to associate different signifiers with the signifieds embedded in one's native natural language. But, in fact, the process is quite different because the linguistic system as a whole determines the values of the signs it contains, and thus the new language has an entirely different set of signifieds from one's native language. When one learns a foreign language, one gradually comprehends the new system of signifieds (concepts), and this sharpens one's understanding of one's own language. One also learns that one's native conceptual system is only one among many possible options, is culturally produced, and thus only *seems* natural.

A second important implication concerns the fact that the meaning of any particular sign in a linguistic system is determined by the other signs existing in the system. Not only is the relation between a single signifier and signified arbitrary, but the signifiers and signifieds change independently as additional signifiers and signifieds become incorporated into the linguistic system. In effect, every sign is related to other signs in the system; structuralism's goal is to clarify these relations as completely as possible. Thus, for Saussure and other structuralists, meaning is not a function of reference, but rather of differential relations among signs.

Saussure's position implies that language has its own distinctive reality that can be studied scientifically. Language need not be reduced to the psychological intentions of speakers; indeed, speakers' intentions are structured by the linguistic system. Individual thoughts and individual speech acts are allegedly functions of these deeper systems. Thus, the notion of individuality so important to the existentialists is threatened by the kinds of system structuralists analyze. Structuralism studies signifying systems as *independent* wholes; it is less concerned with individual uses of these systems.

Saussure also envisioned a general science of signifying systems (semiology) that might develop from his principles for studying natural language.[9] But he did not clarify what such a discipline might look like. Barthes took important steps in this direction. He applied Saussure's principles to dress codes, narrative codes, advertising signs, body language, photography, and cultural myths.

BARTHES

In addition to elaborating the structuralist approach to signifying systems, Roland Barthes (1915–80) experimented with an immense variety of projects in the course of his career. He attempted phenomenological and psychoanalytic criticism, studies of both classical and avant-garde literary texts, analyses of the reading and writing process, and critical assessments of contemporary materials, practices, and myths. Despite a nostalgia for system, he was a fragmentary, aphoristic thinker, and his best books adopt this style. He also wrote most astutely when he had a clear opponent. One of his earliest works, *Writing Degree Zero* (1953), was a direct response to Sartre's *What is Literature?*, and Barthes became famous for his response to an attack from a staid academic critic – *Criticism and Truth* (1966). He liked working with and alongside other texts, as in *A Lover's Discourse* (1977), which allowed him to incorporate many of the best passages in the history of thought about love while also offering a sustained analysis of his own. He was a superb observer, both of contemporary life and texts, but abstract theory was not his strong suit. For all his efforts to articulate a method, most of his criticism demonstrates a strong combination of aesthetic sensitivity and theoretically significant particular insights. He opposed boredom and academicism, making ecstasy an important goal of the critical process. Sometimes his pronouncements were appropriately tentative and measured; often, however, they became self-indulgent and trendy.

Barthes contributes to the development of Saussure's approach in the analysis of contemporary cultural myths and of literature, but he eventually transcends the scientific aspirations of structuralism. He examines a wide variety of symbolic systems using structuralist techniques. His own career reveals many reasons for the emergence of poststructuralism. I will first indicate some of the contributions Barthes makes to structuralism, and later I will examine his final essays to indicate some of structuralism's inadequacies.

Barthes's most direct extension of Saussure's project appears in the short essay, *Elements of Semiology* (1964). In this work, Barthes is honest in admitting the limitations of Saussure's approach, but he also indicates some interesting directions for further research. He had already produced some important initial analyses of contemporary myths and literary works, and he is preparing to embark on a close study of the fashion system using structuralist techniques. His most important book, *S/Z* (1970), is both the culmination of his structuralist research and his transition beyond structuralism.

Barthes endorses Saussure's *langue/parole* (structure/event) distinction both because it makes systematic study of sign systems possible and because it uncovers an autonomous level of social conventions that are resistant to change by individuals even as they unconsciously constrain individual actions. But, unlike Saussure and following Merleau-Ponty, he notes that *parole* (individual uses of language) can potentially transcend the system and thus initiate change. Parole sustains the underlying system as well as providing the possibility of creatively refashioning it.[10] Often, individuals' expressions do become habituated, but this is not a necessary result of underlying structures. Following Jakobson, Barthes notes a variety of linguistic phenomena that challenge the simple *langue/parole* distinction. For example, individuals may possess distinctive idiolects (mini-*langues*); these are systematic patterns of usage unique to themselves or their subculture.[11] Moreover, there are distinctive speech acts that challenge the notion of mere expression. For example, in reporting the assertion of another person, the speaker need not make the assertion herself, but her statement has the form of an assertion (e.g., "Jacob says Marilyn is beautiful").[12] Statements or words can also refer to themselves and thus become paradoxical (e.g., "every statement in this paragraph is false").[13]

Barthes notes that some expressive actions are more constrained than speech – e.g., the meaningfulness of purchasing a car is limited since the consumer does not design the car but must choose from a variety of pre-existing designs. In addition, he notes that a garment system can be examined in a variety of ways – e.g., as *written* about in magazines, as *photographed* (with or without captions), and as *worn*. Certainly, there are rules of completeness and well-orderedness in a wardrobe, but the canonical forms of wardrobe expression are produced by the fashion industry, not by the user.[14] Thus, factors beyond an underlying grammatical system constrain many real-world expressive systems. Moreover, in the richly semic world of advertising, a multiplicity of overlapping systems of meaning exist – images, texts, photographs, film, music, and narrative – and these may have disjointed or even contradictory relations to one another.[15] Expression in these multimedia systems is often determined by a privileged group (e.g., arbiters of fashion); the latitude of the users of such "expressions" is limited because they can only adopt one among a small number of canonical types. Barthes's point is that non-linguistic expressive systems are not always perfect extensions of ordinary language. Such systems often work differently from ordinary language, and the structuralist analysis of such systems must adapt to their multiple, overlapping systems of meaning.

In non-linguistic expressive systems, the relation of the signifier and signified is not always arbitrary, or at least the supposed arbitrariness is compromised in various ways. For example, in the garment system and the food system, the expressive acts (wearing this coat or eating that fruit) have a function that is independent of their semiological meanings. Clothes provide warmth and protection from the weather, and food is necessary for survival. These functions may also influence the choice of expressive acts within these domains; the signifying relation in these systems overlays the functional relation.[16] Barthes notes that there can be degrees of motivation between the signifier and signified in certain systems. For example, on the logos of various corporations, the pictographs may be arbitrary to some extent, but they also attempt to embody key features of the company symbolically. The logos of certain sports teams, for example, graphically portray the ferocity exhibited in the team's play. Simply using certain fonts in a company logo can implicitly suggest the efficiency of the company's operations, or alternatively, using an ancient font can evoke the quaintness of the services offered. Such semiotic systems violate the crucial Saussurian principle of arbitrariness (or unmotivatedness).[17]

Barthes confirms the value of Saussure's two types of structural analysis: syntagmatic and paradigmatic. He notes that Jakobson believes that these two methods – combinative constraints on a string of signifiers and alternate possibilities within associated categories – represent two distinct types of thought, related to metonymy and metaphor.[18] Barthes agrees with this suggestion. Syntagmatic relations concern connections among the terms chosen for expression; paradigmatic relations concern the relation between a chosen term and other possible absent terms that could have been selected. Certain artistic forms are ordered primarily by syntagmatic relations – e.g., pulp novels, newspaper stories, and realist narratives; others are ordered primarily by paradigmatic relations, e.g., aphoristic discourse, thematic criticism, symbolist poetry, and surrealist painting. Both types of relations exist in most non-linguistic sign systems, however. For example, in the garment system, the syntagm is the different elements of a chosen wardrobe, while the paradigm is the types of garment that can be worn on the same part of the body – e.g., different hats or shoes. In interior design, the syntagm is the arrangement of pieces in a room, while the paradigm is the different styles in which each type of object (e.g., divan, side chair, coffee table) can be produced. In the architecture system, the syntagm consists of the parts of the finished building, while the paradigm concerns the possible variations in each of the parts (different types of doors, insulation, roof, exterior facing, etc.).

With respect to the denotative/conative distinction, Barthes is especially interested in the notion of meta-language, a language used to represent and analyze another language. When he explores the various mythological objects in contemporary society, he examines connotation – meaning that is suggested, rather than directly asserted, by the expression. His aim in probing such "myths" is demystification. By uncovering the workings of such connotations, those meanings – which seem so natural to the users of the system – may be subverted.[19]

Barthes offers a variety of structural analyses of particular authors. For example, he explores the grammar that informs the writing of Sade – the basic elements of his tableaux and their rules of combination.[20] He explores the unconscious elements of Michelet's style, especially the contrasting qualities (warmth, dryness, smoothness) that inform his descriptions.[21] And he analyzes the features of the world of Racinean tragedy, the background structures the motivate Racine's plays.[22] In all cases, he concentrates on features other than explicit themes or surface meaning in favor of deeper structures that make such meaning possible. In effect, he shows how to read a wide variety of literary works in imaginative ways, ways that displace the traditional goal of clarifying thematic meaning. The upshot of Barthes's experiments is to show that multiple layers of meaning operate in any literary work and that a variety of codes produce them. He rejects the idea that a text has a single meaning or a single dimension of meaning, and he insists that the plurality of meanings need not coalesce into an organically coherent set of conclusions. Barthes focuses on meaning structures that do not depend on the organizing intention of an author or on the referential function of language. Grasping these multiple layers in a text is essential to achieving an *ecstasy* of reading, as opposed to the mere *pleasure* produced by more conventional, critical readings.[23]

Barthes challenges the central assumptions of academic literary analysis in his strident response to an attack on his book on Racine by Henri Picard. Picard insisted that Barthes's assertions about Racine were unsupported and couched in an impenetrable pseudo-scientific jargon, that his methods invited a dangerous evaluative relativism, and that he exhibited a perverse interest in sexuality. Picard defended the artist's control over the literary work and the value of academic interpretation in transmitting cultural heritage to new generations. Barthes replies to these charges in a variety of ways, but several points are central.[24] First, he shows that the standpoint of the academic critic is plagued by presuppositions and ideology, and Barthes directly attacks this assumed ideology. Second, he suggests that readings are only valuable if they reveal new textual features; otherwise criticism becomes a boring repetition of what is already known. Finally, he differentiates his own project from that of the academic critics. He seeks not a complete interpretation of a particular text, but a science of the conditions of meaning for *any* literary work, thus construing all of literature as a *langue*. His various critical approaches to literature simply offer some first steps toward such a science. Thus, Barthes redirects the focus of literary theory away from a hermeneutics of particular texts – governed by assumptions of authorial control/intention and organic unity – to an elucidation of the background structures that make appreciation of the plural dimensions of textual meaning possible.

In developing this science of literary meaning, however, Barthes rarely seeks to be exhaustive. He reveals a number of codes that contribute to literary meaning. For example, he attempts to isolate the central elements and rules of combination for narrative; he describes the many ways in which the reader responds to a literary text and how these responses eventually enhance meaning; and he defines the literariness of literature. *S/Z*, perhaps his most influential critical book, thoroughly examines a short story by Balzac. In it, he exhibits the process of reading in slow motion. He defines five distinct interpretive codes: the hermeneutic code (terms through which enigmas are proposed, explored, and resolved), the semic code (terms that typify a certain character or location), the symbolic code (terms that indicate more universal meanings), the proairetic code (terms that indicate various sequences of action which eventually constitute the "plot"), and cultural codes (terms which refer to pre-existing extra-textual forms of knowledge and whose comprehension relies on such knowledges, however adequate or valid).[25] He then divides the story into 561 lexias – short strings of text of varying length and complexity – and elucidates the operation of these five codes for each one. He does not detail the results of every code for every lexia, only those codes that seem to reveal important textual operations, and he does not require the various codes to reinforce each other. Indeed they often conflict with one another and produce complex crosscurrents of meaning. Barthes does not seek a phenomenological description of the reading process, but he elaborates the complexity of the interaction of codes involved in reading a classical realist short story. He shows how its conventions operate, how it interrogates itself, and how meaning emerges even if no final thematic conclusion is reached. He shows how these meanings are constructed and produced, but in the process he threatens to transcend the structuralist project because he abandons the search for an underlying system and attends to the complex interactions of various levels of meaning.

LÉVI-STRAUSS

Claude Lévi-Strauss (b. 1908) majored in philosophy but began his teaching career in anthropology in Brazil. He returned to France to serve in the military during World War II, but after the German victory he fled to the US where he taught at the New School for Social Research from 1941 to 1945. There he met Roman Jakobson, a famous structural linguist. He returned to Brazil several times after the war to do research. Eventually he was appointed to a prestigious chair at the Collège de France.

Lévi-Strauss shows how to apply Saussure's and Jakobson's structuralist approaches to the study of cultures. He clarifies the unconscious cognitive operations that make cultural meanings possible – in kinship systems, in myths, in totemism, and in categorial schemes. In order to do this, he examines data from a variety of different cultures and highlights their underlying patterns. He claims to identify universal capacities of the mind that are differently expressed in different cultures,[26] much in the way Chomsky posits a universal grammar that informs the specific grammars of the world's many natural languages. In both cases, these universal structures operate beneath the user's explicit consciousness but nevertheless condition both the production and comprehension of meaning. Lévi-Strauss implies that so-called "primitive" cultures (by which he means "cultures without writing") and more technologically advanced cultures do not differ in their basic cognitive capacities; they merely use these capacities in different ways. He thus challenges the arrogance of Western rationality toward non-Western cultures.[27] Technologically advanced cultures can learn much about their own cognitive capacities through his structural analyses.

Lévi-Strauss does not just study the meanings that organize cultures, but also their various social relationships (especially kinship relations). Many cultural meanings to which he gives special attention – e.g., myths – reveal the mind functioning in relatively unconstrained contexts. Myths are like collective dreams, and both are unconstrained by empirical laws or practical limits. He is rarely interested in the surface meaning of a single myth or in a single social relationship in the culture, but rather in the underlying rules governing a series of myths or the underlying oppositions and laws organizing diverse kinship relationships (e.g., one such linkage is that an opposition exists between the experience of the husband/wife relation and the brother/sister relation such that when one of these is regarded indifferently or as taboo, the other is regarded as significant and trusting[28]). Lévi-Strauss does not try to comprehend every aspect of a culture, only those most amenable to his structuralist principles, and he rarely studies any one culture in depth because its surface meanings allegedly provide no basis for genuine social science.

Lévi-Strauss seeks a scientific approach to the study of culture and systems of meaning, rather than one rooted in an analysis of subjective experiences (which is what he thinks existentialists offer). Nonetheless, his approach is conditioned by his sensibility. For example, he suggests that his books are written passively – in just the way he hypothesizes that most individuals experience cultural meaning.[29] Also, the mood of the book recounting his most moving field experiences, *Tristes Tropiques* (1955), is central to understanding his entire project. It recounts his travels and discoveries, his struggle with the limitations of his own ethnocentrism, and his nostalgia for the dying cultures decimated by Western colonialism and Western anthropologists.[30] He describes the grandeur of these cultures, defending them against Western arrogance. He often reiterates the claim that the logic governing mythic thought is as sophisticated as that governing Western reason. He also exhibits an intellectual's lingering guilt and search for redemption, which surfaced as the colonial system disintegrated. He creates the characteristic structuralist stance: an alien onlooker searching for an underlying logic that is inaccessible to the culture's participants. By implication, he suggests that Western culture's constitutive rules escape its self-consciousness and control.

For Lévi-Strauss, elevating an inquiry into a social *science* is not a function of surviving the challenge of empirical disconfirmation. Rather, it requires building abstract models that simplify the wealth of empirical data, reducing the complexity of the surface observations to simpler units and rules of combination, which exhibit greater intelligibility.[31] His "explanations" of cultural meanings are not causal; instead, they articulate the rules and oppositions by which they are comprehended. The surface data are "explained" as results of oppositions and rules of combination that he takes to operate unconsciously. He claims that his own method of studying humanity's universal capacities is more informative than those used in hermeneutics and phenomenology. He thinks hermeneutics merely reveals surface unities and relationships, while phenomenology concentrates on explicitly conscious processes. There are similarities between his thought and Kant's. Both thinkers see innate concepts as tools for organizing the world.[32] Some critics complain that Lévi-Strauss ignores vast amounts of data about the particular cultures he studies, but his reply is that science must always select its data and perspective in order to make significant progress.[33] He notes that seventeenth-century scientists had to ignore most of the observed data of common sense in order to build the mathematical models and formulas that propelled physics and chemistry to their first major advances and that he seeks similar advances in social theory.

One of Lévi-Strauss's methods is to locate a particular object of study (e.g., a myth, a totem symbolizing a particular social group, a particular kinship relation) in a larger context that defines all the logical possibilities of the basic elements informing it (e.g., all myths containing those elements, all existing totemic symbols, all possible kinship relations). In order to create this system of logical possibilities, he identifies the system's fundamental elements and determines their possible combinations. He is able to explain the significance of a particular object (or combination) by understanding its place in this exhaustive system of possibilities.[34] Constructing a complete system of meanings differs from simply relating the object (e.g., functionally or causally) to other surface phenomena. As Saussure and Barthes showed, the combinations that are *not* present in a particular culture can be as informative as those that are. Also, clarifying the relationship between a specific combination and others (realized perhaps in distant eras or cultures) can better clarify the significance of this combination because its place in the whole system can be elucidated.

Kinship relations were Lévi-Straus's first objects of study, and his central concern was the incest taboo, an almost universal prohibition. Many theorists had tried to explain this taboo by appealing to the biological consequences of inbreeding or to moral injunctions. Instead of concentrating on its prohibition function, Lévi-Strauss notes that it has a positive function of circulating women among different groups, thus creating a basis for continuing social alliances. Potential spouses are divided into "permitted" and "prohibited," and women then become gifts between different clans. This is a unique rationale for this virtually universal social law: the incest taboo becomes a basis for social reciprocity and mutual obligations. Lévi-Strauss develops analogies between the circulation of goods and meanings between groups, and the circulation of women. Each is regulated by its own codes, which are amenable to structuralist analysis.

Lévi-Strauss is also fascinated by myths. His four-volume study, *Introduction to the Science of Mythology* (1964, '67, '68, '71), demonstrates the organizing power of primitive categories, which creates as much order and meaning as the rationality operating in technologically advanced cultures. Myths explore major issues faced by any culture: life/death, youth/age, culture/nature, time/eternity. They try to resolve paradoxes that are concealed from those whose lives are informed by the myths. The resolutions remain implicit because they are not entirely acceptable to everyday morality; they indicate the tragic sacrifices that must be made if cultures are to survive (e.g., that sons must supersede their fathers and that daughters must disobey their families). Only by studying the variations and transformations of the myth does its broader significance – and thus the importance of any particular version – become clear. Many instances explore different organizations of the myth's elements to produce distinctive meanings.[35] When certain elements are changed, other related elements undergo parallel transformations, and only by studying all the myth's versions can the mythologist determine which elements are invariably paired with other elements.

Like Freud, Lévi-Strauss believed that the given material of a myth (or dream) had to be rewritten or reorganized before its inner structure could be discovered. He compares this rearrangement process to reading the score of a symphony. Conductors must read both horizontally (to understand the developing melody) and vertically (to understand how the instruments contrast with each other to produce the multiplicity of tones at any given moment). With respect to myths, this implies that mythologists must not only attend to the developing story (and its possible variations), but also to the possible alternative – and possibly contrapuntal – elements in each phase. Lévi-Strauss strives to hear the myth more completely than the auditor in any given culture, viz., against the backdrop of a full system of oppositions from which the passages of the myth are constituted. He even suggests that different myths have distinctive musical forms: sonata, rondo, toccata, and fugue.[36]

Perhaps a brief example will clarify his procedure. In analyzing the Oedipus myth, Lévi-Strauss (writing with Jakobson) seeks the underlying *langue* (or system) that informs all the particular instances of an individual myth. In order to do this, he isolates fundamental units – often categorial oppositions – and shows how many different variations of a myth can be derived from transformations of these basic oppositions. He discovers such oppositions by comparing all the versions of a myth, thus rejecting the search for an original or true version. He reorganizes the basic elements of the various versions into four columns, which attempt to capture the synchronic oppositions informing the diachronic story. One pair of columns reveal a contrast between the overvaluation and undervaluation of blood relationships, while the other concerns the opposition between natural birth (through parents) and autochthonous self-origination. Lévi-Strauss thinks the central theme of the myth is the struggle to deny one's earthly, natural origins while being forced to acknowledge them by experiencing physical handicaps. Ultimately, the myth tries to resolve the paradox of the one and the many (being born from the earth and from two-distinct parents).[37]

This example illustrates several problems with Lévi-Strauss 's method. First, although the theme he identifies is certainly a possible interpretation of the myth, it is rarely the only one. Second, in reorganizing the myth, the arrangement of elements in their respective categories and even the choice of binary oppositions themselves seem arbitrary, thus introducing a whimsical quality into what offers itself as a rigorous analytic procedure. Third, large portions of the myth are simply ignored by his analysis; entirely different oppositions might emerge if other passages of the myth were taken seriously. These shortcomings plague this early example of his method because Lévi-Strauss did not attempt to relate the Oedipus myth to a system of related myths. In his larger treatises, this is his main enterprise. Still, even there, he relies on intuitions about the natural connections among certain myths, either via theme or cultural function. Once he creates these groupings, he is able to discover underlying formal oppositions, but this can be done with almost any material. He has no way of determining whether the underlying logic he discovers is just his own elaborate projection or whether it really informs the myth. Unlike Chomsky's universal grammar, myth analysis appeals to no everyday cognitive competence that the analyst is trying to formalize. This makes Lévi-Strauss's hypotheses difficult to evaluate.

He believes that history has only the most limited explanatory role, even today. Structuralism looks to synchronic unconscious structures – rather than diachronic principles of development – to illuminate cultures. Nonetheless, he does not entirely dismiss the role of history. He often compares history and myth.[38] In our era, Lévi-Strauss suggests that history has usurped the role of myth. But their functions differ. Myth tries to insure that the future will resemble the past, while history incites the future to supersede the past.

LACAN

Jacques Lacan (1901–81) integrates structural linguistics with Freudian psychoanalysis. He also enriches his reading of Freud by utilizing Alexandre Kojève's (1902–68) lectures on Hegel,[39] which Sartre and Merleau-Ponty also attended. Lacan read Freud with great seriousness and intensity, and he concentrates on Freud's early works while de-emphasizing the later texts, which led to the development of ego-psychology. Though Lacan seeks to preserve the substance of Freud's insights, the spirit and style of his writing is very different. He is playful and ambiguous where Freud would be serious and clear. He is Olympian and dismissive where Freud would be fair to competing views. He erects a self-enclosed theoretical system where Freud would create works in progress. Lacan's most important disagreement with Freud is that he embraces the forces in the unconscious, while Freud remains suspicious of them. Lacan takes consciousness to be riddled with illusory hopes, while Freud takes it to be the sole source of stability. Lacan's ideal is to accept the tensions and complexities of the unconscious, rather than flee or deny them. In some ways, his rejection of coherent selfness is similar to Sartre's, and his alternative is also similar – learning to live with ambiguity, ambivalence, and reduced expectations.

Lacan treats the unconscious as a distinct, independent psychic system, irreducible to biological instincts. He distinguishes drives from instincts, and insists that drives are related to one another like Saussure's signifiers. Unconscious drives are thus similar to a system of word-like sounds that are related according to linguistic rules, rather than perceptual laws (which would dominate if the unconscious consisted of images). When Lacan elucidates the operations of the unconscious, he studies patients' discourse (as did Freud), e.g., their *accounts* of their dreams, their *verbal* associations. Lacan notes that hypnosis operates primarily through the controlling *words* of the hypnotist. And therapeutic breakthroughs occur primarily through *verbal exchanges* between patient and therapist. At every point language dominates the psychoanalytic process.[40] Lacan's initial principle is thus that the unconscious is structured like a language. The unconscious exhibits a different logic from that informing thought – e.g., contradictions coexist, time is illusory, and elements are fluid rather than fixed. The unconscious is not the same as language, and language learning is not an initiation into the unconscious, but both language and the unconscious condition all other in operations of consciousness.

Just as structuralists typically conceive language as a system that conditions individual speech-acts (rather than being created through them), so too does Lacan believe the unconscious conditions speech and action. Neurotic symptoms are like a foreign language that the sufferer fails to comprehend, but nonetheless inhabits.[41] Many actions are triggered by a chain of signifiers, whose meanings the agent is unable to decipher. Lacan stresses the power of signifiers in opposition to meanings (or signifieds); indeed, rather than conceive each signifier as correlated with a unique signified, Lacan believes that the signifier-chain is typically supercharged with polyvalent associations (and thus is overdetermined).[42] Learning language is an initiation into the symbolic dimension – the sphere of the law. This is the second path by which other people (the whole linguistic community and its past) enter into the constitution of subjectivity; they penetrate the structure of the unconscious itself. The first path by which other people constitute the self is the mirror-stage.

The mirror-stage is an early moment in maturation when children become fascinated with their own mirror images, a fascination triggered by their experience of the coherence of their parents' bodies.[43] During the first year of life, the psychic life of the infant is chaotic, and its control of its own body is tenuous. Moreover, it senses its own helplessness even as it rebels against this. But the stable, unified body of the parent provides an ever-present model that enables the infant to fantasize control over its own body – ultimately achieving a unified ego. Unlike Husserl, who believed that the experience of one's own ego's coherence was necessary to experience another ego, Lacan believes that the experience of the other's unified body (as object – as if in a mirror) is necessary to experience the unity of one's own body and oneself.[44] This unified ego is, according to Lacan, an illusion based on a misinterpretation of the other's body and its relation to one's own body. Others' bodies provide the model for this illusory, unattainable ego-ideal. The goal of self-sufficient autonomy – of an independent and domineering relation to the environment – derives from this mirror-stage.[45] The infant's parents may not experience themselves as centered, coherent egos, but this is irrelevant. The parents' apparent coherent bodily responses allow the infant to imagine having control of itself and the world, and this imaginary ideal haunts the adult forever. The irony is that autonomy is often defined in opposition to the influence of other people, when in fact their bodily coherence is necessary to experiencing autonomy as an ideal. The infant becomes divided within itself, constantly in pursuit of an ego-ideal that is unrealizable yet constantly aware of its own weakness and dependency.

Thus, Lacan rejects the unity of the ego in favor of the complexities and tensions of the unconscious. Just as Sartre claims that the ego is an illusion of reflection, Lacan thinks the ego is an illusion pursued because of the other's bodily coherence. Whenever people berate themselves because they lack autonomy, they suffer from this illusion. Because the unified ego can never be achieved, Lacan rejects the school of psychoanalysis that seeks to strengthen the ego (ego-psychology).[46] People make immense sacrifices before the idol of the autonomous self, a hoax that his therapy seeks to shatter. In Sartrean terms, Lacan suggests that the search for centered autonomy is everyone's fundamental project, and yet it is an illusion, a thesis parallel to Sartre's contention that all people seek to become god-like (unifying the kinds of being possessed by consciousness and things). Lacan could say, with Sartre, that as long as humanity pursues this illusion, it is a useless passion – a condition from which Lacanian therapy seeks redemption. The chaotic crosscurrents of desire dominate the unconscious. Lacan neglects to defend this value premise. Even if the centered ego is an illusion, it may be an illusion worth pursuing. Lacan never argues for the opposite claim. Instead he accepts the critical stance of the entire structuralist movement against consciousness and autonomy.

One goal of Lacanian therapy is to wean people from this imaginary fantasy. Lacan also extends the range of psychoanalytic treatment from the neuroses to the psychoses. His therapy seeks to create an acceptance of the patient's separation from the mother, and thus to abandon the fantasy of fusion with the cosmos. This produces an initial sense of loss and mourning. To acknowledge separateness is to choose the chaotic tensions of the unconscious over the illusions of consciousness. This is a moment of truth, an acknowledgment of fate. Unlike Freud, Lacan resists the patient's transference, which reenacts the fantasies of the mirror-stage and simply exacerbates the patient's condition. The therapist's goal is to reflect patients' unconscious processes so that they can be accepted. Lacan's therapy does not operate through the patient's self-knowledge and release of psychic energy, but through an acceptance of limits, a refusal to deny the truth. He was famous for cutting his therapeutic sessions short. His rationale for this is that interruptions of the patient's discourse can reveal the underlying chaos of desire and provoke sudden revelations that patients have avoided.[47]

Recall the second path by which others produce the warp and woof of one's identity – the entrance into language. Lacan suggests that a "position" for "oneself" is already prepared. This position is produced by the network of pronouns, verb tenses, self-referential devices, gendered modification, and linguistic moods. To enter this symbolic sphere is to bind oneself to the linguistic history of one's community, culture, and clan. It is a discursive history that carries the force of law: ancient, traditional, powerful. Following Jakobson, Lacan suggests that the two linguistically based forms of mental operation – metaphor and metonymy – also play an important role in the development of psychic functioning. Two key operations in the unconscious are condensation and displacement; condensation incorporates into one term the energies that infuse many others, while displacement redirects energies from one nexus to different ones. The unconscious is a network of drives that function like a signifying chain of terms. Condensation is an essentially metaphoric process (allowing one term to summarize the whole signifying chain), and displacement is an essentially metonymic process (allowing the energy of one term to dissolve into adjacent terms).[48] Similarly, the emergence of psychic trauma is a metaphoric event, allowing a drive to attach itself to a symptom, while the common process by which new objects are substituted for old fixations is a metonymic process. Because the unconscious operates like a language and often operates through language, Lacan teaches his disciples to master linguistic theory, rhetoric, poetic structure, literary symbols, and verbal tropes. Freud drew on such resources frequently, and Lacan's reinterpretation of Freud stresses the therapeutic value of such knowledge.

ALTHUSSER

Louis Althusser (1918–90) was born in Algeria and studied philosophy at the prestigious École Normale Supérieure. Afterwards, he was appointed to an influential post there which involved tutoring many future philosophy teachers on their qualifying exams. He joined the French Communist Party in 1948, and this undoubtedly influenced his project of returning to a more orthodox reading of Marx, which rejected the importance of the early "humanist" Marx. Althusser died in prison, having been convicted of strangling his wife some years earlier.

He uses the notion of "epistemological break," which was coined by Canguilhem and later elaborated by Foucault, as a principle of interpretation for Marx's corpus. Arguing that Marx entirely abandoned his early humanist writings for a truly scientific treatment of society, Althusser insists that Marx's Hegelian roots and his theory of alienation are irrelevant for any genuine comprehension of his mature project.[49] He develops a "structuralist" version of orthodox Marxism that dismisses the insights of Gramsci, Lukács, the Frankfurt School, and his existential Marxist contemporaries (Sartre, Merleau-Ponty). His structuralism concentrates on the *relationships* among persons, groups, and institutions in order to understand the dynamics of history and to explicate the *mode of production*, a system of relations that is typically invisible to the people governed by it. That the mode of production is amenable to *scientific* explication and invisibly governs every other aspect of society distinguishes Marx's position from others. Like many structuralists, Althusser dismisses the self-conscious experience of individual agents as well as their claim to individual responsibility. Instead he insists that the mode of production is the primary determinant of history and individuality.

Althusser claims that Marx discovered a way to make speculative concepts scientific, a way of transcending ideologies (ethical, political, aesthetic, or religious) to reveal the truth about the governing dynamic of society. Althusser's interpretation avoids economism – which reduces all social dynamics to mere reflections of the changes in the economic forces and relations of production.[50] Instead he argues that different elements of historical societies (religious-ethical, political-legal, biological) can govern all other social relations within a specific era, but which element is dominant is determined by the economic mode of production. Thus, there is a double structuration within any given historical era. The deepest determinant is always that of the mode of production, but the surface relationships in society may be governed by a non-economic factor that is given its importance by the mode of production. This is a subtler version of Marx's canonical position, and it incorporates the "deep structure" metaphor so central to structuralism.

Althusser dismisses the relevance of Marx's early writings entirely. Since the discovery of those texts was crucial to the emergence of the "Western" alternative to orthodox Marxism, he produces an entirely different "reading" of Marx's texts. Indeed, he examines the process of reading in order to show how to read Marx properly. Marx's mature work supposedly offers a *scientific* elucidation of history.[51] A truly scientific understanding of history ignores the self-consciousness of historical agents and instead focuses on the primary motor of history – the mode of production. Althusser's goal is to revise purely ideological theories of history in favor of Marx's scientific one. Despite the obvious influence of Hegel's logic on Marx's magnum opus, *Capital,* Althusser insists that Marx almost entirely abandoned his early dependency on Hegelian methodology and assumptions. Marx allegedly transforms Hegel's speculative concepts into scientific ones.

One reason Althusser dismisses experience is that it is governed by ideological factors that effectively conceal real historical operations. The goal of Marxist analysis is to challenge these ideological factors. The view that people are active, self-determining "subjects" is among the most potent ideological illusions of capitalism.[52] Althusser claims that the important social dynamics within a culture are determined by contradictions within the mode of production. Though he contests Hegel's influence on Marx, he nonetheless believes that many social spheres express these underlying contradictions – a major Hegelian hypothesis. He may not think that the social order expresses the complex dynamic among concepts, but he certainly accepts the expressive relation between the mode of production and the other dimensions of the social order. This part/whole relation remains internal and dialectical, in the sense that a change in any part will produce a corresponding change in the other parts, but Althusser's "whole" is only the complex of relations among the parts; it does not "emerge" from them in an ontological sense. In addition, Althusser rejects the Hegelian idea that the ultimate aim or telos of history is contained

– at least in embryo – in the beginning. Finally, Althusser insists that contradictions among elements of the mode of production form a system, that some contradictions are dominant within the system, and are reflected or expressed in the other contradictions. Thus, although Althusser questions the Hegelian concept of totality, both the notions of contradiction and expressiveness still play a considerable role in his position.

Althusser believes that structuralist Marxism can offer better practical guidance to revolutionary political activity than Hegelian Marxism because it identifies the dominant contradiction at which the mode of production can most effectively be transformed. Revolutionary activity must focus on that nexus. In Gramsci's conception of social totality, every element is equally essential, and thus none can have any political priority over the others. However, this means that attacking any element can produce significant change. Altering one should contribute to changing all the others if it is part of a true totality. Thus, Althusser's alleged advantage over Gramsci may be illusory.

Althusser does see some liberating function in art, at least when it does not serve purely ideological purposes. Genuine art allows people to discover the operations of ideology in everyday experience; it uncovers and reveals those operations in the lives of specific types of persons.[53] Art, however, is impotent when it comes to defeating the operations of ideology; this can be achieved only by "science."

One of Althusser's most influential essays is "Ideology and Ideological State Apparatuses." Here he distinguishes between repressive state apparatuses (police, law, prisons, courts, and government administration) and ideological state apparatuses (education, political parties, religious sects, the family, unions, and some high culture).[54] Repressive state apparatuses ultimately dominate individuals through violence. Ideological state apparatuses dominate people through ideology, and the ruling ideology operates in all ideological state apparatuses (ISAs), however hidden from view. ISAs contribute to the reproduction of relations of the mode of production.[55] In the feudal era, the dominant ISA was the Church; now it is the school, which inculcates the necessary expectations, roles, rules, and skills to maintain the capitalist mode of production indefinitely.[56] It infiltrates all strata of the population and all professions. Because it functions without resistance in an individual's formative years, its effects are long lasting and difficult to alter.

Ideology produces a representation of the imaginary relation of individuals to the real conditions of their existence. It operates not primarily through beliefs (although they play a role), but through ritualized practices. The aim of ideology is not so much to produce false beliefs, but rather to create "subjects" – i.e., to establish a network of rituals in which persons can recognize themselves and achieve some sense of identity. These rituals call to all "subjects" to identify themselves with the rituals, and insofar as they respond to the solicitation of the ideology and perform the rituals, they function like well-oiled machines.[57] Such rituals include dutifully sacrificing one's life to one's job and voting to ratify the status quo. Ideologically dominated subjects thus consent to their subjection by becoming "good performers." With such individuals, repressive state apparatuses become superfluous, for "subjects" function all by themselves.[58]

BARTHES'S TRANSCENDENCE OF STRUCTURALISM

The ultimate goal of structuralism is to reduce surface multiplicity to systematic order using a minimum of contrasting elements and rules of combination. Once Barthes wholeheartedly embraces multiplicity for its own sake, he abandons the structuralist enterprise. The many breaks that structuralists insert between historical stages of systems (e.g., economic, psychic, cultural, linguistic) begin to invade the systems themselves. Barthes realizes that structuralist results are often produced by the investigator's clever organizing devices, rather than by uncovering deeper truths about mind or reality. More and more he abandons his own creative role in organizing his materials, using instead the artificial order of the alphabet.[59] Just as he often opposed dominant theoretical tendencies while structuralism was ascending, so he challenges its assumptions when it becomes dominant. His rejection of authorship in other texts invites him to interrogate his own authorship. Gradually, he seeks to create texts that organize themselves. Simultaneously, his own voice becomes more distinctive, and his authorial standpoint becomes more assured.

A Lover's Discourse (1977) is among the finest of his last books. In it he examines the exquisite sufferings and joys of romantic love – love that shakes people to their foundations. Though he presupposes a psychoanalytic theory of love, he closely examines the variety of experiences that define the total phenomenon.[60] These are organized as phrases that the lover might say to the beloved or sometimes phrases that describe revelatory experiences of the lover. Their arrangement, however, is alphabetical (nearly random), lacking any system or order. Some of these derive from famous philosophical or literary studies of love, and the entire book is a commentary on Goethe's *Sorrows of Young Werther*. Barthes explores the many voices and moods of lovers, their anguish and joys. Though he is clearly moved by the lover's plight, he also seeks to demystify love, questioning the immense investment people make in it.

In addition, he begins to assert explicitly what was always implicit in his essays – the joy of comprehending complex nuances. The earlier distinction between the readerly and writerly text is refashioned as the text of pleasure and the text of ecstasy (in *The Pleasure of the Text*, 1973). Mere pleasure is derived from texts that are conventional and typical, that can be consumed without thinking. Texts of ecstasy produce a revolution in the reader's outlook; they challenge and disconcert.[61] Barthes embraces these dangerous texts. His post-structuralism begins to emerge when he questions his own key distinction – noting that texts of pleasure can contain ecstatic moments and that texts of ecstasy may contain long stretches of mere pleasure. This observation makes the distinction lose its stability.

His autobiography, also organized alphabetically, consists not of a narrative, but a series of vignettes written sometimes in the first person, sometimes in the third person. Barthes realizes how much of a "myth" or cultural institution he has become, and he tries to unmake and refashion that myth as he describes the layers of meaning that have overlaid his name.[62] His final book on photography, *Camera Lucida* (1980) explores many aspects of the image.[63] These final essays are very personal, even though they aspire to universal insights. Gone is Barthes's scientific guise; far more powerful is his effort to see things in new ways, to interrogate both art and experience to discern the fragmentary insights for which he is best remembered. His trajectory is similar to both Foucault's and Derrida's: the more he denied the importance of the human subject, the more personal and distinctive his writing became and the more insistently he asserted his unique aesthetic approach to living. The poststructuralists provide challenging arguments against key assumptions of structuralism, but many passed through a structuralist moment. They abandoned it less because of its theoretical insufficiency than because of its poverty of imagination.

ASSESSMENT

Structuralism is rooted in a specific theory of meaning, the central premise of which is that meaning derives from a system of differences, not independent positive terms. This doctrine is closely related to the definition of a system in gestalt theory and the dialectical notion of totality. This premise is almost certainly one important feature in any correct theory of meaning, even if there may be other elements that are less essential to the structuralist picture. This model allows structuralists to develop a synchronic notion of system-state that can be described and understood independently of previous states of the system. When this system is treated as an underlying explanatory matrix for observable surface phenomena, then structuralism offers an alternative mode of "explanation" for areas of social science to which this notion of system can be applied. The model has met with modest success in linguistics, anthropology, psychoanalysis, psychology, literary theory, and cultural studies. It can yield useful results without relying on positivist causal explanations.

However, the power of these "explanations" varies greatly in the various areas to which structuralism has been applied. Chomsky's reinvigoration of structuralism solidified its usefulness in linguistics. Similarly, Jakobson's phonology had enormous impact and success because the possibilities of the human sound production are finite and can be defined through a limited number of differential elements. But these two successes have proved hard to replicate in other fields. Other areas of human behavior are less amenable to a "grammatical" analysis that derives from potential universal structures of the mind. Lévi-Strauss's theories are especially difficult to evaluate, despite his evident aspirations toward scientificity. The problem is that the structures and systems he identifies provide only one possible organization of the data and, even then, his organization makes questionable assumptions. Barthes's examination of the fashion system is fascinating, but it too fails to exhibit the explanatory power and fecundity of Chomsky's grammatical models.

Structuralism's results are also mixed in literary studies, where the concept of structure has a long history. Vladimir Propp (1895–1970), Algirdas Julius Greimas (1917–92), and Jakobson have made significant contributions to the understanding of specific areas of literary theory. Christian Metz (1931–93) has perhaps made modest contributions to film theory. But these theorists contribute to an established discourse already demonstrating an ability to clarify structure in works of fiction. In addition, the contributions of the structuralists to clarifying particular literary works or to comprehending either the reading or creative writing process are limited. Thus, structuralism's methods seem incapable of standing alone as an approach to literature, but they also are not easily integrated with other types of literary analysis. The structuralist aspiration to provide a comprehensive and exhaustive analysis of the possibilities of literature (from any perspective) seems quixotic, and it often devolves into a proliferation of typologies when it attempts to realize this goal. Similarly the endless cataloguing of possible literary devices often deadens – rather than inspires – readers' love and understanding of texts. Still, when structuralists limit their efforts to examination of particular genres (folktales, symbolist poetry) or even particular authors (as Genette concentrates on Proust), they can make valuable strides both in understanding the target of analysis and in clarifying intermediate level structures that may be useful in other contexts as well.

So even in its areas of its greatest success, substantial reservations can be raised about the overall value of structuralism's achievements. But it exhibits definite weaknesses as well. One weakness concerns the unconscious categorial activity that is invoked to explain a variety of surface phenomena. First, how does the structuralist limit the number of unconscious structures that are posited? Can any observed phenomenon ever require a specific configuration of such structures? How can the claim that particular unconscious structures are universal be tested? What if the posited structures produce poor cognition, e.g., bad inferences or inept thought? Is there any way to transform or improve them in such a case, or are they hard-wired and unchangeable? Another weakness is that structuralists forget that humans must sustain and support the structures that operate through them. This is true even for linguistic rules. Speakers (agents) must reproduce the linguistic structures (laws, norms, categories) in their speech. This moment of reproduction opens the possibility of transforming the structures, not via the utterances of one individual alone, but gradually via the actions of the entire speaking community. This is how art advances, how conventions change, how value systems get enriched. The same process can augment deeply embedded behavioral patterns and categorial structures as well. Structuralism wants to grant an ontological independence to its structures, but few really have such independence. At a given historical moment, certain structures are favored by practical (habituated, embodied) inertia, but nothing can escape potential transformation by collective human activity.

I have acknowledged the ways in which some kinds of structuralism provide useful explanatory models. But many do not. One of these is the strategy of defining a grid that establishes all the logical possibilities and then tries to draw conclusions about the case at hand against this backdrop. The problem here is that unless there is some genuine relationship between the larger system and the various possibilities that define it, the discovery that a case falls in one box of the grid or another produces no illumination or explanatory force. At best, it indicates where the case falls on a typology. But if the investigator arbitrarily constructs the typology, it may have no explanatory relation to the case at hand. Chomsky's structuralism escapes this criticism because his abstract rules summarize a kind of competence that can be tested by observations. This kind of structuralist explanation reveals little about deep structures of the mind or about significant ontological connections among entities. This is why so much structuralist research seems merely diagrammatic – producing endless classificatory schemes that only faintly illuminate particular cases.

Finally, the structuralist rejection of history can have methodological value, if the researcher chooses to concentrate on the interlocking relationships of a system at a given time. Even historical explanations must presuppose some synchronic organization, if only to discover *significant* changes over time. But synchronic explanation also has limits. Diachronic change is no less real than synchronic systemic relations. Often researchers can only discover synchronic relations by observing the way in which the system *changes* as a result of various inputs. Also, the extent to which certain kinds of structure (the unconscious, categorial operations, etc.) can be affected by history is almost certainly an empirical question. Hegel sought to discover the underlying logic of a given system or mentality, but he also argued that temporal changes have a logic of their own as well. The two approaches can strengthen each other, each refining the other's results. The structuralist does not so much disprove the value of historical explanation as show how some order and coherence can still be articulated even when diachronic relations are ignored. Even if systemic transformations are not caused by a single factor, the complex sources of such change can still be discovered and usually are illuminating.

PHILOSOPHIES OF DISPERSION

CHAPTER 9

INTRODUCTION

I distinguish "poststructuralism" from "postmodernism," which is usually taken to incorporate the former term. Postmodernism can best be understood as a theory about the defining features of the "current era" (1980–2001). Poststructuralism, on the other hand, claims that concepts, cognitive frameworks, psychic impulses, social movements, and historical forces typically are dispersed in relation to one another; it thus defends an empirical-metaphysical hypothesis. The word "dispersion" captures a common theme among the major poststructuralists: Foucault, Derrida, and Deleuze. To be dispersed is to become scattered and diffused without pattern. Dispersion is a process as well as a resulting configuration of relationships. It epitomizes Foucault's analysis of the connections among discursive formations (e.g., scholarly disciplines) and power-knowledge practices (e.g., prisoner reform) (skewed – without any organic bonds uniting them); it pictorially symbolizes Derrida's process of *différance* (or dissemination); and it summarizes Deleuze's rhizomatic models. As a process, "dispersion" suggests that the dividing, self-repelling operation is ongoing, unceasing. Things have not simply "fallen apart"; they continue to fall further apart. Philosophies of dispersion conceptualize everything as skewed (in space and time); nothing coalesces or develops into organic unity. Some interpreters mistakenly conclude that they construe everything to be chaotic. In fact, they allow for limited constellations of coherence, but these fragments of order have no hierarchical or expressive relation to each other; nor do they provide any clue to order-fragments existing in other areas. Moreover, this defining metaphor for poststructuralism does not apply merely to concepts or linguistic structures, it characterizes all types of entities and dynamics – from intra-psychic forces to social groups, power's effects, and technological innovations.

Many interpreters treat poststructuralism as primarily a skeptical or critical movement – as deconstruction *incapable* of reconstruction. This view is misleading. Dispersionists do have an affirmative vision even though their common features are more evident in what they negate. They *are* highly critical of past approaches to philosophy (especially Hegel, Freud, phenomenology, and structuralism), but each introduces new philosophical tasks. They aim to hilosophical landscape they inherit, abandoning the aspirations logy, hermeneutics, and structuralism – a search for timeless horitative interpretations, or for underlying structures that organ- nts. Foucault is best understood as a historian of institutions ylum, medical clinic, prison, and confessional) and systems of ally in psychology, but also in philosophy and social theory), ...ions have dramatic philosophical implications. Derrida and Deleuze are professional philosophers, who develop their positions in response to previous philosophers. All three focus on language, exploring pragmatic theories of discourse that differ significantly from structuralist theories.

Perhaps the clearest indication that dispersionists do not abandon truth is their defense of core claims and ideals. They each think they understand the psyche, language, and even ultimate reality (in Derrida's and Deleuze's cases) more adequately than previous philosophers. Foucault seems to reject the notion of ultimate reality, suggesting that conceptual formations (in all their multiplicity and dispersion) *constitute* ultimate reality. Derrida may deny that we can achieve absolute presence to ultimate reality, but he definitely asserts that not only persons but also ultimate reality itself exists in irrevocable dispersion from itself (severing/severed), and is thus unable to achieve reunification. Deleuze also believes ultimate reality is constantly dividing itself, proliferating in unsystematic – but not necessarily random – ways. They each embrace dispersion, and they defend ethical and political ideals consonant with it. Foucault defends an aesthetics of existence that encourages both self-criticism and self-creation. He also defends a local politics of targeted resistance, in which groups seek to refashion specific institutional operations to improve their lot. Derrida rejects standard conceptions of law and justice, but he defends ideals of friendship and ethical responsiveness that acknowledge self-dispersion. Deleuze values a process of becoming that releases the productivity of desire and creates temporary affiliations between groups in order to accomplish specific goals.

CORE CONTRIBUTIONS

Philosophies of dispersion make several major contributions. First, they offer new arguments to show that the mind is not transparent to itself – it exists always at a distance from itself. This follows from Derrida's denial of the possibility of complete self-presence. Foucault reaches the same conclusion by arguing for the existence of rules that *unconsciously* organize and limit what can be said and done in specific contexts. Since agents are blind to these rules, they lack full self-possession. Deleuze arrives at this result by noting that mental operations are integrally connected to other bodies and energy flows in the interpersonal field; for him, individual minds overflow themselves because they are permeable to outside forces. Conscious states can never be treated as self-enclosed or self-sufficient; they function like cogs in larger social machines, the full impact of which cannot be fully transparent to any one individual.

Hence, the dispersionists develop new arguments to support this current of anti-Cartesianism that runs throughout post-Kantian Continental philosophy.

Second, though they reconceive *everything* on the model of dispersed, fragmented, perpetually self-dividing forces, their best example of this model is the *self*. They show that the self consists of multiple voices, rules, drives, and energies, all of which exist in a disharmonious, countervailing relation to one another. This self-disintegration is so great that the ideals of rational autonomy, individual self-sufficiency, and personal coherence seem untenable. They thus mount a serious attack on the defining ideal of selfhood inherited from the Enlightenment. Dispersionists destabilize selfhood further by revealing the powerful role of unconscious operations in knowledge production (Foucault), in writing and speech (Derrida), and in socio-cultural movements (Deleuze). Whether dispersion is a correct model for all reality is arguable, but it does capture the often-tenuous experience of selfhood, at least in recent decades. Although Heidegger and Sartre anticipate this conception of severed selfhood, the dispersionists defend its importance more forcefully. Moreover, unlike the existentialists, they do not recuperate the ideal of self-realization (or self-unification or authenticity) to compensate for this divided condition. Instead, they embrace this condition, claiming that it is a more promising, truer way to live.

Third, the dispersionist model suggests that universal rules are unlikely to gain much purchase on reality. They argue that detailed attention to specific contexts is necessary to make any progress in knowledge. Whether they are examining specific disciplines, rhetorical tropes, linguistic structures, rules governing institutional behavior, or ways of liberating desire, they delimit their claims in order to provide richer illumination. They thus contest the privilege that philosophers have often granted to universal claims. They are also more alive to the operations of contingency and chance in every area of human endeavor, including cognition, thus challenging the traditional philosophical demand for necessary truths. Moreover, they stress the dynamic character of reality and mind, building on models of becoming established by Nietzsche and Bergson. Instead of identifying fundamental principles, primordial structures, or governing operations, they examine surface processes – the process of becoming (Deleuze), the process of *différance* (Derrida), and the dynamics of power (Foucault). Focusing on these processes produces significant changes in traditional ontology. The dispersionists defend the need for these changes.

They note that most linguistic and social distinctions are culturally constituted and sustained, not natural, automatic, necessary, or inevitable. Instead of seeking a science of language, they produce a critique of many typical operations of language, for they believe those operations help sustain the dominant order. They examine how language functions in specific contexts in order to disrupt its naive acceptance. Foucault examines the complex intersection of social and historical forces required to create a new social distinction (e.g., "madness" versus reason). Derrida challenges the binary oppositions implicit in many linguistic distinctions and shows how they often undermine themselves. Deleuze shows how many uses of language (e.g., classification or stereotyping) reinforce cultural and psychoanalytic strategies for subverting desires that might threaten the dominant order. All of them offer strategies for reversing these linguistic effects and provide a finer-grained understanding of their specific operations.

Fourth, the Marxist left was collapsing as poststructuralists became prominent, and collectively they attempt a new critique of the current order and sketch some ideals that might sustain political protest. Their critique concentrates on the operations of power, and their ideals involve acknowledging the claims of minorities – understanding the distinctiveness of their experiences and aspirations. Though their goals continue to be emancipation and justice, dispersionists recognize that these concepts may require different conditions for different groups. They also seek more effective means of social change based on new theories of power's operations. They start from Nietzsche's vision of multiple wills-to-power operating throughout nature, humanity, and culture. They insist that such power is dispersed throughout many sites within society and that it operates in different ways in different contexts. It cannot be reduced to the operations of the state or its police and juridical apparatus. They believe that power anticipates resistance and incorporates its counter-moves into ongoing strategies of domination. They see power operating in every social encounter, arguing that it cannot be bracketed or transcended. Thus, the question is not how to overcome power, but how to manipulate it to produce desired results, how to make conflict productive rather than stultifying. This becomes the dispersionists' main political goal.

Foucault abandons a juridical or legal conception of power in favor of one that stresses the control of behavior through science, supervision, the inculcation of habits, and the imposition of norms. Deleuze concentrates on power's flows, its capacity to produce new connections among people and technological devices, its ability to find alternative routes when seemingly blocked, and its overflow of boundaries. These flows may occasionally interlock in specific contexts, but they never become organic systems, and their connections remain fluid. Power creates temporary group affiliations and keeps refashioning the social field. Deleuze examines how power can be used to liberate desire and enhance the process of becoming. Derrida concentrates on law rather than power. He notes that law strives to codify justice, but always does so imperfectly. He examines law's preconditions and operations in order to achieve better jurisprudence – better approximations of justice and more adaptable, sensitive applications of law to specific contexts. Foucault recommends more strategic thinking in responding to power, perhaps redirecting it to achieve different goals. Derrida challenges the distinctions on which overzealous uses of law depend, stressing the near impossibility of codifying justice. Deleuze seeks ways of stimulating the flow and productivity of desire without reincorporating it into existing structures of domination.

Finally, they mount a forceful critique of many human sciences and philosophical positions. For example, they raise serious objections to Hegel, Marxism, Freud, phenomenology, and structuralism; this critical onslaught represents a common contribution.[1] They also challenge epistemological realism and foundationalism. Foucault challenges the scientific character of many of the human sciences and shows that they have had invidious political implications. He details many ways in which they have disseminated methods of control used in prisons to other social institutions (e.g., schools and factories). Foucault also criticizes the rise of intrusiveness and "pastoral power" among the "helping" professions. Deleuze questions the received truth and value of psychoanalytic dogma, and he uses his rhizome model to challenge paradigms in other human sciences (e.g., linguistics, anthropology). Derrida rejects the general approach of structuralism in the social sciences and linguistics, though he has fewer suggestions for reconstructing these disciplines than either Deleuze or Foucault. Many of his objections to the founding distinctions of philosophy also apply to basic concepts in social science. All the dispersionists rethink many traditional distinctions within Continental philosophy itself and explore new ways of doing philosophy. Though they think philosophy can still be productive, they believe it must assimilate their criticisms before it can continue.

FOUCAULT

Michel Foucault (1926–84) and Jacques Derrida (b. 1930) are among the most prominent Continental philosophers of the late twentieth century. Several important innovations explain why Foucault deserves this acclaim. He develops revolutionary ways of thinking about the historical process (it consists of inexplicable breaks, not incremental progress),[2] about a community's relationship to individuals (both in thought and action, people unconsciously follow anonymous rules[3]), and about the proper interpretation of modernity (instead of a progressive realization of freedom, modernity expands the institutional domination of everyday life[4]). Foucault suggests that instead of rational, self-conscious, autonomous subjects, modern individuals are docile, passive, and normalized – meticulously supervised and controlled by social institutions.[5] He claims that instead of generating deeper comprehension of social life, the human sciences are agents of this domination – refining disciplinary practices inside total institutions (asylums, prisons, clinics) that are intended to "humanize" refractory populations, which have been designated as "abnormal" by "scientific" concepts. Under the guise of compassion and human improvement, the human sciences experiment to find effective methods of controlling subject populations and then transmit these newly minted technologies of power to other supervisory social institutions (schools, factories, armies, and corporations).[6] Foucault also develops a new theory of power in the course of supporting this critical stance toward the present. Finally, he defends two oppositional ideals: the specific intellectual and the self-creator.

His core theme is the complex relationships between knowledge frameworks (rules informing discourses) and ways of structuring human activity (institutions, power relations, and self-produced styles of life). He studies their changes and complex relationships in three historical eras: the Renaissance, the Classical Age (1650–1800), and the Modern Age (1800–1950). Occasionally he sketches possible contemporary developments, but rarely elaborates them in depth. His historical studies create critical distance on the present and motivate a search for alternatives. Even though his theory of history draws on earlier French philosophers of science (e.g., Canguilhem[7]), its implications remain revolutionary even today. After achieving notoriety on the basis of his first four books – *Madness and Civilization* (1960), *Birth of the Clinic* (1963), *The Order of Things* (1964), and *The Archaeology of Knowledge* (1968), Foucault underwent two intellectual shifts. In the first (from 1972 to 1978), his main theoretical focus becomes power – *Discipline and Punish* (1972) and *History of Sexuality, Vol. 1* (1978); he articulates a unique theory of its operations. In the second (from 1978 to 1984), his main focus becomes ethical self-constitution – *The Uses of Pleasure* (1982), *Care of the Self* (1984). In this final period, he focuses on classical Greece and Rome, and he formulates a more constructive vision of his project. I will summarize Foucault's contributions by sketching his theories of history, social distinctions, truth, the human sciences, power, and self-constitution.

Perhaps the most common assumption about human history is that it progresses – both in knowledge and human well-being. Foucault questions this view with "archaeological" studies of specific disciplines and "genealogical" studies of institutions. His archaeologies challenge the claim that knowledge progresses by arguing for epistemological breaks. His genealogies reject the claim that freedom increases by showing instead that domination has become more subtle and widespread. The archaeologies describe configurations of thought and institutional practice in adjacent eras whose differences are so pronounced that hardly any connection – and certainly no progression – seems to exist between them.[8] The central point is that the rules governing a knowledge-formation in one era are often unrelated to its operative rules in the next era. Thus, the history of thought consists of a series of inexplicable "breaks," not gradual, progressive development. Foucault does not actually demonstrate that there are *no* connections across these breaks, but he shows that the discipline's goals, concepts, and rules of evidence are so different in adjacent periods that his discontinuity thesis becomes the only plausible one. These breaks emerge at different times for different fields and typically are unnoticed by practitioners; they must usually be discovered after the fact. Also, within eras, different fields exhibit discontinuous, dispersed relationships to one another. No governing principles inform and organize all human thought *within* an era. Certain sectors of thought may be so organized, but not the whole landscape.[9]

Foucault's thesis of epistemic breaks is different from a related thesis propounded by Kuhn – that periods of normal science are interrupted by brief periods of revolution in which many of the assumptions of the previous period of normal science are explicitly rethought and revised.[10] For Kuhn, periods of revolution arise because of unresolved problems in normal science. Standard strategies of resolving such problems prove unsuccessful, and the anomalies multiply. This leads to revolutionary ferment and explicit re-evaluations until a new paradigm that resolves the anomalies emerges. Then new theories, methods, and standards of evidence become established. On Foucault's understanding, these seismic shifts occur *behind the backs* of the thinkers involved.[11] The changes occur in implicit systems of rules that determine intelligibility and plausibility in knowledge claims. At one time, a particular statement is perfectly plausible and debatable, but 50 years later the same statement becomes so laughable that it cannot be taken seriously. On Foucault's picture, there is no single science of biology, linguistics, or economics (for example); rather, there are diverse intellectual enterprises that constitute the history of each of these disciplines, and later enterprises are not necessarily corrections or improvements of the earlier ones – but are entirely different research programs. These changes are often concealed by similar terminologies and procedures, but the meanings of the terms and the goals of the procedures are completely different.[12]

In the *Order of Things*, for example, Foucault elucidates three distinct principles of order loosely governing thought about language, economics, and natural history since the Renaissance. These principles imply specific methods for understanding events and distinctive standards of truth, but they are rarely explicit in the periods they govern. The ordering principle Foucault discovers in the Renaissance is homology – everything functions as a microcosmic model for the larger macrocosm. Thus, everything is metaphorically connected with everything else, and hermeneutic methods that explicate these symmetries are the favored strategies of explanation.[13] Later, in the Classical Age, the principle of order shifts to well-formed typologies, in which perceptible, surface characteristics are used to organize an empirical field (e.g., life-forms) into static classifications (e.g., biological species). This principle allows many observable properties to be ignored because they are irrelevant to the classification. "Explanation" involves placing each object in its proper place in the classificatory scheme.[14] Still later, in the Modern Age, a new principle of order emerges: imperceptible, underlying governing forces (e.g., grammar, biological drives). These forces are often unknown to individuals yet determine their actions.[15] In the Modern Age, classificatory tables and hermeneutic analogies become irrelevant because its principle of order generates different strategies of explanation, and so methods that produced recognized knowledge in former eras are simply useless in the new era. Similarly, explanatory strategies that are perfectly plausible in the Modern Age would have been incoherent in previous eras. Foucault does not ask how or why these basic principles of order change, but he would reject the claim that they shift because of internal contradictions, since – within its own terms – each principle can resolve apparent problems. One principle of order fades, and another emerges – almost fortuitously.

If proven, these "epistemic breaks" would establish that standards of truth change in inexplicable ways and that every principle of order would have only an historically limited application. Thus, hermeneutics would be outdated because its underlying ordering principle is irrelevant now. Foucault suggests that the concept "man" (an entity that is both subject and object of knowledge) will be defunct as soon as the Modern principle of order is abandoned.[16] Foucault also shows that conceptual change and institutional change are closely related. New principles of order may produce new institutional mechanisms of control, and changes in institutional function may demand new ordering concepts. Though practices and concepts operate on different planes, they cannot be isolated from one another. Foucault is a dispersionist because he believes that institutions and concepts change at different rates and in different directions.

Foucault also challenges the assumption of historical progress by showing that humans are *not* advancing toward greater freedom and rationality. Instead he sees a more precise, insidious domination of populations by diverse social institutions. Moreover, Foucault claims that this increased domination flows from seemingly progressive victories. For example, in eighteenth-century France, as madness became more sharply distinguished from rationality, reason's capacity to learn from madness decreased, and stigmas formerly associated with lepers were transferred first to the mad and then also to the poor, the criminals, and the handicapped with whom they were initially segregated (all embodying forms of "Unreason").[17] Eventually, reason simply silenced these "irrational" modes of existence and regarded them as subhuman – unworthy of sympathy. By the time the category of "insanity" emerged in nineteenth-century medical practice, justifications for exhaustive supervision of the insane had been legitimated, and thus humanely "caring" for the mad meant continuously observing, judging, and policing them.[18] Similarly, as the human sciences (e.g., anthropology, sociology, economics, linguistics, biology, psychology, medicine, public health, and psychoanalysis) developed hypotheses about mental functioning, they used them to create techniques for controlling subject populations, e.g., criminals. In the name of curing social "diseases," the human sciences recommended constant surveillance, positive and negative conditioning, soliciting confessions, etc.[19] Prisons and asylums also supplied helpless subjects on which the human sciences could experiment. As a result, they discovered more potent methods of human control, which were then adopted by other social institutions in order to "improve" humanity: schools, hospitals, factories, the military, and the family. Instead of enhancing autonomy, the human sciences normalized populations into conformity.

Foucault's historical studies share a distinctive perspective. Whether he describes the discontinuities among cognitive frameworks or the subtle operations of power within institutions, he views them from a perspective so remote that they appear alien – as alien as the strangest operations of termites. By describing relatively recent practices from a Martian standpoint, he leaves readers adrift, helplessly confronting human history as a strange, surreal field. Forms of treatment and modes of analysis that seemed illuminating only a few hundred years ago now seem mystifying, even outrageous.[20] His writing thus evokes a parallel experiential confirmation of the breaks he describes. If those practices are so alien now, what will prevent *current* forms of inquiry and *current* institutional operations – both of which *seem* eminently rational – from becoming equally alien in the future? He claims that current practices and modes of thought are arbitrary and contingent; in this way he invites a search for alternatives.

Few claims have become more familiar than those that insist that apparently "natural" distinctions (masculinity/femininity; normal/abnormal; healthy/ill) are socially constructed. Foucault is among the first to examine the processes by which such social distinctions are constituted and maintained. He describes the complicity between knowledge frameworks and institutional operations in sustaining them.[21] They are not merely intellectual products, and they are rarely justified by some "fact of the matter." By studying the history of confinement of the mad or of penal institutions or of medical clinics, Foucault explores the origins and development of the "concepts" of madness, criminality, and public health. He shows how forging a concept often *creates* the class of people which it allegedly just describes, by justifying practices that maintain its isolation. By "create," I do not mean simply "give a name to," but rather *literally produce* as a socially recognized group. Criminals were once "created" by extracting confessions via brutal torture from anyone accused of lawbreaking.[22] These confessions allowed the monarch to inflict vicious punishments (or spontaneous reprieves) on those admitting guilt. Once incarceration rather than execution became the typical punishment for crime, prison administrators invented many practices to "rehabilitate" criminals, but these deepened the control of authorities over criminal behavior.[23] Similarly, classifying someone as "insane" legitimated various treatments that would *drive* many people insane. Thus, establishing a social distinction requires both intellectual justification (often provided by the human "sciences") and institutional supports. The two components reinforce one another, and by criticizing the knowledge claims of the human sciences and the consequences of institutional practices, Foucault challenges such distinctions and their institutional effects.

In his earliest phase, Foucault sought reconciliation between those who impose such distinctions and those who suffer them (the "reasonable" and the "mad," for example).[24] Such reconciliation might occur through Hegelian mutual recognition, requiring (for example) reason to acknowledge its own madness and madness to claim its own rationality. Foucault sought to effect this reconciliation by chastening reason and giving voice to madness. But this Hegelian model assumes that social distinctions can be challenged through altered self-understanding. In his later work, Foucault argues that cognitive-institutional collusion sustains these distinctions through disciplinary practices. On this view, change can only occur through continuously contesting these marginalizing practices. The task then becomes locating the most effective sites of challenge and the most promising strategies for altering power's effects. Full reconciliation is no longer a goal, only compromises in a continuous struggle for power.[25] Foucault's writings strive to realign these social distinctions, though he is sometimes vague about how to alter them (both *in what direction?* and *with what procedures?*). He does insist that effective strategies can only be discovered in each local context and that transforming power relations is always an ongoing struggle.

Foucault also criticizes the "human sciences" for their arrogance. They represent knowledges that are not full-fledged sciences (like physics or chemistry); yet they claim a degree of professionalization that allegedly justifies elaborate technologies of control. By challenging their claims to truth, he hopes to undermine their ability to support these invidious distinctions and methods of domination. Demonstrating that the human sciences undergo significant epistemic breaks is one component of this critique. Another is showing that they fall below the threshold of "scientificity." Discourses can be classified according to four degrees of epistemological adequacy: positivities, knowledges, sciences, and axiomatized systems.[26] At the lowest level are positivities, which have criteria for determining well-formed statements, but which lack verification procedures. At the next level are knowledges, which have criteria for verifying statements' truth as well as their well-formedness. At the third level are sciences, which establish a significant degree of logical coherence among their statements. At the highest level are axiomatized systems, which fully integrate their statements in a deductive system. At present, only some areas of formal logic and mathematics have the highest degree of epistemic adequacy. Foucault claims that most human sciences lie between positivities and knowledges. They seek adequate criteria by which their claims can be validated, but often different "schools of thought" contest the proposed criteria. Foucault notes that the criteria for these degrees of epistemological adequacy may change over time. Nonetheless, despite efforts to model themselves on the natural sciences, the human sciences do not really satisfy the requirements of scientificity.

Foucault thus challenges the human sciences' ability to produce timeless truths, and also doubts whether they are genuine "sciences" – suggesting instead that they qualify only as "positivities." He also accuses them of collusion in the ever-widening domination of human populations.[27] How does this complicity work? By postulating a variety of drives and inner psychic operations, the human sciences give supervisory institutions a target for technologies of control. By examining mechanisms by which these psychic functions can be manipulated, they contribute to such technologies. Thus, if they postulate that the difference between an habitual criminal and a law-abiding citizen is "conscience," then they encourage prisons to instill criminals with consciences through regular monitoring and relentless judgment. If this environment of omnipresent surveillance is enforced consistently, then criminals might internalize the self-monitoring function they allegedly lack. Similarly, if a specific sexual behavior is deemed abnormal and must be uprooted, then psychiatric professionals are urged to intervene and use whatever "treatments" will obliterate it. The deviant's family is also recruited to reinforce "normal" sexual behavior. Foucault believes that defining and institutionally enforcing this ideal of "normalcy" is the central goal of the human sciences and modern bureaucracies. The human sciences thus invent dispositions for power to monitor and supply strategies for producing normalized subjects. They are fully implicated in power's operations.

Sometimes Foucault suggests that the psychic functions postulated by the human sciences are pure myths. Everything happens as if theorists invented these psychic constructs in order to legitimate vigilant control of behavior. The more deeply buried a psychic "complex," the more relentlessly the scientist must intervene to access and shape it. The more complex a psychic disposition, the more points at which specific strategies can alter its course.[28] Sometimes institutions operate through guilt and expiation; sometimes they reshape subjects' behavior directly. Thus, Foucault shows that seeking greater knowledge of "man" has created more effective methods of controlling individuals and national populations (in the case of medicine and public health). The result of these scientific interventions is an ideal of "normalcy" that includes docility, obedience, and self-policing. Foucault notes that the smooth functioning of modern institutions requires normalized individuals.

Throughout this critique, Foucault deploys a distinctive conception of power that challenges the notion dominant in Marxism and political philosophy. There, power is conceived as centralized in the state (or the head of state or in bureaucratic state apparatuses) and as interdictive – preventing certain behaviors by outlawing or forcibly inhibiting them. This analysis allows liberalism to argue that individuals should be guaranteed a sphere protected from state power, as long as they harm no one and obey the laws. This sphere allegedly provides political subjects a space for autonomous self-expression. Against this conception, Foucault argues that power is decentralized – operating at multiple sites and in manifold ways – is not directed from a central authority, often operates at cross purposes, and is primarily productive rather than interdictive in the sense that it shapes and solicits the behavior and habits of its "subjects."[29] For Foucault, there is no protected sphere where power cannot intrude; power influences all behavior in every institutional context. Rather than view power as primarily a legal or political fact, Foucault construes power's goal to be behavioral modification – positive or negative. Thus, any influence that alters human behavior becomes an operation of power. It therefore operates in families, friendships, schools, workplaces, churches, voluntary associations, hospitals, courthouses, and prisons. Foucault believes that state power is often ineffective because it is so remote. Even though threats of force back governmental commands, laws typically concern only behavioral extremes, not its everyday forms. But many apparatuses of power supervise everyday life even though no central organizer coordinates their operations.[30] In every social context, power operates by shaping, defining, punishing, and reinforcing specific types of action. Power achieves its goal when the subject behaves as expected ("normally"); then prohibitions become unnecessary.

Foucault claims that power anticipates resistance. Resistance allows power to refine its strategies and refocus its points of attack.[31] In fact, power is often strengthened by resistance even in smaller-scale institutions, such as prisons, hospitals, factories, and schools. The task of Foucault's analysis of power is to understand its operations in each institutional setting, to describe its results, to evaluate its effects, and to determine whether it can be redirected or challenged. Power's grip cannot be escaped, only redirected.[32] No legally protected sphere can prevent power's penetration. Foucault seeks a critical distance from which power's effects can be evaluated and, if necessary, altered. Combating power requires anticipating its responses in advance and engaging in long-range strategic thinking. Struggles with power rarely achieve complete victories; the battles are never-ending.

Throughout his *oeuvre* Foucault's thought embodies underlying ethical currents, which become explicit and prominent in his final period. His studies of marginalized populations express a barely concealed rage over their absurd treatments by well-meaning "scientists" and professionals. He seeks to reincorporate marginalized experiences and to explore ecstatic states to entice people beyond the limits of the "normal." His historical studies elucidate the forces constituting the present so that it can be refashioned and transformed, thus demonstrating its contingency and malleability. His analysis of power shows how people's concepts, feelings, desires, ideals, and fantasies are socially constructed and thus suggests how they can be reconstructed. Even if people cannot remake themselves entirely, they can target specific elements of their lives for reshaping. Foucault privileges transgression because it facilitates self-transcendence. People must oppose what they are (what power relations have made of them) in order to determine what they want to become.[33] He also defines a new ideal of the committed intellectual – the "specific intellectual" who works in concert with political action groups. Specific intellectuals refuse to accept leadership positions and to tell group members what to do. They provide analyses of specific contexts, challenge mistaken assumptions, and clarify important facts in order to facilitate effective group action.[34] But they encourage groups to pursue their own goals in their own ways. Rather than pursue sweeping cultural revolution, specific intellectuals pursue limited causes and goals. They are subversive without being domineering.

In his third period, Foucault advocates an ethics of self-creation. He invites individuals to take control of their self-constitution. To do this, individuals must create their own goals, habits, and practices of self-shaping. Three ideals that define Foucault's late ethics are *maturity, critique*, and *creativity*. Maturity requires understanding the normalizing processes that govern Western culture in order to circumvent or combat them. Maturity recognizes the limits of conventional morality and develops its own rules. It dismisses mere happiness in the hopes of discovering true joy. Its central goal is to achieve self-mastery – a possibility Foucault seemed to deny during his second period analysis of power. Critique allows individuals to achieve some distance from the institutional practices that dominate their everyday lives and to embrace new options. It uses the alienation his historical studies produce in a positive manner – to motivate revaluation of what one has become. Creativity involves inventing self-concepts, developing goals and strategies of self-realization, and choosing distinctive pleasures. Foucault thus accepts a reconstructed ideal of Enlightenment freedom.[35] It also involves giving a distinctive aesthetic style to one's life.

In his final studies of ethical practices (*The Use of Pleasures* and *Care of the Self*), Foucault examines the ways in which Greek and Roman citizens sought to transform themselves – to gain control over their own behavior, thoughts, desires, and imagination. He formulates a new understanding of ethics and canvasses strategies of self-critique and self-shaping in these early eras. Both the Greeks and the Romans developed elaborate methods of self-analysis, self-control, and self-transformation.[36] Sometimes these "technologies of the self" concerned specific types of relationship (e.g., homoerotic relations between men and boys, husband/wife relationships); sometimes they concerned other issues (health, suitability for leadership). Rather than conceiving ethics as discovering rational justifications for fixed principles, Foucault urges ethicists to create practices that allow people to "work on" themselves in order to become different kinds of person. He believes the Greeks and Romans best exemplified this ethical thinking. Foucault discovers strategies of self-transformation in classical Greece similar to techniques used today (e.g., diaries, meditation, dream analysis, daily diet and exercise regimens). However, Foucault does not embrace Greek or Roman ideals, nor does he sympathize with their ethical dilemmas. Instead, he uses their examples to challenge modern conceptions of ethics that stress principles, confession, duty, justification, and punishment.[37]

Foucault is uninterested in abstract principles that might be shared in different cultures. Although these may resist historical change, describing them fails to capture the ethical tenor and aspirations of particular cultures. Instead, he identifies four elements that undergo significant historical modifications: (1) ethical substance, (2) mode of subjectivization, (3) ethical work, and (4) telos.[38] Ethical substance involves the aspects of oneself to be acted on, reshaped, or transformed (e.g., desires, images, thoughts, or emotions). The mode of subjectivization consists of the sources or powers that motivate the self-transformation (e.g., an idealized self, divine law, natural law, or beautiful form). Ethical work is the specific technologies of self-transformation used to produce the changes (e.g., daily regimens, types of self-analysis, or shaping/renouncing desires). And the telos is the ultimate goal of the enterprise (e.g., purity, freedom, tranquility, or detachment). By clarifying each of these elements for Greek ethics, Roman ethics, Christian ethics, and his own alternative, Foucault elaborates this fourfold analysis.

The Greeks focus on pleasures, seeking a moderation that avoids the extremes of too many or too few. Their telos is immortality and freedom, and their ethical work is voluntary self-mastery.[39] Achieving self-mastery is a prerequisite for leadership. The Romans also focus on pleasures, but they exhibit a greater sense of their dangers, especially to health and to one's vital energies. Unlike the Greeks, they mistrust pleasures, and this mistrust creates a basis for the Christian renunciation of pleasure. The Romans seek purity and calm, and they place great emphasis on self-knowledge, self-examination, and self-testing. The Romans elevated marital partners to co-participants in self-mastery, each serving as an advisor to the other.[40]

The Christian mode of self-constitution – a mode that continues into the Classical and Modern Ages – abandons the self-direction and self-creation so central to ancient ethics.[41] Like Nietzsche, Foucault believes that Christianity is the source of major ethical errors. Greek self-transformation involves a self-perfection or elevation, while Christian self-shaping involves self-abnegation and withdrawal. Christians see the self as evil, full of hidden urges, constantly in need of external monitoring. The Ancients sought to produce earthly examples of excellence, while Christianity demands conformity to God's will. Foucault believes that the Christian postulation of a soul that requires pastoral supervision and regular confession is the first step on the path toward today's docile, normalized subjects. The Greeks allowed for wise mentors, but this relation inspired individuals to create themselves, rather than inviting imposition of harsh dogmas. Christianity's means of enforcement is punishment, while the Ancients at most offered advice that individuals could ignore at their own risk.

For Foucault himself, the ethical substance is life in its pre-personal (non-individuated) flux; the specific goal is to create an artistic style out of one's life; the specific means is critique of the present; and the telos is to think differently, to embody a distinctive voice.[42] Foucault acknowledges that achieving this ideal will require serious self-interrogation because people's "inner selves" are products of power structures that must be challenged. It may require rejecting accepted ethical codes and common-sense ideals; it may involve revising standard ways of responding to other people and to the demands of institutions. Individuals may have to transcend the limits of "decency," perhaps even to embrace extremes. He is skeptical of many of the methods for self-creation and self-critique that have been used in the past: journals, dream analysis, and asceticism. These methods sought greater self-*knowledge*, while Foucault seeks genuine self-transformation.[43] He claims that the processes by which "normal" people are constituted must be dismantled; only then will genuine self-creation become possible.

DERRIDA

Jacques Derrida (b. 1930) writes almost entirely in response to other texts. His positions emerge from close readings and critiques of specific philosophers (e.g., Husserl, Levinas, Plato, Hegel, Marx, and Rousseau), as well as other thinkers (e.g., Freud, Saussure) and novelists (e.g., Jabes, Mallarmé, Kafka, Joyce, Ponge). He has published many books and essays, of which the most notable are *Speech and Phenomena* (1967), *Of Grammatology* (1967), *Writing and Difference* (1967), *Margins of Philosophy* (1972), *Dissemination* (1972), *The Post Card* (1980), *Glas* (1974), *The Truth in Painting* (1978), *Psyche: Inventions of the Other* (1987), *Given Time* (1992), and *Politics of Friendship* (1994). This text-specific, reactive character of his writing makes summarizing his positive views difficult. I will begin by suggesting that he explores one key insight: the claim that nothing can ever be fully present to anything else (even itself) and hence that self-identity (or self-coincidence) is impossible. (Sartre argued for this thesis in the case of human existence, but Derrida extends the claim to everything.) Thus, everything is constantly self-divided and endlessly dividing, unable to achieve internal unity. Many of his essays explore ramifications of this insight because, if it is correct, it threatens many philosophical assumptions and programs. Philosophers often want to believe that facts are given directly to the mind, that the mind can directly encode truths into language, and that speech can be directly understood by all native speakers. Derrida challenges every element of this picture; his theories force a reassessment of the nature of language, mind, and reality. Meaning, expression, and existence are forever haunted by a fluid, self-dividing background that conditions every word, action, or event. Although his position may seem primarily critical, Derrida also develops its constructive aspects.

A *first* approximation of Derrida's insight – that absolute presence to anything is impossible – emerges from the following example. You are looking at the full moon in the night sky. There it is! You think you see the moon itself. But, in fact, you are seeing the moon as it was several minutes prior to your current perception. The actual moon might have been destroyed by an alien warship only seconds before. Thus, there is a temporal gap that separates the emanation of light from the moon and anyone's perception of that light on earth (setting aside, for the moment, the temporal gap between perceiving the light and categorizing it as a perception *of the moon*). This gap between emanation and uptake can be reduced to mere microseconds, but it cannot be eliminated. Any theory of perception (or truth) that requires perceivers to achieve absolute presence to perceived objects requires the impossible.[44] Derrida concludes that perception always grasps a trace (or echo) of the perceived object (and, in addition, self-cognition grasps only a trace or echo of the initial conscious act). Moreover, if the moon itself is only the intersection of all the traces (perceptual and cognitive) it makes possible, then its own internal unity is threatened.

Cartesians might reply that absolute presence can be achieved in at least one case: persons' relationships to their own mental states (their thoughts or feelings, for example). They claim that when people think (or feel), they are absolutely present to their own thoughts (or feelings). Allegedly, there is no temporal gap separating thinking a thought and registering it, feeling and grasping what is felt. Thus, Cartesians claim that the human mind is absolutely self-present, capable of achieving translucent self-identity. Like Hegel and others, Derrida denies this claim. For Derrida, subjects are in no better position concerning their experiences than observers. An unbridgeable gap exists between having a thought and registering it and between experiencing a feeling and knowing it.[45] The actual thought (feeling) is already fading as it is registered; hence, its registration may be imperfect or incomplete. Moreover, the registration requires a complex network of background associations in order to isolate this thought or feeling. This matrix can be loose or fine-grained, but its mesh will condition the precision of the self-comprehension.[46] This matrix easily diffuses into the "original" experience in a way that may make isolating that experience impossible.

Nowhere is this assumption of self-presence more evident than in theories of speaking (as opposed to writing). Many construe thought as inner speech or silent soliloquy. Here, allegedly, expression and understanding coincide; the speaker perfectly comprehends the thought as it is expressed. But Derrida suggests this theory of speech (even inner speech) is mistaken. The articulated speech may inadequately express the speaker's intention, and that intention is gradually achieving clarity in the course of its expression. Speech is always a first draft, often modified by further speech.[47] Only a vague unease guides the speaker toward further self-elucidation. Moreover, that intention itself is not "original" in the sense of primordial; it is motivated by some previous thought or state, which itself has only an incomplete hold on itself, or by some situationally motivated impulse that can be given many interpretations. Speech is thus a constant effort to further complete the speaker's inchoate intent, which only becomes determinate in the process of speaking. This is perhaps more obvious in the case of writing (where writers constantly revise to better express their meanings), but once Derrida's main point is understood, its relevance to speaking is obvious. People constantly reshape and recast their speech in the way writers revise texts. Derrida suggests that people constantly strive to decipher their own meanings in just the way that other people strive to grasp them. Their access to their own "inner" states is as close or distant as another person's access; both try to complete an already unfolding series of expressions: linguistic, gestural, and behavioral.

Derrida sometimes summarizes this claim by saying that writing "precedes" speech, because writing better exhibits the mind's relation to itself. He is opposed to logocentrism: the claim that a self-present *logos* – law, speech, thought, essence, etc. – renders actual expression superfluous and secondary.[48] This formulation makes Derrida's claim seem paradoxical because speech (or thought) seems obviously to precede writing (or any expression). But Derrida claims that expression is essential to intention; neither can exist without the other. The written expression is not simply a copy or externalization of an already formulated speech; writing recasts and refines speech, just as speech constantly recasts "thought." Speakers/subjects are not sufficiently coherent to fully grasp their intentions prior to expression; expression is essential to discovering their thought, just as writing is essential to preserving their speech. Though linguistic theorists have often privileged speech, Derrida shows that writing provides a better model for language use. In addition, writing is frequently criticized because it invites an upsurge of potentially irrelevant associations (because writing, without the limiting condition of speaker's intent, can suggest a variety of arbitrary connections). Derrida notes that such associations are frequently pulsing through writers (or speakers) in the course of writing (speaking), and there is no way of knowing which of them is irrelevant. Some of them *may* clarify the writer/speaker's intent. *No one* has perfect access to an individual's meaning-intention.[49] All anyone can know are expressions and their associations/revisions. These linguistic associations are partly explicated by structuralists (recall the syntagmatic and paradigmatic forms of comprehension), but Derrida believes they are far less organized than structuralists assume. Instead he thinks potentially illuminating associations resonate in many directions. Derrida insists that the mind's relation to itself is like a writer's gradual recovery of a meaning-intention in a text written yesterday.

These reflections show that meaning is not a function of a speaker's intent since that intent takes shape and becomes determinate under the guidance of other factors. Meaning is determined from many directions by context. The complex relations between these manifold contexts and perception, thought, meaning, and reality constitute Derrida's central theme. Philosophy, guided by the early model of Socrates – who never wrote a word – often ignores its own written character. It pretends its insights are directly accessible: in an intuition of essences, in direct contact with the Absolute, or in the recollection of Forms. Philosophy typically delivers a closed, final, indubitable version of truth as a result. Derrida shows, however, that this ideal of philosophy is illusory, that its written character must be acknowledged, and that flaws endemic to writing cannot be expunged.[50] Derrida thus stresses the fragmentary, supplemental character of philosophical work; it cannot organize truth into a perfect system, expressed in a perfectly lucid, unified book. It can only provide a continuing series of commentaries; it cannot produce a transforming epiphany in one radiant moment.

Derrida can now derive some dramatic implications. Essentially, identity cannot exist because everything is fracturing, striving unsuccessfully to retain internal coherence. Instead, there is only a continuous process of dispersion to which Derrida gives many names: *différance*, dissemination, trace.[51] This is true for mental states in relation to their expressions and to the perceived world, and for ordinary entities in relation to themselves. None achieves unity or self-coincidence. An absolute point of origin can never be discovered, and a final endpoint that would complete the unification of all the traces will never emerge. Everything exists at a distance from itself; everything is constantly dividing itself and losing itself further in the very effort to recover itself. People constantly seek self-recovery, but never succeed. They reach temporary plateaus that seem like moments of repose only because so many undercurrents and crosscurrents of dispersion are ignored. Many philosophers resist this conclusion; they try to resuscitate some legitimate concept of self-identity. They search for a distinction that might neutralize Derrida's dissemination process. Derrida's task is to explore these strategies for escaping his conclusions and to prove them unsuccessful. In the process he usually discovers additional kinds of dissemination. His constructive task is to learn how to acknowledge *différance* and abide with it – refusing to deny or repress it. He clarifies its implications for thinking (philosophy), for ethics and politics, and for art, language, and nature.

Derrida takes temporality seriously. Time itself is the medium of dispersion; time severs substances into traces/echoes. Any single "moment" of time is always already a complex of traces in various stages of diffusion and decay. These traces drift and shift chaotically, engaging in a kind of play to which the theorist must learn to conform, rather than dominate or control. Play produces continuous surface transformation that is not random, but is also not formulaic.[52] In using the term "play," Derrida suggests that occasional islands of coherence can dissolve at any time and that theorists must modify their interpretations accordingly.

In his best known essay, "*Différance*," which was initially given as a public lecture, Derrida plays upon the fact that in French the essay's title (a technical term he creates) is pronounced in an exactly similar fashion as the French word "*différence*" (a term with a well-established ordinary meaning). Thus, his voice alone cannot guarantee that the audience properly understands which of the two terms ("*différance*" or "*différence*") he is using. Only the written version of the essay would allow the audience to accurately determine this.[53] The example shows that when auditors listen to another person's speech, they are not directly grasping the meaning as it is uttered; rather, they are interpreting, just as readers interpret written texts. The voice cannot better guarantee the author's meaning than the pen. In both cases context is essential, but context itself is interpreted. The speaker cannot insure that auditors will properly grasp the meaning both because speech can be ambiguous and because speech is only a first draft of the author's meaning. It is constantly being revised in the course of speaking. (Even if a lecture is already written down beforehand, the lecturer often edits and supplements the talk while speaking, adapting the text to the particular audience, occasion, and time limit.) This example also shows that in many cases, the written version is essential to knowing the meaning-intention; without it, the meaning-intention may remain indeterminate.

Derrida then clarifies the process of *différance*, an endless proliferation of contrasts that multiply meanings. It has both a temporal dimension – in which meaning is deferred until the next element in the series emerges (but the series itself is never-ending) – and a spatial dimension – which produces new possibilities of meaning by contrasting terms with each other.[54] *Différance* always operates; it cannot be restrained or eliminated. It is neither an origin nor a result; it is both active and passive, product and production; it describes the functioning of both mental and physical processes. One of Saussure's favorite formulas was that in language there are only differences, no positive terms; in short, the meaning (or identity) of any particular term is determined by its relations to all other terms. Derrida amends this by suggesting that the number of terms affecting the identity of any single term is constantly proliferating, never fixed, and thus that the meaning of every term is constantly under revision.[55] In addition, Derrida generalizes this basic insight to every system, not just linguistic systems or sign systems. Once the full implications of this process of *différance* are understood, many of the founding distinctions of philosophy (and linguistics) implode: sign/referent, speech/writing, thought/expression, presence/absence, active/passive, things/effects, sensible/intelligible, description/interpretation, language/reality, feeling/thought, reason/intuition, truth/illusion, logic/rhetoric, literal/metaphoric, etc.

Derrida acknowledges earlier thinkers who partially anticipated his core insight: Hegel's self-dividing system of concepts, Freud's suggestion that the unconscious constantly breaks into consciousness, Husserl's description of time-consciousness as a complex interweave of protensions and retentions, Heidegger's ontological difference between being and entities, and Levinas's contention that other people challenge one's self-identity. Exploring some of these antecedents may help clarify the nature of *différance*. Husserl, for example, notes that every temporal moment consists of an infinite series of retentions (in the form of retentions of retentions that shade off into the distant past) and of protensions, or expectations for the future (which themselves project further expectations). Thus each "moment" extends into the indefinite past and future, making the experience of temporal continuity and change possible.[56] It also means that each moment is haunted by echoes of times past and times to come – never just itself – continuously pointing beyond itself. Derrida's notion of *différance* as temporal deferral with multiple overlays for every "present" is heavily indebted to Husserl's conception. Husserl's insight reveals the temporal dimension of *différance* – the endless deferral of final meaning. The previous discussion of context reveals its spatial dimension – continuous reference to relevant differences among possible alternative terms.

Another important predecessor is Freud. Derrida's theory of expression (or experience) is already anticipated by Freud's model of a writing pad on which children doodle. The pad causes writing to appear on a cellophane overlay because the stylus causes a wax residue to adhere to the underside of the cellophane surface. The writing can be quickly erased simply by lifting the cover sheet of cellophane, but an imprint of the writing remains on the wax base.[57] Derrida suggests that experience functions in the same way. The underlying wax base is the unconscious, which retains a record of all experiences. The emergence of an experience (or expression) is parallel to the gradual appearance of figures on the pad. Just as the "new" lines arise from records of many other lines made long ago, so the unconscious base infuses the surface experience with manifold related memories (the writing on the pad). Thus even before the experience has fully taken shape there is already a dreamlike supplement from the unconscious that invades the experience as it takes shape. In this way, perception is constantly imbued with memory and fantasy. Thus, when meeting a class for the first time, teachers often experience memory flashes of previous classes and fantasies of possible future successes. There is no absolute perceptual present; experience always carries a series of complex references to other moments of experience within itself, alongside itself, and in its own wake. No moment is ever just itself; every moment is continuously modified by others, just as the lines on the writing pad derive from the traces of all the drawings ever made on it. The underlying network of associations that sustain the process of *différance* is just as essential to the constitution of experience as the subset of features that derive from the "present" moment. Both experience and language are haunted by this complex network of resonant echoes that haunt every present moment. Philosophers often err because they take the present to be prior to the underlying network that makes it possible. Derrida's claim is that experience is possible only through an interaction between the present and an underlying layer of unconscious relations (the wax base of the pad), and this interwovenness constitutes the texture of experience.

One of the many names Derrida gives to his response to other texts is "deconstruction." This term is related to Heidegger's "destruction" of the history of philosophy, which he too thought was overly reliant on the metaphor of presence.[58] Heidegger challenged past distinctions on the basis of the new insights into human existence he achieved in *Being and Time*. Derrida's "deconstruction" is an approach to the reading of philosophical texts which shows that they undermine themselves from within. In its strongest form, it demonstrates that – when read closely and attentively – philosophical essays contain realizations that undermine their main assertions. Many philosophical essays, for example, create distinctions and claim that one term of the resulting opposition is primary, or else they rely on implicit distinctions. But they also acknowledge that the other term of the distinction is equally essential or that the presupposed distinction is problematic. Derrida discovers this "repressed" evidence in the interstices of philosophical essays through a remarkable process of close reading and interrogation.[59] Derrida suggests that philosophers are nearly always subliminally aware of the evidence that will disprove their claims, but they repress it. Deconstruction thus dissolves essays into congeries of tensions and potential contradictions. Derrida believes that many philosophers have glimpsed the deep reality of these irresolvable tensions and conceal their horror by writing philosophy. This explains why Derrida must continually contest the history of philosophy. In effect, it systematically conceals the crucial realizations about presence and *différance* that he seeks to underscore. He also claims that the writing process itself often forces authors to experience *différance* subliminally but that this can produce such anxiety that many writers flee to the safety of canonical conceptions of identity. The constructive side of Derrida's investigations demonstrates ways to abide with these deeper realizations without betraying or fleeing them.

Drawing a distinction is a canonical way to defend philosophical positions. Typically, one side of the distinction is privileged, and this relegates the other side to insignificance. Maintaining both the distinction and the privilege is essential to the position's success. Derrida's "deconstruction" shows that this strategy fails because it seeks to maintain an absolute separation between the two terms. But the two sides are inevitably implicated in one another; neither can exist without the other. In addition, in most cases, drawing the distinction conceals an awareness of this untenability, but this awareness is repressed. Deconstruction uncovers these repressions, and thereby shows that the philosophical text (which asserts the distinction) undermines itself. Thus, deconstruction is a form of internal criticism, akin to the negative moment of Hegel's dialectic. The main difference is that, for Derrida, no synthesis, recovery, or supersession ever occurs. Deconstruction concludes that the two sides of the distinction will mutually challenge one another endlessly without producing any final result.

In his most recent writings, Derrida explores some ethical implications of his position. He claims that ethical decisions are only serious when no well-established rule covers the case. Then the ethical sensitivity, improvisation, and creativity necessary for instituting rules are required.[60] Derrida refuses to lighten the burden of ethical decisions by allowing certain values to be unquestionable or some ends ultimate. Moreover, choosing is never just a momentary decision, but a decision to continue to act – subject to re-evaluation and further insight – in a way that promises the best possible future. A space for questioning ethical assessments is essential, since action must be able to restart and correct itself in the way writing often does. The existence of other people enlivens one's own sense of responsibility, and hospitality – the capacity to live together through continuously rethinking the rules – is a central ethical notion for Derrida.[61] Ethical concepts must be contested and challenged in the same way as other metaphysical concepts. Ethically responsible actions must be mindful of those who are absent – those long dead or still to be born. Laws or maxims never fully or adequately codify the justice or sense of rightness that guides them. Although these insights are tentative and heavily indebted to the phenomenologist Emmanuel Levinas, they indicate some ethical directions Derrida has begun to elaborate.

DELEUZE

Several of Gilles Deleuze's (1925–95) important theoretical books were co-authored with Felix Guatarri (1930–92), a Lacanian therapist who explores connections between individual psyches and cultural/economic systems. These include *Anti-Oedipus* (1972) and *A Thousand Plateaus* (1980), as well as the late work, *What is Philosophy?* (1991). Their books articulate new theories of intrapsychic and social functioning. They challenge the concept of a unified, autonomous subject, and they seek ways of liberating desire that bypass the drive to dominate and be dominated. In addition, Deleuze authored a series of commentaries on other philosophers (e.g., Hume, Nietzsche, Kant, Spinoza, Bergson, and Leibnitz), in which he managed both to inhabit the systems of these philosophers and to use them to develop his own problems and concepts. Deleuze challenged his own theories by mastering these philosophers' contrasting visions, but he also used them to refine his positions. He also produced an early synthesis of his own views in *Difference and Repetition* (1968) and *The Logic of Sense* (1969) and wrote substantial essays on specific arts – *Cinema I and II* (1983/5) – and artists: *Proust and Signs* (1964), *Masochism* (1967) (which examines the writer Leopold von Sacher-Masoch), and *Kafka* (1975). I will discuss the early works and the expository books only insofar as they overlap with the main concerns of his co-authored magnum opus, *Capitalism and Schizophrenia* (of which *Anti-Oedipus* and *A Thousand Plateaus* are the two volumes).

The opening essay of *A Thousand Plateaus* is called "Rhizome"; it introduces Deleuze's distinctive example of the philosophy of dispersion. Rhizomes are plants (e.g., ivies) or other structures (e.g., burrows) that branch in multiple, unexpected directions, creating complex lattice connections. They differ from root-based plants (e.g., trees), which are true organic unities. The roots provide foundations for the rest of the plant. Though they may support many branches, ultimately this diversity emanates from one center, the trunk. Even when tree branches divide, they remain united with the trunk and through it with the roots. Although plurality exists, it is subsumed into an organic unity. Roots produce ordered hierarchies and fixed points of growth. Coherent genetic and structural descriptions can be given to root structures, and root structures can seem internally self-contained. Deleuze believes that root plants constitute the key metaphor informing much Western philosophy. Although that metaphor may have some real-world exemplifications, Deleuze believes the rhizome model better captures most of reality.

In rhizomatic growth, any point on the plant can connect with any other point, but no point is more basic than any other; so there is no hierarchy. *Every* growth in a rhizome is an offshoot; there is no primary trunk or central root from which all the offshoots emanate.[62] In rhizomes, the multiple branchings are independent; they cannot be explained by an underlying unity or reintegrated into a larger whole. The offshoots grow in multiple directions, and there is no way of predicting their growth. If rhizomes' growth is blocked, they simply veer in different directions. They may grow because they are attracted to something (e.g., the sunlight) or because they are repelled by something (e.g., infertile ground), but both attraction and repulsion produce dispersion. External conditions affect the growth of a rhizome; it cannot be self-contained. Rhizomes "begin" in the middle, continue in the middle, and "end" in the middle; they do not have a "life" (origin and end) that genealogists can describe. They follow no single motive, principle, or goal; they exhibit no hierarchy.[63] Rhizomes represent nothing beyond themselves and refer only to themselves. Finally, their parts are interchangeable; all parts can interact with all other parts directly, without the mediation of a central trunk. In order to comprehend rhizomatic development, a new kind of thinking is needed: nomad thought. Nomad thought does not seek origins, goals, principles, systems, unities, or development; it simply traces the twists and turns, spurts and reversals, of the rhizomatic structure.[64] To the extent that rhizomes break rules and codes, nomad thought reinforces this process, rather than reinstituting limits or reimposing a new order. Deleuze argues that rhizomes provide a better model than root plants of how events and processes are actually related to one another. This is a broad empirical hypothesis, and he appeals to current developments in science (chaos theory and fractals) to support it.

Deleuze focuses attention on flux and becoming and on *events*, the analysis of which differs significantly from objects, subjects, or structures. His ontology consists of intensities that transform from potential to actual and have complex, *external* relations to neighboring intensities.[65] These intensities form no coherent system, and they react to many different stimuli. Relations between events and intensities are contingent, rather than necessary. Events exist in dispersion from themselves (e.g., the wind or a waterfall). This model also applies to consciousness, which Deleuze treats as a subjectless, flowing current, existing in duration, but without origin or goal. Consciousness is a moment of the surging and receding life-process. Individuals can personalize this impersonal life-process, but this requires achieving a distinctive style of expression (in speech, writing, thought, or action). This personalization process is the actualization of a potential intensity. Whether in objects or subjects, the expression of these intensities produces qualities – sensible qualities of objects, and feeling-states of subjects; both are emanations from the pre-personal, pre-individuated plane of intensities.[66] Deleuze emphasizes singularities over generalities, instantaneity over permanence, contingency over necessity, and the distinctive over the common.

For Deleuze, the dominant psychic energy is desire and, as the above model might suggest, he construes desire as a productive outpouring of energy, infusing and intensifying desire's object. He rejects the notion that desire expresses lack or emptiness, which must then be compensated by consumption or action.[67] Thus, his conception of desire is fundamentally opposed to Hegel's. In addition, he refuses to construe consciousness as a Freudian internal theater in which purposive "characters" (e.g., id, ego, superego) interact, but rather as a factory that produces connections with other machine-like elements of reality – natural, social, linguistic, or historical. The flow of desire can be routinized or channeled either by habit, power, rules, or dead metaphors.[68] Deleuze's goal is to find ways of releasing desire from these limits and allowing it to flow in new directions, creating new connections. Because desire constitutes the psyche and binds psychic energies to objects, psyches dissolve into their relations with the world, others, groups, and signs. Persons are not merely divided into dispersed roles or groups, but pieces of them split off and bond with many different objects of desire. Desire creates connections on many different plateaus, however, which are often indifferent to intensities on the other planes.[69]

An energy flux of desire creates relationships among various entities, and these relations constitute what Deleuze calls "desiring machines." These are loosely constructed, short-lived entities that exchange intensities of desire, allowing energies to circulate. Desire connects parts of bodies with parts of other bodies, and these interlaced parts become miniature machines – feeding on and powered by each other – often independently of their respective bodies. Moreover, a person's body parts typically function in many different desiring machines; they rarely function as a unified whole. The body is a complex, divided system by which multiple flows of energy traverse each other in many directions; these flows connect parts of the body with other's bodies and devices (e.g., tools, nature).[70] Deleuze thinks these short-lived desiring machines are the proper objects of social and psychological analysis – not isolated intrapsychic processes or the body taken as a self-contained unit or the autonomous ego posited by philosophy – because these are the real units of actual life. In his social and psychological analysis, Deleuze favors an empirical focus, external relations, and restricted generalizations.

The first volume of *Capitalism and Schizophrenia* (*Anti-Oedipus*) shows how larger social structures are related to flows of psychic energy and the desiring machines they produce. It rejects the centrality of Freud's Oedipus complex on the grounds that it restricts the productivity of desire. Deleuze charges psychoanalysis with colluding with capitalism in rigidly channeling flows of desire. He contrasts capitalism with two previous, historical-social orders: primitive culture and the barbarian-despotic orders. The dominant relation in primitive culture is kinship; it orders primitive behavior through harsh cruelty, which gradually makes rule-following and legal systems possible. Kinship systems provide the channels for the flow of goods, prestige, gifts, and women.[71] Barbarian-despotic systems create the state and establish writing as a means of administering the state. Initially the state exhibits fearsome tyranny because the despot models himself on vengeful gods.[72] Bureaucrats execute the will of the despot. Capitalism turns everything into quantities of energy and encourages the free flow of energy across all bodies – dissolving all previous limits to economic development (kinship, caste). Money facilitates the free flow and exchange of all goods and services. Because so many energy currents flow over individuals, everyone has schizophrenic tendencies.[73] Instead of finding this problematic, Deleuze embraces them.

A Thousand Plateaus continues the investigations begun in *Anti-Oedipus*. It examines a series of crucial historical moments in which theory made great leaps forward. It is an exploratory book in which a wide range of concepts are created and deployed. Its intended audience is creative people in the arts, sciences, and politics – not philosophers. Throughout the book, Deleuze examines various theories of language – favoring a pragmatic approach to meaning, rather than a referential or communicative one. He believes that language exhibits all the strains and tensions of individual psyches and desiring-machines. It does not consist of universal rules or structures, but a congeries of jargons and a multiplicity of minor modes.[74] Linguistics typically searches for major modes (modes that govern all linguistic uses; universal rules), and Deleuze thinks this is a quixotic quest. He believes that minor modes are the source of language's creativity. Minor modes are exceptions, islets of distinctive meaning that have no implications beyond themselves. They violate existing rules or codes not to produce new universal rules, but to demonstrate new creativity. Minor modes generate their own limited rules. Minor literatures create their own audiences, initiating sympathetic readers into the unique ways of life they articulate.[75]

Finally, in *What is Philosophy?*, he and Guatarri examine the assumptions that have guided their theories all along. They believe that philosophy is a unique discipline – different from art, science, and logic – in that it creates new concepts that challenge the status quo. It does not produce new propositions (like science) or idealized languages (like logic), or engender new percepts and affects (like art). Instead it creates new concepts, within a "plane of immanence." This plane is a set of dominant assumptions organizing theoretical work in an entire era. Moreover, concepts arise in specific contexts, in relation to definite problems, and express the distinctive voices of their authors. Concepts are deployed and explored through conceptual personae, distinct voices or characters that embody the philosopher's discourse (e.g., Plato's Socrates; Nietzsche's Zarathustra).[76] This diversity of voices allows philosophers to express more aspects of themselves in their conceptual lattices.

Deleuze offers a modest ethics deriving from his philosophy of difference. Central is the task of making oneself worthy of developing events. Events are unique and require unique responses. Precedents rarely provide useful guideposts. Events require determinate responses, and ethical individuals will rise to the occasion.[77] He also seeks to resist fascism in all its forms, challenging flows of desire and social myths and metaphors that support it. Sometimes people desire their own humiliation and enslavement, and thus embrace fascism. Deleuze strives to forestall that option. Although he does not believe that all schizophrenics are ethical models for the rest of humanity, he does credit the schizophrenic process with engendering bursts of creativity and insight that are only later fully understood.[78] In general, extreme experiences reveal nature and society in their wild states, still full of energy and demanding unique responses. He agrees with Foucault that one ethical goal of every individual should be to think differently and embrace self-transformation.

ASSESSMENT

Poststructuralism challenges many of the figures and movements discussed in this book. Its own claims should be scrutinized with the same critical intensity. I will first offer some objections to key points of each of the three main figures, and then conclude by indicating some problems with the movement as a whole.

Some of Foucault's important claims are insufficiently supported. For example, he never demonstrates that there are genuine epistemic breaks, even in the fields that he discusses with care. He provides snapshots of disciplines from a very high altitude, often in 50-year increments. If one examines these increments more closely, one may find transitional thinkers who both fill in gaps and motivate the shifts. Moreover, the real issue is not whether there are breaks, but whether there is genuine progress in these fields. Even if a new approach within a discipline does emerge from an epistemic break, it may still produce major progress in both insight and practical applications. For example, biology has made major strides in understanding genetics and cell development in the last century. Perhaps in the eighteenth and nineteenth centuries, natural history was at a pre-scientific stage, but biology now seems to have achieved the status of a genuine science. The other two fields Foucault examines – linguistics and economics – have at least explored a number of different paradigms, and achieved modest successes in some areas. Epistemic breaks are more common when a cognitive discipline is in a pre-scientific stage; various models and metaphors are explored until a major breakthrough is discovered. Foucault is perhaps right to be skeptical of truths proffered by some of the human "sciences." But his broader claims about the inevitability of epistemic breaks and lack of progress in knowledge of human life are arguable.

Foucault is also no doubt correct to claim that the human sciences have been implicated in many questionable practices, intended and unintended. Their theories have legitimated a number of dubious results, but Foucault's story about power's relationship with the human sciences is also one-sided. To be punished by the guillotine (or by being drawn and quartered) is quite different from being imprisoned for a finite period. To have a right to a jury trial and a defense lawyer and a presumption of innocence were major victories against the frivolous application of monarchical power. Foucault is disdainful of these liberal achievements. They may not constitute a juridical utopia, but they make power more accountable. Moreover, when the politically disenfranchised can demonstrate that existing laws or constitutions support their claims, their struggles become more legitimate and their victories more attainable. Foucault is also critical of the processes of normalization. Cultures give some shape and style to human activity; they set some generally acceptable parameters. Education systems prevent each new generation from having to reinvent the wheel and often help individuals to discover their best talents. Both tasks make human flourishing possible. Finally, Foucault fears the dominance of pastoral power operating in professionalized therapeutic disciplines. But pastoral power is weaker now because people are expected to be autonomous agents and bear some responsibility for their life-choices. If anything, people may feel an absence of guidance in making these choices, rather than suffocation by authorities.

Foucault's theory of power also has flaws. First, it expands the meaning of "power" to include virtually all influences, and thus anything that affects human activity in any way can be construed as power. But some influence is enhancing and liberating, and thus some operations of power in this sense are beneficial. To respond to this objection, some commentators have suggested that Foucault accepts a value-neutral conception of power. But Foucault's critique of modernity is precisely that it multiplies sites of power, makes it more precise and penetrating, etc. Thus, he wants to retain the negative connotations of the classical notion of power (domination). But he is not really entitled to trade on those connotations because he adopts this broadened conception that may avoid those effects. Indeed, Foucault's "power" almost lacks any connection to human intentions and purposes. Any causal influence on human action of any kind becomes an operation of power; these seem to operate independently, like machines. Moreover, some of the institutions that import the "carceral" regime of power, e.g., education and business, produce significant benefits for both individuals and society. So the fact that "power" operates within those institutions may only help them to perform their functions. Foucault's analysis thus casts its net too wide because institutional reformers need to discover the necessary conditions of *invidious* practices, and Foucault's broadened conception fails to illuminate those conditions. It fails to demarcate the crucial operations that must be changed to reshape or terminate an oppressive practice.

Finally, Foucault's ethics is a return to themes in existentialist ethics, with its focus on liberation through transgression, self-criticism, and self-creation. Oddly, his books on Greek and Roman ethics of self-perfection cast little light on methods that might encourage maturity, critique, and creativity in the current era. Foucault recognizes that he is returning to certain Enlightenment themes (thus moderating his critique of the Enlightenment), but his praise of self-creation may contradict his earlier critiques of subjectivization, technologies of the self, and autonomy. One important question is whether transgression of current norms is really necessary for genuine self-creation and the achievement of a mature freedom. Fascists transgress liberal morality, but they are not ethical exemplars. Similarly, even if some forms of self-creation do not transgress the current order, they may still represent significant ethical accomplishments (e.g., a person might breathe new life into virtues deriving from an earlier era or genuinely embody a contemporary ideal to which most only give lip service). Although Foucault ratifies the existentialist's rejection of traditional duties and of utilitarians' calculations, he does not significantly refine their basic ideal.

Derrida's position also has some difficulties. One crucial question is whether *différance* is universally applicable, e.g., to inanimate objects, like rocks. Sartre argues that such objects are self-coincident, providing a dramatic contrast to the being of consciousness. Most of Derrida's arguments target consciousness's relation to itself or to the world. He rarely discusses objects in themselves. Derrida might reply that the dissemination process might apply to physical objects on the sub-atomic level. Would this mean that an ontology of ordinary objects should be abandoned? Another key question is how problematic the phenomenon of dissemination is. Does it imply, for example, that consciousness cannot ever successfully elucidate its own dynamics? Presumably not, because Derrida's own arguments rely on evidence derived from consciousness's self-comprehension (e.g., time-consciousness). Derrida challenges self-*certainty,* but he does not show that self-comprehension is impossible or even typically misleading. He indicates complexities that must not be forgotten, traps that must be avoided, and over-generalizations that are unjustified. By now, nearly *all* claims to knowledge (not just to self-knowledge) are regarded as fallible and revisable; does Derrida show simply that a similar caution is necessary in the sphere of consciousness?

Sometimes Derrida suggests that even writers have only the most minimal grasp of their meaning-intentions. Although he may be correct in thinking that few writers (or speakers) lucidly grasp their exact meaning before commencing to write (or speak), he is wrong in thinking that nothing guides them as they refine and clarify their meanings during revision (or further elaboration). Both writers and speakers have a tentative grasp of their inchoate intentions, which are constantly in the process of self-clarification. Other people can comprehend this intention by seizing it through one's various revisions and clarifications. Writers and speakers discover it when they sense that a new attempt successfully captures their implicit intention, without loss or excess; the need to modify that version then dissipates. Also, Derrida neglects the fact that face-to-face encounters do provide more data for grasping another person's meaning: body language, intonation, responses to questions, etc. These are not always entirely reliable, and writing does afford the opportunity to choose words with precision and care, thus allowing more accurate self-expression than most speech. So I agree with Derrida that one cannot in general privilege speech over writing. But his position minimizes their differences and confuses the factors relevant to each case.

Perhaps the most important question is this: if all of Derrida's claims were accepted, how damaging would this be? Must propositional, predicate, or modal logic be reconceived? Must the ontology of garden-variety objects, states, or processes be recast? Must accepted theories in physics, biology, or sociology be reconsidered? The most damaging implications seem to concern the philosophical understanding of mental states, but Derrida's position may leave the analysis of their objects untouched. I would argue that the problematic implications are less sweeping that seems first apparent, mainly because Derrida himself is able to access experience to provide reasonable arguments in favor of his views. Moreover, one can question the force of his deconstructive methods of reading. His early critiques of Husserl are among his strongest essays. But even the results of other early essays, say in *Of Grammatology*, seem less devastating, and some have argued that his readings of other figures can be as misleading as he claims the arguments supporting logocentrism are. Derrida teaches an new approach to texts, but the power of that approach varies with the text being considered.

Finally, one might register two objections to Derrida's tentative ethical proposals. The ideal of hospitality he imports from Levinas may demand the impossible. (Derrida himself worries about this.) If so, this would locate Derrida in a long line of ethicists – resisted by Nietzsche – who posit impossible goals for humanity, thus inviting a continuing sense of failure for its inability to realize those goals. Levinas suggests that every human being deserves the absolute reverence demanded by his Other, and Derrida seems to accept this position. But perhaps – as Nietzsche again claimed – only a small number of other people deserve such reverence (true friends, for example). Offering such hospitality to everyone may be saintly, but unrealistic, and it may demean true friendship. Second, Derrida suggests that ethics really only becomes serious when no established rule covers the case at hand. But this belittles the wide range of cases in which the ethical agent's task is easier, but is nonetheless still significant. For applying rules *in the best way* is also ethically important; it can be done ineptly, and this can undermine the quality of one's ethical response. So ethics should not concern itself only with cases that demand new principles; ethical creativity is needed when applying existing principles as well. Moreover, Derrida offers very little guidance on how to invent promising new rules that are ethically viable. He indicates an important area for further research, but he does not contribute to it significantly. Although he wants to resist easy generalization, this should not prevent him from offering mid-level suggestions.

Deleuze's main theme is becoming – revolutionary transformation – in individuals and cultures. Perhaps the most important question is whether his metaphysical apparatus is helpful in clarifying the conditions in which becomings are genuinely revolutionary in the best sense. Also, does it even clarify the actual process of becoming? Deleuze's machinic energetics does apply to nature, mind, and society; so it might better integrate these three levels. But is it *equally* illuminating on all these levels? Especially on the social level, I fail to see how Deleuze's concepts will produce deeper understanding of group dynamics and group/individual relationships. Yet Deleuze's own standard for evaluating theories is: what can you do with them? Even if one masters his metaphysics, one may be no better able to guide one's own becomings effectively. If so, this would be a major failing on Deleuze's own criteria.

In addition, Deleuze constantly waffles between claiming that his rhizomatic models are more accurate elucidations of reality and suggesting that the root model and the rhizome models must continually contest each other, without either achieving complete victory. On the latter reading, his position is less incoherent, but also less interesting. It becomes a corrective, possibly a stage that will need further corrections itself, but it is no longer a deep illumination of reality. If both models have validity, then he must clarify the conditions under which the root metaphor is more useful, as well as those under which the rhizome model is more effective.

Deleuze rethinks the entire enterprise of explicating another philosopher. He engages in the expository process in order to transform himself as a philosopher, but he also bends the explicated figure into new shapes, extracting unusual insights from him or her. Undoubtedly his examination of Nietzsche helped Deleuze discover his own positions. But his contributions to a full understanding of Nietzsche are less certain because he ignores elements of Nietzsche's position that contradict his vision. In allowing himself to be assimilated into the philosopher he explicates, Deleuze succeeds in refashioning his own philosophical ideas, but often fails to fairly explicate the target figure.

In addition to these particular reservations, two more general objections to dispersionists theories should be mentioned. First, dispersionists are inept at protecting their own hypotheses from the acids they throw at other theories. What, for example, are the power-knowledge effects and implications of Foucault dispersionist claims? Do Derrida's own master-concepts (e.g., *différance*, dissemination) become unquestioned metaphors to which human experience is forced to conform? Is Deleuze's vision of revolutionary transformation consistent with his own rhizomatic thinking? Critical Marxists have pressed these concerns vigorously, and the responses from dispersionists have been weak.[79] Among the three, Foucault is probably the least consistent at the metatheoretical level (insisting that he has direct unmediated access to past power-knowledge frameworks, while at the same time claiming that every power-knowledge system itself is constituted by unconscious rules and thus that unmediated access to them is impossible). Derrida strives to prevent *différance* from becoming a new metaphysical postulate, but he nonetheless still seems to assume that all reality conforms to his basic picture without much supporting argument. Deleuze seems sometimes to acknowledge that other models of reality are possible (e.g., root structures), but he also seems to think that only rhizomatic thinking is reliable, regardless of what area of reality is examined. Some have claimed that dispersionists' views have unintended political effects, e.g., Foucault's non-normative theory of power actually strengthens the status quo because he abandons any normative basis for establishing alternatives, or Deleuze's machinic complexes describe the insidious ability of the current order to co-opt all revolutionary energies, but provides no truly alternative vision.

The dispersionists claim to offer an alternative ethical vision – a set of ideals more appropriate to dispersed reality. Instead of nostalgically longing for a lost unity, identity, and harmony, they embrace multiplicity, difference, and chaotic ecstasies – on the individual, micro-social, and macro-social levels. They stress an acknowledgment of and respect for difference, an intentional refusal to assimilate others (otherness within oneself, in other people, or in alien cultures). They seek to challenge former value assumptions and stimulate creative thinking about how to acknowledge human differences. Foucault explores an ethic of individual self-criticism and self-refashioning. Derrida recommends a similar ethic of self-criticism, an ascetic process of thinking that acknowledges dispersion and celebrates the play of differences. Deleuze embraces a schizoid, constantly fissioning form of life that pushes momentary intensities to their limits, acknowledges connections with manifold elements in the social field, and resolves the demands of diverse social demands. All this will take them only so far in creating an ethical position.

They all try to reverse the value placed on unity, identity, and harmony by insisting on the positive value in the opposite conditions, values insufficiently appreciated in previous ethical thought. But they are still mainly just reversing the poles of the value oppositions, embracing the opposites of the traditional values. They do not resolve the value oppositions, and they do not acknowledge the value of the traditional qualities they oppose. Thus, they fail to respect difference in that sense. So where they provide an alternative ethical position, the creative insight they offer is less impressive than it first appears. In this area, the French feminist philosophers produce more interesting and creative positions. They take dispersion in more promising directions than did the dispersionists themselves.

FRENCH FEMINIST PHILOSOPHY

Simone de Beauvoir's major treatise, *The Second Sex*, resurrected feminism worldwide after the Second World War. She extended and applied many of Sartre's key existentialist concepts, but she also challenged and revised some of his central claims in *Being and Nothingness*, claims that Sartre himself was later to rethink in light of her contributions. The next generation of French feminists worked in a similar fashion – both incorporating and challenging the central ideas of the dispersionists (especially Derrida and Deleuze). Irigaray and Kristeva start from specific dispersionists' insights, but they develop and apply them in innovative ways, challenging the philosophical tradition just as forcefully and creatively as Derrida and Deleuze. Le Doeuff also criticizes de Beauvoir's deference to Sartre. In addition, several French feminists are practicing psychotherapists, and they produce scathing criticisms of Freud's theories of feminine sexual development and women's experience generally. Their general goal is to articulate the distinctive character of women's experience and to force philosophy to acknowledge its importance.

CORE CONTRIBUTIONS

The four French feminists discussed in this chapter are very different from each other. They challenge each other, but they all seek to clarify how the oppression of women operates. They explore both its ideological and institutional sources. Oppression can operate by creating fixed, submissive identities or by systematically ignoring the distinctive significance of women's experience or by denying women access to institutions that would allow them to develop their own independent perspectives. The range of its analyses of oppression and its suggested solutions are important contributions of this movement.

In addition, they interrogate the role of key theoretical disciplines in maintaining oppression, e.g., philosophy and psychoanalysis. Irigaray launches chastening attacks on both fields, showing that many dominant philosophical assumptions and dichotomies are threatened if the value of women's experience, speech, and writing is acknowledged. She also shows that Freud was almost completely oblivious to women's actual experience. Le Doeuff criticizes the institutional operations of philosophy in universities and schools and its arrogance in relation to other disciplines. De Beauvoir shows how many social scientific disciplines (including psychoanalysis) and literary myths have contributed to maintaining the patriarchal order, and she indicates how pervasively institutions and patterns of thought must be changed if authentic relations between men and women are to be possible. Kristeva challenges the ideal of self-sufficient, autonomous subjectivity, arguing that no one can possibly achieve that ideal, and she explores the ramifications of this claim for the nature of human identity. She challenges many cognitivist assumptions in developmental psychology, especially its obliviousness to the symbiotic relation between mother and child both before and after birth.

Each thinker reveals important, often unacknowledged dimensions of women's experience and shows why they should be taken seriously. Kristeva demonstrates the complex dynamics of speaking in order to challenge the alleged self-certainty and centeredness of speakers. Her study of the symbiotic dependency of children on their mothers challenges the ideals of independence and autonomy. De Beauvoir shows the prices that both men and women pay because women are systematically denigrated, and indicates how women can reclaim their freedom. She examines the many losing strategies women use to transcend their situations, and then she offers a plausible way to transform the situation itself. Irigaray underlines the distinctiveness of women's desire, emotions, selfhood, and their speaking styles with other women, in order to show that women's experience demands a revision of some major postulates of Western thought. Le Doeuff draws on her experience as a philosophy student to articulate the powerful institutional sources of misogyny in philosophy, and she illustrates many distinctive ways women come to know and understand the world that challenge traditional epistemological assumptions.

Several common themes emerge from these various critiques. First, French feminists attack ossified dichotomies that conceal the actual contours of everyone's experience: reason/passion, self/other, thought/perception, mind/body, and cognition/intuition. They seek to show that the apparent boundaries are fluid and that their terms are interdependent. They also show the importance of the second member of the oppositions to the first: the centrality of passion to reason, of others to the constitution of selfhood, of the body to all "mental" operations, etc. In pursuing this, they build on many achievements of previous movements: from Hegel to Dilthey, from Marx to Merleau-Ponty, from Heidegger to Derrida. But they develop their own distinctive arguments for overcoming these oppositions, and they enrich comprehension of everyone's lived experience (male and female) by underlining distinctive elements of women's experience.

Second, they share a genuine Utopian intent, sketching outlines of a potentially more hopeful, bracing, and enlivening world, a world in which men and women respond to each other more vitally, recognize each other's strengths, and transcend outmoded cultural forms. They indicate not only concrete interpersonal ways, but also institutional and cultural ways, of moving toward this Utopian vision. Although they can sometimes seem harsh toward men and masculine-infused assumptions about experience, their vision and proposals are free of resentment, retribution, and arrogance. Indeed, the spirit of their research is exploratory and interrogative; they invite further elaboration, exploration of alternative perspectives, and engaged critical discussion. They seek to provide a viable conception of emancipation and to articulate a variety of other virtues that collectively represent a new ethical vision for human relationships. The fact that their thought is meant to inform political action and policy gives their research incisiveness and relevance that is sometimes lacking in other late-twentieth-century Continental movements.

DE BEAUVOIR

The older of two daughters of an upper-middle-class Parisian family, Simone de Beauvoir's (1908–86) early education was in Catholic girls' schools. She decided to pursue philosophy in 1925, eventually studying under Léon Brunschvicg. Her dissertation examined Leibnitz. She taught at Marseilles, Rouen, and Paris until 1943, when she retired to support herself exclusively by her writing. She wrote novels and a four-volume autobiography in addition to writing philosophy and feminist theory. She used her novels to test and develop her philosophical ideas, arguing that fiction can create new experiences and thus provide new sources of truth. She thinks literature provides a synthesis of the universal and the particular that can often better articulate subtle truths than abstract philosophical analysis. Her lifelong companion was Sartre, though both had several affairs outside their relationship. She was a founding editor of *Les Temps modernes*, and actively contributed to feminist struggles for reform.

She reinvigorated the feminist movement in advanced industrial societies with her important treatise, *The Second Sex* (1949).[1] There she uses Sartre's insights in *Being and Nothingness* and elaborates them in original ways to develop a distinctive theory of women's oppression. She also published a book on existentialist ethics, a project Sartre had promised at the end of his early treatise. In *The Ethics of Ambiguity* (1947),[2] she makes significant advances both in defining an existentialist vision of the human condition and in defending the ideal of authenticity, which informs her goal for relationships between men and women. In addition to her autobiographical works, *Memoirs of a Dutiful Daughter* (1958), *The Prime of Life* (1960), *The Force of Circumstance* (1963), *All Said and Done* (1972), she also wrote essays on many other important topics, including ageing – *The Coming of Age* (1972) – and death – *A Very Easy Death* (1964). Several of her novels are philosophically important, including *She Came to Stay* (1949), *The Mandarins* (1954), and *The Blood of Others* (1945).

De Beauvoir's book on ethics articulates her vision of the human condition: a felt ambiguity between antecedent limits (facticity) and future possibilities (transcendence). People live between a completed past and a future yet to be created; between a self defined by other people and a self-determined, open-ended series of projects; and between a body governed by natural laws and a consciousness limited only by itself. Genuine freedom – or authenticity – requires accepting this ambiguous condition, realizing that humans will never have the substantive identity that objects possess, even though it would relieve them of the burden of creating themselves.[3] Authenticity also requires acknowledging contingencies affecting one's life (either by accepting them or seeking to overcome them), realizing that life is always in process (subject to reinterpretation and re-evaluation), and overcoming the resistances that make projects meaningful. The most common way to abdicate authenticity is to adopt a fixed self-definition, which is experienced as unchangeable and given.[4] Life then feels fated. This experience denies the possibility of self-transformation – of transcending one's situation and redefining one's goals – that is the core of Sartrean freedom. To accept this freedom and all that it implies requires a kind of existential conversion that alters one's experience of values (they are no longer absolute imperatives, but situated, revisable directives that must be re-examined regularly in the light of experience) and of actions (they are never mere performances that concretize a pre-existing individual essence, but they utilize flexible means to achieve ends that must be periodically re-evaluated as the situation changes).[5]

For de Beauvoir, authenticity also involves bearing responsibility for the existing historical situation, which reinforces some institutions and social movements and resists others. In effect, authentic persons refuse to mindlessly reproduce tradition, and recognize that social norms and rules can be revised.[6] They operate through political action groups in order to influence the direction of history, the overall trajectory of which results from millions of human choices. Their responsibility also extends to the future, for they consciously strive to create the world they want future generations to inherit. This broad sense of social responsibility requires comprehending current historical possibilities and assessing existing political resistance. To make their own political efforts as effective as possible, authentic people must track their actions through the many vicissitudes and challenges they encounter. Simply acting and hoping for the best is insufficient, an irresponsible approach to social change.[7] Authentic people are responsible for the long-term effects of their actions as well as for their original intent. De Beauvoir thus defends several conditions of authenticity: a sharper sense of personal responsibility for political actions, for their actual effects and repercussions, and for their regular re-evaluation as situations change.

During this period (1947–8), both Sartre and de Beauvoir sought innovative defenses of the claim that no individual can be fully free unless everyone is free, and thus that one's own freedom depends on liberating others from oppression. Sartre presented his position in *What is Literature?* (1948) and his (then unpublished) *Notebooks for an Ethics* (1983). De Beauvoir offers several original arguments for this crucial principle in her ethics book. First, the social goals of historical agents typically require longer than their own lifetimes to be fully implemented. Thus, if they are to come to fruition, these agents must rely on other people to help complete them. This will happen only if others freely choose to adopt and pursue these goals, and this requires them to make authentic choices. Others can freely take up historical projects only in situations without oppression. Hence overcoming others' oppression is essential to fully realizing one's own long-term social goals.[8] Second, if historical agents accept the freedom of others, they acknowledge that they may adopt a distinct perspective on the world. This forces them to realize that their own perspective is a limited, situated viewpoint, not the only possible one. Thus, grasping the reality of others' freedom helps people see their own limitations more vividly and so makes their own choices more informed.[9] Finally, she offers a Hegelian argument that recalls the dynamic of pure recognition.[10] She claims that when a person achieves authentic recognition by others, then her own freedom and authenticity are ratified and enhanced. People then feel a solidarity of commitment to freedom – a potentially open-ended solidarity that invites inclusion of as yet unrecognized others. This solidarity means that authentic people will take others' goals seriously, helping to realize them if they are compatible with their own aspirations.[11]

De Beauvoir is the first to offer a theory of the psychological emergence of authentic freedom. Unlike Freud, who thought that much of one's character was determined in early childhood, de Beauvoir suggests that the crucial period for the development of authenticity is adolescence. In that phase, many individuals begin to experience the contingency of their own values because they suddenly realize the rational limitations of their parents' values. Adolescents discover that the values that have informed their youth are merely inherited values, which are then intensely scrutinized during this period.[12] Indeed, many adolescents actively reject their parents' values in order to assert their own distinctiveness. Once these parental absolutes disintegrate, then adolescents suddenly experience the freedom (and anxiety) of potential self-determination. They realize that rationality often cannot decide hard cases, that many potentially worthwhile ways of life are incompatible, and that traditional values can be harmful to human flourishing. These facts underline the importance of personal choices. Adolescents thus vividly experience their freedom, and they have the opportunity to commit themselves to authenticity or simply to accept another predetermined code. De Beauvoir insists that authenticity requires a continuing re-evaluation and self-criticism so that the values guiding one's current practice continue to reflect one's deepest experience and best thought.[13] This obligation of self-criticism is distinctive in de Beauvoir; Sartre rarely emphasizes it himself. They both stress that authenticity requires maintaining commitments despite opposition, if the values guiding those commitments have been freely chosen.

She also makes contributions to the theory of self-deception (or bad faith), identifying various approaches to life that are fundamentally self-deceptive: the subperson, the serious person, the nihilist, the adventurer, the passionate person, and the intellectual. Understanding her criticisms of these forms of life can help clarify the conditions of self-deception. *Subpersons* live without affect or passion, without love, desire, or spontaneity. They deny attachment to life even as they continue to live, and de Beauvoir believes that this is deeply self-deceptive. If one chooses to live, then one should engage life with passion and intensity.[14] *Serious persons* regard their values as absolute and refuse to entertain any objections to them. They sacrifice their own freedom to reconsider their value (and everyone else's freedom) to them. This approach to life denies that values are posited through free choices and thus denies the ontological contingency of values.[15] *Nihilists* refuse to act altogether because they believe that nothing can be justified absolutely. They derogate others' actions, justifications, meanings, and aspirations, denying their own talents and dreams as well. Though rejecting values altogether, they deny having any rationale for rejecting them, and thus they live a basic inconsistency. Instead of realizing that living is a process of continuous self-justification through actions, of re-evaluating the values on the basis of which one lives, and striving to live by one's best insights (however fallible and uncertain), nihilists withdraw from life altogether.[16]

Adventurers throw themselves into action without any concern for achieving actual results. Dedicated to the quest itself, they believe that the goal is secondary, even irrelevant. Adventurers adopt goals because actions require goals, but they act as if achieving them is irrelevant. They would rather make a statement than make a difference.[17] Authentic freedom requires adjudicating ends and means, finding effective means to achieve substantive ends, and tracking actions through adversity to insure that they actually achieve their goals. These conditions are necessary for political effectiveness. *Passionate people* are fanatically devoted to their goals and sacrifice everything to them. They are so possessed by goals that they lose all critical distance, all sense of perspective, all consideration of alternatives.[18] Authentic passion requires fortitude in the face of adversity, but it is unafraid to re-examine a goal's importance in particular contexts – when an important victory on a different front might be achieved by delaying action on the more passionate commitment. Finally, the *intellectual*'s flaw is a search for eternal, transcendent truths. That goal requires a viewpoint above and beyond the current historical situation, which easily makes intellectuals oblivious to its specific oppressions.[19] Authentic thinkers realize that most truths are contingent, fallible, revisable, and partial. They may seek to achieve a synthetic perspective by integrating diverse viewpoints, and they identify crucial features of the current historical situation because these features often provide clues to the positive possibilities that can be achieved in the situation.

Thus, many ways of life are flawed because they misunderstand the realities of human agency, the status of values, the relation between ends and means, and the limited and perspectival nature of truth. De Beauvoir also claims that the important Sartrean/Nietzschean value of generosity requires full-fledged equality between persons. Generosity can only be offered and accepted by equals (without incurring resentment or debts). Moreover, her vision of community suggests that everyone gains from the creativity of any single person.[20] Each is challenged and inspired by others' creativity. Most can envision better goals by listening to others' critical questions. De Beauvoir's ideal is a collaborative society in which everyone helps each other transcend oppression and the limitations of their situations, in which each is stimulated by the achievements of the others. This requires reciprocal recognition, which de Beauvoir takes to be essential to equality between the sexes. When both women and men are free, they can create entirely new kinds of values together; neither masculine nor feminine values need dominate.[21] Indeed entirely different kinds of reciprocity and sexual relationships would emerge as institutions are gradually transformed to facilitate freedom.

In *The Second Sex*, de Beauvoir accepts Sartre's early view that the initial encounter between persons involves a struggle to determine which person will dominate by imposing an objectified social identity.[22] This assertion of subjectivity comes with a heavy price, however, because it undermines reciprocal recognition. She thinks this scenario explains the way men have responded to women in many cultures and historical eras. Men create slave-like or stigmatized identities for women. Whatever is "male" is treated as a norm for all humanity.[23] Men establish these subordinate identities because they cannot bear their own freedom; they seek to define themselves in opposition to women, rather than through changing the world directly. Central to de Beauvoir's position, however, is a claim that women are in part responsible for accepting this servile position and refusing to resist it by reclaiming their own subjectivities. To be sure, men are responsible for the initial moment of domination, but women are culpable for allowing it to continue unchallenged.[24] When they do react, they often create similar prisons for the men who care for them, instead of trying to define their own identities. This domination is so pervasive in most cultures that dismantling the social structures that sustain it will require the collaboration of both men and women. An entirely different culture, social and economic system, and ideology will be needed.[25] Men will be able to achieve richer identities in relationships of mutual recognition with women, but they cannot comprehend this until women assert their own equality and make their own contributions to the public world.

De Beauvoir examines alternative explanations for men's suppression of women – derived from biology, Marx, and Freud – and finds them all wanting because they assume that persons are mere objects that can be determined by uncontrollable inner or outer forces. But she insists on the freedom of human beings to posit their own goals, to fashion their own future out of the conditions they inherit, and thus on humanity's transcendence of nature. Biological facts do not predestine women to any particular social condition, since biological facts can invite many possible institutional reactions.[26] (For example, while pregnant, women could be given special privileges.) She also examines the general situation of women – at least in Western culture – by analyzing their patterns of socialization, their typical education, their roles in families, the expectations society has of them, and the paucity of feminine leadership models. She describes some of the universals of female experience, especially during puberty, in sexual relationships, and in marriage. These situational factors, though they do not determine a passive and docile result, certainly encourage it. In addition, society expects women to marry and become mothers, and de Beauvoir is extremely critical of these roles. Marriage virtually institutionalizes the inequality of the wife and consigns her to the status of the husband's possession.[27] Furthermore, after the mother devotes her entire life to raising and caring for children, her mature children typically dismiss her value because they adopt the male-dominated assumptions of their culture. She also analyzes the special paradoxes of women who attempt to succeed in a "man's world" while simultaneously preserving the traditional values of femininity.

In addition to these socialization patterns, women must contend with an elaborate mythology created by men through literary narratives, drama, and the other arts. Men look to women to compensate them for their shortcomings and to support them in moments of weakness. Furthermore, men idealize women in the hopes of finding and magically appropriating the virtues they lack.[28] This mythological thinking allows men to characterize women in contradictory ways with impunity: for example, as virgins and temptresses, as mothers and whores, as muses and nags. This mythology often ensnares women who successfully deflect traditional cultural expectations; by emulating these idealized images, they abdicate their freedom to define themselves. Other women exhaust themselves in challenging this mythology, which only demonstrates their preoccupation with it. Still others benefit from men's tendency to objectify women by presenting them with entrancing, hypnotic objects, thus entrapping the very subjectivity men assert. The mystic, the narcissist, and the high-class prostitute all adopt this strategy, as does the woman in love.[29] But though this approach surreptitiously challenges male domination through a sort of judo maneuver, it still fails to create a self-determining, authentic way of life for women. In none of these cases is reciprocal recognition achieved, and de Beauvoir believes that recognition is the only hope for conquering this system of oppression.

Such reciprocal recognition would make authentic freedom possible for both men and women. Achieving this, however, will require significant institutional as well as interpersonal changes. Her main political principle is that the only public good is whatever contributes to the enhancement of private goods; new institutions that provide new opportunities must be created.[30] Child-rearing and educational practices would have to allow women full opportunity to discover and develop their talents and acquire the intellectual and practical skills necessary to assume social leadership positions. Once they have assimilated this training and developed their talents, women must have the same career options as men. Finally, they must work collectively and collaboratively to create a world more hospitable to women's equality and achievements.[31] De Beauvoir suggests that working collectively to achieve a better future is essential to achieving personal authenticity. Men can participate in this social transformation by supporting women's efforts to create better access to education and professional careers, and by participating in social movements that combat men's more vicious strategies for dominating women. Indeed, perhaps the most appealing feature of de Beauvoir's vision is that men and women can work together to transform the patriarchal system that produces frustration, misery, and inauthenticity for both sexes.

Men gain a false sense of security and self-definition through their objectification of women. They miss the opportunity to create a flexible and authentic identity of their own, and instead merely define themselves in opposition to a fantasy. When they idealize women as possessing virtues they lack, they fail to embody these virtues for themselves.[32] Men must recognize women as subjects and acknowledge their right to self-definition and self-transcendence. Women, for their part, must assert their subjectivity, their intelligence, and their humanity while cultivating their talents and practical understanding of the world. When women's subjectivity is nurtured, they can then recognize men for their achievements and successes, and this recognition will matter more than the false adulation of pacified and prettified objects. This nurturing can be done only through alternative forms of child-rearing and education, and this will require major economic and institutional changes. In addition, women must be capable of controlling their own reproductive fate.[33] De Beauvoir stresses the basic similarities in the condition of men and women, and she believes that these similarities provide a sufficient basis for the mutual recognition that is so essential to women's liberation. This recognition will not undermine diversity or the different values each sex may contribute, but it will allow women to define their own identities. Women's freedom will make possible the liberation of all humanity, for both men and women are slaves in the current patriarchal system.

KRISTEVA

Julia Kristeva (b. 1941) is a literary critic, psychoanalyst, language-acquisition theorist, and existential phenomenologist. Her main theme is the contributions of the body and unconscious drives to linguistic expression. Like Lacan, she is critical of the notion of autonomous subjectivity; but her position is more balanced and nuanced, arguing that unconscious elements supporting order and unity are as important as elements urging transgression and disorder. She appeals to the universal fact of the child's dependence on the mother – both prenatally and after birth – to dispel the myth of the self-sufficient subject, which conceals humanity's dependence on the body and the unconscious. She rejects the label "feminist," but the self-sufficient, autonomous subject is a common target for nearly all the French feminists, and her study of mothering connects her work with several others. She draws on the ideas of Lacan, Derrida, Deleuze, and Foucault, but she also develops her own positions on key issues and synthesizes these ideas in original ways. Her most important books are *Polylogue* (1977; partially translated as *Desire in Language*), *Revolution in Poetic Language* (1974), *Powers of Horror* (1980), *Tales of Love* (1983), *Black Sun* (1987), *Strangers to Ourselves* (1988), *New Maladies of the Soul* (1993), and *Time and Sense: Proust and the Experience of Literature* (1994). Some works focus on particular phenomena (love, depression, foreignness), which Kristeva examines through the lens of many literary texts and other sources. Other works develop theories that interlace child development, language development, and interpersonal development. In addition to poetry and avant-garde writing, she also studies the discourses of madness and religion as ways of attempting to articulate the inexpressible.

Kristeva defends her distance from "feminism" by distinguishing three stages of the movement.[34] In the first stage, the goal is to achieve equal rights based on the similarities between the sexes. This stage is embodied in de Beauvoir's defense of mutual recognition and the joint achievement of authenticity. Kristeva's objection to this strategy is that it overvalues authentic subjectivity and simply accepts the "masculine" goal of autonomy. The second stage involves asserting feminine difference, defining a distinctively feminine identity and defending its value. She links this strategy to Irigaray's valorization of difference, and Kristeva argues that it creates a new, restrictive, essentialist identity for women, even if it differs from masculine autonomy. This new "femininity" is parasitic on masculinity because they are mirror images of each other (e.g., caring/assertive; multiple/singular; diffuse/centered). The third stage anticipates Kristeva's own position, which challenges – even dissolves – all identities and undermines the reign of the autonomous subject altogether.[35] In part, the experience of mothering and of dependence on mothers produces this dissolution. Though many women become mothers, she does not believe they are necessarily best placed to articulate motherhood's significance. She suggests that some male avant-garde writers have captured the implications of mothering better than many women writers.

Many feminists have questioned the political implications of Kristeva's efforts to dissolve unified selfhood. They worry that this will destroy the commitment and character necessary to produce long-term political and institutional change. Moreover, they argue that Kristeva's textual analyses ignore women writers almost completely, thus suggesting that male authors provide better examples of the decentered identity she seeks. Still others suggest that she is overly harsh toward Irigaray, who mounts similar attacks on autonomy.[36] The first charge would be more serious if Kristeva sought to eliminate the experience of self-coherence altogether. But her position is more moderate (she denies that any specific identity necessarily applies to either sex), and this leaves open the possibility that her transformed subjects could alter institutions sufficiently to sustain the dispersed identity she advocates. To the second charge, she would reply that she chooses the most illuminating examples of her vision; since her main point is that both men and women must undergo similar self-dispersion and that both face similar obstacles, there is no reason to privilege women writers. The task is to find authors who understand the necessary changes and whose writings illustrate the best means of achieving them. To the last charge, she would argue that she is not trying to positively revalue femininity in the way that Irigaray is; so she highlights this difference between them. Some women's pregnancies may illustrate the fluid, diffuse, polymorphous subjectivity Kristeva celebrates, but not all pregnant women experience their pregnancies in this way. She emphasizes her position's uniqueness because it is different from Irigaray's.

Kristeva believes other feminists are trying to refurbish the notion of stable identities, and this she resists. She also believes that they presuppose a conception of a feminine essence supposedly embodied in all women, which Kristeva rejects. Moreover, she is more sympathetic with psychoanalysis (both Freudian and Lacanian) than is Irigaray, who condemns Freud's and Lacan's theories of women's character development. In some ways Kristeva is closer to de Beauvoir than to Irigaray. The kind of social and individual transformation she advocates would affect both men and women, and the resulting relationships between them would become radically different.[37] De Beauvoir supports a joint effort to achieve authenticity, which implies both political commitment and social responsibility, but need not presuppose a stable, fixed identity. Kristeva believes that masculine and feminine represent poles within each person, and she aims for a better balance – in which the feminine pole is less repressed – in everyone.[38] Because her main discoveries concern the feminine pole of the psyche and because motherhood plays a central role in her position, she can be legitimately classified with the other feminists. I will present her views on poetic language and psychic development first, and then examine her theories of signification and mothering.

Kristeva examines the simultaneous process of language acquisition and self-development. She explores the process by which the speaking subject emerges, rather than the system of language (or *langue*) in Saussure's sense. Embodiment and especially the manifold drives that exist unconsciously are central to speaking for Kristeva. They provide energy and motivation for speech, and they also threaten to overwhelm the speaker, shattering the rules of discursive coherence. She calls this embodied source of speech the "semiotic." The semiotic includes energy flows and rhythms, drives and residues, which exist prior to the development of the self and even prior to birth. It is formless, chaotic and disordered.[39] It is Kristeva's interpretation of Freud's unconscious and primary process "thinking." It expresses itself in giggles, burbles, baby-talk, gestures, sensations, and sighs. The source of the semiotic lies in the infant's primordial relation to the mother's body prior to birth, which Kristeva calls the "chora." The fetus responds to the mother's moods, dreams, physiological upsets, and actions; these energies provide a pre-linguistic medium that prepares the newborn infant for its continued dependence on the mother's body, to which it responds with uncensored semiotic expressions.[40]

At the opposite end of speech lies what Kristeva calls the "symbolic," which is related to Lacan's conception. The symbolic establishes a separation of subject and object, in which the subject achieves a coherent identity; linguistic grammar and rules of rhetoric are mastered, and the assertive subject-position of enunciation is learned. Once the child has achieved the symbolic level of expression, it can state propositions, take positions, use proper names and demonstratives, and participate in the ongoing dialogue of reason, classification, and judgment. Symbolic discourse becomes possible only because the semiotic is repressed.[41] The semiotic still provides the energy and raw materials for speech, but the symbolic gives it structure and coherence so that interpersonal communication can succeed. The symbolic is the realm of the Oedipal father, while the semiotic is the realm of the nurturing mother. According to Kristeva, the symbolic never completely detaches itself from the semiotic; the semiotic forms a constant undercurrent that can threaten the coherence of the symbolic at any time. Both operate in everyday speech. Without the semiotic there would be nothing specific to say, but without the symbolic there would be no way to communicate it. Between these two necessary conditions of speech lies the "thetic" – the structures that produce the transition from the primitive semiotic to the civilized symbolic.[42] The thetic breaks into the flow of the semiotic and provides initial steps toward the semiotic (e.g., first words, first refusals, first sentences).

Kristeva believes that many processes facilitate this transition; so thetic structures are multiple and complex. Lacan's mirror stage is one structure (first sense of bodily coherence); Freud's Oedipal crisis is another (first challenge to fixated love). Indeed for each step in the development of self-identity and isolation from the object, there is a distinct thetic process. Such world-separation has its source in the birthing process and in the anal stage in which the baby learns to distinguish itself from its own waste products. Thetic structures and the semiotic processes they organize are revealed in avant-garde writing. Close examination of such writing reveals the manner in which the thetic can organize the semiotic on the path to achieving the symbolic (which is constantly threatened by the avant-garde writer). Kristeva's distinctive contribution to literary theory is "semanalysis," which explores the relationships between the thetic and the semiotic as revealed in experimental literary texts.[43] Poetic language constantly challenges symbolic functions and rules, and this process reveals the operation of the thetic, which is virtually indiscernible in ordinary speech.

Moreover, the symbolic never achieves complete victory over the semiotic; its order is precarious. This constant threat to one's sense of completed, autonomous self-identity Kristeva calls "the abject." The body is one threat to the self's coherence. Whenever the unclean or impure elements of the body assert themselves, the abject threatens the person's identity.[44] Thus, even when a distinct, coherent sense of identity emerges, it is never stable because it is constantly threatened from within. The impure reveals the permeability of the boundaries of the self. What appeared to be a sharp boundary (between self and world, self and other) in fact is an open membrane through which foreign elements can pass. Three major impurities are foods, waste products, and sexual difference itself. Impurity is always ambiguous, always inside and outside at once, threatening the ego's claims to independence and autonomy. The body depends on its relationship to external material: foods are necessary to live; waste products must be eliminated to survive, and sexual difference must be maintained to procreate. The abject is a threat that culture must constantly repress and conceal. Religion tries to distract the self from the implications of the abject; art tries to sublimate the abject, and socialization hides it. Yet the abject is never finally defeated, and this means that autonomous selfhood is never fully established. It can only be tentative, temporary.[45] Kristeva values these challenges to selfhood because they maintain contact with the vital powers of life. But she does not want to abandon the symbolic completely; instead she reveals its limits and forces it to acknowledge its dependence on these "maternal" elements: the semiotic, the chora, the thetic, and the abject.

With these basic concepts Kristeva explores the processes by which signification occurs. Drives motivate speech, but they are shaped into coherent discourse by thetic processes. Speaking involves organizing the constantly fluid, amorphous, unconscious urges. The fact that the subject constantly emerges from a threatening medium suggests that living within communal diversity should be manageable. The semiotic breaks into speech periodically, especially in the language of madness, of mysticism, and of avant-garde art, as well as slips and asides. Kristeva rejects the Marxist conception of art, which claims it reflects the underlying economic dynamic of the society. She thinks some linguistic acts can have political effects even if there is no economic basis for them. She also notes that even if economic change often produces artistic upheaval, this may be delayed. Art may act as a stabilizing force when other factors of the culture are threatened. Moreover, she rejects the controlling intention of the artist in the artwork because she believes that art is not primarily a product of explicit self-consciousness. Rather it involves a tentative, slowly evolving order imposed on uncontrollable, unconscious forces.[46] Kristeva's semanalysis closely examines the surface of discourse to reveal the moments when the semiotic breaks into the symbolic's apparently measured order. She thus examines the crosscurrents, tensions, and vortices in discourse. She also identifies textual elements that are not integrated with the main body of the text, floating above its surface logic, disrupting its apparent coherence. Giving free reign to the chaos of the semiotic is risky, however, because a fascist, authoritarian reaction can result, as can a willful embrace of tradition and the status quo. For this reason, she advocates maintaining contact with the semiotic – allowing it to challenge self-certainty – but not abdicating ordered selfhood entirely. She thus seeks a just balance between the masculine and feminine elements of the psyche.

To better understand the implications of accepting these challenges to self-identity, Kristeva examines the process of mothering. Everyone has a mother, since everyone is born. Since in the prenatal period the fetus is radically dependent on the mother's body for nourishment and life, it is never autonomous. Even after birth, however, the infant continues to be dependent. The child's identity is achieved only through painful separation from this primordial symbiosis. The fetus's and infant's development are dominated by the rhythms set by the mother's body and moods.[47] A maternal law organizes the infant's life prior to the law of the father that emerges during the Oedipal crisis. Thus, mothers support order and law as much as chaos and multiplicity. On the other hand, Kristeva insists that fathers play an important nurturing role by supporting the infant when it distinguishes its identity from the mother's. The father facilitates this separation and sustains the infant's tenuous selfhood. On this basis, Kristeva insists that the meanings attached to "mother" and "father" – male and female – are mixed. Both nurture, and both establish limits/laws for the developing child. The mother is thus as much a socializer as the father; mothers are not merely vehicles of nature, and fathers are not only instruments of culture.

Beyond this, Kristeva claims that mothering shatters the sense of identity in the *mother* both because pregnancy befalls the woman and because the experience of carrying a child produces a sense of merging (with the fetus), of fragmenting (of her body into part-objects), and of splitting (of the mother's identifications). Most significant is Kristeva's claim that the newly pregnant woman finds herself identifying both with her own mother and with the developing fetus.[48] Thus, mothering threatens self-identity within mothers. It also underlines her corporeality and animality. This period in the development of the child is the source of the semiotic. In the prenatal period, the fetus is both part of the mother and distinct from her; the whole concept of identity explodes in this experience. Thus, the mother's own sense of autonomy and identity dissolves as she recovers the primordial semiotic condition that Kristeva values. This interfusion of identities is an important source of ethical responsiveness, according to Kristeva. Felt obligations toward the child emerge, and its symbiosis with the mother provides the child with a potential connectedness to others that is never completely lost. If ethics is to be emotionally sustainable after the death of God, the mother-child relation makes this possible.

Kristeva also examines a number of social-psychological phenomena that both elaborate her theory of child development and require close readings of literary texts. For example, she writes books on love, depression, time, and foreignness (or experiencing oneself as a stranger). In these works the value she concedes to the symbolic and to coherent identity emerges more vividly. Love, for example, requires separation from the mother, the experience of distinct selfhood and autonomy, and openness to idealizations of the other. Like Freud, she roots love in the process of transference.[49] Kristeva articulates a different dimension of the father in her theory of love – an imagined father (rather than the Oedipal father) who is the source of the infant's ego-ideal. The father encourages the child to take the first steps toward the symbolic. Kristeva also examines the sources of agape, which nurtures others without seeking any return from them. Melancholy derives from an inability to love that results from damage or interruption of the processes leading to the formation of the ego-ideal or the symbolic in general. She thus notes that the failure to develop some coherent identity can lead to psychic and political disaster. Politically, the lack of selfhood leads to a need for authority figures and an urge toward violence, or else it produces a continuing dependence on leaders. In these studies, Kristeva seeks to define new types of self-identity, rather than to undermine all identity.

IRIGARAY

Luce Irigaray (b. 1930) is a psychotherapist, linguist, and philosopher (holding doctoral degrees in each of these fields); yet she is highly critical of all these disciplines. She rejects the way subjectivity has typically been conceived (as masculine) in the history of Western thought and in psychoanalysis, and she seeks a new vision of embodiment that shatters these masculine paradigms.

Whereas Kristeva owes much to Deleuze's vision of subjectivity, Irigaray draws on Derridean strategies for her critiques, while establishing a completely original alternative. She interprets femininity in ways that underline its distinctive value, power, and specificity. Her most important creative advances are in ethics. Ethics is not even possible until the new kind of subjectivity she calls "feminine" is realized. She has written many fascinating books, the most famous of which are *Speculum of the Other Woman* (1974), *The Sex Which is Not One* (1977), and *Ethics of Sexual Difference* (1984). Irigaray's task is to revalue the feminine – not to denigrate the masculine, but to show the distinctive virtues of the feminine. This strategy grounds both her critical stances to philosophy and psychoanalysis and her constructive stance in ethics. Most recently her position incorporates some new elements. She seeks a new era of thought, language, sexuality, and politics that will result from a recognition and appreciation of sexual difference. Both men and women must create this new world together. Each sex will develop distinctive identities that can allow genuine love and creativity to flourish between them.

Some feminists believe that changing social institutions will be sufficient to overthrow male domination. By contrast, Irigaray asserts that philosophical categories and assumptions play essential roles in the suppression of women, and she insists that a critique of those categories is essential to social transformation. Irigaray challenges existing linguistic categories in order to create new ones that do better justice to the specifics of feminine experience. The feminine is typically defined in a way that makes it dependent on the masculine – either as a complement, an opposite, or a correlative term. These relational characterizations ignore the specific quality of feminine experience.[50] When the feminine is described as equal or correlative, then the distinctiveness of the feminine vanishes completely, and all experience is treated as masculine. When the feminine is defined as complementary to the masculine, then the feminine reaches its perfection only by completing or rectifying the inadequacies of the masculine; it is accorded no positive value on its own. Finally, when the feminine is treated as the opposite of the masculine, then only the masculine is given positive value; the feminine is taken to be impoverished and lacking or, worse, destructive to the "masculine" virtues of reason, order, unity, and equilibrium. Insofar as women are conceived to have experience at all, it is regarded as a degradation of masculine models. Because the notion of subjectivity is so completely infused with masculine elements, Irigaray challenges it in several ways.

The first is to attack the masculine subject's emphasis on *looking* by showing how deeply implicated feminine subjectivity is in *touching*.[51] The spectatorial element in the standard philosophical conception of subjectivity derives either from its transcendental character (i.e., contemplating everyday experience from a remote, otherworldly standpoint) or from a mastery of the world achieved via analysis or practical action. The masculine subject dominates its environment through the look; this is how he organizes the world and expresses himself. Feminine subjectivity, on the other hand, achieves immediacy and intimacy from the caress. The caress meets the world, but does not dominate it. It conforms itself to the world's contours. Moreover, its exhilaration is nearly autoerotic; it need not alter or reshape the world to find excitement in it or to fulfill its desire. The feminine experience of embodiment produces a permanent self-caressing in which the feeling and the felt interanimate each other.[52]

Irigaray's second strategy is to attack the experience of subjectivity directly – exploding it through mystic self-abnegation.[53] Mysticism is excessive, and Irigaray thinks the feminine is wildly excessive. Mysticism discovers the positive elements in the dark night of the soul, in paradox, and in celebratory ecstasy that overcomes selfhood by merging with the cosmos. This disappearance of the subject-object opposition is central to her new vision. This capacity for selfless immersion – for ecstatic multiplicity rather than isolated identity – summarizes her conception of the feminine.

A third strategy involves describing the specific modes of discourse women use in their everyday talk and showing their differences from propositional judgments or assertions. Women's discourse functions differently from the standard tropes of rhetoric and logic studied by philosophy and linguistics. Their talk permits sharing experiences without calling each other to account or requiring justification. Women caress and interpenetrate each other through talking in a way the male modes of rationality, assertion, argument, imperatives, and judgments rarely can.[54] They engage in banter, narratives, and playful explorations, often spoken in half-voice. Thus, in their speech as well, women typically transcend the assertive, domineering self-identity presupposed in the Western philosophical tradition. Her critical examination of that tradition elaborates these initial observations on the distinctiveness of feminine experience.

According to Irigaray, philosophy leads other disciplines in repressing the feminine: by denying its distinctiveness, by ignoring birthing and mothering, and by assimilating everything foreign and alien into narcissistic reflections of male subjectivity.[55] Some of her positions develop those of the phenomenologist Emmanuel Levinas, but she takes the alien other to be distinctively feminine rather than transcendent and infinite. Like Levinas, she rejects the concept of subjectivity that claims complete autonomy and independence from the world, that justifies and grounds itself through isolated self-reflection, and that assimilates everything by taking possession of it through knowledge or desire. Like Levinas, she seeks to force the "assimilators" in philosophy to take other-ness or difference seriously, to be challenged and moved by it, and to respect its distinctiveness. She also explores in greater depth what Levinas calls the "elements" of being: air, water, fire, and earth.[56] Irigaray's "other," however, is palpable and present – feminine sexuality itself, while Levinas's other is radically transcendent, almost unknowable.

In addition, philosophy operates with distinctions that typically (mis)interpret the masculine/feminine division: reason/passion, culture/nature, subject/object, intellect/sensibility, and mind/body. Generally, the first, "masculine" term in these oppositions dominates the second "feminine" term. Irigaray's purpose is to undermine these dichotomies first by analyzing the distinctive character of the repressed term and then by demonstrating that its value equals the supposedly dominant term. She does not simply reverse the value hierarchy, however, by elevating the repressed term to dominate the originally favored one. Such a strategy would replicate the mistake of classical philosophy. By demonstrating the specific character and value of the feminine, she forces philosophy to reconsider both the nature of the opposition and the status of both terms.[57] She discovers some strategies for shattering these classical oppositions by studying the speech and cognition of hysterics. She suggests that their speech is intelligible if interpreted as expressing an entirely different kind of experience from that assumed by the dominant model of subjectivity.

She also challenges the way philosophy dominates other disciplines by claiming it can supply their logical and epistemological foundations. By insisting that feminine experience is independent and does not require any contrast to masculine experience, she shows that the feminine need not be grounded on the masculine. The masculine subject pretends to speak for everyone – to achieve as a universal standpoint – when in fact he represents only one mode of experience.[58] By showing that many different types of experience, relationships with people, and orientations to the world exist, she undermines the supremacy of the masculine stance. She thus restricts its universality, demonstrating that no one group can legitimately claim to speak for all. If philosophers attend to the differences she highlights in feminine experience and relationships, then they will be forced to rethink the masculine's hegemony of other standpoints. Irigaray thus captures some distinctive features of the feminine – its disruptive excess, multiplicity, and fluidity. Women act as mediators, creatively interweaving participants into harmony without threatening their integrity.

While she offers a penetrating reconsideration of many philosophical dichotomies, Irigaray adopts a vituperative, contemptuous stance toward classical psychoanalytic theories of women's psychological development. Freud's essay on female development, in which he postulates penis envy in all women, is notoriously problematic. Irigaray relentlessly deconstructs the essay, showing that feminine development must be rethought completely.[59] She conclusively demonstrates that Freud assumed that little girls will follow the same psychic patterns as little boys. Then Freud realized that little girls would lack any motivation to abandon their attachments to their mothers and to enter the Oedipal phase, which he regards as essential to the development of the superego – morality, justice, and culture. This implies that girls will remain trapped in the narcissistic phase of sexual development, rather than internalizing moral codes. Irigaray shows how women can enter into and accept the symbolic order, but they do so on their own terms and in their own way. Women relate to laws and norms differently than men, valuing relationships to specific persons, rather than universal duties. But they also respond more completely and sensitively to other people's needs instead of blindly obeying principles regardless of the situation.

Irigaray shows that Freud presupposes a panoply of unsubstantiated male prejudices. He *deduces* how feminine development *must* occur, given his understanding of masculine development, rather than studying how it does occur.

She suggests that Freud postulates penis envy in little girls because of male anxiety about castration when they see female genitalia. For example, Freud explicitly says that the clitoris is a degenerate or inferior version of the penis. This is clearly a masculine way of viewing things, but neither Freud nor Lacan seem capable of conceiving women's sexual organs in any other way. Similarly, the male experience of orgasm is regarded as the paradigm of all legitimate sexual pleasure, a paradigm that Irigaray caustically dismisses. The feminine experience of orgasm is multiple and dispersed throughout the body. There are many sites of stimulation, and women's sexual organs offer constant auto-stimulation because the lips of the labia constantly caress each other.[60] Feminine sexual pleasure is polymorphous, fluid, varied, multiple, and constantly evolving. Compared with the richness described by Irigaray, the masculine experience of orgasm seems colorless and ephemeral.

Still another problem concerns the manner in which a woman's sexual object-choice allegedly shifts from the mother to the father. Freud offers no convincing motivation for this change. Irigaray charges that Freud misunderstands the distinctive relationships between mothers and daughters, and she indicates various ways in which this relationship can be productive and supportive.[61] In adult love, Freud posits still another asymmetry: the little boy is allowed to return to his first love (the mother), and romantic love is a recuperation of his mother's affection. But the little girl's "normal" development requires her to "cathect" the world of men, thus abandoning her first love forever. The resulting sense of abandonment can lead women to hate other women and even themselves. They come to devalue their own distinctiveness. She believes that Freud's theory of feminine development has such invidious implications that it must be dismissed altogether and that a new beginning is required. Because Irigaray creates a robust conception of the feminine, she articulates many ways in which child-rearing enhances feminine identity. When mothers become over-protective or domineering, she thinks they are trying to satisfy a masculine vision of motherhood that would answer every demand the child makes. Irigaray insists that mothers must abandon this phallic interpretation of maternal goodness for a notion of giving and caring that offers itself without reserve, but does not dominate the child (male or female). Mothers must allow their own experience to interweave with that of their children, but reject assimilating the child narcissistically.[62] Then daughters can learn to accept their dependence and acknowledge their debts without feeling any resulting guilt. Irigaray suggests that the source of the masculine subject's demand for autonomy and omnipotence derives from his inability to acknowledge this debt to his mother.

These remarks about mothers' relationships with their daughters foreshadow some of the main points of Irigaray's ethical theory. Her first principle is that others' differences must be celebrated, rather than obliterated. Otherness must not be assimilated or denied.[63] The denial of difference stifles the denier's identity because it cannot be challenged or enriched. The proper relation to other people is wonder – awe at their distinctiveness and specificity. The ethical person responds to others' calls. Their existence makes an appeal, and the quality of the response expresses the respondent's ethical character.[64] The second principle is that giving oneself to another should be done without expectation of return or imposition of obligations. This is a distinctively feminine way of offering love, which nurtures and energizes others, rather than possessing or dominating them. Irigaray thinks that ethical relationships between the sexes are possible if their distinctiveness is recognized. Women can no longer be treated as reflections, doubles, antagonists, or mythic opposites of men. They are not merely men's vessels: wombs, homemakers, or appendages. Women must learn to appreciate each other. When men can meet women in a way that acknowledges their differences and value, then a mutual ethical attitude of wonder becomes possible.

In addition, Irigaray has attempted to articulate different visions of the cosmos and feminine models of a deity. She is not trying to refurbish the notion of God, but she realizes that humans project ego ideals into the cosmos as gods, and she believes that existing models of God are exclusively masculine.[65] God the Father, Son, and Holy Spirit: all masculine. Also, Western theism is typically monotheistic rather than polytheistic; its God is omnipotent and omniscient, rather than limited and perspectival. A feminine God would relate to humankind through the voice, rather than through the objectifying, all-knowing eye. This voice would call to humanity, urging people to rise to their best possibilities. In addition to re-envisioning God, Irigaray examines the four elements that combine to constitute all created things: air, earth, water, and fire. Change and attraction (love) are central principles by which these elements relate to one another. Though each element is as fundamental as the others (because they each have distinctive properties), they also combine in ways that allow the properties of each to be retained, rather than annihilated. She explores distinctive types of subjectivity that would be constituted by various elements, thus providing a basis for respecting their differences. This cosmic vision also rejects the urge for domination and self-aggrandizement.

LE DOEUFF

Michèle Le Doeuff's (b. 1948) tone is more moderate than that of Kristeva or Irigaray, and her essays are more convincing because of this. She insists that there are many different types and sites of philosophy, many different kinds of reason, many different kinds of women, and many different programs for feminists.[66] She pulls no punches in rejecting types of philosophy and rationality that are antagonistic to women, and she traces many subtle ways in which women have been marginalized by, as well as excluded from, philosophy. Not just by individual philosophers (who, for example, have claimed that women are incapable of reason, are secondary humans, are vegetative and passive, like primitives, children, and commoners), but by the entire institution of philosophy which has created many distinctions essential to excluding women from full humanity. Her main target is a certain vision of philosophy – a self-sufficient, autonomous, self-generating, master discipline that seeks to dictate to all other discourses. She also challenges the institutional organization of philosophy – its dependence on universities, its reliance on master-disciple relationships, and its subtle diminishing of women by regarding them as midwives or acolytes. Not only her tone, but also the scope of her claims is measured, and she rarely asserts more than she can show. Her position avoids the temptations she identifies in traditional philosophy; it is inclusive, careful, and acknowledges its reliance on other disciplines and forms of thought. She has published several important books: *The Philosophical Imaginary* (1980), *Hipparchia's Choice* (1989), and *The Sex of Knowing* (1998). The first examines the central role that images and metaphors play in philosophy, especially in the Renaissance. The second critically examines the disciplinary realities of philosophy and de Beauvoir's long-term relationship with Sartre. I will restrict my discussion to selected features of the first two books.

Le Doeuff notes that nearly every philosophical text makes use of illustrative images at crucial junctures. The task of her first book is to study how these images function. Traditionally, philosophy prides itself on its austere rational argumentation, its reliance on only the most pristine epistemic standards. For this reason, the inclusion of such illustrative images is surprising, and typically they are treated as secondary devices that allow the average person to ascend to the philosophical standpoint. But Le Doeuff argues that in many cases such images indicate a moment of uncertainty, an unjustified leap in the discussion that is concealed by using the image.[67] Reason alone is rarely able to produce conviction, and when reason falters, philosophers unhesitatingly call on poetry and rhetoric. Le Doeuff reads philosophical texts as closely as Derrida, but she is less reductive in diagnosing their problems. She thinks that images operate in a variety of ways in philosophy, but they all mask weaknesses in purely rational arguments. Typically, philosophy tries to repress alternative discourses (e.g., poetry, science, final causes, analogies, rhetoric, etc.); this self-constituting division also separates the masculine from the feminine.[68] This is why philosophy's relation to women is so problematic. Whenever philosophy claims complete autonomy and self-sufficiency, its dependence on alternative forms of discourse soon emerges, and these limitations are only reluctantly acknowledged.

Philosophy thus seeks to reject its "opposite" even when it desperately needs it. To conceal this dependency, philosophy insists that such images are offered only for the benefit of the uninitiated (e.g., children, the naive person), or it may claim that they are remnants of an era that was proto-philosophical (mythic or primitive) and thus has yet to be purified of such images.[69] But Le Doeuff shows that these cover stories are misleading and that philosophy cannot avoid using images, metaphors, and non-rational rhetorical strategies. This dependency shows that one dream of philosophy – of becoming an entirely self-sufficient, self-generating discourse – cannot be realized. Philosophy is one kind of discourse among others. It cannot dominate other discourses, and it cannot function as a master discourse.[70] Le Doeuff insists that the time has come for philosophy to acknowledge the importance of the sciences, of poetry and art, and of countless other kinds of knowledge. Moreover, these images and metaphors are not limited to specific writers. An entire tradition of developing, revising, and commenting on previous philosophical images and poetic gestures exists. Often weaknesses in the tradition infect new philosophical thought at these junctures. When philosophers use images, their weaknesses, anxieties, evasions, and self-doubts become transparent. Through close study of such images, Le Doeuff is able to fashion a supple and robust form of philosophical critique. Her deconstructions are often more convincing than Derrida's playful maneuvers.

This antagonistic relation to alien, non-rational elements of discourse embodies traditional philosophy's attitude toward the feminine and the institution's characteristic treatment of women. Close examination of philosophic texts reveals a shocking series of images whenever the feminine is discussed and an array of problematic metaphors that carry gender connotations. Knowledge is nearly always figured as masculine penetration into virgin territory and thus excludes women from the capacity to know. Throughout history, philosophers have been prominent misogynists, and they have nearly always depended on poetic images to defend their sexist ideologies.[71] Although women have not been entirely excluded from philosophy (consider Diotima, Hypatia, Queen Christina, and Héloïse), they have been treated as acolytes and disciples, rather than creative original minds in their own right.[72] Typically, women are venerated for their power to inspire male philosophers. Perhaps the most dominant myth in philosophy is that a mentor must transmit it, and women have always been subordinates in this relationship. Historically, they have not been given adequate education or opportunity to develop their philosophical abilities. Their access to publishers, teaching employment, and the best educational programs has been severely restricted. They are not recommended to the best jobs, and their interpretive subtlety makes their official exams and essays easy to fail because they do not pretend to "master" the text.[73] To the extent that women have contributed to philosophy, supposedly this has been through their elaboration of their male mentors' insights. They are permitted to comment and expand, but not to create in their own right, and this is hardly to participate in philosophy at all. These assumptions sharply contrast with those typically applied to men, who are expected to overthrow their mentors as they refashion the elder's system. Le Doeuff takes de Beauvoir to task for her self-subordination to Sartre, suggesting that she reinforced women's marginalization in philosophy despite her evident talent. This position of devoted adulation that is assigned to talented women in philosophy provides compensation both for the knowledge that the mentor's philosophical system cannot be self-legitimating and for the current marginality of philosophy in relation to the sciences.[74]

Le Doeuff's primary focus in *The Philosophical Imaginary* and other writings is the Utopian tradition, especially during the Renaissance. She offers close analyses of both More's and Bacon's Utopias. She finds in the Utopian tradition the same dream that animates the rest of philosophy – the dream of self-sufficiency, autonomy, and autarchy. Utopias seem to stand apart from the rest of the world and declare independence from the human condition as such.

Instead of offering genuine political theories, she interprets Utopias as attempts to reorganize all of society around new types of school. These schools will allegedly produce more adequate and effective knowledges and refashion human nature in the process. Utopias express the will to power of intellectuals, who seek to subordinate all other institutions to thought and to produce a complete cultural transformation through educational reform.[75] And indeed most Utopias anticipated significant institutional changes in education, e.g., the creation of learned societies in Britain and the rise of state-sponsored research organizations in France. Utopian fantasies are one device by which Renaissance humanism subverted religious control over education and the rest of society. Foucault begins many of his genealogies of modernity with the Renaissance, and Le Doeuff studies the formation of the concepts of masculine and feminine within philosophy in these Utopian texts. She acknowledges, however, that Plato and More at least gave women relatively equal status in their Utopias. Only in the eighteenth century did Utopians abandon this ideal. In this same era, philosophy sought to distinguish itself from other discourses and elevate itself over them. Le Doeuff sees a deep connection between these two events.

Hipparchia's Choice is a meditation on the relation of women and philosophy with special attention to Simone de Beauvoir's relationship with Sartre.[76] De Beauvoir declared herself a writer primarily and refused the title of creative philosopher, even though she introduced important ethical notions into Sartre's existentialist framework.[77] Le Doeuff also admires de Beauvoir for her ability to transform the Sartrean ontological framework into an historically relevant manifesto that allowed women everywhere to seek major social and ideological change. Oddly, de Beauvoir was better able to create a sense of outrage at women's condition because she did not identify herself as an oppressed woman. Her high-altitude perspective allowed her to better describe women's condition and to represent it as malleable. She used Sartre's universalistic theory to understand a much more specific set of oppressive conditions and to reveal some ways to overcome them. Le Doeuff credits de Beauvoir with making central alterations in Sartre's postulates to produce a more situated and embodied form of freedom and agency. De Beauvoir thus represents an approach to philosophy that Le Doeuff seeks both to challenge and to emulate.

But Le Doeuff's book also examines many other facets of women's experience of the institution of philosophy: its modes of teaching, writing, thinking, and testing. She argues that women have much to contribute to current philosophy, especially to finding a non-hegemonic manner of relating to other disciplines and a more collaborative approach to research. She tries to diagnose the current condition of philosophy: its theoretical weaknesses, its unwillingness to acknowledge its limits, its need to reject the pristine guise of the a priori and enter into joint investigations with the sciences, its need to read its canonical texts with greater care and sensitivity.[78] She also warns women against thinking that academic jobs are the only places to do philosophy in the future. She urges women to pursue the historical study of philosophy more carefully;

there, women's reading skills will be better appreciated. She also urges that children's capacities for and relation to philosophy be further explored. Philosophy permeates the entire intellectual milieu; one cannot really escape or dismiss it if one is a serious thinker. One can only patiently challenge its distinctions and deflate its arrogance.

Notoriously, philosophers promulgate myths of the feminine; allegedly women are forces of disorder, chaos, darkness, the abyss, and the underworld (at least among the upper classes; among the lower classes, the mythology is entirely different: women are orderly, sensible, and skilled at managing everyday demands). These myths must be made explicit and challenged, and the mainstream intellectual reliance on them must be eliminated. Finally, philosophers must present their ideas with greater humility, as suggestions to be developed rather than closed systems that must either be accepted or rejected in their entirety. Her prescriptions are cautious, but plausible. They do not pretend to introduce a new millennium in philosophy, but they do attempt to indicate promising ways out of its current impasse.

COMPARISONS

Though the dispersionists would attack the Hegelianism implicit in de Beauvoir's notion of pure recognition between the sexes, in general they would approve of the uses made of their strategies by the succeeding generation of French feminist philosophers. Though some might argue that de Beauvoir's authentic interhuman relation involves too much assimilation, she would insist that authentic recognition acknowledges and respects the difference of the other even as it affirms solidarity. Moreover, she lucidly articulates the historical situation of women and the ways in which ideologies and institutions collude to maintain it, and she is unafraid to challenge women to recover their own freedom, instead of waiting for it to be returned to them. Just as de Beauvoir develops and contributes to Sartre's theories, the other French feminists also develop and contribute to many key insights of the dispersionists. Collectively they demonstrate the political potential of theories of dispersion.

For example, Irigaray develops and transforms Derrida's deconstructive methods when she challenges many of the dichotomies that she thinks derive from the masculine-feminine opposition (reason/passion, subject/object, mind/body, will/instinct). However, she does not merely unsettle the oppositions; she reveals the value of the suppressed side of the dichotomy, even as she questions the legitimacy of a sharp distinction. Neither does she reverse the dominance of the two terms by insisting on the supremacy of the previously denigrated term. With a Hegelian flourish she tries to show how passions constitute the basis for reason, how the lived, sensuous, tactile body makes various cognitive capacities possible, how the subject dissolves into the object at least in certain iconic experiences, like mysticism. With Derridean deconstruction, the result seems to be stalemate, uncertainty, or endless see-saw in which each term challenges the other and priority becomes impossible to establish. Irigaray draws positive conclusions and demonstrates important truths through her deconstructive efforts.

Kristeva stresses decentered subjectivity, excessive unbounded desire, and interdependence and symbiosis, which links her position with Deleuze's rhizomatic metaphors and his similar challenges to Freud. Just as Deleuze embraces rhizomatic interconnections, so too does Kristeva insist on interdependent symbiosis, especially between mother and child. In addition, they both appeal to avant-garde literature to clarify and legitimate their positions. Kristeva, however, is aware of the potential conservative reaction to extreme forms of this position, and she strives to block that reaction by defending more plausible, less extreme versions that nonetheless are sufficient to challenge the autonomous, self-sufficient, rational subject that she wants to contest. Kristeva also makes important contributions to the analysis of key emotions, e.g., love, depression, madness, abjection, using the entire history of thought to enrich those analyses, while Deleuze is more interested in rethinking individual philosophers in a way that clarifies his own concepts and claims.

De Beauvoir anticipates some of Foucault's efforts to illuminate the ways in which institutions operate in local contexts to reinforce invidious power relations, and Le Doeuff continues this emphasis by criticizing the institutions of academia – especially of university-centered philosophy programs – in marginalizing and diminishing the intellectual capacities of women. Just as Foucault is attentive to the subtle ways power organizes itself in asylums, prisons, and medical clinics, Le Doeuff closely studies education generally and philosophy in particular with a similar eye to the operations of power. However, Le Doeuff's claims are more measured and careful, more plausible and testable, and her efforts to rethink the role of philosophy as an intellectual discipline actually discover a positive function for it. Foucault seems to seek a successor discipline to philosophy, whether it is the historical study of discursive formations or institutional analyses of the micro-strategies of power or ideological analyses of the ways subjects constitute themselves. The analyses of both de Beauvoir and Le Doeuff provide guidelines for institutional change in a way that Foucault often neglects.

Moreover, almost surreptitiously, the French feminists recuperate the project of experiential phenomenology because comprehending the distinctive contours and contributions of feminine experience is so essential to their project. On the basis of the renewed analysis of experience in each of these thinkers, there emerge significant ramifications for ethics (Irigaray), epistemology (Le Doeuff), philosophy of language (Kristeva), developmental psychology, and art. Thus, in many ways French feminist philosophers improve on the insights of the dispersionists and show how they can be used to overcome oppression.

ASSESSMENT

Though some of the claims these thinkers make about distinctive feminine forms of experience seem correct, others deserve more careful scrutiny. For example, many experiences based on mothering are unlikely to be shared by men, but men's identities may be stretched and made more inclusive through the experience of fathering. But in sexual desire and fulfillment, men have experiences analogous to the complexities described by Irigaray. The caress, multiple sites of stimulation, and a sense of opening to and enfolding the other are equally important in male sexuality. Once their eyes are opened by the insightful analyses of experience these thinkers provide, men will discover many parallel insights that confirm them. This coalescence will only strengthen the broad acceptance of the vision of experience (overcoming dichotomies, the importance of the body) offered by the feminists. These overlapping zones of contact will qualify the claims to feminine distinctiveness claimed by some of these thinkers. Beyond this, the claim that there are distinctive forms of feminine experience must be distinguished from the claim that such forms are better or preferable forms. The latter claim requires separate argument, and often it needs better defense than is often provided. Too easily, one claim simply is taken to imply the other.

Some of the disagreements among these figures are contradictory, and some decision between them may be necessary. Their positions do not always supplement each other. Perhaps some strategies for cultural transformation are best pursued first, and others can come later, but the basic disagreement between de Beauvoir's goal of pure recognition based on the experience of commonness and Irigaray's goal of reciprocity based on the experience of difference needs resolution. Similar critical discussion is needed concerning whether the goal should be an overcoming of self-sufficient identity altogether (Kristeva), or the pursuit of different kinds of identities that allow respect and recognition, but retain some experience of difference (Irigaray). On the other hand, some key thrusts of the movement are compatible and should be pursued together. The institutional analysis provided by de Beauvoir and supplemented by Le Doeuff identifies key targets for overcoming sexism, but so too do the conceptual deconstruction and critique of philosophical methodologies developed by Irigaray and Le Doeuff. Both types of transformation are necessary: changing institutions and changing patterns of thought; when successful, they should reinforce one another and achieve greater effect than either approach pursued in isolation.

From de Beauvoir to Le Doeuff, the politics of these thinkers depends on the key premise that for one (person or group) to be free, all (persons or groups) must be free. In this way they enlist the efforts of everyone to overcome oppression. Each thinker has a different way of defending this key premise, but in order to produce the commitment and continuity they seek, the principle could perhaps be given still stronger defense. At least they explore the deeper social connections that would make that defense feasible.

Finally, while most of these thinkers show how both sexes can contribute to achieving the overall goal of enriching each other's lives, one dimension of de Beauvoir's analysis has too often been ignored by the later contributors – viz., her emphasis on the ways women collude with their own subordination. This emphasis is less central in the other thinkers, and for this reason, they are less helpful in showing ways in which women can transform themselves in achieving these goals. Men still have immense work to do on themselves and on the institutions they typically lead to make the necessary contributions to achieving these goals. But de Beauvoir's analysis shows many ways in which women could reclaim their own lives. Both sexes have much to do to achieve more authentic lives, but the later French feminists indicate additional values that can enrich the lives of both sexes: a holism in understanding persons, a stress on context and ethical sensitivity rather than principles and abstract rules in ethics, an acceptance of a more interdependent, mutually defining form of relatedness among persons and between humanity and nature. In this way, the French feminists provide some defense of new substantive ethical and political goals that was missing in existentialism and poststructuralism.

POSTMODERNISM

SOME DISTINCTIONS

Postmodernism seeks to clarify the unique features of the current era, including its economy, politics, art, social relations, technology, and forms of knowledge. Its central claim is that the current era – which is taken to begin either in 1945, after World War II, or in 1960, with the coming of age of a new generation – is qualitatively different from the preceding one (modernity). Postmodernists believe these differences are so significant that new modes of thought are required to comprehend them. They *describe* its unique features, but rarely try to *explain* them. Some postmodernists – notably Lyotard and Rorty[1] – examine changes in philosophical and scientific assumptions. Others, notably Baudrillard and Jameson,[2] elucidate changes in culture – especially the arts, social life, and technology. Many postmodernists' fascination with the current age is so great that they seem reluctant to criticize it. Their most vocal critics are Marxists, who believe postmodernists' conclusions are merely ideological offshoots of a new mode of capitalist production – global capitalism. My concluding assessment will consider these Marxist criticisms. I will limit the discussion in this chapter to France's major postmodernist thinkers, Lyotard and Baudrillard.

Lyotard is primarily concerned with theory in the postmodern era. In *The Postmodern Condition: A Report on Knowledge* (1979), he compares knowledge in the modern period with the contemporary era. Another important text, *The Differend* (1983), offers foundations for and explores solutions to problems highlighted in the earlier book. Lyotard seeks to clarify procedures that might provide just adjudications of conflicts among types of discourse that lack common standards. This is his dominant theme. Lyotard's major books also include *Discourse, Figure* (1971) and *Libidinal Economy* (1974). Some features of Lyotard's thought resemble those of Deleuze; I will ignore these in order to focus on his contributions to postmodernism. Baudrillard analyzes contemporary culture – describing important shifts in art, everyday life, politics, and the experience of reality. His major theme is the emergence of hyperreality – images so compelling that they transfix subjectivity. Though often dogmatic and self-indulgent, his observations still can be illuminating.

Many scholars categorize under a single heading the three figures I have called "philosophers of dispersion" and the figures discussed here. I think this is a mistake because they exhibit significant differences. Perhaps clarifying them will provide a rationale for my approach. The postmodernists have different theoretical aspirations, adopt a different attitude, and respond differently to the philosophical tradition.

The philosophers of dispersion neglect the postmodernists' central question: what are the distinctive features of the current era? Foucault thinks this is a significant question, but offers little by way of an answer. He thinks the current era is unique, but he sketches its outlines only negatively. His claim that discursive formations are skewed in relation to one another is transhistorical, not restricted simply to the current era. In addition, neither Derrida nor Deleuze believe that *différance* or rhizomes are unique to the contemporary era. They claim these are fundamental, unchanging features of ultimate reality. Postmodernists deny that such metaphysical hypotheses are defensible. They confine their claims to the current era, eschewing transhistorical theories. When postmodernists address dispersionists' issues, they often reach different conclusions. For example, Lyotard celebrates speech and desire as if he were ignorant of Derrida's critique of presence. Baudrillard's victory of the object over the subject ignores Deleuze's theory of desiring-machines, in which subject and object are interlocked. Both Lyotard and Deleuze seek to release desire, but Deleuze's goal is this-worldly while Lyotard seeks to reach inexpressible transcendence. Thus, the theoretical goals and key claims of these two groups of theorists differ.

Second, the philosophers of dispersion provide greater critical perspective on the present era. Derrida thinks deconstruction applies just as forcefully to contemporary theorists and concepts as to classical ones; Foucault establishes a critical distance on virtually every era – including the present; and Deleuze invents concepts that reshape contemporary political, social, and aesthetic dynamics. The postmodernists seem captivated by the current era, almost embracing it – even if hesitantly and with some embarrassment. They explore few alternatives and write as if major change is unlikely. Though both postmodernists and poststructuralists stress the importance of differences and local knowledges, poststructuralists aim for substantial social change. Postmodernists have unusually modest political goals. Their critique of meta-narratives and truth makes justifying revolutionary political programs difficult. Even if they hope for genuine change, their theories limit their ability to legitimate it. Thus, the political aspirations of the two movements are dramatically different.

Finally, philosophers of dispersion conduct intense examinations of the past history of philosophy. Postmodernists, however, exhibit limited interest in past philosophical systems. Lyotard utilizes Kant, and Baudrillard criticizes Marx in his early period, but they do not interrogate the whole philosophical tradition like Derrida and Deleuze, or the range of human sciences like Foucault. In addition, the postmodernists seem philosophically lightweight (unlike the dispersionists) because their claims are more tentative and less justified. Postmodernists may be less interested in the past because they think that the present era transcends it. This implies that past philosophies would offer few clues to present realities. Dispersionists believe that learning from past errors is essential to rethinking philosophy's future. They *demonstrate* flaws in past systems, rather than simply *proclaiming* a new era.

CORE CONTRIBUTIONS

Perhaps the postmodernists' most important contributions are their focal questions. What are the distinctive features of the current era? And what are their philosophical implications? Answering these questions is difficult because, by hypothesis, the features involved are new and may elude current concepts. Elucidating them requires sharp intuition. Lyotard calls it "grasping the sublime" because the theorist must articulate what has rarely been recognized. Fully comprehending their implications is no easier. New concepts may require new research methods, and these must be tested. Past questions/positions may be superseded, and this must be recognized. Postmodernists follow Foucault in thinking that the current era cannot be derived from or explained by previous ones; it emerges from a "break." This is why they focus on descriptions rather than explanations or depth interpretations, which would invariably reduce the present to the past.

The most significant features of the current era identified by the postmodernists are the dissolution of belief in meta-narratives, the fragmentation of knowledges and selfhood, and the hyperreal. They reject the credibility of meta-narratives which suggest that history is developing toward some goal, claiming both that such meta-narratives no longer command assent and that important counter-evidence to them exists. History is not unfolding in the direction of greater truth (Enlightenment), freedom (Hegel), socialism (Marx), or economic productivity (capitalists).[3] The terrible wars of the twentieth century cast doubts on these meta-narratives, which also *contributed* to the destruction because soldiers believed history was "on their side." The loss of belief in these teleological narratives produces intellectual disorientation similar to the loss of faith in God. This explains the absence of larger political programs in Lyotard and Baudrillard. Such visions have had detrimental historical effects.

This dissolution of meta-narratives is connected with the fragmentation of knowledges. Instead of valuing a unified science or a Hegelian system, Lyotard favors limiting the truth and legitimacy of each discourse to its own distinctive sphere. Each thus becomes a specific "game" with its own rules for adequate/inadequate moves. For Lyotard, the central question is how these diverse, self-contained discourses should be adjudicated when they conflict.[4] He further fractures Kant's types of reason in the three *Critiques*. Kant suggested that science, ethics, and aesthetics operate in distinct spheres and thus must be evaluated differently, each on its own terms. Lyotard simply generalizes this move to many types of discourses. In effect, Lyotard reintroduces problems that Hegel and other Continental philosophers sought to resolve after Kant. The tradition has come full circle.

Baudrillard's core insight concerns the hyperreal, the sense that the everyday world is a pale imitation of a fantasy-infused realm constructed by technology and advertising. He suggests that the experience of reality is *constructed*; some experiences have higher coefficients of reality. Virtual worlds and riveting media-engendered fantasies often exhibit high coefficients of reality. The hyperreal drains energy and will from individuals, leaving them impotent – at the mercy of larger social and technological forces.[5] Subjectivity's powers thus disintegrate. Hyperreality engenders experiential disorientations that rival the theoretical disorientations resulting from the decline of meta-narratives.

Despite their deflationary stances, postmodernists continue to theorize, even if in a more tentative spirit that acknowledges the contingent, limited grounds for their own positions. They adopt criteria of adequacy appropriate to their specific tasks, and their observations remain open to challenge and correction. Postmodernists are not radical skeptics in the sense that they deny the search for local truths (limited truths within restricted spheres of inquiry), but they do reject universal and transhistorical truths. This theoretical caution contrasts with the bold visions of the dispersionists, whose belief in dispersion is often belied by their larger theoretical aspirations. Postmodernists acknowledge the full implications of intellectual and cultural dispersion.

Both Lyotard and Baudrillard believe that art perspicuously exhibits postmodern realities. Lyotard claims that avant-garde artists discern defining features of the new era and thus elucidate the ineffable. They also enrich the concept of reality by discovering its unseen dimensions and by providing improvisational models – rules of construction that gradually disclose their own logic – for postmodern thought to emulate. Art uncovers unique events; testifying to such events is one of Lyotard's central goals.[6] Baudrillard also believes that art anticipates new cultural developments. The hyperreal, seduction, and fatal strategies first emerge in contemporary art. Art thus makes crucial trends explicit. Both postmodernists seek to emulate visionary artists' ability to illuminate the current era.

In addition to these positive features, postmodernists share two additional properties deriving from their rejection of modernism: doubts about reason and modest political aspirations. Modernists claimed that reason is shared by all humans regardless of their cultural background, is capable of uncovering important philosophical truths, and can produce improvements in the human condition through technological advances. Postmodernists question these claims. They offer reservations about technological developments (e.g., their benefits are questionable, and they have unintended consequences). They show that reason is fragmented into a multiplicity of conflicting discourses; they claim that no single, universal decision procedure can insure justice among disputants operating within different discourses. They note that the assumption of common rationality has often been used to silence minorities because majorities claim to know minorities' best interests. Baudrillard forsakes rational responses to the hyperreal because its power transcends rational support and is immune to critique. Finally, both appeal to claims deriving from current scientific research (chaos theory, entropy theory) that challenge modernists' conceptions of reason.

Modernists also sought revolutionary political change – Utopia on earth. With the dissolution of Marxism and doubts about liberal rights, clear political goals become harder to define. Postmodernists challenge the grounds for modernist political revolutions. For example, feminism depends on the truth of a narrative about patriarchy (and most minority movements depend on narratives about majority oppression). If such narratives are no longer viable, then the political legitimacy of these movements becomes questionable. Postmodernist politics favors temporary alliances and limited goals, encouraging local groups to pursue their own agendas. It rejects universal justifications for grand political programs and questions whether resurrecting such "grand politics" would be desirable. Because postmodernists tentatively embrace the current era, they do not propose major alternatives or explore Utopian possibilities. They celebrate the Utopian elements within the current order. They reject the view that a single class or group has the capacity to revolutionize contemporary life for the betterment of all. Any group always acts from specific interests. Some of these should perhaps be encouraged; others discouraged. Both Lyotard and Baudrillard seek to preserve the possibility of a genuinely transforming political event, but both seem unable to articulate its justification or direction.

Postmodernism presents itself as a vanguard movement – elaborating the most current social trends. It values the new for its own sake, rejecting tradition, normalcy, and stasis. Its mood is exuberant discovery – celebrating the features of a world still being born. Critics of the current order will see postmodernists as little more than its publicists. If that order is corrupt, its advocates will be stained by that corruption.

LYOTARD

Jean-François Lyotard's (1924–98) thought falls into two distinct periods: an early period, heavily influenced by Deleuze, running from *Discourse/Figure* to *Libidinal Economy*, and a second period, featuring a linguistic turn and offering a theory of postmodern knowledge. The main text of the second period is *The Differend*, and its main question is how to justly formulate disputes between linguistic practices that have no common ground. Lyotard explores the contemporary implications of the plurality and incommensurability of language games (or "phrase regimes"). Here the key text is his most famous book, *The Postmodern Condition: A Report on Knowledge*, on which I will concentrate. In both periods Lyotard explores the ineffable using studies of avant-garde art. In the later period, he examines political dilemmas by examining events that are central to one discourse but which cannot be described in another discourse because the rules governing it exclude those events (e.g., testimony about the holocaust offered to those who deny it ever occurred).

In his early period Lyotard explores features of reality that cannot be reduced to language or linguistic structure. He uses a Deleuzean concept of desire – undifferentiated energy – that explodes existing linguistic frameworks, searching or yearning for what cannot yet be spoken. He also notes that figures (e.g., diagrams, line drawings) cannot be reduced to discourse. Drawings do not abide by conceptual rules; they are more open-ended and fanciful and can be completed in many different ways. In addition, efforts to paraphrase or interpret poems may capture some of their meanings, but they can never fully capture the poem's meanings and effects. A surplus will always resist adequate linguistic articulation.[7]

Even in the early period, Lyotard highlights potential conflicts between justice and truth. He thinks attempts to justify particular value judgments will typically ignore relevant competing claims or conflicting desires. Justice requires that one try to incorporate these complexities, but linguistic efforts to express truth in propositions can rarely do this. He hopes to formulate ways of making particular value judgments without appealing to universal rules, which will nonetheless address the complexities of the particular context. This remains a central problem for Lyotard throughout his career.

His book-length interview with Jean-Loup Thébaud, *Just Gaming* (1979), functions as a transition to Lyotard's second period. Lyotard notes that a distinctive feature of the current age is its patchwork of minority discourses. For him, justice requires rejecting theories that ignore the differences among these discourses, accepting the rules of each, and respecting the right of all participants to contest or reinterpret the rules. Justice then requires acknowledging the integrity of each discourse, refusing to subsume it under other dominant discourses.[8] Prescriptions must respect each discourse's rules because they provide the criteria for legitimating value judgments. Prescriptions cannot be defended by factual appeals because prescription is a fundamentally different type of language game from description.[9] Cultures nonetheless possess appropriate procedures for validating value judgments. Plausible challenges can only be mounted from within, through paradox and internal contradiction. There is no master discourse or absolute perspective that can generate definitive criticisms of local practices or genres. Lyotard's nascent ethics demands sensitivity to specific contexts, rejects abstract rules, and seeks to negotiate value conflicts in creative ways.[10]

The Differend provides a philosophical foundation for the situation he describes in *The Postmodern Condition*. A differend differs from a disagreement, which arises within a language game and can be resolved by appealing to its internal standards. A differend is a conflict between two incommensurable language games.[11] Formulating and resolving differends demands creative insight because the rules of one practice conceal and distort those of the other. Lyotard defines justice as the capacity to attest to such disputes without doing violence to either. There can never be a simple formula for resolving differends; each must be considered in its own context, and not all can be resolved. Resolutions that work in one context may not work in others. Lyotard calls moves in a language game "phrases" (e.g., making a statement, asking a question). His central thesis is: to phrase is necessary (silence is a move), how to phrase is contingent.[12] Responding to a phrase interprets it by situating it in a particular genre. Genres are rules for linking phrases; they constitute particular language games. Every phrase is a response to a previous phrase, and most responses simply assimilate phrases to existing genres. Lyotard underlines the originality of new phrases because they can shatter or refashion existing genres. In the postmodern era, the typical situation involves a plurality of incommensurable genres.

The technical apparatus Lyotard creates allows him to explore the distinctive genre of prescriptions or norms. Norms demand certain kinds of response; if made in a particular context by the right person, the necessary response should be forthcoming because the norm is regarded as legitimate. Modernity attempted to rationally justify norms. If this project succeeds, then the norm's legitimacy is shifted to its justification; if it fails, then the norms seem illegitimate.[13] In any event the status of prescriptions changes. Lyotard suggests that the legitimacy that sustains ethical claims may be beyond rational justification and that the study of differends may permit a better understanding of normativity. One task of postmodern thought is to rectify the damage that modernist attempts to justify norms have done.

The Postmodern Condition further examines incommensurable discourses. There Lyotard's main point is that meta-narratives – theories about the necessary direction and goal of history – no longer inspire confidence. Just as Nietzsche declared the death of God, so Lyotard declares the death of meta-narratives, an event with a similar impact. Whether meta-narratives are invoked to support the sciences (revelation of truth), political movements (emancipation of humanity), or artistic movements (achieving deeper vision), they no longer provide the legitimacy they did in the modern era.[14] Because faith in meta-narratives has been shattered, the postmodern condition of the sciences and other cultural discourses is isolation. They are indifferent, disparate linguistic practices. The goal of a unified science is abandoned. Though some may claim that science legitimates itself with practical results, not all sciences (e.g., the human sciences) produce such results, and, more importantly, Lyotard claims that their real justification is "performativity" – the degree to which their results stimulate *further research* (as opposed to the actual practical benefits).[15]

Postmodern culture is characterized by the same linguistic disintegration as the sciences – fractured into diverse, irreducible, and sometimes incommensurable linguistic genres. Each genre has its own distinctive rules. Society consists of congeries of micro-practices, which operate independently of the others, e.g., academic disciplines.[16] Lyotard greets this fact with both distress and enthusiasm. His distress arises because there is no longer any way to regulate or challenge the legitimacy of science on ethical or political grounds (in the name of justice). For example, the new technology of cloning has stimulated many new research programs. But when non-scientists raise moral questions about this practice – especially about the cloning of human beings – scientists ignore them because ethics is a foreign discourse. Scientists qua scientists rarely engage in moral evaluation. They embrace cloning because performativity, by definition, stimulates creative theorizing, the primary purpose of research. Lyotard is enthusiastic because diffuse discourses cannot obliterate each other. Justice requires that their proponents tolerate each other. He thus embraces diversity in intellectual programs and rejects the search for a unifying synthesis. New knowledge will derive from paralogies – the discovery of internal paradoxes that induce creative changes.[17]

Lyotard notes some additional features of postmodern knowledge. The loss of faith in meta-narratives impacts every area of culture, not just science. Art, government, and society undergo crises of legitimacy as well. This produces special problems for philosophy and the university because philosophy supplied the meta-narratives and the university transmitted them. Both philosophy and the university thus lose their primary function and must be reconceived.[18] An additional factor affecting knowledge in the postmodern era is the rise of remote computer storage (e.g., hard disks, CD-ROMs, DVD). In the modern era, the goal of the intellectual was to master and integrate as many disciplines as possible; this is no longer feasible because of the exponential growth of knowledge. Instead, fields of inquiry are isolated, and integrative metaphors are more difficult to establish. The postmodern goal is to learn how to access the stored knowledge necessary to solve specific problems, not to assimilate and integrate all knowledge. Lyotard hypothesizes that future wars will be fought over access to computerized databanks, not over territory or ideology.[19]

In addition to describing this general crisis of legitimation, Lyotard analyzes the process of legitimation. Law provides a natural point of departure. Laws are legitimate if legislators are authorized to create them; when the legislator is legitimate (in democracies: legally elected), then the law is typically accepted.[20] This issue of legitimation is also important in value theory (including politics, religion, art). The question is how to win others' recognition. Not every linguistic practice (e.g., exclamations, imperatives, or performatives) seeks truth; so truth cannot be a general criterion of legitimation.[21] Each distinct evaluative practice (e.g., art criticism, legal testimony, political debate, ethical decision-making, and religious ritual) has its own legitimation criteria. Justice requires respecting these different standards. For some theorists – e.g., Habermas – legitimation requires consensus. For Lyotard, it is an agonistic process. Individuals struggle for recognition with those whose goals and agendas may conflict.[22]

Different types of social bond arise from communal practices in the modern and postmodern eras. The modern era's ideal society was an organic community. Each member felt integrated in the whole, and the community's traditions provided common roles and background. In the postmodern period, people belong to many diverse communities, which makes organic integration unrealistic. Members adopt distinct group identities for each specific community, and some groups may not even involve face-to-face contact (e.g., people may communicate via computers or remote conferencing). These multiple involvements promote diverse perspectives; postmodern social life involves strife among them. Lyotard predicts that temporary contracts will supplant permanent commitments in the postmodern era: in marital and sexual relations, in business, in research groups, in professional relations, and in politics.[23] Such contracts allow greater flexibility, more productive use of each person's skills, and greater mutual gain for lower individual cost.

PARALOGIES: THE DISCOVERY OF INTERNAL PARADOXES THAT LEAD TO CHANGE

Lyotard clarifies the conditions that legitimate knowledge claims. When he compares narratives with scientific theories, his goal is not to reject one using the standards of the other, but to insist that each must be evaluated on its own terms.[24] Narrative is not inferior because it is unscientific, and science is not soulless because it offers no moral. Narrative legitimates itself by appealing to storytelling traditions. Science justifies itself by showing that it yields truth, remains open to all participants, and revises its conclusions when sufficient counter-evidence emerges. Democracy appeals to similar criteria: it remains open to competing arguments and changes direction when the majority of citizens demand it. For Lyotard, this implies that democracy is no less legitimate than science. The disintegration of meta-narratives allows evaluative discourses to achieve cultural parity with science.

When pressed, scientists seek legitimacy by claiming to control nature and to produce technological inventions. Philosophy and the university, however, cannot appeal to these practical benefits to legitimate their activities. Philosophical speculation produces few practical results and no longer vindicates meta-narratives; thus it fails both as science and as narrative.[25] The postmodern task of philosophy is to find new modes of expression by which disputes between contradictory linguistic practices can be comprehended. Philosophy must creatively produce standpoints from which opposing discourses can acknowledge each other. This requires innovative leaps that may transform both practices. Politically, Lyotard urges intellectuals to renounce the terror and authoritarianism that the drive for total unification of knowledge produces. He insists that the diverse knowledge practices are irreducible.

Lyotard believes that the university has similar legitimation problems. It no longer transmits truth or tradition; instead it produces professionals to fill specific roles. Also, the professor is dying. Computers and expert software will soon teach more effectively than professors, and research teams can produce better knowledge, more quickly, than individual professors.[26] Lyotard predicts that the university will become a series of interdisciplinary research institutes organized around specific societal problems or research topics. It will also train students to perform defined intellectual functions for the professions. Its most important function, however, will be to nurture synthetic minds that can establish connections across various language games and research projects. Their goal will not be to integrate all knowledge, but rather to discover common models and assumptions informing diverse practices that might be missed by specialists. Thus, the fate of philosophy and the university will continue to be intertwined, and the university will enhance the skills most needed by philosophy.

Finally, Lyotard explores the concept of "paralogy." Paralogy promotes creative leaps beyond existing frameworks. It highlights tensions, oppositions, or paradoxes within a linguistic practice that motivate creative thought.[27] He thinks many advances in science arise in this fashion; for example, paradoxes in quantum theory, chaos theory, and mathematics have all contributed to recent innovations. This attention to disharmony provides similar inspiration in contemporary art. Creative reinterpretation emerges from appreciating internal oppositions in artworks. Lyotard advocates paralogy as an intellectual method because it leads to fruitful advances. He rejects political or intellectual movements that oppose paralogy.

BAUDRILLARD

Jean Baudrillard (b. 1929) elucidates several distinctive features of postmodern culture. He highlights postmodern humanity's relationship to objects, images, signs, commodities, the media, and society. He can be insightful on key features of current experience even if his evidence is sketchy. Like Lyotard, his primary focus is on description, but he also formulates theories that illuminate this new era. His thinking develops in three phases. In the first, he updates Marxism with insights about consumer society gained from recent sociology. Further reflection leads him to question Marxism's ability to comprehend both early cultures and postmodern society. He discovers key features of primitive cultures – gifts and rituals – that challenge Marx's theory of production. In the second, he explores the current functioning of signs, media, and "simulacra," and analyzes *hyperreality* – fantasy-infused images (e.g., advertising images) that are experienced as more real than the everyday perceptual world. He also examines postmodern society – especially the indifferent masses – and suggests two possible responses to postmodern discontents: seduction and fatal strategies. The third phase adopts an aphoristic style and explores metaphysical issues, e.g., subject-object, being-appearance.

In his first period, Baudrillard responds to Marxism, first by revising it to account for a new set of phenomena, and later by rejecting it because it cannot adequately comprehend either pre-modern or postmodern societies. This phase's writings include *The System of Objects* (1968), *The Society of Consumption* (1970), *For a Critique of the Economy of the Sign* (1972), and *The Mirror of Production* (1973). These show how the current system of commodities takes on supplementary meanings that must be analyzed independently of the production system. He combines insights from Marx and structuralism to elucidate a new phase of capitalism that centers on consumption rather than production. Consumption bonds people to the capitalist system and legitimates work. Advertising infuses objects with symbolic meanings that inflate their value, eclipsing their use-value. People's desires and fantasies become enthralled with these meaning-enriched consumer goods.[28] The materiality of products and the labor involved in producing them become irrelevant to their value.

Their exchange-value is also superseded by these artificially induced meanings. Baudrillard believes that both enjoyment and usefulness become less important in this era of capitalism. Few actually enjoy the objects they purchase, and their consumption rarely satisfies genuine needs. At best, people enjoy the purchasing, not the products, and even that is often experienced as a mindless ritual. Baudrillard notes that advertising fantasies conceal the numbness most people experience in consumption and implant codes that command spending. The production system is no longer the primary site of subservience;

rather the system of consumption dominates everyone (rich and poor alike). This mesmerizing power of objects remains a consistent theme throughout Baudrillard's career.[29]

Baudrillard gradually becomes more disenchanted with Marxism, eventually rejecting it altogether. Crucial to this change is his study of early cultures, *Symbolic Exchange and Death* (1976). Once he decides that Marx's materialist theory of history cannot account for pre-modern cultures, he becomes more confident in claiming that it also cannot account for postmodern culture. It thus applies only to the modern period. Early cultures were based on symbolic exchange – gifts that celebrate and affirm the status of each participant and exhibit a generosity that transcends utilitarian gain.[30] He draws on the research of Marcel Mauss (1872–1950) and Georges Bataille (1897–1962) in his analysis of pre-modern cultures. Bataille stresses the role of excess, superabundance, and ritualized offerings. In this period, Baudrillard hopes for a return to such generosity. He notes special moments when spontaneous reciprocity emerges in contemporary culture, only to be subverted and co-opted by capitalism. In spontaneous, reciprocal generosity, Baudrillard discovers an ideal against which to evaluate modern and postmodern social relations. Symbolic exchanges express deeper social bonds than those produced by capitalism, which typically involve exploiting others for personal gain.

He uses this analysis of early cultures to re-examine Marx's theories of praxis, alienation, and production.[31] Baudrillard questions whether production and exchange – as these functions operate in capitalism – existed in pre-modern cultures. Although objects are made, they are not "produced"; their relation to their creators is personal, and profit is not the reason they are created. Social relations are based on gifts and recognition – on the spontaneous expression of emotion – rather than on contracts that insure a "fair" exchange. If anything, the participants in a gift-exchange exhibit lavish generosity, offering more than could ever be returned. Objects are not "used" in the same indifferent way; their ritual significance outweighs their pragmatic value. Pre-modern cultures do not experience a division between nature and spirit that motivates technological domination of nature. Neither scarcity, nor law, nor repression is necessary, because gifts, community customs, and rituals provide alternatives. Since alienation is absent, the basis of Marx's critique is lacking. Pre-modern people's ordinary lives also challenge Marxist assumptions: embodying cyclic repetition rather than linear progression, an acceptance of destruction and death as well as joy in creation and renewal, and festivals of Dionysian excess. Baudrillard suggests that Marx's objection to capitalism – that it perverts use-values with market exchange-values – simply misses early cultures' indifference to *either* of these values. Thus, there is no Marxist "mode of production" in these cultures.

He then argues that Marx's concept of use-value is abstracted from – and thus dependent on – exchange value. Marx's socialist ideal – which involves returning to genuine use-values – would not be an alternative to capitalism at all; it would merely render capitalism more efficient and just. Instead of socialism, Baudrillard envisions a postmodern culture that would emulate early societies. In the *Mirror of Production* he connects the struggles of minority groups to this possibility. He argues that workers can no longer produce cultural transformation. Only those outside the system of production – minorities, students, and women – can create such change.[32] He questions the viability of political revolution, calling for a cultural and social transformation instead.

In his second period, Baudrillard develops his own innovative analysis of postmodern society and culture. Its important texts include *In the Shadow of Silent Majorities* (1978), *On Seduction* (1979), *Simulacra and Simulations* (1981), *Fatal Strategies* (1983), and *The Ecstasy of Communication* (1987). His central point is that postmodern culture produces an altered sense of reality. Images and signs become so inflated as a result of fashion, art, and advertising that they become hyperreal. Hyperreal images shimmer with an urgency that eclipses everything else. Everyday life becomes colorless and anemic next to these meaning-infused images disseminated by the media.[33] Baudrillard cites beautiful fashion models who render ordinary people bland by comparison, television characters who overshadow hometown analogs (doctors, lawyers, co-workers, neighbors), designer homes in architecture magazines that make actual houses seem like homeless shelters, the movie-star aura that asphyxiates the real people who are stars, and televised political or athletic events that outdo the actual event (because of replays, multiple angles, and immediate commentaries). Fictions not originating in reality but producing real effects because they are accepted as real are also hyperreal. The simulacra in such cases define the real.[34] Examples include mutually assured destruction scenarios in simulations of nuclear war or political metaphors like "the evil empire" or the "red menace." The hyperreal transforms everyone's sense of reality, dominating more insidiously than the nightmarish visions of dystopian thinkers like Huxley or Orwell because it seems so normal. Baudrillard resists this dystopian interpretation of the postmodern hyperreal, however. He celebrates it – articulating the exhilaration people feel in its presence and clarifying the mechanisms by which it operates.

Baudrillard believes that the relation of the copy (or simulacrum) to the represented object undergoes three major historical shifts before reaching the postmodern era, and language undergoes parallel changes. Initially, the copy refers to an original object and is treated as a counterfeit version of it.[35] In this phase, language is primarily referential, and the sense of reality inheres only in the perception of the original object. Then, in the stage of industrial mass production, the proliferation of "copies" conceals the fact that there is no original object at all, only a set of design specifications. In this stage, language becomes ideological, often pretending to refer to actual events which never existed, and key terms circulate like counterfeit money – without any referents at all. Constant repetition legitimates them, forcing everyone to act as if they have referents. In addition, science erodes human confidence in the everyday perceived world by reducing events to formulas. The scientist's technical terms (e.g., force and energy) seem genuinely real – even if they are unobservable and purely hypothetical – while perceived objects become epiphenomenal. In the third stage, the signs and images become the primary reality, better than any original. This is the era of the hyperreal.[36] Examples that demonstrate the superiority of the copy are computer programs, genetic cloning, xerography, and audio reproduction. This manufactured reality only further distances people from everyday perception. Later Baudrillard identifies a fourth stage, which he calls a "fractal" or "viral" stage of the simulacrum. Here, signs and codes are endlessly replicated without any purpose or rationale. The simulacra dominate subjectivity, which can only submit to the self-sustaining dynamic of virtual reality.[37] War, the economy, and personalities all become virtual (war games, economic models, digital avatars), and the virtual world dominates so completely that living becomes superfluous.

The postmodern era includes the third and fourth stages: the hyperreal and the viral. With the loss of any distinction between the image (simulacrum) and "reality," many other distinctions dissolve (or "implode") as well. If the image is everything, then the accessible surface exhausts all content. No depth can clarify or explain the surface.[38] Baudrillard infers that only effects exist; causes become extraneous postulates, and gradually cause-effect thinking is abandoned. Events happen; they can be more or less intense or fascinating, but they cannot be interpreted or explained. Shimmering surfaces distract and seduce people: their responses are anticipated, programmed, guided (laugh tracks on television shows, advertising imperatives, authorless homilies that everyone reiterates).[39] This relentless programming produces insufferable boredom and irrational violence. The violence may be momentary, but its effects can be catastrophic.

Baudrillard contrasts the second and third eras of simulation by suggesting that postmodernity is an era of screens (film, television, computer) rather than stages (theaters, legislative chambers).[40] Facing the stage, an audience is present at something directly, yielding drama. Watching television (and movie and computer) screens, the audience is only indirectly present at events. When screens mediate events, their impact is reduced. Emotional responses become cooler because audiences remain less invested. Filmmaking tricks allow natural laws to be suspended so that perceptual expectations are shattered. Screened events become pure spectacle. They extend the reach of sensation, but eliminate the need for response. Thanks to CNN, audiences can witness the dismantling of the Berlin Wall or bombing in Belgrade. Now, even when people *directly* participate, their response remains televisual – distantly affectless. People speak to each other as if they were being interviewed on talk shows. This produces isolation, withdrawal, and anxiety. The dominance of screens thus alters peoples' relation to each other as well as to reality; screens may eventually become the preferred mode of communication.[41]

Baudrillard also analyzes postmodern social life. He thinks society and sociality have dissolved, leaving a mass called the silent majority. Since few participate in developing events (most see only the version edited for television), the experience of group action – collectively determined purposive action in pursuit of a common goal – disappears. The experience of sociality disappears simultaneously. The masses learn indifference to the clamoring onslaught of images.[42] To Baudrillard this passivity is a *positive* fact; it shows that the masses can refuse the role assigned to them by advertising.[43] They may not imagine an alternative role, but their indifference resists stereotypical responses. Because social life dissipates, the state, power, and economic class become less important. The masses need not fight power with power because they counteract their screens with passive resistance. Though many theorists might lament such passivity, Baudrillard declares it an effective challenge to the hyperreal. When the masses remain inert and silent, they demonstrate strength. Mass inertia deflects power's imperatives and resists cultural mobilization. A mass cannot act as a collective subject (because it cannot become a unified group), and it cannot be objectified or manipulated (because it does not respond).[44] It can be probed through surveys or modeled with statistics, but it cannot be controlled. When society dissolves, the masses retreat to domesticity and private life, abandoning political Utopia, ideologies, and power strategies. The masses deflate political power by ignoring it. Another factor undermining social life is terrorism (or random violence). Terrorists act blindly, without any effective political goal other than to propagate fear; they also undermine community.[45]

As the social implodes, so does personal selfhood. Affectlessness and enervation become so pervasive that the central philosophical problem becomes proving one's own existence, not the world's.[46] Baudrillard anticipates that the boundaries between self and image will dissolve and that the hyperreal will dominate subjectivity completely. The audience's place is already prepared; their responses already programmed. They become placeholders, replicating the experience of average viewers, each reacting like the others. People either flee from this exposure (and withdraw) or embrace it (selling their life-stories to talk shows). A new inertia and muteness (or anxiety and garrulousness) infect everyone. Since people wait for the screened synopsis of an event before responding to it, screens dominate their reactions. Just as screens control action, the hyperreal governs imagination. Screened images become so potent that human imagination atrophies. Since everything has already been imagined, people become stupefied. Since everything is screened repeatedly, overexposure is endemic. Despite their endless programming, audiences voraciously consume screened images. Even desire dissolves, and sexual responses become automated. Browbeaten by the endless flow of images, most people abandon evaluation and reflection. Since everything has already happened, the natural reaction is: "Been there! Done that! End of story!" Whatever motivated critical, active subjectivity in the past is neutralized by the fateful flow of screened images.[47] Hyperreality thus dominates everyone.

This universal accessibility and continuous repetition of events becomes obscene. Baudrillard compares this process to pornographic movies, which show endless repetition of naked humans in various combinations and positions. These repetitive, superfluous naked bodies evoke minimal response.[48] Sex becomes insufferably boring under such exposure. Actual physical contact with (and genuine desire for) another person becomes passé. Baudrillard claims that only the pose, the invitation, or the evocative tableau produce real stimulation. Some part of the body must be covered or hidden for eroticism to rekindle; mystery becomes an essential element of seduction. Because images are repeatedly screened in precisely the way sex is overexposed, the world itself becomes neutral and bleached. People retreat from all stimulation. Indifference becomes their best defense against incessant solicitations.[49]

Baudrillard suggests two responses to this obscenity: seduction and fatality. Seduction revivifies some elements of symbolic exchange, especially ritual, challenge, and reversibility (to seduce, one must allegedly be seduced – just as to give gifts, one must be given gifts). He opposes seduction to obscene overexposure; it conceals, evokes mystery, and projects unpredictability. Seduction is "cool," manifesting only a desire to provoke another's desire; it requires a reciprocal interaction of scripted challenges and precise responses.[50] Its reciprocity approximates a duel because it makes demands disproportionate to the apparent meaning of its actions. It is a ritual, an initiation into a process that neither partner fully understands or controls, requiring playfulness, curiosity, and exploration. Both partners become giddy or ecstatic through seduction; it becomes shared madness.

Historically, seduction has informed relationships between the sexes, and Baudrillard criticizes feminism because it has inhibited seduction's rebirth. Baudrillard opposes seduction to desire, pleasure, production, and truth. He values seduction over these alternatives because it is riskier and challenges both sexes to live dangerously.[51] Women have often dominated the game of seduction even if men have tended to dominate production. The feminist story of patriarchal oppression ignores this dominance altogether. By seeking greater power and pleasure, feminists abandon seduction, and Baudrillard believes this neuters both sexes. Far from enhancing difference, feminism abandons crucial differences between the sexes. The liberation it advocates undermines women's power of seduction and reduces the challenge of the feminine. He thus views feminism's rise as catastrophic, sullying postmodernity's best hope for recapturing the spirit of symbolic exchange.[52]

Fatality is Baudrillard's second response to the obscene. It meets postmodern reality on its own terms. Fatality describes both a condition of the world (natural and social) and a response to that condition (fatal strategies versus banal strategies). Rationality, referential truth, history, and causation best illuminate the first historical era of simulation (industrial capitalism); they are already problematic in the second era (consumer capitalism) because they express the will and intelligence of subjects. Baudrillard believes that the "object" (the natural world and postmodern cultural reality) has now seized the initiative. Though fatality does imply destiny, it is not fatalism. It allows for chance, chaos, and randomness, and this uncertainty makes the object seductive. Fatality foreshadows the event's end in its beginning; it is cyclic rather than linear.[53] Destiny arrives without being created or produced by anyone, though it can be delayed, and it may involve reversal (the universe first expands, then contracts, and then expands again in endless cycles). Objects or events become both enigmatic and domineering.

Fatal strategies involve mirroring the object's dynamic, doubling it to drive it to excess and triggering premature reversal. In this way, the subject participates in the object, responding to its seduction by seducing in turn. The object (like the masses) is silent, unresponsive, and inert. Fatal strategies mirror that pose.[54] *Banal* strategies, on the other hand, attempt to reassert the power of the subject, a recipe for failure in the postmodern period. The goal of fatal strategies is provocative: to be more seductive than the seductive world. They offer no protest or critique; instead, they play the game of seduction in new ways, using judo-like responses – indirect, cool, uninvolved, without any certainty of success – but also without illusion.[55] Fatal strategies seduce the world into heightened existence.

Thus, in this period, Baudrillard sketches his portrait of postmodernity: the hyperreal, the dominance of screens, the end of sociality and selfhood, and the rise of obscene overexposure. He also suggests two responses: seduction and fatal strategies.

Books relevant to Baudrillard's third period include *America* (1986), *Cool Memories I and II* (1987 and 1990), *The Transparency of Evil* (1990), *The Illusion of the End* (1992), and *The Perfect Crime* (1994). His thought develops in two directions during this period: toward more concrete insights (examining political and cultural developments and new trends in art and social life) and toward a more abstract, encompassing framework. The latter involves explorations of basic philosophical categories, e.g., illusion/reality, being/appearance, object/subject, and identity/difference, which extend and deepen his previous positions. He also considers new theoretical approaches and personal responses to postmodernity. This metaphysical direction is best realized in *The Perfect Crime*.

The major theme of *The Perfect Crime* is that just as modernity murdered illusion by elevating the value of reality, so postmodernity murders reality by celebrating hyperreality. Instead of suffering from a lack of reality, postmodernity suffers from its excess – ecstatic reality.[56] Both the modern experience of reality and postmodern experience of hyperreality are opposed to *illusion*, the experience of the world in the era of symbolic exchange. Illusion exists because subjects can never be absolutely present to objects.[57] When the world's illusoriness became unbearable, reality provided reassurance – banishing the world's mystery and arbitrariness. The increase of meaning, information, and knowledge continues to "dis-illusion" the world; hence, Baudrillard opposes this ongoing avalanche of meaning/reality.[58] He notes that the *modern* experience of reality is only possible in cultures operating at medium speed. When a culture's experience of time is too slow, the sense of reality (and causation and linearity) does not crystallize; when it is too fast, linearity and causation are replaced by repetition and fatality.[59] Baudrillard is amazed that modernity's sense of reality has been so tenacious in the face of current physics, which abandons it entirely.

He also examines the nature of Being as well as the Nothing that existed prior to matter (the void prior to the Big Bang) and the relation of objects to subjects. One reason why he thinks the world itself is seductive is that, as Heidegger claimed, Being withdraws behind appearances, never showing itself fully. Baudrillard imagines the original void to be homogenous, symmetrical, and perfect – a pure illusion. Matter emerges by breaking the symmetry, producing imperfection.[60] Humans expand this imperfection by creating the sense of reality and then hyperreality – continuing to annihilate the Void. Baudrillard believes that the cosmos will cycle through infinite expansions and contractions; its immortality thus will overshadow humanity's mortality. Humanity's apparent drive to self-annihilation may be due to shame over its mortality (if we cannot live forever, let's end it now!).[61] The artifacts and technologies that humans create become autonomous, eventually operating independently of human guidance. "Objects" refers to postmodern hyperreal objects which dominate postmodern subjects. Virtual reality uses people as appendages. As artificial intelligence replaces natural intelligence, human thought may become unnecessary. Humans may abandon forms of thought that cannot be comprehended by computers. Because they are no longer used, such thought-capacities will wither. Technology may atrophy human powers, rather than extending them.[62] Objects will gradually impose their own forms and demands over subjects. Postmodern "objects" are sovereign and inherently meaningless, resisting human efforts to find meaning and to will change. They change at their own pace.

Baudrillard also reinterprets the significance of Derrida's *différance*. He agrees that the severing of Being from itself and of consciousness from itself are inevitable, but notes that such internal divisions are needed for survival and comprehension. Complete identity – the absolute simultaneity and transparency of everything to everything else – would annihilate all thought and all distinction. Thus, the dream of absolute presence is a dream of the subject's death.[63] Thought needs delay and distance to operate; they allow contemplative consideration of options. So does symbolic exchange; gifts should never be reciprocated immediately; the proper return-gift requires careful selection.[64] Perception involves unifying multiple appearances; no single perspective exhausts its content. Persons must transcend themselves to appreciate otherness. The more postmodern speeds approximate simultaneity, the more anti-human postmodern life becomes. The more postmodern life is lived in real time – during which everything is recorded and screened – the more obscene the world becomes. The more the medium becomes hi-definition (television, hi-fi, digital languages, genetic codes, and artificial intelligence), the less content there is to the message.[65] To accept the play of differences would be to abandon the demand for reality (and hyperreality) and embrace illusion. *Différance* is thus humanity's only hope because it preserves mystery and the possibility of seduction.

Baudrillard rejects the value of critical thought because it is impotent against the hyperreal, which eludes its oppositional concepts. If the world redoubled itself in response to modernity's critical thought, then postmodern thought must now redouble itself to outsmart the hyperreal.[66] Baudrillard's new form of radical thought mirrors the hyperreal's excess – embracing illusion, meaninglessness, and the void. This thought uses irony to outdo the complacency of Being. Instead of allowing a coy reality to confirm all hypotheses, thus neutralizing thought, it makes inflated claims to force reality to reveal itself by disconfirming them. This radical thought plays with reality, laughs at it, seduces it, forges reversible concepts that will capture its reversible processes.[67]

It refuses to decipher mystery and acknowledges illusion at the heart of reality – returning to the world more than it receives. Baudrillard's model for responding to the world is Andy Warhol – ironic without being contemptuous, agnostic (suspending belief), without pathos, enigmatic but innocent, without masks. Warhol's art conceals his own contribution, erasing his own will and creativity. It offers no Utopia, no idealization of art, creativity, or subjectivity; instead it presents pure objects – without essence or transfiguration – resistant to meaning and idealization.[68]

If these brief remarks sketch Baudrillard's "system," his notes in *America* provide fresh observations. He develops new metaphors for postmodern life while traveling through America, and he finds many aspects of America emblematic of postmodern reality. Among the metaphors are the desert, the freeway, speed, astral culture, and fractal era. The desert southwest evokes the radical indifference of objects to postmodern subjects.[69] Speeding along a freeway embodies the constant change that prevents taking reality too seriously. Astral culture is untethered to specific locales; it surrounds people even though they are constantly moving.[70] The fractal era is focused on touch rather than sight, on surfaces rather than depth, and on mobility rather than constancy. The Grand Canyon stimulates Baudrillard's discovery of the astral perspective, revealing the void via the finitude of human existence.[71] Running marathons confirm his sense that postmodern people need to prove their own existence; runners' goals are simply to finish, to declare their presence at the event. He marvels at the coexistence of extreme differences (in ethnic groups, in architecture, in moral ideals, in incomes) in America.

Insofar as Baudrillard regards America as an emblem of the postmodern, he both embraces and fears it, calling it at once Utopia and anti-Utopia. He finds *naïveté*, immersion in the present, extravagance, and pure simulation.[72] Americans rarely look beyond the surface, rarely anticipate irony or deception, but this means they have no sense of mystery. He finds social life dominated by vacuous smiles that deflect serious contact or connection; he believes this kind of insularity foreshadows the postmodern future. Americans live in the perpetual present – without awareness of historical precedent or continuity – almost entirely without memory. This allows individuals to remake themselves continually, abandoning past identities. Yet it also allows them to meet situations without presuppositions and discover practical solutions others might overlook. He admires the federal system that allows decentralized social experiments; in contrast, he laments Europe's slavishness to the universal state and its central bureaucracy.[73] But he is aghast at the extravagant excesses in wealth and poverty, hope and violence, hatred and indifference. America's anti-Utopian features include its lack of culture and its indifference to quality.[74] Its immersion in simulation is reflected in the way it offers itself as a model to the world. Americans simply assume other countries want to emulate them. This renders American military power secondary. Americans offer only bracketed belief in their political leaders, the same belief postmodern masses offer to advertisers.[75] America remains indifferent to its rising level of poverty and homelessness, hoping these problems will disappear.

I have only sampled Baudrillard's many concrete observations – usually offered in coy aphorisms. The work in the third period provides broader perspectives to buttress his analysis of postmodernity and elaborates additional supporting observations.

ASSESSMENT

Assessing postmodernism requires answering several questions, Are postmodernists' descriptions of contemporary experience, culture, and thought accurate? Do they capture long-term trends? Is their embrace of these developments justified? Are there defensible, achievable alternatives to them? I will indicate some problems in Lyotard and in Baudrillard separately before considering some flaws common to both.

Lyotard faces several difficulties. First, he does not defend the claim that meta-narratives no longer engender confidence. Many people still rely on them (religious sects, revolutionary movements, and believers in scientific-technological progress). Although these movements may have to reconsider their philosophical foundations if Lyotard is correct, meta-narratives still play a significant role in them. Second, current science is less fragmented than he suggests. Physics is striving to unify the forces it postulates into a single overarching theory. Genetics has unified many sub-disciplines in biology. Many disciplinary sub-fields are reconstituting themselves into larger cross-disciplinary workgroups in the hope of producing greater theoretical coherence. For example, current cognitive science integrates neurophysiology, cognitive psychology, artificial intelligence, computer science, and philosophy of mind; and cultural studies integrates theoretical disciplines and research programs within the humanities and social sciences. Third, the claim that meta-narratives have lost the power to legitimate themselves risks becoming a self-contradictory meta-narrative itself. Fourth, meta-narratives are probably less central to ongoing research, and thus their decline may be less important than Lyotard believes. Finally, Lyotard's willingness to embrace divergence for its own sake remains puzzling; different linguistic practices can achieve working compromises or even consensus without becoming a single all-embracing, total theory/genre.

Lyotard identifies a central issue – the mediation of conflicting linguistic practices. But he assumes, rather than demonstrates, an unbridgeable incommensurability in evaluative standards across discourses. This assumption may be incorrect. Even when it is accurate, acknowledging the rights of each standard may be at best a useful first step, but this step alone will produce few actual adjudications. How, for example, would he resolve a modernist-based challenge to postmodern values? How does attesting to each side help adjudicate the challenge? What is the point of attesting to the difference?

Baudrillard offers daring descriptions, but often inflates his claims beyond plausibility – overgeneralizing and exaggerating. Many people have experienced the hyperreal, but most ignore it during the practical workday and dismiss it during most of their lives. Some may become mesmerized by screens, but most simply find modest release from everyday anxieties in them. Can he defend the claim that the social is dissolving in an era of active social movements? Perhaps communities are being reconstituted outside the electoral system. Many experience his sense of fatalism, but they also resist it and find ways to live responsively, without illusions. Most recognize the temptations of apathy and affectlessness that he describes, but many overcome them and live intensely, especially if they find a self-expressive pursuit. Many sense that imaginative alternatives to the current order are few, but at least some continue to search for them. Any serious description of personal stances on the current era would have take account of differences among classes, nationalities, races, genders, and perhaps other human types; it would need to be less impressionistic and draw on better empirical evidence.

Baudrillard's metaphysical positions are parasitic on other well-known doctrines (e.g., Heidegger's and Derrida's). He offers few new arguments for them, and his evidence remains derivative. His use of the American landscape is inventive, and his descriptions clarify many of his ideas, but they hardly justify them, since counter-evidence to his major points is readily apparent. Midwestern cornfields evoke a different mood than does the desert southwest. Even when Baudrillard appreciates America, the basis for his evaluation seems elusive. The force of his descriptions is supposed to underwrite his evaluative conclusions, but one can agree with the descriptions and reject the evaluations. Even if objects are dominant, their powers should perhaps be resisted. Can Warhol's vacuity really provide a model for responding to the current era? Also, when the source of his evaluative judgments is explicit (e.g., symbolic-exchange cultures), the rationale for maintaining them in the current era is unclear. Why would reinstituting symbolic exchange be culturally valuable? Finally, his specific proposals (e.g., seduction, fatal strategies) seem arbitrary and unlikely to prove beneficial. What plausibility they have derives from being the only options considered.

Though each theorist faces distinct problems, they also share certain successes and failures. Though they may be insufficiently critical of recent developments, they should be applauded for challenging dubious conservative critiques of them. Still, their unreflective endorsement of these changes is smug and unjustified. Change is not good for its own sake, and often they seem to suggest it is. Moreover, the sheer complexity of postmodernist culture calls for a more measured evaluative response that assesses both the enrichment and decadence of postmodern developments. The infatuation with screens, for example, may well induce mindlessness, but the attention to differences produces intellectual refinement. Each trend has to be evaluated on its own merits. Their endorsement of the whole configuration is a global response that postmodernists should question. Such concrete assessments require defensible criteria, however, and their most devastating failure is neglecting to provide them. Even postmodernists' vague endorsement of new social movements (e.g., minority rights) is unwarranted because they offer no basis on which to praise or condemn them.

Some postmodernists associate global, unifying theories with totalitarianism, thus discouraging systematic theory. This connection is problematic, however. The relentlessness with which a theory is believed (and imposed) differs from its scope and degree of coherence. Broad, unifying theories can remain subject to revision and be applied judiciously or experimentally, and sharply delimited theories can be held dogmatically or imposed blindly. Often totalitarian regimes force populations to follow their ideologies, but this does not prove that all systematic theories are imposed on helpless masses. Sometimes ideological uniformity emerges indirectly and despite acknowledgment of diversity because ideas are not taken seriously. This lack of critical discussion may even be encouraged by the belief that all opinions are equivalent and resolution of disagreements impossible. Then people tend to embrace accepted opinion, without coercion, regardless of its generality. Testing the generality of a theory is a way of taking it seriously, determining the limits of its applicability. Thus, systematic thinking can make theorists humble, rather than overzealous.

Moreover, the postmodernists' insistence on divergence (incommensurability) and the death of the subject can be seen as totalizing and overreaching. Some fundamental philosophical disputes may be resolvable. Postmodernists offer nothing to refute this possibility. And subjectivity may be reorganizing itself, recovering an interactive, co-constituting relation with the world. Postmodernists too easily generalize their own partial insights.

Postmodern descriptions assign a central role to art – defining the culture's direction and mood. Postmodernists are keen observers of current artistic trends, and they take art to be revelatory of experiential shifts. One may wonder, however, whether contemporary art – on their own theory – can bear this weight. If all of culture is splintered, can any artist be regarded as exemplary? Artistic trends in the current era are diverse and many-faceted. Serious attention to them would require a more thorough examination, rather than a scattershot citation of examples. Moreover, the postmodernist belief that art is revelatory seems almost nostalgic, even pre-modern. Their own position should disallow privileging any one sphere of culture in this way.

Politically, postmodern theories are minimalist. Although their insistence on local differences and alliance politics can be salutary, it hardly substitutes for a programmatic vision. They do not need all-encompassing or indubitable theories to provide direction or criteria for evaluating current trends. The philosophical task is to guide – not follow – historical developments. After all, Nietzsche hoped to create a new era in human history. Nothing guarantees success, but postmodernists' embrace of the present almost insures failure. Many other Continental movements have also lacked a political vision, but postmodernism aspires to define a new era. Politically, they seem to be victims of the very impotence they document because they abandon both critique and imaginative vision almost entirely. Marxism at least had the courage to challenge current developments and to propose alternatives. Postmodernism's abdication of these tasks leaves people directionless.

Moreover, the depth and permanence of the trends postmodernists describe are uncertain. Already, after only a modest economic expansion (1993–2000), the gloominess surrounding postmodernism seems misplaced. Moreover, even at their most penetrating, postmodern descriptions capture only a fraction of contemporary life. They do not address, for example, personal relationships, community institutions, the positive possibilities of the media (e.g., the internet, public television, and community radio), or current education. Also, many promising political developments are overlooked: the receding grip of bureaucratic totalitarian systems in Eastern Europe, worldwide improvement on environmental reform, and corporate managers' willingness to include the workforce in improving productivity and determining policy. Although these trends require critical scrutiny, they are no less significant than the hyperreal or sectors of incommensurability. Foucault suggests that elucidating the present is perhaps the hardest of philosophical tasks,[76] and postmodernism makes only rudimentary beginnings.

Nietzsche's perspectivism shows that rejecting foundationalism does not require abandoning truth altogether. Researchers in the humanities, in social and biological sciences, in art, and in science can be fallabilisitic in their claims, acknowledge their standpoints' partiality, and still produce intersubjectively verifiable results. Even if meta-narratives no longer produce conviction, researchers may still make progress (and not just within paradigms, either). Moreover, just because no new paradigm or meta-narrative has emerged does not prove that none ever will or that it must be invidiously oblivious to the concrete if it does. Postmodernism commits intellectual hubris when it denies this possibility. Beyond this, researchers can benefit from this absence of a universal paradigm: it encourages more thorough examination of alternatives, invites serious discussion of competing options, and permits an experimentalism that can produce unexpected results.

Postmodernists often take Nietzsche as a source of inspiration. But Nietzsche's critique of the present is more trenchant and better grounded than anything they offer. Moreover, Nietzsche envisions and justifies a positive program for cultural change. If Continental postmodernism is to rise to its potential, these tasks must be resurrected anew.

CONCLUSIONS

In the course of this book, I have sought to achieve several goals. In addition to clear, comprehensible, and reliable expositions of the main figures and movements in post-Kantian Continental philosophy, I have identified their major contributions (in the "Core Contributions" sections), often indicated some useful comparisons with other movements (in the "Comparisons" sections), and suggested some possible objections and questions to explore (in the "Assessments" sections).

In this conclusion, I will pursue four further tasks in order to provide additional perspective. First, I will suggest some important strengths of the Continental tradition as a whole. Second, I will highlight some crucial areas of disagreement among these movements and thus the issues around which the future of Continental philosophy may be decided (I call them "Decision-points").[1] Third, I will indicate some of Continental philosophy's general contributions to specific fields in philosophy (e.g., ethics, metaphysics). I believe the current task of Continental philosophers (wherever they happen to reside) is to use the collective resources of this tradition to address the major issues of philosophy, and I hope the synoptic review offered here will facilitate this. No doubt new movements and new trends will emerge, but I do not expect them to supplant the major achievements of this tradition. In the meantime, there is much productive work to be done that can utilize the innovations of these figures. Finally, I will respond to various objections philosophers of dispersion have made to key Continental figures and movements. These responses will further demonstrate that the basic thrust of this book – to encourage a re-examination and reimagination of all these movements and figures – is warranted.

STRENGTHS AND ACHIEVEMENTS

I begin with some strengths and achievements of Continental philosophy. These can be organized into four main groups: a systematic approach; an examination of some central features of human life, an exploration of key evaluative issues of the times, and a distinctive approach to language and the linguistic dimension of philosophy. One can argue that these factors characterize many of the movements discussed in this book, but I will concentrate here on explaining why I think they are strengths and what they mean.[2]

Partly because they react against Kant's rigid dichotomies and partly because they believe philosophical questions are fundamentally interlocked, Continental philosophers favor systematic treatments over isolated discussions of specific issues and, for the most part, they rely on a conception of totality or holism in understanding culture, history, and human life. Probably the most evident difference between Continental and Anglo-American approaches to philosophy is this disagreement about the value of system versus isolated analysis of specific issues, even though a growing sense of holism in philosophy of mind and language is emerging in recent Analytic philosophy. Largely because of the influence of Hegel, Continental thinkers' thought-systems rarely become abstract or disconnected from everyday life. Hegel strove to capture the "concrete universal" in all of his systematic treatments, the concepts that illuminate the distinctive features of the whole. Other Continental philosophers have followed him. They clarify the subtleties of a phenomenon even as they trace its deeper connections to related phenomena. They examine an entire network of issues, rather than isolating one. Thus, they do not allow their aspiration toward system to overshadow lived reality. Nor do they dismiss careful discussion of specific issues or the value of distinctions and analysis; they simply maintain a broader systematic awareness as well. The value of this approach is that it allows philosophers to test their positions in many different spheres to determine their fecundity and potential problems. Such systematic thinking emulates science's demand to test a theory in many different contexts.

This embrace of systematic thinking takes several forms. I have already mentioned the Continental tradition's sense of the interconnectedness of philosophical questions. Nearly everyone who attempts creative work in philosophy senses these deeper connections, even if they are difficult to articulate. Beyond this, their answers to specific questions often benefit from exploring the variety of viewpoints that emerge when implications are developed. Thus, many pursue Nietzschean perspectivism, attempting to see phenomena with many eyes at once, rather than relying on a single perspective or method. In addition, Continental philosophers regularly rethink the history of thought and culture in order to understand the current situation more deeply and completely. This tendency also descends from Hegel, and it produces the broader canvas on which Continental thought typically operates. One value of this historical perspective is that it improves prescriptions for present problems because they may have parallels in other eras or because their sources are better understood. Another benefit of this perspective is its revelation that certain strategies have already been tried and found wanting, and this can also improve chances of finding more effective alternatives. Still another kind of systematic awareness operates when Continental philosophers seek to explore the real life implications of their innovations. They realize philosophy has important everyday life applications, and they strive to make these explicit. When these applications are illuminating, this type of systematic awareness is beneficial.

Finally, Continental philosophers typically treat phenomena holistically (at whatever level: mental, personal, interpersonal, social, cultural, or historical). In some areas these totalities may be looser, but the systematic character of Continental thought ultimately derives from the sense that life (and every sphere it encompasses) is a totalization in process, a developing whole whose parts are deeply interconnected. Even when this picture is challenged (e.g., in post-structuralism), the dispersion hypothesis is extended to all sectors and thus is taken to characterize all reality.

This systematic impulse gives Continental philosophy a different relationship to the empirical sciences from the one that other traditions of philosophy adopt. They do not dismiss science, but they are not in awe of it either. They understand science to be an extension of philosophy (often having emerged from earlier philosophical investigations) that never fully escapes its philosophical roots. They thus learn from the sciences while also retaining a critical perspective. Each science operates within its own, sometimes limited, philosophical assumptions and conceptual framework. These can be interrogated and sometimes productively revised by attentive philosophical examination, especially if it acknowledges the value and achievements of the science involved. Even when Anglo-American philosophers saw philosophy as an independent discipline involving conceptual analysis, they often picture it as subservient to science, as merely preparatory to science's serious knowledge-creation. Continental philosophers refuse to cede this accolade to the sciences even when they respect scientific achievements. There are risks in this approach since, if the knowledge one incorporates into one's philosophical system is superseded, then one's system may be correspondingly weakened. But at least one's results bear on the actual scientific thought of the era.

A second strength of Continental philosophy is its careful examination of some central features of human life. We are, after all, human, and any philosophical tradition that can provide deeper understanding of human existence is to be valued both for its own sake and for its ability to contribute to better living and more incisive self-understanding. Here is a brief survey of some of the key areas explored by the Continental tradition: the primacy of practical life and freedom; the sociality of human existence; the centrality of time consciousness and of embodiment; emotions, moods and feelings; imagination; factors operating beneath explicit consciousness – whether these are psychic instincts, economic forces of production, conceptual frameworks, or taken-for-granted cultural norms and understandings; and selfhood and individuality. These features are examined not only in existentialism and philosophical anthropology, but also in nearly all other Continental movements.

Although Continental philosophy does not dismiss cognition and theoretical knowledge, it often subsumes them as types of purposive action. Continental philosophy is often anti-Platonic because it contends that Plato overvalued reason and deliberation. When they see reason as essential, Continental philosophers invariably broaden their conception of it (as Hegel and hermeneutic thinkers do). Because their conception of reason is richer, they are less obsessed with formal logic. They believe creative thought cannot be formalized, and their goal is genuine creativity. Hegel had to produce an entirely new kind of logic to capture the complex paths along which human thought actually develops. Others – like Marx, Nietzsche, and Heidegger – simply see practice as more pervasive, necessary, and universal than reason. Reason is treated as just one type of goal-directed activity.

Giving primacy to practice insures that the analysis and value of freedom are central issues in Continental philosophy. The Continental tradition challenges contemporary culture because it subverts genuine freedom. Many Continental philosophers reject the liberal notion of freedom, which involves making choices in a context of minimal obstacles. Instead they elaborate a conception of freedom that integrates social life and requires genuine self-expression, making freedom's achievement more difficult in practice.

The anti-Platonic or anti-cognitive dimension of Continental philosophy has produced an intense exploration of human emotions, both in general and for particular types. Schopenhauer and Nietzsche stress the primacy of the conative dimension of human life and explore the dynamics of emotions like resentment, pride, sympathy, and self-hatred. Both insist that the entire psyche is organized around the passions. Heidegger provides a penetrating analysis of the pervasiveness of moods and their relationship to a person's sense of possibility and self-understanding. Scheler believes emotions provide a distinctive insight into value and offers subtle analyses of sympathy, resentment, shame, love, and suffering. Sartre also offers a general analysis of emotions that interprets them as ineffective forms of action. Merleau-Ponty sees them as deeply interwoven into the dynamics of the lived-body's relationship to the world. Thus, Continental philosophy has begun to redress the balance between reason and passion in philosophy, demonstrating that emotions play a pervasive role in human life.

While many Continental philosophers value individuality, they do not oppose this to the essential sociality that defines all human life. Hegel and Marx take interpersonal recognition to be necessary to any genuine solidarity and individuality; it is the social sustenance of individuality. Nietzsche takes his distinctive version of friendship to be necessary for full self-realization. Freud claims that the internalization of parental dictates is essential to humanity's moral conscience. Scheler claims that children literally share the thoughts, feelings, and values of their families and that this openness to mental "infection" continues throughout our lives. Heidegger takes an individual's cultural background to constitute her average everyday mode of existence and the starting point for achieving of authenticity. Thus, authentic selfhood is only a modification of established forms of life. Sartre takes the Other's look to create an unavoidable dimension/definition of oneself, which is then contested in many types of human relationships. These are just a few Continental thinkers who articulate ways in which other people constitute human life and selfhood.

Selfhood does not only have social dimensions, however. It is essentially related to one's projects and chosen tasks, to reflection on one's past, to tacit self-awareness and explicit self-monitoring. Insofar as selfhood is essentially related to self-consciousness and introspection, the German Idealists extensively explored its sources. Selfhood may also involve an idealized vision of oneself that haunts one's self-evaluation and one's actions, the object of shame and esteem. It includes one's most valued character traits and distinctive talents, which constitute Nietzsche's conception of self-perfection. It may also require tacit memory and an implicit experience of unity across time. Selfhood can be elusive, and poststructuralists have argued it is a false ideal, a trap that enslaves. These examples show that Continental philosophy has explored many elements and dimensions of individuality and selfhood, a study that complements its exploration of essential social relations in human life.

Equally important is lived temporality, whether it is forward-looking toward the future or backward-looking toward the past or simply concerned with the flux of the present. Human life is essentially temporal and thus historical. Similarly, human life is essentially embodied, and the lived body possesses practical know-how, directly grasps cultural meanings, and expresses the whole person. From Nietzsche and Freud to Husserl and Merleau-Ponty and on toward Foucault and the French feminists, humans are conceived as essentially embodied, and though poststructuralists may challenge the personal and historical unity provided by lived time, they acknowledge its flux and the importance of embodiment. Indeed Foucault thinks that the modern institutional domination of the lived body (by schools, corporations, prisons, clinics, and asylums) is tantamount to total oppression. Again, in part because of Plato's high evaluation of contemplation and Descartes's dismissiveness toward a merely "mechanical" body, Continental philosophy has had to resuscitate its importance.

Finally, even if many Continental figures have stressed lived experience, few have forgotten the dimensions of human life that operate beneath conscious awareness, whether these are background cultural norms or subconscious drives. Structuralists and poststructuralists stress the centrality of underlying cognitive rules that organize all experience. Nietzsche, Freud and their psychoanalytically oriented successors highlight unconscious drives. Nietzsche also argues that many emotional factors and one's orientation to a situation operate beneath explicit awareness. Hegelians and Marxists explicate structures of history, technology, and culture that operate often without the comprehension of individuals who are governed by them. Perhaps one of the most urgent questions in the tradition is how to integrate insights discovered from the analysis of lived experience with these unconscious factors. The two kinds of feature need not be incompatible, but the way they work together needs more careful discussion.

A third strength of Continental philosophy is its willingness to face the difficult value questions of the times. The crises of Western culture certainly exist; this tradition strives to address them, and in this way contributes to cultural advance. First, it identified the emerging problem of nihilism early (with Nietzsche), and it has sought effective answers to this challenge ever since. Nihilism is the sense that life has lost all meaning and value in the wake of God's death and the inability to provide absolute justification for basic human values. Nietzsche's general answer to this problem is that humans have to prove their own value, individually and collectively, and Continental philosophers have examined various transformation strategies for elevating and perfecting humanity. In effect, they have continued Nietzsche's quest. Second, Nietzsche's project of revaluing all values has forced Continental philosophers to examine the weaknesses and destructiveness of Western culture and attitudes, and they have not flinched from penetrating indictments of contemporary culture and politics. Nor do they remain content with mere criticism, for they also sketch alternative futures, ways that humanity might achieve a richer culture that better supports human flourishing. Definitive answers on these questions have not yet been achieved, but at least the questions are taken seriously, instead of being buried in indifference. These projects scrutinize some of the guiding ideals of modernity – reason, equality, fraternity, and liberty. Continental philosophers' critical efforts provide a counter-weight to the arrogance of many Western attitudes.

Finally, Continental philosophy has not been oblivious to the core issues that dominate the Anglo-American tradition, viz., clarifying language's nature and philosophical implications. This topic is important because neither philosophy nor developed thought can exist without language; so understanding its operations is crucial to achieving philosophy's goals. Foucault, Derrida, and Lyotard all provide a thorough examination of the operations of language, and show how their conceptions both subsume and supersede previous theories. Although both traditions have at times harbored suspicions about the value of ordinary language, the strategy of seeking a perfected or idealized language has not been pursued in Continental philosophy. Perhaps Continental figures believe that an entirely new system of concepts is needed; perhaps they believe that the effort to formalize logic simply reiterates many of the mistakes embedded in ordinary language. Whatever the reason, they lack the confidence in formalization schemes that Anglo-American philosophers appreciate. Earlier figures, like Nietzsche, Gadamer, Hegel, Merleau-Ponty, and Habermas, note how essential language is to interpersonal understanding and social relationships, as well as thought. Moreover, they attend to the ways in which language operates in philosophy itself: its reliance on metaphor, distinctions and dichotomies, and special rhetorical forms (e.g., dialogue, meditation, treatise). The way language develops philosophical insights is often distinctive, and at least Continental philosophers attempt to gain some degree of self-understanding about this. They establish a more self-reflective and self-critical stance toward their own formulations, and this allows them to achieve a degree of openness to challenge from other standpoints. Still no Continental philosopher has attempted the attentive study of philosophical insights embedded in inherited ordinary language offered by J. L. Austin. This is one area in which Continental approaches to language could be profitably supplemented.

Thus Continental philosophy makes some distinctive contributions to the study of language, in addition to exploring important value issues of the era, essential features of human life, and offering a systematic treatment of philosophical issues. This approach seems at once more relevant to issues of everyday life and more intellectually searching, earnestly pursuing the ramifications of its creative insights.

DECISION-POINTS

Here I will indicate some core issues that divide the major thinkers within this tradition, issues on which no synthesis or compromise is likely to be forthcoming and thus issues on which the future of the discipline may depend. I will discuss them under two general rubrics: metaphysical-epistemological-methodological issues and value issues. Within the first set, I will elucidate five decision-points: dialectic versus dispersion; ahistorical essence versus variation; interpretation versus description; expanded reason versus irrationalism; and realities versus illusions concerning the self. Within the values set, I will clarify three decision-points: embracing versus challenging the ideals of modernity; the capacity of higher culture to promote self-perfection; and foundational issues in value theory. Among the more disturbing facts is that these basic disputes are rarely debated seriously. Partisans adopt one alternative without seriously examining evidence for the other side. Indeed, too often these decision-points are gulfs across which opponents shout, rather than issues subject to analysis and argument. Although I cannot attempt to provide answers to these controversies here, my goal is to pose them properly.

Several decision-points are metaphysical disputes. Perhaps the most important of these is the contest between those who favor some version of a dialectical model of reality and thought (Hegel, Marx, Sartre, Merleau-Ponty) and those who completely reject this model (e.g., Foucault, Derrida, Deleuze). The issue involves at least three disagreements. The first question is whether history has an underlying pattern and whether this pattern ultimately yields progress. Both Hegel and Marx insist that there is a pattern and that it does produce progress, whereas Foucault insists that there are fundamental historical breaks that shatter all patterns, and thus that progress is illusory; discourses within one era are incommensurate with those in another. The pattern and progress features of this issue are actually independent, for there may be progress even if there is no inherent pattern, and there may be a pattern that constantly produces regress. Moreover, dialectics does not anticipate a simple linear pattern; rather, it expects moments of negation and moments of transcendence that eventually produce higher unifications. The second question is whether various movements and discourses within an era have an organic or disparate relation to one another. The dialecticians hold that at least some degree of organic coherence operates within eras, while Foucault and perhaps Deleuze (with his rhizome model) defend a claim of dispersion. On this issue, historical eras might, at least in principle, differ; some may exhibit a high degree of coherence and organicity and others less so. The third question is whether there are *any* totalities or organic systems (those with internal relations among their parts) (and whether thought systems are best understood using this metaphor). Obviously, organic systems themselves are prime candidates for instantiating the dialectical model, but Merleau-Ponty insists that the metaphor also captures the relation between persons and their environments (natural, cultural, and linguistic). Hermeneutics also posits a weak organic relation between interpreters and their backgrounds. Indeed Foucault suggests a similar background coherence between institutional rules and their subjects. On this question, if Derrida's concepts of *différance*, supplement, copula (etc.) describe a fundamental metaphysical fact, then he will probably be the strongest challenger to the dialectical model. Here, too, the real issue concerns the breadth of application of the organic-dialectical versus the dispersionist model. Each side has its favored examples; both pictures could be more fully tested against realities they do not usually consider. Moreover both sides win adherents by claiming that significant political and ethical implications flow from their positions. These claims also need more detailed scrutiny.

A second decision-point concerns whether there are ahistorical essences either in human nature or in nature as a whole that are unaffected by differences in culture, historical period, race, sex, or environment. On this issue phenomenologists and structuralists as well as Nietzsche (will to power) and Freud (basic drives that seek pleasure and destruction) stand on one side (essentialism), while the dialecticians (Hegel, Marx, Marxists), poststructuralists, and postmodernists typically stand on the other (anti-essentialism). Most members of the hermeneutic tradition straddle this opposition by claiming that interpretation is an essential, invariant human capacity, but that it is shaped and influenced by background, context, and history at every point. One could argue that Hegel (the struggle for recognition, freedom) and Marx (productive activity) also posit a small number of invariant, essential features even though they may assume different forms in different eras. Among phenomenologists, Husserl insists that intentionality is an invariant feature of mental acts, and he is opposed to the idea that the laws of logic might vary across cultures and historical eras. Moreover, the existential phenomenologists isolate "existentials" or invariant structures by which human beings are related to the practical environment (being-in-the-world), to themselves (self-interrogation, self-definition), and to other people (the They-self; the look), regardless of culture or era. Structuralists identify invariant cognitive operations governing meaning-production and comprehension; these processes do not vary by culture or era. On the other side stand Foucault, who attacks all constants and invariants, and those hermeneutic thinkers who believe every feature of the mind is conditioned by its social and intellectual background, which varies historically. Most poststructuralists believe that dispersion is an essential feature of reality itself, not a purely contingent fact.

Positions on this question can be articulated on both a general and a specific level. Those on either side have to give some plausible evidence for thinking that cultural and intellectual factors either do or do not organize the mind all the way down. On the specific level, one has to consider each proposed invariant capacity or structure to determine whether in fact it has been invariant across eras, cultures, and human types. Empirical research on non-Western cultures as well as remote historical eras should prove instructive. Probably some invariant structures do exist, but their value implications may need careful assessment. Still each specific proposed invariant structure must be taken on its merits, despite the general arguments on the matter. Here, as on many other questions, the general arguments are only as strong as the particular cases that support them. Essentialism need not be invidious (as is often claimed), but establishing an essentialist claim is a difficult task.

A third metaphysical-epistemological decision-point is related to the second. It concerns whether mind's relation to reality (e.g., nature, other people, history, or one's own occurrent mental states) invariably is interpretive in the sense that it is mediated by structures (foreground or background) that alter that reality (or one's access to it), or whether one can have purely descriptive, unmediated access to that reality. On this issue, most phenomenologists and philosophers who accept a robust concept of intuition (e.g., Bergson, Schopenhauer, and Husserl) believe that unmediated access is possible, while Nietzsche, most hermeneutic thinkers, and Derrida fall on the other side. Others, such as Foucault and Marx, think that the people they analyze can only have mediated access to reality, while also believing that they, as investigators, can have unmediated access to the conceptual schemes or socio-economic systems conditioning those they investigate. Some phenomenologists, like Husserl, think one typically has unmediated access to one's own states of mind, while others, like Sartre, think such access is *possible* (when reflection is purified) but not *typical*. Moreover, those who claim one's access is always necessarily mediated differ on how damaging this fact is. Nietzsche, for example, thinks that one's relation to anything is always perspectival (and thus oversimplifying) but that one can compensate for these simplifications by examining a variety of perspectives on the same phenomenon. This may not provide the unvarnished truth, but it can produce a gradually more adequate grasp of truth.

One argument, typically taken to definitively demonstrate the truth of the mediated-access position, is that all claims about reality must be formulated in language; hence language always mediates one's access to that reality. This argument is not unassailable, however, since one might state or report one's unmediated access in language in a fully adequate fashion without the structure of the language corrupting one's access to reality. One might, for example, report the color of an object, the psychological state that one is experiencing, or the goal one is seeking without the language in which that report is given corrupting one's access to the phenomena. The researcher's powers of description are tested here, not the opacity of language itself. One relies on concepts, but the concepts themselves need not distort one's experience. On this issue, too, both general and specific arguments must be closely examined. On the one hand, defenders of the mediated-access position must show that any *possible* claim for unmediated access is wrong, and this requires refuting existing, as well as possible future, proposals. They must also show that the mediated access is epistemologically invidious. If the medium is diaphanous, then no adulteration will occur. Also, the tensions within split positions (like Foucault's), which hold that access to discursive formations can be unmediated (at least retrospectively) but also claim such formations condition access to reality for agents within them, must be resolved. On the other hand, those defenders of unmediated access must not only provide convincing examples; they must also show why linguistic (or other) factors do not corrupt one's intuitions of reality once described. At stake in this issue is the significance and possibility of intuition.

A fourth metaphysical decision-point pits those who believe that reason must be enhanced in order to be able to comprehend complex, multidimensional, or exotic sectors of reality against those who think reason's limitations are too great to encompass them. In this debate, Hegel, Nietzsche, hermeneutics, and phenomenology (the enhancers) stand opposed to poststructuralists (especially Foucault) and Lyotard (and possibly Marx) (the deflators). In Continental philosophy the claim that the discursive reason used in deductive and inductive logic is sufficient to clarify all spheres of reality is viewed with skepticism. Moreover, at the birth of Continental philosophy Kant insisted that pure reason (i.e., metaphysical speculation) had to be confined within specific limits, and he asserted that practical ethics and aesthetic judgment might involve distinct types of reason. Those who seek to enhance reason are simply following this lead. For example, Hegel developed dialectical reason to comprehend history's stages of development (as well as mind's); Scheler explored a logic of emotions; Merleau-Ponty a logic of perception; and Nietzsche a just adjudication of perspectives. Each tried to enhance the powers of reason to do justice to a refractory area. On the other side, Foucault contends that there are definite epistemic breaks within the history of thought and that arguments and evidence cannot bridge such divisions because what constitutes evidence for one position will be irrelevant to another, and because the assumptions and rules governing knowledge in the new discursive formation will be incommensurate with those in the former one. Lyotard also claims that certain issues are not subject to rational adjudication because the assumptions informing each position are too disparate. These deflators have reintroduced skeptical difficulties about reason that still must be answered.

A related issue concerning reason involves its role in psychic functioning. Here the opposition is between thinkers who take rational autonomy both as an ideal and a real possibility in opposition to those that think the psyche is governed by factors alien to reasons or rational rules. On the irrationalist side stand Marx, Nietzsche, Freud, Bergson, Scheler, Sartre, Foucault, and Deleuze, while on the rationalist side stand Hegel, Husserl, and Habermas. Those who argue against the psychic hegemony of reason do so from a variety of different standpoints. Some argue that ideologies or power-knowledge frameworks or drives undermine any attempt to achieve purely rational self-control. Others argue that emotions provide a more primordial access to reality, while still others argue that reason is the servant of the will or drives or life-force. Those who claim that reason at least *can* become master of its own house acknowledge that its victory requires a strenuous effort to overcome background influences (both unconscious and emotional), and even then the battle is never completely won.

The two interpretations of this decision-point are not identical, and the larger skeptical implications that follow from insisting on the limits of reason in the first case do not necessarily obtain in the second. Nietzsche provides an important example here. He thinks that drives and the will (which itself consists of many complex factors) dominate the human psyche, and thus he rejects the very possibility of a completely objective standpoint, but this does not prevent him from asserting that various drive-based perspectives can correct and supplement one another in such a way that a more complete truth can be achieved. At stake in this issue is whether philosophy can contribute to the solutions of psychic conflicts, since reason – even in an expanded sense – is its primary tool.

A fifth decision-point is really a series of issues concerning the variety of capacities associated with human selfhood and agency, e.g., consciousness, self-consciousness, will, reflection, imagination, memory, individuality, and self-transformation. One issue is which of these capacities are essential to agency; another is whether there is or can be an autonomous self. There are probably as many distinct analyses of selfhood as there are movements in the tradition; all of them adopt diverse stances on the importance and value of the various capacities listed above. Husserl, for example, places great premium on time-consciousness, while Sartre highlights a person's fundamental project. Nietzsche, however, challenges the importance of both consciousness and self-consciousness without thereby rejecting the possibility of genuine self-transformation through consciously organizing and stylizing one's drives. Foucault virtually dismisses the will and the intellect as independent sources of initiative, but he too, in his last phase, seems to allow some capacity for self-transformation resulting from self-critique. Thus, although nearly everyone agrees that the transcendental ego must be rejected, many disputes exist concerning the nature and constitution of the empirical ego. The issue of autonomy is important in Continental philosophy because many movements claim that the self is socially constituted to some degree. Such social constitution typically compromises autonomy (and its related notions of self-sufficiency and self-mastery). One question is whether autonomy is possible at all; another is whether it is worth pursuing since it often isolates people from their surroundings and their cohorts.

A second group of decision-points concern value issues. This group includes debates about the value of modernity (and Enlightenment ideals), about cultural institutions, and about the foundations of value theory. These decision-points concern which direction to pursue, how to do it most effectively, and how to justify the transformation.

Perhaps the most important issue in this group concerns the revaluation of modernity's basic values, e.g., reason, happiness, liberty, equality, and fraternity. Here Hegel, Marx, and Habermas stand at one extreme (fundamentally enthusiastic about the possibilities of modernity) and Nietzsche and Heidegger at the other extreme (deeply skeptical about the basic directions of modernity – while seeking some alternative), with a variety of thinkers enthusiastic about some of these values, but less so about the others (e.g., Sartre, Foucault). Those antagonistic to modernity can be forward-looking (e.g., Nietzsche) or backward-looking (e.g., Heidegger), and many postmodernist theorists do not actually revalue, but instead often embrace, many features of the present (e.g., Baudrillard). Those seeking to revalue modernity's dominant values must produce a coherent method and rationale for doing this. Those who value modernity sometimes believe its core ideals are subverted by the dominant political-economic order; thus, they take the social realities of modernity to be in "contradiction" with its founding ideals and seek to create alternative institutions to better realize them. Their justificatory task is less demanding because a consensus favoring these values already exists. The critical-Utopian stance described as a strength above derives from Continental efforts to force current institutions to make good on their promises or to transform modernity's values into something more defensible.

Equally important is the effort to clarify the effectiveness of various institutions in achieving some future, more promising culture. Some relevant institutions are the state, the arts, popular movements, and philosophy. The disputes concern whether these institutions can produce genuine change and which among them are most effective. Some are sharply critical of the state (Marx, Nietzsche), while others think a reorganization of the state can make a significant contribution to a better future (Hegel). Others minimize the state's role and produce an alternative analysis of institutional power practices that must be opposed and transformed by local popular movements (Foucault, Deleuze). Some believe that art can make significant contributions not just to raising consciousness of the need for cultural change, but in directing and imagining this change (Nietzsche, Marcuse). Marx himself and perhaps Freud are more skeptical of the transformative power of art. Marx and the poststructuralists question the pretensions of philosophy to discover and justify positive change, while Hegel and Nietzsche believe philosophers have a central creative role in making the transition to a more promising future through retrospective comprehension, cultural diagnosis, and value creation. Marx thinks only revolutionary activity which gains control of the means of production will establish lasting change, while some poststructuralists and feminists believe that revising thought can be the lever of cultural transformation. The issue here is not just the most effective strategies for change, but the most effective target for change, the institutions around which contemporary culture revolves.

Finally, the thinkers in this tradition offer various strategies to support the value assessments that underlie these recommendations. On this issue there is not so much direct opposition as a plurality of positions, the relationships among which are unexplored. Hegel, for example, roots many of his value assessments in the historical process itself. Nietzsche defends his ideals naturalistically – as enhancing self-organization (power) already operative in the life-process. Scheler grounds his value assessments in an emotional intuition that illuminates an objective hierarchy of values and governs the aspirations of culture and persons. The existentialists defend a conception of authenticity that expresses itself within a tradition and self-consciously defines its goals, while maintaining a lucid awareness of reality. Levinas and Buber locate their ideals in a specific relation to other people that conditions the entire experience of value. None of these positions is necessarily incompatible with the others, but they are quite different. Future work in the tradition on the sources of value assessment will benefit from a close examination and critique of these attempts.

These eight issues – dialectic versus dispersion, essences versus history, interpretation versus description, expanded reason versus irrationalism, the possibilities and limits of selfhood, the revaluation of modernity's values, the role of specific institutions in achieving cultural transformation, and the sources of value assessment – provide a map of decision-points that begins to delineate the current space of Continental philosophy.

SPECIFIC FIELD CONTRIBUTIONS

Most needed today perhaps is an effort by current Continental thinkers to use the many insights already achieved to address various current philosophical problems, perhaps in cooperation with the Analytic (or Anglo-American) tradition. In an effort to show how this project might be pursued, I shall indicate some contributions of Continental thought to various fields of philosophical research: ethics, politics, aesthetics, metaphysics and epistemology, philosophy of mind (or philosophical anthropology), social theory, and the nature of philosophy itself. In these brief sections, I will not attempt to be exhaustive, but rather suggestive. I indicate some significant contributions, but each area could be given a much fuller elaboration. I will begin with contributions to value theory and continue with the more theoretical areas of philosophy.

In ethics, Continental philosophers depart from the two dominant approaches in the Analytic tradition: consequentialism and deontology. Perhaps consequentialism has been shunned because it is difficult to apply in practice (because consequences are hard to predict and the range of people affected is hard to pinpoint), or because its typical analysis of goodness (happiness or pleasure) is too limited to be taken seriously. Kantian deontology is considered too formalistic and too arbitrary, too easily tethered to an acceptance of the status quo, and too antithetical to the emotional and interpersonal affiliations that give ethical life its motivation and content. The tradition of virtue ethics (Aristotle), which is being resurrected in Analytic ethics, was revitalized in Continental philosophy by Nietzsche through his perfectionism and ethics of character. He roots his constructive ethics naturalistically in a theory of life (two key Nietzschean values are life-enhancement and life-affirmation), aesthetically (the value of creativity), and intrinsically in the value of self-development toward something higher, nobler, and personally fulfilling. Nietzsche believes that there are various types of people and that different types should pursue distinct sets of virtues. Indeed, that ethically serious people find their own energizing virtues is central to Nietzsche's vision. He also develops a theory of untimeliness and self-challenge which puts one's natural talents and early ideals through an intense testing process, which both strengthens those that survive and insures some degree of mastery over (even) one's virtues. Beyond this, he subjects the values of received moralities to a severe critique, thus facilitating a revaluation of values, a project that will determine which values most contribute to human flourishing and to the successful development of different human types. In general, both Nietzsche's critical and constructive ethics seek to defuse the threat of nihilism, a threat still not taken seriously enough by many Analytic ethicists.

At least four other major contributions to ethical theory can be identified.[3] First, though the goal of Hegel's politics and ethics is self-realizing freedom that recognizes itself in its social, political, and natural environments, his point of departure is existing customs, social norms, roles, and ways of life. Alasdair MacIntyre elaborates a position like this when he tries to demonstrate a necessary relation between personal identity, institutional practices, and narrative life history. Hegel believes that "ethics" cannot really be separated from social institutions, and he explicates the important phenomenon of interpersonal recognition to elaborate both a social ideal of solidarity and a basis for mutual self-enhancement. Thus, he examines the social preconditions of flourishing, as well as identity-formation.

Scheler develops a value realism rooted in the "vision" that human emotions make possible. He also offers subtle analyses of ethically significant emotions – like sympathy, shame, resentment, and love – and examines their ethical implications. He believes that emotions attune people to an objective value hierarchy, only segments of which are compelling for each individual. Thus, to appreciate the entire hierarchy individuals and cultures must learn to co-experience the value-attunements of other individuals and cultures. Among Analytic ethical theorists, perhaps Michael Stocker's position lies closest to Scheler's. Scheler also stresses the central role of model persons in human flourishing, and he shows the importance of ethical tenor (which circumscribes the values to which each person is drawn) to personal identity by showing that even the will is constrained by a person's tenor. Thus, one cannot even describe persons' identities without knowing the value-constellation that governs their basic moral tenors.

In addition, Levinas and Buber attempt to root ethical values in face-to-face personal relations. Levinas believes that the source of ethical obligation is direct responsiveness to the distinctiveness of the other, which must be acknowledged, whether this is expressed in powerlessness or assertiveness. For Levinas, this ethical relation is even more fundamental than the experience of being itself. On the other hand, Buber thinks that a distinctive "I–Thou" relationship enables reciprocity and mutual enhancement among persons without merging them. He contrasts this with the more typical "I–It" relationship, in which another person is used, objectified, or dismissed and thus becomes merely a function of one's own pursuits. Levinas insists on the *asymmetry* between the other and the self (when the obligation to the Other is uppermost, I can only respond to it), while Buber holds that the responses each person makes to the other are *symmetrical* (i.e., both achieve I–Thou, or both remain in I–It).

Both thinkers, however, locate the heart of ethical life in the dynamic of these fundamental interpersonal relations, rather than in principles, motives, consequences, self-perfection, or communal norms.

Finally, Heidegger and Sartre develop a distinctive ideal of personal responsibility they call authenticity, though the conditions each believes essential to achieving it differ. Initially, Sartre's ideal is formal: simply acknowledging one's implicit value commitments, comprehending one's situation clearly, and acknowledging responsibility for one's choices. Heidegger's version involves an assessment of and affiliation with one strand of one's historical tradition as well as acknowledging death as an ever-present possibility so that one's choices are made resolutely. In his *Notebooks for an Ethic*, Sartre tries to build some substantive value commitments into his notion of authenticity; these include a dedication to the freedom of others, spontaneity, and truthfulness. Foucault elaborates Sartre's ideal of personal freedom and responsibility by arguing that it can be won only by constantly challenging the existing social order and through continuous self-critique. This critical and self-critical stance is also stressed by Western Marxist thinkers, who think it is required to prevent being co-opted by advanced capitalism and to challenge ideological distortions to which one may have succumbed. These are some of the distinctive Continental contributions to ethical theory.

In political theory Continental philosophers also explore unique positions. Hegel's notion of pure recognition functions as an important political value for human communities, and Hegel shows how the state can make positive contributions to the realization of citizens' freedom. He also stresses the role of unions and professional associations in the representation of group interests and the value of an independent bureaucracy to resolve conflicts among such groups. Though Marx is highly critical of the bourgeois state (because he believes it is merely a tool for the wealthy), later Marxists develop a more complex and sympathetic analysis of culture and the state, showing that challenges to the dominant ideology are necessary if serious social transformation is to occur. Nietzsche challenges many modern political ideals, such as equality and democracy; instead he would pursue a meritocracy, whose leaders would stimulate and oversee a cultural renaissance that would contribute to a more widespread achievement of self-perfection among citizens. Hermeneutic thinkers conceive of law as a self-organizing, self-transforming system that requires constant reinterpretation in order to remain vital and to inform new social practices. Sartre views the state as an institution that can render the collective action of groups inert and ineffective; only if various action-groups acknowledge common purposes can there be a basis for consent to and legitimation of an institution that aims to realize those purposes. Foucault and other poststructuralists question the importance of state power, suggesting that power operates in virtually every social context, and thus must be contested at local sites if significant social change is to occur. Lyotard attempts to examine how conflicts among divergent groups that share no common values might be resolved. He offers no general formulas for such resolution, but at least focuses attention on this important political issue. Thus, the Continental tradition is rich in both specific insights and in new formulations of key political problems.

Continental movements place major importance on art and thus make insightful contributions to aesthetics. Hegel believes art has both a cultural and metaphysical function. It presents the guiding principle of the culture/era in sensuous form, and it contributes to mankind's coming to consciousness of its role in history. It may not express this principle and this place as perspicuously as philosophy can, but it is accessible to more people than is philosophy. Hegel's treatise on aesthetics discusses the achievements of art throughout history and the role of art in culture and in mankind's development; it thus opens entirely new questions for aesthetics. Western Marxists are vitally aware of the potentially liberating function of art (also of the deadening function of some art); they make the ideological role of art a central issue. For early Nietzsche, different arts are expressions of fundamental life-forces (e.g., the Dionysian and the Apollonian), and art can contribute to resolving cultural contradictions. Along with the entire Romantic movement, Nietzsche strives to understand the conditions and transformative potential of creative expression of all kinds, especially music. Hermeneutics takes the interpretation of art as its central theme and makes it the central paradigm for elucidating the general processes of interpretation. Both Heidegger and Sartre make art central to their larger philosophical tasks: for the revelation of being in Heidegger, and for demonstrating how the authentic freedom of one person requires and appeals to the authentic freedom of others (e.g., artist and audience). This reciprocity provides Sartre with a model for revising his social ontology and theory of groups. Structuralism examines the internal logic that governs various genres of art and the process of creation itself. Poststructuralism challenges the importance of authors/creators, suggesting that their creative processes are mysterious for both themselves and their interpreters. Even postmodernism looks to art to reveal many distinctive features of the present age: its loss of orientation in space and time, its affectlessness, its celebration of surfaces, and its contributions to the hyperreal. Thus, the whole tradition makes art central to the definition of larger philosophical issues, and in the process introduces some entirely new questions for aesthetics.

In metaphysics and epistemology, Hegel is the first to try to show that an underlying logic – called dialectic – informs nature, concepts, history, social life, and individual development. He also develops the notion of internal critique by which a position is shown to fail on its own standards, rather than on the external ones a critic might impose. He suggests that, to be known, any entity or process must express itself, thus denying direct access of the mind to itself, and he tries to demonstrate how everyday consciousness can make the transition to the viewpoint of philosophy in order to verify these rather sweeping claims. Nietzsche suggests that minds know the world only through perspectives, which typically simplify the phenomena. Thus full knowledge (and the elucidation of truth) requires multiplying perspectives and carefully adjudicating the contributions of each one. Knowledge therefore always involves complex procedures of interpretation and evaluation; it is a hard-won achievement that cannot be taken for granted. Hermeneutics also insists on the importance of interpretation in achieving knowledge, but it does not relativize knowledge just because of this. Indeed, interpretation contributes to knowledge by integrating diverse factors requiring synthesis and articulating standards for knowing in specific spheres, e.g., history, art, law, social life, and individual psychology, and by uncovering new questions for study. Phenomenologists do not only elucidate the preconditions for knowledge, they also develop complex metaphysical views about the mind's relation to being (Heidegger and Sartre), value (Scheler), pre-reflective experience (Sartre and Merleau-Ponty), to the perceived world (Merleau-Ponty), and other people (Sartre and Levinas). Both existentialists and philosophical anthropologists illuminate the place of humanity in nature with great subtlety. Although many Continental philosophers remain diffident toward the achievements of empirical science, both Merleau-Ponty and the philosophical anthropologists attempt to integrate their studies with critically examined findings from empirical science. They provide one example of how philosophy and science can operate cooperatively. Poststructuralists challenge the view that an underlying logic governs the development of knowledge and that criteria of truth develop in rational, intelligible ways. They represent a re-emergence of skepticism that future movements in Continental philosophy will have to answer. Finally, though A. N. Whitehead is usually given credit for developing "process" metaphysics, the entire Continental tradition – from Hegel to Nietzsche to Bergson to Deleuze – must share credit for this distinctive metaphysical position. I have only indicated a few highlights of the tradition's contributions in these areas.

With respect to the philosophy of mind, I have already mentioned Continental thinkers' clarification of some distinctive features of human life above. These challenge Cartesian assumptions about subjectivity, and this theme organizes many of the tradition's contributions. Not only do they insist that social relations constitute many essential features of individuals (and thus persons cannot be conceived as hermetic, isolated atomic units), they suggest that many unconscious factors organize the operations of the mind (and thus that the mind is not self-transparent) and that the mind and the body cannot be conceived as two independent spheres operating on entirely different principles. They also explore many implicit factors that underlie a person's relationship with the world, from everyday practices and institutions, to skills (know-how), to the operations of the lived body, to linguistic and culture structures and norms. Continental philosophers have struggled to understand the centrality of time in the constitution of consciousness, from Kant (who construes time as a form of intuition imposed on all sensations), to Hegel (who sees time as the medium for the expression and self-understanding of both selfhood and the Absolute), to Nietzsche (whose notion of eternal recurrence plays a central role in his ethics); from Husserl (who showed how both the future and the past are contained in every present) and Bergson (who develops a distinctive conception of time as flux), to Heidegger, Sartre, Merleau-Ponty (all of whom see time as essential to the structure of personhood), time and time-consciousness have been closely analyzed. Finally, the interlocked issues of freedom and the achievement of selfhood have been explored in Kant, Hegel, Marx, Nietzsche, Bergson, the existentialists, and even the poststructuralists.

Philosophy of history is a discipline virtually invented by Continental philosophers, who have regularly redefined its tasks. Hegel thinks that underlying patterns operate in many sectors of history – of social institutions, of art, of thought, of ethical standpoints – and he uses the notion of "dialectic" to clarify these patterns. Marx, the Western Marxists, Sartre, and Merleau-Ponty all attempt to develop Hegel's conception of dialectic and rethink its continuing relevance to historical study. Marxism provides a more reductive picture of historical development than Hegel, but it allows Marxists to better identify necessary social changes because it identifies economic production as the causal principle governing existing institutions. Nietzsche offers a mixed verdict on the study of history, suggesting that it can enhance or debilitate life, contributing to the vitality or decadence of culture. Dilthey examines the preconditions of any historical understanding and shows that the purposiveness of human agents requires a different kind of explanation than that offered in the natural sciences. Sartre amplifies Dilthey's position in his presentation of the progressive-regressive method, an approach that requires that the components of an historical event be identified (the regressive side) and then the manner in which they combine to produce the event must be reconstructed (the progressive side). Both structuralists and poststructuralists challenge the dialectical approach to history, showing that it may better be conceived as a series of historical breaks, rather than regular moments of negation and supersession. Foucault works out an alternative way of understanding the operations of history, one that requires studying institutional norms and background conceptual schemes, rather than individual human projects. These discussions of the nature of history and the preconditions of historical study have been lively and intense. Most work on this topic in other traditions is derivative from major Continental insights.

Finally, rethinking the tasks and possibilities of philosophy itself has been a central project of the Continental tradition. Several important supplements have been explored. One is the effort to refashion the social-political conditions of human existence by engaging in a critique of the present and envisioning alternatives. Although Hegel seems to deny that he is making recommendations for the future, his system explores some still-to-be-achieved conditions for social and individual self-realization. Marx pursues this Hegelian project by envisioning a total alternative to capitalism itself in order to make possible less alienated and more fulfilled lives. Nietzsche rejects the mediocratization and decadence of much modern life, and he shows how this might be redressed through enhanced self-perfection and a reconstitution of high culture and grand politics. He also thinks philosophers should become value legislators for the future as well as physicians to the various ailments of contemporary culture. Sartre shows that his goal of individual authenticity does have social implications, and he envisions a society of activist groups in constant interaction – forming alliances, engaging in conflicts – creating the future of humanity. Habermas's ideal society may not be that different from Sartre's, but Sartre argues that rational discussion is only a small element of the kinds of interaction between political groups in a society. French feminist philosophers imagine a society that has overcome patriarchy and that highlights the value of women's approaches to the world. Poststructuralism challenges the present as forcefully as recent Marxism, but only hints at the kind of society that might escape these criticisms, while postmodernism is perhaps too mesmerized by the present to provide a genuinely critical perspective. Nonetheless, many Continental movements exhibit this Utopian impulse.

Other projects for philosophy are also explored. Hegel provides a comprehensive assessment of the present condition of culture by exploring its history and logic. Although some areas of philosophy (philosophy of art, of science, etc.) might still attempt such a study, few attempt to integrate these assessments into a systematic comprehension of the present, but our present may require such an effort. Nietzsche sought to discover deeper truths by justly assessing a multiplicity of perspectives (from different fields – psychology, sociology, physiology, history – and with different styles of examination – artistic, moralistic, poetic, scientific, linguistic). He thus offers a different model by which philosophy can contribute to human knowledge. Some movements strive to clarify essential preconditions of certain human capacities – conditions of understanding in hermeneutics, conditions of human existence in existentialism, conditions of specific types of mental states in phenomenology – while others attempt to forge entirely new concepts to articulate a new metaphysical understanding of reality (e.g., Deleuze, Derrida, Bergson, Nietzsche). Some movements attempt to reconceive the notion of science in order to show that philosophy can operate on the same plane as the empirical sciences, while others adopt entirely different models of knowledge (art, self-consciousness, life) and model philosophy's epistemological goals on that kind of knowledge. Finally, many Continental movements exhibit a tendency toward suspicion and react to contemporary developments accordingly. Some are suspicious of modern ideals (Nietzsche), some of the metaphysics of presence (Heidegger, Derrida), some of the operations of the unconscious (Schopenhauer, Freud), and some of language's claims to reveal the world (Foucault, Lyotard). These forms of "hermeneutics of suspicion" constitute a recurring background and point of departure for the philosophical efforts in some Continental movements. They refuse to allow common-sense assumptions to reign supreme, and their systematic vision derives from efforts to respond to such suspicions.

DISPERSIONIST CHALLENGES TO THE TRADITION: A RESPONSE

The dispersionists collectively contest many previous movements in Continental philosophy. In retrospect, some of their criticisms are probably overstated, but they had significant effects at the time, and these effects still remain entrenched today. Throughout this book I have attempted to demonstrate the viability, subtlety, and value of the many different movements and figures in Continental philosophy. In order to buttress this stance, I will respond to some of the more important dispersionists' critiques of their forerunners. I will not attempt to defend every figure, but instead will concentrate on the three figures/movements with whom the dispersionists were most harsh: Hegel, phenomenology, and humanism (which plays a significant role in hermeneutics, existentialism, and philosophical anthropology). The dispersionists also sometimes forget that they bear important debts to many of the movements they criticize, and I will indicate these in passing. I shall summarize their main objections and offer some brief responses. The goal of this section is to underline what should already be evident from the main chapters of the book: all the movements in this tradition are still viable today, and they all deserve to be reconsidered both for insights into contemporary issues and for their inventive efforts to solve the problems they inherited.

Hegel

Dispersionists are anti-Hegelian because they reject the dialectical development of history, in which later stages transcend – but retain the best features of – earlier stages. They agree that any entity is an unstable concatenation of forces that typically negates itself, but they reject Hegel's claim that such self-division is eventually overcome and unity re-established at a higher level. Derrida and Deleuze take this self-division to be ongoing; stable unity is never achieved and never existed. Foucault accepts that intellectual formations in specific eras may exhibit temporary unity, but these periods of coherence do not last and are never recovered once lost. Epistemic breaks divide different forms of order and methods of producing knowledge, and thus create different eras in the history of disciplines. Thus, the criteria of truth, evidence, and plausibility at least for the human sciences are incongruent in different eras. Though Hegel could agree with this, he would argue that the transitions between eras exhibit distinctive logical patterns and can be rationally reconstructed; Foucault denies this.

Hegel can reply to this objection in several different ways. First, unlike Foucault, he actually demonstrates his transitions in a variety of areas (from forms of life in the *Phenomenology of Spirit* to logical categories in the *Logic* to stages of history and the development of social institutions and forms of art and religion). Foucault only sketches his epistemic breaks by examining disciplines in snapshots taken over broad spans of time. He does not look for transitional figures or intermediate positions in the disciplines he studies. Though he does show that major differences in methods and criteria within specific disciplines exist, he does not demonstrate that definitive breaks occur (i.e., that there are no intermediate positions that can explain the transitions). Neither does Hegel show that his patterns of supersession will *always* occur. Typically, he discovers these patterns retrospectively; so he makes no effort to predict historical developments using them. He does make most of his transitions intelligible, and he does not argue for a single pattern by which all historical development occurs. Foucault's stance may challenge Hegelians to more firmly establish these patterns of supersession, and Hegel's position may force Foucault's advocates to defend their claim of epistemic breaks more carefully. Certainly historical development does not have to always follow either pattern, and this disagreement can only make serious thought about such developments more informed and sophisticated.

Hegel's second reply is that neither Deleuze nor Derrida presents sufficient evidence that re-emergent syntheses are impossible; indeed, they merely suggest that the dispersion metaphor might apply to more phenomena than one might expect. Again, Hegel *demonstrates* many instances in which a significant synthesis emerges from the internal division and opposition of many different types of phenomena. Moreover, Hegel does not have just one model of reunification or synthesis; the higher-level resolution can emerge in a variety of ways. Derrida and Deleuze present their hypothesis almost as a priori assertions, though they do offer some examples to clarify their general picture. Basically, they are not entitled to present their hypothesis as a metaphysical principle (or master concept) because they deny that any such metaphysical principle can be valid. If this debate were to continue, perhaps Hegelians could usefully examine Derrida's key deconstructions in order to see whether the opposition-contestation between his dichotomies must be interminable. Perhaps they can show how a Hegelian resolution might emerge. Similarly, Derrideans might challenge some of Hegel's supersession claims to determine whether the reunification really is achieved. As with Foucault, there is a legitimate dispute here, but the dispersionists have not refuted Hegel's position because they lack convincing evidence for the universality of their hypotheses.

Hegel's third reply is that his supersessions are not necessarily transparent to those whom they reunify; much is hidden from the historical actors themselves. Indeed, he claims that only through retrospection do most of these higher-level unities become evident. Moreover, he does not deny that suffering, tragedy, and death occur, claiming only that some degree of progress occurs despite these prices. Thus, his reunifications are hard-won achievements, not necessary exemplifications of a formal law. In addition, the loss of an old standpoint is a loss of an entire form of life (including forms of social organization, art, religion, and cognition). Real historical change does occur. Hegel's claim is simply that it is not random or unintelligible and that the process of overcoming the former forms creates the outlines of the new form.

Derrida's method of deconstruction has affinities with Hegel's procedure of internal criticism. Both find the tensions in an existing position, and show that, on analysis, the position undermines itself. But Derrida rejects Hegel's claim that this self-dissolution leads toward a new position. Instead he argues that the opposition is interminable. All dispersionists reject Hegel's claim that "absolute knowledge" – and thus a coherent, linked system of concepts – is possible. Derrida attacks Hegel's systematic claims by questioning the relationships of the prefaces and introductions to his system; they allegedly adopt a standpoint that is both inside and outside the system itself. Derrida also tries to neutralize Hegel's ability to incorporate positions critical of Hegel's position into his system (and thus prevent his own – Derrida's – position from being so incorporated). Here Derrida's fear is that Hegel's position is *too complete* – including all opposing views – and thus unable to allow any innovative developments.

The difference between Derrida and Hegel here is that Derrida revels in stalemate while Hegel seeks genuine resolutions. Again, abstract arguments are helpless to resolve this dispute; one has to scrutinize whether Hegel's resolutions succeed and determine whether Derrida's specific stalemates can be broken. Hegel does *not* argue that all oppositions can be resolved, but, taking all his books collectively, he produces a remarkable number of resolutions in all areas (e.g., forms of life, concepts, history, institutions, art, and forms of inquiry). Derrida seems to enjoy leaving reason to flail helplessly on the cross of its own distinctions, but his strategies and results wear thin very quickly. Derrida's playful games become maneuvers one wants to defeat – just to show that thought can be serious and make a difference. Beyond this, Hegel does not necessarily seek a closed system. I believe he would want to expand his system as history develops further, creating new possibilities of thought, life, and culture. He did anticipate some of the major objections to his view (e.g., Kierkegaard in the "Unhappy Consciousness" section[4] and perhaps Derrida himself in the "Skepticism" section[5]), but he does not pretend to anticipate everything. Nor does he *force* phenomena into his framework; he prides himself on adhering to the specific contours of the positions he discusses and meets them on their own ground. Here too Hegel's position not only withstands Derrida's doubts, but also shows how Derrida can be critically investigated.

Hegel would also allow that his retrospective stance is neither inside nor outside his system, but he does not take this to be an objection. In the *Phenomenology*, the retrospective perspective has undergone the experiences that are taking place, and thus can intelligently comment on them as it reconsiders and recollects their connections. The relationships it identifies are there, but not visible to the consciousness undergoing the development because it enters into each new stage naively. Thus, this objection is a red herring. On the vexed issue of the nature of Hegel's absolute knowledge, Hegel means "all-encompassing" (no longer partial or incomplete) by "absolute," but one can at least interpret him as realizing that historical innovation and development will continue even though his system reaches its conclusion. He can argue that for the historical developments up to his era his system is absolute, and he undoubtedly does think this. But he can acknowledge that historical development will continue, and his system will then require expansion to include the newly emerging forms of life and culture. He certainly did not believe social life had reached its apotheosis; much is still required to achieve the institutions sketched in the *Philosophy of Right*.

The real difference between Hegel and Derrida concerns their aspirations. Derrida offers a modest ethics and politics, but his vision of philosophy's ability to contribute to the birth of a new world is restrained and guarded. Hegel saw that something genuinely new was on the horizon, and he sought to create a logic and a philosophical method to comprehend it. Derrida's contributions are primarily critical. Hegel's retrospective understanding is no less critical, but it is also offers a creative vision – solutions to age-old problems from which a new culture might develop. If anyone's method seems formalistic or diagrammatic, it is Derrida's. He attacks self-presence, but even when he is successful, it is a one-note attack. Hegel's critical discussions are more variegated and supple, and he strives for something more than mere criticism.

Deleuze argues, against Hegel, that any final goal, end, or result would represent death – an end to becoming and the final exhaustion of desire. He also rejects Hegel's claim that desire expresses lack, rather than productive energy. Instead of assimilating the world, Deleuze's desire creates manifold, but temporary, connections with its objects, allowing transfers of energy that can provoke dramatic leaps to new levels of existence. Deleuze's concept of "experience" is similar to Hegel's, but for him experiences are intermittent, contingent, and unexpected. They cannot be ordered into patterns because they escape all pattern and logic, producing unpredictable consequences. He embraces transformative experience as much as Hegel, but he claims it happens less regularly and predictably than Hegel believes.

I have already suggested that Hegel's system many not be closed or completed in the way Deleuze fears. If history produces a new stage, then his system would have to expand to account for it; it thus may not reach a final end in the way Deleuze suggests. Hegel agrees with Deleuze that becoming is essential to fundamental reality, and he agrees that "experiences" involve shifts to higher planes. He simply insists that experiences cohere and that they do not happen arbitrarily or randomly. Deleuze offers no real evidence for his claim; it is an empirical hypothesis. Hegel, on the other hand, shows numerous instances in which experience functions in the way he suggests. He need not claim that everyone follows this pattern because not everyone takes his or her experience (and their criteria for evaluating it) seriously. Finally, although Deleuze may have a valid objection against the notion of desire in the Self-consciousness section of the *Phenomenology*,[6] Hegel explores other world-orientations (e.g., pleasure and social harmony) that do not presuppose this consciousness of lack. Lack is a very common mode of desire, but Deleuze is correct in suggesting the existence of a more self-expressive conception. I would simply argue that this more self-expressive conception of one's fundamental relation to the world in fact exists in Hegel's discussion of "Pleasure and Necessity"[7] and in his analysis of the Greek world's social roles and laws.[8] Greek social roles provide self-identity in the Greek world (and thus enable direct self-expression), and pleasure becomes the medium in which one expresses a sense of harmony with the world.

Both Merleau-Ponty and Sartre had already reinterpreted Hegel's dialectic in compelling new ways, showing that it still has significant applications.[9]

The dispersionists' challenge forces one to reconsider the real implications of Hegel's system and allows one to appreciate its power. If one examines those challenges carefully, they do not have the force the dispersionists believed them to have. Hegel's positions also reveal potential problems in the dispersionists' fundamental assumptions. One appreciates Hegel's achievements more fully because these objections encourage careful attention to his actual execution.

Phenomenology

The dispersionists also offer a critique of phenomenology. They not only question Husserl's search for certainty and his transcendental standpoint; they also reject existential phenomenology's efforts to clarify structures of everyday experience. Though he respects Husserl's rigor and clarity, Derrida challenges phenomenology at a vulnerable point: the power of consciousness to accurately describe itself and to elucidate its essential structures. Although Derrida does not show that reflective consciousness *cannot* articulate pre-reflective life, he does suggest that phenomenology cannot be certain of reflection's accuracy because unbridgeable gaps exist between experience and its registration and between registration and description. Sartre saw this problem when he noted that reflective consciousness *typically* falsifies pre-reflective experience. Derrida's question to Sartre is: can reflective consciousness ever be fully purified? Derrida also rejects Husserl's claim that consciousness is directly present to itself. Husserl reiterates Western philosophy's long-standing reliance on presence (and self-presence). Without this capacity for full self-presence, Derrida claims that consciousness exists in a hall of mirrors, out of which it cannot escape and in which it is constantly lost. Derrida also faults Husserl for requiring a seemingly endless series of reductions while still exhibiting reservations about the foundations of phenomenology.

In reply, I first should admit that Derrida's essays on Husserl are among his best. Thus, if I can raise doubts about the overall power of his attack here, then similar questions can probably be raised against many of his other deconstructions. The crucial point is that even if there are gaps, they may not be unbridgeable. Husserl can suggest that every experience is developed by descriptions made of it. In effect, the experience is not separated into a moment of presence and a moment of description, but the description realizes the experience in a certain direction, a direction already implicit in the experience.[10] Many descriptions may be possible, but the ones that resonate with the experience most completely are most likely to be revealing. This reply can be used both by Husserl and by the existential phenomenologists; they can simply refuse to accept the absolute separation between experience and description that Derrida posits. Good descriptions creatively articulate experiences, bringing them into relief and sharpening their distinctiveness. They also compensate for outmoded, common-sense ways of understanding experience by producing new concepts and new comprehensions. Similar illuminations can emerge from another person's effort to describe one's experience; they may achieve a resonance with it that highlights distinctive features that were concealed. Phenomenological self-descriptions operate in a similar way. They uncover, rethink, and resonate all at once; they do not presuppose or require privileged access to the experience being described.

Sartre could certainly have been clearer about how purifying reflection works, but he does say that it reverses the illusions introduced by impure reflection, which objectifies pre-reflective experience and creates various phantom psychic objects.[11] For Sartre, the capacity to lucidly describe one's experience does not develop automatically or easily. It involves a stance that is both immersed in and outside of the experience at once, and thus is similar to Husserl's reduction. Although Sartre believes that every conscious act is non-positionally conscious of itself, he denies that this kind of "self-presence" (which he insists is also a kind of self-distance) produces knowledge. It grounds the possibility of purifying reflection, but does not insure it will happen. Purifying reflection allows the contours of pre-reflective experience to become explicit; it lets experience become lucid to itself instead of forcing it into pre-established categories. For Sartre, the distance that reflection introduces does not necessarily conceal or veil; it can highlight and reveal. Both Sartre and Husserl could argue that Derrida has to acknowledge some capacity for accurate experiential description because his own analysis of consciousness (as *différance*) relies on this. Derrida could not defend his own position without some ability to accurately describe experience.

The flaw in Derrida's argument is to claim that there are only two alternatives: either perfect, pellucid presence of consciousness to itself or complete absence of consciousness from itself in a hall of mirrors. But neither of these options ever obtains. Consciousness can produce revealing descriptions and thus achieve deeper self-comprehension, even if its accuracy is never complete or certain and must be verified and reassessed with new illuminating descriptions. And, sometimes, consciousness can become so distant from itself that its self-descriptions may simply reiterate the hackneyed, pedestrian self-comprehension that has become sedimented as common sense. Most efforts to creatively describe one's experience achieve some insight, but most can also be developed further through additional descriptive efforts. Phenomenology continually corrects itself, but it also makes definite progress in understanding the variety of structures and types of experience. Greater exposure to insightful phenomenological descriptions can be enlivening and deepening. Even Derrida's challenges to phenomenology can be enlivening and deepening in this way.

Foucault also challenges the efficacy of phenomenology by rejecting the importance it gives to consciousness and arguing that the rules that regulate both cognitive operations and institutional practices are largely unconscious. These rules are not universal structures of human nature, but instead are socially sustained, even if they are not consciously legislated by any group. They operate in the background, governing action and thought, and they mutate behind people's backs. Foucault suggests that experience is culturally produced and that individuals are often passive spectators of their own actions. He argues, in effect, that whatever is phenomenologically accessible is epiphenomenal;

clarifying the unconscious rules that determine what can be said and done in a particular era is more important.

One reply to this stance is that if the rules are socially sustained, they must be accessible because those who transgress the rules must be corrected. Even if the rules cannot be fully articulated as such, one must be able to see when they are violated and apply them in practice. This would imply that some kind of access to them must be possible and thus that eventually they could be effectively described (not just through historical retrospection, but through imagining various possible cases in which they would be violated in present circumstances). Thus, the introspective access to such rules would not be direct, but a methodology similar to Husserl's eidetic variation could provide some access – even for one's own era. Moreover, Foucault's argument does not contest the claim that experience can be described effectively; he merely suggests that such descriptions are less important than they seem. Whether this is so depends on the purpose of one's inquiry. Foucault's archaeology may be a respectable enterprise, but it does not undermine the value or significance of phenomenology. Foucault acknowledges that his own method is retrospective; phenomenology may be able to reveal the rules governing disciplines in this era. Foucault's historical analysis thus may be supplemented by phenomenological techniques.

Foucault's real challenge to phenomenology concerns the universality and historical relativity of its results. Phenomenologists describe what they take to be universal structures of experience. Foucault's questions can be an important corrective to inflated phenomenological claims. But Foucault relies on descriptions of lived experience to render his historical claims precise. He uses Merleau-Ponty's conception of the lived body, for example, to better understand how power controls individuals. Foucault's discussion of historical variations in punishments does not undermine Merleau-Ponty's comprehension of the body; it elaborates other elements of the person that constituted power's targets in previous eras (e.g., the association of ideas, confessional torture, and the spectacle of the beheaded body). Similarly, Foucault's emphasis on surveillance develops Sartre's analysis of the other's look, which is only confirmed when Foucault shows the look has even harsher effects in the current era.

Humanism

Finally, the dispersionists oppose humanism, the view that there is an unchanging essence shared by human beings (e.g., rational thought, ontological freedom, a transcendental ego), an essence that commands respect and justifies human rights. Humanism allegedly values individual persons because they instantiate humanity's essence – not because of their distinctive virtues. Dispersionists identify humanism with Enlightenment ideals (because freedom, equality, and fraternity define humanity's essential features), and acknowledge that they may even have had some liberating effects in the eighteenth century. But Foucault claims that humanism has since been exploited by disciplinary powers that seek to increase control and surveillance of everyday life. Instead of protecting individuals from the incursion of power, it invites ever more strident supervision of humanity because it posits features of the psyche that can be controlled only through constant analysis and intrusive monitoring. Though humanism values the growth of subjectivity, Foucault claims that subjectivity typically involves *subjugation* because subjects must learn to scrutinize, categorize, criticize, and control their own behavior. Subjects are created when they internalize the functions of judge, confessor, watchman, and interrogator.

The first reply to this anti-humanism is that there may be some essential features of human beings, even if Foucault is right about how they have been used. Moreover, the existentialists do not think essential features of the human condition are static or fixed; most attempt to clarify some features that can be transformed (e.g., the shift from inauthentic to authentic existence). Against Foucault, the features most stressed are not subjectivity and consciousness, but temporality, freedom, embodiment, and situatedness. Moreover, humanists do not necessarily need to ground an ethics of rights in these essential features because other, perhaps stronger, defenses of human rights are possible. Existential ethics involves *acknowledging* these essential features – abiding with them, rather than denying or ignoring them. It focuses on self-perfection, rather than on one's treatment of others – just as Foucault's own ethics does. Existentialists acknowledge ways in which humans may be largely passive in relation to some essential features (e.g., Sartre's social self and Heidegger's worldhood or moods), but they need not be passive in relation to all such features (e.g., transcendence, embodiment). In addition, to the extent that Foucault reversed himself in favor of Enlightenment self-critique and self-transformation, his attack on humanism must be seriously qualified or revised. Finally, even if there was a rise of surveillance and hidden forms of domination in the nineteenth century, the extent to which humanist ideals are implicated in this development is arguable. Intrusiveness is facilitated by the postulation of unconscious forces, but Foucault is no stranger to positing unconscious factors (rules, forces); his own theory may emulate the alleged flaws in humanism in this respect. And his claim that humanist subjectivity really involves self-monitoring that colludes with existing systems of power is dubious. *Critical* subjectivity typically *challenges* existing power practices. Any conception of liberation presupposes a conception of selfhood, and Foucault's rejection of the latter raises doubts about his effectiveness in achieving the former.

Foucault's challenge to "humanism" is primarily a challenge to the claims that reason, the psyche, the ego, and autonomy are universal features of human beings. He either wants to reject these features altogether or argues that they have radically different forms in different eras (reason, for example). Existential philosophers have already raised these objections before Foucault, however. They forcefully attack the existence of the ego and of autonomy and of the psyche; Sartre especially realizes that much mischief has been perpetrated with these concepts. Foucault tells this story in greater historical detail, but his main points about these alleged essential features are not new. More importantly, rejecting *these* features does not eliminate the possibility that some important universal features exist, and Heidegger, Sartre, and the philosophical anthropologists defend some plausible proposals for such features. The kind of argument Foucault develops simply does not yield the conclusion he wants to prove.

Derrida challenges humanism's right to say "We," its assumption that all others are like "Us." In assimilating others in this way, humanism allegedly obliterates important cultural differences and contributes to the political-economic domination of the West. Humanism thus colludes in marginalizing alien cultures by incorporating them into the family of "man." Derrida believes that overcoming humanism will require insightful deconstructive work because much classical metaphysics contributes to humanism's ascendancy. For Derrida, humanity is essentially fragmented; its unity cannot be assumed.

The humanist reply here has two parts. First, to achieve genuine reciprocal recognition between diverse people or groups is a significant social achievement; it specifically refuses to ignore differences among the parties recognized. It produces harmony among people without eradicating their diversity. Second, Derrida's insistence that other people are different or distinct from oneself does not guarantee their safety. If they are stigmatized or excommunicated or treated as an alien threat, their difference may be a motivation to destroy them, reduce them to slaves, or at least treat them with disdain. The political issues are not necessarily resolved either by humanist recognition among people or by Derridean differentiation. The task is to find enabling orientations toward other people whether one identifies with them or differentiates oneself from them. Each of these stances can lead in disastrous directions.

Foucault also identifies several paradoxes surrounding humanism's concept of "self." First, the relationship between the transcendental ego that is the alleged source of freedom and the empirical ego that is determined by causal relations is never clarified. Allegedly the transcendental ego guarantees autonomy, but autonomy must express itself empirically, and if all empirical contexts are dominated by power and by implicit rules governing thought and action, then autonomy is lost.[12] Second, the self's creative abilities depend on language, life-force, and labor; but these elements transcend and condition individuals. Insofar as persons are speakers, workers, or organisms, they are subject to forces they cannot control. The very forces that allow subjectivity to express itself undermine the self's autonomy. Insofar as these forces are supra-personal, science must explain their operations; hence the fields of economics, linguistics, and biology dominate the modern era. But the more these forces are understood, the less space for free subjectivity there is. Both paradoxes allegedly produce contradictions within the humanist subject. Rather than attempt to resolve these problems, Foucault suggests that the entire framework of humanism be jettisoned. In its place he describes a situated, rule-following creature that can sometimes achieve distance on its practices through criticism of the present and that may attempt to live differently and creatively as a result.

One reply to this line of criticism suggests that Foucault himself presupposes the conception of liberation he criticizes. If Foucault has an ideal, it is defining oneself in opposition to present intellectual frameworks and practices of power. This requires some capacity to distance oneself from dominating forces, and this is what "autonomy" allows. Indeed all the dispersionists support some such ideal of liberation, the very ideal central to the humanist position. Second, humanists (at least in existential philosophy and hermeneutics) need not depend on a transcendental subject; they situate persons in relation to many conditioning forces and cognitive backgrounds. Humanists do not assume that consciousness automatically has the ability to control these forces, though they contend that it can sometimes do so. The dispersionists admit this. When they are most strident, dispersionists want to dissolve humanity into mere effects or expressions of the forces influencing it, but they flee these conclusions when they formulate their own ethics. The dispersionists provide no better resolution to this problem than the humanists. Obviously, these larger forces have some effect on human action, but they do not operate independently. Human agents sustain them and can transform them. The transcendental ego is not required to defend a viable conception of human agency.

In this conclusion I have drawn the threads of the book together in several different ways. I first indicated the strengths of the Continental tradition as a whole, thus defending it against those still prone to dismissing it altogether. Second, I articulated some important "decision-points," issues that will determine the future direction of this tradition. Third, I suggested a few of the important applications to various specific fields in philosophy that can be developed from a careful review of the positions discussed in this book. Finally, I buttressed the overall thrust of the project by defending key movements or figures in this tradition from overrated poststructuralist attacks. Hopefully this will allow all the movements discussed here to be taken seriously because they make valuable contributions. Our task as students of this tradition is to use its resources to address current philosophical problems, newly emerging social crises, and gradually surfacing cultural aspirations.

NOTES

INTRODUCTION

1 I drew heavily on standard secondary sources to compose these vignettes in addition to whatever dispositional knowledge of the source texts I retained. Especially helpful were John Hermann Randall, *The Career of Philosophy*, vols. 1 and 2 (New York: Columbia University Press, 1961) and relevant articles in Paul Edwards (ed.), *The Encyclopedia of Philosophy* (New York: Macmillan, 1967) and relevant chapters in Frederick Copleston, *A History of Philosophy* (New York: Image/Doubleday, 1963). I will not provide detailed source text references for these vignettes. Where I relied on additional secondary sources, I will indicate this below. Let me say again that these short sections are meant as sketches, not as detailed expositions.

2 On Rousseau, I benefited from the Introduction in *Rousseau: Selections*, ed., intro, and notes by Maurice Cranston (New York: Macmillan, 1988).

3 In discussing Herder I have benefited from Michael Forster's excellent introduction to Herder's *Philosophical Writings* (Cambridge: Cambridge University Press, 2002), which he also edited and translated.

4 On Fichte, Schelling, and Hölderlin, I benefited from Terry Pinkard, *German Philosophy 1760–1860* (Cambridge: Cambridge University Press, 2002) and from relevant articles in Karl Ameriks, *Cambridge Companion to German Idealism* (Cambridge: Cambridge University Press, 2000).

CHAPTER 1 HEGEL

1 G. W. F. Hegel, *Phenomenology of Spirit*, trans. A. V. Miller (Oxford: Oxford University Press, 1977); hereafter PS.

2 G. W. F. Hegel, *Encyclopedia of Philosophical Sciences*; vol. 1: *Logic*; vol. II: *Philosophy of Nature*; vol. III: *Philosophy of Spirit*, trans. William Wallace (based on the 1830 edn.) (Oxford: Oxford University Press, 1975); hereafter E I, E II, E III, respectively.

3 G. W. F. Hegel, *Philosophy of Right*, trans. T. M. Knox. (Oxford: Oxford University Press, 1967); hereafter PR.

4 G. W. F. Hegel, *Early Theological Writings*, trans. T. M. Knox (Philadelphia: University of Pennsylvania Press, 1948).

5 G. W. F. Hegel, *Hegel's Science of Logic*, trans. A. V. Miller (London: George Allen & Unwin, 1969).

6 For an extensive and fascinating philosophical biography of Hegel, see Terry Pinkard, *Hegel* (Cambridge: Cambridge University Press, 2002).
7 PS, section 80. Throughout these references to Hegel's texts, numerals refer to *section* numbers, not page numbers, except where explicitly indicated via "p." or "pp."
8 PS, 84.
9 PS, 85 and 87.
10 PS, 86.
11 PS, 87.
12 PS, 89.
13 This becomes evident, finally, in PS, 680–1.
14 PS, 680.
15 PS, 90–9.
16 PS, 100–4; 105–10.
17 PS, 111–31.
18 PS, 132–65.
19 PS, 166–230.
20 PS, 231–437.
21 PS, 438–76.
22 PS, 477–670.
23 PS, 684–747.
24 PS, 775–87.
25 PS, 788–97.
26 PS, 83–4.
27 PS, 59 makes this point about "argumentative thinking."
28 PS, 87.
29 The following discussion encapsulates a more extended treatment I gave in an earlier work: William Schroeder, *Sartre and His Predecessors: The Self and the Other* (London: Routledge & Kegan Paul, 1984), pp. 66–74.
30 These sections are PS, 166–73, 174–7, 178–84, and 185–96 respectively.
31 PS, 167.
32 PS, 168–72.
33 PS, 177, 178, and 184.
34 This reading seems a more plausible interpretation of PS, 176.
35 PS, 174.
36 PS, 175.
37 PS, 175.
38 One can see this both from the way sections 178–84 are introduced in 177 and concluded in 185.
39 PS, 177.
40 PS, 178–9.
41 PS, 180.
42 PS, 181.
43 PS, 181–2.
44 PS, 184.
45 PS, 186–7. I use gendered pronouns in this section simply to distinguish master and slave. Needless to say, members of either sex can assume the master or slave roles.
46 PS, 188.

47 PS, 189.
48 PS, 190–1.
49 PS, 192–3.
50 PS, 194–6.
51 G. W. F. Hegel (1975) *Lectures on the Philosophy of World History: Introduction*, trans. H. B. Nisbet (Cambridge: Cambridge University Press, 1975), p. 28; hereafter PH.
52 PH, pp. 31–3.
53 PH, p. 53; see also pp. 134, 138.
54 PH, pp. 126–30.
55 PH, pp. 149–51.
56 PH, pp. 54 and 129–31 sketch these stages briefly, which I summarize here. Hegel develops these sketches at length in the main sections of the text.
57 PH, pp. 141–2.
58 PR, 4 and 7.
59 PR, 15.
60 PR, 26–30, 33; see also E III, 485–7.
61 E III, 469 and 486; PR, 31.
62 PR 40, 38.
63 PR, 44–6.
64 PR, 51.
65 PR, 241–2.
66 PR, 244–5.
67 PR, 99–103.
68 PR, 106–8.
69 PR, 136–9.
70 PR, 141–52.
71 PR, 148–9.
72 PR, 156–7.
73 PR, 162–4, 173, 175.
74 PR, 182–7.
75 PR, 249–56.
76 PR, 257–8.
77 PR, 272–3, 279–81.
78 PR, 301–3, 306–12.
79 PR, 289–90, 294.
80 PR, 295, 297.
81 PR, 322–5.
82 PR, 331–40.
83 PS, 682–3; see also E III, 572 and G. W. F. Hegel, *Hegel's Aesthetics: Lectures on Fine Art*, vol. I, trans. T. M. Knox (Oxford: Oxford University Press, 1975), p. 7; hereafter PFA.
84 PFA, pp. 72–3; PS, 700–1 and 727–9.
85 E III, 562.
86 E III, 558.
87 E III, 561–2; PFA, pp. 79–81, 86–9, 517–19.
89 PFA, pp. 10–11, 77–9, 84–5, 427–31.
90 E III, 562; PFA, pp. 79–81, 86–9, 517–19.
91 PFA, pp. 604–11.
92 My brief discussion in this section is heavily indebted to a superb book on the subject by Willem de Vries, *Hegel's Theory of Mental Activity* (Ithaca, NY: Cornell

University Press, 1988); hereafter HTMA. I recommend this book to anyone seeking to understand Hegel's views on this topic.

93 HTMA, pp. 36–7 and 45–6.
94 E III, 378.
95 E III, 381.
96 E III, 400–1.
97 E III, 407–8.
98 E III, 409–10.
99 E III, 441–5.
100 E III, 446–9.
101 E III, 452–4.
102 E III, 455–7.
103 E III, 459–64.
104 E III, 465–8.
105 PS, 69.
106 PS, 68–70, 49, 6–10.
107 PS, 50–1, 15–16.
108 PS, 58–60.
109 PS, 42–6.
110 PS, 60–6.
111 PS, 17–19, 23–7, 36–7, 47.
112 PS, 12–13, 28–30.
113 PS, 2–5, 20–2, 38–9.
114 PS, 54–7.
115 PS, 32–4, 52–3, 47.

CHAPTER 2 MARX AND WESTERN MARXISM

1 Karl Marx, "Theses on Feuerbach" (1845), in *Karl Marx: Essential Writings*, ed. Frederic L. Bender (New York: Harper & Row, 1972), p. 155 (thesis 11); hereafter MEW.
2 Karl Marx, *Karl Marx: Early Writings* (1844), trans. and ed. T. B. Bottomore (New York: McGraw-Hill, 1963), pp. 120–2, 168–74; hereafter EW.
3 EW, pp. 122–4.
4 EW, pp. 124–6.
5 EW, pp. 126–9.
6 EW, p. 129.
7 EW, p. 129.
8 EW, pp. 130–4.
9 EW, pp. 70–5, 181, 187.
10 EW, pp. 86–7.
11 EW, pp. 73, 137–9.
12 EW, pp. 152–60, 176, 200–6.
13 EW, pp. 157–62.
14 Hegel of course does recognize the historical importance of economic factors, but he sees additional conditioning factors as well. Marx's way of characterizing their differences is misleading.
15 MEW, pp. 152, 154.
16 MEW, pp. 153.
17 MEW, pp. 154, 180–1.
18 MEW, pp. 161–3, 170–2.

19 MEW, pp. 162, 178.
20 MEW, pp. 172–3.
21 MEW, pp. 177, 182–5, 240–53.
22 MEW, pp. 301–26.
23 MEW, pp. 162, 175, 200–1.
24 MEW, pp. 204–7.
25 MEW, pp. 178–80.
26 MEW, pp. 166, 209–11.
27 MEW, pp. 166–8, 185–7, 211–14.
28 MEW, pp. 168–70, 187–94, 214–18.
29 MEW, pp. 193–200.
30 MEW, pp. 301–26.
31 MEW, pp. 328–34.
32 MEW, pp. 367–85.
33 MEW, pp. 252–3.
34 MEW, pp. 398–406; see also MEW, pp. 389–98.
35 MEW, pp. 261–3.
36 In this brief section on the historical transition between Marx and Western Marxism, I am compressing a story told more elegantly and completely in Perry Anderson, *Considerations on Western Marxism* (London: Verso, 1979).
37 I have chosen to discuss Althusser's brand of Marxism in chapter 8 on structuralism.
38 Antonio Gramsci, *Selections from the Prison Notebooks*, trans. Quentin Hoare and Geoffrey Nowell Smith (New York: International Publishers, 1971), p. 360; hereafter PN.
39 PN, pp. 349–50, 36–61, 366.
40 PN, pp. 330, 333, 346, 418.
41 PN, pp. 12–13, 369–71, 376–7.
42 PN, p. 365.
43 PN, pp. 366–7, 370–1, 392.
44 PN, pp. 108–10, 229–35, 238–9.
45 PN, p. 344.
46 PN, pp. 351, 353–4.
47 PN, pp. 352–3, 360.
48 Max Horkheimer (1974) *Critical Theory: Selected Essays*, trans. Matthew J. O'Connell. (n.p.: Herder and Herder/New York: Seabury, 1974), pp. 194–5, 197–201, 206–8, 210; hereafter CT.
49 Max Horkheimer, "The State of Contemporary Social Philosophy and the Tasks of the Institute for Social Research" (1931), in Stephen Eric Bronner and Douglas Kellner (eds.), *Critical Theory and Society* (New York: Routledge, 1989), pp. 236–7, 241; hereafter SC.
50 CT, pp. 226–7, 246–7.
51 SC, pp. 31–2.
52 SC, pp. 25, 33–5.
53 CT, pp. 210–12, 213–14, 216.
54 CT, pp. 222–3, 250–1.
55 CT, pp. 219, 229, 246.
56 I discuss Heidegger's contributions to several Continental movements in chapters 5, 6, and 7.
57 See the discussion of authenticity in chapter 7 below.

58 See the discussion of Freud in chapter 3 below.
59 Herbert Marcuse, "The Concept of Essence," in *Negations*, trans. Jeremy J. Shapiro (Boston, MA: Beacon Press, 1968), pp. 67–87.
60 Marcuse's discussion of Freud is in Herbert Marcuse, *Eros and Civilization* (Boston, MA: Beacon Press, 1955).
61 Herbert Marcuse, *An Essay on Liberation* (Boston, MA: Beacon Press, 1969), pp. 57–70; hereafter EL.
62 EL, p. 6.
63 Herbert Marcuse, *One Dimensional Man* (Boston, MA: Beacon Press, 1964), pp. 8–16; hereafter ODM.
64 ODM, pp. 4–8.
65 ODM, pp. 19–21; EL, pp. 64–70.
66 ODM, pp. 2–4; EL, pp. 23–6, 87–9.
67 EL, pp. 26–37.
68 Jürgen Habermas, "The Tasks of a Critical Theory of Society," in Stephen Eric Bronner and Douglas Kellner, *Critical Theory and Society* (New York: Routledge, 1989), pp. 295–7; hereafter CTS.
69 CTS, pp. 293–4, 301–2.
70 CTS, pp. 302–4.
71 CTS, pp. 304–8.
72 Jürgen Habermas, *Moral Consciousness and Communicative Action*, trans. Christian Lenhardt and Shierry Weber Nicholsen (Cambridge, MA: MIT Press, 1990), pp. 14–20; hereafter MC.
73 Jürgen Habermas, *Knowledge and Human Interests*, trans. Jeremy J. Shapiro (Boston, MA: Beacon Press, 1971), pp. 274–300; hereafter KHI.
74 Jürgen Habermas, *Philosophical Discourse of Modernity*, trans. Frederick Lawrence (Cambridge, MA: MIT Press, 1987), pp. 294–326; hereafter PDM. See also Jürgen Habermas, *Communication and the Evolution of Society*, trans. and intro Thomas McCarthy (Boston, MA: Beacon Press, 1979), pp. 50–64; hereafter CES.
75 Still even Habermas can produce pretty flawed interpretations of his opponents, as is shown in PDM.
76 He is more reliable in his discussions of his antecedents in social theory. See Jürgen Habermas, *Theory of Communicative Action*, 2 vols., trans. Thomas McCarthy (Boston, MA: Beacon Press, 1984/7).
77 KHI, pp. 311–15.
78 Jürgen Habermas, *The Structural Transformation of the Public Sphere*, trans. Peter Burger and Frederick Lawrence (Cambridge, MA: MIT Press, 1989), pp. 27–42, 51–5, 117–28.
79 CTS, pp. 297–9. See also Jürgen Habermas, *Legitimation Crisis*, trans. Thomas McCarthy (Boston, MA: Beacon Press, 1993), pp. 45–91.
80 CES, pp. xiii–xix, 65–8.

CHAPTER 3 LIFE-PHILOSOPHY AND UNCONSCIOUS FORCES

1 Arthur Schopenhauer, *The World as Will and Representation* (1818), 2 vols., trans. E. F. J. Payne (New York: Falcon's Way Press/Dover Publications, 1958/66), i, pp. 110–11; 275; hereafter WR.
2 WR i, pp. 100–3, 109, 162; WR ii, 197.

3 WR i, pp. 111–14; WR ii, pp. 573–81, 634–6.
4 WR I, pp. 112–14; WR ii, pp. 371, 490–2.
5 These four patterns of rationality are given extended treatment in Arthur Schopenhauer, *The Fourfold Root of the Principle of Sufficient Reason* (1913), trans. E. F. J. Payne, intro Richard Taylor (La Salle, IL: Open Court, 1974).
6 WR i, pp. 174–6.
7 WR i, pp. 389–93, 404–5, 410–12; WR ii, pp. 611–13.
8 WR ii, pp. 531–60.
9 WR i, pp. 185–7, 194–5; WR ii, pp. 376–91.
10 WR ii, pp. 238–9. See also Arthur Schopenhauer, *Prize Essay on the Freedom of the Will* (1841), trans. E. F. J. Payne, ed. Gunther Zöller (Cambridge: Cambridge University Press, 1999), pp. 44–51; hereafter FW.
11 WR i, pp. 195–200, 242–55, 379–80.
12 WR i, pp. 260–7.
13 WR i, pp. 271–4. See also Arthur Schopenhauer, *On the Basis of Morality* (1841), trans. E. F. J. Payne, intro Richard Taylor (Indianapolis, IN: Bobbs-Merrill, 1965), p. 83; hereafter BM.
14 BM, pp. 138–48, 148–67.
15 WR i, pp. 408–12; WR ii, pp. 636–9; BM, p. 213.
16 WR i, pp. 277–86; WR ii, pp. 486–93.
17 Sigmund Freud, *The Origins of Psychoanalysis*, trans. Eric Mosbacher and James Strachey (New York: Basic Books, 1954). The crucial unpublished essay dates from 1895.
18 Sigmund Freud, *An Outline of Psychoanalysis* (1940), trans. and ed. James Strachey (New York: W.W. Norton, 1949), pp. 1–5, 20–1, 54–5; hereafter OP.
19 OP, pp. 3, 55–8.
20 OP, pp. 3–4, 62–4.
21 OP, pp. 4–8.
22 OP, pp. 40–4. See also Sigmund Freud, *Five Lectures on Psychoanalysis* (1910), trans. James Strachey (New York: W.W. Norton, n.d.), pp. 12–15; hereafter FL.
23 OP, pp. 17–19; FL, pp. 12–18.
24 FL, p. 33.
25 OP, pp. 26–8. See also Sigmund Freud, *The Interpretation of Dreams* (1900), trans. and ed. James Strachey (New York: Avon, 1965), pp. 155–66, 588–611; hereafter ID.
26 OP, 22–3; FL, pp. 34–8.
27 OP, pp. 24–6; ID, pp. 311–74.
28 OP, p. 90; FL, pp. 43–5.
29 OP, pp. 10–12.
30 OP, p. 10.
31 OP, pp. 12, 45–51.
32 OP, pp. 45–6.
33 OP, pp. 46–9.
34 OP, pp. 50–1.
35 Sigmund Freud, "Female Sexuality" (1931), in *Sexuality and the Psychology of Love*, trans. Joan Riviere (New York: Macmillan/Collier, 1963), pp. 194–211.
36 OP, pp. 29–30.
37 OP, p. 30.
38 OP, pp. 31–3.

39 OP, p. 32.
40 OP, pp. 34–5; FL, p. 53.
41 OP, pp. 35–7; FL, pp. 54–5.
42 OP, pp. 32, 36–7.
43 OP, pp. 30–9.
44 Sigmund Freud, *Civilization and Its Discontents* (1930), trans. James Strachey (New York: W.W. Norton, 1961), pp. 23–8, 33–5; hereafter CD.
45 CD, pp. 48–51, 56–60, 66–9.
46 CD, pp. 60–3.
47 CD, pp. 42–5.
48 CD, pp. 88–92.
49 Sigmund Freud, *Group Psychology and the Analysis of the Ego* (1921), trans. and ed. James Strachey (New York: Liveright, 1967), pp. 49, 54–6; hereafter GP.
50 GP, pp. 32–6.
51 Sigmund Freud, *The Freud Reader*, ed. Peter Gay (New York: W.W. Norton, 1989), pp. 436–43.
52 Sigmund Freud, *The Future of an Illusion*, trans. James Strachey (New York: W.W. Norton, 1961), pp. 16–20, 30–3; hereafter FI. See also CD, pp. 21–3, 29–30.
53 FI, pp. 54–6.
54 Henri Bergson, *Creative Evolution* (1907), trans. Arthur Mitchell (New York: Henry Holt/Mineola, NY: Dover, 1911/1988), pp. 329–43; hereafter CE. My references are to the Dover paperback edition. See also Henri Bergson, *The Creative Mind* (1934), trans. Mabelle L. Andison (New York: Philosophical Library, 1946), pp. 188–94; hereafter CM.
55 CM, pp. 14–22, 146–8. See also Henri Bergson, *Time and Free Will*, trans. F. L. Pogson. (New York: Macmillan/Harper & Row, 1910/1960), pp. 104–7; hereafter TF.
56 CE, pp. 247–53.
57 CM, pp. 30–7, 159–62.
58 TF, pp. 14–15, 43–4, 99–101.
59 CM, pp. 124–9, 197–200.
60 CE, pp. 87–97.
61 CE, pp. 88–9, 98–101, 135.
62 CE, pp. 51, 133–4, 263–8.
63 CE, pp. 135–51, 184–5.
64 TF, pp. 159–70.
65 TF, pp. 222–40.
66 TF, pp. 129–39.
67 Henri Bergson, *Matter and Memory*, trans. Nancy Margaret Paul and W. Scott Palmer (New York: Zone, 1991), pp. 78–88; hereafter MM.
68 MM, pp. 127–34.
69 Henri Bergson, *The Two Sources of Morality and Religion*, trans. R. Ashley Audra and Cloudesley Brereton (New York: Henry Holt/Doubleday, 1935/n.d.), pp. 85–95, 267–71; hereafter TS. My references are to the Doubleday/Anchor paperback edition.
70 TS, pp. 35–8, 49, 55.
71 TS, pp. 33–5, 38, 45–8, 55, 228.
72 TS, pp. 212–16.
73 TS, pp. 230–1, 234–5.

'etzsche also provides an alternative to Darwin's theories.

ıopenhauer insists that it is possible in aesthetic contemplation, but this is a rare achievement.

CHAPTER 4 NIETZSCHE (1844–1900)

1 F. Nietzsche, *The Gay Science*, trans. Walter Kaufmann (Random House, New York, 1974), sect. 125; hereafter GS. All numbered references to Nietzsche's works in this chapter are to section numbers or to part and section numbers, not to page numbers.

2 F. Nietzsche, *Schopenhauer as Educator* in *Untimely Meditations*, trans. R. J. Hollingdale (Cambrdige: Cambridge University Press, 1983), sect. 3; hereafter SE. See also F. Nietzsche, *Thus Spoke Zarathustra*, in *The Portable Nietzsche*, trans. Walter Kaufmann (New York: Viking, 1954), Book III, ch. 12, sect. 3; hereafter Z, III, 12, 3.

3 Z, I, 2 and 3.

4 Z, I, 7.

5 Z, I, 4.

6 F. Nietzsche, *The Birth of Tragedy*, in *Basic Writings of Nietzsche*, trans. Walter Kaufmann (New York: Modern Library, 1968), sect. 25; hereafter BT. See also F. Nietzsche, *Beyond Good and Evil*, in *Basic Writings of Nietzsche*, trans. Walter Kaufmann (New York: Modern Library, 1968), sects. 44, 208, and 213; hereafter BGE.

7 F. Nietzsche, *Ecce Homo* in *Basic Writings of Nietzsche*, trans. Walter Kaufmann (New York: Modern Library, 1968), Preface, sect. 3; hereafter EH.

8 Z, I, 1; III, 12.

9 Z, I, 5.

10 F. Nietzsche, (1968) *On the Genealogy of Morals* in *Basic Writings of Nietzsche*, trans. Walter Kaufmann (New York: Modern Library, 1968), Essay III, sect. 12; hereafter GM, III, 12.

11 BGE 61, 213. See also GM, III, 9 and F. Nietzsche, *Daybreak*, trans. R. J. Hollingdale (Cambridge: Cambridge University Press, 1982), 43, 432; hereafter D. Compare with F. Nietzsche, *The Will to Power*, trans. Walter Kaufmann (New York: Random House, 1967), 976; hereafter WP.

12 F. Nietzsche, *Human, All Too Human*, trans. R. J. Hollingdale (Cambridge: Cambridge University Press, 1986), Book I, sect. 243; hereafter HAH, I, 243. Book II is also called *Mixed Opinions and Maxims*, and Book III is also called *The Wanderer and His Shadow*. See also D, 52.

13 BGE, 295.

14 BGE, 211.

15 GS, 343; see also Z, IV, 6; HAH I, 243.

16 GS, 347.

17 This was Nietzsche's project throughout his career. It emerges in his goal of self-perfection in *Schopenhauer as Educator*; it develops in his elaboration of the "free spirit" in *Human, All Too Human*, of the *Übermensch* in *Zarathustra*, and of "new philosophers" in *Beyond Good and Evil*. These conceptions have different accents, but each develops the previous vision.

18 Z, I, 3.

19 Z, II, 4.

20 Z, II, 5; see also D, 202.

21 Z, I, 3.
22 Z, III, 10.
23 GS, 290; see also D, 346.
24 Z, I, 5. See also F. Nietzsche, *Twilight of Idols*, in *The Portable Nietzsche*, trans. Walter Kaufmann (New York: Viking, 1954), sect. V, 2; hereafter TI. Major parts in this text are numbered in roman numerals, starting with the Preface.
25 GM, I, 10–11.
26 Z, Preface, 5.
27 WP, 22–3.
28 I take Nietzsche's ideal in *Zarathustra* to incorporate the moments from his earlier discussion of self-perfection in *Schopenhauer as Educator*, sect. 1.
29 Z, I, 22.
30 Z, I, 6.
31 HAH, II, 89; GS, 116.
32 HAH, I, 70; D, 13, 202, 236, 252.
33 D, 215.
34 Z, I, 14, 22.
35 GS, 143; D, 404.
36 HAH, III, 44.
37 HAH, I, 228; D, 107; GS, 117.
38 GM, I, 4–7, 11.
39 GM, I, 10, 13–14.
40 BGE, 219.
41 HAH, II, 90; D, 9.
42 Z, II, 13; Z, IV, 13; see also HAH, I, 220.
43 GS, 335.
44 HAH, II, 89; GS, 116; BGE, 62.
45 BGE, 221; see also D, 55, 194.
46 Z, II, 7.
47 What follows is my own interpretation of Nietzsche's approach to the revaluation of values. For a different, equally useful analysis, see E. E. Sleinis, *Nietzsche's Revaluation of Values* (Urbana, IL: University of Illinois Press, 1994).
48 D, 164, 453. See also F. Nietzsche, *The Antichrist*, in *The Portable Nietzsche*, trans. Walter Kaufmann (New York: Viking, 1954), sect. 57; hereafter A.
49 SE, 1; Z, I, 1.
50 Z, I, 5.
51 GS, 290.
52 D, 462; HAH, I, 394; HAH, II, 191; HAH, III, 5–6.
53 EH, II, 10; Z, EH, III, 12, 15; TI, IX, 49.
54 Z, I, 22.
55 Z, III, 12; see also Z, II, 12, 13.
56 GS, 341; see also Z, III, 2, 14–16.
57 Z, II, 12; see also D 548.
58 Z, I, 1.
59 EH, III; BT, 2.
60 F. Nietzsche, "The Birth of Tragedy," in *Basic Writings of Nietzsche*, trans. Walter Kaufmann (New York: Modern Library, 1968), sects. 1–2; hereafter BT.
61 BT, 7, 16, 18.
62 BT, 3–4.
63 BT, 3, 5, 24.

64 Z, II, 17.
65 GS, 370.
66 GS, 370.
67 HAH, III, 96; TI, IX, 11. See also, HAH, II, 177.
68 F. Nietzsche, *On the Uses and Disadvantages of History for Life* in *Untimely Meditations*, trans. R. J. Hollingdale (Cambridge: Cambridge University Press, 1983), sects. 1 and 5; hereafter UDHL.
69 UDHL, 2.
70 UDHL, 2.
71 UDHL, 3.
72 UDHL, 3.
73 UDHL, 6.
74 UDHL, 1. 7.
75 F. Nietzsche, *The Philosopher: Reflections on the Struggle Between Art and Knowledge* in *Philosophy and Truth*, ed. and trans. D. Breazeale (Atlantic Highlands, NJ: Humanities Press, 1979), sect. 46.
76 SE, 5–6.
77 BGE, 229.
78 SE, 1.
79 BGE, 208, 258, 272; see also A, 57.
80 F. Nietzsche, "Homer's Contest," in *The Portable Nietzsche*, trans. Walter Kaufmann (New York: Viking, 1954).
81 SE, 6.
82 Z, I, 14; see also HAH, 228.
83 BGE 259, 263; HAH, I, 93.
84 HAH, I, 446, 473.
85 HAH, II, 317.
86 BGE, 16, 281; see also GS, 322; HAH, I, 65.
87 GS, 354.
88 GS, 11, 333.
89 GS, 290; see also, Z, I, 1; HAH, I, Preface.
90 BGE, 19.
91 Z, I, 4.
92 Z, I, 4; BGE, 225; see also WP, 674, 701.
93 BGE, 19.
94 Z, I, 6.
95 BGE, 22, 14.
96 GM, III, 12.
97 BGE, 39; EH, Preface, 5–6.
98 BGE, 16, 20.
99 BGE, 16; see also D, 47.
100 HAH, I, 2; see also WP 407, 408.
101 GM, III, 12; GM III, 9.
102 BGE, 211.
103 BGE, 211.
104 Z, I, 1; HAH, I, Preface.
105 BGE, 295.

CHAPTER 5 HERMENEUTICS

1 Friedrich Ast (1808/1990) *Hermeneutics* (selections), trans. Dora Van Franken, in Gayle L. Ormiston and Alan D. Schrift, *The Hermeneutic Tradition* (Albany, NY: State University of New York Press, 1990), p. 43; hereafter HT. This is an extremely useful collection of materials from the main figures in this movement.
2 HT, pp. 43–4, 45, 48.
3 HT, pp. 51–3.
4 Friedrich Schleiermacher (1805, 1809/10), *Aphorisms on Hermeneutics* (selections) and (1819) *The Hermeneutics: Outline of 1819 Lectures* (selections), trans. Roland Haas and Jan Wojcik, in HT.
5 HT, pp. 71, 77, 95–6, 97.
6 HT, pp. 64, 66, 76, 79, 86–7.
7 HT, pp. 92–4, 98.
8 HT, pp. 64, 73, 77, 94.
9 HT, pp. 95–6.
10 HT, pp. 93–4, 97.
11 HT, pp. 61.
12 HT, pp. 62–3.
13 HT, pp. 88–9.
14 Wilhelm Dilthey, *Selected Writings*, ed, trans., and intro. by H. D. Rickman (Cambridge: Cambridge University Press, 1976), pp. 260–1, 89–90, 225; hereafter SW.
15 Wilhelm Dilthey, *The Rise of Hermeneutics* (1990), trans. Fredric Jameson, in HT, pp. 102. See also SW, 260–1.
16 SW, pp. 258, 262, 90, 96–7, 221–2.
17 SW, pp. 226–8.
18 HT, pp. 101; SW, pp. 224–5.
19 SW, pp. 89, 211–12.
20 SW, pp. 89, 94–5.
21 SW, pp. 93–4.
22 SW, pp. 92, 95.
23 Sartre was later to call such patterns of personal development "fundamental projects." See chapter 7.
24 SW, p. 91. Elaborating such a hierarchy is a goal of the later movement called Philosophical Anthropology, discussed below in chapter 7.
25 SW, pp. 210–12.
26 SW, pp. 208–10.
27 SW, pp. 216.
28 SW, pp. 214–15.
29 HT, p. 103; SW, pp. 218–20.
30 SW, pp. 220–1.
31 SW, pp. 258, 208, 226.
32 Martin Heidegger, *Being and Time*, trans. John Macquarrie and Edward Robinson (New York: Harper & Row, 1962), sect. 1; hereafter BT. All references to this text will be to *section* number, not page number.
33 BT, 3.
34 BT, 4.
35 BT, 3.
36 BT, 4.
37 BT, 5.

38 BT, 5.
39 BT, 12.
40 BT, 15.
41 BT, 16.
42 BT, 2, 9.
43 Worldhood (12–24); Being-with and *Das Man* (25–7); Being-in (28–38).
44 BT, 9.
45 BT, 27.
46 BT, 74.
47 BT, 2, 32.
48 BT, 3.
49 BT, 28.
50 Much of my exposition below abbreviates Hubert Dreyfus's helpful discussion in his *Being in the World* (Cambridge, MA: MIT Press, 1991).
51 BT, 29.
52 BT, 31.
53 BT, 34.
54 BT, 32.
55 BT, 32.
56 BT, 33.
57 Hans-Georg Gadamer, *The Universality of the Hermeneutic Problem* (1976), in HT, pp. 148, 152. See also Hans-Georg Gadamer, *Truth and Method*, ed. Garett Barden and John Cumming (New York: Seabury Press, 1975), pp. 319–21, 334–7, 337–9; hereafter TM.
58 HT, pp. 148–50; TM, pp. 244–5.
59 HT, pp. 151–2; TM 267–9, 326–7.
60 HT, p. 152; TM, pp. xxiii, 324–5, 330, 340–1.
61 HT, pp. 156–7; TM, pp. 261–67, 271–2, 324–5.
62 TM, pp. 316–19, 340–1, 358–9.
63 TM, pp. 272–4, 337–41.
64 HT, 156.
65 TM, pp. 332–3.
66 HT, pp. 152–4; TM, pp. 328–9.
67 Emilio Betti, *Hermeneutics as the General Methodology of the Geistwissenschaften* (1972; selections), trans. Josef Bleicher, in HT, pp. 164, 171–5, 186–7.
68 HT, pp. 182–4.
69 HT, pp. 192–4.
70 HT, pp. 184–5.
71 HT, pp. 161–4, 172–3, 188.
72 HT, pp. 160–2, 165.
73 HT, pp. 188–91.
74 HT, pp. 163–4, 168–9.
75 HT, pp. 165–6.
76 HT, pp. 167–8, 193–4.
77 William R. Schroeder, "A Teachable Theory of Interpretation," in Cary Nelson (ed.), *Theory in the Classroom* (Champaign, IL: University of Illinois Press, 1986), pp. 9–44.
78 Stanley Cavell, *Pursuits of Happiness* (Cambridge, MA: Harvard University Press, 1981), pp. 1–42.

79 Cavell thinks romantic comedies of remarriage and the melodramas of the unknown woman are adjacent in this way. See Stanley Cavell, *Contesting Tears* (Chicago, IL: University of Chicago Press, 1996), pp. 3–30.

CHAPTER 6 PHENOMENOLOGY

1 Edmund Husserl, *Cartesian Meditations*, trans. Dorian Cairns (The Hague, Netherlands: Martinus Nijhoff, 1960), sects. 7–8; hereafter CM. All references to this text will be to *section* numbers.
2 Max Scheler, "The Philosopher's Outlook," in *Philosophical Perspectives*, trans. Oscar A. Haac (Boston: Beacon Press, 1958).
3 Martin Heidegger, *Being and Time*, trans. John Macquarrie and Edward Robinson (New York: Harper & Row, 1962), sects. 12–13, 15; hereafter BT. All further references to this text will be to *section* numbers.
4 Jean-Paul Sartre, *Transcendence of the Ego*, trans. Forrest Williams and Robert Kirkpatrick (New York: Noonday, 1957), pp. 71–91; hereafter TE.
5 Jean-Paul Sartre, *Being and Nothingness*, trans. Hazel E. Barnes (New York: Philosophical Library, 1956), pp. 553–66; hereafter BN.
6 Maurice Merleau-Ponty, *Phenomenology of Perception*, trans. Colin Smith (London: Routledge & Kegan Paul, 1962), pp. xvii–xxi; hereafter PP.
7 Emmanuel Levinas, *Totality and Infinity*, trans. Alphonso Lingis (Pittsburgh, PA: Duquesne University Press, 1969), pp. 194–240; hereafter TI.
8 CM, 3–5.
9 BT, 3–4.
10 CM, 14, 17.
11 Max Scheler, "Idealism-Realism," in *Selected Philosophical Papers*, trans. David R. Lachterman (Evanston, IL: Northwestern University Press, 1973); hereafter SPP.
12 BN, pp. ix–xvii.
13 PP, pp. 3–13.
14 BN, pp. 171–204.
15 BN, pp. 557–74; PP, pp. 410–33.
16 Max Scheler, *The Nature of Sympathy*, trans. Peter Heath (Hamden, CN: Archon, 1954), pp. 260–4; hereafter NS. See also Max Scheler, "Ordo Amoris" (1973), in SPP.
17 Jean-Paul Sartre, *Critique of Dialectical Reason*, vol. 1, trans. Alan Sheridan-Smith, ed. Jonathan Ree (London: New Left Books, 1976); hereafter CDR.
18 CM, 3–5, 7, 9, 12.
19 See Maurice Merleau-Ponty, *The Structure of Behavior*, trans. Alden L. Fischer (Boston: Beacon Press, 1963).
20 BN, pp. 47–70.
21 PP, pp. 142–53.
22 CM, 14–17.
23 Alfred Schutz, *Phenomenology of the Social World*, trans. George Walsh and Frederick Lehnert (Evanston, IL: Northwestern University Press, 1967), pp. 45–96.
24 BT, 2.
25 BT, 29–34.
26 BN, pp. 155–60.
27 CM, 6–9.
28 CM, 1–3, 10–11.

29 CM, 5–9, 24.
30 CM, 14, 17.
31 CM, 34–6.
32 CM, 25–9.
33 CM, 36–41.
34 CM, 43.
35 CM, 30–3, 41.
36 CM, 43.
37 CM, 44–7.
38 CM, 45–7.
39 CM, 51.
40 CM, 50, 52.
41 CM, 53–4.
42 CM, 51.
43 CM, 55.
44 CM, 56–8.
45 NS, pp. 213–33.
46 NS, p. 244.
47 NS, pp. 244–6.
48 NS, pp. 246–7.
49 NS, pp. 252–3, 260–1.
50 NS, pp. 261–2.
51 BT, 26.
52 BT, 26.
53 BT, 27.
54 BT, 26.
55 BN, pp. 250–2.
56 BN, pp. 259–68.
57 BN, pp. 268–9.
58 BN, pp. 361–4.
59 BN, pp. 557–75.
60 PP, pp. vii–xxi.
61 PP, pp. 3–65.
62 PP, pp. 73–97.
63 PP, pp. 148–53, 174–201.
64 PP, pp. 299–354.
65 PP, pp. 207–41.
66 PP, pp. 334–45.
67 PP, pp. 177–84.
68 PP, pp. 358–65.
69 Maurice Merleau-Ponty, "An Unpublished Text," in *The Primacy of Perception*, ed. James M. Edie (Evanston, IL: Northwestern University Press, 1964), pp. 10–11; hereafter PriP.
70 This is amply demonstrated in the footnotes to both SB and PP.
71 Roman Ingarden, *The Literary Work of Art*, trans. George M. Grabowicz (Evanston, IL: Northwestern University Press, 1973).
72 Maurice Merleau-Ponty, "Eye and Mind" (1964), in PriP, pp. 159–90.
73 Mikel Dufrenne, *The Phenomenology of Aesthetic Experience*, trans. Edward S. Casey, Albert A. Anderson, Willis Domingo, and Leon Jacobson (Evanston, IL: Northwestern University Press, 1973).

74 R. D. Laing, *Knots* (New York: Pantheon, 1970); Erving Goffman, *Interaction Ritual* (New York: Anchor, 1967).

75 Martin Buber, *I and Thou*, trans. Walter Kaufmann (New York: Charles Scribner's Sons, 1970).

76 Eugene Minkowski, *Lived Time*, trans. Nancy Metzel (Evanston, IL: Northwestern University Press, 1970).

77 Max Scheler, *Formalism in Ethics and a Non-Formal Ethic of Value*, trans. Manfred Frings and Roger L. Funk (Evanston, IL: Northwestern University Press, 1973).

78 Nicolai Hartmann, *Ethics*, vol. 2, trans. Stanton Coit, Introduction by J. H. Muirhead (London: George Allen & Unwin, 1932).

79 Jean-Paul Sartre, *Search for a Method*, trans. Hazel E. Barnes (New York: Alfred A. Knoft, 1963).

CHAPTER 7 EXISTENTIALISM AND PHILOSOPHICAL ANTHROPOLOGY

1 Sartre discusses the importance of pre-reflective experience in his early essay, "Transcendence of the Ego." Jean-Paul Sartre, *Transcendence of the Ego*, trans. Forrest Williams and Robert Kirkpatrick (New York: Farrar, Straus, and Giroux, 1957), pp. 45–9; hereafter TE. Heidegger highlights this dimension of human life in his discussions of Being-in-the-World and of phenomenology in his *Being and Time*, trans. John Macquarrie and Edward Robinson (New York: Harper & Row, 1962), sects. 4, 7, and 12; hereafter BT. All references to this text will be to *section* numbers.

2 BT, 65–9, 79, 82. Jean-Paul Sartre, *Being and Nothingness: An Essay in Phenomenological Ontology*, trans. Hazel E. Barnes (New York: Philosophical Library, 1956), pp. 124–9; hereafter BN.

3 BT, 43.

4 BT, 14, 16; BN, 124–9. Jean-Paul Sartre, *Emotions: Outline of a Theory*, trans. Bernard Frechtman (New York: Philosophical Library, 1948), pp. 56–64; hereafter E.

5 BT, 15.

6 BN, pp. ix–lxvii, 200–4.

7 BT, 50–3, 61–2.

8 BN, pp. 55–70.

9 BN, pp. 29–45; BT, 40.

10 BN, p. lxvi; BT, 38.

11 BN, pp. 553–6.

12 Søren Kierkegaard, *The Present Age*, trans. Alexander Dru (New York: Harper & Row, 1962), pp. 36–41; hereafter PA.

13 Kierkegaard's discussion of these types of life appears in Søren Kierkegaard, *Either/Or*, vols. 1 and 2, trans. Walter Lowrie (Garden City, NY: Doubleday & Co., 1959); hereafter E/O; Søren Kierkegaard, *Stages on Life's Way*, trans. Walter Lowrie (New York: Schocken, 1967); hereafter SLW; and Søren Kierkegaard, *Fear and Trembling*, trans. Walter Lowrie (Garden City, NY: Doubleday & Co., 1954); hereafter FT.

14 Hegel stresses the importance of internal critical of evaluating forms of life in his *Phenomenology of Spirit*, trans. A. V. Miller (Oxford: Oxford University Press, 1977), sects. 84–6; hereafter PS. All references to this text will be to *section* numbers.

15 PS, 87.

16 G. W. F. Hegel, *Philosophy of Right*, trans. T. M. Knox. (Oxford: Oxford University Press, 1967), sects. 198, 243–5; hereafter PR.

17 Hegel indicates the rough nature of this structure in PS, 85–6.

18 PA, pp. 42–5.

19 PA, pp. 35–8.

20 This is clearest in SLW.

21 This is one of the key charges against "reflection" in PA, pp. 37–9, 77–9.

22 Some support for this view exists in both PR and PS, but there is support for more complex readings as well. Hegel does think that social life and culture are essential to a viable individual ethic.

23 Richard Schacht offers an insightful analysis of these subtypes in "Kierkegaard's Phenomenology of Spiritual Development," in his *Hegel and After* (Pittsburgh, PA: University of Pittsburgh Press, 1975), pp. 135–74; hereafter HA. I have drawn on this essay in the discussion below.

24 This type of life is described in "Diary of a Seducer," in E/O i, pp. 297–440.

25 E/O i, pp. 322–3, 330–1.

26 E/O i, pp. 304–5.

27 E/O ii, pp. 234–6.

28 PS, 360–5.

29 The commitment to marriage is the paradigm of the ethical type of life.

30 E/O ii, 345–56. See also Søren Kierkegaard, *Concluding Unscientific Postscript*, trans. David F. Swenson, Introduction and Notes Walter Lowrie (Princeton, NJ: Princeton University Press, 1941), pp. 404–6; 516–18; F/T, pp. 84–8; hereafter CUP.

31 These values inform the entire discussion of PA.

32 FT, pp. 64–72, 89–91; CUP, pp. 191–5, 206.

33 FT, pp. 47, 81–2; CUP, p. 290.

34 This case is discussed at length in FT.

35 CUP, pp. 230–1, 340–3.

36 CUP, pp. 175, 217, 228. See also Richard Schacht, "Kierkegaard on 'Truth is Subjectivity' and 'The Leap of Faith'," in HA.

37 BT, 1–4.

38 BT, 15.

39 Thus, presence-at-hand is a degenerate form of readiness-to-hand (BT, 15); being-alone is a degenerate form of being-with (BT, 26); and theory is only one type of practice (BT, 13).

40 BT, 16.

41 BT, 15.

42 BT, 13.

43 BT, 4, 9.

44 BT, 9.

45 BT, 59.

46 BT, 12.

47 BT, 25.

48 BT, 14–15.

49 BT, 16, 18.

50 BT, 26.

51 BT, 26.

52 BT, 36–7.

53 BT, 40–1, 62.
54 BT, 16, 18.
55 BT, 9, xx (60).
56 BT, (61).
57 BT, 65, 74.
58 BT, 65–74.
59 BT, 74.
60 BN, pp. lxiv–lxvi.
61 BN, pp. lxvi, 199–201.
62 BN, pp. 353–6. See also Jean-Paul Sartre, "Existentialism is a Humanism," in *Existentialism from Dostoevsky to Sartre*, ed. Walter Kaufmann (Cleveland, OH: World Publishers, 1956), pp. 290–1; hereafter EH.
63 BN, pp. 481–553.
64 This approach to facticity emerges most clearly in Jean-Paul Sartre, *Critique of Dialectical Reason*, vol. 1, trans. Alan Sheridan-Smith, ed. Jonathan Ree (London: New Left Books, 1976), pp. 153–97; hereafter CDR.
65 BN, pp. 29–32.
66 Sartre describes several patterns of self-deception in BN, pp. 55–67.
67 These conclusions emerge vividly from Sartre's play, *The Flies*. See also EH, pp. 291–4.
68 BN, pp. lxii–lxvi.
69 BN, pp. lxv–lxvi, 66–7.
70 BN, pp. lx–lxii.
71 BN, pp. 282–97.
72 BN, pp. 57–63.
73 BN, pp. 57–63.
74 BN, pp. 84–105.
75 BN, pp. 481–553.
76 BN, pp. 29–35.
77 BN, pp. 75–9.
78 For an elaboration of this point, see Christina Howells, "Sartre and the Deconstruction of the Subject" in Howells, Christina (ed.) *The Cambridge Companion to Sartre* (Cambridge: Cambridge University Press, 1992), pp. 318–52.
79 BN, pp. 160–7; TE, pp. 71–91.
80 BN, pp. 285–9.
81 BN, pp. 361–4.
82 BN, pp. l–lvi.
83 BN, pp. 260–3.
84 BN, pp. 155–61.
85 Jean-Paul Sartre, *Nausea*, trans. Lloyd Alexander (New York: New Directions, 1949).
86 BN, 357–9.
87 E, pp. 53–91.
88 BN, pp. 563–75.
89 BN, pp. 573–4.
90 BN, pp. 571–3.
91 Included in these biographies are books on Baudelaire, Genet, Mallarmé, and Flaubert. Jean-Paul Sartre, *Baudelaire*, trans. Martin Turnell (New York: New Directions, 1950). Jean-Paul Sartre, *Saint Genet*, trans. Bernard Frechtman (New York: George Braziller, 1963). Jean-Paul Sartre, *Mallarmé*, trans. Earnest Sturm

(University Park, PA: Pennsylvania State University Press, 1988). Jean-Paul Sartre, *The Family Idiot*, trans. Carol Cosman (Chicago, IL: University of Chicago Press, 1981–93).

92 Jean-Paul Sartre, *The Words*, trans. Bernard Frechtman (New York: George Braziller, 1964).

93 BN, pp. 597–600, 626–8.

94 See CDR.

95 BN, pp. 408–12.

96 BN, pp. 70, 412.

97 Jean-Paul Sartre, *What is Literature*? trans. Bernard Frechtman (Cambridge, MA: Harvard University Press, 1988), pp. 48–69; hereafter WL.

98 Jean-Paul Sartre, *Notebooks for an Ethics*, trans. David Pellauer (Chicago, IL: University of Chicago Press, 1992), pp. 274–89.

99 See Jean-Paul Sartre, *Search for a Method*, trans. Hazel Barnes (New York: Knopf, 1963).

100 Max Scheler, *Man's Place in Nature*, trans. Hans Meyerhoff (New York: Beacon Press/Noonday, 1961); hereafter MPN.

101 Max Scheler, "Man and History" in *Philosophical Perspectives*, trans. Oscar A. Haac (Boston: Beacon, 1958); hereafter MH.

102 These four positions are discussed in MH, pp. 69–89.

103 MH, pp. 82–93.

104 Max Scheler, "Man in the Age of Adjustment," in *Philosophical Perspectives*, trans. Oscar A. Haac (Boston: Beacon, 1958), pp. 100–22; hereafter MAA.

105 MPN, pp. 9–12.

106 MPN, pp. 10–14.

107 MPN, p. 15.

108 MPN, pp. 14, 52–3.

109 MPN, pp. 28–9.

110 MPN, p. 16.

111 MPN, pp. 20–1.

112 MPN, pp. 22–6.

113 MPN, pp. 26–7.

114 MPN, pp. 29–30.

115 MPN, pp. 36–41.

116 MPN, pp. 37–40, 43, 46.

117 MPN, pp. 40–1, 64.

118 MPN, p. 41.

119 MPN, p. 47.

120 MPN, p. 48.

121 MPN, pp. 49–55.

122 MPN, pp. 57, 64–5, 81.

123 MPN, pp. 66–71.

124 MPN, pp. 83–7.

125 Kurt Goldstein, *Human Nature in the Light of Psychopathology* (New York: Schocken, 1963); hereafter HN. Kurt Goldstein, *The Organism* (New York: Zone Books, 1995); hereafter O.

126 HN, pp. 10–12; O, pp. 173–200.

127 HN, pp. 28, 209–10.

128 HN, pp. x–xii; 28–9; O, pp. 26–7.

129 HN, pp. 23–6, 203–6.

130 HN, pp. 11, 140–5; O, pp. 95–6.
131 HN, pp. 11–13; O, pp. 101–2.
132 HN, pp. 15, 172–84; O, pp. 265–83.
133 HN, pp. 15–21.
134 HN, pp. 24–5; O, pp. 307–8.
135 O, pp. 23–6.
136 O, pp. 240–64.
137 HN, pp. 51–61.
138 HN, pp. 133–8; O, pp. 380–2.
139 HN, pp. 23–8.
140 O, pp. 307–8; 314–16.
141 Arnold Gehlen, *Man: His Nature and Place in the World*, trans. Clare McMillan and Karl Pillemer (New York: Columbia University Press, 1988), pp. 13, 24–31; hereafter M.
142 M, pp. 30–1.
143 M, pp. 32–7.
144 M, pp. 27–31, 333–40.
145 M, pp. 28–9, 354–62.
146 Arnold Gehlen, *Man in the Age of Technology*, trans. Patricia Lipscomb (New York: Columbia University Press, 1980), pp. 8–22; hereafter MAT.
147 MAT, pp. 115–16.
148 MAT, pp. 106–9; M 392–3.
149 M, 237–42.

CHAPTER 8 STRUCTURALISM

1 Ferdinand de Saussure, *Course in General Linguistics*, trans. Wade Baskin, ed. Charles Bally and Albert Sechehaye (New York: Philosophical Library/McGraw-Hill, 1959/66), pp. 8–11; hereafter CGL. My references are to the McGraw-Hill paperback edition.
2 CGL, pp. 13–20, 71–4.
3 CGL, pp. 65–7.
4 CGL, pp. 67–9.
5 CGL, pp. 111–20.
6 CGL, pp. 120–2.
7 CGL, pp. 87–91, 98–102.
8 CGL, pp. 122–7.
9 CGL, pp. 15–17.
10 Roland Barthes, *Elements of Semiology and Writing Degree Zero*, trans. Annette Lavers and Colin Smith (London: Jonathan Cape, 1967; Boston: Beacon Press, 1970), pp. 15–17; hereafter ES.
11 ES, pp. 21–2.
12 ES, pp. 22–3.
13 ES, pp. 22–3.
14 ES, pp. 25–30.
15 ES, pp. 30–4.
16 ES, pp. 41–2.
17 ES, pp. 31–2, 50–4.
18 Roman Jakobson, *Language in Literature*, ed. Krystyna Pomorski and Stephen Rudy (Cambridge, MA: Harvard University Press, 1987), pp. 109–14.

19 Roland Barthes, "Myth Today," in *Mythologies*, trans. Annette Lavers (New York: Hill and Wang, 1972), pp. 109–59.
20 Roland Barthes, *Sade, Fourier, Loyola*, trans. Richard Miller (New York: Hill and Wang, 1976), pp. 15–37, 122–71.
21 Roland Barthes, *Michelet*, trans. Richard Howard (New York: Hill and Wang, 1987).
22 Roland Barthes, *On Racine*, trans. Richard Howard (New York: Hill and Wang, 1964).
23 Roland Barthes, *Pleasure of the Text*, trans. Richard Howard (New York: Hill and Wang, 1975); hereafter PT.
24 Roland Barthes, *Criticism and Truth*, trans. and ed. Katrine Pilcher Keuneman (Minneapolis, MN: University of Minnesota Press, 1987).
25 Roland Barthes, *S/Z*, trans. Richard Miller (New York: Hill and Wang, 1974), pp. 18–20; hereafter SZ.
26 Claude Lévi-Strauss, *Myth and Meaning* (Toronto: University of Toronto Press/New York: Schocken Books, 1978/79), New York, pp. 18–20; hereafter MM. My references are to the Schocken edition.
27 Claude Lévi-Strauss, *The Savage Mind* (London: Weidenfelt and Nicholson Ltd/ Chicago, IL: University of Chicago Press, 1966), chs. 1 and 2; hereafter SM. My references are to the University of Chicago edition. See also Claude Lévi-Strauss, *Structural Anthropology*, trans. Claire Jacobson and Brooke Grundfest Schoepf (New York: Basic Books/Anchor Books, 1963/67), pp. 226–7; hereafter SA. My references are to the Anchor edition.
28 SA, pp. 38–49.
29 MM, pp. 3–4.
30 Claude Lévi-Strauss, *Tristes Tropiques*, trans. John and Doreen Weightman (New York: Atheneum, 1974).
31 MM, pp. 8–10. See also SA, pp. 247–8.
32 Lévi-Strauss comments on this connection explicitly in his *The Raw and the Cooked*, trans. John and Doreen Weightman (New York: Harper & Row, 1969), pp. 10–12; hereafter RC.
33 SA, pp. 31–2.
34 SA, pp. 203–28; see also RC, pp. 1–5.
35 This idea is developed throughout RC.
36 MM, pp. 44–54. These musical forms govern the organization of RC, as an examination of the table of contents will show.
37 SA, pp. 209–27.
38 MM, 34–44.
39 Alexander Kojève, *Introduction to the Reading of Hegel*, trans. James H. Nichols, Jr., ed. Allan Bloom (New York: Basic Books, 1969).
40 Jacques Lacan, *Écrits*, trans. Alan Sheridan (New York: W.W. Norton, 1977), pp. 49, 59; hereafter E.
41 E, pp. 68–70.
42 E, pp. 153–5.
43 E, pp. 2–4.
44 E, pp. 4–6.
45 E, pp. 6–7, 41–3.
46 E, p. 64.
47 E, pp. 44–6.
48 E, pp. 155–9.
49 Louis Althusser, *For Marx*, trans. Ben Brewster (New York: Allen Lane, Penguin Press/Random House, 1969/70), pp. 30–9; hereafter FM.

50 Louis Althusser and Étienne Balibar, *Reading Capital*, trans. Ben Brewster (London: New Left Books, 1970), pp. 185–6. See also, FM, pp. 200–9.
51 FM, pp. 12–14.
52 Louis Althusser, *Lenin and Philosophy*, trans. Ben Brewster (New York: Monthly Review Press, 1971), pp. 170–4; hereafter LP.
53 FM, pp. 149, 232.
54 LP, pp. 140–5.
55 LP, pp. 146–57.
56 LP, pp. 152–3.
57 LP, pp. 165–70.
58 LP, pp. 172–6, 180–3.
59 This is how Barthes organizes most of his last books, e.g., *Lover's Discourse, Pleasure of the Text*, and *Barthes by Barthes*.
60 Roland Barthes, *A Lover's Discourse*, trans. Richard Howard (New York: Hill and Wang, 1978).
61 PT, pp. 19–22, 24–5, 40–1, 44, and 51–3.
62 Roland Barthes, *Roland Barthes*, trans. Richard Howard (New York: Hill and Wang, 1977).
63 Roland Barthes, *Camera Lucida*, trans. Richard Howard (New York: Hill and Wang, 1981).

CHAPTER 9 PHILOSOPHIES OF DISPERSION

1 I consider these objections in the fourth section of the Conclusions, pp. 363–73.
2 Michel Foucault, *The Order of Things*, trans. A. M. Sheridan-Smith (New York: Random House/Vintage, 1970/73), pp. xii–xiii, xxii–xxiv; hereafter OT. References to this book are to the Vintage paperback.
3 OT, pp. xi, xiv, xx–xxii.
4 Michel Foucault, *Discipline and Punish*, trans. Alan Sheridan (New York: Pantheon, 1977), pp. 298–306; hereafter DP.
5 DP, pp. 136–41, 170–84.
6 DP, pp. 294–308.
7 See, e.g., Georges Canguilhem, *The Normal and the Pathological*, trans. Carolyn R. Fawcett and Robert S. Cohen (New York: Zone Books, 1989); and Georges Canguilhem, *Ideology and Rationality in the History of the Life Sciences*, trans. Arther Goldhammer (Cambridge, MA: MIT, 1988).
8 Michel Foucault, *Archaeology of Knowledge*, trans. A. M. Sheridan-Smith (New York: Pantheon, 1972), pp. 7–12, 169–77; hereafter AK.
9 AK, pp. 37–9, 138–40.
10 Thomas Kuhn, *The Structure of Scientific Revolutions* (Chicago, IL: University of Chicago Press, 1962).
11 OT, pp. 217–21.
12 AK, pp. 72–6, 160–2.
13 OT, pp. 17–44.
14 OT, pp. 50–76.
15 OT, pp. 250–300.
16 OT, pp. 303–43, 386–7.
17 Michel Foucault, *Madness and Civilization*, trans. Richard Howard (New York: Random House/Vintage, 1965/73), pp. 38–64; hereafter MC. References to this book are to the Vintage paperback.

18 MC, pp. 218–28, 232–40.

19 DP, pp. 231–56; MC, pp. 260–9; Michel Foucault, *Birth of the Clinic*, trans. A. M. Sheridan-Smith (New York: Random House/Vintage, 1973/75), pp. 107–22; hereafter BC. References to this book are to the Vintage paperback.

20 DP, pp. 248–56; MC, pp. 241–55.

21 DP, pp. 22–30, 209–17, 271; Michel Foucault, *History of Sexuality*, trans. Robert Hurley (New York: Random House, 1978), pp. 135–59; hereafter HS.

22 DP, pp. 32–69.

23 DP, pp. 170–94.

24 MC, pp. ix–xi.

25 DP, pp. 248–56, 272–92.

26 AK, pp. 181–4, 186–92.

27 DP, pp. 23–4, 27–8, 218–28; MC, pp. 247–69.

28 DP, pp. 29–31, 170–94.

29 DP, pp. 218–28.

30 DP, pp. 192–4. See also Michel Foucault, *Power/Knowledge*, trans. Colon Gordon et al., ed. Colin Gordon (London/New York: Harvester/Pantheon, 1980), p. 142; hereafter PK.

31 PK, p. 142.

32 PK, pp. 143–5.

33 Michel Foucault, *The Foucault Reader*, ed. Paul Rabinow (New York: Pantheon, 1984), pp. 42–7; hereafter FR.

34 PK, pp. 126–33.

35 FR, pp. 32–50.

36 Michel Foucault, *The Use of Pleasure*, trans. Robert Hurley (New York: Random House, 1985), pp. 78–93, 109–24, 166–84; hereafter UP. Michel Foucault, *The Care of the Self*, trans. Robert Hurley (New York: Random House, 1986), pp. 17–35, 81–95, 124–43, 249–54; hereafter CS.

37 FR, pp. 344–7.

38 UP, pp. 25–32.

39 UP, pp. 14–24, 33–95.

40 CS, pp. 69–80, 145–85.

41 CS, pp. 235–40; FR, pp. 353–6, 358–9, 366–70.

42 FR, pp. 47–50.

43 FR, pp. 351–2, 354–5. Michel Foucault, *Ethics, Subjectivity, and Truth*, trans. Robert Hurley, ed. Paul Rabinow (New York: New Press, 1997), pp. 286–7, 300–1.

44 Jacques Derrida, *Speech and Phenomena*, trans. David B. Allison, Preface by Newton Garver (Evanston IL: Northwestern University Press, 1973), pp. 60–9, 99–104; hereafter SP.

45 SP, pp. 48–59.

46 SP, pp. 82–7.

47 SP, pp. 74–84.

48 SP, pp. 99–104. Jacques Derrida, *Of Grammatology*, trans. Gayatri Chakravorty Spivak (Baltimore, MD: Johns Hopkins University Press, 1974/76), pp. 3–10, 17–26; hereafter OG.

49 SP, pp. 32–47; OG, pp. 65–73.

50 Jacques Derrida, *Margins of Philosophy*, trans. Alan Bass (Chicago IL: University of Chicago Press, 1982), pp. 177–205.

51 Jacques Derrida, "Différance" (1973), in SP, pp. 129–31, 138–42, 149–56.

52 Jacques Derrida, *Writing and Difference*, trans. and intro. Alan Bass (Chicago, IL: University of Chicago Press, 1978), pp. 285–93; hereafter WD. SP, pp. 135–6.
53 SP, pp. 129–38.
54 SP, pp. 136–40.
55 SP, pp. 140–2.
56 Edmund Husserl, *The Phenomenology of Internal Time Consciousness*, trans. James Churchill, ed. Martin Heidegger (Bloomington, IN: Indiana University Press, 1964).
57 WD, pp. 196–9, 215–31.
58 Martin Heidegger, *Being and Time*, trans. John Macquarrie and Edward Robinson (New York: Harper & Row, 1962), sect. 6.
59 See SP.
60 Jacques Derrida, "The Force of Law," in Druscilla Cornell, et al. (eds.), *Deconstruction and the Possibility of Justice* (London: Routledge, 1992).
61 Jacques Derrida, *The Politics of Friendship*, trans. George Collin (London: Verso, 1997), pp. 138–93.
62 Gilles Deleuze and Felix Guatarri, *A Thousand Plateaus*, trans. Brian Massumi (Minneapolis, MN: University of Minnesota Press, 1987), pp. 6–8; hereafter TP.
63 TP, pp. 8–11.
64 TP, pp. 12–16, 25, 53–4, 361–74, 380–3.
65 Gilles Deleuze, *Difference and Repetition*, trans. Paul Patton (New York: Columbia University Press, 1994), pp. 228–46; hereafter DR.
66 DR, pp. 234–9.
67 Gilles Deleuze and Felix Guatarri, *Anti-Oedipus*, trans. Robert Hurley, Mark Seem, and Helen L. Lane (Minneapolis, MN: University of Minnesota Press, 1983), pp. 1–8; hereafter AO.
68 AO, pp. 36–41.
69 TP, pp. 21–5, 398–401.
70 AO, pp. 36–41, 322–5, 340–2.
71 AO, pp. 145–53.
72 AO, pp. 192–216.
73 AO, pp. 222–61.
74 TP, pp. 103–10.
75 Gilles Deleuze and Felix Guatarri, *Kafka: Toward a Minor Literature*, trans. Dana Polan (Minneapolis, MN: University of Minnesota Press, 1986), pp. 16–27.
76 Gilles Deleuze and Felix Guatarri, *What is Philosophy?* trans. Hugh Tomlinson and Graham Burchell (New York: Columbia University Press, 1994), pp. 2–8, 15–34, 61–84.
77 Gilles Deleuze, *The Logic of Sense*, trans. Mark Lester with Charles Stivale, ed. Constantin Boundas (New York: Columbia University Press, 1990), pp. 142–53.
78 AO, pp. 322–82.
79 For a good example, see Terry Eagleton, *The Illusions of Postmodernism* (Oxford: Blackwell, 1996).

CHAPTER 10 FRENCH FEMINIST PHILOSOPHY

1 Simone de Beauvoir, *The Second Sex*, trans. H. M. Parshley (New York: Alfred A. Knopf, 1953/New York: Bantam, 1961); hereafter SS. My references are to the Bantam paperback edition.

2 Simone de Beauvoir, *The Ethics of Ambiguity*, trans. Bernard Frechtman (New York: Philosophical Library, 1948/New York: Citadel, 1964); hereafter EA. My references are to the Citadel paperback edition.
3 EA, pp. 13–17, 156–9.
4 EA, pp. 7–8.
5 EA, pp. 14–15, 25–6, 122–8, 145–6.
6 EA, pp. 118–25.
7 EA, pp. 133–8.
8 EA, pp. 70–3.
9 EA, pp. 62–3, 118–20.
10 I summarize Hegel's discussion of pure recognition above in chapter 1, pp. 38–9.
11 EA, pp. 60, 66–7, 82.
12 EA, pp. 39–43.
13 EA, pp. 76–8, 132–4.
14 EA, pp. 42–6.
15 EA, pp. 47–52.
16 EA, pp. 52–7.
17 EA, pp. 58–62.
18 EA, pp. 63–6.
19 EA, pp. 68–70.
20 EA, pp. 135–6, 144–5.
21 EA, pp. 142–3; SS, pp. xxvii, 688–9.
22 SS, pp. xvii–xviii, 675–7.
23 SS, p. xvi.
24 SS, pp. xx–xxi.
25 SS, pp. 681–6.
26 SS, pp. 674–5.
27 SS, pp. xxix, 400–55.
28 SS, pp. 185–235.
29 SS, pp. 592–637.
30 SS, p. xxvii.
31 SS, pp. 681–4, 686.
32 SS, pp. 675–7.
33 SS, pp. 654–6.
34 Julia Kristeva, "Women's Time," in Richard Kearney and Mara Rainwater (eds.), *The Continental Philosophy Reader* (London: Routledge, 1996), pp. 384–5; hereafter WT.
35 WT, pp. 385, 397–9.
36 Some of these objections are mentioned in Elizabeth Grosz, *Sexual Subversions* (Sydney, Australia: Allen & Unwin, 1989); hereafter Ssub. I have benefited from her discussions of Kristeva, Irigaray, and Le Doeuff.
37 Since the mid-1990s, Irigaray herself has been moving in this direction.
38 WT, 396–8.
39 Julia Kristeva, *Revolution in Poetic Language*, trans. Margaret Waller, intro. Leon S. Roudiez (New York: Columbia University Press, 1984), pp. 24–5; hereafter RPL.
40 RPL, pp. 25–7, 40–1.
41 RPL, pp. 24, 43–5, 66–7, 81.
42 RPL, pp. 58–60, 62–6, 70–1.

43 This method is illustrated in various essays in Julia Kristeva, *Desire in Language*, trans. Thomas Gora, Alice Jardine, and Leon S. Roudiez (New York: Columbia University Press, 1980); hereafter DL.
44 Julia Kristiva, *Powers of Horror*, trans. Leon S. Roudiez (New York: Columbia University Press, 1982), pp. 1–6, 9–10; hereafter PH.
45 PH, pp. 12–15.
46 PH, pp. 16–17, 18–26.
47 DL, 337–8.
48 DL, pp. 239–40.
49 Julia Kristeva, *Tales of Love*, trans. Leon S. Roudiez (New York: Columbia University Press, 1987), pp. 6–12.
50 Luce Irigaray, *The Sex Which Is Not One*, trans. Catherine Porter with Carolyn Burke (Ithaca, NY: Cornell University Press, 1985), pp. 68–70; hereafter SNO.
51 SNO, pp. 25–6, 78–80. See also Luce Irigaray, *An Ethics of Sexual Difference*, trans. Carolyn Burke and Gillian C. Gill (Ithaca, NY: Cornell University Press, 1993), pp. 121–2; hereafter ESD.
52 Both Merleau-Ponty and Levinas explore this aspect of the caress as well.
53 ESD, pp. 17–19.
54 ESD, pp. 138–41.
55 SNO, pp. 74–5.
56 See, for example, ESD, p. 127 and SNO, pp. 101–18. Also Luce Irigaray, *Marine Love of Friedrich Nietzsche*, trans. Gillian C. Gill (New York: Columbia University Press, 1991) and Luce Irigaray, *The Forgetting of Air in Martin Heidegger*, trans. M. B. Mader (Austin, TX: University of Texas Press, 1999). There is precedent for this kind of analysis in the work of Gaston Bachelard and Emmanuel Levinas.
57 SNO, pp. 78–80.
58 SNO, p. 80.
59 Luce Irigaray, *Speculum of the Other Woman*, trans. Gillian C. Gill (Ithaca, NY: Cornell University Press, 1985), pp. 13–129; hereafter SOW.
60 SNO, pp. 24–5, 28–30, 77–8.
61 ESD, pp. 101–11.
62 ESD, pp. 76–7.
63 ESD, pp. 5–7, 127.
64 ESD, pp. 74–5, 81–2.
65 ESD, pp. 85–94.
66 Michèle le Doeuff, "Ants and Women or Philosophy Without Borders," in A. Phillips Griffiths (ed.), *Contemporary French Philosophy* (Cambridge: Cambridge University Press, 1987), pp. 41, 45–6, 49–50, 53–4; hereafter AW.
67 Michèle le Doeuff, *The Philosophical Imaginary*, trans. Colin Gordon (London: Athlone/Continuum, 1989/2002), pp. 2–6, 12, 18–19; hereafter PI.
68 AW, pp. 51–2; PI, pp. 1–2, 103–4.
69 PI, pp. 6–7.
70 PI, pp. 112, 114–16, 118, 124, 126–7.
71 AW, p. 41.
72 PI, pp. 102–5; AW, p. 51.
73 PI, pp. 101, 120–4.
74 PI, pp. 117–20.
75 Ssub, p. 201.

76 Michèle le Doeuff, *Hipparchia's Choice*, trans. Trista Selous (Oxford: Basil Blackwell, 1991).
77 See the discussion of de Beauvoir's *Ethics of Ambiguity* above.
78 PI, pp. 124–8.

CHAPTER 11 POSTMODERNISM

1 Richard Rorty is an American philosopher who has an insightful grasp of many issues in the Continental tradition. He sees himself in the pragmatist tradition, and so is not further discussed here. Three of his important books are *Consequences of Pragmatism* (Minneapolis, MN: University of Minnesota Press, 1982); *Philosophy and the Mirror of Nature* (Princeton, NJ: Princeton University Press, 1979); and *Contingency, Irony, and Solidarity* (Cambridge: Cambridge University Press, 1989).
2 Fredric Jameson is among the foremost American Marxist literary theorists of his generation. He has made significant contributions to postmodernist theory and is a trenchant critic of the era it describes. His most important book in this area is *Postmodernism, or The Cultural Logic of Late Capitalism* (Durham, NC: Duke University Press, 1991).
3 Jean-François Lyotard, *The Postmodern Condition: A Report on Knowledge*, trans. Geoff Bennington and Brian Massumi (Minneapolis, MN: University of Minnesota Press, 1984), pp. 31–41; hereafter PMC.
4 This is a central theme in Jean-François Lyotard, *The Differend: Phrases in Dispute*, trans. Georges Van Den Abbeele (Minneapolis, MN: University of Minnesota Press, 1988), pp. xi–xvi and sects. 1–27; hereafter D. All further references to this text will be to *section* numbers.
5 Jean Baudrillard, *Selected Writings*, ed. Mark Poster (Stanford, CA: Stanford University Press, 1988), pp. 143–7; hereafter SW.
6 The analysis of events is a central theme of Jean-François Lyotard, *Peregrinations: Law, Form, Event* (New York: Columbia University Press, 1988). See also PC, p. 81.
7 Gary Gutting, *French Philosophy in the Twentieth Century* (Cambridge: Cambridge University Press, 2001), pp. 318–21.
8 Jean-François Lyotard and Jean-Loup Thébaud, *Just Gaming*, trans. Wlad Godzich (Minneapolis, MN: University of Minnesota Press, 1985), pp. 95–100; hereafter JG.
9 JG, pp. 50–1.
10 JG, pp. 73–5.
11 D, 12–14, 21–4.
12 D, 25, 99, 101–3, 136.
13 D, 174–7.
14 PMC, pp. 37–41.
15 PMC, pp. 41–7.
16 PMC, pp. 10, 18–20.
17 PMC, pp. 60–7.
18 PMC, pp. 47–53.
19 PMC, pp. 50–2.
20 PMC, p. 89.
21 PMC, pp. 29–31.
22 PMC, pp. 65–7.
23 PMC, p. 66.
24 PMC, pp. 26–7.

25 PMC, pp. 38–41.
26 PMC, pp. 49–53.
27 PMC, pp. 60–1.
28 Jean Baudrillard, *Selected Writings*, ed. Mark Poster (Stanford, CA: Stanford University Press, 1988), pp. 21–2, 30–1, 43–6; hereafter, SW).
29 SW, pp. 34–5, 46, 49–51.
30 Jean Baudrillard, *Symbolic Exchange and Death*, trans. Iain Hamilton Grant, intro. Mike Gane (London: Sage, 1993), pp. 1–3, 131–6; hereafter SED.
31 SW, pp. 98–105, 128–35; SED, pp. 9–38.
32 Douglas Kellner, *Jean Baudrillard* (Stanford, CA: Stanford University Press, 1989), pp. 46–7.
33 SW, pp. 143–7, 166–7. Jean Baudrillard, *The Ecstasy of Communication*, trans. Bernard and Caroline Schutze, ed. Slyvere Lotringer (New York: Semiotext(e), 1988), pp. 15–18; hereafter EC.
34 Jean Baudrillard, *Simulations*, trans. Paul Foss, Paul Patton, and Philip Beitchman (New York: Semiotext(e), 1983), pp. 1–4.
35 SW, 135–47.
36 Jean Baudrillard, *Fatal Strategies*, trans. Philip Beitchman and W. G. J. Niesluchowski, ed. Jim Fleming (New York: Semiotext(e)/Pluto, 1990), pp. 7–15; hereafter FS.
37 FS, pp. 181–91; EC, pp. 86–95.
38 EC, pp. 11–14, 36–44.
39 EC, pp. 15–18.
40 EC, pp. 11–14.
41 EC, pp. 14–18.
42 Jean Baudrillard, *In the Shadow of Silent Majorities . . . or the End of the Social*, trans. Paul Foss, Paul Patton, and John Johnston (New York: Semiotext(e), 1983), pp. 1–6, 9; hereafter SSM.
43 SSM, pp. 13–14.
44 SSM, pp. 19–29.
45 SSM, pp. 48–54.
46 EC, pp. 29–31.
47 SSM, pp. 7–8, 18–19.
48 EC, pp. 21–7.
49 SSM, pp. 21–4.
50 EC, pp. 57–63.
51 EC, pp. 57–61.
52 Jean Baudrillard, *Seduction*, trans. Brian Singer (New York: St. Martin's Press, 1990), pp. 79–97; hereafter S.
53 EC, pp. 80–3, 86–9.
54 FS, pp. 111–15.
55 S, pp. 157–70.
56 Jean Baudrillard, *The Perfect Crime*, trans. Chris Turner (London: Verso, 1996), pp. 1–5; hereafter PC.
57 PC, pp. 6–7.
58 PC, pp. 16–21.
59 PC, pp. 45–9.
60 PC, pp. 60–3.
61 PC, pp. 42–4.
62 PC, pp. 36–41.

63 PC, pp. 64–7.
64 PC, pp. 30–1.
65 PC, pp. 28–30.
66 PC, pp. 64–70, 94–105.
67 PC, pp. 104–5.
68 PC, pp. 77–84.
69 Jean Baudrillard, *America*, trans. Chris Turner (London: Verso, 1988), pp. 3–11, 121–4; hereafter A.
70 A, pp. 52–4.
71 A, pp. 3–4.
72 A, pp. 76–8.
73 A, pp. 80–5.
74 A, pp. 88–98.
75 A, pp. 108–11.
76 Oddly, Hegel would agree with Foucault on this point.

CONCLUSIONS

1 I used material from these first two sections to compose parts of my "Afterword," in S. Critchley and W. R. Schroeder (eds.), *A Companion to Continental Philosophy* (Oxford: Blackwell, 1998), pp. 616–25, 629–35.
2 I try to show how extensively they apply to the different movements in my "Afterword" to *A Companion to Continental Philosophy*; the list of strengths has evolved to some extent.
3 A more elaborate version of this section on ethics can be found in William R. Schroeder, "Continental Ethics," in H. LaFollette (ed.), *The Blackwell Guide to Ethical Theory* (Oxford: Blackwell, 2000), pp. 375–99.
4 G. W. F. Hegel, *Phenomenology of Spirit*, trans. A. V. Miller (Oxford: Oxford University Press, 1977), sects. 207–30; hereafter PS. All references to this text are to *section* numbers.
5 PS, 203–7.
6 One could even argue that one experience of desire in this section (PS, 175–6) implies a harmony with the desired object, a sense that it embodies oneself. Appropriating the desired object is meant to prove or confirm this harmony.
7 PS, 360–6.
8 PS, 446–63.
9 Sartre does this in his masterful *Critique of Dialectical Reason*, while Merleau-Ponty does it in his theory of institutions and his understanding of history.
10 In this reply I am adapting a response to this problem made by Eugene Gendlin, "How Philosophy Cannot Appeal to Experience and How it Can," in David Michael Levin (ed.), *Language Beyond Postmodernism* (Evanston, IL: Northwestern University Press, 1997), pp. 3–41.
11 This is the main argument of Jean-Paul Sartre, *Transcendence of the Ego*, trans. F. Williams and R. Kirkpatrick (New York: Noonday, 1957).
12 In passing one should note that this is a well-known problem with Kant's position that Hegel and many other humanist thinkers in the tradition have tried to solve. Foucault himself has no solution except to abandon the concept of autonomy altogether.

BIBLIOGRAPHY

Where appropriate, the first date listed in an entry is the date of original publication of that work.

INTRODUCTION

Selected works by pre-Kantian philosophers in translation

Descartes, René, *Discourse on Method; Passions of the Soul* (1637; 1649), vol. 1 of *The Philosophical Writings of Descartes*, trans. J. Cottingham et al., 2 vols. (Cambridge: Cambridge University Press, 1985).

Diderot, D., *Rameau's Nephew and Other Works*, trans. J. Barzun and R. Bowen (Indianapolis, IN: Hackett, 2001).

—— *Selected Works of Diderot*, ed. and intro L. G. Crocker, trans. D. Coltman (New York: Macmillan, 1966).

Herder, J. G., *Philosophical Writings*, trans. and ed. M. Forster (Cambridge: Cambridge University Press, 2002).

Hume, D., *A Treatise of Human Nature* (1737), ed. L. A. Selby-Bigge and P. H. Nidditch (Oxford: Clarendon Press, 1975).

—— *Enquiries*, ed. L. A. Selby-Bigge and P. H. Nidditch (Oxford: Clarendon Press, 1978).

Rousseau, J.-J., *The Discourses and Other Early Political Writings*, ed. and trans. V. Gourevitch (Cambridge: Cambridge University Press, 1997).

—— *Émile, or On Education* (1762), trans. A. Bloom (New York: Basic Books, 1979).

—— *The Reveries of a Solitary Walker* (1782), trans. C. E. Butterworth (New York: Harper & Row, 1979).

—— *The Social Contract and Other Political Writings*, ed. and trans. V. Gourevitsch (Cambridge: Cambridge University Press, 1997).

Spinoza, B., *A Spinoza Reader: The Ethics and Other Works*, ed. and trans. E. Curley (Princeton, NJ: Princeton University Press, 1994).

—— *The Political Works*, trans. A. G. Wernham (Oxford: Clarendon Press, 1958).

Voltaire, *Selections*, ed. Paul Edwards (New York: Macmillan, 1989).

Selected works by Immanuel Kant in translation

Lectures on Ethics (1775–), trans. P. Heath (Cambridge: Cambridge University Press, 1997).

—— *Critique of Pure Reason* (1st edn. 1781; 2nd edn. 1787), trans. N. Kemp Smith (New York: St. Martins, 1965).

—— *Groundwork of the Metaphysics of Morals* (1785), *Critique of Practical Reason* (1788), and *Metaphysics of Morals* (1797), trans. M. Gregor, in *Immanuel Kant: Practical Philosophy* (Cambridge: Cambridge University Press, 1996).

—— *Critique of the Power of Judgment* (1790), trans. P. Guyer and E. Matthews (Cambridge: Cambridge University Press, 2000).

—— *Religion Within the Boundaries of Mere Reason* (1793), trans. G. di Giovanni (Cambridge: Cambridge University Press, 1996).

Selected works by German Idealists in translation

Fichte, Johann Gottleib, *Attempt at a Critique of All Revelation* (1792; 1793), trans. G. Green (New York: Cambridge University Press, 1978).

—— *Early Philosophical Writings*, trans. and ed. B. Breazeale (Ithaca, NY: Cornell University Press, 1988).

—— *Science of Knowledge* (1795), trans. P. Heath and J. Lachs (New York: Appleton-Century-Crofts, 1970).

—— *Foundations of Natural Right* (1796–7), ed. F. Neuhouser, trans. M. Baur (Cambridge: Cambridge University Press, 2000).

—— *Foundations of Transcendental Philosophy* (1796–9), trans. and ed. D. Breazeale (Ithaca, NY: Cornell University Press, 1992).

—— *The Vocation of Man* (1800), trans. P. Preuss (Indianapolis, IN: Hackett, 1987).

—— *A Crystal Clear Report to the General Public Concerning the Actual Essence of the Newest Philosophy: An Attempt to Force the Reader to Understand* (1801), trans. J. Botterman and W. Rash, in E. Behler (ed.) *Philosophy of German Idealism* (New York: Continuum, 1987).

—— *Addresses to the German Nation* (1808), trans. R. F. Jones and G. H. Turnbull, ed. G. A. Kelly (New York: Harper & Row, 1968).

Hölderlin, F., *Essays and Letters on Theory*, ed. and trans. T. Pfau (Albany, NY: State University of New York Press, 1988).

Novalis (Friedrich von Hardenberg), *Philosophical Writings*, trans. and ed. M. Mahony Stoljar (Albany, NY: State University of New York Press, 1997).

Schelling, F. W. J., *The Unconditional in Human Knowledge: Four Early Essays* (1794–96), trans. F. Marti (Lewisburg, PA: Bucknell University Press, 1980).

—— *Ideas for a Philosophy of Nature* (1797), trans. E. E. Harris and P. Heath (Cambridge: Cambridge University Press, 1988).

—— *System of Transcendental Idealism* (1800), trans. P. Heath (Charlottesville, VA: University Press of Virginia, 1978).

—— *Bruno, or On the Nature and Divine Principle of Things* (1802), trans. and ed. M. G. Vater (Albany, NY: State University of New York Press, 1984).

—— *On University Studies* (1803), trans. E. S. Morgan and Nietzsche Guterman (Athens, OH: Ohio University Press, 1966).

—— *The Philosophy of Art* (1801; 1804), trans. and ed. D. W. Stott (Minneapolis, MN: University of Minnesota Press, 1989).

—— *Philosophical Inquires in the Nature of Human Freedom* (1809), trans. J. Gutmann (Chicago, IL: Open Court, 1936).

—— *Ages of the World* (1813), trans. F. D. Bolmon (New York: AMS Press, 1942).

Further reading

Ameriks, K. (ed.), *The Cambridge Companion to German Idealism* (Cambridge: Cambridge University Press, 2000).

Beiser, F. C., *German Idealism: The Struggle against Subjectivism, 1781–1801* (Cambridge, MA: Harvard University Press, 2002).

Bowie, A., *Schelling and Modern European Philosophy* (London: Routledge, 1993).

Copleston, F., *A History of Philosophy*, 9 vols. (Westminster, MD: Newman Press, 1963–75; pb., New York: Doubleday/Image, 1964–75).

Klemm, D. and Zöller, G., *Figuring the Self: Subject, Absolute, and Others in Classical German Philosophy* (Albany, NY: State University of New York Press, 1997).

Pinkard, T., *German Philosophy 1760–1860: The Legacy of Idealism* (Cambridge: Cambridge University Press, 2002).

Randall, J. H., *The Career of Philosophy*, 2 vols. (New York: Columbia University Press, 1962).

CHAPTER 1 HEGEL

Works by Hegel in translation

Hegel, G. W. F., *The Difference Between Fichte and Schelling's System of Philosophy* (1801), trans. H. S. Harris and Walter Cerf (Albany, NY: State University of New York Press, 1977).

—— *Faith and Knowledge* (1802), trans. Walter Cerf and H. S. Harris (Albany, NY: State University of New York Press, 1977).

—— *Natural Law* (1802–3), trans. T. M. Knox, intro H. B. Acton (np: University of Pennsylvania Press, 1975).

—— *Phenomenology of Spirit* (1807), trans. A. V. Miller (Oxford: Oxford University Press, 1977).

—— *Science of Logic* (1812–16; 2nd edn. 1832), trans. A. V. Miller (London: George Allen & Unwin, 1969).

—— *Philosophy of Right* (1820), trans. T. M. Knox (Oxford: Oxford University Press, 1952).

—— *Logic* (1830), trans. William Wallace; in Part I of the *Encyclopedia of the Philosophical Sciences* (Oxford: Clarendon Press, 1975).

—— *Philosophy of Nature* (1830), trans. A. V. Miller; in Part II of the *Encyclopedia of the Philosophical Sciences* (Oxford: Clarendon Press, 1970).

—— *Philosophy of Mind* (1830), trans. William Wallace and A. V. Miller; in Part III of the *Encyclopedia of the Philosophical Sciences* (Oxford: Clarendon Press, 1971).

—— *Aesthetics: Lectures on Fine Art* (1835), trans. T. M. Knox; 2 vols. (Oxford: Oxford University Press, 1975).

—— *Philosophy of History* (1840), trans. J. Sibree (New York: Dover, 1956).

—— *Lectures on the Philosophy of World History: Introduction* (1840), trans. H. B. Nisbet, intro Duncan Forbes (Cambridge: Cambridge University Press, 1975).

—— *Lectures on the History of Philosophy* (1840), trans. E. S. Haldane and Frances H. Simson; 3 vols. (Lincoln, NE: University of Nebraska Press, 1995).

—— *Lectures on the Philosophy of Religion* (1993) trans. R. F. Brown et al., ed. Peter C. Hodgson; 3 vols. (Berkeley, CA: University of California Press, 1984–7).

—— *Three Essays, 1793–95*, trans. Peter Fuss and John Dobbins (Notre Dame, IN: University of Notre Dame Press, 1984).

—— *Early Theological Writings* (1907), trans. T. M. Knox, intro Richard Kroner (Chicago, IL: University of Chicago Press, 1948).

Further reading

Avineri, S., *Hegel's Theory of the Modern State* (Cambridge: Cambridge University Press, 1972).

Beiser, F. C. (ed.), *The Cambridge Companion to Hegel* (Cambridge: Cambridge University Press, 1993).

Burbidge, J., *On Hegel's Logic: Fragments of a Commentary* (Atlantic Highlands, NJ: Humanities Press, 1981).

De Vries, W. A., *Hegel's Theory of Mental Activity* (Ithaca, NY: Cornell University Press, 1988).

Harris, H. S., *Hegel's Development*, 2 vols.; vol. 1: *Toward the Sunlight, 1770–1801* (Oxford: Clarendon Press, 1972); vol. 2: *Night Thoughts (Jena 1801–1806)* (Oxford: Clarendon Press, 1983).

—— *Hegel's Ladder*, 2 vols.; vol. 1: *The Pilgrimage of Reason*; vol. 2: *The Odyssey of Spirit* (Indianapolis, IN: Hackett, 1997).

Hyppolite, J., *Genesis and Structure of Hegel's Phenomenology of Spirit* (1946), trans. S. Cherniak and J. Heckman (Evanston, IL: Northwestern University Press, 1974).

Kojève, A., *Introduction to the Reading of Hegel* (1947), trans. J. H. Nichols, ed. A. Bloom (New York: Basic Books, 1969).

Pinkard, T., *Hegel: A Biography* (Cambridge: Cambridge University Press, 2000).

—— *Hegel's Phenomenology: The Sociality of Reason* (Cambridge: Cambridge University Press, 1994).

Pippin, R. and Hoffe, O. (eds.), *Hegel on Ethics and Politics* (Cambridge: Cambridge University Press, 2003).

Solomon, R. C., *In the Spirit of Hegel* (Oxford: Oxford University Press, 1983).

Taylor, C., *Hegel* (Cambridge: Cambridge University Press, 1975).

Williams, R., *Hegel's Ethics of Recognition* (Berkeley: University of California Press, 1997).

CHAPTER 2 MARX AND WESTERN MARXISM

Selected works by Marx in translation

Marx, Karl, *Essential Writings*, ed. F. L. Bender (New York: Harper & Row, 1972).

—— *Critique of Hegel's Philosophy of Right* (1843), trans. and ed. J. O'Malley (Cambridge: Cambridge University Press, 1970).

—— *Early Writings* (1844), trans. and ed. T. B. Bottomore (New York: McGraw Hill, 1963).

—— and Engels, F., *The German Ideology, Parts I and II* (1846/1932), ed. R. Pascal (New York: International Publishers, 1947).

—— *The Poverty of Philosophy* (1847) (Peking, China: Foreign Language Press, 1978).

—— *The Eighteenth Brumaire of Louis Bonaparte* (1853) (New York: International Publishers, 1963).

—— *Grundrisse, Foundations of a Critique of Political Economy* (1857–8/1953), trans. Martin Nicolaus (New York: Vintage, 1973).

—— *Capital, Vol. 1* (1867), ed. F. Engels (New York: International Publishers, 1967).

Further reading

Avineri, S., *The Social and Political Thought of Karl Marx* (Cambridge: Cambridge University Press, 1971).

Carver, T., *Marx's Social Theory* (Oxford: Oxford University Press, 1982).

—— (ed.), *The Cambridge Companion to Marx* (Cambridge: Cambridge University Press, 1991).
Elster, J., *Making Sense of Marx* (Cambridge: Cambridge University Press, 1985).
Heilbroner, R. L., *Marxism: For and Against* (New York: W. W. Norton, 1980).
Robinson, J., *An Essay on Marxist Economics* (London: Macmillan, 1942).
Sweezy, P., *The Theory of Capitalist Development* (New York: Monthly Review Press, 1942).
Woolf, J., *Why Marx Today?* (Oxford: Oxford University Press, 2002).

Selected works by Gramsci in translation

Gramsci, Antonio: *Selections from the Prison Notebooks*, trans. and ed. Q. Hoare and G. Nowell Smith (New York: International Publishers, 1971).
—— *Further Selections from the Prison Notebooks*, trans. and ed. D. Boothman (London: Lawrence & Wishart, 1995).
—— *Selections from his Cultural Writings*, ed. D. Forgas and G. Nowell Smith (London: Lawrence & Wishart, 1985).
—— *Selections from the Political Writings 1910–20*, trans. and ed. Q. Hoare (London: Lawrence & Wishart, 1977).
—— *Selections from the Political Writings 1921–26*, trans. and ed. Q. Hoare (London: Lawrence & Wishart, 1978).
—— *Letters from Prison*, ed. L. Lawner (New York: Harper & Row, 1973).
—— *History, Philosophy, and Culture in the Young Gramsci*, trans. P. Molajoni et al., ed. P. Calvacante and P. Piccone (St. Louis, MO: Telos Press, 1975).
—— *The Modern Prince and Other Writings*, trans. L. Marks (New York: International Publishers, 1957).

Selected works by Horkheimer in translation

Horkheimer, Max, *Critical Theory: Selected Essays* (1968), trans. M. J. O'Connell (New York: Herder & Herder, 1972).
—— and Adorno, T. W., *Dialectic of the Enlightenment* (1944), trans. J. Cumming (New York: Seabury, 1972).
—— *Eclipse of Reason* (Oxford: Oxford University Press, 1974).
—— *Critique of Instrumental Reason*, trans. M. J. O'Connell and others (New York: Seabury, 1974).
—— *Between Philosophy and Social Science*, trans. G. F. Hunter et al. (Cambridge, MA: MIT Press, 1995).

Selected works by Marcuse

Marcuse, Herbert, *Negations* (1934–8/1965), trans. Jeremy J. Shapiro (Boston, MA: Beacon Press, 1968).
—— *Reason and Revolution* (Oxford: Oxford University Press, 1941; repr. Boston, MA: Beacon Press, 1960).
—— *Eros and Civilization: A Philosophical Inquiry Into Freud* (Boston, MA: Beacon Press, 1955).
—— *Soviet Marxism* (New York: Columbia University Press, 1958; 2nd edn. 1988).
—— *One Dimensional Man* (Boston, MA: Beacon Press, 1964; 2nd edn. 1991).
—— *An Essay on Liberation* (Boston, MA: Beacon Press, 1969).
—— *Counterrevolution and Revolt* (Boston, MA: Beacon Press, 1972).

—— *Studies in Critical Philosophy* (Boston, MA: Beacon Press, 1973).
—— *The Aesthetic Dimension* (Boston, MA: Beacon Press, 1978).
—— *Technology, War, and Fascism*, ed. D. Kellner (London, Routledge, 1997).

Selected works by Habermas in translation

Habermas, Jürgen: *The Structural Transformation of the Public Sphere* (1962), trans. P. Burger and F. Lawrence (Cambridge, MA: MIT Press, 1989).
—— *Theory and Practice* (1963), trans. J. Viertel (Boston, MA: Beacon Press, 1973).
—— *On the Logic of the Social Sciences* (1967), trans. S. Nicholsen and J. Stark (Cambridge, MA: MIT Press, 1988).
—— *Toward a Rational Society* (1968), trans. J. Shapiro (Boston, MA: Beacon Press, 1970).
—— *Knowledge and Human Interests* (1968), trans. J. Shapiro (Boston, MA: Beacon Press, 1971).
—— *Legitimation Crisis* (1973), trans. T. McCarthy (Boston, MA: Beacon Press, 1975).
—— *Communication and the Evolution of Society* (1976), trans. T. McCarthy (Boston, MA: Beacon Press, 1979).
—— *The Theory of Communicative Action* (1981), 2 vols., trans. T. McCarthy (Boston, MA: Beacon Press, 1984).
—— *Moral Consciousness and Communicative Action* (1983), trans. C. Lenhardt and S. Nicholsen (Cambridge, MA: MIT Press, 1990).
—— *The Philosophical Discourse of Modernity* (1985), trans. F. Lawrence (Cambridge, MA: MIT Press, 1987).
—— *Postmetaphysical Thinking* (1988), trans. W. M. Hohengarten (Cambridge, MA: MIT Press, 1992).
—— *Autonomy and Solidarity* (1986, 1992), ed. Peter Dews, rev. and enlarged edn. (London: Verso, 1992).
—— *Justification and Application: Remarks on Discourse Ethics* (1991), trans. C. Cronin (Cambridge, MA: MIT Press, 1993).
—— *Between Facts and Norms: Contributions to a Discourse Theory of Law and Democracy* (1992), trans. W. Rehg (Cambridge, MA: MIT Press, 1995).

Further reading

Adorno, T., *Negative Dialectics* (1966), trans. E. B. Ashton (New York, Continuum, 1992).
—— *Aesthetic Theory* (1970), trans. R. Hullot-Kentor (Minneapolis, MN: University of Minnesota Press, 1998).
Anderson, P., *Considerations on Western Marxism* (London: Verso, 1979).
Benhabib, S., *Critique, Norm, Utopia* (New York: Columbia University Press, 1986).
Benjamin, W., *Illuminations* (1955), trans. H. Zohn; ed. with intro by H. Arendt (New York: Harcourt, Brace, and World, 1968).
—— *Reflections*, trans. Edmund Jephcott (New York: Harcourt, Brace, Jovanovich, 1978).
Bloch, E., *The Principle of Hope* (1957), 3 vols. (Oxford: Blackwell, 1986).
Bronner, S. E. and Kellner, D. (eds.), *Critical Theory and Society* (New York: Routledge, 1989).
Fraser, N., *Unruly Practices* (Minneapolis, MN: University of Minnesota Press, 1989).
Geuss, R., *The Idea of a Critical Theory* (Cambridge: Cambridge University Press, 1981).
Jameson, F., *Marxism and Form* (Princeton, NJ: Princeton University Press, 1971).
Jay, M., *Marxism and Totality* (Berkeley, CA: University of California Press, 1984).

Kellner, D., *Critical Theory, Marxism, and Modernity* (Baltimore, MD: Johns Hopkins University Press, 1989).

—— *Herbert Marcuse and the Crisis of Marxism* (Berkeley, CA: University of California Press, 1984).

Lefèbvre, H., *Everyday Life in the Modern World* (1968), trans. S. Rabinovitch (New York: Harper & Row, 1971).

Lukács, G., *History and Class Consciousness* (1968), trans. Rodney Livingstone (London: Merlin, 1971).

—— *The Ontology of Social Being*, 3 vols., trans. David Fernbach (London: Merlin, 1978–80).

McCarthy, T., *The Critical Theory of Jürgen Habermas* (Cambridge, MA: MIT Press, 1978).

Rehg, W., *Insight and Solidarity: The Discourse Ethics of Jürgen Habermas* (Berkeley, CA: University of California Press, 1994).

CHAPTER 3 LIFE PHILOSOPHY AND THE UNCONSCIOUS

Selected works by Schopenhauer in translation

Schopenhauer, Arthur, *On the Fourfold Root of the Principle of Sufficient Reason* (1813), trans. E. J. F. Payne, intro R. Taylor (La Salle, IL: Open Court, 1974).

—— *The World as Will and Representation* (1818), 2 vols., trans. E. J. F. Payne (New York: Falcon's Way Press, 1958; ppk: Dover, 1966).

—— *On the Basis of Morality* (1841), trans. E. J. F. Payne, intro Richard Taylor (Indianapolis, IN: Bobbs-Merrill, 1965).

—— *Prize Essay on the Freedom of the Will* (1841), trans. E. F. J. Payne, ed. Günther Zöller (Cambridge: Cambridge University Press, 1999).

—— *Parerga and Paralipomena: Short Philosophical Essays* (1851), trans. E. J. F. Payne (Oxford: Oxford University Press, 1974).

—— *Manuscript Remains in Four Volumes*, trans. E. F. J. Payne (London: Berg, 1988).

Selected works by Freud in translation

Freud, Sigmund, *The Standard Edition of the Complete Psychological Works of Sigmund Freud*, ed. James Strachey (London: Hogarth Press, 1953–71).

—— and Breuer, J., *Studies in Hysteria* (1895), trans. J. Strachey, intro A. A. Brill (Boston, MA: Beacon Press, 1964; orig. 1937).

—— *The Origins of Psychoanalysis: Letters to Wilhelm Fleiss, Drafts, and Notes, 1887–1902*, trans. E. Mosbacher and J. Strachey, eds. M. Bonaparte, A. Freud, and E. Kris (New York: Basic Books, 1954).

—— *The Interpretation of Dreams* (1900), trans. and ed. J. Strachey (New York: Avon, 1965).

—— *Three Essays on the Theory of Sexuality* (1905), trans. and ed. J. Strachey (New York: Avon, 1962/1965).

—— *Five Lectures on Psychoanalysis* (1910), trans. J. Strachey (New York: W.W. Norton, n.d.).

—— *Introductory Lectures on Psychoanalysis* (1917), trans. Joan Riviere (London: George Allen & Unwin, 1922).

—— *Group Psychology and the Analysis of the Ego* (1921), trans. and ed. J. Strachey (New York, Liverright, 1967).

—— *The Ego and the Id* (1923), trans. Joan Riviere, ed. J. Strachey (New York: W.W. Norton, 1962).
—— *Future of an Illusion* (1927), trans. J. Strachey (New York: W.W. Norton, 1961).
—— *Civilization and Its Discontents* (1930), trans. J. Strachey (New York: W.W. Norton, 1961).
—— "Female Sexuality" (1931), trans. Joan Riviere, in *Sexuality and the Psychology of Love* (New York: Macmillan/Collier, 1963).
—— *An Outline of Psychoanalysis* (1940), trans. and ed. J. Strachey (New York: W.W. Norton, 1949).
—— *The Freud Reader*, ed. Peter Gay (New York: W.W. Norton, 1989).

Selected works by Bergson in translation

Bergson, Henri, *Time and Free Will* (1889), trans. F. L. Pogson (London: Macmillan, 1910).
—— *Matter and Memory* (1896), trans. Nancy M. Paul and W. S. Palmer (New York: Zone, 1991).
—— *Laughter: An Essay on the Meaning of the Comic* (1900), trans. C. Brereton and F. Rothwell (London: Macmillan, 1911).
—— *Creative Evolution* (1907), trans. A. Mitchell (New York: Henry Holt, 1911; Mineola, NY: Dover, 1988).
—— *Two Sources of Morality and Religion* (1932), trans. R. Ashley Audra and C. Brereton (New York: Henry Holt, 1935).
—— *The Creative Mind* (1934), trans. M. Andison (New York: Philosophical Library, 1946).

Further reading

Atwell, J. E., *Schopenhauer: The Human Character* (Philadelphia, PA: Temple University Press, 1990).
Dilman, I., *Freud: Insight and Change* (Oxford: Basil Blackwell, 1988).
Gardiner, P., *Schopenhauer* (Harmondsworth: Penguin, 1963).
Gay, P., *Freud, A Life for Our Time* (New York: W.W. Norton, 1988).
Grünbaum, A., *The Foundations of Psychoanalysis: A Philosophical Critique* (Berkeley: University of California Press, 1984).
Hamlyn, D. W., *Schopenhauer* (London: Routledge & Kegan Paul, 1980).
Kofman, S., *The Enigma of Woman: Woman in Freud's Writings* (Ithaca, NY: Cornell University Press, 1985).
Kolakowski, L., *Bergson* (Oxford: Oxford University Press, 1985).
Lacey, A. R., *Bergson* (London: Routledge, 1989).
Lear, J., *Love and Its Place in Nature: A Philosophical Interpretation of Freudian Psychoanalysis* (New York: Farrar, Straus, and Giroux, 1990).
Neu, J., *The Cambridge Companion to Freud* (Cambridge: Cambridge University Press, 1991).
Pribham, K. and Merton, G., *Freud's "Project" Reassessed* (London: Hutchinson, 1976).
Ricoeur, P., *Freud and Philosophy: An Essay on Interpretation* (New Haven, CN: Yale University Press, 1970).
Simmel, G., *Schopenhauer and Nietzsche*, trans. H. Lorskandl (Amherst, MA: University of Massachusetts Press, 1986).
Wollheim, R., *Sigmund Freud* (New York: Viking, 1971).
—— *Freud: A Collection of Critical Essays* (Garden City, NY: Anchor, 1974).
—— and Hopkins, J. (eds.), *Philosophical Essays on Freud* (Cambridge: Cambridge University Press, 1982).

CHAPTER 4 NIETZSCHE (1844–1900)

Selected works by Nietzsche in translation

Nietzsche, F., *The Birth of Tragedy* (1872), trans. Walter Kaufmann (New York: Random House, 1966).

—— *Untimely Meditations* (includes *David Strauss, the Confessor and the Writer* (1873); *On the Uses and Disadvantages of History for Life* (1874); *Schopenhauer as Educator* (1874); and *Richard Wagner in Bayreuth* (1876)), trans. R. J. Hollingdale (Cambridge: Cambridge University Press, 1983).

—— *Human, All Too Human* (1878) (includes *Assorted Opinions and Maxims* (1879) and *The Wanderer and His Shadow* (1880)), trans. R. J. Hollingdale (Cambridge: Cambridge University Press, 1986).

—— *Daybreak: Thoughts on the Prejudices of Morality* (1881), trans. R. J. Hollingdale (Cambridge, Cambridge University Press, 1982).

—— *The Gay Science* (1882), trans. W. Kaufmann (New York: Vintage, 1974).

—— *Thus Spoke Zarathustra, A Book for All and None* (1883–5), trans. W. Kaufmann (New York: Viking/Penguin, 1954).

—— *Beyond Good and Evil, Prelude to a Philosophy of the Future* (1886), trans. W. Kaufmann (New York: Random House, 1966).

—— *On The Genealogy of Morality, A Polemic* (1887), trans. and intro Maudmarie Clark and Alan J. Swensen (Indianapolis, IN: Hackett, 1998).

—— *The Case of Wagner, A Musician's Problem* (1888), trans. W. Kaufmann (New York: Random House, 1966).

—— *Twilight of the Idols, Or How to Philosophize with a Hammer* (1889), trans. W. Kaufmann (New York: Viking/Penguin, 1954).

—— *The Antichrist* (1895), trans. W. Kaufmann (New York: Viking/Penguin).

—— *Nietzsche Contra Wagner* (1895), trans. W. Kaufmann (New York: Viking/Penguin, 1954).

—— *Ecce Homo, How One Becomes What One Is* (1908), trans. Walter Kaufmann (New York: Random House, 1967).

—— *The Will to Power*, trans. W. Kaufmann and R. J. Hollingdale (New York, Random House, 1968).

—— *Philosophy and Truth, Selections from Nietzsche's Notebooks of the Early 1870s*, trans. and ed. D. Breazeale (Atlantic Highlands, NJ: Humanities Press, 1979).

—— *Writings from the Late Notebooks*, trans. Kate Sturge, ed. Rüdiger Bittner (Cambridge: Cambridge University Press, 2003).

Further reading

Brobjer, T., *Nietzsche's Ethics of Character* (Uppsala: Dept. of History of Science and Ideas, Uppsala University, 1995).

Clark, M., *Nietzsche on Truth and Philosophy* (Cambridge: Cambridge University Press, 1990).

Deleuze, G., *Nietzsche and Philosophy*, trans. Hugh Tomlinson (New York: Columbia University Press, 1983).

Fink, E., *Nietzsche's Philosophy*, trans. G. Richter (London: Continuum, 2003).

Kaufmann, W., *Nietzsche: Philosopher, Psychologist, Antichrist*, 3rd edn., rev. and enlarged (New York: Vintage, 1968).

Lampert, L., *Nietzsche's Task* (New Haven, CN: Yale University Press, 2001).

—— *Nietzsche's Teaching* (New Haven, CN: Yale University Press, 1986).

Magnus, B., *Nietzsche's Existential Imperative* (Bloomington, IN: Indiana University Press, 1978).

May, S., *Nietzsche's Ethics and His "War on Morality"* (Oxford: Clarendon Press, 1999).

Morgan, G., *What Nietzsche Means* (Cambridge, MA: Harvard University Press, 1941).

Richardson, J., *Nietzsche's System* (Oxford: Oxford University Press, 1996).

—— and Leiter, B. (eds.), Nietzsche (Oxford: Oxford University Press, 2001).

Schacht, R., *Nietzsche* (London: Routledge & Kegan Paul, 1983).

—— (ed.), *Nietzsche, Genealogy, Morality* (Berkeley, CA: University of California Press, 1994).

Sleinis, E. E., *Nietzsche's Revaluation of Values* (Urbana, IL: University of Illinois Press, 1994).

White, A., *Within Nietzsche's Labyrinth* (London: Routledge, 1990).

CHAPTER 5 HERMENEUTICS

Collections

Ormiston, G. L. and Schrift, A. D. (eds.), *The Hermeneutic Tradition: From Ast to Ricoeur* (Albany, NY: State University of New York Press, 1990).

—— *Transforming the Hermeneutic Context: From Nietzsche to Nancy* (Albany, NY: State University of New York Press, 1990).

Selected works by Schleiermacher in translation

Schleiermacher, Friedrich, *Hermeneutics and Criticism and Other Writings* (1838), trans. and ed. A. Bowie (Cambridge: Cambridge University Press, 1998).

—— *Hermeneutics: The Handwritten Manuscripts* (1959), trans. J. Duke and J. Fortsman, ed. H. Kimmerle (Missoula, MT: Scholars Press, 1977).

Selected works by Dilthey in translation

Dilthey, Wilhelm: *Selected Works*: vol. 1: *Introduction to the Human Sciences* (1989), vol. 4: *Hermeneutics and the Study of History* (1996), vol. 5: *Poetry and Experience* (1985), eds. R. Makkreel and F. Rodi (Princeton, NJ: Princeton University Press).

—— *Meaning in History*, ed. and intro. H. D. Rickman (London: George Allen & Unwin, 1961)

—— *Selected Writings*, tr., ed., and intro. H. D. Rickman (Cambridge: Cambridge University Press, 1976).

—— *Descriptive Psychology and Historical Understanding*, trans. R. Zaner and K. L. Heiges (The Hague: Martinus Nijhoff, 1977).

—— *The Essence of Philosophy* (1924; 2nd edn. 1957), trans. S. A. Emery and W. T. Emery (New York: AMS Press, 1969).

Selected works by Heidegger in translation

See listing for chapter 7 below

Selected works by Gadamer in translation

Gadamer, Hans-Georg, *Truth and Method* (1960), ed. G. Barden and J. Cumming (New York: Seabury, 1975; 2nd rev. edn., New York: Crossroad, 1990).

—— *Philosophical Hermeneutics*, trans. and ed. David E. Linge (Berkeley: University of California Press, 1976).
—— *Reason in the Age of Science* (1976), trans. F. G. Lawrence (Cambridge, MA: MIT Press, 1981).
—— *The Relevance of the Beautiful and Other Essays*, trans. N. Walker, ed. R. Bernasconi (Cambridge: Cambridge University Press, 1986).
—— *Literature and Philosophy in Dialogue*, trans. and intro. R. H. Paslick (Albany, NY: State University of New York Press, 1994).

Further reading

Altieri, C., *Act and Quality: A Theory of Literary and Humanistic Understanding* (Amherst, MA: University of Massachusetts Press, 1981).
Barnes, A., *On Interpretation: A Critical Analysis* (Oxford: Basil Blackwell, 1986).
Betti, E., *Die Hermeneutik als Allgemeine Methodik der Geistewissenschaften* (Tübingen: J. C. B. Mohr, 1972).
Bleicher, J., *Contemporary Hermeneutics: Hermeneutics as Method, Philosophy, and Critique* (London: Routledge, 1980).
Bubner, R., *Essays in Hermeneutics and Critical Theory*, trans. E. Matthews (New York: Columbia University Press, 1987).
Cavell, Stanley, *Pursuits of Happiness* (Cambridge, MA: Harvard University Press, 1981).
—— *Contesting Tears* (Chicago, IL: University of Chicago Press, 1996).
Eco, U., *Interpretation and Overinterpretation* (with Rorty, R., Culler, J., and Brooke-Rose, C.), ed. Stefan Collini (Cambridge: Cambridge University Press, 1992).
Forster, M., *Gadamer and Practical Philosophy: The Hermeneutics of Moral Confidence* (Atlanta, GA: Scholars Press, 1991).
Geertz, C., *The Interpretation of Culture* (New York: Basic Books, 1973).
—— *Local Knowledge: Further Essays in Interpretive Anthropology* (New York: Basic Books, 1985).
Grondin, J., *Introduction to Philosophical Hermeneutics* (New Haven, CN: Yale University Press, 1974).
Hiley, D., Bohman, J., and Shusterman, R. (eds.), *The Interpretive Turn: Philosophy Science, Culture* (Ithaca, NY: Cornell University Press, 1991).
Hoy, D., *The Critical Circle: Literature and History in Contemporary Hermeneutics* (Berkeley, CA: University of California Press, 1978).
Makkreel, R., *Dilthey: Philosophy of the Human Studies* (Princeton, NJ: Princeton University Press, 1992).
Nelson, Cary, *Theory in the Classroom* (Champaign, IL: University of Illinois Press, 1986).
Nicholson, G., *Seeing and Reading* (Atlantic Highlands, NJ: Humanities Press, 1984).
Pettit, P. (ed.), *Action and Interpretation: Studies in the Philosophy of the Social Sciences* (Cambridge: Cambridge University Press, 1978).
Rickman, H. P. (ed.), *Dilthey Today: A Critical Appraisal of the Contemporary Relevance of His Work* (New York: Greenwood, 1988).
Ricoeur, P., *The Conflict of Interpretation: Essays in Hermeneutics* (1969), trans. W. Domingo et al., ed. D. Ihde (Evanston, IL: Northwestern University Press, 1974).
—— *Interpretation Theory: Discourse and the Surplus of Meaning* (Fort Worth, TX: Texas Christian University Press, 1976).
—— *Hermeneutics and the Human Sciences*, trans. and ed. J. B. Thompson (Cambridge: Cambridge University Press, 1981).
Smith, N., *Strong Hermeneutics: Contingency and Moral Identity* (London: Routledge, 1997).

Tuttle, H. N., *Wilhelm Dilthey's Philosophy of Historical Understanding: A Critical Analysis* (Leiden: E. J. Brill, 1969).

Warnke, G., *Gadamer: Hermeneutics, Tradition, and Reason* (Stanford, CA: Stanford University Press, 1987).

—— *Justice and Interpretation* (Cambridge, MA: MIT Press, 1993).

Weinsheimer, J., *Philosophical Hermeneutics and Literary Theory* (New Haven, CN: Yale University Press, 1991).

CHAPTER 6 PHENOMENOLOGY

Selected works by Husserl in translation

Husserl, Edmund, *Logical Investigations*, 2 vols. (1900), trans. J. N. Findlay (London: Routledge & Kegan Paul, 1970).

—— *The Idea of Phenomenology* (1907/58), trans. W. Alston and G. Nakhnikian (The Hague, Netherlands: Martinus Nijhoff, 1964).

—— *On the Phenomenology of the Consciousness of Internal Time* (1893–1917), trans. J. B. Brough (Dordrecht, Holland: Kluwer, 1990).

—— *Ideas Pertaining to a Pure Phenomenology and to a Phenomenological Philosophy, Book I* (1913), trans. F. Kersten (The Hague: Martinus Nijhoff, 1983).

—— *Cartesian Meditations* (1929/50), trans. Dorian Cairns (The Hague: Martinus Nijhoff, 1960).

—— *Experience and Judgment* (1948), trans. J. Churchill and K. Ameriks (Evanston, IL: Northwestern University Press, 1970).

—— *The Crisis of European Sciences and Transcendental Phenomenology* (1954), trans. D. Carr (Evanston, IL: Northwestern University Press, 1970).

Selected works by Scheler in translation

Scheler, Max, *Ressentiment* (1912), trans. W. W. Holdheim, intro. L. A. Coser (New York: Free Press, 1961).

—— *The Nature of Sympathy* (1913), trans. P. Heath, intro. W. Stark (London: Routledge & Kegan Paul, 1954; repr. Hamden, CN: Archon, 1970).

—— *Formalism in Ethics and a Non-Formal Ethic of Value* (1913–16), trans. M. Frings and R. Funk (Evanston, IL: Northwestern University Press, 1973).

—— *Selected Philosophical Essays*, trans. and intro. D. Lachterman (Evanston, IL: Northwestern University Press, 1973).

—— *Man's Place in Nature* (1928), trans. and intro. H. Meyerhoff (New York: Noonday, 1961).

—— *Philosophical Perspectives* (1929), trans. Oscar Haac (Boston, MA: Beacon Press, 1958).

—— *Person and Self-Value*, ed., partial trans., and intro. M. Frings (Dordrecht, Netherlands: Martinus Nijhoff, 1987).

Selected works by Heidegger in translation

See listing for chapter 7 below

Selected works by Sartre in translation

See listing for chapter 7 below

Selected works by Merleau-Ponty in translation

Merleau-Ponty, Maurice, *The Structure of Behavior* (1942), trans. A. L. Fisher (Boston, MA: Beacon Press, 1963).
—— *Phenomenology of Perception* (1945), trans. C. Smith (London: Routledge & Kegan Paul, 1962).
—— *The Primacy of Perception* (1947–61), trans. A. B. Dallery, ed. J. M. Edie (Evanston, IL: Northwestern University Press, 1964).
—— *Humanism and Terror* (1947), trans. J. O'Neill (Boston, MA: Beacon Press, 1969).
—— *Sense and Non-Sense* (1948), trans. H. L. Dreyfus and P. Allen Dreyfus (Evanston, IL: Northwestern University Press, 1964).
—— *The Adventures of the Dialectic* (1955), trans. J. Bien (Evanston, IL: Northwestern University Press, 1973).
—— *Signs* (1960), trans. R. C. McCleary (Evanston, IL: Northwestern University Press, 1964).
—— *Prose of the World* (1950–1/1969), trans. J. O'Neill (Evanston, IL: Northwestern University Press, 1973).
—— *The Visible and the Invisible* (1959–61/1964), trans. A. Lingis, ed. C. Lefort (Evanston, IL: Northwestern University Press, 1968).

Selected works by Levinas in translation

Levinas, E., *The Theory of Intuition in Husserl's Phenomenology* (1930), trans. A. Orianne (Evanston, IL: Northwestern University Press, 1973).
—— *Existence and Existents* (1947), trans. A. Lingis (The Hague: Martinus Nijhoff, 1978).
—— *Time and the Other* (1947), trans. R. Cohen (Pittsburg, PA: Duquesne University Press, 1987).
—— *Totality and Infinity* (1961), trans. A. Lingis (Pittsburg, PA: Duquesne University Press, 1969).
—— *Difficult Freedom* (1963), trans. S. Hand (London: Athlone, 1990).
—— *Discovering Existence with Husserl* (1967), trans. R. Cohen and M. B. Smith (Evanston, IL: Northwestern University Press, 1998).
—— *Otherwise Than Being or Beyond Essence* (1974; 2nd edn. 1978), trans. A. Lingis (The Hague: Martinus Nijhoff, 1981).
—— *Ethics and Infinity* (1982), trans. R. Cohen (Pittsburgh, PA: Duquesne University Press, 1985).
—— *Collected Philosophical Papers*, trans. A. Lingis (Dordrecht: Martinus Nijhoff, 1987).
—— *Basic Philosophical Writings*, ed. A. Peperzak, S. Critchley, and R. Bernasconi (Indianapolis, IN: Indiana University Press, 1996).

Further reading

Brentano, F., *Psychology from an Empirical Standpoint* (1874), trans. A. C. Rancurello, et al. (London: Routledge & Kegan Paul, 1973).
Buber, M., *I and Thou* (1922), trans. Walter Kaufmann (New York: Charles Scribner's Sons, 1970).
Dillon, M., *Merleau-Ponty's Ontology* (Bloomington, IN: Indiana University Press, 1988).
Dreyfus, H., with Hall, H., *Husserl Intentionality and Cognitive Science* (Boston, MA: MIT Press, 1982).

Dufrenne, Mikel, *The Phenomenology of Aesthetic Experience* (1953) (Evanston, IL: Northwestern University Press, 1973).

Follesdal, D., *Husserl and Frege* (Oslo: Aschehoug Press, 1958).

Frings, M., *Max Scheler* (Pittsburgh, PA: Duquesne University Press, 1965; 2nd edn., Milwaukee, WI: Marquette University Press, 1996).

Hammond, M., Howarth, J., and Keat, R., *Understanding Phenomenology* (Oxford: Blackwell, 1991).

Hartmann, N., *Ethics*, 3 vols. (1926), vol. 1: *Moral Phenomena*; vol. 2: *Moral Values*; vol. 3: *Moral Freedom*, trans. S. Coit, intro. J. H. Muirhead (London: George Allen & Unwin, 1932).

Ingarden, Roman: *The Literary Work of Art* (1965), trans. G. M. Grabowicz (Evanston, IL: Northwestern University Press, 1973).

—— *The Cognition of the Literary Work of Art* (1968), trans. R. Crowley and K. Olson (Evanston, IL: Northwestern University Press, 1973).

Kelly, E., *Structure and Diversity: Studies in the Phenomenological Philosophy of Max Scheler* (Dordrecht, Netherlands: Kluwer, 1997).

Mallin, S., *Merleau-Ponty's Philosophy* (New Haven, CN: Yale University Press, 1979).

Meinong, A., *On Emotional Presentation* (1917), trans. M. Schubert Kalsi (Evanston, IL: Northwestern University Press, 1972).

Minkowski, E., *Lived Time* (1933), trans. N. Metzel (Evanston, IL: Northwestern University Press, 1970).

Mohanty, J. N., *Transcendental Phenomenology* (Oxford: Basil Blackwell, 1989).

Pfänder, A., *Phenomenology of Willing and Motivation*, trans. H. Speigelberg (Evanston, IL: Northwestern University Press, 1967).

Schutz, A., *Phenomenology of the Social World* (1932) trans. G. Walsh and F. Lehnert (Evanston, IL: Northwestern University Press, 1967).

—— and Luckmann, T., *Structures of the Lifeworld* (1975) (trans. R. Zaner and H. T. Engelhardt, Jr. (Evanston: IL: Northwestern University Press, 1973).

Sokolowski, R., *Husserlian Meditations: How Words Present Things* (Evanston, IL: Northwestern University Press, 1974).

—— *Introduction to Phenomenology* (Cambridge: Cambridge University Press, 2000).

Spiegelberg, H., *The Phenomenological Movement: A Historical Introduction*, 2 vols. (The Hague: Martinus Nijhoff, 1971).

Stein, E., *On the Problem of Empathy* (1917), trans. W. Stein, 2nd edn. (The Hague: Martinus Nijhoff, 1970).

CHAPTER 7 EXISTENTIALISM AND PHILOSOPHICAL ANTHROPOLOGY

Selected works by Kierkegaard in translation

Kierkegaard, Søren, *Fear and Trembling* (1843) and *The Sickness Unto Death* (1849), trans. W. Lowrie (Princeton, NJ: Princeton University Press, 1954).

—— *Either/Or*, 2 vols. (1843), trans. W. Lowrie (Garden City, NY: Doubleday & Co, 1959).

—— *Philosophical Fragments* (1844), trans. H. V. and E. H. Hong (Princeton, NJ: Princeton University Press, 1985).

—— *The Concept of Dread* (1844), trans. W. Lowrie (Princeton, NJ: Princeton University Press, 1957).

—— *Stages on Life's Way* (1845), trans. W. Lowrie (New York: Schocken, 1967).

—— *The Present Age* (1846), trans. A. Dru (New York: Harper & Row, 1962).
—— *Concluding Unscientific Postscript* (1846), trans. D. Swenson, intro. W. Lowrie (Princeton, NJ: Princeton University Press, 1941).
—— *Works of Love* (1847), trans. H. V. and E. H. Hong (Princeton, NJ: Princeton University Press, 1962).

Selected works by Heidegger in translation

Heidegger, Martin, *Being and Time* (1927), trans. J. Macquarrie and Robinson, E. (New York: Harper & Row, 1962).
—— *The Basic Problems of Phenomenology* (1927/75), trans. A. Hofstadter (Bloomington, IN: Indiana University Press, 1982).
—— *The Essence of Reasons* (1928), trans. T. Malick (Evanston, IL: Northwestern University Press, 1969).
—— *The Fundamental Concepts of Metaphysics* (1929–30/83), trans. W. McNeill and N. Walker (Bloomington, IN: Indiana University Press, 1995).
—— *Introduction to Metaphysics* (1935/53), trans. R. Mannheim (New Haven, CN: Yale University Press, 1959).
—— *Basic Concepts* (1941/81), trans. G. Aylesworth (Bloomington, IN: Indiana University Press, 1993).
—— *What is Called Thinking?* (1951–2/54), trans. F. D. Wieck and J. G. Gray (New York: Harper & Row, 1968).
—— *What is Philosophy?* (1955), trans. J. T. Wilde and W. Klubach (New Haven, CN: College and University Press, 1968).
—— *The Principle of Reason* (1955–6/57), trans. R. Lilly (Bloomington, IN: Indiana University Press, 1991).
—— *Pathmarks* (1967), ed. W. McNeill (Cambridge: Cambridge University Press, 1998).
—— *Basic Writings*, 2nd edn., ed. D. Krell (New York: Harper & Row, 1992).

Selected works by Sartre in translation

Sartre, Jean-Paul, *Transcendence of the Ego* (1936), trans. F. Williams and R. Kirkpatrick (New York: Noonday, 1957).
—— *Nausea* (1938), trans. L. Alexander (New York: New Directions, 1949).
—— *Emotions: Outline of a Theory* (1939), trans. B. Frechtman (New York: Philosophical Library, 1948).
—— *Psychology of the Imagination* (1940), trans. B. Frechtman (New York: Philosophical Library, 1948, and Washington Square, 1966).
—— *Being and Nothingness* (1943), trans. H. E. Barnes (New York: Philosophical Library, 1956).
—— *Existentialism is a Humanism* (1946) in W. Kaufmann (ed.), *Existentialism from Dostoevsky to Sartre* (Cleveland, OH: World, 1956).
—— *Anti-Semite and Jew* (1946), trans. G. J. Becker (New York: Schocken, 1974).
—— *Baudelaire* (1947), trans. M. Turnell (New York: New Directions, 1950).
—— *What is Literature?* (1948), trans. B. Frechtman et al. (Cambridge, MA: Harvard University Press, 1988).
—— *Truth and Existence* (1948/89), trans. A. van den Hoven (Chicago, IL: University of Chicago Press, 1992).
—— *Notebooks for an Ethics* (1947–8/83), trans. D. Pellauer (Chicago, IL: University of Chicago Press, 1992).

—— *Saint Genet* (1952), trans. B. Frechtman (New York: George Braziller, 1963).

—— *Mallarme* (1953/86), trans. E. Sturm (University Park, PN: Pennsylvania State University Press, 1988).

—— *Search for a Method* (1957), trans. H. Barnes (New York: A.A. Knopf, 1963).

—— *Critique of Dialectical Reason*, 2 vols. (1960/1985): vol. 1: *Theory of Practical Ensembles*, trans. A. Sheridan-Smith (London: New Left Books, 1976); vol. 2: *The Intelligibility of History*, trans. Q. Hoare (London: Verso, 1991).

—— *The Words* (1964), trans. B. Frechtman (New York: George Braziller, 1964).

—— *The Family Idiot* (3 vols., 1971–2), trans. C. Cosman (in 5 vols.), (Chicago, IL: University of Chicago Press, 1981, 1987, 1989, 1991, 1993).

Selected works by Scheler in translation

See listing for chapter 6 above

Selected works by Goldstein

Goldstein, Kurt, *The Organism* (1934) (New York: Zone Books, 1995).

—— *Human Nature in the Light of Psychopathology* (1940) (New York: Schocken, 1963).

—— *Language and Language Disturbances* (New York: Grune and Stratton, 1948).

—— *Selected Papers*, ed. A. Gurwitsch et al. (The Hague: Martinus Nijhoff, 1971).

Selected works by Gehlen in translation

Gehlen, Arnold, *Man: His Nature and Place in the World* (1950), trans. C. McMillan and K. Pillemer (New York: Columbia University Press, 1988).

—— *Man in the Age of Technology* (1957), trans. P. Lipscomb (New York: Columbia University Press, 1980).

Further reading

Aronson, R., *Sartre's Second Critique* (Chicago, IL: University of Chicago Press, 1987).

Barnes, H., *Sartre and Flaubert* (Chicago, IL: University of Chicago Press, 1981).

Cassirer, E., *An Essay on Man* (New Haven, CN: Yale University Press, 1944).

Conant, J., "Putting Two and Two Together: Kierkegaard and Wittgenstein and the point of view for their work as authors," in T. Tessin and M. von der Ruhr (eds.), *Philosophy and the Grammar of Religious Belief* (Basingstoke: Macmillan, 1995).

Dreyfus, H., *Being in the World* (Cambridge, MA: MIT Press, 1991).

Evans, C. S., *Passionate Reason: Making Sense of Kierkegaard's Philosophical Fragments* (Bloomington, IN: Indiana University Press, 1992).

Fell, J., *Emotion in the Thought of Jean-Paul Sartre* (New York: Columbia University Press, 1965).

—— *Heidegger and Sartre: An Essay on Being and Place* (New York: Columbia University Press, 1979).

Flynn, T., *Sartre and Marxist Existentialism* (Chicago, IL: University of Chicago Press, 1984).

Gerassi, J., *Jean-Paul Sartre: Hated Conscience of His Century* (Chicago, IL: University of Chicago Press, 1989).

Grene, M., *Approaches to a Philosophical Biology* (New York: Basic Books, 1968).

Guignon, C. (ed.), *The Cambridge Companion to Heidegger* (Cambridge: Cambridge University Press, 1993).

Hannay, A., *Kierkegaard* (London: Routledge, 1982).
Howells, C., *The Necessity of Freedom* (Cambridge: Cambridge University Press, 1988).
—— *The Cambridge Companion to Sartre* (Cambridge: Cambridge University Press, 1992).
Kaufmann, W., *Existentialism from Dostoevsky to Sartre*, ed. W. Kaufmann (Cleveland, OH: World, 1956).
McBride, W., *Sartre's Political Theory* (Bloomington, IN: Indiana University Press, 1991).
Plessner, H., *Laughing and Crying* (3rd edn. 1961), trans. J. S. Churchill and M. Grene (Evanston, IL: Northwestern University Press, 1970).
Pöggeler, O., *Martin Heidegger's Path of Thinking* (1963), trans. D. Magurshak and S. Barber (Atlantic Highlands, NJ: Humanities Press, 1987).
Polyani, M., *Personal Knowledge* (London: Routledge & Kegan Paul, 1958).
Schacht, R., *Hegel and After* (Pittsburgh, PA: University of Pittsburgh Press, 1975).
Schilder, P., *Mind: Perception and Thought* (New York: Columbia University Press, 1942).
Schilpp, P. A. (ed.), *The Philosophy of Jean-Paul Sartre* (La Salle, IL: Open Court, 1981).
Taylor, Mark C., *Journeys to Selfhood: Hegel and Kierkegaard* (Berkeley: University of California Press, 1980).
Westphal, M., *Becoming a Self: A Reading of Kierkegaard's "Concluding Unscientific Postscript"* (West Lafayette, IN: Purdue University Press, 1996).
Wider, K. V., *The Bodily Nature of Consciousness: Sartre and Contemporary Philosophy of Mind* (Ithaca, NY: Cornell University Press, 1997).

CHAPTER 8 STRUCTURALISM

Selected works by Saussure in translation

De Saussure, Ferdinand, *Course in General Linguistics* (1916), trans. Wade Baskin (New York: McGraw-Hill, 1959).

Selected works by Barthes in translation

Barthes, Roland, *Writing Degree Zero* (1953) and *Elements of Semiology* (1964), trans. A. Lavers and C. Smith (London: Jonathan Cape, 1967; pbk, Boston, MA: Beacon Press, 1970).
—— *Michelet* (1954), trans. R. Howard (New York: Hill and Wang, 1987).
—— *Mythologies* (1957), trans. A. Lavers (London: Jonathan Cape / New York: Hill and Wang, 1972).
—— *On Racine* (1960), trans. R. Howard (New York: Hill and Wang, 1964).
—— *Criticism and Truth* (1966), trans. K. P. Denneman (Minneapolis, MN: University of Minnesota Press, 1987).
—— *The Fashion System* (1967), trans. M. Ward and R. Howard (New York: Hill and Wang, 1983).
—— *S/Z* (1970), trans. R. Miller (New York: Hill and Wang, 1974).
—— *Sade, Fourier, and Loyola* (1971), trans. R. Miller (New York: Hill and Wang, 1976).
—— *The Pleasure of the Text* (1973), trans. R. Miller (New York: Hill and Wang, 1975).
—— *Roland Barthes* (1975), trans. R. Howard (New York: Hill and Wang, 1977).
—— *A Lover's Discourse* (1977), trans. R. Howard (New York: Hill and Wang, 1978).
—— *Camera Lucida* (1980), trans. R. Howard (New York: Hill and Wang, 1981).

Selected works by Lévi-Strauss in translation

Lévi-Strauss, Claude, *The Elementary Structures of Kinship* (1949), trans. J. H. Bell and J. von Sturmer, ed. R. Needham (Boston, MA: Beacon Press, 1969).

—— *Tristes Tropiques* (1955), trans. J. and D. Weightman (New York: Atheneum, 1974).

—— *Structural Anthropology* (1958), trans. C. Jacobson and B. G. Schoepf (New York: Basic Books, 1963; pb. Anchor, 1967).

—— *Totemism* (1962), trans. R. Needham (Boston, MA: Beacon Press, 1963).

—— *The Savage Mind* (1962), trans. unknown (London: Weidenfelt and Nicholson and Chicago, IL: University of Chicago Press, 1966).

—— *The Raw and the Cooked: Introduction to a Science of Mythology,* vol. 1 (1964), trans. J. and D. Weightman (New York: Harper & Row, 1969).

—— *From Honey to Ashes: Introduction to a Science of Mythology,* vol. 2 (1967), trans. J. and D. Weightman (New York: Harper & Row, 1973).

—— *The Origin of Table Manners: Introduction to a Science of Mythology,* vol. 3 (1968), trans. J. and D. Weightman (New York: Harper & Row, 1978).

—— *The Naked Man: Introduction to a Science of Mythology,* vol. 4 (1971), trans. J. and D. Weightman (New York: Harper & Row, 1981).

—— *Structural Anthropology,* vol. 2 (1973), trans. J. and D. Weightman (New York: Basic Books, 1976).

—— *Myth and Meaning* (Toronto: University of Toronto Press, 1978; repr. New York: Schocken, 1979).

—— *The View from Afar* (1983), trans. J. Neugroschel and P. Hoss (New York: Basic Books, 1985).

Selected works by Lacan in translation

Lacan, Jacques, *The Language of the Self: The Function of Language in Psychoanalysis* (1953), trans. A. Wilden (Baltimore, MD: Johns Hopkins University Press, 1968).

—— *The Seminar of Jacques Lacan.* Book I: *Freud's Papers on Technique* (1953–4), ed. J.-A. Miller, trans. J. Forrester (New York: W.W. Norton, 1988).

—— *The Seminar of Jacques Lacan.* Book II: *The Ego in Freud's Theory and in the Technique of Psychoanalysis* (1954–5), ed. J.-A. Miller, trans. S. Tomaselli; notes J. Forrester (New York: W.W. Norton, 1988).

—— *The Seminar of Jacques Lacan.* Book III: *The Psychoses* (1955–6), ed. J.-A. Miller, trans. R. Grigg (New York: W.W. Norton, 1993).

—— *The Seminar of Jacques Lacan.* Book VII: *The Ethics of Psychoanalysis* (1959–60), ed. J.-A. Miller, trans. D. Porter (New York: W.W. Norton, 1992).

—— *Ecrits* (1966), trans. A. Sheridan (New York: W.W. Norton, 1977).

—— *Feminine Sexuality* (1966, 1968, 1975), trans. J. Rose, ed. J. Mitchell and J. Rose (New York: W.W. Norton, 1982).

—— *The Four Fundamental Concepts of Psychoanalysis* (1973), ed. J.-A. Miller, trans. A. Sheridan (New York: W.W. Norton, 1977).

Selected works by Althusser in translation

Althusser, Louis, *For Marx* (1965), trans. B. Brewster (New York: Random House, 1970).

—— *Lenin and Philosophy* (1969), trans. B. Brewster (New York: Monthly Review Press, 1971).

Althusser, L. and Balibar, E., *Reading Capital* (1969), trans. B. Brewster (London: New Left Books, 1970).

Further reading

Caws, P., *Structuralism: The Art of the Intelligible* (Atlantic Highlands, NJ: Humanities Press, 1988).

Culler, J., *Structuralist Poetics* (Ithaca, NY: Cornell University Press, 1975).

Dosse, F., *History of Structuralism*, 2 vols. Vol. 1: *The Rising Sign, 1945–1966* (1991); vol. 2: *The Sign Sets (1967–present)* (1992), trans. D. Glassman (Minneapolis, MN: University of Minnesota Press, 1997).

Eco, U., *A Theory of Semiotics* (Bloomington, IN: Indiana University Press, 1976).

Genette, G., *Narrative Discourse: An Essay in Method* (1972), trans. J. E. Lewin (Ithaca, NY: Cornell University Press, 1980).

—— *Figures of Literary Discourse*, trans. A. Sheridan, intro. M.-R. Logan (New York: Columbia University Press, 1982).

—— *The Architext: An Introduction* (1979), trans. J. E. Lewin (Berkeley, CA: University of California Press, 1992).

—— *Narrative Discourse Revisited* (1983), trans. J. E. Lewin (Ithaca, NY: Cornell University Press, 1988).

Greimas, A. J., *On Meaning* (1970, 1983), trans. P. J. Perron and F. H. Collins, intro P. J. Perron (Minneapolis, MN: University of Minnesota Press, 1987).

—— *The Social Sciences: A Semiotic View*, trans. P. J. Perron and F. H. Collins (Minneapolis, MN: University of Minnesota Press, 1990).

—— and J. Fontanille, *The Semiotics of Passions* (1991), trans. P. J. Perron and F. H. Collins (Minneapolis, MN: University of Minnesota Press, 1993).

Hartmann, G., *Beyond Formalism* (New Haven, CN: Yale University Press, 1970).

Hjelmslev, L., *Language: An Introduction*, trans. F. J. Whitfield (Madison, WI: University of Wisconsin Press, 1970).

Jakobson, R., *Main Trends in the Science of Language* (New York: Harper & Row, 1970/73).

—— *Verbal Art, Verbal Sign, Verbal Time*, ed. K. Pomorska and S. Rudy (Oxford: Blackwell, 1985).

—— *Language in Literature*, ed. K. Pomorska and S. Rudy (Cambridge, MA: Harvard University Press, 1987).

Jameson, F., *The Prison House of Language: A Critical Account of Structuralism and Russian Formalism* (Princeton, NJ: Princeton University Press, 1972).

Lane, M. (ed.), *Introduction to Structuralism* (New York: Basic Books, 1970).

Mauss, M., *The Gift* (1921), trans. I. Cunnison, intro. E. E. Evans-Pritchard (New York: W.W. Norton, 1967).

Nasio, J.-D., *Five Lessons on the Psychoanalytic Theory of Jacques Lacan* (1992), trans. D. Pettigrew and F. Raffoul (Albany, NY: State University of New York Press, 1998).

Pettit, P., *The Concept of Structuralism: A Critical Analysis* (Berkeley, CA: University of California Press, 1975).

Piaget, J., *Elements of Genetic Epistemology* (1950), trans. E. Duckworth (New York: Columbia University Press, 1970).

—— *Behavior and Evolution* (1976), trans. D. Nicholson-Smith (New York: Pantheon, 1978).

—— *Structuralism* (1968), trans. and ed. C. Maschler (New York: Basic Books, 1970).

Propp, V., *Morphology of the Folktale* (1966) (Austin, TX: University of Texas Press, 1968).

Serres, M., *Hermes: Literature, Science, Philosophy* (1968), trans. J. V. Harari and D. F. Bell (Baltimore, MD: Johns Hopkins University Press, 1982).

—— *The Parasite* (1980), trans. L. Schehr (Baltimore, MD: Johns Hopkins University Press, 1982).

Todorov, T., *The Fantastic: A Structural Approach to a Literary Genre* (1970), trans. R. Howard (Ithaca, NY: Cornell University Press, 1973).

—— *Theories of the Symbol* (1977), trans. C. Porter (Ithaca: NY: Cornell University Press, 1982).

White, H., *Metahistory* (Baltimore, MD: Johns Hopkins University Press, 1973).

CHAPTER 9 PHILOSOPHIES OF DISPERSION

Selected works by Foucault in translation

Foucault, Michel, *Madness and Civilization* (1961; 2nd edn. 1972), trans. R. Howard (New York: Pantheon, 1965).

—— *Birth of the Clinic* (1963), trans. A. Sheridan (New York: Random House, 1973; pb. Vintage, 1975).

—— *The Order of Things: An Archaeology of the Human Sciences* (1966), trans. A. M. Sheridan-Smith (New York: Random House, 1970; pb. Vintage, 1973).

—— *The Archaeology of Knowledge* (1969), trans. A. Sheridan (New York: Random House, 1972).

—— *Discipline and Punish* (1975), trans. A. Sheridan (New York: Pantheon, 1977).

—— *The History of Sexuality*. Vol. 1: *An Introduction* (1976), trans. R. Hurley (New York: Random House, 1978).

—— *The Use of Pleasure: The History of Sexuality*. Vol. 2 (1984), trans. R. Hurley (New York: Random House, 1985).

—— *The Care of the Self: The History of Sexuality*. Vol. 3 (1984), trans. R. Hurley (New York: Pantheon, 1986).

—— *Language, Counter-memory, Practice-Selected Essays and Interviews by Michel Foucault*, trans. D. F. Bouchard and S. Simon, ed. D. F. Bouchard (Ithaca, New York: Cornell University Press, 1977).

—— *Power/Knowledge*, trans. C. Gordon et al., ed. C. Gordon (New York: Pantheon, 1980).

—— *The Foucault Reader*, ed. P. Rabinow (New York: Pantheon, 1984).

—— *The Essential Works of Foucault 1954–1984* (1994), 3 vols. Vol. 1: *Ethics, Subjectivity, and Truth*, trans. R. Hurley et al., ed. P. Rabinow; vol. 2: *Aesthetics, Method, Epistemology*, trans. R. Hurley et al., ed. J. D. Faubion; vol. 3: *Power*, trans. R. Hurley et al., ed. J. D. Faubion (New York: New Press, 1997, 1998, 2000).

Selected works by Derrida in translation

Derrida, Jacques, *Of Grammatology* (1967), trans. G. Spivak (Baltimore, MD: Johns Hopkins University Press, 1976).

—— *Speech and Phenomena* (1967), trans. D. Allison (Evanston, IL: Northwestern University Press, 1973).

—— *Writing and Difference* (1967), trans. A. Bass (Chicago, IL: University of Chicago Press, 1978).

—— *Dissemination* (1972), trans. B. Johnson (Chicago, IL: University of Chicago Press, 1981).

—— *Margins of Philosophy* (1972), trans. A. Bass (Chicago, IL: University of Chicago Press, 1982).

—— *Glas* (1974), trans. J. Leavey and R. Rand (Lincoln, NE: University of Nebraska Press, 1986).

—— "Force of Law: The 'Mystical Foundations of Authority'" (1994), trans. M. Quaintance, in D. Cornell, et al. (eds.), *Deconstruction and the Possibility of Justice* (New York: Routledge, 1992).

—— *Given Time I: Counterfeit Money* (1991), trans. P. Kamuf (Chicago, IL: University of Chicago Press, 1992).

—— *The Gift of Death* (1992), trans. D. Willis (Chicago, IL: University of Chicago Press, 1995).

—— *Specters of Marx* (1993), trans. P. Kamuf, intro. B. Magnus and S. Cullenberg (New York: Routledge, 1994).

—— *The Politics of Friendship* (1994), trans. G. Collins (New York: Verso, 1997).

—— *Of Hospitality* (1997), trans. R. Bowlby (Stanford, CA: Stanford University Press, 1997).

—— *Adieu: To Emmanual Levinas* (1997), trans. P.-A. Brault and M. Naas (Stanford, CA: Stanford University Press, 1999).

—— *A Derrida Reader*, ed. P. Kamuf (London: Harvester, 1991).

Selected works by Deleuze in translation

Deleuze, Gilles, *Nietzsche and Philosophy* (1962), trans. H. Tomlinson (New York: Columbia University Press, 1983).

—— *Proust and Signs* (1964), trans. R. Howard (New York: George Braziller, 1972).

—— *Masochism* (1967), trans. J. McNeil (New York: George Braziller, 1971).

—— *Difference and Repetition* (1968), trans. P. Patton (New York: Columbia University Press, 1994).

—— *Expressionism in Philosophy: Spinoza* (1968), trans. M. Joughin (New York: Zone Books, 1990).

—— *The Logic of Sense* (1969), trans. M. Lester and C. Stivale, ed. C. Boundas (New York: Columbia University Press, 1990).

—— *Cinema 1: The Movement Image* (1983), trans. H. Tomlinson and B. Habberjam (Minneapolis, MN: University of Minnesota Press, 1986).

—— *Cinema 2: The Time-Image* (1985), trans. H. Tomlinson and R. Galeta (Minneapolis, MN: University of Minnesota Press, 1989).

—— *Foucault* (1986), trans. S. Hand (Minneapolis, MN: University of Minnesota Press, 1988).

Deleuze, G. and Guatarri, F., *Captalism and Schizophrenia*, 2 vols. Vol. 1: *Anti-Oedipus* (1972), trans. R. Hurley et al.; vol. 2: *A Thousand Plateaus* (1980), trans. B. Massumi (Minneapolis, MN: University of Minnesota Press, 1983 and 1987).

—— *Kafka: Toward a Minor Literature* (1975), trans. D. Polan (Minneapolis, MN: University of Minnesota Press, 1986).

—— *What is Philosophy?* (1991), trans. H. Tomlinson and G. Burchell (New York: Columbia University Press, 1994).

Further reading

Armstrong, T. J. (ed.), *Michel Foucault: Philosopher* (1989), trans. T. J. Armstrong (New York: Routledge, 1992).

Badiou, A., *Deleuze: The Clamor of Being* (1997), trans. L. Burchill (Minneapolis, MN: University of Minnesota Press, 2000).

Canguilhem, G., *The Normal and the Pathological* (1966), trans. C. R. Fawcett with R. S. Cohen, intro. M. Foucault (New York: Zone Books, 1989).

—— *Ideology and Rationality in the History of the Life Sciences* (1977), trans. A. Goldhammer (Boston, MA: MIT Press, 1988).

Critchley, S., *The Ethics of Deconstruction: Derrida and Levinas* (Oxford: Basil Blackwell, 1992).

Davidson, A., *Foucault and His Interlocutors* (Chicago, IL: University of Chicago Press, 1996).

Dreyfus, H. and Rabinow, P., *Michel Foucault: Beyond Structuralism and Hermeneutics* (Chicago, IL: University of Chicago Press, 1982; 2nd edn. 1983).

Ellis, J., *Against Deconstruction* (Princeton, NJ: Princeton University Press, 1989).

Gasché, R., *The Tain in the Mirror: Derrida and the Philosophy of Reflection* (Cambridge, MA: Harvard University Press, 1986).

Frank, M., *What is Neostructuralism?* (1983), trans. R. Grey and S. Wilke (Minneapolis, MN: University of Minnesota Press, 1989.

Gutting, G., *Michel Foucault's Archaeology of Scientific Reason* (Cambridge: Cambridge University Press, 1989).

—— (ed.), *The Cambridge Companion to Foucault* (Cambridge: Cambridge University Press, 1994).

Hardt, M., *Gilles Deleuze: An Apprenticeship in Philosophy* (Minneapolis, MN: University of Minnesota Press, 1993).

Honneth, A., *The Critique of Power: Reflective Stages in a Critical Social Theory* (Cambridge, MA: MIT Press, 1991).

Howells, C., *Derrida* (Cambridge: Polity, 1999).

Kofman, S., *Lectures de Derrida* (Paris: Galilée, 1984).

Norris, C., *Derrida* (Cambridge, MA: Harvard University Press, 1987).

Patton, P., *Deleuze: A Critical Reader* (Oxford: Basil Blackwell, 1996).

CHAPTER 10 FRENCH FEMINIST PHILOSOPHY

Selected works by de Beauvoir in translation

De Beauvoir, Simone, *She Came To Stay* (1943), trans. Y. Moyse and R. Senhouse (Cleveland, OH: World Publishing, 1954).

—— *The Blood of Others* (1945), trans. R. Senhouse and Y. Moyce (New York: Knopf, 1948).

—— *All Men Are Mortal* (1946), trans. L. M. Friedman (Cleveland, OH: World Publishing, 1955).

—— *The Ethics of Ambiguity* (1947), trans. B. Frechtman (New York: Philosophical Library, 1948; pb. Citadel, 1964).

—— *The Second Sex* (1949), trans. H. M. Parshley (New York: Knopf, 1953; pb. Bantam, 1961).

—— *The Mandarins* (1954), trans. L. M. Friedman (Cleveland, OH: World Publishing, 1957).

—— *Memoirs of a Dutiful Daughter* (1958), trans. J. Kirkup (Cleveland OH: World Publishing, 1959).

—— *The Prime of Life* (1960), trans. P. Green (Cleveland OH: World Publishing, 1962).

—— *Force of Circumstance* (1963), trans. R. Howard (New York: Putnam, 1964/65).
—— *A Very Easy Death* (1964), trans. P. O'Brian (New York: Putnam, 1966).
—— *The Woman Destroyed* (1968), trans. P. O'Brian (New York: Putnam, 1969).
—— *Coming of Age* (1970), trans. P. O'Brian (New York: Putnam, 1972).
—— *All Said and Done* (1972), trans. P. O'Brian (New York: Putnam, 1974).
—— *Adieux: A Farewell to Sartre* (1981), trans. P. O'Brian (New York: Pantheon, 1984).

Selecteed works by Kristeva in translation

Kristeva, Julia, *About Chinese Women* (1974), trans. A. Barrows (New York: Marion Boyars, 1977).
—— *Revolution in Poetic Language* (1974), trans. M. Waller (New York: Columbia University Press, 1984).
—— *Desire in Language* (partial translation of *Polylogue*, 1977), trans. T. Gora, A. Jardine, L. Roudiez, ed. L. Roudiez (New York: Columbia University Press, 1980).
—— *Powers of Horror* (1980), trans. L. Roudiez (New York: Columbia University Press, 1982).
—— *Tales of Love* (1983), trans. L. Roudiez (New York: Columbia University Press, 1987).
—— *Black Sun: Depression and Melancholy* (1987), trans. L. Roudiez (New York: Columbia University Press, 1989).
—— *Strangers to Ourselves* (1989), trans. L. Roudiez (New York: Columbia University Press, 1991).
—— *Nations Without Nationalisms* (1990), trans. L. Roudiez (New York: Columbia University Press, 1993).
—— *New Maladies of the Soul* (1993), trans. R. Guberman (New York: Columbia University Press, 1995).
—— *Time and Sense: Proust and the Experience of Literature* (1994), trans. R. Guberman (New York: Columbia University Press, 1996).
—— *The Crisis of the European Subject*, trans. S. Fairfield (New York: The Other Press, 2000).
—— *The Sense and Nonsense of Revolt* (1996), trans. J. Herman (New York: Columbia University Press, 2000).
—— *Intimate Revolt: Powers and Limits of Psychoanalysis* (1997), trans. J. Herman (New York: Columbia University Press, 2002).
—— *Hannah Arendt* (1999), trans. R. Guberman (New York: Columbia University Press, 2001).
—— *Melanie Klein* (1999), trans. R. Guberman (New York: Columbia University Press, 2001).
—— *The Julia Kristeva Interviews*, ed. R. Guberman (New York: Columbia University Press, 1996).
—— *The Portable Kristeva*, ed. K. Oliver (New York: Columbia University Press, 1998).

Selected works by Irigaray in translation

Irigaray, Luce, *Speculum of the Other Woman* (1974), trans. G. C. Gill (Ithaca, NY: Cornell University Press, 1985).
—— *The Sex Which Is Not One* (1977), trans. C. Porter (Ithaca, NY: Cornell University Press, 1985).
—— *Marine Love of Friedrich Nietzsche* (1980), trans. G. Gill (New York: Columbia University Press, 1991).

—— *Elemental Passions* (1981), trans. J. Collie and J. Still (New York: Routledge, 1992).

—— *The Forgetting of Air in Martin Heidegger* (1983), trans. M. Mader (Austin, TX: University of Texas Press, 1999).

—— *An Ethics of Sexual Difference* (1984), trans. C. Burke and G. Gill (Ithaca, NY: Cornell University Press, 1993).

—— *To Speak is Never Neutral* (1985), trans. G. Schwab (New York: Routledge, 2000).

—— *Sexes and Genealogies* (1987), trans. G. Gill (New York: Columbia University Press, 1993).

—— *Thinking the Difference: For a Peaceful Revolution* (1989), trans. A. Martin (New York: Routledge, 1994).

—— *Je, tu, nous: Toward a Culture of Difference* (1990), trans. C. Burke and G. Gill (New York: Routledge, 1993).

—— *I Love to You* (1992), trans. A. Martin (New York: Routledge, 1996).

—— *Democracy Begins Between Two* (1994), trans. K. Anderson (New York: Routledge, 2001).

—— *To Be Two* (1997), trans. M. Rhodes and M Cocito-Monoc (New York: Routledge, 2000).

—— *Between East and West: From Singularity to Community* (1999), trans. S. Pluhácek (New York: Columbia University Press, 2002).

—— *The Way of Love* (2000), trans. H. Bostic and S. Pluhácek (London: Continuum, 2002).

Selected works by Le Doeuff in translation

Le Doeuff, Michèle, *The Philosophical Imaginary* (1980), trans. C. Gordon (London: Athlone, 1989; pb. Continuum, 2002).

—— "Ants and Women, or Philosophy Without Borders," in A. P. Griffiths, *Contemporary French Philosophy* (Cambridge: Cambridge University Press, 1987).

—— *Hipparchia's Choice* (1989), trans. T. Selous (Oxford: Basil Blackwell, 1991).

—— *The Sex of Knowing* (1998), trans. K. Hamer and L. Code (New York: Routledge, 2003).

Further reading

Arp, K., *The Bonds of Freedom* (Chicago, IL: Open Court, 2001).

Bergoffen, D. B., *The Philosophy of Simone de Beauvoir: Gendered Phenomenologies, Erotic Generosities* (Albany, NY: State University of New York Press, 1997).

Braidotti, R., *Patterns of Dissonance: A Study of Women in Contemporary Philosophy* (London: Polity, 1991).

Card, C., *The Cambridge Companion to Simone de Beauvoir* (Cambridge: Cambridge University Press, 2003).

Chanter, T., *Ethics of Eros: Irigaray's Rewriting of the Philosophers* (London, Routledge, 1995).

Cixous, H. and Clement, C., *The Newly Born Woman* (1975), trans. B. Wing (Minneapolis, MN: University of Minnesota Press, 1986).

Cixous, H., *The Hélène Cixous Reader*, ed. S. Sellers (New York: Routledge, 1994).

Delphy, C., *Close to Home: A Materialist Analysis of Women's Oppression* (Amherst, MA: University of Massachusetts Press, 1984).

Deutscher, M. (ed.), *Michèle Le Doeuff: Operative Philosophy and Imaginary Practice* (Amherst, NY: Humanity Books, 2000).

Grosz, E., *Sexual Subversions* (Sydney, Australia: Allen and Unwin, 1989).

Guillaumin, C., *Racism, Sexism, Power, and Ideology* (New York: Routledge, 1995).
Kofman, S., *The Enigma of Woman*, trans. C. Porter (Ithaca, NY: Cornell University Press, 1985).
—— *Nietzsche and Metaphor* (1972), trans. D. Large (Stanford, CA: Stanford University Press, 1993).
—— *Smothered Words* (1987), trans. M. Dobie (Evanston, IL: Northwestern University Press, 1998).
Moi, T., *Sexual/Textual Politics* (London: Methuen, 1985; pb. Routledge, 1988).
—— (ed.), *French Feminist Thought: A Reader* (Oxford: Basil Blackwell, 1988).
—— *Simone de Beauvoir: The Making of an Intellectual Woman* (Oxford: Blackwell, 1994).
Oliver, K., *Reading Kristeva: Unraveling the Double-Bind* (Bloomington, IN: Indiana University Press, 1993).
Schwartzer, A. (ed.), *After the Second Sex: Conversations with Simone de Beauvoir* (University Park, PA: Pennsylvania State University Press, 1995).
Smith, A., *Julia Kristeva: Speaking the Unspeakable* (New York: Stylus Press, 1998).
Whitford, M., *Luce Irigaray: Philosophy of the Feminine* (London: Routledge, 1991).

CHAPTER 11 POSTMODERNISM

Selected works by Lyotard in translation

Lyotard, Jean-François, *Phenomenology* (1954), trans. B. Beakley (Albany, NY: State University of New York Press, 1991).
—— *Libidinal Economy* (1974), trans. I. Hamilton Grant (Bloomington, IN: Indiana University Press, 1993).
—— (with J. L. Thébaud), *Just Gaming* (1979), trans. W. Godzich (Minneapolis, MN: University of Minnesota Press, 1985).
—— *The Postmodern Condition: A Report on Knowledge* (1979), trans. G. Bennington and B. Massumi (Minneapolis, MN: University of Minnesota Press, 1984).
—— *The Differend: Phrases in Dispute* (1983), trans. G. Van Den Abbeele (Minneapolis, MN: University of Minnesota Press, 1988).
—— *The Postmodern Explained* (1986), trans. D. Barry et al., ed. J. Pefanis and M. Thomas (Minneapolis, MN: University of Minnesota Press, 1993).
—— *The Inhuman* (1988), trans. G. Bennington and R. Bowlby (Cambridge: Polity/ Stanford, CA: Stanford University Press, 1991).
—— *Peregrinations: Law, Form, Event* (New York: Columbia University Press, 1988).
—— *Postmodern Fables* (1993), trans. G. Van Den Abbeele (Minneapolis, MN: University of Minnesota Press, 1997).
—— *The Lyotard Reader*, ed. A. Benjamin (Oxford: Blackwell, 1989).

Selected works by Baudrillard in translation

Baudrillard, Jean, *The System of Objects* (1968), trans. J. Benedict (London: Verso, 1996).
—— *Consumer Society: Myths and Structures* (1970), intro. G. Ritzer (London: Sage, 1998).
—— *For a Critique of the Political Economy of the Sign* (1972), trans. C. Levin (St. Louis, MO: Telos, 1981).
—— *The Mirror of Production* (1973), trans. and intro. M. Poster (St. Louis, MO: Telos, 1975).

—— *Symbolic Exchange and Death* (1976), trans. I. H. Grant, intro Mike Gane (London: Sage, 1993).
—— *Seduction* (1979), trans. B. Singer (New York: St. Martin's Press, 1990).
—— *Simulations* (1981), trans. P. Foss et al. (New York: Semiotext(e), 1983).
—— *Fatal Strategies* (1983), trans. P. Beitchman and W. G. J. Niesluchowski (New York: Semiotext(e)/Pluto, 1990).
—— *America* (1986), trans. C. Turner (London: Verso, 1988).
—— *Cool Memories 1980–85* (1987), trans. C. Turner (London: Verso, 1990).
—— *The Ecstasy of Communication* (1987), trans. B. and C. Schutze, ed. Slyvere Lotringer (New York: Semiotext(e), 1988).
—— *The Transparency of Evil* (1990), trans. J. Benedict (London: Verso: 1993).
—— *Cool Memories II 1987–1990* (1990), trans. C. Turner (Durham, NC: Duke University Press, 1996).
—— *The Gulf War Did Not Take Place* (1991), trans. P. Patton (Bloomington, IN: Indiana University Press, 1995).
—— *The Illusion of the End* (1992), trans. C. Turner (Stanford, CA: Stanford University Press, 1994).
—— *The Perfect Crime* (1995), trans. C. Turner (London: Verso, 1996).
—— *Impossible Exchange* (1999), trans. C. Turner (London: Verso, 2001).
—— *Vital Illusion*, ed. J. Witwer (New York: Columbia University Press, 2000).
—— *Selected Writings*, ed. M. Poster (Stanford, CA: Stanford University Press, 1988).
—— *Revenge of the Crystal*, ed. and trans. P. Foss and J. Pefanis (London: Pluto, 1990).

Further reading

Bauman, Z., *Intimations of Postmodernity* (New York: Routledge, 1992).
—— *Postmodernity and its Discontents* (New York: New York University Press, 1997).
Debord, G., *The Society of the Spectacle* (Detroit, MI: Black and Red, 1976).
Jameson, F., *Postmodernism, or the Cultural Logic of Late Capitalism* (Durham, NC: Duke University Press, 1991).
Giddens, A., *The Consequences of Modernity* (Cambridge: Polity, 1990).
Foster, H. (ed.), *The Anti-Aesthetic* (Port Townsend, WA: Bay Press, 1983).
Harraway, D., *Simians, Cyborgs, and Women* (London: Routledge, 1991).
Kellner, D., *Jean Baudrillard* (Stanford, CA: Stanford University Press, 1989).
Kellner, D. and Best, S., *Postmodern Theory: Critical Interrogations* (New York: Guilford, 1991).
—— *The Postmodern Turn* (New York: Guilford, 1997).
Nicholson, L. (ed.): *Feminism/Postmodernism* (London: Routledge, 1990).
Pefanis, J., *Heterology and the Postmodern* (Durham, NC: Duke University Press, 1991).
Pippin, R., *Modernism and a Philosophical Problem* (Oxford: Blackwell, 1991).
Rorty, R., *Philosophy and the Mirror of Nature* (Princeton, NJ: Princeton University Press, 1979).
—— *Consequences of Pragmatism* (Minneapolis, MN: University of Minnesota Press, 1982).
—— *Contingency, Irony, and Solidarity* (Cambridge: Cambridge University Press, 1989).
Soja, E., *Postmodern Geographies* (London: Verso, 1989).
—— *Postmetropolis: Critical Studies of Cities and Regions* (Oxford: Blackwell, 2000).
Toulmin, S., *Cosmopolis* (New York: The Free Press, 1990).
Turner, B. (ed.), *Theories of Modernity and Postmodernity* (London: Sage, 1990).
Vattimo, G., *The End of Modernity* (Cambridge: Polity, 1988).

INDEX

Numbers in **bold** indicate significant discussion of the topic